Understanding DB2®

DB2® BOOKS

DB2® Universal Database V8 for Linux, UNIX, and Windows Database Administration Certification Guide, Fifth Edition
Baklarz and Wong

DB2® for Solaris
Bauch and Wilding

Understanding DB2®
Chong, Liu, Qi, and Snow

Integrated Solutions with DB2®
Cutlip and Medicke

High Availability Guide for DB2®
Eaton and Cialini

DB2® Universal Database V8 Handbook for Windows, UNIX, and Linux
Gunning

DB2® SQL PL, Second Edition
Janmohamed, Liu, Bradstock, Chong, Gao, McArthur, and Yip

DB2® Universal Database for OS/390 V7.1 Application Certification Guide
Lawson

DB2® for z/OS® Version 8 DBA Certification Guide
Lawson

DB2® Universal Database V8 Application Development Certification Guide, Second Edition
Martineau, Sanyal, Gashyna, and Kyprianou

DB2® Universal Database V8.1 Certification Exam 700 Study Guide
Sanders

DB2® Universal Database V8.1 Certification Exam 703 Study Guide
Sanders

DB2® Universal Database V8.1 Certification Exams 701 and 706 Study Guide
Sanders

The Official Introduction to DB2® for z/OS®, Second Edition
Sloan

Advanced DBA Certification Guide and Reference for DB2® Universal Database v8 for Linux, UNIX, and Windows
Snow and Phan

DB2® Express
Yip, Cheung, Gartner, Liu, and O'Connell

DB2® Version 8
Zikopoulos, Baklarz, deRoos, and Melnyk

ON DEMAND COMPUTING BOOKS

Business Intelligence for the Enterprise
Biere

On Demand Computing
Fellenstein

Grid Computing
Joseph and Fellenstein

Autonomic Computing
Murch

WEBSPHERE BOOKS

IBM® WebSphere®
Barcia, Hines, Alcott, and Botzum

IBM® WebSphere® Application Server for Distributed Platforms and z/OS®
Black, Everett, Draeger, Miller, Iyer, McGuinnes, Patel, Herescu, Gissel, Betancourt, Casile, Tang, and Beaubien

Enterprise Java™ Programming with IBM® WebSphere®, Second Edition
Brown, Craig, Hester, Pitt, Stinehour, Weitzel, Amsden, Jakab, and Berg

IBM® WebSphere® and Lotus
Lamb, Laskey, and Indurkhya

IBM® WebSphere® System Administration
Williamson, Chan, Cundiff, Lauzon, and Mitchell

Enterprise Messaging Using JMS and IBM® WebSphere®
Yusuf

MORE BOOKS FROM IBM PRESS

Developing Quality Technical Information, Second Edition
Hargis, Carey, Hernandez, Hughes, Longo, Rouiller, and Wilde

Building Applications with the Linux Standard Base
Linux Standard Base Team

An Introduction to IMS™
Meltz, Long, Harrington, Hain, and Nicholls

Understanding DB2®

Learning Visually with Examples

DB2® Information Management Software

Raul F. Chong
Clara Liu
Sylvia F. Qi
Dwaine R. Snow

IBM Press
Pearson plc
Upper Saddle River, NJ • Boston • Indianapolis • San Francisco
New York • Toronto • Montreal • London • Munich • Paris • Madrid
Capetown • Sydney • Tokyo • Singapore • Mexico City
www.phptr.com/ibmpress

The authors and publisher have taken care in the preparation of this book, but make no expressed or implied warranty of any kind and assume no responsibility for errors or omissions. No liability is assumed for incidental or consequential damages in connection with or arising out of the use of the information or programs contained herein.

IBM Press Program Manager: Tara Woodman, Ellice Uffer
IBM Press Consulting Editor: Susan Visser
Cover design: IBM Corporation
Published by Pearson plc
Publishing as IBM Press

Library of Congress Cataloging-in-Publication Data

Understanding DB2® : learning visually with examples / Raul F. Chong ... [et al.].
    p. cm.
  Includes bibliographical references and index.
  ISBN 0-13-185916-1 (hardcover : alk. paper)
  1. Relational databases. 2. IBM Database 2. I. Chong, Raul F.

  QA76.9.D3U55 2005
  005.75'65--dc22

                                            2004028592

IBM Press offers excellent discounts on this book when ordered in quantity for bulk purchases or special sales, which may include electronic versions and/or custom covers and content particular to your business, training goals, marketing focus, and branding interests. For more information, please contact:

    U. S. Corporate and Government Sales
    1-800-382-3419
    corpsales@pearsontechgroup.com

For sales outside the U. S., please contact:

    International Sales
    international@pearsoned.com

    Pearson Education, Inc.
    Rights and Contracts Department
    One Lake Street
    Upper Saddle River, NJ 07458

ISBN 0-13-185916-1
Text printed in the United States on recycled paper at Courier in Westford, Massachusetts.
First printing, January 2005

Raul would like to thank his parents, Elias and Olga Chong, for their support, love, and understanding; and to his siblings, Alberto, David, Patricia, and Nancy. Their examples of success and perseverance encouraged Raul to continue with the hard work of writing and completing this book.

Clara would like to thank her family—Louis, Christina, and Esther—for their endless love and support. Most of all, Clara wants to thank Heison for being patient and understanding when she spent numerous late nights and weekends writing this book.

Sylvia would like to thank her parents for their love and support throughout the years. And also to her husband, Michael, for his endless support, love, patience, and understanding.

Dwaine would like to thank Linda Snow and Alyssa Bergman for their support, love, and understanding during the hours that were spent writing this book.

Contents

Chapter 4 **Using the DB2 Tools**   **107**

Chapter 5 Understanding the DB2 Environment, DB2 Instances, and Databases   153

Chapter 6   Configuring Client and Server Connectivity   193

Chapter 7   Working with Database Objects   243

Chapter 13 **Developing Database Backup and
Recovery Solutions**   **537**

Chapter 16   Database Performance Considerations   643

Foreword

I t is a great pleasure and privilege to be asked to write the foreword for this book. It is also somewhat of a surprise—although I've worked with DB2 for many years, I certainly wouldn't consider myself an expert. I'm just a DB2 user, and my shop is no different from many other DB2 shops—lots of databases to manage, high availability is a business imperative, and data security is on everyone's mind.

DB2 UDB Version 8.2, codenamed "Stinger," is as buzzworthy as the name suggests. This latest release of DB2 UDB for Linux, UNIX, and Windows contains a wide variety of new features, designed to speed application development and make administrative tasks easier. While exciting, there's something about it that's a little intimidating as well. That's where this book comes in—it demystifies DB2, and serves as an excellent reference, whether you are relatively new to DB2 or preparing for certification.

Take Chapter 3, for example. As everyone who has ever installed DB2 knows, there are many variables that can affect the outcome of the process, and each platform will be slightly different. The same is true when installing FixPaks. Chapter 3 is devoted exclusively to the installation process, and provides many graphs and examples, as well as practical troubleshooting tips for common errors, all in a format that is very easy to follow. Each chapter is presented in this same straightforward manner, but I think my personal favorite is Chapter 14, The DB2 Process Model. During problem determination, the DBA may encounter an impressive array of running processes, and sometimes may enter the dreaded **kill -9** command against some of them in an effort to resolve the problem. This is often the worst thing to do. Chapter 14 explains the DB2 processes and the interaction between them, as well as how they are affected by DB2 settings, so the DBA can understand what's running and why.

This book is an excellent reference and is a compilation of exactly the kind of information that DBAs need to have at their fingertips. The authors have drawn on their collective experience in the DB2 development lab and with many DB2 customers to produce this book. It has earned a place on the must-read list of every DB2 professional.

—Sandy Smith
President, International DB2 Users Group (IDUG)
Director of Data Management, Hewitt Associates

Preface

I n the world of information technology today, it is more and more difficult to keep up with the skills required to be successful on the job. This book was developed to minimize the time, money, and effort required to learn DB2 Universal Database (DB2 UDB) for Linux, UNIX, and Windows. The book visually introduces and discusses the latest version of DB2 UDB, Version 8.2. The goal with the development of DB2 was to make it work the same regardless of the operating system on which you choose to run it. The few differences in the implementation of DB2 UDB on these platforms are explained in this book.

WHO SHOULD READ THIS BOOK?

This book is intended for anyone who works with databases, such as database administrators (DBAs), application developers, system administrators, and consultants. This book is a great introduction to DB2, whether you have used DB2 before or you are new to DB2. It is also a good study guide for anyone preparing for the IBM DB2 Universal Database Version 8 Certification exams 700 (DB2 UDB Family Fundamentals) and 701 (DB2 UDB Database Administration), or the DB2 UDB Version 8.1 Database Administration upgrade exam, number 706.

This book will save you time and effort because the topics are presented in a clear and concise manner, and we use figures, examples, case studies, and review questions to reinforce the material as it is presented. The book is different than many others on the subject because of the following.

1. **Visual learning:** The book relies on visual learning as its base. Each chapter starts with a "big picture" to introduce the topics to be discussed in that chapter. Numerous graphics are used throughout the chapters to explain concepts in detail. We feel that figures allow for fast, easy learning and longer retention of the material. If you forget some of the concepts discussed in the book or just need a quick refresher, you will not need to read the entire chapter again. You can simply look at the figures quickly to refresh your memory. For your convenience, some of the most important figures are provided in color on the CD-ROM accompanying this book. These figures in color can further improve your learning experience.

2. **Clear explanations:** We have encountered many situations when reading other books where paragraphs need to be read two, three, or even more times to grasp what they are describing. In this book we have made every effort possible to provide clear explanations so that you can understand the information quickly and easily.

3. **Examples, examples, examples:** The book provides many examples and case studies that reinforce the topics discussed in each chapter. Some of the examples have been

taken from real life experiences that the authors have had while working with DB2 customers.

4. **Sample exam questions:** All chapters end with review questions that are similar to the questions on the DB2 Certification exams. These questions are intended to ensure that you understand the concepts discussed in each chapter before proceeding, and as a study guide for the IBM Certification exams. Appendix A contains the answers with explanations.

GETTING STARTED

If you are new to DB2 and would like to get the most out of this book, we suggest you start reading from the beginning and continue with the chapters in order. If you are new to DB2 but are in a hurry to get a quick understanding of DB2, you can jump to Chapter 2, DB2 at a Glance: The Big Picture. Reading this chapter will introduce you to the main concepts of DB2. You can then go to other chapters to read for further details.

If you would like to follow the examples provided with the book, you need to install DB2. Chapter 3, Installing DB2, gives you the details to handle this task.

A WORD OF ADVICE

In this book we use figures extensively to introduce and examine DB2 concepts. While some of the figures may look complex, don't be overwhelmed by first impressions! The text that accompanies them explains the concepts in detail. If you look back at the figure after reading the description, you will be surprised by how much clearer it is.

This book only discusses DB2 UDB for Linux, UNIX, and Windows, so when we use the term DB2, we are referring to DB2 UDB on those platforms. DB2 UDB for iSeries, DB2 UDB for OS/390 and z/OS, and DB2 UDB for VM and VSE are mentioned only when presenting methods that you can use to access these databases from an application written on Linux, UNIX, or Windows. When DB2 UDB for iSeries, DB2 UDB for OS/390 and z/OS, and DB2 UDB for VM and VSE are discussed, we refer to them explicitly.

CONVENTIONS

Many examples of SQL statements, DB2 commands, and operating system commands are included throughout the book. SQL keywords are written in uppercase bold. For example: Use the **SELECT** statement to retrieve data from a DB2 database.

DB2 commands are shown in lowercase bold. For example: The **list applications** command lists the applications connected to your databases.

You can issue many DB2 UDB commands from the Command Line Processor (CLP) utility, which accepts the commands in both uppercase and lowercase. In the UNIX operating systems, program names are case-sensitive, so be careful to enter the program name using the proper case. For example, on UNIX, **db2** must be entered in lowercase. (See Appendix B, Use of Uppercase Versus Lowercase in DB2, for a detailed discussion of this.)

Database object names used in our examples are shown in italics. For example: The *country* table has five columns.

Italics are also used for variable names in the syntax of a command or statement. If the variable name has more than one word, it is joined with an underscore. For example: **CREATE SEQUENCE** *sequence_name*

Where a concept of a function is new in DB2 Version 8.2, we signify this with an icon as follows.

Note that the DB2 UDB Version 8.1 Certification Exams do not cover Version 8.2 material.

CONTACTING THE AUTHORS

We are interested in any feedback that you have about this book. Please contact us with your opinions and inquiries at udb2book@ca.ibm.com.

Depending on the volume of inquires, we may be unable to respond to every technical question but we'll do our best. The DB2 newsgroup at comp.databases.ibm-db2 is another great way to get assistance from IBM employees and the DB2 user community. Finally, for more information on this book, be sure to visit www.phptr.com/title/0131859161.

Acknowledgments

Raul, Clara, Sylvia, and Dwaine would like to thank Linda Snow for the tremendous effort that she gave in helping us to ensure that this book is accurate, easy to read, and easy to understand. Linda's comments made a huge impact on improving this book for our readers, and we thank her very much.

Michael Dang worked hard to ensure the technical accuracy of the book; we thank him for his valuable contributions.

Susan Visser provided guidance and invaluable help throughout the whole process of planning, writing, and publishing the book. Without her help, this book would never have been completed as smoothly as it has been.

We would also like to thank Magie Liu, Scott J. Martin, Amyris Rada, and Bill Wilkins for their comments and suggestions.

About the Authors

Raul F. Chong is a DB2 Information Developer with the Application Development Solutions team at the IBM Toronto Lab. He has recently taken over this new role and is responsible for developing sample programs and DB2 documentation for Web Services and CLI. Raul has seven years of experience at IBM, three of them in DB2 Technical Support helping and resolving customer problems on the Linux, UNIX, Windows, OS/390, and z/OS platforms, and four years as a consultant specializing in database application development, performance tuning, and migrations from other relational database management systems to DB2. Raul has taught many DB2 technical workshops, published numerous articles, and has contributed to the DB2 Certification exam tutorials. Raul holds a B.S. in computer science from the University of Toronto and is a DB2 Certified Solutions Expert in both DB2 Administration and Application Development. Raul is also a coauthor of the book *DB2® SQL PL: Essential Guide for DB2® UDB on Linux®, UNIX®, Windows®, i5/OS™, and z/OS®*.

Clara Liu works for the IBM Toronto Laboratory as a database consultant. In the past five years Clara has worked with a wide variety of IBM partners and customers on projects utilizing DB2 Universal Database. She specializes in database application development and integration of new technologies with DB2. She is also the coauthor of two other books: *DB2® Express: Easy Development and Administration* and *DB2® SQL PL: Essential Guide for DB2® UDB on Linux®, UNIX®, Windows®, i5/OS™, and z/OS®*. In addition to working with DB2, Clara has several on-going projects, such as "Scuba Diving 101" and "Karaoke in the Basement."

Sylvia Qi is a senior DB2 Support Analyst at the IBM Toronto Lab. She has over five years of working experience in the DB2 engine and tools areas, supporting customers worldwide. Sylvia is also a contributing author to IBM developerWorks, the IBM technical resource Web site. Sylvia holds a B.S. in computer science from McGill University and is an IBM Certified Solution Expert in DB2 Administration.

Dwaine R. Snow is a senior product manager for DB2 UDB for Linux, UNIX, and Windows and focuses on competitive technologies. Dwaine has worked with DB2 UDB for the past fourteen years, as part of the development team focusing on the database engine and tools, the development of the DB2 Certification program, and as part of the lab-based consulting team. Dwaine has presented at conferences worldwide, contributed to the DB2 tutorial series, and has written a number of articles and coauthored books on DB2 including the *Advanced DBA Certification Guide and Reference for DB2® Universal Database for Linux, UNIX, and Windows, DB2® UDB for Windows, The DB2® Cluster Certification Guide*, and the second edition of the *DB2® Certification Guide for Linux, UNIX, and Windows*. Dwaine is a DB2 Certified Solutions Expert in both Database Administration and Application Development as well as a Certified Advanced

Database Administrator—DB2 Universal Database V8.1 for Linux, UNIX, and Windows. He has also worked extensively onsite with customers in planning and implementing both transaction-based and data warehouse systems.

AUTHOR PUBLICATIONS

Chong, Raul. "Getting Started with DB2 for z/OS and OS/390 Version 7 for DB2 Distributed Platform Users." www.ibm.com/software/data/developer. July 2002.

————. "Leverage Your Distributed DB2 Skills to Get Started on DB2 UDB for the iSeries (AS/400)." www.ibm.com/software/data/developer. October 2002.

————. "Backup and Recovery: DB2 V8.1 Database Administration Certification Prep, Part 6 of 6." www.ibm.com/software/data/developer. May 2003.

————. *DB2® SQL PL, Second Edition: Essential Guide for DB2® UDB on Linux™, UNIX®, Windows™, i5/OS™, and z/OS®*. Upper Saddle River, N.J.: Prentice Hall, 2005.

Liu, Clara. *DB2® SQL Procedural Language for Linux™, UNIX®, and Windows™*. Upper Saddle River, N.J.: Prentice Hall, 2002.

————. "Migrate DB2 V7 Databases to DB2 V8.1." www.ibm.com/software/data/developer. March 2004.

————. *DB2® SQL PL, Second Edition: Essential Guide for DB2® UDB on Linux™, UNIX®, Windows™, i5/OS™, and z/OS®*. Upper Saddle River, N.J.: Prentice Hall, 2005.

————. *DB2® Express: Easy Development and Administration*. Upper Saddle River, N.J.: Prentice Hall, 2005.

Qi, Sylvia. "An introduction to DB2 UDB Backup Solution with Veritas NetBackup." www.ibm.com/software/data/developer. February 2004.

————. "The DB2 UDB Memory Model." www.ibm.com/software/data/developer. June 2004.

————. "DB2 Universal Database Commands by Example." www.ibm.com/software/data/developer. June 2004.

Snow, Dwaine. *DB2® Universal Database Certification Guide, Second Edition*. Upper Saddle River, N.J: Prentice Hall, 1997.

————.*DB2 UDB® Cluster Certification Guide*. Upper Saddle River, N.J: Prentice Hall, 1998.

————. *The Universal Guide to DB2® for Windows NT*. Upper Saddle River, N.J.: Prentice Hall, 1999.

————. *Advanced DBA® Certification Guide and Reference for DB2® Universal Database V8 for Linux, UNIX, and Windows*. Upper Saddle River, N.J: Prentice Hall, 2004.

CHAPTER 1

Introduction to DB2 UDB

D ATABASE 2 (DB2) Universal Database (UDB) for Linux, UNIX, and Windows is a relational database management system (RDBMS) developed by IBM. Version 8.2, available since September 2004, is the most current version of the product, and the one discussed in this book.

In this chapter you will learn about:

- The history of DB2
- The DB2 portfolio of information management products
- How DB2 is developed
- DB2 server editions and clients
- How DB2 is packaged for developers
- Syntax diagram conventions

1.1 A BRIEF HISTORY OF DB2

Since the 1970s, when IBM Research invented the Relational Model and the Structured Query Language (SQL), IBM has developed a complete family of RDBMS software. Development started on mainframe platforms such as Virtual Machine (VM), Virtual Storage Extended (VSE), and Multiple Virtual Storage (MVS). In 1983, DB2 for MVS Version 1 was born. "DB2" was used to indicate a shift from *hierarchical* databases—like the Information Management System (IMS) popular at the time—to the new *relational* databases. DB2 development continued on mainframe platforms as well as on distributed platforms.[1] Figure 1.1 shows some of the highlights of DB2 history.

---

1. Distributed platforms, also referred to as **open system platforms**, include all platforms other than mainframe or midrange operating systems. Some examples are Linux, UNIX, and Windows.

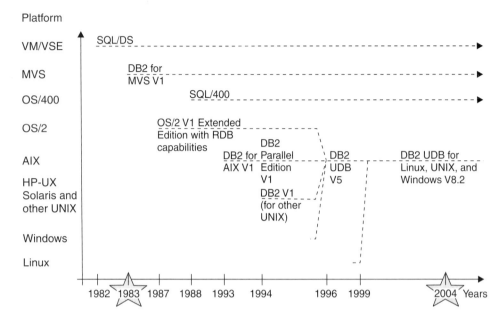

Figure 1.1   DB2 timeline

In 1996, IBM announced DB2 UDB Version 5 for distributed platforms. With this version, DB2 was able to store all kinds of electronic data, including traditional relational data, as well as audio, video, and text documents. It was the first version optimized for the Web, and it supported a range of distributed platforms—for example, OS/2, Windows, AIX, HP-UX, and Solaris—from multiple vendors. Moreover, this universal database was able to run on a variety of hardware, from uniprocessor systems and symmetric multiprocessor (SMP) systems to massively parallel processing (MPP) systems and clusters of SMP systems. IBM included the term "Universal" in the name to represent the new capabilities of this version. All versions of DB2 on distributed platforms and on MVS, AS/400, VM, and VSE have adopted the name DB2 UDB.

Today, DB2 represents a portfolio of information management products. Table 1.1 shows the DB2 Information Management portfolio and the product offerings under each classification. To specifically refer to database servers, "UDB" needs to be added to the name, as in **DB2 UDB**. In most books and documents, including this one, the terms "DB2" and "DB2 UDB" are used interchangeably. Unless otherwise noted, when we use any one of these terms in this book, we are referring to DB2 running on Linux, UNIX, or Windows.

Table 1.1   DB2 Information Management Products

Information Management Products	Description	Product Offerings
Database Servers	Store electronic data and enable the sharing of information across multiple platforms.	IBM DB2 UDB IBM Informix IBM IMS IBM Red Brick Warehouse IBM U2 IBM Cloudscape
DB2 Business Intelligence	Help customers collect, prepare, manage, analyze, and extract valuable information from all data types to help them make more insightful business decisions faster.	DB2 Warehouse Manager IBM DB2 Information Integrator DB2 OLAP Server DB2 Intelligent Miner DB2 Text Miner DB2 Search Extender DB2 UDB Data Warehouse Edition DB2 Cube Views Query Patroller
DB2 Content Management	Manage content (unstructured data) such as images, digital media, word processing documents, and Web content.	IBM DB2 Content Manager IBM DB2 CommonStore IBM DB2 CM OnDemand IBM DB2 Document Manager IBM DB2 Records Manager
DB2 Information Integration	Bring together distributed information from heterogeneous environments. Companies view their information as if it was all residing in one place.	IBM DB2 Information Integrator IBM DiscoveryLink for Life Sciences
DB2 and IMS Tools	Automate functions to help companies reduce administrative costs.	IMS & DB2 Tools & Utilities DB2 Multiplatform Tools

1.2 DB2 SOFTWARE AND THE IBM E-BUSINESS ON-DEMAND MODEL

IBM's on-demand business model is based on the definition of an on-demand business. An **on-demand business**, as indicated on the IBM on-demand Web site, is "an enterprise whose business processes—integrated end to-end across the company and with key partners, suppliers and customers—can respond with speed to any customer demand, market opportunity, or external threat." To support the on-demand model, IBM uses the e-business framework shown in Figure 1.2.

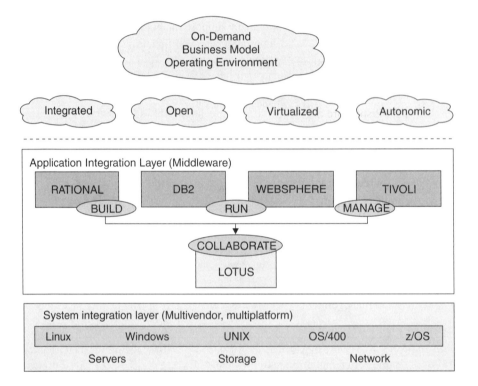

Figure 1.2   The IBM e-business framework

In Figure 1.2 the dotted line divides the logical concepts at the top with the physical implementation at the bottom. Conceptually, the IBM e-business framework is based on the on-demand business model operating environment, which has four essential characteristics: it is integrated, open, virtualized, and autonomic. These characteristics are explained later in this section.

Below the dotted line shows how this environment is implemented by the suite of IBM software products.

- Rational is the "build" brand; it is used to develop software.
- DB2 and WebSphere are the "run" brands; they store and manipulate your data and manage your applications.

- Tivoli is the "manage" brand; it integrates, provides security, and manages your overall systems.
- Lotus is the "collaborate" brand used for integration, messaging, and collaboration across all the other brands.

The IBM DB2 software brand plays a critical role in the on-demand operating environment. All elements of the DB2 portfolio are developed with the four essential characteristics of the on-demand business model in mind.

- **Integrated:** DB2 software has built-in support for both Microsoft and Java development environments. It is also integrated into WebSphere, Tivoli, Lotus, and Rational products. In addition, the DB2 family has cross-platform capabilities and can be integrated natively with Web services and message-queuing technologies. It also provides support for heterogeneous data sources for both structured and unstructured information.
- **Open**: DB2 software allows for different technologies to connect and integrate by following standards. Thus, it provides strong support for the Linux operating system and for Java, XML, Web services, grid computing, and other major industry applications.
- **Virtualized**: Grid computing technology, a type of distributed computing, collects and shares resources in a large network to simulate one large, virtual computer. DB2 software products support grid computing technology through federation and integration technologies. Both of these are discussed in more detail later in this chapter.
- **Autonomic**: An autonomic computing system manages, repairs, and protects itself. As systems become more complex, autonomic computing systems will likely become essential. DB2 software provides self-tuning capabilities, dynamic adjustment and tuning, simple and silent installation processes, and integration with Tivoli for system security and management.

The bottom of Figure 1.2 shows the operating systems in which the IBM software suite can operate: Linux, UNIX, Windows, OS/400[2], and z/OS; and below that, the servers, storage, and network represent the actual hardware used to support the framework.

1.3 DB2 UDB EDITIONS

DB2 UDB for Linux, UNIX, and Windows (sometimes referred to as **LUW**) is developed using the C/C++ language; more than ninety percent of the code is common among these platforms. The remaining code is unique to take full advantage of the underlying platform architecture; however, the database functionality on all of these platforms is the same.

Like any other C/C++ application, DB2 is written in separate modules—.c/.C source files—that have been separately compiled to obtain object files (.o files). These object files are later linked to obtain an executable file. Figure 1.3 shows a *simplified* view of how each edition is built.

---

2. The next generation of OS/400 is called IBM i5/OS.

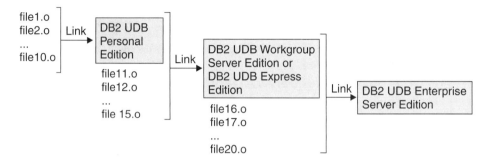

Figure 1.3   How DB2 editions build on top of each other

As you can see in Figure 1.3, each edition (other than DB2 UDB Everyplace, which is not shown in the figure) builds on top of the other by linking modules or object files that contain additional functionality. The core of the DB2 UDB code is common across all editions, which greatly benefits application development. For example, if you are developing an application for the DB2 UDB Personal Edition, this application will also work on the DB2 UDB Workgroup Server Edition, the DB2 UDB Express Edition, and the DB2 UDB Enterprise Server Edition on any of the supported platforms.

From the above explanation, it should be clear that the DB2 LUW editions are mainly packaging and licensing distinctions that let you choose the appropriate features or functions you need for the right price. The underlying technology is always DB2, so choose the appropriate edition based on the features and functions you need and which server(s) DB2 will be running.

> **N O T E**   DB2 UDB for OS/390 and z/OS, DB2 UDB for VM/VSE, and DB2 UDB for iSeries use a different code base than DB2 LUW. Note, however, that the Linux operating system extends across all of IBM's servers: xSeries, eSeries, pSeries, iSeries, and zSeries. DB2 UDB for Linux on all of these server platforms is the same. Thus, DB2 UDB for Linux on zSeries uses the same code base and is licensed in the same way as DB2 UDB for Linux on an xSeries (Intel) platform.

> **N O T E**   Refer to Appendix C, IBM Servers, for a description of the xSeries, eSeries, pSeries, iSeries, and zSeries servers.

Figure 1.4 illustrates the different editions and the types of servers they typically run on. DB2 takes advantage of all the processing power it is given, and the figure also shows that DB2 is a scalable product. With the exception of DB2 UDB Everyplace, the functions, features, and benefits of an edition shown on the bottom of the figure are included in each subsequent edition as you move up the figure. The following sections provide more detail on the functionality of each edition.

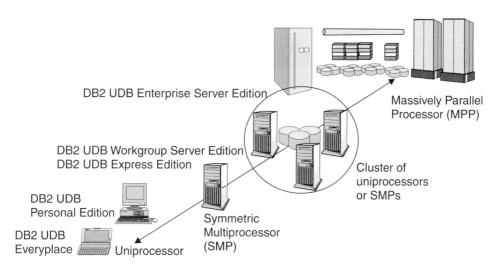

Figure 1.4   DB2 UDB editions

1.3.1 Everyplace Edition

As its name implies, the DB2 UDB Everyplace edition can run anywhere, anytime, in all kinds of small devices like personal digital assistants (PDAs), handheld computers, embedded devices, and laptops. DB2 UDB Everyplace, though only about 200K in size, is a true RDBMS that uses a subset of the DB2 UDB server SQL functionality. While database maintenance operations and some specific features like triggers are not supported, DB2 UDB Everyplace does include the DB2 UDB Everyplace Mobile Application Builder tool to develop, deploy, and support e-business applications. If you know how to code an application for a DB2 UDB server edition, you know how to code for DB2 UDB Everyplace. Applications can be developed using ODBC, CLI, JDBC, and .NET.

Typically, users of DB2 UDB Everyplace store information in the mobile database and later replicate it to a back-end database server using the DB2 UDB Everyplace Sync Server installed on another machine.

This edition supports operating systems that run on mobile devices.

- Embedded Linux
- Java 2 Micro Edition (J2ME) devices
- Microsoft Windows CE/PocketPC
- Palm OS
- QNX Neutrino
- Symbian
- Windows 32-bit operating systems

DB2 UDB Everyplace can be licensed as a fully synchronized environment or as a standalone embedded database.

1.3.2 Personal Edition

The DB2 UDB Personal Edition (PE) is a complete product for a single user. It has all the functionality of a database server, including the administration graphical tools, as well as audio, image,
spatial, and video extenders. While this edition can also be used as a client to connect to other DB2
servers, it does not support database connections from other computers. Only Windows and Linux
operating systems, which are the most commonly used platforms in *personal* computers, support the
DB2 UDB Personal Edition.

Figure 1.5 shows the DB2 UDB PE installed on Machine 2. The local DB2 client (the client
component of Machine 2) can connect to the DB2 UDB PE server on Machine 2, but the remote
DB2 client in Machine 1 cannot connect to the server on Machine 2 because DB2 UDB PE does
not accept remote (inbound) connections. The figure also shows the DB2 UDB PE on Machine 2
as the remote client to other DB2 UDB server editions installed on machines 3, 4, and 5.

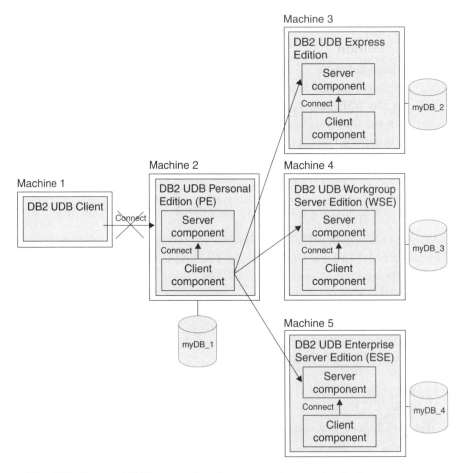

Figure 1.5   DB2 Personal Edition as a (local) server and a remote client

> **N O T E** A DB2 UDB database is considered a server when it can accept inbound client connections for data retrieval purposes. Hence, DB2 UDB Personal Edition is not considered a DB2 UDB server.

1.3.3 Workgroup Server Edition

The DB2 UDB Workgroup Server Edition (WSE) is a full-function database server designed for deployment in a department or small business environment. Linux, UNIX, and Windows platforms support the DB2 UDB WSE running on at most four CPU servers with a 32-bit operating system. It comes under two licensing models.

1. Licensing per user (ideal for applications with just a few users)
2. Licensing per processor (ideal for applications with many users, like a Web application)

This edition is referred to as Workgroup Server Unlimited Edition (WSUE) when using the per-processor licensing model because an unlimited number of users are allowed.

1.3.4 Express Edition

The DB2 UDB Express Edition, a low-cost, full-function database server, is ideal for a business that requires a database, but has minimal in-house database skills. This edition provides the same support as DB2 UDB WSE, but it also features one-click installation, enhanced self-management, and other ease-of-use features. Businesses developing applications that require a database can embed DB2 UDB Express Edition as part of their solution.

The supported operating systems for this edition are Windows and Linux (on Intel and AMD), running at most on two CPU 32-bit SMP hardware computers.

1.3.5 Enterprise Server Edition

The Enterprise Server Edition (ESE) is the most complete database server offering. It provides unparalleled scalability, accessibility, and extensibility features, as well as full 64-bit support, and is the edition of choice for most enterprises. It provides the same functionality as DB2 UDB WSE, but also includes DB2 Connect functionality, which provides licensed access for a single user to connect to host systems like DB2 UDB for iSeries or DB2 UDB for OS/390 and z/OS (zSeries).

DB2 UDB ESE includes the database partitioning feature (DPF), which allows you to partition your data within a single server or across multiple servers running the same operating system. This means that your databases can grow to sizes that are limited only by the number of servers available. DPF can be used when you buy the corresponding DPF license.

You can use DB2 UDB ESE in SMP systems, and DB2 UDB ESE with DPF can be used in either SMP or clustered server systems. The supported operating system platforms are Linux, UNIX, and Windows. Figure 1.6 summarizes all the DB2 editions and features.

DB2 UDB Everyplace
- Supported platforms: Palm OS, J2ME, Symbian, Windows, CE/Pocket PC, any 32-bit operating system, Neutrino. Embedded Linux
- True RDBMS, mainly for mobile users
- Supports applications written in ODBC, CLI, JDBC, .NET

DB2 UDB Personal Edition (PE)
- Supported platforms: Linux and Windows
- Supported users: 1 user
- Supported hardware: uniprocessors
- Fully functional RDBMS
- Does not accept remote client connections, only local
- Comes with the Administration Client
- Can work as a remote client to other servers
- Comes with audio, image, spatial, and video extenders for a single user
- Supports applications written in ODBC, CLI, JDBC, .NET

DB2 UDB Express Edition
- Supported platforms: Linux and Windows
- Supported users: Ideal for companies with 100 to 1,000 employees
- Supported hardware: Up to 2-way 32-bit SMP systems
- Fully functional RDBMS
- As a server, accepts remote and local client connections
- Comes with the Administration Client
- Can work as a remote client to other servers
- Comes with audio, image, spatial, and video extenders
- Includes easy to use features:
  - One-click installation
  - Self managing features
  - Minimal maintenance
- Supports applications written in ODBC, CLI, JDBC, .NET

DB2 UDB Workgroup Server Edition (WSE)
- Supported platforms: Linux, UNIX, and Windows
- Supported users: Ideal for a departmental or small business environments
- Supported hardware: Up to 4-way 32-bit SMP systems
- Fully functional RDBMS
- As a server, accepts remote and local client connections
- Comes with the Administration Client
- Can work as a remote client to other servers
- Comes with audio, image, and video extenders
- Optional
  - Net Search
  - Spatial extenders
- Supports applications written in ODBC, CLI, JDBC, .NET

DB2 UDB Enterprise Server Edition (ESE)
- Supported platforms: Linux, UNIX, and Windows
- Supported users: Ideal for large enterprise environments
- Supported hardware: uniprocessors, SMP, cluster of uniprocessor/SMP, and MPP systems
- Fully functional RDBMS
- As a server, accepts remote and local client connections
- Comes with the Administration Client
- Can work as a remote client to other servers
- Can work as a client to most systems (DB2 for z/OS and OS/390, DB2 for iSeries, DB2 for VM/VSE) as it includes DB2 Connect capability
- Comes with audio, image, and video extenders
- Optional:
  - Net Search and Spatial extenders
  - Data Links Manager
  - Warehouse Manager
  - Intelligent Miner
  - Database Partitioning Feature (DPF)
- Supports applications written in ODBC, CLI, JDBC, .NET

Figure 1.6 Summary of DB2 editions and features

1.4 DB2 UDB CLIENTS

To connect from a client machine to a DB2 UDB database server machine, you usually need to install DB2 UDB client software on the client machine. This isn't always required; for example, this isn't necessary for a JDBC application using the type 4 driver running on the client machine. We provide more detail about connectivity scenarios in Chapter 6, Configuring Client and Server Connectivity.

A DB2 UDB client installed on a different machine than the DB2 UDB server is known as a **remote client**. A remote client can establish communication to the server using any of these supported communication protocols: TCP/IP, NetBIOS (Windows only), APPC (IBM environments only), and Named Pipes (Windows only).

If the DB2 UDB client is installed on the same machine as a DB2 UDB server, then it is known as a **local client** and it connects to the server using inter-process communication (IPC) on the same machine. Note that since all DB2 UDB servers come with a local client component, you don't need to install the DB2 UDB client separately after installing a DB2 UDB server. Figure 1.7 shows local and remote clients. Client Machine 1 and 2 are remote clients with the DB2 UDB client code installed and are accessing Server Machine A, which has a DB2 UDB server installed. The DB2 UDB server has a client component that is the local client.

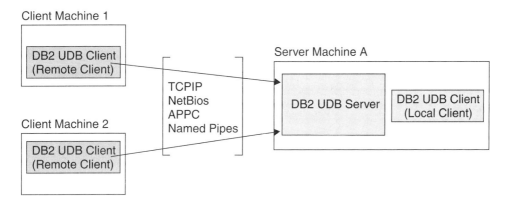

Figure 1.7   Local and remote DB2 UDB clients

There are four types of DB2 UDB clients:

- Thin clients
- Runtime clients
- Administration clients
- Application development clients

A **thin client**, also known as a **dumb terminal**, is a machine with no operating system or DB2 client code. All libraries and modules required to fulfill a request are loaded from a server having this code, including the DB2 client code. Figure 1.8 shows an example of thin clients. The DB2 client box represents the runtime, administration, or application development client.

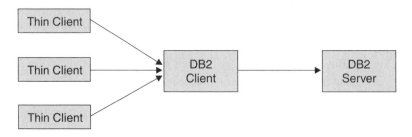

Figure 1.8   A thin client

Each DB2 client, other than the thin client, is built on top of the other types of clients. A **runtime client** has the minimum basic requirements to connect to DB2 servers and to provide basic client functionality. The **administration client** comes with everything the runtime client has, plus graphical administration tools. The **application development client** includes all of the functionality of the administration client, plus development tools and libraries. Figure 1.9 illustrates this client progression.

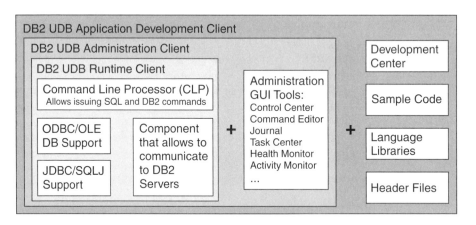

Figure 1.9   The DB2 Clients

V8.2 **1.5 "TRY AND BUY" VERSIONS**

Prior to Version 8.2, most Try and Buy versions of any of the DB2 UDB editions had a 90-day evaluation period. With Version 8.2, a new educational Try and Buy version provides a six-month evaluation period. The CD-ROM provided with this book includes the DB2 UDB ESE six-month Try and Buy version. Other than this time limitation, the Try and Buy version contains all the features of a fully licensed version. During or after the Try and Buy period you can buy a permanent license by calling 1-800-IBM-SERV. An IBM representative will direct you to the License Key Center. After the purchase, when you receive the license file, you can use it to upgrade the Try and Buy version to the fully licensed product level without reinstalling it. Use the following command from a Command Line Processor window to install the license file:

```
db2licm -a file_name
```

where *file_name* stands for the name of the license file, which normally has a .lic extension.

Issuing the **db2licm -l** command lists the software products installed in your machine and the current license. After adding the license, the Expiry Date field will have a value of *Permanent*. Chapter 3, Installing DB2, discusses more about the **db2licm** command and the License Center.

> **N O T E** Licensing policies, as well as the evaluation period, are subject to change. The information in this section is accurate as of the time this book was written.

1.6 HOST CONNECTIVITY

DB2 Connect is the software product containing the licensed files required to communicate from a DB2 distributed client, also known as the **DRDA Application Requester**, to a host DB2 server, a **DRDA Application Server**. (DRDA—Distributed Relational Database Architecture— is the standard that defines formats and protocols for providing transparent access to remote data.) Host DB2 servers include DB2 UDB for z/OS and OS/390, DB2 UDB for VM/VSE, and DB2 UDB for iSeries. DB2 Connect also includes a DB2 runtime client.

As indicated earlier, if you install DB2 UDB ESE there is no need to install DB2 Connect since DB2 UDB ESE comes with a DB2 Connect component.

> **N O T E** DB2 Connect software is only required when communicating from a workstation to a host; it is *not* required in the other direction (from a host to a workstation).

DB2 Connect comes in two main flavors.

- The Personal Edition supports the direct connection of one DB2 client to multiple host DB2 servers.
- The Enterprise Edition supports the connection of multiple DB2 clients to multiple host DB2 servers via a DB2 Connect server.

1.7 FEDERATED SUPPORT

Federation allows you to query and manipulate data stored on other servers and in other RDBMSs. When you issue an SQL statement in a federated environment, you may actually be accessing information from multiple databases and potentially multiple RDBMSs (see Figure 1.10).

Federated support is included in DB2 when the other databases being accessed are part of the IBM DB2 family, that is, another DB2 database or an Informix database. For accessing databases from other vendors, refer to the IBM DB2 Information Integrator product described in section 1.9.

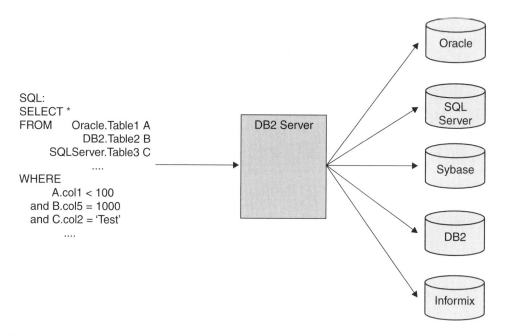

Figure 1.10   DB2 federation

1.8 REPLICATION SUPPORT

Replication lets you propagate data to different servers to keep different databases synchronized. Data changes captured at one server are later applied to another (target) server, as illustrated in Figure 1.11. In the figure, the first box shows the source server and the fourth box

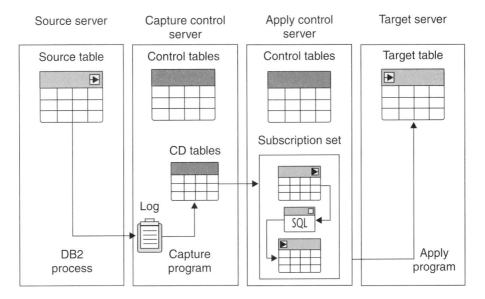

Figure 1.11 DB2 replication environment

shows the target server. The second and third boxes contain the "capture" and "apply" components, respectively.

DB2 UDB has built-in support for replication when source and target databases are part of the IBM family, which includes Informix. For databases from other vendors, such as Oracle or SQL Server, the IBM DB2 Information Integrator software is required.

1.9 IBM DB2 INFORMATION INTEGRATOR

The IBM DB2 **Information Integrator** (**II**) provides federated support by masking databases from IBM or different vendors as if they were part of the same database. The II uses wrappers to communicate with and retrieve data from these other data sources; II encapsulates any conversions required from the source database and presents them to the target database as tables.

The Replication Edition of IBM DB2 Information Integrator supports the propagation of data between DB2 UDB, Microsoft SQL Server, Oracle, and others.

1.10 SPECIAL PACKAGE OFFERINGS FOR DEVELOPERS

Two special offerings are available for application developers.

- The DB2 Personal Developer's Edition (PDE), for Linux and Windows platforms, comes with DB2 UDB Personal Edition, DB2 Connect Personal Edition, and all the DB2 clients.

- The DB2 Universal Developer's Edition (UDE), for Linux, UNIX, and Windows platforms, comes with all server editions, with the exception of the database partitioning feature and optional extenders. In addition, all the DB2 clients are also provided.

Both editions come at a reduced price, and are restricted to the development, evaluation, demonstration, and testing of application programs. Figure 1.12 shows most of the software provided with each offering. For a detailed listing of the features included with each offering, refer to the DB2 for Linux, UNIX, and Windows main Web page at http://www.ibm.com/software/data/db2/udb/.

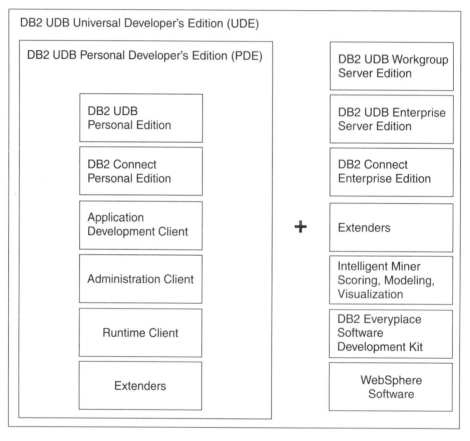

Figure 1.12   Special package offerings for application developers

1.11 DB2 SYNTAX DIAGRAM CONVENTIONS

DB2 supports a comprehensive set of statements for data access and manipulation. These statements are documented online in the DB2 Information Center, which gives you access to all information about DB2 UDB as well as major DB2 features and components. It can be conveniently accessed by using a browser, as shown in Figure 1.13. The DB2 Information Center is also available through the Internet at http://publib.boulder.ibm.com/infocenter/db2help.

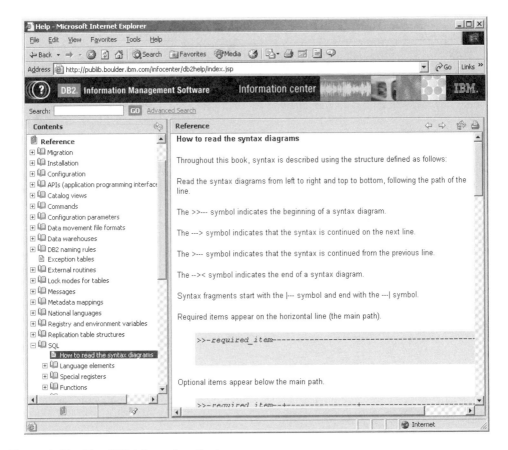

Figure 1.13   The DB2 Information Center

You can find the syntax of the statements we introduce in this book in the DB2 Information Center. Understanding how to read the syntax diagrams will help you use the numerous options available with many of the statements.

Syntax diagrams are all read from left to right and top to bottom following the path of each line. Table 1.2 summarizes a few of the most commonly used symbols in a syntax diagram.

Table 1.2   Summary of Some Symbols Used in Syntax Diagrams

Symbol	Description
`>>---`	Indicates the beginning of a syntax diagram.
`--->`	Indicates that the syntax is continued on the next line.
`>---`	Indicates that the syntax is continued from the previous line.
`--->< `	Indicates the end of a syntax diagram.

When a mandatory field is required, it appears on the horizontal line (the main path) like this.

```
>>-mandatory_field------------------------------------><
```

Optional fields appear below the main path.

```
>>-mandatory_field--+---------------+-----------------><
                    '-optional_field-'
```

If an optional field appears above the main path, it means that it is the default option.

```
                    .-default_field-.
>>-mandatory_field--+---------------+-----------------><
                    '-optional_field-'
```

If two or more mandatory choices are available, one of the mandatory choices will appear in the main path, and the rest will appear in a stack. You must choose one of these options.

```
>>-mandatory_field--+-mandatory_choice1-+--------------><
                    '-mandatory_choice2-'
```

An arrow returning to the left, above the main line, indicates an option can be repeated. In this example, repeated options are separated by one or more blanks.

```
                       .----------------.
                       V                |
>>-mandatory_field----repeatable_field-+---------------><
```

If the repeat arrow contains a comma, you must separate repeated items with a comma.

```
                       .-,--------------.
                       V                |
>>-mandatory_field----repeatable_field-+---------------><
```

You now know how to read syntax diagrams in the DB2 manuals. Browse through the DB2 online documentation and review some examples there.

1.12 CASE STUDY

John recently graduated from Pennsylvania State University, where he learned DB2 UDB as part of the IBM Scholars' program, a program that provides DB2 UDB for free to teach database skills.

While at school, he worked with the DB2 UDB Enterprise Server Edition installed in a pSeries machine at the university computer lab. He was given SYSADM authority, and he was able to see connections from many different clients to all created databases using the `list applications` command. John wanted to develop a Java application using the JDBC type 2 application driver, so he downloaded and installed the six-month Try and Buy version of DB2 UDB Personal Edition. After he installed this edition, he realized that only the Administration client was included, but that he needed the application development (AD) client for some library and header files to develop the program. Fortunately, all DB2 UDB clients are free of charge, so he downloaded the AD client from the IBM DB2 support Web site (see the Resources section at the end of this book), and he was then able to build, test, and run his application against the DB2 UDB Personal Edition on his laptop. Since the client and database server were both on his laptop, he was dealing with a local client connection.

John wanted to test whether his application would work as a remote client, so he used the client software that comes with DB2 UDB Personal Edition to test his application against the database he had created earlier on the university's pSeries computer. This also worked, and John was feeling like a DB2 guru.

Eager to show his program to his colleagues, he emailed the executable to his friend Peter, who had just bought a new laptop with Microsoft Windows XP Professional Edition installed. Peter detached the file and tried to run the application against John's database on the University's pSeries server. After spending a few hours trying to figure out why he couldn't, he dropped by John's place. John realized that Peter had to install a DB2 client, as this is a requirement for JDBC type 2 programs. Given that Peter was neither going to develop a new program nor administer a database, John asked Peter to download the runtime client from the IBM Web site. He also asked him to issue a few commands to set up the connectivity between the client and the server . . . and voila, the program successfully ran. Peter then asked John to perform the test from his laptop against the database on John's laptop, but John said it would not work because he had installed DB2 UDB Personal Edition, which is not a database server, and it cannot accept inbound remote client connections.

After the graduation ceremony, John received a PDA as a gift from his dad. His dad had heard John praise DB2, so he had had DB2 Everyplace installed on the PDA. Since John was going to take six months off to travel before looking for a job, John decided to take his PDA with him rather than his laptop. John's account at the university was going to be active for the next nine months, so while he was traveling he could connect to his "old" database on the pSeries and use his application (which he had installed on his PDA) to transfer information about all the friends he met and places he visited during his trip. This way he was able to save information in another place should he lose his PDA.

After his trip, John applied for a position at a medium-sized company in his hometown. To prepare for his interview, John again tested the program he had written against his laptop database, but the Try and Buy evaluation period had expired. John figured that he would always need DB2 UDB on his laptop, so he decided to buy the permanent license. When John received the license file after the purchase, he installed it on his laptop with the command `db2licm -a filename`. Once this problem was resolved, John showed his program during the job interview and was immediately hired.

Company ABC, which was using DB2 UDB Workgroup Server Edition, asked John to modify his application so that it would connect to a DB2 UDB for z/OS host machine. John responded that he did not need to make any modifications, but since DB2 UDB Workgroup Server Edition does not come with the DB2 Connect software component, either the company needed to purchase this software, or obtain the DB2 UDB Enterprise Server Edition. Given that the ABC company was a software development company, John suggested purchasing the DB2 Universal Developer's Edition (UDE), as it would be cheaper and has all of the software for all DB2 UDB editions. If ABC company wanted to use DB2 in a production environment, they would not be able to use DB2 UDE, but would have to buy the appropriate license.

Company ABC was also interested in the DB2 UDB Express Edition, because one of their applications needs a database to be embedded as part of their solution. Other than John, there are not many skilled DB2 personnel in the company, so DB2 UDB Express is also ideal because of its ease-of-use features.

Three months after John was hired, he was promoted. John is well on his way to a very successful career with DB2 UDB!

1.13 SUMMARY

This chapter introduced DB2 and its history. IBM pioneered relational database management systems and invented SQL. IBM's technology in the relational management system area has been around for more than twenty years. Its legacy is visible in the DB2 product line, which now represents a portfolio of information management products: database management software, business intelligence software, content management software, information integrator software, and DB2 and IMS tools.

You also learned about the types of clients and servers available with DB2. Although different editions are available to provide varying functionality, the core DB2 product is the same; therefore, application development on any edition will work on all editions. The various editions allow you to choose the functions that best suit your needs.

The chapter also discussed federated support, replication, the IBM DB2 Information Integrator, and packaging options available for application developers. These packaging options allow developers to obtain DB2 software at a reduced price.

1.14 REVIEW QUESTIONS

1. IBM added the term "Universal" to the DB2 name with Version 5 of the product. Why was this term added?

2. Which five software brands support the IBM on-demand strategy?

3. Can an application developed for DB2 UDB Personal Edition work with DB2 UDB Enterprise Server Edition?

4. Is DB2 Connect required to connect from a DB2 for z/OS client to a DB2 for Linux, UNIX, and Windows server?

5. Why would DB2 UDB WSUE be more appropriate than DB2 UDB WSE for a Web application with an average of 1,000 users?

6. Is IBM DB2 Information Integrator required to set up a federation environment between a DB2 server and an Informix server?

7. Provide an example when replication support may be required.

8. Does DB2 for Linux, UNIX, and Windows have one single file that is used for installation in any of these platforms?

9. What does the database partitioning feature (DPF) allow you to do?

10. What should you do if your Try and Buy period expires and you would like to buy a permanent license?

11. Which of the following products is the minimum required on the Windows client to *run* a DB2 application accessing a DB2 database on UNIX?
    A. DB2 ESE
    B. DB2 Personal Edition
    C. DB2 Connect
    D. DB2 Runtime Client

12. Which of the following products is required to *write* a DB2 application using JDBC?
    A. Thin Client
    B. Runtime Client
    C. Administration Client
    D. Application Development Client

13. Which of the following products does not allow applications to connect to its databases from remote clients?
    A. DB2 Express
    B. DB2 Personal Edition
    C. DB2 Enterprise Server Edition
    D. DB2 Workgroup Server Edition

14. Which of the following products is *not* considered a DB2 server?
    A. DB2 UDB Workgroup Server Edition
    B. DB2 UDB Workgroup Server Unlimited Edition
    C. DB2 UDB Personal Edition
    D. DB2 UDB Enterprise Server Edition

15. Which of the following DB2 clients provide the DB2 graphical administration tools?

    A. Thin client

    B. Application Development client

    C. Thick client

    D. Runtime client

16. Which of the following DB2 editions is the most appropriate for sales personnel who need a basic database to store contacts and business leads made during business trips?

    A. DB2 Everywhere

    B. DB2 Satellite Edition

    C. DB2 Everyplace

    D. DB2 Personal Edition

17. A software development company would like to test an application that connects to both DB2 for LUW as well as DB2 for z/OS. Which of the following would suit its needs the best?

    A. DB2 UDB Enterprise Server Edition

    B. DB2 UDB Workgroup Server Edition

    C. DB2 Connect Enterprise Edition

    D. DB2 UDE

18. Which of the following products can run on a zSeries server?

    A. DB2 UDB for Linux, UNIX, and Windows

    B. DB2 UDB for iSeries

    C. DB2 Connect

    D. IBM DB2 Information Integrator

19. Which of the following products allows ten clients to connect from DB2 LUW to DB2 for z/OS?

    A. DB2 UDE

    B. DB2 PDE

    C. DB2 UDB

    D. DB2 LUW

20. Which of the following products can be used to collect, prepare, and analyze your data to allow you to make better business decisions?

    A. DB2 Content Manager

    B. DB2 Warehouse Manager

    C. IBM DB2 Information Integrator

    D. DB2 LUW

CHAPTER **2**

DB2 at a Glance:
The Big Picture

This chapter is like a book within a book: it covers a vast range of topics that will provide you not only with a good introduction to DB2 core concepts and components, but also with an understanding of how these components work together and where they fit in the "DB2 puzzle." After reading this chapter you should have a general knowledge of the DB2 architecture that will help you better understand the topics discussed in the next chapters. Subsequent chapters will revisit and expand what has been discussed here.

In this chapter you will learn about:

- SQL statements and DB2 commands
- DB2 tools
- The DB2 environment
- Federation
- The database partitioning feature

You work with DB2 by issuing SQL statements and DB2 commands. To issue these statements and commands, you use DB2 tools. The DB2 tools interact with the DB2 environment by passing these statements and commands to the DB2 server for processing. This is shown in Figure 2.1.

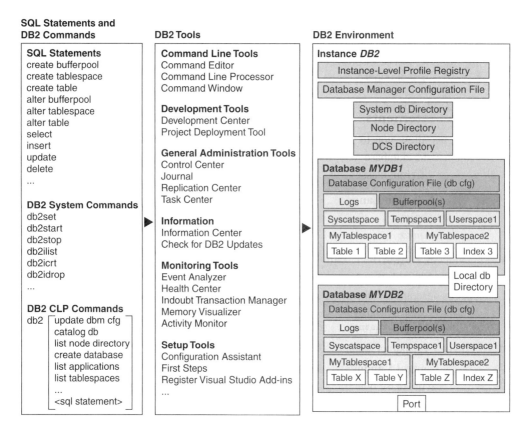

Figure 2.1   Overview of DB2

2.1 SQL STATEMENTS AND DB2 COMMANDS

SQL is the standard language used for retrieving and modifying data in a relational database. An SQL council formed by several industry leading companies determines the standard for these SQL statements, and the different relational database management systems (RDBMSs) follow these standards to make it easier for customers to use their databases. This section introduces the different categories of SQL statements and presents some examples.

DB2 commands are directives specific to DB2 that allow you to perform tasks against a DB2 server. There are two types of DB2 commands:

- System commands
- Command Line Processor (CLP) commands

> **N O T E** SQL statements and DB2 commands can be specified in uppercase or lowercase. However, in Linux/UNIX some of the commands are case-sensitive; see Appendix B for a detailed explanation of the use of uppercase versus lowercase in DB2.

2.1.1 SQL Statements

SQL statements allow you to work with the data stored in your database. The statements are applied against the database you are connected to, not against the entire DB2 environment. There are three different classes of SQL statements.

- **Data Definition Language (DDL)** statements create, modify, or drop database objects. For example:

```
CREATE INDEX ix1 ON t1 (salary)
ALTER TABLE t1 ADD hiredate DATE
DROP VIEW view1
```

- **Data Manipulation Language (DML)** statements insert, update, delete, or select data from the database objects. For example:

```
INSERT INTO t1 VALUES (10,'Johnson','Peter')
UPDATE t1 SET lastname = 'Smith' WHERE firstname = 'Peter'
DELETE FROM t1
SELECT * FROM t1 WHERE salary > 45000
```

- **Data Control Language (DCL)** statements grant or revoke privileges or authorities to perform database operations on the objects in your database. For example:

```
GRANT   select ON employee TO peter
REVOKE update ON employee FROM paul
```

> **N O T E** SQL statements are commonly referred to simply as "statements" in most RDBMS books. For detailed syntax of SQL statements, see the *DB2 UDB SQL Reference* manual.

> **N O T E** The file *Command_and_SQL_Examples.pdf* on the CD-ROM accompanying this book includes a list of all SQL statements and DB2 commands and has examples for each one.

2.1.2 DB2 System Commands

You use DB2 system commands for many purposes, including starting services or processes, invoking utilities, and configuring parameters. Most DB2 system commands do not require the instance—the DB2 server engine process—to be started (instances are discussed later in this chapter). DB2 system command names have the format

```
db2x
```

where *x* represents one or more characters. For example:

```
db2start
db2set
db2icrt
```

> **NOTE**   Many DB2 system commands provide a quick way to
> obtain syntax and help information about the command by using the
> **-h** option. For example, typing **db2set -h** displays the syntax of the
> **db2set** command, with an explanation of its optional parameters.

2.1.3 DB2 Command Line Processor (CLP) Commands

DB2 CLP commands are processed by the CLP tool (introduced in the next section). These commands typically require the instance to be started, and they can be used for database and instance monitoring and for parameter configuration. For example:

```
list applications
create database
catalog tcpip node
```

You invoke the Command Line Processor by entering **db2** at an operating system prompt. If you enter **db2** and press the Enter key, you would be working with the CLP in interactive mode, and you can enter the CLP commands as shown above. On the other hand, if you don't want to work with the CLP in interactive mode, prefix each CLP command with **db2**. For example:

```
db2 list applications
db2 create database
db2 catalog tcpip node
```

Many books, including this one, display CLP commands as db2 *CLP_command* for this reason. Chapter 4, Using the DB2 Tools, explains the CLP in greater detail.

> **NOTE**   On the Windows platform, **db2** must be entered in the
> DB2 Command Window, not at the operating system prompt. The DB2
> Command Window and the DB2 CLP are discussed in detail in Chapter
> 4, Using the DB2 Tools.

> **NOTE**   A quick way to obtain syntax and help information about a
> CLP command is to use the question mark (**?**) character followed by
> the command. For example:
>
> db2 ? catalog tcpip node
>
> or just
>
> db2 ? catalog
>
> For detailed syntax of a command, see the *DB2 UDB Command Reference* manual.

2.2 DB2 TOOLS OVERVIEW

Figure 2.2 shows all the tools available from the IBM DB2 menu. The IBM DB2 menu on a Windows system can be typically displayed by choosing **Start > Programs > IBM DB2**. On a Linux/UNIX system, the operating system's graphical support needs to be installed. DB2's graphical interface looks the same on all platforms. This section briefly introduces the tools presented in the IBM DB2 menu. Chapter 4 covers these tools in more detail, but for now simply familiarize yourself with them.

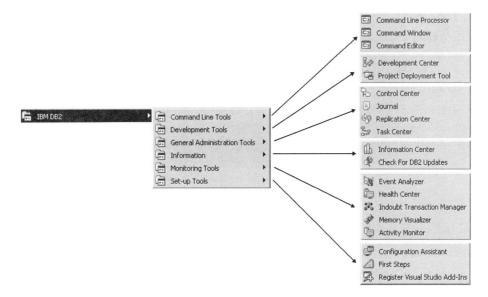

Figure 2.2   The IBM DB2 menus

2.2.1 Command Line Tools

Command line tools, as the name implies, allow you to issue DB2 commands and SQL statements from a command line interface. The two text-based interfaces are the Command Line Processor (CLP) and the Command Window. The Command Window is available only on Windows, while the CLP is available on all other platforms.

The Command Editor is a graphical interface tool that provides the same functionality as the text-based tools—and more. It also has the ability to invoke the Visual Explain tool, which shows the access path for the query.

2.2.2 Development Tools

Development tools allow developers to easily write and test stored procedures and user-defined functions, as well as to deploy them to different databases. DB2 provides two development tools.

- The **Development Center** provides developers with an environment where they can develop and test database application objects like stored procedures.
- The **Project Deployment Tool** lets developers deploy their Development Center project to another database.

2.2.3 General Administration Tools

The general administration tools allow database administrators (DBAs) to manage their database servers and databases from a central location.

- The **Control Center** is the most important of these tools. Not only does it support the administration of DB2 database servers on the Linux, UNIX, and Windows platforms, but also on the OS/390 and z/OS platforms. From the Control Center, database objects can be created, altered, and dropped. The tool also comes with several advisors to help you configure your system more quickly.
- The **Journal** tool can help investigate problems in the system. It tracks error messages and scheduled tasks that have been executed.
- The **Replication Center** lets you set up and manage your replication environment. Use DB2 replication when you want to propagate data from one location to another.
- The **Task Center** allows you to schedule tasks to be performed automatically. For example, you can arrange for a backup task to run at a time when there is minimal database activity.

2.2.4 Information Tools

The Information menu provides easy access to the DB2 documentation. The **Information Center** provides a fast and easy method to search the DB2 manuals. You can install the Information Center locally on your computer or intranet server, or access it via the Internet. Use the **Check for DB2 Updates** menu option to obtain the most up-to-date information about updates to the DB2 product.

2.2.5 Monitoring Tools

To maintain your database system, DB2 provides several tools that can help pinpoint the cause of a problem or even detect problems proactively before they cause performance deterioration.

- The **Event Analyzer** processes the information collected by an event monitor based on the occurrence of an event. For example, when two applications cannot continue their processing because the other is holding resources they need, a deadlock event occurs. This event is captured by an event monitor, and you can use the Event Analyzer to examine the captured data related to the deadlock and help resolve the contention. Some other events that can be captured are connections to the database, buffer pool activity, table space activity, table activity, SQL statements, and transactions.
- The **Health Center** detects problems before they happen by setting up thresholds which when exceeded cause alert notifications to be sent. The DBA can then choose to execute a recommended action to relieve the situation.

- The **Indoubt Transaction Manager** can help resolve issues with transactions that have been prepared but have not been committed or rolled back. This is only applicable to two-phase commit transactions.
- The **Memory Visualizer** tool lets you track the memory used by DB2. It plots a graph so you can easily monitor memory consumption.
- The **Activity Monitor** allows you to monitor application performance and concurrency, resource consumption, and SQL statement execution for a database. You can more easily diagnose problems with the reports this tool generates.

2.2.6 Setup Tools

The Setup tools help you configure your system to connect to remote servers, provide tutorials, and install add-ins to development tools.

- **First Steps** is a good starting point for new DB2 users who wish to become familiar with the product. This tool allows you to create a sample database and provides tutorials that help you familiarize yourself with DB2.
- The **Configuration Assistant** allows you to easily configure your system to connect to remote databases and to test the connection.
- The **Register Visual Studio Add-Ins** menu item lets you add a plug-in into Microsoft Visual Studio so that DB2 tools can be invoked from Visual Basic, Visual C++, and Visual InterDev. In each of these Microsoft development tools, the add-in inserts the DB2 menu entries into the tool's View, Tools, and Help menus. These add-ins provide Microsoft Visual Studio programmers with a rich set of application development tools to create stored procedures and user-defined functions designed for DB2.

2.2.7 Other Tools

The following are other DB2 tools that are not invoked directly from the DB2 menus.

- The **License Center** summarizes the licenses installed in your DB2 system and allows you to manage them.
- **Visual Explain** describes the access plan chosen by the DB2 optimizer, the brain of DB2, to access and retrieve information from tables.
- **SQL Assist** aids new users who are not familiar with the SQL language to write SQL queries.
- The **Satellite Administration Center** helps you set up and administer both satellites and the central satellite control server.

2.3 THE DB2 ENVIRONMENT

Several items control the behavior of your database system. We first describe the DB2 environment on a single-partition database, and in section 2.6, Database Partitioning Feature, we expand the material to include concepts relevant to a multipartition database system (we don't want to overload you with information not required at this stage in the chapter).

Figure 2.3 provides an overview of the DB2 environment. Consider the following when you review this figure:

- The figure may look complex, but don't be overwhelmed by first impressions! Each item in the figure will be discussed in detail in the following sections.
- Since we reference Figure 2.3 throughout this chapter, *we strongly recommend that you bookmark page 31.* Alternatively, since this figure is available in color as a GIF file on the CD-ROM provided with this book (Figure_2_3.gif), consider printing it.
- The commands shown in the figure can be issued from the Command Window on Windows or the operating system prompt on Linux/UNIX. Chapter 4, Using the DB2 Tools, describes equivalent methods to perform these commands from the DB2 graphical tools.
- Each arrow points to a set of three commands. The first command in each set (in blue if you printed the figure using a color printer) inquires about the contents of a configuration file, the second command (in black) indicates the syntax to modify these contents, and the third command (in purple) illustrates how to use the command.
- The numbers in parentheses in Figure 2.3 match the superscripts in the headings in the following subsections.

2.3.1 An Instance[1]

In DB2, an instance provides an independent environment where databases can be created and applications can be run against them. Because of these independent environments, databases in separate instances can have the same name. For example, in Figure 2.3 the database called *MYDB2* is associated to instance *DB2*, and another database called *MYDB2* is associated to instance *myinst*. Instances allow users to have separate, independent environments for production, test, and development purposes.

When DB2 is installed on the Windows platform, an instance named *DB2* is created by default. In the Linux and UNIX environments, if you choose to create the default instance, it is called *db2inst1*.

To create an instance explicitly, use:

```
db2icrt instance_name
```

To drop an instance, use:

```
db2idrop instance_name
```

To start the current instance, use:

```
db2start
```

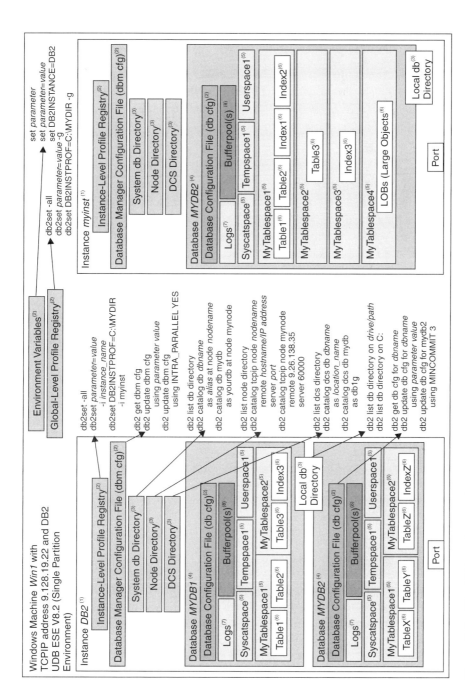

Figure 2.3 The DB2 environment

To stop the current instance, use:

```
db2stop
```

When an instance is created on Linux and UNIX, logical links to the DB2 executable code are generated. For example, if the machine in Figure 2.3 was a Linux/UNIX machine and the instances *DB2* and *myinst* were created, both of them would be linked to the same DB2 code. A logical link works as an alias or pointer to another program. In Windows, there is a shared install path, and all instances access the same libraries and executables.

2.3.2 The Database Administration Server

The Database Administration Server (DAS) is a daemon or process running on the database server that allows for remote graphical administration from remote clients using the Control Center. If you don't need to administer your DB2 server using a graphical interface from a remote client, you don't need to start the DAS. There can only be one DAS per server machine regardless of the number of instances on the machine. Note that the DAS needs to be running at the database server you are planning to administer remotely, not at the DB2 client.

To start the DAS, use the command:

```
db2admin start
```

To stop the DAS, use the command:

```
db2admin stop
```

2.3.3 Configuration Files and the DB2 Profile Registries[2]

Like many other RDBMSs, DB2 uses different mechanisms to influence the behavior of the database management system. These include:

- Environment variables
- DB2 profile registry variables
- Configuration parameters

2.3.3.1 Environment Variables

Environment variables are defined at the operating system level. On Windows you can create a new entry for a variable or edit the value of an existing one by choosing **Control Panel** > **System** > **Advanced Tab** > **Environment Variables**. On Linux and UNIX you can normally add a line to execute the script **db2profile** (Bourne or Korn shell) or **db2cshrc** (C shell) (provided after DB2 installation), to the instance owner's .login or .profile initialization files.

The DB2INSTANCE environment variable allows you to specify the current active instance to which all commands apply. If DB2INSTANCE is set to *myinst*, then issuing the command **CREATE DATABASE mydb** will create a database associated to instance *myinst*. If you wanted to create this database in instance *DB2*, you would first change the value of the DB2INSTANCE variable to *DB2*.

Using the Control Panel (Windows) or the user profile (Linux/UNIX) to set the value of an environment variable guarantees that value the next time you open a window or session. If you only want to change this value temporarily while in a given window or session, you can use the operating system **set** command on Windows, or **export** on Linux/UNIX. The command

```
set DB2INSTANCE=DB2 (on Windows)
```

or

```
export DB2INSTANCE=DB2 (on Linux and UNIX)
```

sets the value of the DB2INSTANCE environment variable to *DB2*. A common mistake when using the command is to leave spaces before and/or after the equal sign (=)—no spaces should be entered.

To check the current setting of this variable, you can use any of these three commands:

```
echo %DB2INSTANCE% (Windows only)
set DB2INSTANCE
db2 get instance
```

For a list of all available instances in your system, issue the following command:

```
db2ilist
```

2.3.3.2 The DB2 Profile Registry

The word "registry" always causes confusion when working with DB2 on Windows. The DB2 profile registry variables, or simply the DB2 registry variables, have no relation whatsoever with the Windows Registry variables. The DB2 registry variables provide a centralized location where some key variables influencing DB2's behavior reside.

> **N O T E**   Some of the DB2 registry variables are platform-specific.

The DB2 Profile Registry is divided into four categories.

- The DB2 instance-level profile registry
- The DB2 global-level profile registry
- The DB2 instance node-level profile registry
- The DB2 instance profile registry

The first two are the most common ones. The main difference between the global-level and the instance-level profile registries, as you can tell from their names, is the level to which the variables apply. Global-level profile registry variables apply to all instances on the server. As you can see from Figure 2.3, this registry has been drawn outside of the two instance boxes. Instance-level profile registry variables apply to a specific instance. You can see separate instance-level profile registry boxes inside each of the two instances in the figure.

To view the current DB2 registry variables, issue the following command from the CLP:

```
db2set -all
```

You may get output like this:

```
[i] DB2INSTPROF=C:\PROGRAM FILES\SQLLIB
[g] DB2SYSTEM=PRODSYS
```

As you may have already guessed, `[i]` indicates the variable has been defined at the instance level, while `[g]` indicates that it has been defined at the global level.

The following are a few other commands related to DB2 Registry variables.

To view all the registry variables that can be defined in DB2, use this command:

```
db2set -lr
```

To set the value of a specific variable (in this example, DB2INSTPROF) at the global level, use:

```
db2set DB2INSTPROF="C:\PROGRAM FILES\SQLLIB" -g
```

To set a variable at the instance level for instance *myinst*, use:

```
db2set DB2INSTPROF="C:\MY FILES\SQLLIB" -i myinst
```

Note that for the above commands, the same variable has been set at both levels: the global level and the instance level. When a registry variable is defined at different levels, DB2 will always choose the value at the lowest level, in this case the instance level.

For the **db2set** command, as with the **set** command discussed earlier, there are no spaces before or after the equal sign.

Some registry variables require you to stop and start the instance (**db2stop/db2start**) for the change to take effect. Other registry variables do not have this requirement. Refer to the *DB2 UDB Administration Guide: Performance* for a list of variables that have this requirement.

2.3.3.3 Configuration Parameters

Configuration parameters are defined at two different levels: the instance level and the database level. The variables at each level are different (not like DB2 registry variables, where the same variables can be defined at different levels).

At the instance level, variables are stored in the Database Manager Configuration file (dbm cfg). Changes to these variables affect all databases associated to this instance, which is why Figure 2.3 shows a Database Manager Configuration file box defined per instance and outside the databases.

To view the contents of the Database Manager Configuration file, issue the command:

```
db2 get dbm cfg
```

To update the value of a specific variable, use:

```
db2 update dbm cfg using parameter value
```

For example:

```
db2 update dbm cfg using INTRA_PARALLEL YES
```

With Version 8, many of the Database Manager Configuration parameters are now "configurable online," meaning the change is dynamic—you don't need to stop and start the instance. The file *ConfigurationParameters.pdf* included on the CD-ROM accompanying this book provides a short description of the Database Manager Configuration parameters and indicates whether they are configurable online.

At the database level, parameter values are stored in the Database Configuration file (db cfg). Changes to these parameters only affect the specific database. In Figure 2.3 you can see there is a Database Configuration file box inside each of the databases defined.

To view the contents of the Database Configuration file, issue the command:

```
db2 get db cfg for dbname
```

For example:

```
db2 get db cfg for mydb2
```

To update a value of a specific variable, use:

```
db2 update db cfg for dbname using parameter value
```

For example:

```
db2 update db cfg for mydb2 using MINCOMMIT 3
```

With Version 8 many of these parameters are configurable online, meaning that the change is dynamic, and you no longer need to disconnect all connections to the database for the change to take effect. The file *ConfigurationParameters.pdf* included on the book's CD-ROM provides a short description of the Database Configuration parameters and indicates whether they are configurable online.

2.3.4 Connectivity and DB2 Directories[3]

In DB2, directories are used to store connectivity information about databases and the servers on which they reside. There are four main directories, which are described in the following subsections. The corresponding commands to set up database and server connectivity are also included; however, many users find the Configuration Assistant graphical tool very convenient to set up database and server connectivity.

Chapter 6, Configuring Client and Server Connectivity, discusses all the commands and concepts described in this section in detail, including the Configuration Assistant.

2.3.4.1 System Database Directory

The system database directory (or system db directory) is the main "table of contents" that contains information about all the databases to which you can connect from your DB2 system. As you can see from Figure 2.3, the system db directory is stored at the instance level.

To list the contents of the system db directory, use the command:

```
db2 list db directory
```

Any entry from the output of this command containing the word *Indirect* indicates that the entry is for a local database, that is, a database that resides on the database server on which you are working. The entry also points to the local database directory indicated by the *Database drive* item (Windows) or *Local database directory* (Linux/UNIX).

Any entry containing the word *Remote* indicates that the entry is for a remote database—a database residing on a server other than the one on which you are currently working. The entry also points to the node directory entry indicated by the *Node name* item.

To enter information into the system database directory, use the **catalog** command:

```
db2 catalog db dbname as alias  at node nodename
```

For example:

```
db2 catalog db mydb    as yourdb at node mynode
```

The **catalog** commands are normally used only when adding information for remote databases. For local databases, a catalog entry is automatically created after creating the database with the **CREATE DATABASE** command.

2.3.4.2 Local Database Directory

The local database directory contains information about databases residing on the server where you are currently working. Figure 2.3 shows the local database directory overlapping the database box. This means that there will be one local database directory associated to all of the databases residing in the same location (the drive on Windows or the path on Linux/UNIX). The local database directory does not reside inside the database itself, but it does not reside at the instance level either; it is in a layer between these two. (After you read section 2.3.10, The Internal Implementation of the DB2 Environment, it will be easier to understand this concept.)

Note also from Figure 2.3 that there is no specific command used to enter information into this directory, only to retrieve it. When you create a database with the **CREATE DATABASE** command, an entry is added to this directory.

To list the contents of the local database directory, issue the command:

```
db2 list db directory on drive / path
```

where **drive** can be obtained from the item *Database drive* (Windows) or **path** from the item *Local database directory* (Linux/UNIX) in the corresponding entry of the system db directory.

2.3.4.3 Node Directory

The node directory stores all connectivity information for remote database servers. For example, if you use the TCP/IP protocol, this directory shows entries such as the host name or IP address of the server where the database to which you want to connect resides, and the port number of the associated DB2 instance.

To list the contents of the node directory, issue the command:

```
db2 list node directory
```

To enter information into the node directory, use:

```
db2 catalog tcpip node node_name
    remote hostname or IP_address
    server service_name or port_number
```

For example:

```
db2 catalog tcpip node mynode
    remote 192.168.1.100
    server 60000
```

You can obtain the port number of the remote instance to which you want to connect by looking at the SVCENAME parameter in the Database Manager Configuration file of that instance. If this parameter contains a string value rather than the port number, you need to look for the corresponding entry in the TCP/IP services file mapping this string to the port number.

2.3.4.4 Database Connection Services Directory

The Database Connection Services (DCS) directory contains connectivity information for host databases residing on a zSeries (z/OS or OS/390) or iSeries (OS/400) server. You need to have DB2 Connect software installed unless the server you are working on has DB2 UDB Enterprise Server Edition (ESE) installed. DB2 ESE comes with DB2 Connect support built in.

To list the contents of the DCS directory, issue the following command:

```
db2 list dcs directory
```

To enter information into the DCS directory, use:

```
db2 catalog dcs db dbname as location_name
```

For example:

```
db2 catalog dcs db mydb as db1g
```

2.3.5 Databases[4]

A database is a collection of information organized into interrelated objects like table spaces, tables, and indexes. Databases are closed and independent units associated to an instance. Because of this independence, objects in two or more databases can have the same name. For example, Figure 2.3 shows a table space called *MyTablespace1* inside the database *MYDB1* associated to instance *DB2*. Another table space with the name *MyTablespace1* is also used inside the database *MYDB2*, which is also associated to instance *DB2*.

Since databases are closed units, you cannot perform queries involving tables of two different databases in a direct way. For example, a query involving *Table1* in database *MYDB1* and *TableZ* in database *MYDB2* is not readily allowed. For an SQL statement to work against tables of different databases, you need to use *federation* (see section 2.4, Federation).

You create a database with the command **CREATE DATABASE**. This command automatically creates three table spaces, a buffer pool, and several configuration files, which is why this command can take a few seconds to complete.

> **N O T E**   While **CREATE DATABASE** looks like an SQL statement, it is considered a DB2 CLP command.

2.3.6 Table Spaces[5]

Table spaces are logical objects used as a layer between logical tables and physical containers. **Containers** are where the data is physically stored in files, directories, or raw devices. When you create a table space, you can associate it to a specific buffer pool (database cache) and to specific containers.

Three table spaces—the catalog (SYSCATSPACE), system temporary space (TEMPSPACE1), and the default user table space (USERSPACE1)—are automatically created when you create a database. The catalog and the system temporary space can be considered system structures, as they are needed for the normal operation of your database. The catalog contains **metadata** (data about your database objects) and must exist at all times. Some other RDBMSs call this structure a "data dictionary."

> **N O T E**   Do not confuse the term "catalog" in this section with the `catalog` command mentioned earlier; they have no relationship at all.

A system temporary table space is the work area for the database manager to perform operations, like joins and overflowed sorts. There must be at least one system temporary table space in each database.

The USERSPACE1 table space is created by default, but you can delete it. To create a table in a given table space, use the **CREATE TABLE** statement with the **IN** *table_space_name* clause. If a table space is not specified in this statement, the table will be created in the first user-created table space. If you have not yet created a table space, the table will be created in the USERSPACE1 table space.

Figure 2.3 shows other table spaces that were explicitly created with the **CREATE TABLESPACE** statement (in brown in the figure on the CD-ROM). Chapter 8, The DB2 Storage Model, discusses table spaces in more detail.

2.3.7 Tables, Indexes, and Large Objects[6]

A **table** is an unordered set of data records consisting of columns and rows. An **index** is an ordered set of pointers associated with a table, and is used for performance purposes and to ensure uniqueness. Nontraditional relational data, such as video, audio, and scanned documents, are stored in tables as large objects (LOBs). Tables and indexes reside in table spaces. Chapter 8 describes these in more detail.

2.3.8 Logs[7]

Logs are used by DB2 to record every operation against a database. In case of a failure, logs are crucial to recover the database to a consistent point. See Chapter 13, Developing Backup and Recovery Solutions, for more information about logs.

2.3.9 Buffer Pools[8]

A **buffer pool** is an area in memory where all index and data pages other than LOBs are processed. DB2 retrieves LOBs directly from disk. Buffer pools are one of the most important objects to tune for database performance. Chapter 8, The DB2 Storage Model, discusses buffer pools in more detail.

2.3.10 The Internal Implementation of the DB2 Environment

We have already discussed DB2 registry variables, configuration files, and instances. In this section we illustrate how some of these concepts physically map to directories and files in the Windows environment. The structure is a bit different in Linux and UNIX environments, but the main ideas are the same. Figures 2.4, 2.5, and 2.6 illustrate the DB2 environment internal implementation that corresponds to Figure 2.3.

Figure 2.4 shows the directory where DB2 was installed: H:\Program Files\IBM\SQLLIB. The SQLLIB directory contains several subdirectories and files that belong to DB2, including the binary code that makes DB2 work, and a subdirectory is created for each instance that is created on the machine. For example, in Figure 2.4 the subdirectories DB2 and MYINST correspond to the instances *DB2* and *myinst* respectively. The DB2DAS00 subdirectory corresponds to the DAS.

At the top of the figure there is a directory H:\MYINST. This directory contains all the databases created under the H: drive for instance *myinst*. Similarly, the H:\DB2 directory contains all the databases created under the H: drive for instance *DB2*.

Figure 2.5 shows an expanded view of the H:\Program Files\IBM\SQLLIB\DB2 directory. This directory contains information about the instance *DB2*. The db2systm binary file contains the database manager configuration (dbm cfg). The other two files highlighted in the figure (db2nodes.cfg and db2diag.log) are discussed later in this book. For now, the description of these files in the figure is sufficient. The figure also points out the directories where the system database, Node, and DCS directories reside. Note that the Node and DCS directories don't exist if they don't have any entries.

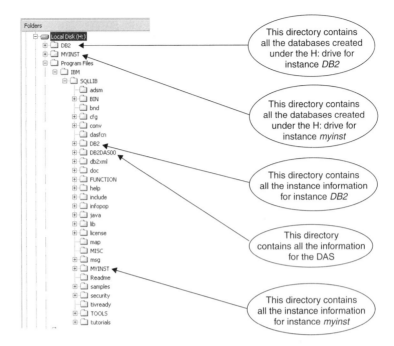

Figure 2.4 The internal implementation environment for DB2 for Windows

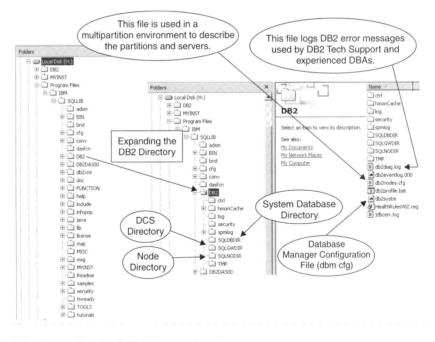

Figure 2.5 Expanding the DB2 instance directory

In Figure 2.6, the H:\DB2 and H:\MYINST directories have been expanded. The subdirectories SQL00001 and SQL00002 under H:\DB2\NODE0000 correspond to the two databases created under instance *DB2*. To map these directory names to the actual database names, you can review the contents of the local database directory with this command:

```
list db directory on h:
```

Chapter 6, Configuring Client and Server Connectivity, shows sample output of this command. Note that the local database directory is stored in the subdirectory SQLDBDIR. This subdirectory is at the same level as each of the database subdirectories; therefore, when a database is dropped, this subdirectory is not dropped. Figure 2.6 shows two SQLDBDIR subdirectories, one under H:\DB2\NODE0000 and another one under H:\MYINST\NODE0000.

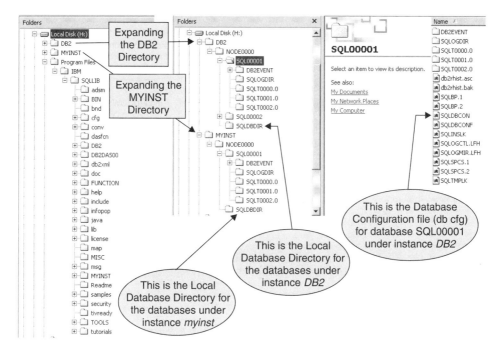

Figure 2.6   Expanding the directories containing the database data

Knowing how the DB2 environment is internally implemented can help you understand the DB2 concepts better. For example, looking back at Figure 2.3 (that one you should have printed!), what would happen if you dropped the instance *DB2*? Would this mean that databases *MYDB1* and *MYDB2* are also dropped? The answer is no. Figure 2.4 clearly shows that the directory where the instance information resides (H:\Program Files\IBM\SQLLIB\DB2) and the directory where the data resides (H:\DB2) are totally different. When an instance is dropped, only the subdirectory created for that instance is dropped.

Similarly, let's say you uninstall DB2 at a given time, and later you reinstall it on the same drive. After reinstallation, can you access the "old" databases created before you uninstalled DB2 the first time? The answer is yes. When you uninstalled DB2, you removed the SQLLIB directory, therefore the DB2 binary code as well as the instance subdirectories were removed, but the databases were left untouched. When you reinstall DB2, a new SQLLIB directory is created with a new default DB2 instance; no other instance is created. The new DB2 instance will have a new empty system database directory (db2systm). So even though the directories containing the database data were left intact, you need to explicitly put the information in the DB2 system database directory for DB2 to recognize the existence of these databases. For example, if you would like to access the MYDB1 database of the *DB2* instance, you need to issue this command to add an entry to the system database directory:

```
catalog db mydb1 on h:
```

If the database you want to access is MYDB2 that was in the *myinst* instance, you would first need to create this instance, switch to the instance, and then issue the `catalog` command as shown below.

```
db2icrt myinst
set DB2INSTANCE=myinst
catalog db mydb2 on h:
```

It is a good practice to back up the contents of all your configuration files as shown below.

```
db2 get dbm cfg > dbmcfg.bk
db2set -all > db2set.bk
db2 list db directory > systemdbdir.bk
db2 list node directory > nodedir.bk
db2 list dcs directory > dcsdir.bk
```

Notice that all of these commands redirect the output to a text file with a .bk extension.

> **CAUTION** The purpose of this section is to help you understand the DB2 environment by describing its internal implementation. We strongly suggest that you *do not tamper with the files and directories discussed in this section.* You should only modify the files using the commands described in earlier sections.

2.4 FEDERATION

Database federated support in DB2 allows tables from multiple databases to be presented as local tables to a DB2 server. The databases may be local or remote; they can also belong to different RDBMSs. While Chapter 1 briefly introduced federated support, this section provides an overview of how federation is implemented.

First of all, make sure that your server allows federated support: The database manager parameter FEDERATED must be set to YES.

DB2 uses NICKNAME, SERVER, WRAPPER, and USER MAPPING objects to implement federation. Let's consider the example illustrated in Figure 2.7.

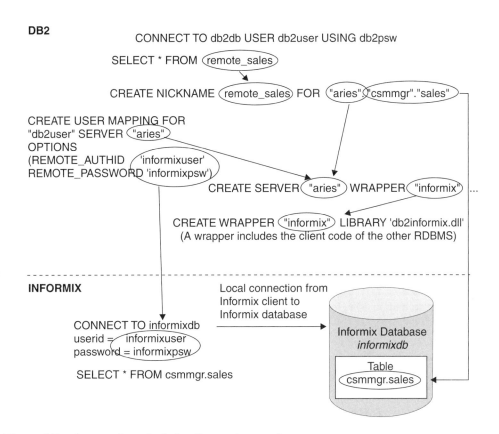

Figure 2.7   An overview of a federation environment

The DB2 user *db2user* connects to the database *db2db*. He then issues the statement:

```
SELECT * FROM remote_sales
```

The table **remote_sales**, however, is not a local table but a **nickname**, which is a pointer to a table in another database, possibly in another server and from a different RDBMS. A nickname is created with the **CREATE NICKNAME** statement, and requires a SERVER object (*aries* in the example) and the schema and table name to be accessed at this server (*csmmgr.sales*).

A SERVER object is associated to a WRAPPER. A wrapper is associated to a library that contains all the code required to connect to a given RDBMS. For IBM databases like Informix, these wrappers or libraries are provided with DB2. For other RDBMSs, you need to obtain the IBM DB2 Information Integrator software. In Figure 2.7, the wrapper called *informix* was created, and it is associated to the library *db2informix.dll*.

To access the Informix table *csmmgr.sales*, however, you cannot use the DB2 user id and password directly. You need to establish a mapping between the DB2 user id and an Informix user id that has the authority to access the desired table. This is achieved with the **CREATE USER MAPPING** statement. Figure 2.7 shows how the DB2 user *db2user* and the Informix user *informixuser* are associated with this statement.

2.5 CASE STUDY: THE DB2 ENVIRONMENT

> **NOTE**   Several assumptions have been made in this case study and the rest of the case studies in this book, so if you try to follow them some steps may not work for you. If you do follow some or all of the steps in the case studies, we recommend you use a test computer system.

You recently attended a DB2 training class and would like to try things out on your own laptop at the office. Your laptop is running Windows 2000 and DB2 UDB Enterprise Server Edition has been installed. You open the Command Window and take the following steps.

1. First, you want to know how many instances you have in your computer, so you enter:

   ```
   db2ilist
   ```

2. Then, to find out which of these instances is the current active one, you enter:

   ```
   db2 get instance
   ```

   With the **db2ilist** command, you found out there were two instances defined on this computer, *DB2* and *myinst*. With the **db2 get instance** command, you learned that the *DB2* instance is the current active instance.

3. You would now like to list the databases in the *myinst* instance. Since this one is not the current active instance, you first switch to this instance temporarily in the current Command Window:

   ```
   set DB2INSTANCE=myinst
   ```

4. You again issue **db2 get instance** to check that *myinst* is now the current instance.

5. To list the databases defined on this instance you issue:

   ```
   db2 list db directory
   ```

   This command shows that you only have one database (*MYDB2*) in this instance.

6. You want to try creating a new database called *TEMPORAL*, so you execute:

   ```
   db2 create database temporal
   ```

   The creation of the database takes some time because several objects are created by default inside the database. Issuing another **list db directory** command now shows two databases: *MYDB2* and *TEMPORAL*.

7. You connect to the *MYDB2* database (**db2 connect to mydb2**) and check which tables you have in this database (**db2 list tables for all**). You also check how many table spaces are defined (**db2 list tablespaces**).

8. Next, you want to review the contents of the database configuration file (db cfg) for the *MYDB2* database:

   ```
   db2 get db cfg for mydb2
   ```

9. To review the contents of the Database Manager Configuration file (dbm cfg) you issue:

```
db2 get dbm cfg
```

10. At this point, you want to practice changing the value of a dbm cfg parameter, so you pick the INTRA_PARALLEL parameter which has a value set to YES. You change its value to NO as follows:

```
db2 update dbm cfg using INTRA_PARALLEL NO
```

11. You learned at the class that this parameter is not "configurable online," so you know you have to stop and start the instance. Since there is a connection to a database in the current instance (remember you connected to the *MYDB2* database earlier from your current Command Window), DB2 will not allow you to stop the instance. Enter the following sequence of commands:

```
db2 terminate (terminates the connection)
db2stop
db2start
```

And that's it! In this case study you have reviewed some basic instance commands like **db2ilist** and **get instance**. You have also reviewed how to switch to another instance, create and connect to a database, list the databases in the instance, review the contents of the database configuration file and the database manager configuration file, update a database manager configuration file parameter, and stop and start an instance.

2.6 DATABASE PARTITIONING FEATURE

In this section we introduce you to the database partitioning feature (DPF) available on DB2 UDB Enterprise Server Edition (ESE). DPF lets you partition your database across multiple servers or within a large SMP server. This allows for scalability, since you can add new machines and spread your database across them. That means more CPUs, more memory, and more disks from each of the additional machines for your database!

DB2 UDB ESE with DPF is ideal to manage large databases, whether you are doing data warehousing, data mining, online analytical processing (OLAP), or working with online transaction processing (OLTP) workloads. You do not have to install any new code to enable this feature, but you must purchase the license before enabling the database partitioning feature. Users connect to the database and issue queries as usual without the need to know the database is spread among several partitions.

Up to this point, we have been discussing a single partition environment, and all of those concepts apply to a multipartition environment as well. We will now point out some implementation differences and will introduce a few new concepts, including database partitions, partition groups, and the coordinator partition, that are relevant only to a multipartition environment.

N O T E   Prior to Version 8, DB2 UDB ESE with DPF was known as DB2 UDB Enterprise-Extended Edition (EEE).

2.6.1 Database Partitions

A **database partition** is an independent part of a partitioned database with its own data, config-uration files, indexes, and transaction logs. You can assign multiple partitions across several physical servers or to a single physical server. In the latter case, the partitions are called **logical partitions** and they can share the machine's resources.

A single-partition database is a database with only one partition. We described the DB2 environ-ment for this type of database in section 2.3, The DB2 Environment. A **multipartition database** (also referred to as a **partitioned database**) is a database with two or more database partitions. Depending on your hardware environment, there are several topologies for database partitioning. Figure 2.8 shows configurations of physical partitions, one partition per machine. The illustra-tion at the top of the figure shows an SMP machine with one partition (single-partition environ-ment). This means the entire database resides on this one machine. The illustration at the bottom

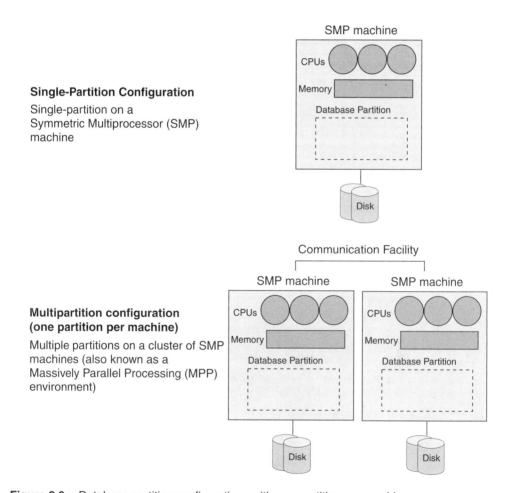

Figure 2.8 Database partition configurations with one partition per machine

shows two SMP machines, one partition per machine (multipartition environment). This means the database is split between the two partitions.

> **NOTE** In Figure 2.8, the symmetric multiprocessor (SMP) systems could be replaced by uniprocessor systems.

Figure 2.9 shows multipartition configurations with multiple partitions per machine. Unlike Figure 2.8 where there was only one partition per machine, this figure illustrates two (or more) partitions per machine.

Multipartition Configurations Partitions (several partitions per machine)

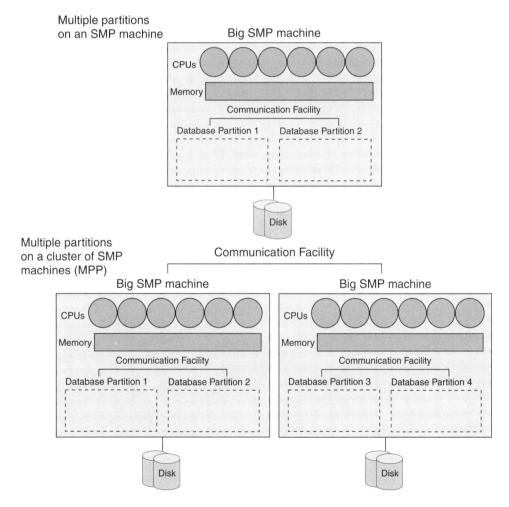

Figure 2.9 Database partition configurations with multiple partitions per machine

> **N O T E**   Prior to Version 8, the term "node" was used instead of "database partition." In Version 8, some commands will accept this term for compatibility with scripts written in previous versions of DB2.
>
> Also, note that the *node directory* concept described in section 2.3.4.3, Node Directory, has no relationship whatsoever to the *database partition* concept, even though the term "node" is used.

To visualize how a DB2 environment is split in a DPF system, Figure 2.10 illustrates a partial reproduction of Figure 2.3, and shows it split into three physical partitions, one partition per server. (We have changed the machine in the original Figure 2.3 to use the Linux operating system instead of the Windows operating system.)

> **N O T E**   Since we reference Figure 2.10 throughout this section, *we recommend that you bookmark page 49.* Alternatively, since this figure is available in color on the CD-ROM provided with this book (Figure_2_10.gif), consider printing it.

In Figure 2.10, the DB2 environment is "split" so that it now resides on three servers running the same operating system (Linux, in this example). The partitions are also running the same DB2 version, but it is important to note that different FixPak levels are allowed. This figure shows where files and objects would be located on a new installation of a multipartition system.

It is also important to note that all of the machines participating in a DPF environment have to be interconnected by a high-speed communication facility that supports the TCP/IP protocol. TCP/IP ports are reserved on each machine for this "interpartition" communication. For example, by default after installation, the services file on Linux (/etc/services) is updated as follows (assuming you chose to create the *db2inst1* instance):

```
DB2_db2inst1           60000/tcp
DB2_db2inst1_1         60001/tcp
DB2_db2inst1_2         60002/tcp
DB2_db2inst1_END       60003/tcp
db2c_db2inst1          50000/tcp
```

This also depends on the number of partitions on the server. By default, ports 60000 through 60003 are reserved for interpartition communication. You can update the services file with the correct number of entries to support the number of partitions you are configuring.

When the partitions reside on the same machine, communication between the partitions still requires this setup. You force interpartition communication to be performed in memory by setting the DB2 registry variable DB2_FORCE_FCM_BP to YES.

For a DB2 client to connect to a DPF system, you issue **catalog** commands at the client to populate the system and node directories. In the example, the port number to use in these commands is 50000 to connect to the *db2inst1* instance, and the host name can be any of the servers

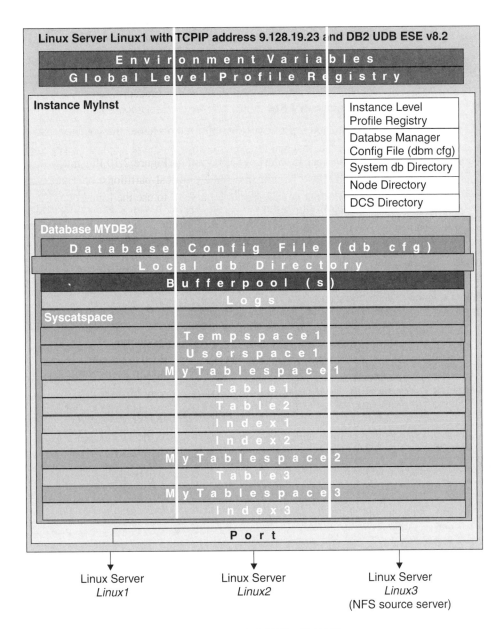

Figure 2.10 The DB2 environment in DB2 UDB ESE with DPF

participating in the DPF environment. The server used in the `catalog` command becomes the coordinator, unless the DBPARTITIONNUM option of the `connect` statement is used. The concept of coordinator is described later in this section. Chapter 6, Configuring Client and Server Connectivity, discusses the `catalog` command in detail.

> **N O T E**   Each of the servers participating in the DPF environment
> have their own separate services file, but the entries in those files that
> are applicable to DB2 interpartition communication must be the same.

2.6.2 The Node Configuration File

The node configuration file (db2nodes.cfg) contains information about the database partitions
and the servers on which they reside that belong to an instance. Figure 2.11 shows an example of
the db2nodes.cfg file for a cluster of four UNIX servers with two partitions on each server.

In Figure 2.11, the partition number, the first column in the db2nodes.cfg file, indicates the number that identifies the database partition within DB2. You can see that there are eight partitions in
total. The numbering of the partitions must be in ascending order, can start from any number,
and gaps between the numbers are allowed. The numbering used is important as it will be taken
into consideration in commands or SQL statements.

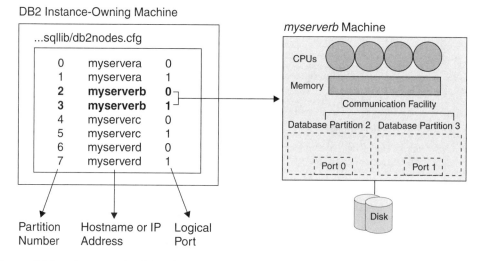

Figure 2.11   An example of the db2nodes.cfg file

The second column is the hostname or TCP/IP address of the server where the partition is created.

The third column, the logical port, is required when you create more than one partition on the
same server. This column specifies the logical port for the partition within the server and must be
unique within a server. In Figure 2.11, you can see the mapping between the db2nodes.cfg
entries for partitions 2 and 3 for server *myserverb* and the physical machine implementation.
The logical ports must also be in the same order as in the db2nodes.cfg file.

The fourth column in the db2nodes.cfg file, the netname, is required if you are using a high-
speed interconnect for interpartition communication or if the resourcesetname column is used.

The fifth column in the db2nodes.cfg file, the resourcesetname, is optional. It specifies the operating system resource that the partition should be started in.

On Windows, the db2nodes.cfg file uses the *computer name* column instead of the *resourcesetname* column. The *computer name* column stores the computer name for the machine on which a partition resides. Also, the order of the columns is slightly different: partition number, hostname, computer name, logical port, netname, and resourcesetname.

The db2nodes.cfg file must be located

- Under the SQLLIB directory for the instance owner on Linux and UNIX
- Under the SQLLIB*instance_name* directory on Windows

In Figure 2.10 this file would be on the Linux3 machine, as this machine is the Network File System (NFS) source server, the server whose disk(s) can be shared.

On Linux and UNIX you can edit the db2nodes.cfg file with any ASCII editor or use DB2 commands to update the file. On Windows, you can only use the **db2ncrt** and **db2ndrop** commands to create and drop database partitions; the db2nodes.cfg file should not be edited directly.

For any platform, you can also use the **db2start** command to add and or remove a database partition from the DB2 instance and update the db2nodes.cfg file using the **add dbpartitionnum** and the **drop dbpartitionnum** clauses respectively.

2.6.3 An Instance in the DPF Environment

Partitioning is a concept that applies to the database, not the instance; you partition a database, not an instance. In a DPF environment an instance is created once on an NFS source server machine. The instance owner's home directory is then exported to all servers where DB2 is to be run. Each partition in the database has the same characteristics: the same instance owner, password, and shared instance home directory.

On Linux and UNIX, an instance maps to an operating system user; therefore, when an instance is created, it will have its own home directory. In most installations /home/*user_name* is the home directory. All instances created on each of the participating machines in a DPF environment must use the same name and password. In addition, you must specify the home directory of the corresponding operating system user to be the same directory for all instances, which must be created on a shared file system. Figure 2.12 illustrates an example of this.

In Figure 2.12, the instance *myinst* has been created on the shared file system, and *myinst* maps to an operating system user of the same name, which in the figure has a home directory of /home/myinst. This user must be created separately in each of the participating servers, but they must share the instance home directory. As shown in Figure 2.12, all three Linux servers share /home/myinst, and it resides on a shared file system local to Linux3. Since the instance owner directory is locally stored on the Linux3 machine, this machine is considered to be the DB2 **instance-owning server**.

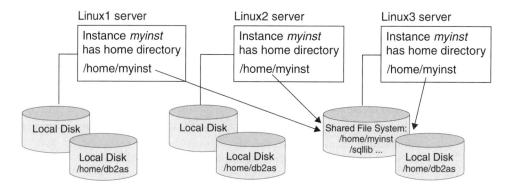

Figure 2.12   An instance in a partitioned environment

Figure 2.12 also shows that the Database Administration Server user db2as is created locally on each participating server in a DPF environment. There can only be one DAS per physical server regardless of the number of partitions that machine contains. The DAS user's home directory cannot be mounted on a shared file system. Alternatively, different userids and passwords can be used to create the DAS on different machines.

> **N O T E**   Make sure the passwords for the instances are the same on each of the participating machines in a DPF environment, otherwise the partitioned system will look like it is hanging because the partitions are not able to communicate.

2.6.4 Partitioning a Database

When you want to partition a database in a DPF environment, simply issue the **CREATE DATABASE** command as usual. For example, if the instance owner home directory is /home/myinst, when you execute this command:

```
CREATE DATABASE mydb2
```

the structure created is as shown in Figure 2.13.

```
/home
    /myinst
        /NODE0000
            /SQL00001
        /NODE0001
            /SQL00001
        /NODE0002
            /SQL00001
```

Figure 2.13   A partitioned database in a single file system

If you don't specify a path in your **CREATE DATABASE** command, by default the database is created in the directory specified by the database manager configuration parameter DFTDBPATH, which defaults to the instance owner's home directory. This partitioning is not optimal because all of the database data would reside in one file system that is shared by the other machines across a network.

We recommend that you create a directory with the same name, locally in each of the participating machines. For the environment in Figure 2.12, let's assume the directory /data has been created locally on each machine. When you execute the command:

```
CREATE DATABASE mydb2 on /data
```

the following directory structure is automatically built for you:

/data/*instance_name*/NODE*xxxx*/SQL*yyyyy*

The /data directory is specified in the **CREATE DATABASE** command, but the directory must exist *before* executing the command. *instance_name* is the name of the instance; for example, *myinst*. NODE*xxxx* distinguishes which partition you are working with, where *xxxx* represents the number of the partition specified in the db2nodes.cfg file. SQL*yyyyy* identifies the database, where *yyyyy* represents a number. If you have only one database on your system, then *yyyyy* is equal to 00001; if you have three databases on your system, you will have different directories as follows: SQL00001, SQL00002, SQL00003. To map the database names to these directories, you can review the local database directory using the command:

```
list db directory on /data
```

Inside the SQL*yyyyy* directories are subdirectories for table spaces, and within them, files containing database data—assuming all table spaces are defined as system-managed space (SMS).

Figure 2.14 illustrates a partitioned database created in the /data directory

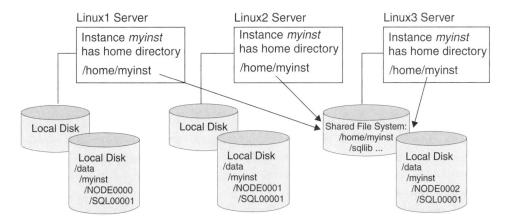

Figure 2.14   A partitioned database across several file systems

> **N O T E**   Before creating a database, be sure to change the value of
> the dbm cfg parameter DFTDBPATH to an existing path created locally
> with the same name on each of the participating machines of your DPF
> system. Alternatively, make sure to include this path in your **CREATE
> DATABASE** command. Similarly, to create the SAMPLE database, spec-
> ify this path in the command:
>
> ```
> db2sampl path
> ```

Partitioning a database is described in more detail in Chapter 8, The DB2 Storage Model.

2.6.5 Configuration Files in a DPF Environment

As shown in Figure 2.10, the Database Manager Configuration file (dbm cfg), system database
directory, node directory, and DCS directory are all part of the instance-owning machine and are
not partitioned. What about the other configuration files?

- Environment variables: Each participating server in a partitioned environment can have different environment variables.
- Global-level profile registry variable: This is stored in a file called default.env that is located in a subdirectory under the /var directory. There is a local copy of this file on each server.
- Database configuration file: This is stored in the file SQLDBCON that is located in the SQL*yyyyy* directory for the database. In a partitioned database environment, a separate SQLDBCON file is created for each partition in every database.
- The local database directory: This is stored in the file SQLDBDIR in the corresponding directory for the database. It has the same name as the system database directory, which is located under the instance directory. A separate SQLDBDIR file exists for each partition in each database.

> **C A U T I O N**   We strongly suggest you do *not* manually edit any of
> the DB2 configuration files. You should modify the files using the com-
> mands described in earlier sections.

> **N O T E**   The values of the global-level profile registry variables,
> database configuration file parameters, and local database directory
> entries should be the same for each database partition.

2.6.6 Logs in a DPF Environment

The logs on each database partition should be kept in a separate place. The database configuration parameter *Path to log files* (LOGPATH) on each partition should point to a local file system,

not a shared file system. The default log path in each partition includes a NODE000*x* subdirectory. For example, the value of this parameter in the DPF system shown in Figure 2.10 could be:

- For Partition 0: /datalogs/db2inst1/NODE0000/SQL00001/SQLOGDIR/
- For Partition 1: /datalogs/db2inst1/NODE0001/SQL00001/SQLOGDIR/
- For Partition 2: /datalogs/db2inst1/NODE0002/SQL00001/SQLOGDIR/

To change the path for the logs, update the database configuration parameter NEWLOGPATH.

2.6.7 The Catalog Partition

As stated previously, when you create a database, several table spaces are created by default. One of them, the catalog table space SYSCATSPACE, contains the DB2 system catalogs. In a partitioned environment SYSCATSPACE is not partitioned, but resides on one partition known as the **catalog partition**. The partition from which the **CREATE DATABASE** command is issued becomes the catalog partition for the new database. All access to system tables must go through this database partition. Figure 2.10 shows SYSCATSPACE residing on server Linux1, so the **CREATE DATABASE** command was issued from this server.

For an existing database, you can determine which partition is the catalog partition by issuing the command **list db directory**. The output of this command has the field *Catalog database partition number* for each of the entries, which indicates the catalog partition number for that database.

2.6.8 Partition Groups

A **partition group** is a logical layer that provides for the grouping of one or more database partitions. A database partition can belong to more than one partition group. When a database is created, DB2 creates three default partition groups, and these partition groups cannot be dropped.

- **IBMDEFAULTGROUP**: This is the default partition group for any table you create. It contains all database partitions defined in the db2nodes.cfg file. This partition group cannot be modified. Table space USERSPACE1 is created in this partition group.
- **IBMTEMPGROUP**: This partition group is used by all system temporary tables. It contains all database partitions defined in the db2nodes.cfg file. Table space TEMPSPACE1 is created in this partition.
- **IBMCATGROUP**: This partition group contains the catalog tables (table space SYSCATSPACE). It only includes the database's catalog partition. This partition group cannot be modified.

To create new database partition groups, use the **CREATE DATABASE PARTITION GROUP** statement. This statement creates the database partition group within the database, assigns database partitions that you specified to the partition group, and records the partition group definition in the database system catalog tables.

The following statement creates partition group *pgrpall* on all partitions specified in the db2nodes.cfg file:

```
CREATE DATABASE PARTITION GROUP pgrpall ON ALL DBPARTITIONNUMS
```

To create a database partition group *pg23* consisting of partitions 2 and 3, issue this command:

```
CREATE DATABASE PARTITION GROUP pg23 ON DBPARTITIONNUMS (2,3)
```

Other relevant partition group statements/commands are:

- **ALTER DATABASE PARTITION GROUP** (statement to add or drop a partition in the group)
- **DROP DATABASE PARTITION GROUP** (statement to drop a partition group)
- **LIST DATABASE PARTITION GROUPS** (command to list all your partition groups; note that IBMTEMPGROUP is never listed)

2.6.9 Buffer Pools in a DPF Environment

Figure 2.10 shows buffer pools defined across all of the database partitions. Interpreting this figure for buffer pools is different than for the other objects, because the data cached in the buffer pools is not partitioned as the figure implies. Each buffer pool in a DPF environment holds data only from the database partition where the buffer pool is located.

You can create a buffer pool in a partition group using the **CREATE BUFFERPOOL** statement with the **DATABASE PARTITION GROUP** clause. This means that you have the flexibility to define the buffer pool on the specific partitions defined in the partition group. In addition, the size of the buffer pool on each partition in the partition group can be different. The following statement will create buffer pool *bpool_1* in partition group *pg234*, which consists of partitions 2, 3, and 4.

```
CREATE BUFFERPOOL bpool_1 DATABASE PARTITION GROUP pg234
       SIZE 10000
       EXCEPT ON DBPARTITIONNUM (3 TO 4) SIZE 5000
```

Partition 2 in partition group *pg234* will have a buffer pool *bpool_1* defined with a size of 10,000 pages, and Partitions 3 and 4 will have a buffer pool of size 5,000 pages.

As an analogy, think of it as if you were issuing the **CREATE BUFFERPOOL** statement on each partition separately, with the same buffer pool name for each partition but with different sizes. That is:

- On partition 2: **CREATE BUFFERPOOL bpool_1 SIZE 10000**
- On partition 3: **CREATE BUFFERPOOL bpool_1 SIZE 5000**
- On partition 4: **CREATE BUFFERPOOL bpool_1 SIZE 5000**

Note that we use these statements only to clarify the analogy; they will not work as written. Executing each of these commands as shown will attempt to create the same buffer pool on all partitions. It is not equivalent to using the **DATABASE PARTITION GROUP** clause of the **CREATE BUFFERPOOL** statement.

Buffer pools can also be associated to several partition groups. This means that the buffer pool definition will be applied to the partitions in those partition groups.

2.6.10 Table Spaces in a Partitioned Database Environment

You can create a table space in specific partitions, associating it to a partition group, by using the **CREATE TABLESPACE** statement with the **IN DATABASE PARTITION GROUP** clause. This allows users to have flexibility as to which partitions will actually be storing their tables. In a partitioned database environment with three servers, one partition per server, the statement:

```
CREATE TABLESPACE mytbls IN DATABASE PARTITION GROUP pg234
      MANAGED BY SYSTEM USING ('/data')
      BUFFERPOOL bpool_1
```

creates the table space *mytbls*, which spans partitions 2, 3, and 4 (assuming *pg234* is a partition group consisting of these partitions). In addition, the table space is associated with buffer pool *bpool_1* defined earlier. Note that creating a table space would fail if you provide conflicting partition information between the table space and the associated buffer pool. For example, if *bpool_1* was created for partitions 5 and 6, and table space *mytbls* was created for partitions 2, 3, and 4, you would get an error message when trying to create this table space.

2.6.11 The Coordinator Partition

In general, each database connection has a corresponding DB2 agent handling the application connection. An **agent** can be thought of as a process (Linux/UNIX) or thread (Windows) that performs DB2 work on behalf of the application. There are different types of agents. One of them, the coordinator agent, communicates with the application, receiving requests and sending replies. It can either satisfy the request itself or delegate the work to multiple subagents to work on the request.

The **coordinator partition** of a given application is the partition where the coordinator agent exists. You use the **SET CLIENT CONNECT_NODE** command to set the partition that is to be the coordinator partition. Any partition can potentially be a coordinator, so in Figure 2.10 we do not label any particular partition as the coordinator node. If you would like to know more about DB2 agents and the DB2 process model, refer to Chapter 14, The DB2 Process Model.

2.6.12 Issuing Commands and SQL Statements in a DPF Environment

Imagine that you have twenty physical servers, with two database partitions on each. Issuing individual commands to each physical server or partition would be quite a task. Fortunately, DB2 provides a command that executes on all database partitions.

2.6.12.1 The db2_all command

Use the **db2_all** command when you want to execute a command or SQL statement against all database partitions. For example, to change the db cfg parameter LOGFILSIZ for the database *sample* in all partitions, you would use:

```
db2_all ";db2 UPDATE DB CFG FOR sample USING LOGFILSIZ 500"
```

When the semicolon (;) character is placed before the command or statement, the request runs in parallel on all partitions.

> **NOTE** In partitioned environments, the operating system command **rah** performs commands on all servers simultaneously. The **rah** command works per server, while the **db2_all** command works per database partition. The **rah** and **db2_all** commands use the same characters. For more information about the **rah** command, refer to your operating system manuals.

2.6.12.2 Using Database Partition Expressions

In a partitioned database, database partition expressions can be used to generate values based on the partition number found in the db2nodes.cfg file. This is particularly useful when you have a large number of database partitions and when more than one database partition resides on the same physical machine, because the same device or path cannot be specified for all partitions. You can manually specify a unique container for each database partition or use database partition expressions. The following example illustrates the use of database partition expressions.

On Linux/UNIX, here are sample contents of a db2nodes.cfg file:

```
0      myservera      0
1      myservera      1
2      myserverb      0
3      myserverb      1
```

This shows two servers with two database partitions each. The command:

```
CREATE TABLESPACE ts2
  MANAGED BY DATABASE USING
  (file '/data/TS2/container $N+100' 5000)
```

creates the following containers:

- /data/TS2/container100 on database partition 0
- /data/TS2/container101 on database partition 1
- /data/TS2/container102 on database partition 2
- /data/TS2/container103 on database partition 3

You specify a database partition expression with the argument **$N** (note that there must be a space before **$N in** the command). Table 2.1 shows other arguments for creating containers. Operators are evaluated from left to right, and **%** represents the modulus (the remainder of a division). Assuming the partition number to be evaluated is 3, the value column in Table 2.1 shows the result of resolving the database partition expression.

Table 2.1   Database Partition Expressions

Database Partition Expressions	Example	Value
[blank]$N	$N	3
[blank]$N+[number]	$N+500	503
[blank]$N%[number]	$N%2	1
[blank]$N+[number]%[number]	$N+15%13	5
[blank]$N%[number]+[number]	$N%2+20	21

2.6.13 The DB2NODE Environment Variable

In section 2.3, The DB2 Environment, we talked about the DB2INSTANCE environment variable used to switch between instances in your database system. The DB2NODE environment variable is used in a similar way, but to switch between partitions on your DPF system. By default, the active partition is the one defined with the logical port number of zero (0) in the db2nodes.cfg file for a server. To switch the active partition, change the value of the DB2NODE variable using the **SET** command on Windows and the **export** command on Linux/UNIX. Be sure to issue a **terminate** command for all connections from any partition to your database after changing this variable or the change will not take effect.

Using the settings for the db2nodes.cfg file shown in Table 2.2, you have four servers, each with two logical partitions. If you log on to server *myserverb*, any commands you execute will affect partition 2, which is the one with logical port of zero on that server, and the default coordinator partition for that server.

Table 2.2   Sample Partition Information

Partition	Server Name	Logical Port
0	myservera	0
1	myservera	1
2	myserverb	0
3	myserverb	1
4	myserverc	0
5	myserverc	1
6	myserverd	0
7	myserverd	1

If you would like to make partition 0 the active partition, make this change on a Linux/UNIX system:

```
DB2NODE=0
export DB2NODE
db2 terminate
```

> **N O T E**   You must issue the **terminate** command, even if there aren't any connections to any partitions.

Note that partition 0 is on server *myservera*. Even if you are connected to *myserverb*, you can make a partition on *myservera* the active one. To determine which is your active partition, you can issue this statement after connecting to a database:

```
db2 "values (current dbpartitionnum)"
```

2.6.14 Partitioning Maps and Partitioning Keys

By now you should have a good grasp of how to set up a DPF environment. It is now time to understand how DB2 distributes data across the partitions. Figure 2.15 shows an example of this distribution.

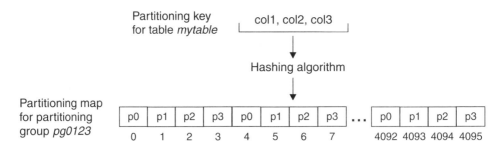

Figure 2.15   Distributing data rows in a DPF environment

A **partitioning map** is an internally generated array containing 4096 entries for multipartition database partition groups or a single entry for single-partition database partition groups. The partition numbers of the database partition group are specified in a round-robin fashion in the array.

A **partitioning key** is a column (or group of columns) that determines the partition on which a particular row of data is physically stored. You define a partitioning key explicitly using the **CREATE TABLE** statement with the PARTITIONING KEY clause.

When you create or modify a database partition group, a partitioning map is associated with it. A partitioning map in conjunction with a partitioning key and a hashing algorithm determine which database partition will store a given row of data.

For the example in Figure 2.15, let's assume partition group *pg0123* has been defined on partitions 0, 1, 2, and 3. An associated partitioning map is automatically created. This map is an array with 4096 entries containing the values 0, 1, 2, 3, 0, 1, 2, 3. . . . (note that this is shown in Figure 2.15 as p0, p1, p2, p3, p0, p1, p2, p3 . . . to distinguish them from the array entry numbers). Let's also assume table *mytable* has been created with a partitioning key consisting of columns col1, col2, and col3. For each row, the partitioning key column values are passed to the hashing algorithm, which returns an output number from 0 to 4095. This number corresponds to one of the entries in the array that contains the value of the partition number where the row is to be stored. In Figure 2.15, if the hashing algorithm had returned an output value of 7, the row would have been stored in partition *p3*.

2.7 CASE STUDY: DB2 WITH DPF ENVIRONMENT

Now that you are familiar with DPF, let's review some of the concepts discussed using a simple case study.

Your company is expanding, and it recently acquired two other firms. Since the amount of data will be increased by approximately threefold, you are wondering if your current single-partition DB2 database server will be able to handle the load, or if DB2 with DPF will be required. You are not too familiar with DB2 with DPF, so you decide to play around with it using your test machines: two SMP machines running Linux with four processors each. The previous DBA, who has left the company, had installed DB2 UDB ESE with DPF on these machines. Fortunately, he left a diagram with his design, shown in Figure 2.16.

Figure 2.16 is a combined physical and logical design. When you validate the correctness of the diagram with your system, you note that database *mydb1* has been dropped, so you decide to rebuild this database as practice. The instance *db2inst1* is still there, as are other databases. These are the steps you follow.

1. Open two telnet sessions, one for each server. From one of the sessions you issue the commands **db2stop** followed by **db2start**, as shown in Figure 2.17.

   The first thing you note is that there is no need to issue these two commands on each partition; issuing them on any partition once will affect all partitions. You also can tell that there are four partitions, since you received a message from each of them.

2. Review the db2nodes.cfg file to understand the configuration of your partitions (see Figure 2.18). Using operating system commands, you determine that the home directory for instance *db2inst1* is /home/db2inst1. The db2nodes.cfg file is stored in the directory /home/db2inst1/sqllib.

   Figure 2.18 shows there are four partitions, two per server. The server host names are *aries* and *saturn*.

3. Create the database *mydb1*. Since you want partition 0 to be your catalog partition, you must issue the **CREATE DATABASE** command from partition 0. You issue the statement **db2 "values (current dbpartitionnum)"** to determine which partition is currently active and find out that partition 3 is the active partition (see Figure 2.19).

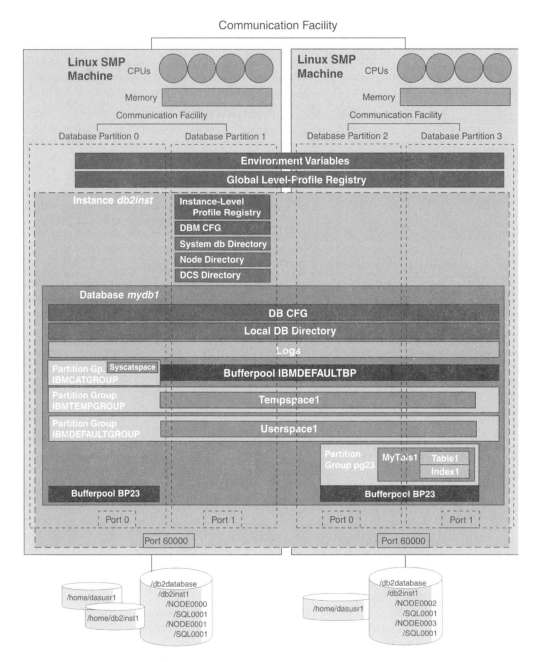

Figure 2.16   DB2 UDB ESE with DPF design

```
[db2inst1@aries db2inst1]$ db2stop
05-18-2004 23:44:42    3   0   SQL1064N  DB2STOP processing was successful.
05-18-2004 23:44:43    1   0   SQL1064N  DB2STOP processing was successful.
05-18-2004 23:44:44    2   0   SQL1064N  DB2STOP processing was successful.
05-18-2004 23:44:44    0   0   SQL1064N  DB2STOP processing was successful.
SQL1064N  DB2STOP processing was successful.

[db2inst1@aries db2inst1]$ db2start
05-18-2004 23:44:51    1   0   SQL1063N  DB2START processing was successful.
05-18-2004 23:44:51    0   0   SQL1063N  DB2START processing was successful.
05-18-2004 23:44:52    3   0   SQL1063N  DB2START processing was successful.
05-18-2004 23:44:53    2   0   SQL1063N  DB2START processing was successful.
SQL1063N  DB2START processing was successful.

[db2inst1@aries db2inst1]$
```

Figure 2.17   Running the db2stop and db2start commands

```
[db2inst1@aries sqllib]$ pwd
/home/db2inst1/sqllib

[db2inst1@aries sqllib]$ more db2nodes.cfg
0 aries.myacme.com 0
1 aries.myacme.com 1
2 saturn.myacme.com 0
3 saturn.myacme.com 1

[db2inst1@aries sqllib]$
```

Figure 2.18   A sample db2nodes.cfg file

```
[db2inst1@saturn db2inst1]$ db2 "values (current dbpartitionnum)"

1
-----------
          3

  1 record(s) selected.
```

Figure 2.19   Determining the active partition

4. Next, you change the DB2NODE environment variable to zero (0) as follows (see Figure 2.20):

```
DB2NODE=0
export DB2NODE
db2 terminate
```

```
[db2inst1@saturn db2inst1]$ DB2NODE=0
[db2inst1@saturn db2inst1]$ export DB2NODE
[db2inst1@saturn db2inst1]$ db2 terminate
DB20000I  The TERMINATE command completed successfully.

[db2inst1@saturn db2inst1]$ db2 list applications
SQL1611W  No data was returned by Database System Monitor. SQLSTATE=00000

[db2inst1@saturn db2inst1]$ db2 create db mydb1 on /db2database
DB20000I  The CREATE DATABASE command completed successfully.

[db2inst1@saturn db2inst1]$ db2 connect to mydb1

   Database Connection Information

 Database server        = DB2/LINUX 8.1.2
 SQL authorization ID    = DB2INST1
 Local database alias    = MYDB1

[db2inst1@saturn db2inst1]$ db2 "values (current dbpartitionnum)"

1
-----------
          0

  1 record(s) selected.

[db2inst1@saturn db2inst1]$
```

Figure 2.20   Switching the active partition, then creating a database

In the **CREATE DATABASE** command you specify the path, /db2database in this example, which is an existing path that has been created locally on all servers so that the data is spread across them.

5. To confirm that partition 0 is indeed the catalog partition, simply issue a **list db directory** command and look for the *Catalog database partition number* field under the entry for the *mydb1* database. Alternatively, issue a **list tablespaces** command from each partition. The SYSCATSPACE table space will be listed only on the catalog partition.

6. Create partition group *pg23* on partitions 2 and 3. Figure 2.21 shows how to accomplish this and how to list your partition groups. Remember that this does not list IBMTEMPGROUP.

7. Create and manage your buffer pools. Issue this statement to create buffer pool *BP23* on partition group *pg23*:

   ```
   db2 "create bufferpool BP23 database partition group pg23 size 500"
   ```

```
[db2inst1@saturn db2inst1]$ db2 "create database partition group pg23 on
dbpartitionnum (2 to 3)"
DB20000I  The SQL command completed successfully.

[db2inst1@saturn db2inst1]$ db2 "list database partition groups"

DATABASE PARTITION GROUP
---------------------------
IBMCATGROUP
IBMDEFAULTGROUP
PG23

  3 record(s) selected.

[db2inst1@saturn db2inst1]$
```

Figure 2.21   Creating partition group pg23

Figure 2.22 shows this statement. It also shows you how to associate this buffer pool to another partition group using the **ALTER BUFFERPOOL** statement.

To list your buffer pools and associated partition groups, you can query the SYSCAT.BUFFERPOOLS catalog view, also shown in Figure 2.22.

```
[db2inst1@saturn db2inst1]$ db2 "create bufferpool BP23 database partition group
pg23 size 500"
DB20000I  The SQL command completed successfully.

[db2inst1@saturn db2inst1]$ db2 "alter bufferpool BP23 add database partition group
IBMCATGROUP"
DB20000I  The SQL command completed successfully.

[db2inst1@saturn db2inst1]$ db2 "select bpname, ngname from syscat.bufferpools"

BPNAME                                              NGNAME
------------------------------------------------------------------------------
IBMDEFAULTBP                                        -

BP23                                                PG23

BP23                                                IBMCATGROUP

  3 record(s) selected.

[db2inst1@saturn db2inst1]$
```

Figure 2.22   Managing buffer pools

Note that a buffer pool can be associated with any partition group. Its definition will be applied to all the partitions in the partition group, and you can specify different sizes on the partitions if required.

8. Create the table space *mytbls1*:

```
db2 "create tablespace mytbls1 in database partition group pg23
        managed by system using ('/data') bufferpool bp23"
```

9. Create table *table1* in table space *mytbls1* with a partitioning key of col1 and col2:

```
db2 "create table table1 (col1 int, col2 int, col3 char(10))
        in mytbls1
        partitioning key (col1, col2)"
```

10. Create the index *index1*. Note that this doesn't have any syntax specific to a DPF environment:

```
db2 "create index index1 on table1 (col1, col2)"
```

The index will be constructed on each partition for its subset of rows.

11. Test the **db2_all** command to update the database configuration file for all partitions with one command. Figure 2.23 shows an example of this.

```
[db2inst1@aries sqllib]$ db2 get db cfg for mydb1 | grep LOGFILSIZ
 Log file size (4KB)                        (LOGFILSIZ) = 1000
[db2inst1@aries sqllib]$ db2_all "db2 update db cfg for mydb1 using LOGFILSIZ 500"

DB20000I  The UPDATE DATABASE CONFIGURATION command completed successfully.
aries.myacme.com: db2 update db cfg for mydb1 using LOGFILSIZ 500 completed ok

DB20000I  The UPDATE DATABASE CONFIGURATION command completed successfully.
aries.myacme.com: db2 update db cfg for mydb1 using LOGFILSIZ 500 completed ok

DB20000I  The UPDATE DATABASE CONFIGURATION command completed successfully.
saturn.myacme.com: db2 update db cfg for mydb1 using LOGFILSIZ 500 completed ok

DB20000I  The UPDATE DATABASE CONFIGURATION command completed successfully.
saturn.myacme.com: db2 update db cfg for mydb1 using LOGFILSIZ 500 completed ok
[db2inst1@aries sqllib]$ db2 get db cfg for mydb1 | grep LOGFILSIZ
 Log file size (4KB)                        (LOGFILSIZ) = 500
[db2inst1@aries sqllib]$
```

Figure 2.23   Using db2_all to update the db cfg file

And that's it! In this case study you have reviewed some basic statements and commands applicable to the DPF environment. You reviewed the **db2stop** and **db2start** commands, determined and switched the active partition, and created a database, a partition group, a buffer pool, a table space, a table with a partitioning key, and an index. You also used the **db2_all** command to update a database configuration file parameter.

2.8 SUMMARY

This chapter provided an overview of the DB2 core concepts using a "big picture" approach. It introduced SQL statements and their classification in Data Definition Language (DDL), Data Manipulation Language (DML), and Data Control Language (DCL).

DB2 commands are classified into two groups—system commands and CLP commands—and several examples were provided, like the command to start an instance, `db2start`.

You need an interface to issue SQL statements and commands to the DB2 engine. This interface was provided by using the DB2 tools available with the product. Two text-based interfaces were mentioned, the Command Line Processor (CLP) and the Command Window. The Control Center was noted as being the most important administration graphical tool.

The chapter introduced the concepts of instances, databases, table spaces, buffer pools, logs, tables, indexes, and other database objects in a single partition system. There are different levels of configuration for the DB2 environment: the environment variables, the DB2 registry variables, and the configuration parameters at the instance (dbm cfg) and database (db cfg) levels. DB2 has federation support for queries using tables from other databases in the DB2 family. The chapter also covered database partition, catalog partition, coordinator node, and partitioning map on a multipartition system.

Two case studies reviewed the single-partition and multipartition environments respectively, which should help you understand the topics discussed in the chapter.

2.9 REVIEW QUESTIONS

1. How are DB2 commands classified?
2. What is a quick way to obtain help information for a command?
3. What is the difference between the Information Center tool and simply reviewing the DB2 manuals?
4. What command is used to create a DB2 instance?
5. How many table spaces are automatically created by the **CREATE DATABASE** command?
6. What command can be used to get a list of all instances on your server?
7. What is the default instance that is created on Windows?
8. Is the DAS required to be running to set up a remote connection between a DB2 client and a DB2 server?
9. How can the DB2 environment be configured?
10. How is the local database directory populated?
11. Which of the following commands will start your DB2 instance?
    A. startdb
    B. db2 start
    C. db2start
    D. start db2
12. Which of the following commands will list all of the registry variables that are set on your server?
    A. db2set –a
    B. db2set –all

Chapter 2 • DB2 at a Glance: The Big Picture

C. db2set –lr

D. db2set -ltr

13. Say you are running DB2 on a Windows server with only one hard drive (C:). If the DB2 instance is dropped using the **db2idrop** command, after recreating the DB2 instance, which of the following commands will list the databases you had prior to dropping the instance?

    A. list databases

    B. list db directory

    C. list db directory all

    D. list db directory on C:

14. If the **list db directory on C:** command returns the following:

```
Database alias                        = SAMPLE
Database name                         = SAMPLE
Database directory                    = SQL00001
Database release level                = a.00
Comment                               =
Directory entry type                  = Home
Catalog database partition number     = 0
Database partition number             = 0
```

which of the following commands must be run before you can access tables in the database?

    A. catalog db sample

    B. catalog db sample on local

    C. catalog db sample on SQL00001

    D. catalog db sample on C:

15. If there are two DB2 instances on your Linux server, *inst1* and *inst2*, and if your default DB2 instance is *inst1*, which of the following commands allows you to connect to databases in the *inst2* instance?

    A. export inst2

    B. export instance=inst2

    C. export db2instance=inst2

    D. connect to inst2

16. Which of the following DB2 registry variables optimizes interpartition communication if you have multiple partitions on a single server?

    A. DB2_OPTIMIZE_COMM

    B. DB2_FORCE_COMM

    C. DB2_USE_FCM_BP

    D. DB2_FORCE_FCM_BP

17. Which of the following tools is used to run commands on all partitions in a multipartition DB2 database?

    A. db2_part

    B. db2_all

    C. db2_allpart

    D. db2

18. Which of the following allows federated support in your server?
    A. db2 update db cfg for federation using FEDERATED ON
    B. db2 update dbm cfg using FEDERATED YES
    C. db2 update dbm cfg using NICKNAME YES
    D. db2 update dbm cfg using NICKNAME, WRAPPER, SERVER, USER MAPPING YES

19. Which environment variable needs to be updated to change the active logical database partition?
    A. DB2INSTANCE
    B. DB2PARTITION
    C. DB2NODE
    D. DB2PARTITIONNUMBER

20. Which of the following statements can be used to determine the value of the current active database partition?
    A. values (current dbpartitionnum)
    B. values (current db2node)
    C. values (current db2partition)
    D. values (current partitionnum)

## CHAPTER 3

Installing DB2

N ow that you have an overview of DB2, the next step is to install it. In this chapter we walk you through the DB2 installation process on the Windows, Linux, and UNIX platforms with step-by-step installation instructions. For the latest information about DB2 installation system requirements, see

http://www.ibm.com/software/data/db2/udb/sysreqs.html

In this chapter you will learn about:

- The various DB2 installation methods
- The user IDs and groups required to install DB2
- Installing DB2 using the DB2 Setup Wizard
- Installing DB2 in a distributed environment using the Silent install method
- Installing DB2 licenses
- Installing DB2 FixPaks

3.1 DB2 INSTALLATION: THE BIG PICTURE

Table 3.1 lists the two methods for installing DB2 on Windows and the four methods for installing DB2 on Linux/UNIX.

The **DB2 Setup Wizard** provides an easy-to-use graphical interface for installing DB2. In addition to creating a DB2 instance and required user IDs, it also sets up some initial configuration parameters. It guides you through the installation tasks listed in Figures 3.1 and 3.2. After the installation is completed, DB2 is ready for use. We recommend that you use this installation method.

Table 3.1   Installation Methods by Operating Systems

Installation Method	Windows	Linux/UNIX
DB2 Setup Wizard	Yes	Yes
Silent install	Yes	Yes
`db2_install` script	No	Yes
Native operating system install tools	No	Yes

Imagine you have to install DB2 on thousands of machines. Although the DB2 Setup Wizard is easy to use, it is an interactive tool, which means you have to physically sit in front of the screen and input values when the wizard prompts you. As you can imagine, if you have to install DB2 on many machines, this process is extremely time-consuming. To avoid this, DB2 offers the **Silent install** method. The key to this installation method is the **response** file, a text file that contains setup and configuration values. You pass this file to the DB2 setup program as input, and then the setup program installs DB2 according to the values specified in the response file, unattended.

The **db2_install script** (only available on Linux/UNIX platforms) uses the operating system's native installation utility to install DB2. The **db2_install** script prompts for a DB2 product keyword and then installs all components for the DB2 product you specify. You cannot select or deselect components or specify the language to be used. The **db2_install** script does not perform user and group creation, instance creation, or configuration; it simply installs the DB2 components onto your system. You might prefer this method of installation if you want to customize the instances and their configurations yourself.

Installing DB2 using your operating system's **native installation tools** provides the greatest control over the installation process, but it is also more difficult than the other installation methods. This method is only available on Linux and UNIX platforms. When installing a particular DB2 product, you have to ensure that the required components are installed and that component dependencies are maintained. This requires advanced knowledge of both DB2 and your operating environment. You must manually perform user and group creation, instance creation, and configuration.

Figures 3.1 and 3.2 give you an overview of the various installation methods on the Windows and Linux/UNIX platforms respectively. The figures also list the items that the DB2 Setup Wizard creates. We recommend using the DB2 Setup Wizard for all platforms, and we focus on that method in this chapter.

3.2 REQUIRED USER IDS AND GROUPS

Figures 3.1 and 3.2 show that you create several user IDs and user groups that DB2 needs to operate when installing DB2. This section discusses the basic requirements of those user IDs and groups, which are different for Windows and Linux/UNIX.

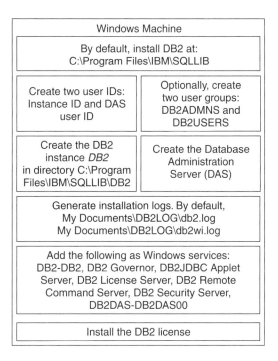

Figure 3.1   The big picture: DB2 installation on Windows

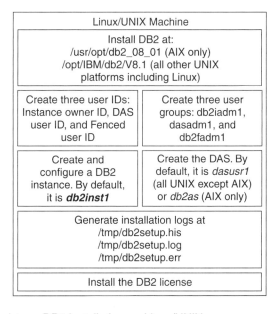

Figure 3.2   The big picture: DB2 installation on Linux/UNIX

3.2.1 User IDs and Groups Required for Windows

In addition to needing an **installation user ID** to install the DB2 product on Windows, to operate DB2 you need two other user IDs.

- The **Instance owner** owns and controls the DB2 instance.
- The **DB2 Administration Server** (DAS) **user** runs the DB2 administration server service on your system. The DB2 GUI tools also use this ID to perform administration tasks against the local server database instances and databases.

Table 3.2 describes these user IDs in more detail.

Table 3.2   User IDs and Groups for DB2 on Windows

	Installation User ID	Instance Owner User ID	DAS User ID
Authority of the User ID	A local or domain user account that is part of the administrator group on the server where you are installing DB2. You can also use the built-in Local System account to run the installation for all products except DB2 UDB Enterprise Server Edition. If you want to have the DB2 Setup Wizard create a domain user account for the Instance owner or the DAS user, the installation ID must have authority to create domain user accounts.	A local or domain user account that belongs to the administrator group on the server.	A local or domain user account that belongs to the administrator group on the machine. The built-in Local System account can also be used.
When to Create It	Before installation.	Before installation, or during installation by the DB2 Setup Wizard. Either way, the necessary rights will be granted during the installation process.	Same as Instance Owner User ID.
Rights Granted During Installation	Not applicable.	• Act as part of the operating system. • Debug programs. • Create a token object. • Increase quotas. • Lock pages in memory. • Log on as a service. • Replace a process-level token.	Same as Instance Owner User ID.

3.2.2 IDs and Groups Required for Linux/UNIX

On Linux/UNIX, you need to log on as a root user to perform DB2 installation. In addition, you need three users and three groups to operate DB2.

- The DB2 instance **Instance owner** is created in the instance owner home directory. This user ID controls all DB2 processes and owns all file systems and devices used by the databases contained within the instance.
- The **Fenced user** runs fenced user-defined functions (UDFs) and stored procedures. Fenced UDFs and stored procedures execute outside of the address space used by the DB2 instance and therefore cannot interfere with the execution of the instance. If you do not need this level of security, for example, in a test environment, you can use the instance owner as your fenced user.
- The same as on Windows, the **DAS user** runs the DB2 Administration Server process on your system. This user ID is also used by the DB2 GUI tools to perform administration tasks against the local server database instances and databases.
- Three separate user groups must also be created for the Instance Owner, the Fenced User, and the DAS user.

Table 3.3 describes these user IDs and groups in more detail.

Table 3.3   User IDs and Groups Required for Installing DB2 on UNIX Platforms

	Instance Owner User ID	Fenced User ID	DAS User ID
When to Create It	If the system is running NIS or similar security software, and you plan to create a DB2 instance during the DB2 installation process, then you must create this ID prior to installing DB2. See section 3.2.3, Creating User IDs and Groups if NIS Is Installed in Your Environment (Linux/UNIX Only), for more information. Otherwise: • During installation when using the DB2 Setup Wizard or Silent install. • After installation when using the `db2_install` script or native OS install tool.	Same as Instance Owner User ID.	Same as Instance Owner User ID.

continues

Table 3.3   User IDs and Groups Required for Installing DB2 on UNIX Platforms *(Continued)*

	Instance Owner User ID	Fenced User ID	DAS User ID
Default User ID Created by DB2 Installer	db2inst1 If *db2inst1* already exists, the DB2 installer will then search for the user *db2inst2*. If that user doesn't exist, it will then create that user. If that user does exist, the DB2 installer will continue its search (*db2inst3*, *db2inst4*, and so on) until it finds an available user.	db2fenc1 Uses the same algorithm as Instance Owner User ID.	• db2as (AIX only) • dasusr1 (all other Linux/UNIX platforms). Uses the same algorithm as Instance Owner User ID.
Example Primary Group Name	db2iadm1	db2fadm1	dasadm1
Example Secondary Group Name	dasadm1	Not applicable.	db2iadm1

3.2.3 Creating User IDs and Groups if NIS Is Installed in Your Environment (Linux/UNIX Only)

NIS is a secure and robust repository of information about network entities, such as users and servers, which enables the efficient administration of enterprise client/server networks. Administration tasks such as adding, removing, and reassigning systems and users are facilitated by modifying information in NIS. **NIS+** is a more mature version of NIS with better support for security issues and very large work groups.

If you have NIS or a similar security component installed on your machine, you must create the users and groups listed in Table 3.3 *manually before* installing DB2, because the DB2 installation scripts attempt to update objects that are under the control of the security packages. NIS prevents DB2 from doing those updates.

Keep the following restrictions in mind if you are using NIS or NIS+.

- You must create groups and users on the NIS server before installing DB2.
- You must add the primary group of the instance owner to the secondary DAS group. Likewise, you must add the primary DAS group to the secondary group for the instance owner.
- On a DB2 ESE system, before you create an instance, you must create an entry for the instance in the etc/services file. For example, if you want to create an instance for the user *db2inst1*, you require an entry similar to the following:

```
DB2_db2inst1    50000/tcp
```

> **N O T E**   These considerations hold true for any environment in
> which an external security program does not allow the DB2 installation
> or instance creation programs to modify user characteristics.

3.3 INSTALLING DB2 USING THE DB2 SETUP WIZARD

The DB2 Setup Wizard uses a step-by step-method to guide you through the installation process, perform the tasks listed in Figure 3.1, and keep an installation log. Refer to the documentation that comes with DB2 for the complete installation instructions. The following steps highlight the main points. Note that there are different first steps for Windows and Linux/UNIX, but that the procedure is mostly the same. For simplicity, we have used screen shots from the Windows installation in this section.

3.3.1 Step 1 for Windows: Launch the DB2 Setup Wizard

To start the installation of DB2 on Windows, you must log on to the system with a user ID that belongs to the local Administrators group and has the *Act as part of the operating system* advanced user right.

1. First, make sure to close all programs so that the installation program can update files as required.
2. Insert the DB2 CD-ROM. If enabled, the auto-run feature automatically starts the DB2 Setup Launchpad and the window shown in Figure 3.3 appears.

From the launchpad, you have the option to view the installation prerequisites and the release notes, or to proceed directly to the installation. Select *Install Products* and then select the DB2 product to install.

The DB2 Setup Wizard will determine your system's language and launch the setup program in that language. If you want to run the setup program in a different language, or if the setup program fails to start automatically, you can start the DB2 Setup Wizard manually and use the **/i** option to specify a language. To start the DB2 Setup Wizard manually, change to the CD-ROM drive and double-click on *setup*. Alternatively, click on **Start > Run**. In the Open field, enter the following command:

```
x:\setup /i language
```

where:

> **x** represents your CD-ROM drive, and **language** is the territory identifier for your language (for example, **EN** for English).

If the **/i** flag is not specified, the installation program will run in the default language of the operating system. You can also click *Browse*, change to the CD-ROM drive, and run *Setup*.

Continue with step 2.

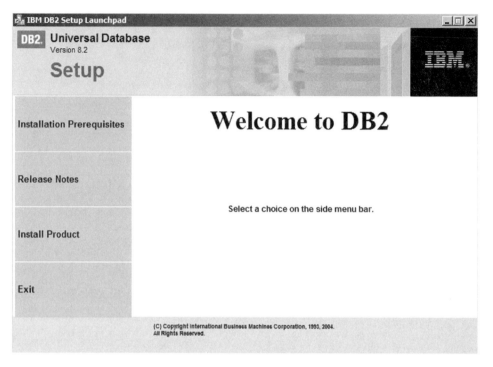

Figure 3.3   The DB2 Setup Launchpad

3.3.2 Step I for Linux/UNIX: Launch the DB2 Setup Wizard

The DB2 Setup Wizard is also available on Linux/UNIX platforms. You must have X-Windows software capable of rendering a graphical user interface for the DB2 Setup Wizard to run this on your machine. Do one of the following:

- To install DB2 on Linux/UNIX platforms, log on as a root user and mount the CD-ROM.
- On Linux, HP-UX, and AIX 4.3.3, enter the **db2setup** command from the CD-ROM drive to start the DB2 Setup Wizard.
- For Solaris and AIX 5L, you need to copy the file *product name*.tar.Z, where *product name* represents the product you are installing, to a file system on the server with a size of at least 2GB. Then enter:

```
zcat product_name.tar.Z | tar -xf - ; ./product_name/db2setup
```

For example, if the product name for DB2 Enterprise Server Edition is *ese*, enter the following command:

```
zcat ese.tar.Z | tar -xf - ; ./ese/db2setup
```

You will see the same DB2 Setup Launchpad as shown in Figure 3.3. Continue with step 2.

3.3.3 Step 2: Choose an Installation Type

As shown in Figure 3.4, you can select one of three installation types.

- **Typical** installs all required components as well as components that are used most often, such as ODBC support and the DB2 GUI tools. The DB2 instance and the DAS will be created and customized during installation.
- **Compact** installs only the required DB2 components plus ODBC support. The DB2 instance and the DAS will be created and customized during installation.
- **Custom** installs all required components, but gives you the flexibility to pick and choose which tools to install. You can also choose whether to create the DB2 instance and the DAS.

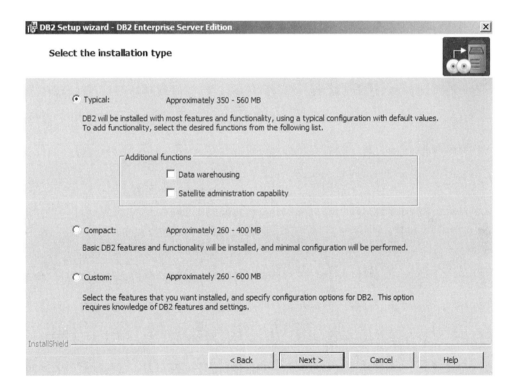

Figure 3.4   Selecting the installation type

3.3.4 Step 3: Choose Whether to Generate a Response File

As mentioned earlier, a response file allows you to perform DB2 installation on other computers in an unattended mode (refer to section 3.4, Silent Install Using a Response File, for information on how to do this).

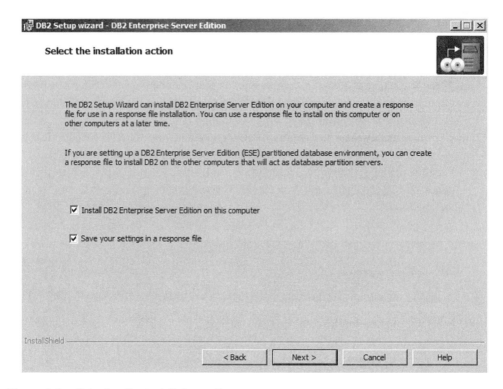

Figure 3.5   Selecting the installation action

If you need to install DB2 with the same configuration on other computers, it is a good idea to create a response file by selecting the Save your settings in a response file option (see Figure 3.5).

3.3.5 Step 4: Indicate Whether This Machine Will Be Part of a Partitioned Database Environment

If this machine will be part of a partitioned database environment, select the *Partitioned database environment* option, then indicate whether this is going to be the instance owning machine, that is, where the DB2 instance will be created (see Figure 3.6).

3.3.6 Step 5: Specify the Installation Folder

By default, DB2 will be installed in C:\Program Files\IBM\SQLLIB (see Figure 3.7). You can specify another drive and directory if you wish.

1. Click on the *Disk space* button to check that there is sufficient disk space to perform the installation.

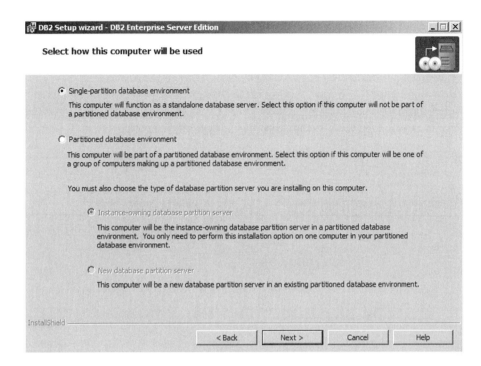

Figure 3.6 Selecting how this computer will be used

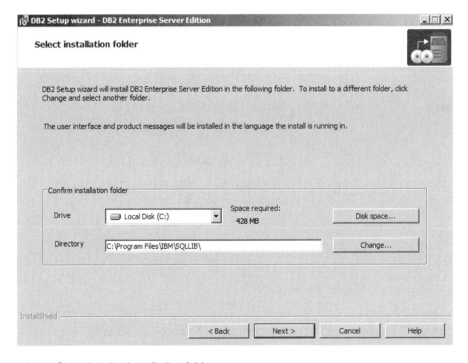

Figure 3.7 Selecting the installation folder

3.3.7 Step 6: Set User Information for the DB2 Administration Server

The DAS is a special service needed to support the DB2 graphical administration tools and assist with administrative tasks on local and remote DB2 servers. Each server can have only one DAS. During the installation the DAS is configured to start when the operating system is started.

You can specify either a local user or a domain user. If specifying a domain user, click on the domain drop down list and choose the domain. Otherwise, leave it blank. If the user does not already exist, it will be created and granted the appropriate rights. If the user already exists, DB2 will grant it the appropriate rights.

If you are creating a domain user, the user ID you are using for this installation must belong to the administrator group of the domain.

Click on *Next* to proceed.

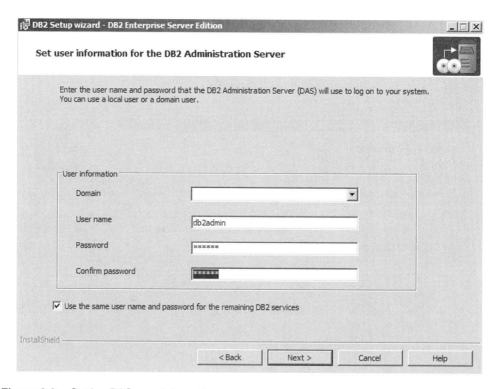

Figure 3.8   Setting DAS user information

3.3.8 Step 7: Enable the Alert Notification Feature

You can configure the DAS to send e-mail or pager notifications to administrators should certain conditions occur, such as a disk becoming full. The contact list can be stored on either the local machine or a remote machine (see Figure 3.9).

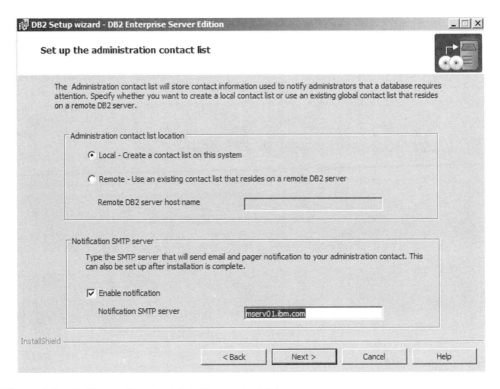

Figure 3.9   Setting up the administration contact list

- **Local** stores the contact list on this server only. This list can be used by other computers in a partitioned environment.
- **Remote** stores the contact list on a remote machine. In partitioned environments, we
  recommend storing the contact list on the instance-owning machine for easy access.

To send the notification, select the Enable notification option and specify the hostname of the
mail (SMTP) server. If you don't want to specify the SMTP server at this time, you can do this
after the installation. (Refer to **UPDATE ADMIN CONFIG** command in the *DB2 UDB Command
Reference* manual.)

3.3.9 Step 8: Create and Configure the DB2 Instance

By default, a DB2 instance named *DB2* will be created. The DB2 Setup Wizard automatically
detects the communication protocols configured on the server and generates communication
parameter values for the instance to use, for each detected protocol (see Figure 3.10).

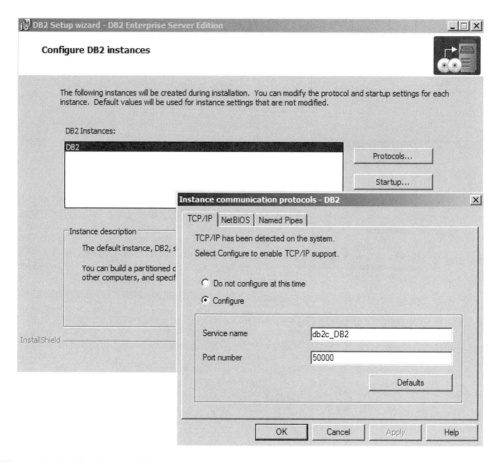

Figure 3.10   Configuring the DB2 instance and its communication protocols

Click the *Protocols* button to display the settings for each protocol. Figure 3.10 shows a list of the supported protocols on Windows: TCP/IP, NetBIOS, and Named Pipes. If a protocol is installed and configured correctly, the Configure option will be checked. Otherwise, the Do not configure at this time option will be checked. You can use the default values or enter different values.

The server needs a port number to accept connections from remote DB2 clients using TCP/IP. The clients will connect to the server through this port. If configured, the *x*:\WINNT\System32\ drivers\etc\services file will be updated, where *x* represents the Windows install directory.

The service name is the name that is associated with the port number in the services file. If you want to specify a different port number, make sure that this number does not already exist in the services file, because you cannot use the same port for two different applications.

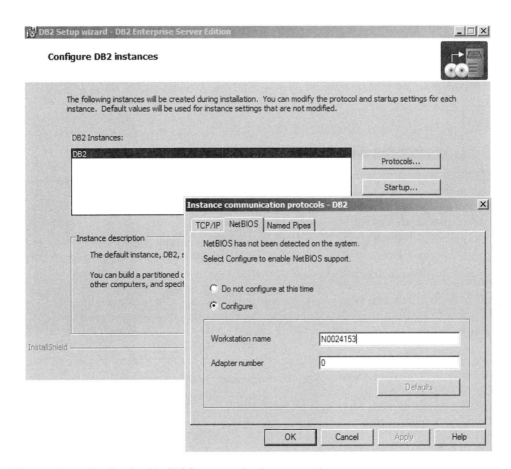

Figure 3.11 Configuring NetBIOS communication protocol

Figure 3.11 shows that NetBIOS has been detected as well, and shows the workstation name of the DB2 server on the network. The server's NetBIOS name must be unique on the network.

The Adapter number is the logical LAN adapter number that is used for the NetBIOS connection.

If you do not wish to configure a protocol at this time, choose *Do not configure at this time*. Figure 3.12 shows that the Name Pipes protocol is not going to be configured.

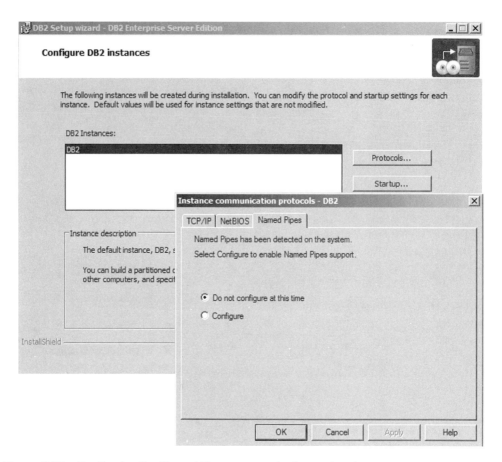

Figure 3.12   Configuring the Named Pipes communication protocol

You can choose to start the DB2 instance automatically during system startup. If you prefer to start it manually (using the **db2start**command) select the *Do not autostart the instance* option (see Figure 3.13).

3.3.10 Step 9: Create the DB2 Tools Catalog

The DB2 tools catalog consists of several tables that store information for use by the Task Center and the Journal. We will talk about these tools in Chapter 4, Using the DB2 Tools. If you plan to use these tools, it is a good idea to create the tools catalog now; if not, you can create the tools catalog later using the **CREATE TOOLS CATALOG** command (see Figure 3.14).

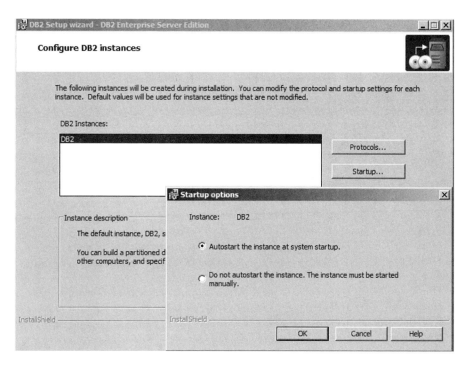

Figure 3.13   Configuring startup options for the DB2 instance

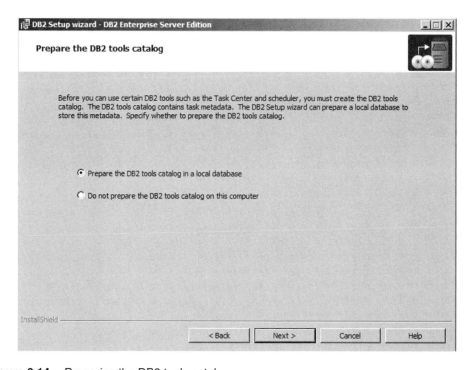

Figure 3.14   Preparing the DB2 tools catalog

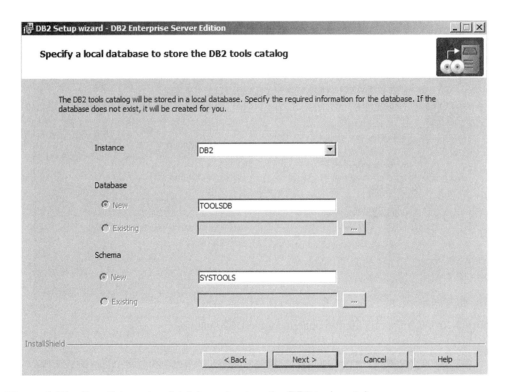

Figure 3.15   Specifying a local database to store the DB2 tools catalog

If you choose to create the tools catalog now, you need to create a database in which to store the catalog information (see Figure 3.15). The default database name is *TOOLSDB*, with a default schema *SYSTOOLS*. You can specify different names if you wish.

3.3.11 Step 10: Specify a Contact for Health Monitor Notification

The health monitor automatically tracks database performance. When a health indicator notices an alarm or warning level, it sends an alert to the contact specified in Figure 3.16.

3.3.12 Step 11: Enable Operating System Security for DB2 objects (Windows Only)

The DB2 Setup Wizard in Version 8.2 has a new security feature, which, if enabled, creates two user groups in the operating system security system (see Figure 3.17). Their default names are DB2ADMNS and DB2USERS.

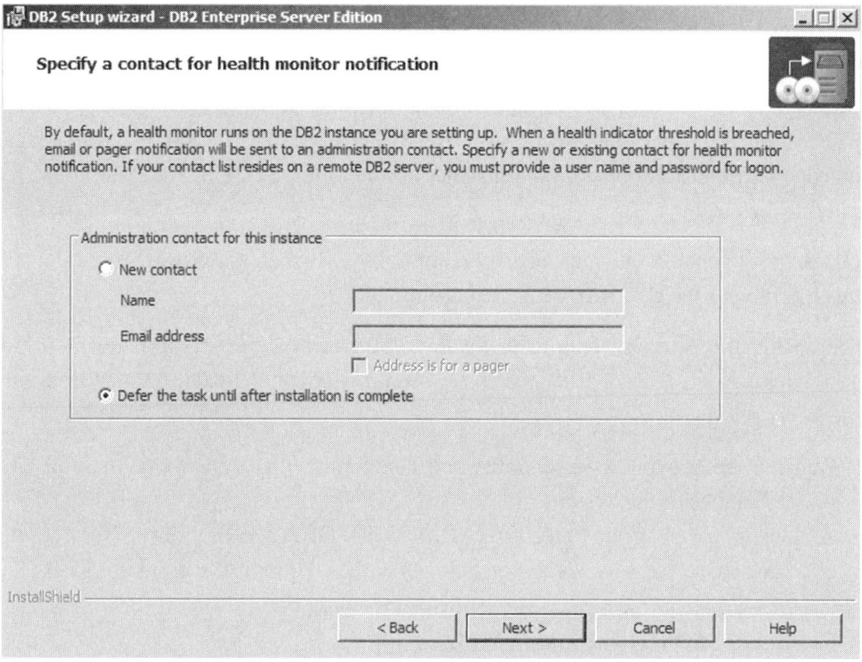

Figure 3.16 Specifying a contact for the health monitor notification

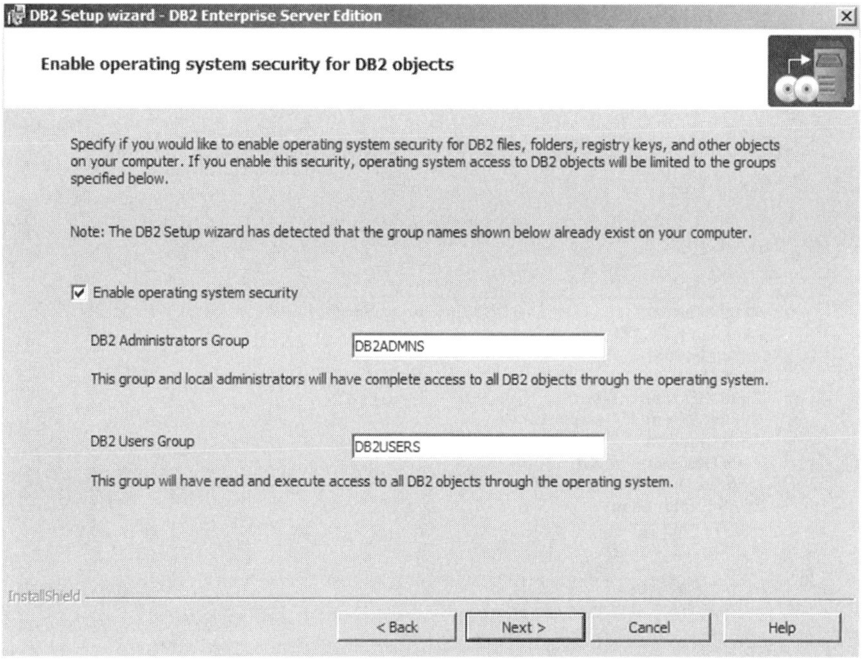

Figure 3.17 Enabling operating system security for DB2 objects

After successfully completing a DB2 installation, you can add users to the DB2ADMNS or the DB2USERS groups to give them access to DB2. Users in the DB2ADMNS groups have complete control over all DB2 objects in the instance; users in the DB2USERS group have read and execute authorities only.

If you choose not to enable the new security feature now, you can still do so after the installation completes by running the **db2secv82.exe** command.

Once you enable this security feature using the **db2secv82.exe** command, you have two options for backing out. Note that if there have been *any* changes made to the system you must use the second option.

- Run the **db2secv82.exe** command again immediately *without* making any additional changes to the system.
- Add the *Everyone* group to the DB2ADMNS and DB2USERS groups. This does not actually back it out, but since everyone belongs to these groups, the grouping loses its effect.

3.3.13 Step 12: Start the Installation

Just before starting the installation, the DB2 Setup Wizard displays a window summarizing the components that are going to be installed (see Figure 3.18). If you specified in step 3 to save

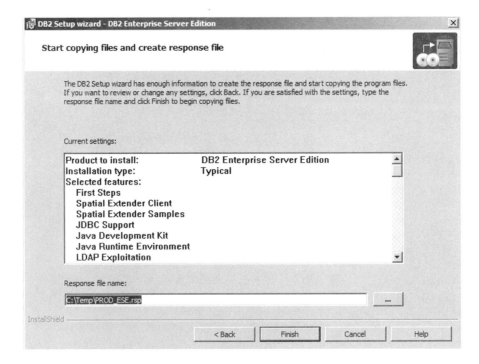

Figure 3.18   Component summary and response file location

your setting in a response file, the file information displays. Specify the location and name for the response file. Review this window carefully. Click on *Back* to make any changes; click *Finish* to start the installation.

Figure 3.19 shows the window that displays when the DB2 installation is complete. Read the list of recommended steps and click Finish to exit the DB2 Setup Wizard.

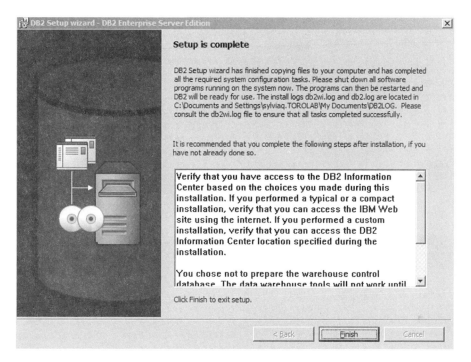

Figure 3.19   Setup complete

When you exit the DB2 Setup Wizard, after a successful DB2 installation, the First Steps dialog is automatically launched (see Figure 3.20). From this menu, you have the option to create a sample database, create your own database, check for DB2 updates, or exit First Steps.

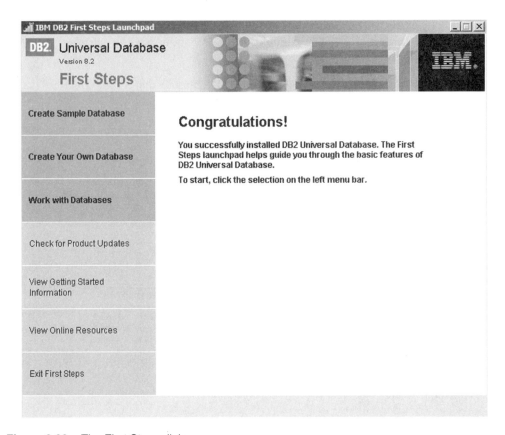

Figure 3.20   The First Steps dialog

3.4 SILENT INSTALL USING A RESPONSE FILE

When you need to install DB2 on a number of computers, you may want to install it using a response file to reduce the amount of work involved. With a response file, you can install DB2 unattended, which is why it is called Silent install. This installation method is available on all supported platforms.

A response file is a text file with the extension *.rsp*. It specifies configuration and setup parameters such as the destination directory (Windows only) and the products and components to install. It can also be used to:

- Create instances
- Set up global DB2 registry variables
- Set up the database manager configuration

Figure 3.21 shows a response file, *db2ese.rsp*, which can be used to perform a DB2 ESE server installation on Windows.

```
PROD=ENTERPRISE_SERVER_EDITION
LIC_AGREEMENT=ACCEPT
FILE=C:\Program Files\IBM\SQLLIB\
INSTALL_TYPE=TYPICAL

LANG=EN
DAS_CONTACT_LIST=LOCAL

DATABASE=TOOLS_DB
TOOLS_CATALOG_DATABASE=TOOLS_DB
TOOLS_CATALOG_SCHEMA=SYSTOOLS
TOOLS_DB.DATABASE_NAME=TOOLSDB

INSTANCE=DB2

TOOLS_DB.INSTANCE=DB2
TOOLS_DB.LOCATION=LOCAL
DB2.NAME=DB2
DEFAULT_INSTANCE=DB2
DB2.SVCENAME=db2c_DB2
DB2.DB2COMM=TCPIP
DB2.PORT_NUMBER=50000
DB2.AUTOSTART=YES
DB2.USERNAME=db2admin
DB2.PASSWORD=232259330271417239
ENCRYPTED=DB2.PASSWORD
DAS_USERNAME=db2admin
DAS_PASSWORD=232259330271417239
ENCRYPTED=DAS_PASSWORD
DB2_EXTSECURITY=YES
DB2_USERSGROUP_NAME=DB2USERS
DB2_ADMINGROUP_NAME=DB2ADMNS
```

Figure 3.21   A response file (created by the DB2 Setup Wizard)

As shown in Figure 3.21, a response file consists of keywords and their values. For example, the *PROD* keyword specifies the DB2 product you are installing. The *FILE* keyword specifies the install location, and the *INSTALL_TYPE* keyword specifies whether to perform a *TYPICAL* install, a *COMPACT* install, or a *CUSTOM* install. These are the values you would have to enter interactively if you were installing DB2 using the DB2 Setup Wizard.

3.4.1 Creating a Response File

There are three ways to create a response file for your installation.

- Using the DB2 Setup Wizard to save the setup and configuration data.
- Modifying a sample response file to create a custom response file.
- Using the response file generator (Windows only).

3.4.1.1 Creating a Response File Using the DB2 Setup Wizard

If you use the DB2 Setup Wizard to install DB2, you have the option to create a response file (refer back to step 3). This response file will record all the parameters you input to the DB2 Setup Wizard, and you can use this file to perform installation on other computers. The DB2 Setup Wizard created the response file shown in Figure 3.21.

3.4.1.2 Creating a Custom Response File Using a Sample Response File

You can manually edit the response file created by the DB2 Setup Wizard or the sample response files provided on the DB2 CD-ROM. Each DB2 product has sample response files. They are

```
* General Options
* -----------------
PROD                = ENTERPRISE_SERVER_EDITION
INSTALL_OPTION      = SINGLE_PARTITION
*FILE               = C:\Program Files\IBM\SQLLIB
*INSTALL_TYPE       = TYPICAL, COMPACT, or CUSTOM (default=TYPICAL)
*TYPICAL_OPTION     = BLANK, DATA_WAREHOUSE, or SATELLITE_ADMIN
(default=BLANK)
*LANG               = BR (default=Operating System Language)
*COMP               = SYSTEM_BIND_FILES

* General information for instance to be created
* ------------------------------------------------
INSTANCE            = DB2
DEFAULT_INSTANCE    = DB2
DB2.NAME            = DB2
*DB2.TYPE           = ESE, WSE, CLIENT, STANDALONE or SATELLITE

* Default Instance Logon Settings
* --------------------------------
*DB2.USERNAME       = char(30) [char(20) for Windows NT]
*DB2.DOMAIN         = char(14)
*DB2.PASSWORD       = char(14)

* Default Instance Auto-start Option
* -----------------------------------
*DB2.AUTOSTART      = YES or NO (default=YES)

* Default Instance TCP/IP port number
* -------------------------------------
*DB2.PORT_NUMBER    = 1024 - 65535

* Administration Server Logon Settings
* --------------------------------------
*DAS_USERNAME       = char(30) [char(20) for Windows NT]
*DAS_DOMAIN         = char(14)
*DAS_PASSWORD       = char(14)
```

Figure 3.22 A sample Windows response file

located at the *cd-rom*/db2/*platform*/samples directory (where *cd-rom* represents the location of the installable version of DB2). Figure 3.22 shows a sample Windows response file.

All the entries in the sample response files are commented out with asterisks (*). You need to remove the asterisks to activate the entries. The possible values are listed to the right of the equal sign.

3.4.1.3 Creating a Response File Using the Response File Generator (Windows Only)

The **response file generator utility**, `db2rspgn`, creates a response file from an existing installed and configured DB2 product.

The syntax for `db2rspgn` is:

```
db2rspgn -d x:\path [-i instance] [-noctlsrv] [-nodlfm]
```

where:

-**d** specifies the directory for a response file and any instance files. This parameter is required.

x represents the disk drive.

-**i** (optional) specifies a list of instances for which you want to create a profile. The default is to generate an instance profile file for all instances.

-**noctlsrv** (optional) indicates that an instance profile file will not be generated for the Control Server instance.

`-nodlfm` (optional) indicates that an instance profile file will not be generated for the Data Links File Manager instance.

For example,

```
db2rspgn d:\temp
```

will generate two files in the *d:\temp* directory. One is the response file, *db2ese.rsp* (assuming DB2 UDB ESE is the product installed), and the other file is *DB2.INS*, which contains information such as the registry variables and database manager configurations.

3.4.2 Installing DB2 Using a Response File on Windows

To perform a DB2 installation using a response file, use the **setup** command.

```
cd-rom/setup [/L log_file]
    /U response_file [/T trace_file] [/F]
```

where:

> **cd-rom** represents the location of the DB2 installable image.

> **/L** (optional) specifies the fully qualified log file name, where setup information and any errors occurring during setup are logged. If you do not specify the log file's name, DB2 names it *db2.log* and puts it in the *My Documents/db2log* folder.

> **/U** specifies the full path name of the response file.

> **/T** (optional) specifies the full path name of a file to trace install information.

> **/F** (optional) forces all DB2 processes before installation. If any DB2 processes are running when the DB2 setup command is issued, the installation of DB2 cannot occur. Use this option to stop all DB2 processes so installation can be started.

For example:

```
setup /U d:\temp\db2ese.rsp
```

3.4.3 Installing DB2 Using a Response File on Linux/UNIX

To perform a DB2 installation using a response on Linux/UNIX, use the **db2setup** command:

```
cd-rom/db2setup -r response_file
```

where:

> **cd-rom** represents the location of the DB2 install image.

> **response_file** represents the full path name of the response file.

For example:

```
db2setup -r /usr/tmp/db2ese.rsp
```

3.5 INSTALLING DB2 MANUALLY (LINUX/UNIX ONLY)

DB2 supports two additional methods for installing DB2 on Linux and UNIX.

- Using the operating system's native install tool
- Using the `db2_install` script

These two methods require a certain level of operating system knowledge. Tasks such as user and instance creation and configuration that would be performed for you by the DB2 Setup Wizard or during a response file installation must be performed after the product is installed. We do not recommend using either of these methods if you are new to DB2.

3.5.1 Installing DB2 Using the Native Operating System Install Tool

When installing DB2 using an operating system's native install tool, it is important to identify the required, typical, and optional DB2 components for the product that you want to install. Each DB2 product's CD-ROM provides a file that lists the components available for installation. The component list is in a file called *ComponentList.htm* and is located in the */db2/platform* directory on the CD-ROM (where *platform* is the platform on which you are installing).

You can use the following native operating system install tools to install DB2.

- smit on AIX
- swinstall on HP-UX
- rpm on Linux
- pkgadd on Solaris

3.5.2 Installing DB2 Using the db2_install Script

The `db2_install` script is in the root directory on your DB2 Version 8 product CD-ROM. The `db2_install` script prompts you for one of the keywords shown in Table 3.4 (depending upon which DB2 product you are installing). Enter the keyword for the product you want to install. If you specify more than one product keyword, separate the keywords with spaces.

> **NOTE** For Solaris you have the option of specifying a different base directory for the DB2 installation. The default base directory for the Solaris operating environment is /opt. If you choose to install DB2 to a different base directory, links will be set up for the default DB2 installation directory, /opt/IBM/db2/V8.1. Parts of the product are dependent upon the default installation directory. Creating links allows DB2 to physically exist on a base directory other than /opt.

Table 3.4   Keywords Used by the db2_install Script

DB2 Product	Keyword
DB2 Administration Client	DB2.ADMCL
DB2 Application Development Client	DB2.ADCL
DB2 Connect Enterprise Edition, DB2 Connect Unlimited Edition, and DB2 Connect Application Server Edition	DB2.CONEE
DB2 Connect Personal Edition	DB2.CONPE
DB2 Cube Views	DB2.CUBE
DB2 Data Links Manager	DB2.DLM
DB2 Enterprise Server Edition	DB2.ESE
DB2 Express Edition or DB2 Express Edition Processor Option	DB2.EXP
DB2 Information Integrator Non-Relational Wrappers	DB2.LSDC
DB2 Information Integrator Relational Wrappers	DB2.RCON
DB2 Personal Edition	DB2.PE
DB2 Query Patroller	DB2.QP
DB2 Run-Time Client	DB2.RTCL
DB2 Spatial Extender	DB2.GSE
DB2 Warehouse Manager	DB2.WM
DB2 Workgroup Server Edition and DB2 Workgroup Server Unlimited Edition	DB2.WSE

3.6 INSTALLING A DB2 LICENSE

Licenses are automatically installed if you installed the DB2 product using the DB2 Setup Wizard or response file. If you installed DB2 using the `db2_install` script or the operating system's native install tools, you need to install the licenses manually.

There are two ways you can install a DB2 license: using the GUI License Center or the `db2licm` command.

3.6.1 Installing a DB2 Product License Using the License Center

The License Center is a GUI tool you can use to display, add, remove, or change a license. To start the License Center from the Control Center, click on the icon that looks like a key and a user (see Figure 3.23).

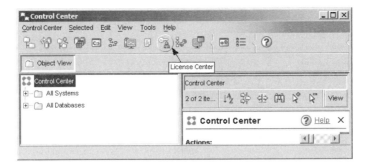

Figure 3.23   Starting the License Center from the Control Center

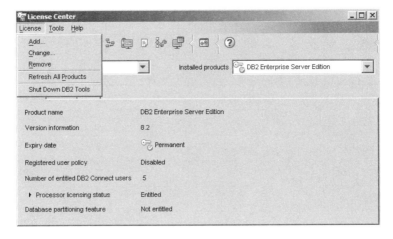

Figure 3.24   The License Center

Figure 3.24 shows the License Center.

If a license is already installed, it will be displayed. If not, you have to add a license using the **License > Add** menu option.

3.6.2 Installing the DB2 Product License Using the db2licm Command

You can also install the license by using the **db2licm** command.

On Linux/UNIX, you can either log in as a root user or an instance owner to install a license.

As an instance owner use:

```
db2instance_path/adm/db2licm -a filename
```

As a root user type:

```
/usr/opt/db2_08_01/adm/db2licm -a filename (on AIX)
/opt/IBM/db2/V8.1/adm/db2licm -a filename (on all other UNIX platforms and Linux)
```

On Windows, type:

```
db2instance_path\adm\db2licm -a filename
```

where:

> *db2instance_path* is where the DB2 instance was created.

> *filename* is the full pathname and filename for the license file that corresponds to the product you purchased.

The license file is located in the /db2/license directory at the root directory of the product's CD-ROM.

For example, on AIX, if the CD-ROM is mounted in the /cdrom directory and the name of the license file is db2dlm.lic, the command to use would be:

```
/usr/opt/db2_08_01/adm/db2licm -a /cdrom/db2/license/db2dlm.lic
```

After running the **db2licm** command, the DB2 product license key information is contained in the nodelock file in one of the following directories.

- For AIX: /var/ifor
- For HP-UX, Linux, or Solaris Operating Environment: /var/lum.
- For Windows: DB2PATH/sqllib/license

3.7 INSTALLING DB2 IN A DPF ENVIRONMENT

In a DPF environment with multiple physical machines, each of the participating machines must have DB2 installed locally. To ease the installation of DB2 on other machines, we recommend you create a response file when you install DB2 on the first machine. Once this response file is created, you can transfer the file to the other machines and run a Silent installation (see section 3.4, Silent Install Using a Response File, for details).

The DB2 install code from the installation CD-ROM can reside on a shared disk, from which you proceed to install DB2 locally onto each participating computer, as illustrated in Figure 3.25.

The Linux2 machine in Figure 3.25 has a disk onto which the install code from the installation CD-ROM has been copied. This disk is set up so that it can be shared by the other two machines, Linux1 and Linux3. From each of the machines you can execute the **db2setup** command to install DB2 locally; therefore, each machine will have its own local directory /opt/IBM/db2/ V8.1 containing the DB2 installed binaries. Installing DB2 locally on the Linux2 machine and sharing the installed binaries with Linux1 and Linux3 is not supported.

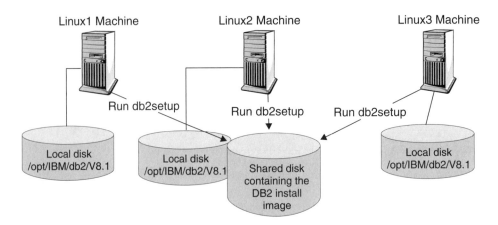

Figure 3.25   Installing DB2 in a DPF environment

> **N O T E**   On Linux, the DB2 installed binaries are locally stored in
> directory /opt/IBM/db2/V8.1. On other platforms DB2 is installed in
> other directories. Use the **db2level** command to determine where
> the installed code has been locally installed in your machine.

3.8 INSTALLING DB2 FIXPAKS

A DB2 **FixPak** provides fixes to program defects. A fix to a program defect is also known as an
Authorized Program Analysis Report (APAR). A FixPak may also provide new functionality.
FixPaks are normally available every three months. There are two kinds of DB2 FixPaks: regular
and alternate FixPaks. We will describe these in the next sections.

3.8.1 Applying a Regular DB2 FixPak (All Supported Platforms and Products)

Regular FixPaks provide cumulative fixes that are applied on top of other regular FixPaks, or
the base DB2 code also known as the **generally available** (**GA**) code.

When you apply a DB2 regular FixPak, you are in fact refreshing the DB2 code by overwriting
some or all of the DB2 programs. You then need to reestablish the links to an existing instance
using the **db2iupdt** program on Linux/UNIX (but not on Windows). Figure 3.26 shows an
example of what happens after applying FixPak 8 to DB2 UDB Version 8.2.

After applying a new FixPak, the code in the DB2 installation directory is replaced with the new
code from the FixPak. All the instances should be updated using **db2iupdt** to reestablish their
links to the new code. However, the data in the databases remains unchanged.

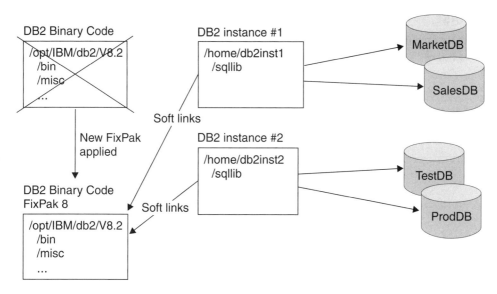

Figure 3.26 Applying a DB2 FixPak

3.8.2 Applying an Alternate FixPak (Available on DB2 ESE and on UNIX Platforms Only)

For each regular FixPak x, there is an **alternate** FixPak x. You can download the alternate Fix-Paks from the same location as regular FixPaks. Let's look at the following example to understand the purpose of an alternate FixPak.

Your production environment is running DB2 Version 8 FixPak x and has been running with no problems. Now a new FixPak y has just been released. You would like to upgrade your system to the FixPak y level. However, without having tested it, you cannot be sure FixPak y will work with your current applications. You have no spare system on which to test this new FixPak. What can you do?

With alternate FixPaks, you can install the new FixPak on the same system without having to remove your current FixPak. You can now test the new features in FixPak y while FixPak x continues to support your production environment. This is referred to as DB2's **Multiple FixPak** (**MFP**) support.

An alternate FixPak contains the same cumulative fixes as a regular FixPak, but they are built into the product. You do not apply an alternate FixPak on top of any existing FixPak, regular or alternate. Instead, you install alternate FixPaks on a different path than the existing DB2 installation; therefore, an alternate FixPak is treated as a different version of the product.

> **N O T E**   Each DB2 FixPak comes with a README file and Release Notes. The README file contains installation instructions. The Release Notes contain detailed information about what has changed in the Fix-Pak, including any new functionality.

3.9 CASE STUDY

Your company has chosen DB2 as their RDBMS, and would like you to install DB2 Enterprise Server Edition (ESE) on a Windows machine. You have DB2 UDB Personal Edition (PE) with FixPak 8 installed on that machine, since you were learning DB2 on your own time. To install DB2 UDB ESE, you do not need to uninstall the DB2 UDB PE; you just need to install DB2 UDB ESE on top of DB2 UDB PE. When you run the DB2 ESE **setup** command, the installation goes through, but you receive the warning message shown in Figure 3.27.

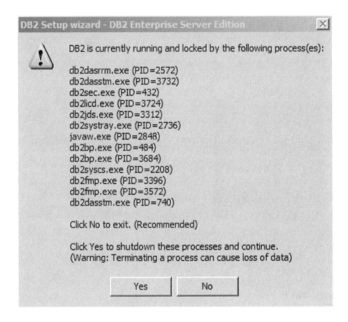

Figure 3.27   Shutting down processes on Windows

You click on *Yes*, as you were using DB2 PE for training purposes. After this, the installation successfully completes.

Next you issue the command **db2licm -l** to confirm you installed the right product and to review the license status. Figure 3.28 shows the output of the command.

The response confirms that you have DB2 ESE installed, but now you realize it is a Try and Buy copy. You tell this to your manager, who calls the 1-800-IBM-SERV number to buy a permanent license.

Next, you issue the **db2level** command to ensure you are at the latest FixPak. Figure 3.29 shows the command's output.

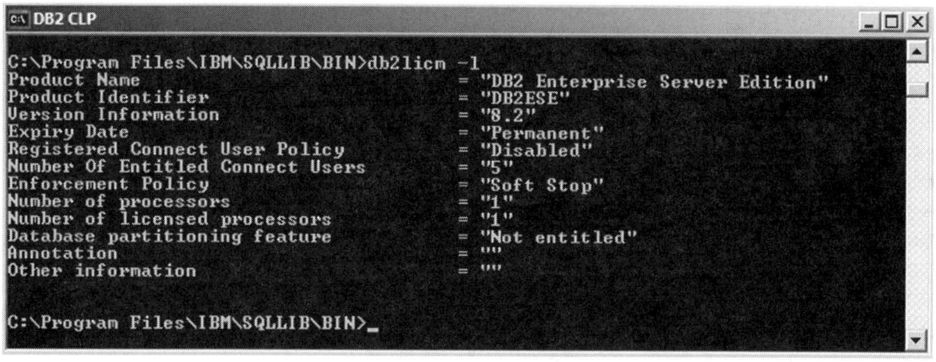

Figure 3.28   Output from the db2licm command

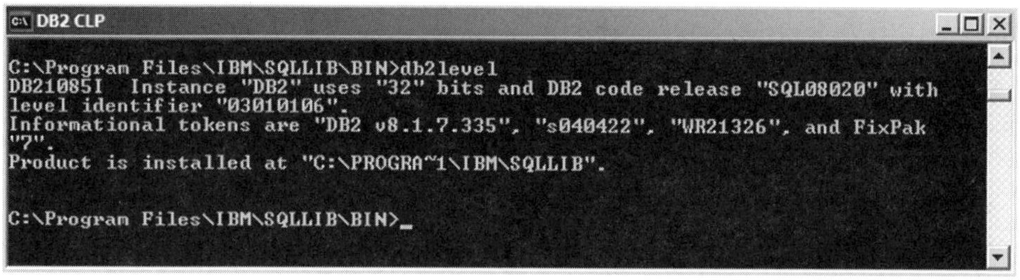

Figure 3.29   Output of the db2level command

You notice the FixPak level is 7. Since you know the latest FixPak is 8, you go to the IBM Support Web site and download FixPak 8. Because you are working on the Windows platform, only regular FixPaks are available; alternate FixPaks are not an option. Figure 3.30 shows the DB2 Technical support Web site.

> **N O T E**   At the time this book was written, FixPak 8 for DB2 Version 8.2 was not available. We use this FixPak number hypothetically to illustrate how to work with FixPaks.

> **N O T E**   Web site content changes constantly. The DB2 Technical Support Web site may change in the future or may not look as shown in Figure 3.30.

After applying FixPak 8, you again issue the **db2level** command to confirm it now shows the right FixPak level.

Now your company is ready to start working with DB2!

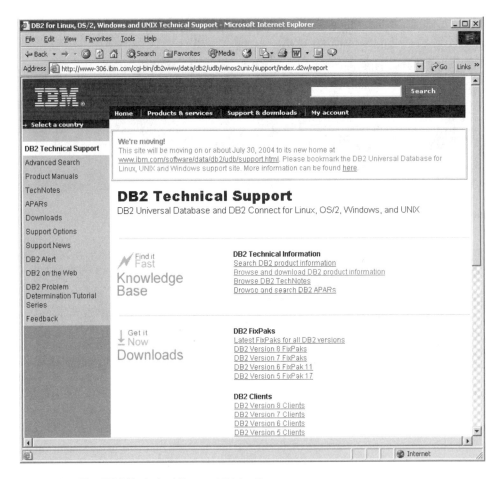

Figure 3.30   The DB2 Technical Support Web site

3.10 Summary

In this chapter we discussed four DB2 installation methods:

- Using the DB2 Setup Wizard
- Using a response file
- Using the **db2_install** script
- Using native operating system install tools

The first two methods are available on all supported platforms; the last two are only available on Linux/UNIX platforms. The recommended method to install DB2 is by using the DB2 Setup Wizard. If you use the DB2 Setup Wizard or the response file methods, you have the choice to create a DB2 instance and the DAS during installation. The instance owner user ID and the DAS user ID are also created. If you use the other two methods, you must manually create the user

IDs and the instance after the installation is completed. If you use the native operating system install tool to perform the install, you must install the DB2 license manually.

To install DB2 in a DPF environment with multiple machines, the recommended installation method is the Silent install. Copy the DB2 install image from the CD-ROM to a shared disk, then run the DB2 setup program from each machine to install DB2 locally.

There are two different types of DB2 FixPaks: the regular DB2 FixPaks and the alternate DB2 FixPaks. Both types of FixPaks contain fixes to APARs. However, the alternate FixPak lets you maintain different FixPak levels of DB2 for the same version.

3.11 REVIEW QUESTIONS

1. What DB2 installation methods are available on Windows?
2. What DB2 installation methods are available on Linux/UNIX?
3. What is the name of the default instance created by the DB2 Setup Wizard during installation on Linux/UNIX?
4. What is the purpose of a DB2 alternate FixPak?
5. On Linux/UNIX, where are installation logs generated by default? Can you redirect them to a different location?
6. On Windows, where are installation logs generated by default? Can you redirect them to a different location?
7. Two user groups are optionally created on Windows during a DB2 install. What are they?
8. What command needs to be run after you install a DB2 FixPak on Linux or UNIX?
9. What user rights are granted to an instance owner during installation on Windows?
10. What authority must a user have to install DB2 on Windows?
11. Which of the following is a valid method for installing DB2 on Windows?
    A. The db2_install script
    B. The DB2 Setup Wizard
    C. The db2setup.exe program
    D. Using the operating system's Add or Remove program utility under the Control Panel
12. Which of the following allows you to install DB2 unattended?
    A. The db2_install script
    B. The DB2 Setup Wizard
    C. A response file
    D. Smitty on AIX
13. Which of the following is the TCP/IP port the DB2 Setup Wizard uses to configure the default DB2 instance during installation (assuming TCP/IP is enabled on the system)?
    A. 6000
    B. 20000
    C. 50000
    D. 5000

14. What authority is required for a user to install DB2 on Linux/UNIX?
    A. Instance owner authority
    B. DAS user authority
    C. Local Administrator authority
    D. Root authority

15. Which of the following user IDs is used by the DB2 GUI tools to perform administration tasks against the local server database instances and databases?
    A. The DAS user ID
    B. The instance owner user ID
    C. The fenced user ID
    D. The DB2 user ID

16. Which of the following is *not* a valid method of creating a response file on Windows?
    A. Using the DB2 Setup Wizard to save the setup and configuration data
    B. Using the db2_install script to save the setup and configuration data
    C. Using the response file generator
    D. Modifying one of the sample response files that are provided

17. During installation, which of the following methods prompts you to enter the product keyword (e.g., DB2.ESE, DB2.WSE) for the product you want to install?
    A. The DB2 Setup Wizard
    B. A response file install
    C. The db2_install script
    D. Smitty on AIX

18. Which of the following commands should be used to install DB2 on Linux/UNIX using a response file?
    A. db2setup –r *response_file*
    B. setup /U *response_file*
    C. install –r *response_file*
    D. response_install /U *response_file*

19. Which of the following *cannot* be used to install a DB2 license?
    A. The db2licm command
    B. The DB2 License Center
    C. The DB2 Setup Wizard
    D. The db2_install script

20. Which of the following is the recommended method when installing DB2 in a DPF environment with multiple machines?
    A. Using the DB2 Setup Wizard
    B. Using a response file
    C. Using the db2_install script
    D. Using the operating system's native install tools

## CHAPTER 4

Using the
DB2 Tools

H ow do you work with DB2? How do you issue SQL queries and enter DB2 commands? Are there graphical tools that can make your administration tasks easier? The answer to all of these questions is *yes*. DB2 provides a wide range of tools, both graphical and command driven, to help you work with DB2.

In this chapter you will learn about:

- Database command line tools
- Application development tools
- Database administration tools
- The DB2 information center
- Monitoring tools

4.1 DB2 TOOLS: THE BIG PICTURE

Figure 4.1 shows most of the DB2 tools available from the **IBM DB2** menu on the Windows platform and the sequence of items to click to start them. These same tools (except the Command Window) are available on the Linux and UNIX platforms.

The tools that you see in Figure 4.1 are of two types: command driven and non-command driven. In the next section you will learn about command-driven tools, and in section 4.4, General Administration Tools, you will be presented with the non-command-driven tools, which are available only using a graphical interface. In most cases you can perform the same DB2 commands and SQL statements using either type of tools.

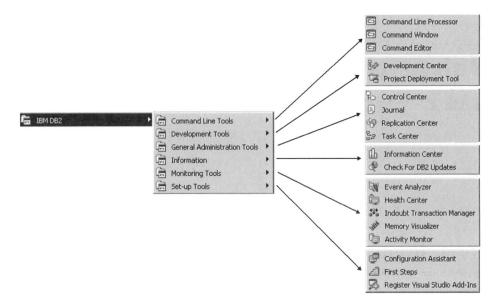

Figure 4.1   The IBM DB2 menu

4.2 THE COMMAND LINE TOOLS

All DB2 operations are invoked by DB2 commands or SQL statements. For example, to back up a database, you use the **BACKUP DATABASE** command. To create a table, you use the **CREATE TABLE** SQL statement. All of these commands and SQL statements can be entered using the command line tools.

The command line tools consist of the Command Line Processor (CLP), the Command Window (Windows platform only), and the Command Editor. Since they are command driven, you must have some knowledge of DB2 commands and SQL statements to use them.

> **N O T E**   In this chapter we use **DB2 commands** to refer to both types of commands: DB2 system commands and DB2 CLP commands. When a section is only applicable to a given type of command, it will be explicitly indicated. Refer to section 2.1, SQL Statements and DB2 Commands, for an explanation about the differences between these two types of commands.

4.2.1 The Command Line Processor and the Command Window

The DB2 CLP and the DB2 Command Window are text-based tools used to interact with the DB2 engine. Figure 4.2 shows the relationship between the CLP and the Command Window.

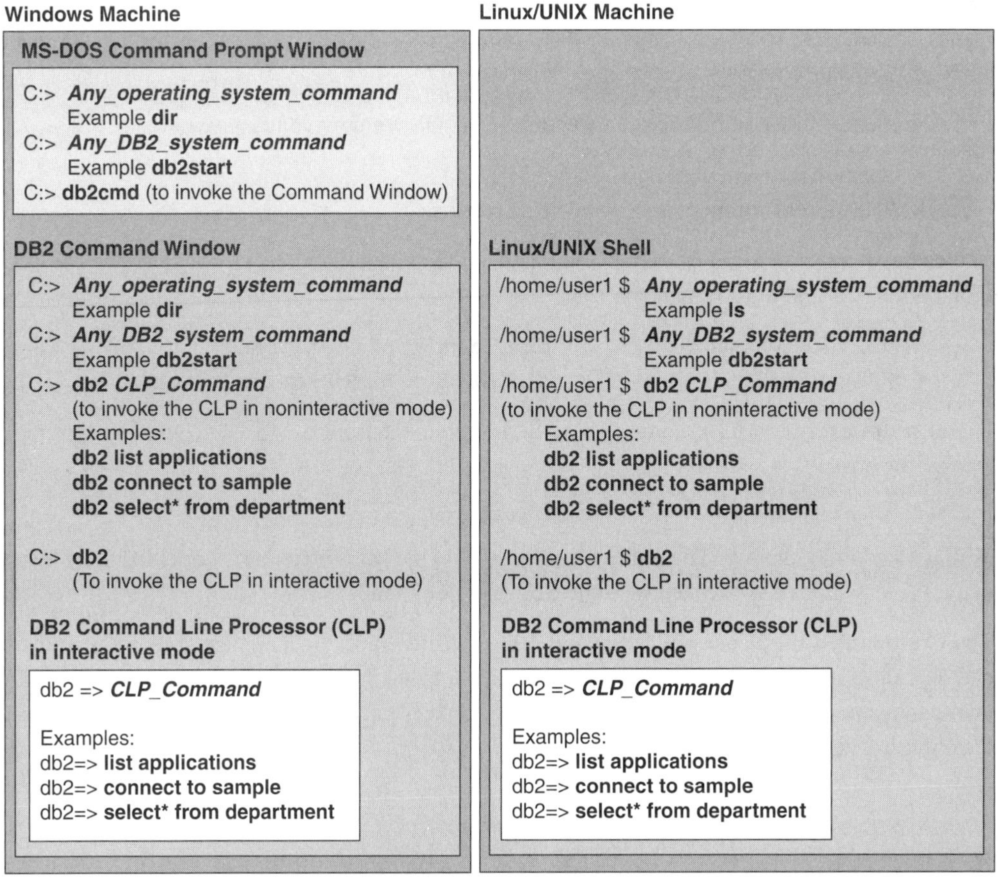

Windows Machine   **Linux/UNIX Machine**

MS-DOS Command Prompt Window

C:> *Any_operating_system_command*
    Example **dir**
C:> *Any_DB2_system_command*
    Example **db2start**
C:> **db2cmd** (to invoke the Command Window)

DB2 Command Window   **Linux/UNIX Shell**

C:> *Any_operating_system_command*   /home/user1 $ *Any_operating_system_command*
    Example **dir**   Example **ls**
C:> *Any_DB2_system_command*   /home/user1 $ *Any_DB2_system_command*
    Example **db2start**   Example **db2start**
C:> **db2** *CLP_Command*   /home/user1 $ **db2** *CLP_Command*
    (to invoke the CLP in noninteractive mode)   (to invoke the CLP in noninteractive mode)
    Examples: Examples:
    db2 list applications   **db2 list applications**
    db2 connect to sample   **db2 connect to sample**
    db2 select* from department   **db2 select* from department**

C:> **db2**   /home/user1 $ **db2**
    (To invoke the CLP in interactive mode)   (To invoke the CLP in interactive mode)

DB2 Command Line Processor (CLP)   **DB2 Command Line Processor (CLP)**
in interactive mode   **in interactive mode**

db2 => *CLP_Command*   db2 => *CLP_Command*

Examples: Examples:
db2=> **list applications**   db2=> **list applications**
db2=> **connect to sample**   db2=> **connect to sample**
db2=> **select* from department**   db2=> **select* from department**

Figure 4.2   The Command Line Processor versus the Command Window

Compare each line in the Windows machine versus the Linux/UNIX machine. The equivalent line in each machine has been aligned in the figure.

The **Command Window** is only available on Windows; this is due to some architecture differences in Windows versus Linux and UNIX. If you are familiar with the Linux and UNIX platforms, you can think of the Command Window on Windows as the Linux/UNIX shell. Figure 4.2 illustrates this: the commands and statements inside the DB2 Command Window box on the left side of the figure are equivalent to the ones inside the Linux/UNIX shell box on the right side of the figure.

To start the Command Window, click on **Start > Programs > IBM DB2 > Command Line Tools > Command Window** (see Figure 4.1). Alternatively, to invoke the Command Window from an MS-DOS window, issue the command **db2cmd**. This command spawns another window which displays *DB2 CLP* in the title bar. Note that the Command Window looks like any MS-DOS window except for this title bar.

From a MS-DOS window, you can perform operating system commands and DB2 system commands but not DB2 CLP commands or SQL statements. However, you can perform all of these from a Command Window.

For example, as shown in Figure 4.2, from the MS-DOS window you can execute:

- Operating system commands: `dir`
- DB2 system commands: `db2start`

You can also perform these from the Command Window, and in addition you can perform DB2 CLP commands and SQL statements:

- DB2 CLP command: `db2 list applications`
- SQL statements: `db2 SELECT * FROM department`

If you try to execute a CLP command or SQL statement from a MS-DOS window, you will receive the error:

`DB21061E Command line environment not initialized`

as illustrated in Figure 4.3. The figure also shows how the same statement works from the Command Window after it is invoked with the **db2cmd** command.

The **Command Line Processor** is an application written in the C language containing embedded SQL. It provides you with a text-based interface to the DB2 engine that lets you issue CLP commands and SQL statements. The CLP executable is called **db2** and it is stored under the ...sqllib/bin directory.

Figure 4.3   Invoking the Command Window from a MS-DOS command prompt

> **N O T E**   We recommend that you learn how to use the Command
> Line Processor, as it is the common tool available with all DB2 versions
> and clients.

4.2.1.1 Methods to Work with the CLP

There are three ways to issue a DB2 command or SQL statement with the CLP: interactive
mode, non-interactive mode, and non-interactive mode using a file as input. These methods are
discussed in the following sections.

Method 1: Interactive Mode

You start the CLP in interactive mode by clicking on **Start > Programs > IBM DB2 > Command
Line Tools > Command Line Processor** (see Figure 4.1). Alternatively, from the Command
Window or Linux/UNIX shell, you start the CLP in interactive mode by entering **db2** and press-
ing Enter as shown in Figure 4.4.

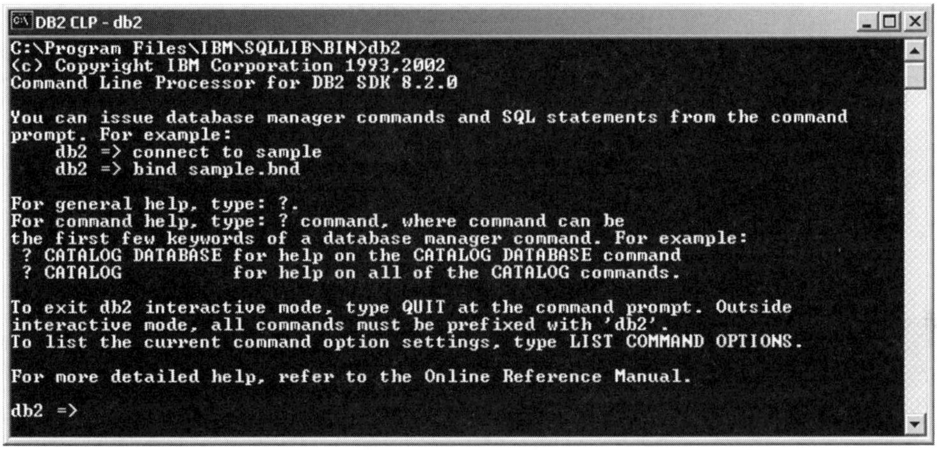

Figure 4.4   Figure 4.4 The Command Line Processor in interactive mode

After you invoke the CLP in interactive mode, a few messages will appear on the screen, and
then your command prompt will change to **db2 =>**. This prompt indicates that you are in interactive mode and that you can type any DB2 CLP command or SQL statement.

Table 4.1 lists some common CLP interactive mode commands. The underlined letter in the
command shows the shortcut that you can use to invoke the command.

Figure 4.5 shows a few examples of the commands in Table 4.1 in action.

Table 4.1   Useful CLP Commands for Working with the CLP in Interactive Mode

Command	Explanation	Example
history	Lists the last 20 commands entered and prefixes each with a number. The maximum number of commands kept in memory can be customized with the DB2 registry variable DB2_CLP_HISTSIZE (see Chapter 5 for information about DB2 registry variables).	`history`
runcmd <*n*>	Reexecutes command number *n* from the list given by the `history` command. If *n* is not specified (or *n* = -1), the previous command is invoked.	To reexecute the third command in the history list: `r 3`
edit <*n*>	Edits the command number *n* using an editor defined by the DB2 registry variable DB2_CLP_EDITOR. If not set, this uses the vi editor on Linux/UNIX and Notepad on Windows.	To edit the fifth command in the history list: `e 5`
Exclamation mark (!)	This is the escape character that lets you issue operating system commands from within the CLP interactive mode	`!dir`

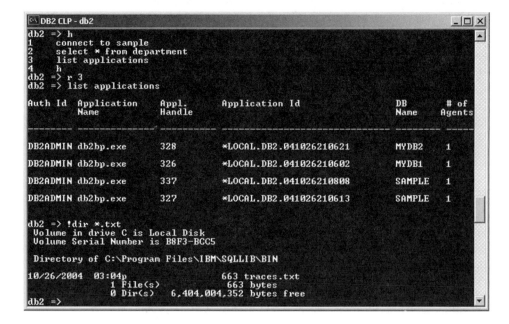

Figure 4.5   Examples of CLP commands in interactive mode

Method 2: Non-interactive Mode

To work with the CLP in non-interactive mode is equivalent to working with the DB2 Command Window (on Windows) or the Linux/UNIX shell. If you start the CLP in interactive mode, entering the **quit** command takes you to the CLP in non-interactive mode. In this mode you need to prefix the CLP command or SQL statement with the **db2** executable. For example:

```
db2 connect to sample
db2 list applications all
db2 select * from employee
```

Using this method you can execute operating system commands in addition to DB2 commands and SQL statements from the same window or session.

> **N O T E**   References to the Command Window and the CLP on Windows platforms are sometimes used interchangeably in DB2 books to indicate the use of a command line interface as opposed to a GUI tool.

Many DB2 users prefer to work in this environment because they can use some shortcut key strokes, such as pressing the up arrow key to repeat the last commands on Windows, or to take advantage of operating system mechanisms like piping the output of the CLP to the **more** command on Linux and UNIX to display the output in portions.

Every time you issue the **db2** executable, a "CLP session" is created where a front-end process is invoked. This takes the rest of the statement as input and then closes the process. For example, when you issue:

```
db2 list db directory
```

db2 invokes a CLP front-end process that takes **list db directory** as input. Once the CLP digests this command, it implicitly issues the **quit** command to end the CLP front-end process. The front-end and back-end processes are discussed in more detail later in this chapter.

Figure 4.6 shows the CLP in non-interactive mode.

When invoking the CLP in non-interactive mode, double quotes (") enclosing the CLP command or SQL statement may be required if these contain special characters that the operating system may interpret as wildcard characters. This is especially important on Linux and UNIX platforms. If double quotes are not used, the error message DB2 reports will vary depending on where the wildcard character is used in the statement. For example, if you issue this statement:

```
db2 select * from employee
```

you *may* receive the following error message, since the asterisk (*) is a wildcard character:

```
SQL0104N An unexpected token "*" was found following "select "
```

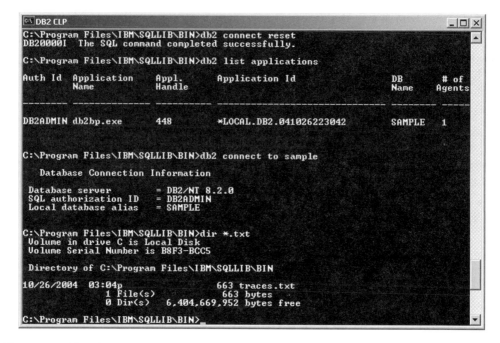

Figure 4.6   The Command Line Processor in non-interactive mode

Use double quotes to avoid parsing errors:

```
db2 "select * from employee"
```

A more deceiving example occurs when you use the greater than (>) character. For example, the statement:

```
db2 select lastname from employee where salary > 10000
```

will be first parsed by the operating system, which will interpret **> 10000** as the redirection of the output to the file *10000*. After executing the above statement, your current directory will have a new file with the name *10000* containing a DB2 syntax error message because only **select lastname from employee where salary** was passed to DB2. Again, to resolve this problem, make sure to enclose the statement in double quotes:

```
db2 "select lastname from employee where salary > 10000"
```

Method 3: Non-interactive Mode Using a File as Input

The CLP can use a file containing one or more CLP commands or SQL statements and process them one after the other. This is ideal to develop DB2 database scripts. For example, Figure 4.7 shows the contents of the file *myInput.txt*, which we will use as input to the CLP.

Usetwodashes
forcomments

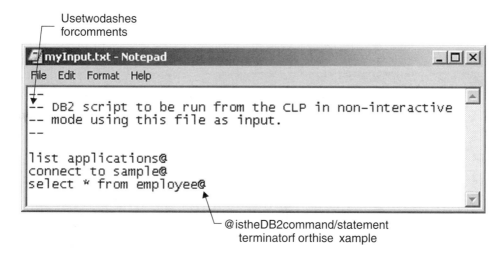

@istheDB2command/statement
terminatorf orthise xample

Figure 4.7   Input file to be used by the CLP

To execute this DB2 script file, the **-f** command option (for *file*) followed by the file name is required to indicate to the CLP that this file contains the input. (CLP command options are described in detail in the next section.) If the input file contains a statement terminator character, the **-t** command option (for *terminator*) is required to indicate a terminator character is present. By default, the statement terminator is a semicolon (**;**). If you want to use a different terminator, the **–d***character* option (for *delimiter*) indicates which delimiter character is being used as the terminator. Use the **-v** option (for *verbose*) to echo the command you are executing. Figure 4.8 provides an example of invoking the CLP using these command options.

> **N O T E**   The input file must be a text file. Be aware that invisible characters may cause the DB2 CLP to fail processing the file. If using the Notepad application on Windows, for example, saving the text file with Unicode encoding rather than ANSI encoding will cause this error:
>
> `DB21007E End of file reached while reading the command.`

If you prefix each of the CLP commands with **db2** (the CLP executable) in a file and remove the terminator characters, you are effectively converting this file into an operating system script rather than a DB2 script. Depending on the operating system, you may have to make additional modifications. For example, on Windows, you need to use **rem** for comments. You may also need to change the file name so that the *.bat* extension is used. Figure 4.9 shows this for the file *myOS_Input.bat*.

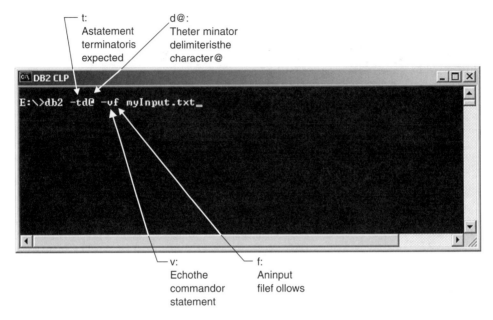

Figure 4.8   Invoking the CLP in non-interactive mode using a file as input

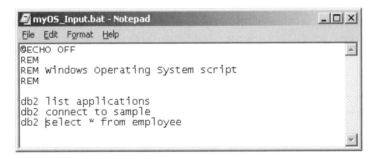

Figure 4.9   Invoking DB2 CLP commands and SQL statements in a Windows script file

On Linux and UNIX platforms, use the pound sign (#) for comments. You may also need to change the permissions of the file so that it is executable. Typically you can use this command to change the file permissions:

```
chmod +x myOS_Input.txt
```

Figure 4.10 shows the same script for a Linux or UNIX platform.

> **N O T E**   DB2 scripts do not accept parameters, but operating system scripts do. In other words, if you need to invoke your scripts with parameters, you need to use operating system scripts.

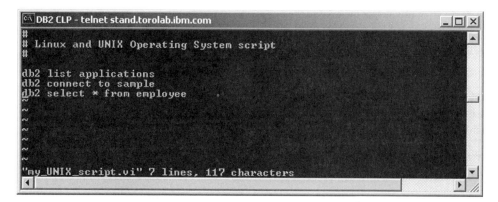

Figure 4.10   Invoking DB2 CLP commands and SQL statements in a Linux/UNIX script file

4.2.1.2 CLP Command Options

The CLP is just another program designed to interact with DB2. Like many other programs, the CLP has been designed to accept several parameter options. The CLP command `list command options` displays the available CLP command option parameters (see Figure 4.11).

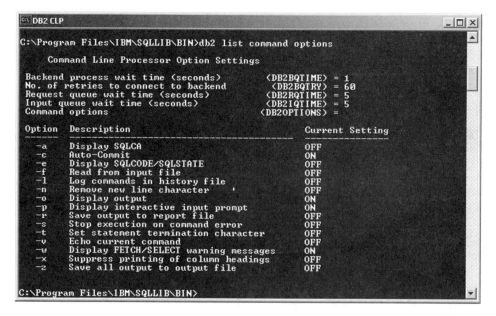

Figure 4.11   CLP command options

To turn on an option, use a dash (-) in the command line. To turn off an option, use a plus symbol (+). Some options are on (or off) by default. For example, to enable autocommit, invoke the CLP as follows:

```
db2 -c insert into employee (firstnme) values ('Raul')
```

After you execute this command, a **COMMIT** statement is automatically issued because autocommit is enabled. (As you can see in Figure 4.11, the Auto-Commit option was already on by default, so including **-c** in the above example is not necessary.)

To disable autocommit, invoke the CLP as follows:

```
db2 +c insert into employee (firstnme) values ('Raul')
```

Note that specifying a command option in the **db2** command applies only to that session of the CLP. Issuing the **db2** command without an option will use the default command option values, or the ones contained in the DB2OPTIONS registry variable, which we discuss later in this section.

You can also change a command option when working with the CLP in interactive mode using the following command:

```
update command options using option value option value...
```

Figure 4.12 shows an example where the **v** option (verbose) is used. This option causes the command or statement to be repeated or echoed when executed as discussed earlier. In Figure 4.12, note that the **SELECT * FROM department** statement is echoed.

If you would like the changes to your CLP options effective across all your CLP sessions, you can set the DB2OPTIONS registry variable with the desired options. In the command:

```
db2set db2options="-v -z myfile.log"
```

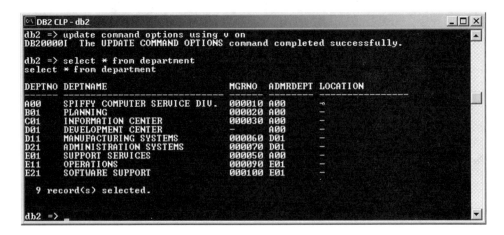

Figure 4.12   The CLP in interactive mode

the DB2OPTIONS registry variable is set so that any command executed will be echoed (**-v** option), and the output will be spooled in the file *myfile.log* (**-z myfile.log** option). The changes take effect immediately for the current session and any other new CLP sessions that you start.

To reset the values to the default, issue this command:

```
db2set db2options=
```

DB2 registry variables are explained in detail in Chapter 5, Understanding the DB2 Environment, DB2 Instances, and Databases.

4.2.1.3 Obtaining Help Information from the CLP

One of the most useful CLP commands is the help command represented by a question mark (**?**). This command provides help on SQL error codes (SQLCODE), DB2 messages, and CLP command syntax. For example:

```
db2 ? SQL0104N
db2 ? DB21004E
db2 ? list applications
```

In addition, using the help command by itself displays the entire list of CLP commands, as shown in Figure 4.13.

```
DB2 CLP                                                                    _ □ ×
C:\Program Files\IBM\SQLLIB\BIN>db2 ?
db2 [option ...] [db2-command | sql-statement |
    [? [phrase | message | sqlstate | class-code]]]
option: -a, -c, -e{c|s}, -finfile, -lhistfile, -o, -n, -p, -rreport, -s,
        -t, -td;, -v, -w, -x, -zoutputfile.
db2-command:
  ACTIVATE DATABASE         GET/UPDATE DB CFG          RECONCILE
  ADD CONTACT               GET/UPDATE DBM CFG         RECOVER
  ADD CONTACTGROUP          GET DBM MONITOR SWITCHES   REDISTRIBUTE DB PARTITION
  ADD DATALINKS MANAGER     GET DESCRIPTION FOR HEALTH REFRESH LDAP
  ADD DBPARTITIONNUM        GET NOTIFICATION LIST      REGISTER
  ARCHIVE LOG               GET HEALTH SNAPSHOT        REORG INDEXES/TABLE
  ATTACH                    GET INSTANCE               REORGCHK
  AUTOCONFIGURE             GET MONITOR SWITCHES       RESET ADMIN CFG
  BACKUP DATABASE           GET RECOMMENDATIONS        RESET ALERT CFG
  BIND                      GET ROUTINE                RESET DB CFG
  CATALOG APPC NODE         GET SNAPSHOT               RESET DBM CFG
  CATALOG APPN NODE         HELP                       RESET MONITOR
  CATALOG DATABASE          HISTORY                    RESTART DATABASE
  CATALOG DCS DATABASE      IMPORT                     RESTORE DATABASE
  CATALOG LDAP DATABASE     INITIALIZE TAPE            REWIND TAPE
  CATALOG LDAP NODE         INSPECT                    ROLLFORWARD DATABASE
```

Figure 4.13   Output of the command db2 ?

> **N O T E**   The help (**?**) command can display CLP command syntax, but not SQL statement syntax. Refer to the *DB2 UDB SQL Reference* manual for SQL statement syntax.

Figure 4.14 shows other examples of the help (**?**) command.

```
DB2 CLP                                                              _ □ x
C:\Program Files\IBM\SQLLIB\BIN>db2 ? list applications
LIST APPLICATIONS [FOR DATABASE database-alias]
[AT DBPARTITIONNUM db-partition-number] GLOBAL] [SHOW DETAIL]

NOTE: From the operating system prompt, prefix commands with 'db2'.
      Special characters MAY require an escape sequence (\), for example:
      db2 \? change database
      db2 ? change database xxx comment with \"text\"

C:\Program Files\IBM\SQLLIB\BIN>
C:\Program Files\IBM\SQLLIB\BIN>
C:\Program Files\IBM\SQLLIB\BIN>db2 ? sql0104


SQL0104N An unexpected token "<token>" was found following
         "<text>".  Expected tokens may include:
         "<token-list>".

Explanation:

A syntax error in the SQL statement was detected at the specified
token following the text "<text>".  The "<text>" field indicates
the 20 characters of the SQL statement that preceded the token
that is not valid.

As an aid to the programmer, a partial list of valid tokens is
```

Figure 4.14   The CLP help (?) command

4.2.1.4 Line Continuation

There are two ways to use line continuation from the CLP: with the backslash character and with the delimiter terminator character.

Method 1: Using the Backslash (\) Character

You can use the backslash (\ ) character in either interactive or non-interactive mode. Figure 4.15 shows an example using interactive mode first, followed by a non-interactive mode example.

Notice that after entering \ and pressing Enter, the prompt changes to:

```
db2 (cont.) =>
```

Method 2: Using a Delimiter Terminator Character with the CLP in Interactive Mode

Using this method, the CLP is invoked in interactive mode using the terminator delimiter option. For example:

```
db2 -td!
```

After entering this command and pressing Enter, the CLP is invoked in interactive mode. You can wrap commands onto multiple lines until you type the terminator character, which is the exclamation mark (!) in the example shown in Figure 4.16.

Use this method when you have statements that include carriage returns. If you copy and paste one of these statements into the CLP, the carriage returns will cause the statement to continue in another line, which is acceptable, because the CLP processes the command after the terminator character is entered.

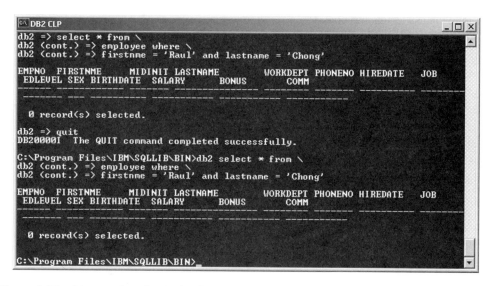

Figure 4.15   Line continuation in the CLP using the backslash continuation character

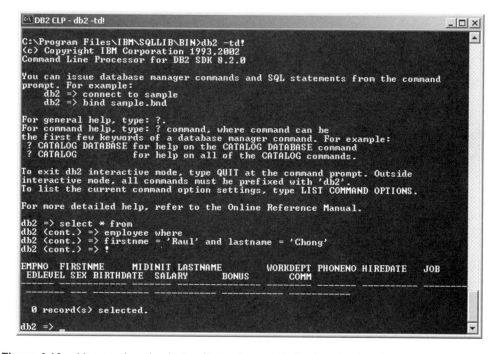

Figure 4.16   Line continuation in the CLP using a delimiter termination character in interactive mode

The following statement has one carriage return character after **staff** and one after **Edwards**; therefore, use method 2 to start the DB2 CLP in interactive mode:

```
select * from staff
where name = 'Edwards'
and job = 'Sales'
```

After you copy and paste the statement into the CLP, enter the terminator character and press Enter to execute it.

4.2.1.5 The CLP Front-end and Back-end Processes

The CLP has both front-end and a back-end processes. The front-end allows you to perform actions without connecting to a database. For example, issuing the command:

```
db2 list db directory
```

does not require a connection to a database. Depending on the operation, the instance need not be started either.

The back-end process is needed when you perform actions against a database. The back-end process is created when you connect to the database in a CLP session and can be identified by the application name *db2bp*. Figure 4.17 shows the output of the **list applications** command, which shows this process (or thread in Windows) indicating a connection to the *sample* database.

Figure 4.17   The CLP back-end process

To remove the connection to a database, issue the **connect reset** statement, the **terminate** command, or the **disconnect** statement. **Connect reset** and **terminate** will work even if the process is in the middle of a unit of work. **Disconnect** only works when there is no active unit of work. Closing a window or session without previously issuing a **terminate** command will close the CLP application and front-end process and remove the connection to the database, but does not guarantee that the back-end process will be terminated.

> **NOTE**   The **terminate** command is the only one that guarantees the back-end process is indeed terminated. Even if the **list applications** command does not display the *db2bp* back-end process running, use the **terminate** command to be certain.

It is important to make sure that the back-end process is terminated because in some circumstances a change to a parameter, environment variable, or DB2 registry variable will not take effect until this is performed. For example, in a multi-partition environment, the DB2NODE environment variable is used to indicate which partition is the coordinator. After changing the value of this variable, you must issue a **terminate** command for it to take effect.

> **NOTE** We recommend issuing a **terminate** command before a **db2stop** command. This prevents the back-end process from maintaining an attachment to an instance that is no longer active.

V8.2 ## 4.2.2 The Command Editor

The **Command Editor** is the graphical user interface (GUI) version of the Command Line Processor. The Command Editor offers several other functions in addition to those provided by the CLP and the Command Window.

- The ability to execute multiple DB2 commands and SQL statements interactively and simultaneously. With the CLP, only one command at a time can be executed interactively. If you want to execute multiple commands, you have to save them in a text file and execute the file with the **-f** option as explained in section 4.2.1.1, Methods to Work with the CLP.
- The ability to save all the commands you typed in the Command Editor window to a file or as a task to be executed from the Task center.
- The ability to display a Visual Explain output of the access path chosen by the DB2 optimizer for an SQL statement. The Visual Explain tool is discussed in the next section.
- The ability to display results in well-formatted tables.

> **NOTE** The Command Editor in Version 8.2 replaces the Command Center used in previous DB2 versions. The Command Editor provides the same functionality as the Command Center but has a simplified interface.

You can start the Command Editor either from the IBM DB2 menu or from the Control Center. (We will talk about the Control Center in section 4.4, General Administration Tools.) Alternatively, the command **db2ce** starts it from a command line prompt.

Figure 4.18 shows the start screen of the Command Editor. The Target field is empty until you click on the *Add* button, which displays the Specify Target window. Select a Target type from the pull-down menu, and the database you want to work with in the Available targets pull-down menu.

The Command Editor makes an implicit connection to the database you have chosen, and you can then start entering your commands from the command input window (see Figure 4.19).

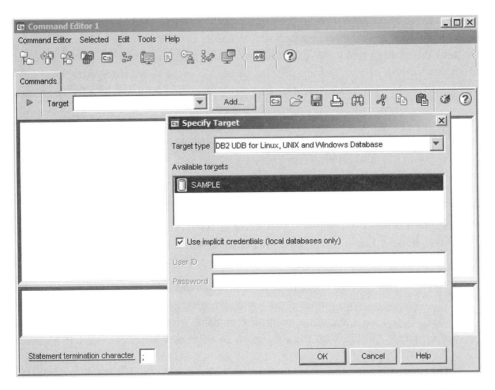

Figure 4.18   The Command Editor lets you choose the database you want to work with

Figure 4.19 shows the three tabs associated with views in the Command Editor. The tab selected in Figure 4.19 is for the Commands view. This view displays all the commands you have entered. If you want to execute several commands or statements at once, make sure to delimit them with the character specified in the Statement terminator character field (at the bottom of the window). If you entered several commands or statements in the Command Input window, but would like to execute only a particular one, highlight it. Then you have the following options.

- To execute the command and produce the results, click on the *Execute* button 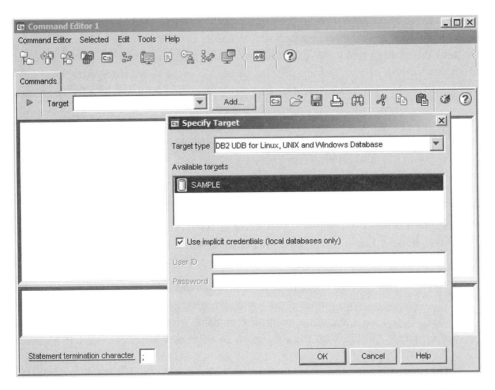.
- To execute the command, produce the results, and the access plan, click on the *Execute and Access Plan* button .
- To produce the access plan but not execute the command, click on the *Access Plan* button .

If you chose to execute the command, the results are nicely displayed in a table in the Query Results view, as shown in Figure 4.20.

You can directly perform updates by clicking on the corresponding value and making the desired change in the Query Results view. To add or delete an entire row, click the *Add Row* or *Delete*

Executes the command, produces the results and access plan.

Saves all the commands in the Command Input window to a file or to the Task Center.

Executes the command and produces results.

Produces the access plan only. Does not execute the command.

SQL Assist Tool helps you construct your SQL Statements.

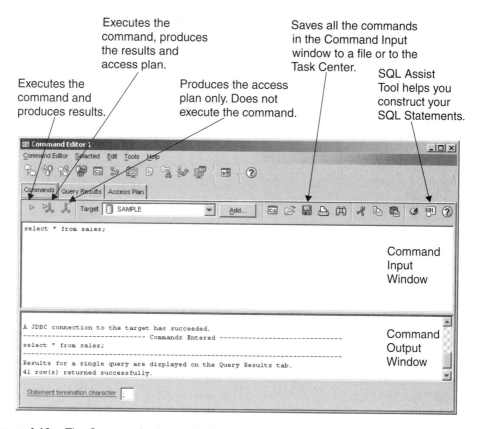

Figure 4.19   The Commands view in the Command Editor

Row button respectively. All of these changes are not permanent unless you click on the *Commit* button. If you want to cancel your changes, click on the *Roll Back* button.

If you chose either of the other two options that produce the access plan, a tool called **Visual Explain** is invoked. The next section explains this tool in more detail.

4.2.2.1 Visual Explain

DB2 provides an SQL facility that stores in "explain" tables detailed information about how DB2 will access the data to satisfy a query request. For example, the information in these explain tables may show that DB2 will scan the table sequentially, or it may show that the data will be accessed through the indexes associated to the table. The method to access the data that DB2 chooses is called the **access plan**, and the particular component of DB2 that makes this decision is called the **DB2 optimizer**, which can be considered the "brain" of DB2. To analyze the access plan, you can use text-based tools like the `db2exfmt` and the `db2expln` command line tools; however, it is often useful to display this information in a graph. Use **Visual Explain** to graphically display an access plan for a query.

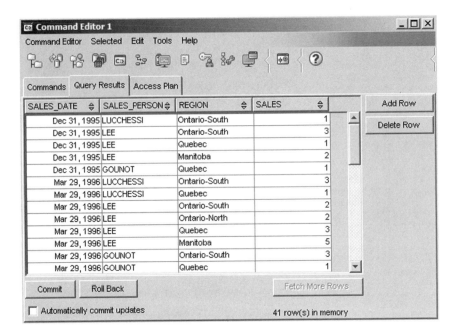

Figure 4.20   The Query Results view in the Command Editor

You can invoke Visual Explain from the Command Editor. Simply enter an SQL statement in the Command Editor's Command Input window, and then press either the *Execute and Access Plan* button or the *Access Plan* button. Figure 4.21 shows the Visual Explain output of the query `select * from sales`. In this particular example, the DB2ADMIN.SALES table is accessed using a table scan (TBSCAN) with a cost of 13.07 timerons. Visual Explain can also be invoked from the Control Center; see Chapter 16, Database Performance Considerations, for more details.

4.3 DEVELOPMENT TOOLS

The development tools help you build and deploy stored procedures, user-defined functions, and structured types. There are two tools that fall into this category: the Development Center and the Project Deployment tool.

4.3.1 The Development Center

The Development Center is included with both the Application Development Client and with all DB2 UDB server edition products. This tool helps you build, debug, and test application objects that are stored in the database server, such as stored procedures, user-defined functions (UDFs), and structured types.

Stored procedures allow you to move part of the application logic to the database, providing a centralized location from which you can maintain your code. Because the logic runs at the data-

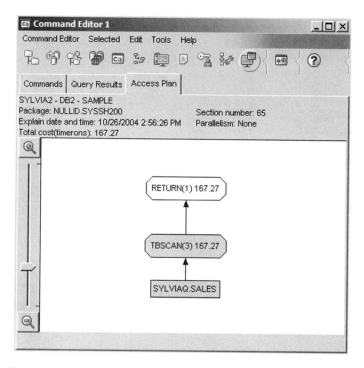

Figure 4.21   The Access Plan view in the Command Editor

base server, stored procedures improve performance by reducing network traffic. UDFs let you extend the SQL language and built-in functions with your own logic. You can write a UDF in C/C++, Java, or SQL Procedural Language to perform operations within any SQL statement that returns a single scalar value or a table. Structured types are useful for modeling objects that have a well-defined structure with attributes, each of which has a data type.

As you can see in Figure 4.22, the Development Center has two view tabs. The *Project View* tab contains your project with all the stored procedures, UDFs, or structured types stored locally in your machine. The *Server View* tab displays the stored procedures, UDFs, or structured types that were built successfully, and thus are stored on the database server.

4.3.2 The Project Deployment Tool

When you develop application objects with the Development Center, you can export them to a file as an export script or a project, and deploy them to another (target) database using the Project Deployment Tool, which walks you through several steps. Figure 4.23 shows the step where you have to choose the stored procedures you want to deploy from a list of procedures available in the *SAMPLE* database.

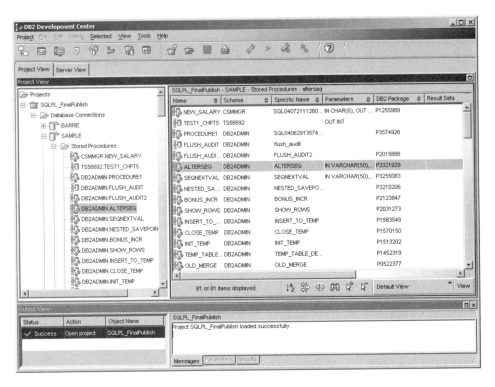

Figure 4.22   The Development Center

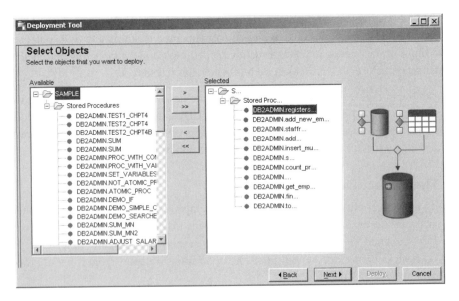

Figure 4.23   The Project Deployment Tool

4.4 GENERAL ADMINISTRATION TOOLS

The tools available under **General Administration Tools** in the DB2 menu are GUI-based. If you are unfamiliar with DB2 commands or SQL statements, the tools in this section allow you to perform all kinds of database administration tasks without having to enter one single DB2 command!

The General Administration Tools consist of the Control Center, the Journal, the Replication Center, and the Task Center.

4.4.1 The Control Center

As mentioned in Chapter 2, DB2 at a Glance: The Big Picture, the **Control Center** is the most important DB2 GUI administration tool. It provides the following functions.

- A complete picture of all your instances and databases on local and remote systems, including host systems (OS/390 and z/OS platforms). This helps you visualize how your instances and databases are structured.
- Management of your federated database systems (federation was briefly discussed in Chapter 2).
- Most database operations, which you would otherwise have to perform using DB2 commands.
- A launchpad for all other GUI tools.
- Many wizards and advisors, which can make your database administration tasks a lot easier.

You can start the Control Center in three different views, as shown in Figure 4.24.

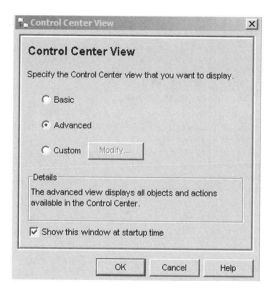

Figure 4.24   The Control Center Views

The **Basic** view only shows databases residing locally on the server; it doesn't display instances. The **Advanced** view shows everything: all instances and databases on both the local system and remote systems (if connections have been configured). The **Custom** view allows you to tailor the Object Tree and the object actions to your specific needs.

Figure 4.25 shows the Control Center Advanced view. The **Object Tree** displays the tree structure on your local and remote systems, and the **Contents** pane provides more detail about the specific item selected. The **Object Details** pane displays details and actions that can be performed for the selected object.

For example, in Figure 4.25 the Tables folder in the Object Tree is selected, so the Contents pane displays the list of tables. Since the EMPLOYEE table is selected, the Object Details pane shows the table structure as well as other actions like the Create New Table action.

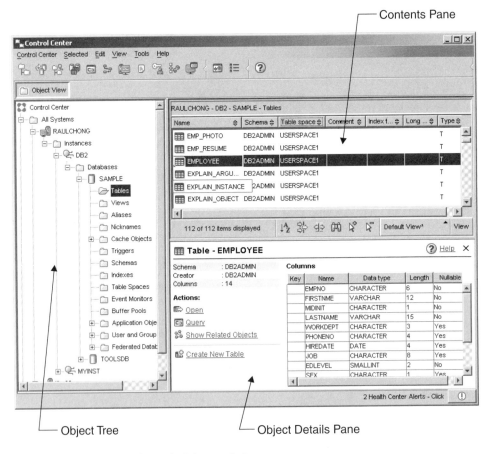

Figure 4.25   The Control Center's Advanced view

You can perform many tasks from the Control Center by right-clicking an object to display its list of operations. Figure 4.26 shows the list of available operations for the database named *SAMPLE*.

As shown in Figure 4.26, **Drop**, **Connect**, **Backup**, and **Restore** are among the many available database operations you can perform in the Control Center.

You can also start most of the GUI tools shown in the IBM DB2 menu from the Control Center. Figure 4.27 displays the Control Center toolbar contents. To start the GUI tool, click its toolbar icon.

The Control Center offers several wizards and advisors. They can assist you in many tasks such as backing up a database, creating a table, and setting up high-availability disaster recovery databases. These wizards and advisors are launched by selecting **Tools** > **Wizards** in the Control Center.

Figure 4.28 shows the list of available wizards and advisors.

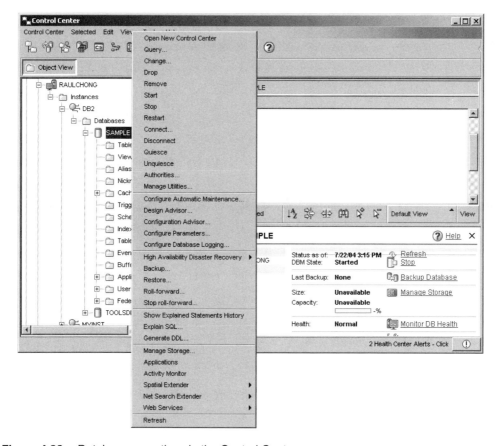

Figure 4.26 Database operations in the Control Center

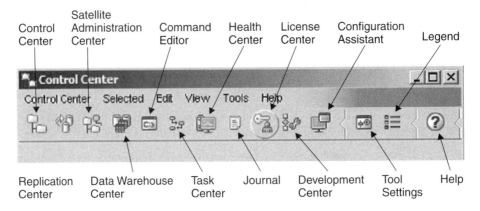

Figure 4.27 The Control Center's Toolbar

Figure 4.28 Wizards and advisors available in the Control Center

4.4.2 The Journal

The **Journal** tool keeps track of all scheduled tasks performed, DB2 recovery information, DB2 administration tools messages, and Notification log records. Should you need to investigate a problem, you can use this tool to find out what happened. Figure 4.29 shows the Messages view in the Journal.

4.4.3 The Replication Center

The **Replication Center** lets you set up and manage your replication environment. The required steps can be easily followed by using the Replication Center Launchpad. Use DB2 replication when you want to propagate data from one location to another.

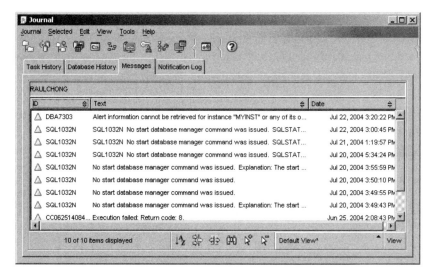

Figure 4.29 The Journal

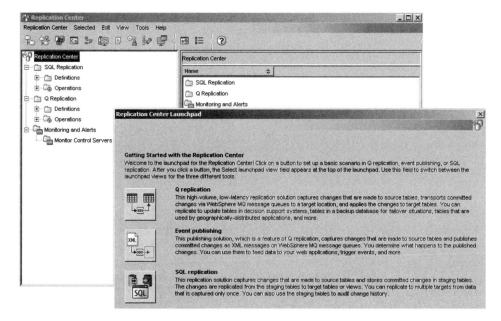

Figure 4.30 The Replication Center

4.4.4 The Task Center

The **Task Center** lets you schedule your jobs to run at a chosen time. You could use the Task Center to back up your database daily at 3:00 a.m. when there is no activity on your system. You can also set up the Task Center to take different actions on successful execution of a task and another action on an unsuccessful execution. For example, the Task Center can send you an e-mail if the operation was successful and can page you if it was not. Figure 4.31 shows the Task Center.

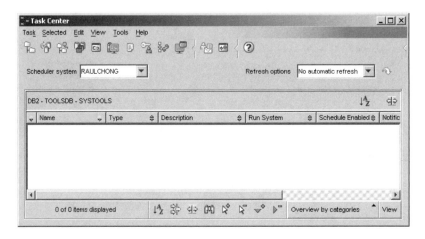

Figure 4.31   The Task Center

> **N O T E**   The TOOLSDB database must exist for the Journal and the Task Center to work correctly. You can create this database during the installation process or create it manually using the **CREATE TOOLS CATALOG** command.

4.5 INFORMATION TOOLS

The **Information** menu (see Figure 4.1) provides access to all DB2 documentation.

4.5.1 Information Center

The **Information Center** gives you access to all DB2 documentation. It comes with a very fast search engine allowing you to search on any given topic. The DB2 Information Center can be accessed in three different ways.

- Dynamically through the Internet (at http://publib.boulder.ibm.com/infocenter/db2help).
- Locally on the database server after installing the DB2 Information Center from a separate CD.
- Through a designated server on your company's intranet. The DB2 Information Center must be installed on that server.

- Figure 4.32 shows the Information Center accessed through the Internet. On the left panel there is a list of topics from which you can choose. Each of these topics can be drilled down to subtopics, and selecting a specific subtopic makes the contents panel on the right side display more information. At the top left corner of the Information Center, you will find the *Search* field. Use this field to input any topic or keyword that you want to search in the DB2 manuals. Then click on the *GO* button.

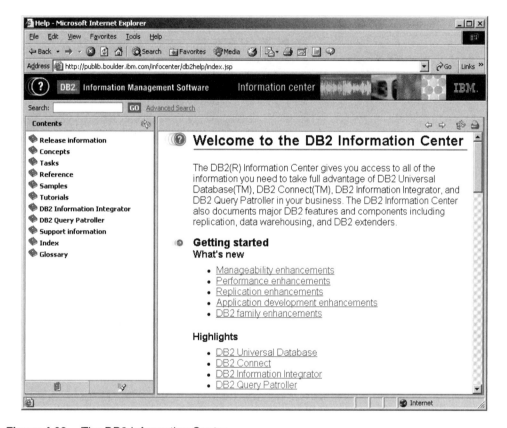

Figure 4.32   The DB2 Information Center

V8.2 **4.5.2 Checking for DB2 Updates**

The Information Center Web site (shown in Figure 4.32) is periodically updated with new and current documentation; however, if you have installed the Information Center locally, make sure to check for updates regularly. Use the **Check For DB2 Updates** option in the DB2 menu (see Figure 4.1) to launch the InstallShield Update Service, which is shown in Figure 4.33. From this site you can download the refreshed DB2 Information Center image and install it on your server. You can also obtain information about updates to the DB2 code and news about DB2 in general.

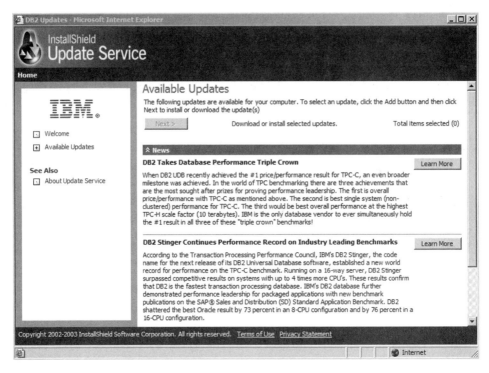

Figure 4.33   Checking for DB2 updates

4.6 MONITORING TOOLS

As a database administrator, it is important to have a good understanding of your database environment. Some of the things you need to know are the kinds of activities that are happening on the system, the database workload, and memory usage. The **Monitoring tools** watch the database based on the criteria you provide and generate reports.

The graphical Monitoring tools consist of the Activity Monitor, Event Analyzer, Health Center, Indoubt Transaction manager, and the Memory Visualizer. In addition, DB2 Version 8.2 introduces a new command line Monitoring tool called **db2pd**.

V8.2 4.6.1 The Activity Monitor

The **Activity Monitor** helps you monitor the performance of your application and database by tracking monitor data. Among other things, it can help you monitor application concurrency, resource consumption, SQL statement usage, and lock-waiting situations.

You can start the Activity Monitor either from the DB2 menu or using the **db2am** command. When you start the Activity Monitor, the Set Up Activity Monitor Wizard appears. This wizard prompts you to select from a set of predefined monitoring tasks, as shown in Figure 4.34.

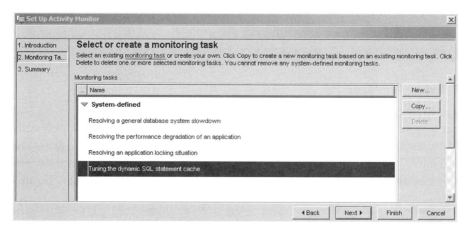

Figure 4.34   The Set Up Activity Monitor Wizard

The data that is monitored depends on the monitoring task you select, which can be either pre-defined by DB2 or user-defined. After setting up your Activity Monitor, you can produce a report. The report shows the results of the selected monitoring task.

Figure 4.35 shows a sample report produced by the Activity Monitor, based on the selected monitoring task *Tuning the dynamic SQL statement cache*. In Figure 4.35, each executed dynamic SQL statement is listed in the left-most column. The other columns display the system resources that have been consumed. Click on the *Details and Recommendations* tab to get more information on the selected report.

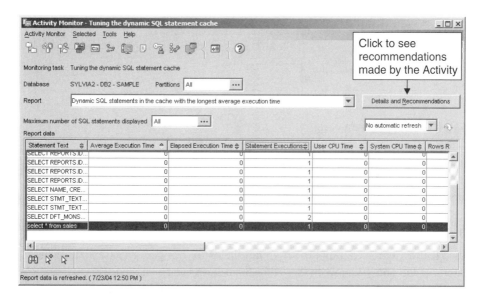

Figure 4.35   An Activity Monitor report

To use the Activity Monitor, you must set the following database manager configuration (DBM CFG) parameters to ON: DFT_MON_BUFPOOL, DFT_MON_LOCK, DFT_MON_SORT, DFT_ MON_ STMT, DFT_MON_ TIMESTAMP, AND DFT_MON_UOW.

4.6.2 Event Analyzer

You use Event Monitors for troubleshooting performance problems. After creating an Event Monitor with the **CREATE EVENT MONITOR** statement, the output file produced (normally with an .EVT extension) can be analyzed with the **Event Analyzer**. You can also create Event Monitors in the Control Center by right-clicking on the *Event Monitors* folder for a selected database and choosing **Create**. They can later be analyzed with the Event Analyzer, as shown in Figure 4.36.

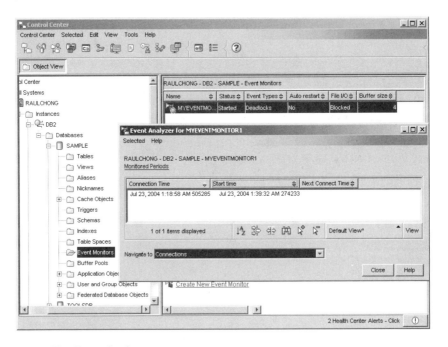

Figure 4.36   The Event Analyzer

In Figure 4.36, the Event Monitor *evmon1* was created to detect deadlock events. The Event Analyzer is showing two time periods for which this type of information was collected. Event Monitors are discussed in more detail in Chapter 16, Database Performance Considerations.

4.6.3 Health Center

Use the **Health Center** GUI tool to set up thresholds for key performance and database health indicators, and to notify you when these thresholds have been exceeded. This tool provides rec-ommendations and allows you to take action to correct the problem. In other words, you can have the database manage itself! Figure 4.37 shows the Health Center.

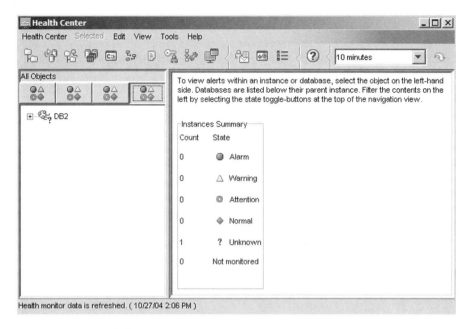

Figure 4.37   The Health Center

4.6.4 Indoubt Transaction Manager

You can use the **Indoubt Transaction Manager** to help resolve transactions left in an indoubt state during two-phase commit processing. An **indoubt transaction** is one that has been prepared but has not been committed or rolled back. This can happen if an error occurs while processing statements against any database in a transaction that updates multiple databases. You can right-click on a transaction and then choose to Forget, Commit, or Rollback the transaction.

Figure 4.38 shows the Indoubt Transaction Manager with no indoubt transactions listed.

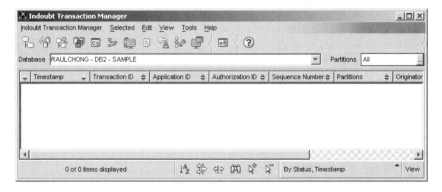

Figure 4.38   The Indoubt Transaction Manager

4.6.5 The Memory Visualizer

The **Memory Visualizer** tool helps you track and graphically display the memory used by DB2. The tool can help you detect memory problems. You can also modify the memory settings within the tool. Chapter 15, The DB2 Memory Model, discusses the memory usage by DB2 and the **db2mtrk** memory tracker tool, which is a text-based tool equivalent to the Memory Visualizer. Figure 4.39 shows the Memory Visualizer. In the figure, the buffer pools and Lock Manager Heap are being plotted in the graph at the bottom of the window every five seconds. In both cases, the graph shows a straight line indicating the memory usage for these two is not increasing.

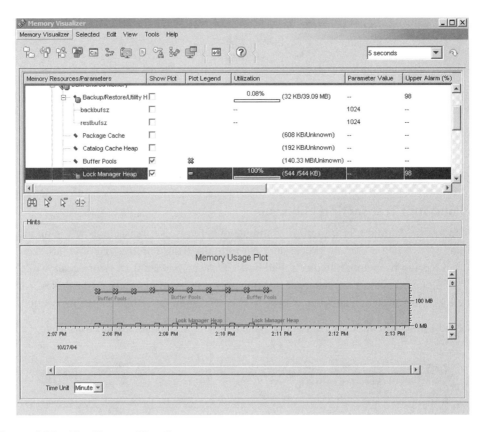

Figure 4.39   The Memory Visualizer

V8.2   4.6.6 The db2pd Tool

The **db2pd** tool is a command line tool that retrieves statistics, including memory usage statistics, from a running DB2 instance or database. For example:

- To display the operating system information, issue

```
db2pd -osinfo
```

- To display all instance-related information, issue

  `db2pd -inst`

- To display all database-related information to the *sample* database, issue

  `db2pd -db sample`

Use the **db2pd -help** command to display all the available options. This tool is not available through the graphical interface.

4.7 SETUP TOOLS

The **Setup Tools** get you started with DB2 by creating the *sample* database. They also help you configure connections to remote databases. The Setup Tools consist of the First Steps, Configuration Assistant, and Register Visual Studio Add-Ins.

4.7.1 First Steps

The IBM DB2 **First Steps** tool is a good starting point for new DB2 users who want to get familiar with the product. Figure 4.40 shows the operations you can perform using this tool.

The *Create Sample Database* option creates a database called *sample* on your local system. The *sample* database is provided with the DB2 product for testing and learning purposes. It comes

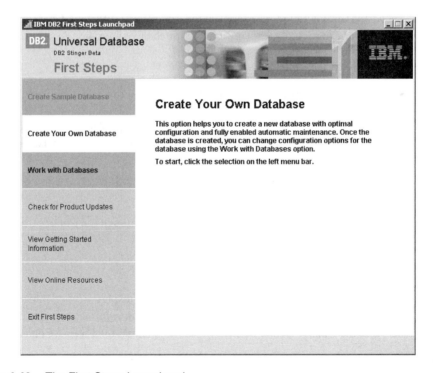

Figure 4.40   The First Steps Launchpad

with a set of predefined tables. You can work with this database just like any other database. The equivalent DB2 command to create this *sample* database is **db2sampl**.

The *Create Your Own Database* option walks you through several steps to create your own new database, configured for optimal performance. You can specify the name of the database and the location where it is going to be created. The equivalent DB2 command to create a new database is **create database** and is discussed in Chapter 8, The DB2 Storage Model. After the database is created, you can create tables using the Control Center or SQL statements. The SQL statements to create database objects are described in Chapter 7, Working with Database Objects.

The *Work with Databases* option simply launches the Control Center, so you can see your databases and perform operations on them.

The other options in the IBM DB2 First Steps Launchpad are self-explanatory.

4.7.2 The Configuration Assistant

The Configuration Assistant helps you:

- Set up connections to databases residing on remote servers using the Add Database Wizard.
- Configure connection properties for local databases.

Figure 4.41 shows the Configuration Assistant and the Add Database Wizard. Chapter 6, Configuring Client and Server Connectivity, explains how to use the Configuration Assistant in detail.

4.7.3 Register Visual Studio Add-Ins

When you select the **Register Visual Studio Add-Ins** menu item (the last item in the **IBM DB2** menu shown in Figure 4.1.), it adds a plug-in into Microsoft Visual Studio so that DB2 tools can be invoked from Visual Basic, Visual C++, and Visual InterDev (see Figure 4.42). The add-in inserts the DB2 menu entries into each of these Microsoft development tool's **View**, **Tools**, and **Help** menus.

4.8 OTHER TOOLS

This section describes some additional tools that are available through the Control Center or the Command Editor but not from the IBM DB2 menu.

4.8.1 License Center

You use the **License Center** to install a new license and to display license information for installed products (the **db2licm** command provides equivalent information). You launch the License Center from the Control Center toolbar. Figure 4.43 shows the License Center.

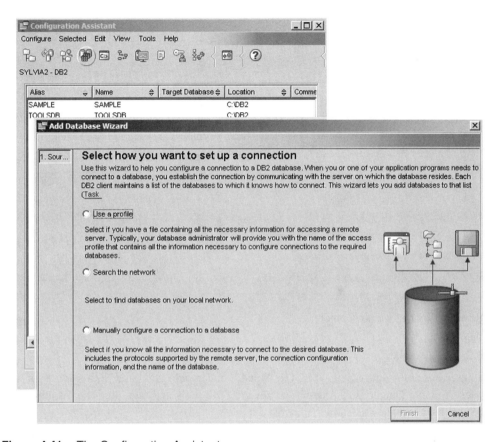

Figure 4.41   The Configuration Assistant

Figure 4.42   Visual Studio Add-Ins

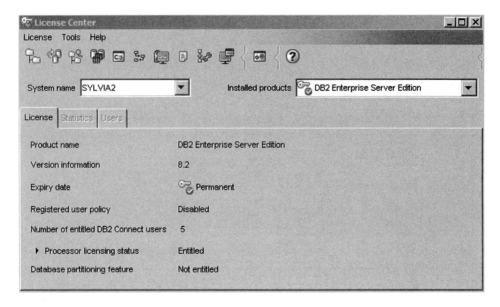

Figure 4.43   The License Center

4.8.2 SQL Assist

If you are not proficient in SQL, the **SQL Assist** tool can help you build SQL statements step-by-step. You can launch SQL Assist from several DB2 tools and then plug the resulting SQL statement back into the DB2 tool that invoked it.

You can launch SQL Assist from the Command Editor, Control Center, Replication Center, Data Warehouse Center, and Development Center. Figure 4.44 shows SQL Assist after being launched from the Command Editor.

4.8.3 Satellite Administration Center

The **Satellite Administration Center** is a tool that provides centralized administrative support for satellites. A **satellite** is a DB2 server that is a member of a group of similar DB2 servers, each running the same application and with similar configurations. You launch the Satellite Administration Center from the DB2 Control Center toolbar (see Figure 4.45).

The Satellite Administration Center stores its information in the **satellite control database** (SATCTLDB). This database records, among other things, which satellites are in the environment, the group each satellite belongs to, and which version of the end-user application a satellite is running. This database is on a DB2 server known as the **Satellite Control Server**. To set up and maintain its database configuration, each satellite connects to the satellite control database to download the batches that correspond to its version of the end-user application. The satellite executes these batches locally, then reports the results back to the satellite control database.

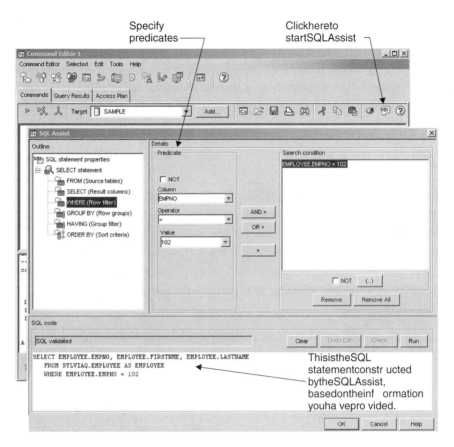

Figure 4.44 SQL Assist

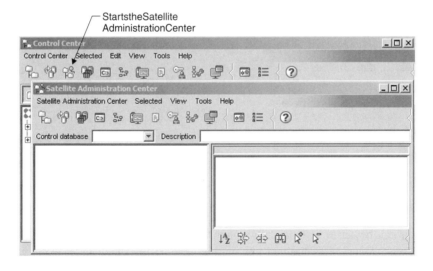

Figure 4.45 The Satellite Administration Center

This process of downloading batches, executing them, and then reporting the results of the batch execution is known as **synchronization**. A satellite synchronizes to maintain its consistency with the other satellites that belong to its group and are running the same version of the end-user application. For more information about how to install and administer a satellite environment, refer to the Resources section at the end of this book.

4.9 TOOL SETTINGS

All of the graphical tools that you can invoke through the Control Center, including the Control Center itself, have a menu for setting up the general tool characteristics. If you select **Tools > Tools Settings** from any of these tools, the window shown in Figure 4.46 is displayed. Note that each tool invokes the same Tools Setting window.

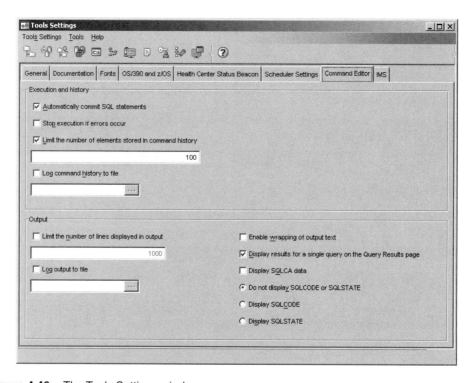

Figure 4.46   The Tools Settings window

In Figure 4.46, the *Command Editor* tab is selected. You can see that under this tab the Command Editor can be set to automatically commit SQL statements (autocommit is enabled by default). When autocommit is disabled, you must issue the **COMMIT** statement explicitly to commit SQL statements. There are many other settings that you can change under the other tabs, and we encourage you to explore them yourself.

4.10 CASE STUDY

You recently installed the Try and Buy version of DB2 Personal Edition on your Windows laptop. During the installation, the *DB2* instance was created. Now you want to start using DB2 by creating a database. Since you are new to DB2, you decide to use the DB2 First Steps tool (see Figure 4.40).

You click on *Create Sample Database* from the First Steps Launchpad. After the *sample* database is created, you click on *Work with Databases*, which launches the Control Center.

From the Control Center, choose the *Advanced* view and then expand the *Object Tree* to display the *sample* database and all its database objects (see Figure 4.25).

The *sample* database already has a set of tables defined in it. However, you decide to create a table of your own. To do so, you right-click on the *Tables* folder in the *Object Tree* and choose *Create*. This launches the Create Table Wizard, which will guide you through the process of creating a table. You are presented with the following pages.

- Identify the schema and name for the new table: In the *Table schema* field, enter the user ID you logged in with. We will discuss the significance of schemas in Chapter 7, Working with Database Objects; for now it is sufficient to enter your user ID. In the *Table name* field, enter the name of the table you want to create, say *Table1*.
- Change column definitions for the new table: Click *Add* to add columns one at a time. In the *Column name* field, enter the name of the first column for *Table1*, for example, *Col1*. Choose the data type from the pull-down menu, say *INTEGER*. You could create more columns by repeating this step, but one column is sufficient for now.

There are other windows in which you can define the properties of other database objects. However, completing the above two windows is enough to create the table. Click on the *Finish* button to create the table.

Table1 is displayed under the *Tables* folder once it is created (all tables are displayed in the Contents pane of the Control Center—see Figure 4.25). To display the contents of the table, right-click on the table name and choose *Open*. Since nothing has been inserted into *Table1*, no contents are displayed. To insert a row into the table, click on the *Add Row* button and enter a value under *Col1*. Click the *Commit* button to apply the changes (see Figure 4.47).

Your colleague, who is a DB2 expert, drops by your office and offers his help for any problems you may have. You tell him you would like to explore the Activity Monitor. He says you first need to turn on the DFT_MON_STMT database manager parameter to start collecting information that will be displayed by the Activity Monitor (database manager parameters are discussed in detail in Chapter 5, Understanding the DB2 Environment, DB2 Instances, and Databases). He quickly turns this on for you.

Next, you start the Activity Monitor and choose the *sample* database in the *Introduction* page. You see the four predefined functions of the Activity Monitor (see Figure 4.34). You decide to

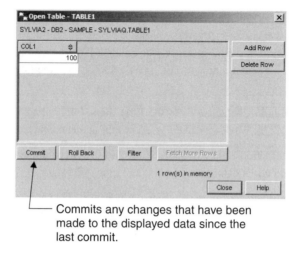

Commits any changes that have been
made to the displayed data since the
last commit.

Figure 4.47   Inserting a row into a table

monitor dynamic SQL statements performed on this database. Therefore, you highlight the *Tuning the dynamic SQL statement cache* option and click *Next*.

Figure 4.48 lists the SQL statement items that the Activity Monitor checks. Click *Finish* to complete the Activity Monitor definition and you see the window shown in Figure 4.49.

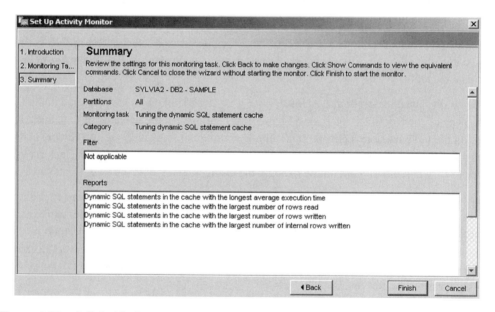

Figure 4.48   Activity Monitor summary page

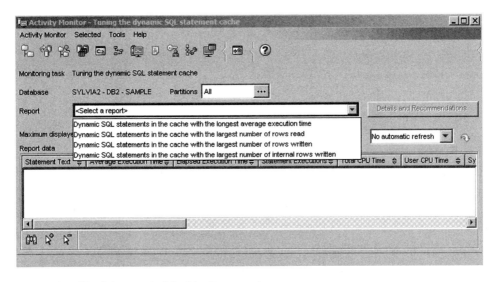

Figure 4.49   Obtaining an Activity Monitor report

To obtain the Activity Monitor report, select one of the four options listed. The Activity Monitor starts monitoring all dynamic SQL statements being executed on the database. If there are users connected to the database, all the dynamic SQL statements they submit will be monitored. Figure 4.50 shows an Activity Monitor report on *Dynamic SQL statements in the cache with the largest number of rows read.*

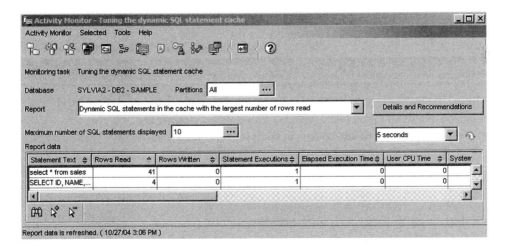

Figure 4.50   The Activity Monitor report

If there are no other users connected to the system, you can generate some SQL statements yourself. The simplest way to do that from the Control Center is to right-click on a table name and
choose *Open* to display its contents. This is equivalent to the following SQL statement:

```
SELECT * FROM table_name
```

Though you have not finished exploring all the DB2 tools, this exercise has made you realize
how easy to use and powerful they are!

4.11 SUMMARY

This chapter introduced all the tools that are available in DB2. They come in two categories: the
command-driven and the non-command-driven tools. All of the non-command-driven tools are
GUI Tools. To use the command line tools you need to have some knowledge of DB2 commands
and SQL statements. If you aren't familiar with these, the GUI tools come in handy.

The Command Line tools include the Command Line Processor (CLP), the Command Window
(only on the Windows platform), and the Command Editor. Among the GUI tools, the most powerful one is the Control Center. From the Control Center you can launch other tools and administer your instances and databases. In addition, the Control Center facilitates your administration
tasks with wizards and advisors.

The Application Development tools help you build, test, debug, and deploy stored procedures,
user-defined functions (UDFs), and structured types.

The monitoring tools keep track of your databases according to criteria you provide and generate
reports. They are handy for investigating performance problems and setting benchmarks for your
database.

4.12 REVIEW QUESTIONS

1. Which of the DB2 tools can be used to schedule SQL scripts in DB2?
2. The DB2 Command Window is only available on Windows. What is the equivalent tool
   on the Linux/UNIX platforms?
3. Which registry variable needs to be changed to set **autocommit** to off permanently
   for the CLP?
4. When is it handy to start the CLP in interactive mode with a different terminator character as in **db2 -td!**?
5. Which command is necessary to guarantee the CLP back-end process is terminated?
6. How can Visual Explain be invoked?
7. Which tool can be used to develop SQL user-defined functions?
8. Can the Control Center be used to administer DB2 for iSeries databases?
9. It's 9:00 a.m. and you would like to investigate a problem that happened at 3:00 a.m.
   Where do you look for more information?
10. How can you obtain the most current information about a given DB2 topic?

11. Which two of the following tools can be used to execute SQL statements against a DB2 database?

   A. Command Window
   B. Command Editor
   C. Command Line Processor
   D. Command Processor
   E. db2cc

12. Which of the following is the default termination character for files processed by the DB2 CLP?

   A. :
   B. ;
   C. |
   D. $

13. If you have the following CLP input file named *samp.sql*, how many commits will occur during the processing of the **db2 -tvf samp.sql** command?

```
connect to sample;
select * from org;
select * from dept;
connect reset;
```

   A. 0
   B. 1
   C. 2
   D. 3
   E. 4

14. The Health Center will alert you when:

   A. A row is deleted from a table
   B. You run the load tool
   C. You exceed a defined threshold on performance characteristics
   D. An SQL statement fails because of incorrect syntax

15. Which of the following tools will give you information about the memory used by DB2 and your DB2 applications?

   A. db2memlist
   B. Memory Visualizer
   C. db2mv
   D. Memory Center
   E. db2mtrk

16. If you have the following CLP input file named *samp.sql*, how many commits will occur during the processing of the **db2 +c -tvf samp.sql** command?

```
connect to sample;
select * from org;
select * from dept;
```

    A. 0

    B. 1

    C. 2

    D. 3

    E. 4

17. If you have the following CLP input file named *samp.sql*, which of the commands below will run this file successfully?

```
connect to sample@
select * from org@
select * from dept@
connect reset@
```

    A. db2 –t@f samp.sql

    B. db2 -td@ -f samp.sql

    C. db2 -t@ -f samp.sql

    D. db2 -td@f samp.sql

18. If your application receives the SQL code -911, which of the following commands can be used to get its description?

    A. db2 ? -911

    B. db2 ? 911N

    C. db2 ? SQL-911

    D. db2 ? SQL911N

19. Which of the following commands *cannot* be run from the CLP in interactive mode?

    A. History

    B. Edit

    C. Runcmd

    D. Repeat

20. Which two of the following *can* be performed from the CLP in interactive mode?

    A. db2 ? SQL911N

    B. db2stop

    C. list applications

    D. select * from staff

## CHAPTER 5

Understanding the DB2 Environment, DB2 Instances, and Databases

Y ou need to understand the DB2 environment and the concepts of DB2 instances and databases to work effectively with DB2. DB2 instances and the DB2 environment control many factors that influence DB2's behavior by using configurable parameters at different levels and locations.

In this chapter you will learn about:

- The big picture of the DB2 Environment, DB2 instances, and databases
- The environment variables
- The DB2 registry variables
- How to manage and configure a DB2 instance
- How to manage and configure the Database Administration Server
- How to manage and configure databases
- Instance and database design considerations

5.1 THE DB2 ENVIRONMENT, DB2 INSTANCES, AND DATABASES: THE BIG PICTURE

Figure 5.1 illustrates the different levels in which you can configure your DB2 environment. You can use

- Environment variables at the operating system level
- The DB2 profile registry variables at the operating system and instance levels
- The Database Manager (DBM) Configuration file at the instance level
- The database configuration file at the database level

In the following sections you will learn in detail how to work with all of these variables.

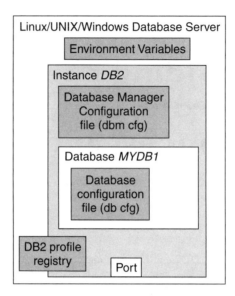

Figure 5.1   The big picture of the DB2 environment, instances, and databases

> **NOTE** DB2 provides several levels of configuration that allow
> users to control the DB2 environment with more flexibility. Starting
> with Version 8, DB2 provides the **Configuration Advisor** graphical
> tool, which can set parameter values based on your answers to simple
> questions about your system. Chapter 16, Database Performance Con-
> siderations, discusses this tool in more detail.

5.2 THE DB2 ENVIRONMENT

The DB2 environment consists of environment variables and DB2 profile registry variables.
These manage, monitor, and control the behavior of a DB2 system.

5.2.1 Environment Variables

You set the **environment variables** at the operating system level. Most environment variables
applicable to DB2 are set automatically during the DB2 installation. For example, the PATH
environment variable is updated to point to the DB2 executable code directory.

The two most important environment variables applicable to DB2 are

- DB2INSTANCE, which determines the active instance in your machine, and
- DB2NODE, which determines the active database partition in a multi-partitioned
  environment.

To review the contents of an environment variable like DB2INSTANCE, you can do the following.

On Windows:

```
echo %DB2INSTANCE%
```

or

```
set DB2INSTANCE
```

On Linux/UNIX:

```
export | grep DB2INSTANCE
```

or

```
set | grep DB2INSTANCE
```

To change the value of an environment variable *temporarily*, use the **set** operating system command on Windows or **export** on Linux/UNIX as shown in the following examples.

On Windows:

```
set DB2INSTANCE=myinst
```

On Linux/UNIX it would depend on the shell that is used:

- For the Korn shell:
  ```
  DB2INSTANCE=myinst
  export DB2INSTANCE
  ```
- For the Bourne shell:
  ```
  export DB2INSTANCE=myinst
  ```
- For the C shell:
  ```
  setenv DB2INSTANCE myinst
  ```

This setting will be lost after you close the window or end the session.

> **NOTE** A common mistake when using the **set** (Windows) or **export** (Linux/UNIX) commands is to leave spaces before and/or after the equal sign (=). No spaces must be used!

To create a new or modify an existing environment variable *permanently*, you can do the following.

- On Windows platforms, use the Control Panel. Figure 5.2 shows an example using Windows 2000 and the environment variable DB2INSTANCE. In the figure, *System* was selected followed by the *Advanced* tab, and then the *Environment Variables* button.
- On Linux and UNIX platforms you can permanently change an environment variable by adding the **export** command in the .login or .profile startup scripts. However, rather than making this change directly, edit the script that comes with DB2 to set up the default DB2 environment, and then invoke this script from .login or .profile. DB2

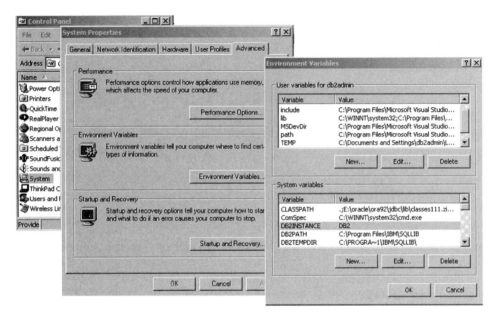

Figure 5.2   Setting an environment variable permanently in Windows

provides the scripts **db2profile** (for the Bourne and Korn shells) and **db2cshrc** (for the C shell), which contain all the required commands to set up this default DB2 environment. These script files are located under the *INSTHOME*/sqllib directory, where *INSTHOME* represents the instance owner's home directory.

Figure 5.3 shows part of the **db2profile** script. Note that the DB2INSTANCE environment variable is set in the script file.

```
##########################################################################
# NAME:     db2profile
#
# FUNCTION: This script sets up a default database environment for
#           Bourne shell or Korn shell users.
#
# USAGE:    . db2profile
#           This script can either be invoked directly as above or
#           it can be added to the user's .profile file so that the
#           database environment is established during login.
#
#           #### DO NOT EDIT THIS FILE ####
##########################################################################

# Default DB2 product directory
DB2DIR="/opt/IBM/db2/V8.1"
```

Figure 5.3   Part of the db2profile script file for a Linux/UNIX machine *(continues)*

```
# Function to avoid repetitive environment variable entries
AddtoString()
{
  var=$1
  addme=$2
  awkval='$1 != "'${addme?}'"{print $0}'
  newval=`eval echo \\${$var} | awk "${awkval?}" RS=:`
  eval ${var?}=`echo $newval | sed 's/ /:/g'`:${addme?}
  unset var addme awkval newval
}

#---------------------------------------------------------------------
# DB2INSTANCE [Default null, values: Any valid instance name]
# Specifies the instance that is active by default.
#---------------------------------------------------------------------
DB2INSTANCE=db2inst1
export DB2INSTANCE

INSTHOME=/home/db2inst1
#---------------------------------------------------------------------
# First remove any sqllib entries from the user's path.
# Add the directories:
#   INSTHOME/sqllib/bin  - database executables
#   INSTHOME/sqllib/adm  - sysadm executables
#   INSTHOME/sqllib/misc - miscellaneous utilities
# to the user's PATH.
#---------------------------------------------------------------------

AddtoString PATH ${INSTHOME?}/sqllib/bin
AddtoString PATH ${INSTHOME?}/sqllib/adm
AddtoString PATH ${INSTHOME?}/sqllib/misc
export PATH

#---------------------------------------------------------------------
# UDB Extender initialization
#---------------------------------------------------------------------
if [ -f ${INSTHOME}/dmb/dmbprofile ]; then
    . ${INSTHOME}/dmb/dmbprofile
fi

#---------------------------------------------------------------------
# The following variables are used for JDBC support
#---------------------------------------------------------------------
CLASSPATH=${CLASSPATH:-""}

if [ -f ${INSTHOME?}/sqllib/java/db2java.zip ]; then
    AddtoString CLASSPATH ${INSTHOME?}/sqllib/java/db2java.zip
fi
...
```

Figure 5.3 Part of the db2profile script file for a Linux/UNIX machine *(continued)*

For the DB2 instance owner, a line to invoke the **db2profile/db2cshrc** script file is automatically added during the instance creation. If you work with DB2 but are not the instance owner, add the following line to your .login or .profile startup scripts:

`. INSTHOME/sqllib/db2profile`   (for Bourne and Korn shells)

or

`source INSTHOME/sqllib/db2cshrc` (for C shell)

Executing the above commands will guarantee that your database environment is configured to use DB2.

5.2.2 DB2 Profile Registries

Most DB2-specific information is stored in a centralized repository called the **DB2 profile registry**. Depending on the operating system platform where DB2 is installed, variables stored in the DB2 profile registries may be different. The DB2 profile registry variables are commonly referred to as **DB2 registry variables**.

> **NOTE**   The word "Registry" always causes confusion when working with DB2 on the Windows platform. The DB2 profile registry variables have no relationship to the Windows registry variables.

The DB2 profile registry consists of the following registries.

- The DB2 Instance-Level Profile Registry: Variables set at this level apply only to a specific instance.
- The DB2 Global-Level Profile Registry: Variables set at this level apply globally to all instances.
- The DB2 Instance Node-Level Profile Registry: Variables at this level apply to a specific partition in a multi-partitioned environment.
- The DB2 Instance Profile Registry: Contains a list of all instances in the system. The command **db2ilist**, which lists all instances in a system, uses this registry as input.

> **NOTE**   All variables in the DB2 registries *except* those in the DB2 Instance Profile Registry are the same. The difference is at which level you set the variable. For example, you can set the DB2COMM registry variable at the instance-level, global-level, or node-level profile registries.

The DB2 registries are stored as binary or text files in different locations depending on the operating system. To modify these registries, do not edit these files directly; instead, use the **db2set** command. Figure 5.4 shows the **db2set** command with the **-all** option, which lists all of the currently set DB2 profile registry variables.

Figure 5.4   The db2set -all command

Notice that each registry variable is prefixed with a letter in square brackets. This indicates in which level the variable is set.

- **[i]** indicates the variable has been set at the DB2 Instance-Level Profile Registry using the **-i** option (which is the default). For example, in Figure 5.4 *[i] DB2COMM= appc,tcpip,npipes* was set using the following command in instance *myinst*:

  ```
  db2set DB2COMM=appc,tcpip,npipes -i myinst
  ```

- **[g]** indicates the variable has been set at the DB2 Global-Level Profile Registry using the **-g** option. This setting applies to all instances defined on the DB2 server. For example, in Figure 5.4, *[g] DB2COMM=netbios* was set using this command:

  ```
  db2set DB2COMM=netbios -g
  ```

- **[e]** indicates a DB2 registry variable has been set as an environment variable using the **set** command (Windows) or **export** command (Linux/UNIX). For example, in Figure 5.4 *[e] DB2COMM=tcpip* was set using this command:

  ```
  set DB2COMM=tcpip
  ```

Although most DB2 registry variables can be set as an environment variable, we recommend setting them as DB2 registry variables using the **db2set** command. Changes to DB2 registry variables do not require a server reboot, while changes to environment variables may require a reboot.

To set a registry variable at the DB2 instance node-level profile registry level, use a command with this syntax:

```
db2set registry_variable=value -i instance_name partition_number
```

> **N O T E**   Like the **set** operating system command, do not leave spaces before and/or after the equal sign (=) when using the **db2set** command.

In Figure 5.4 the DB2COMM registry variable was set three times with different values each at the [e], [i], and [g] levels. When a registry variable is defined at different levels, DB2 will choose the value using this search order.

1. Environment variable set using the **set/export** operating system commands.
2. DB2 Instance Node-Level Profile Registry
3. DB2 Instance-Level Profile Registry
4. DB2 Global-Level Profile Registry

Based on this search order, for the example in Figure 5.4, the value *tcpip* for the DB2COMM registry variable is the one that takes precedence as it has been set temporarily at the environment level.

Table 5.1 summarizes other options commonly used with the **db2set** command.

Table 5.1   Common db2set Command Options

Command	Explanation
db2set -all	Lists all the currently set DB2 registry variables
db2set -lr	Lists all the DB2 registry variables that can be set
db2set -h	Displays help information about the **db2set** command
db2set *DB2_registry_variable=*	Deletes a variable from the DB2 registry. Note that a blank space follows the equal sign (=).

Some registry variables require that you stop and start the instance (**db2stop/db2start**) for the change to take effect. Refer to the *DB2 UDB Administration Guide: Performance* for a list of variables that have this requirement.

5.3 THE DB2 INSTANCE

From a user's perspective, a **DB2 instance** provides an independent environment where database objects can be created and applications can run. Several instances can be created on one server, and each instance can have a multiple number of databases, as illustrated in Figure 5.5.

Because of these independent environments, one instance cannot "see" the contents of another instance; therefore, objects of two or more different instances can have the same name. In Figure 5.5, the database called *MYDB1* is associated with instance *Development*, and another database also called *MYDB1* is associated with instance *Test*. Instances allow users to have different environments for production, test, and development purposes. In addition, independent environments let you perform instance and database operations without affecting other instances. For example, if you stop and start the instance *Test*, the other two instances are not affected.

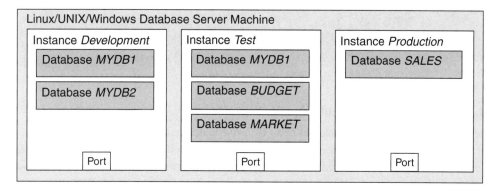

Figure 5.5   A DB2 instance from a user's perspective

From an architectural perspective, an instance serves as a layer between the DB2 binary code and the user database objects. It is important to understand that this is just an association of the DB2 code to the database objects. There is a common misconception among new DB2 users that dropping an instance also drops the databases associated to that instance; this is not necessarily true. When an instance is dropped, the association to the user databases is broken, but it can later be reestablished, as discussed in Chapter 2, DB2 at a Glance: The Big Picture.

Figure 5.6 shows an example of two instances in a Linux/UNIX environment. Databases *MarketDB* and *SalesDB* are associated to instance *#1*. Databases *TestDB* and *ProdDB* are associated to instance *#2*. Each instance has its own configuration files. In this example, both instances are pointing to the same DB2 binary code for Version 8.2 using **soft links**. On Linux and UNIX, a soft link behaves like an alias to another file. Soft links are also referred to as **symbolic links** or **logical links**.

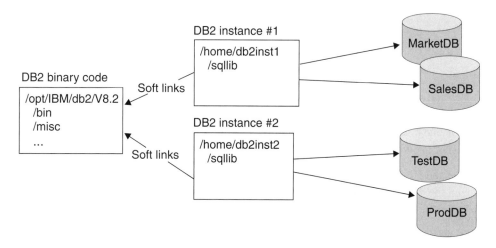

Figure 5.6   The DB2 instance in Linux/UNIX from an architectural perspective

> **N O T E**   On Linux and UNIX, soft links are used as pointers from
> the instance *sqllib* directory to the DB2 binary code. On Windows,
> there is a shared install path and all instances access the same libraries
> and executables.

5.3.1 Creating DB2 Instances

When you install DB2 on the Windows platform, an instance called *DB2* is created by default. On Linux and UNIX you can choose to create the default instance during the installation, change the instance owner's name, or not create an instance so that you can create one later. If you choose to create the default instance on these platforms, this instance is named *db2inst1*. DB2 will create an operating system user with the same name as the instance. This user is known as the **instance owner**.

You can also create new, additional instances on your server using the **db2icrt** command.

Figure 5.7 summarizes the **db2icrt** command and provides examples.

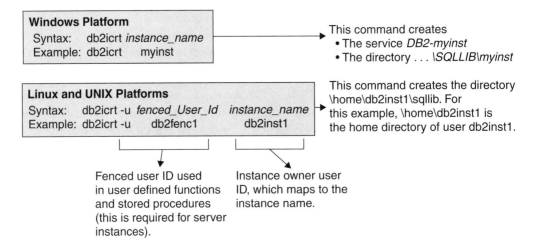

Figure 5.7   The db2icrt command

On Windows the **db2icrt** command can be run by a user with Local Administrator authority. The command creates a subdirectory under the SQLLIB directory with the name of the instance just created. In addition, a Windows service *DB2 - instance_ name* will be created.

On Linux and UNIX you must have root authority or else you need to have the system administrator run the **db2icrt** command for you. You can either use the fully qualified path name to the program or change into the directory to run this command as shown below:

- Run the command **/opt/IBM/db2/v8.1/instance/db2icrt**
  (or **/usr/opt/IBM/db2/v8.1/instance/db2icrt** on AIX)

or

- Change into the directory /opt/IBM/db2/v8.1/instance
  (or /usr/opt/IBM/db2/v8.1/instance on AIX) and then invoke the **db2icrt** command.

In addition, on Linux and UNIX, the instance name must match an existing operating system user ID, which becomes the instance owner. This operating system user must exist prior to executing the `db2icrt` command. The `db2icrt` command will create the subdirectory *sqllib* under the home directory of this user.

DB2 on Linux and UNIX also requires a fenced user to run stored procedures and user-defined functions (UDFs) as fenced resources, that is, in a separate address space other than the one used by the DB2 engine. This ensures that problems with these objects do not affect your database or instance. If you are not concerned about this type of problems, you can use the same ID for the fenced user and the instance owner.

> **N O T E** The terms *instance* and a *DB2 instance* are used interchangeably. On Windows, the default name of the DB2 instance is *DB2*. This sometimes confuses new DB2 users.

5.3.2 Creating DB2 64-bit Instances

You need to have the correct DB2 version and operating system to create 64-bit instances. At this time only AIX 5L, HP-UX, and the Solaris Operating Environment support this.

To create a 64-bit instance, include the **-w** option. For example:

```
db2icrt -w 64 -u db2fenc1 my64inst
```

creates a 64-bit instance called *my64inst* and uses a fenced id of *db2fenc1*.

5.3.3 Creating Client Instances

In general, when we talk about instances in this book we are referring to server instances: fully functional instances created at the DB2 server where your database resides. There are other types of instances that can be created. One of them, the **client instance**, is a scaled down version of a server instance. A client instance cannot be started or stopped, and databases cannot be created in this type of instance.

You create a DB2 client instance using the **-s** option. For example:

```
db2icrt -s CLIENT myclinst
```

creates the client instance *myclinst*. On Linux/UNIX, the operating system user *myclinst* must exist before executing this command. On Windows, an instance does not map to a user ID, so this would not be a requirement.

On a Windows client, the entire machine is considered the DB2 client regardless of the user. On a Linux/UNIX client machine the DB2 client is associated to an operating system user.

You need to have a client instance if you have two physically separate Linux/UNIX machines, one containing the DB2 client code (assume it is an application server machine) and the other one containing the DB2 server code (the DB2 server machine). Although the client machine contains the DB2 client code, a client instance must be created that will associate it to a given operating system user. Logging on as this user lets you perform the commands required to set up connectivity to the DB2 server machine. In this example, if the client and server resided on the same machine, there would be no need to create a client instance, because the operating system user used as the client can "source" the instance owner profile in sqllib/db2profile as described in section 5.2.1, Environment Variables.

5.3.4 Creating DB2 Instances in a Multi-Partitioned Environment

In a multi-partitioned environment, an instance is only created once: in the machine where the disks to be shared by the other partitions reside. The instance owner's home directory is then exported to all the servers participating in the multi-partitioned environment (see Chapter 2, DB2 at a Glance: The Big Picture).

> **N O T E**   You can only create a multi-partitioned database if you have DB2 UDB Enterprise Server Edition (ESE) installed and you have purchased the database partitioning feature (DPF). The DPF is a paper-only license that you need to acquire; you do not need to install any additional products to use this feature.

5.3.5 Dropping an Instance

You can drop an instance if you no longer require it. Before you drop an instance, make sure that it is stopped, and that all memory and inter-process communications (IPCs) owned by the instance have been released. You can then run the **db2idrop** command to drop the DB2 instance. For example, to drop the instance *myinst*, use the command:

```
db2idrop myinst
```

> **N O T E**   On Linux and UNIX, you can use the **ipclean** command to remove all IPCs associated with the ID that runs the command.

5.3.6 Listing the Instances in Your System

You can list all instances on your server using the **db2ilist** command. On Windows you can run this command from any Command Window. On Linux and UNIX you need to change into the path where DB2 was installed to run this command.

Alternatively, you can list your instances using the DB2 Control Center. Figure 5.8 shows the steps that are needed.

1. Right-click on the Instances folder.
2. Choose **Add Instance**.
3. Click on the *Discover* button.

Clicking on *Discover* displays a list of all available instances. You can then select the desired instance(s) to add to the Control Center.

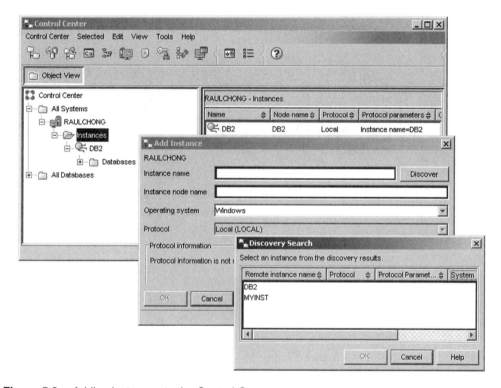

Figure 5.8 Adding instances to the Control Center

N O T E You cannot create an instance from the Control Center. You can only add an existing instance to the Control Center so it can be displayed and managed more easily with this tool.

5.3.7 The **DB2INSTANCE** Environment Variable

The environment variable DB2INSTANCE determines the active instance. It is particularly important to have this variable set correctly when you have multiple instances in the same DB2 server. For example, if you have two instances, *myinst1* and *myinst2*, and DB2INSTANCE is set to *myinst2*, any command you execute will be directed to the *myinst2* instance.

Because DB2INSTANCE is an operating system environment variable, you set its value like any other environment variable for your operating system, as discussed in section 5.2.1, Environment Variables. Figure 5.9 illustrates setting the DB2INSTANCE environment variable temporarily in the Windows platform using the **set** operating system command. It also illustrates the methods used to determine its current value.

The **get instance** command works on any platform. The other methods were described in section 5.2.1, Environment Variables.

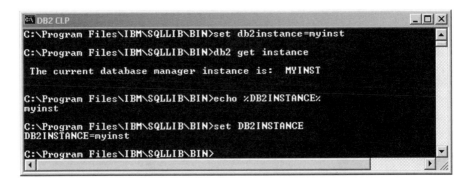

Figure 5.9   Working with the DB2INSTANCE variable

5.3.8 Starting a DB2 Instance

An instance must be started to work with it. You can choose to start the instance manually or automatically every time you reboot your machine. To start an instance manually, use the **db2start** command. On Windows, since DB2 instances are created as services, you can also start an instance manually using the **NET START** command. To start an instance automatically on Windows, look for the service corresponding to the DB2 instance by opening the Control Panel, choosing the *Administration Tools* folder, and then double-clicking on *Services*. A Services window similar to the one displayed in Figure 5.10 will appear.

Several DB2 services are listed in Figure 5.10. All of the DB2 services can be easily identified as they are prefixed with *DB2*. For example, the service *DB2 - MYINST* represents the instance *MYINST*. The service *DB2 - DB2-0* represents the instance named *DB2* (highlighted in the figure). The *0* in the service name represents the partition number. As you can see from the figure, this service is set up to be manually started, so you would need to execute a **db2start** command every time the system is restarted for the DB2 instance to be able to work with your databases.

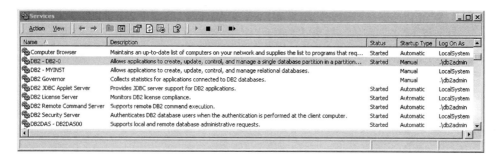

Figure 5.10   Windows services for DB2

You can set up the instance to be automatically started by right-clicking on the *DB2 - DB2-0* service and choosing **Properties** from the drop-down menu. Once the Properties panel appears, you can change the *Startup type* from *Manual* to *Automatic* (see Figure 5.11).

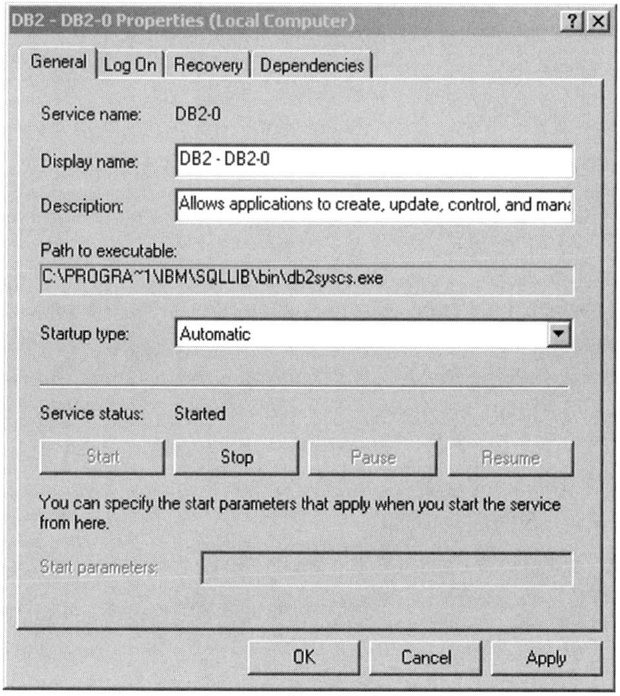

Figure 5.11   Service properties for the instance *DB2*

On Linux and UNIX, to automatically start the DB2 instance every time the server is started, use the **db2iauto** command. To set up the *db2inst1* instance to be started automatically, run the command:

```
db2iauto -on db2inst1
```

> **N O T E**   If you are setting up your system for High Availability failover, you *should not* set up the instance to be started automatically.

When you run the **db2start** command on your Linux or UNIX server, a number of processes start. If you run the **ps -ef** command you will notice a db2sysc process that is associated with the instance owner's ID. This is the DB2 main system controller for the instance. DB2 processes are discussed in more detail in Chapter 14, The DB2 Process Model.

In a multi-partitioned environment you only need to run the **db2start** command once, and it will start all of the partitions defined in the db2nodes.cfg file. Notice in the output of the **db2start** command below that there is one message returned for each partition, and each message has the partition number associated with it in the third column. Since the instances are started in parallel, they are not likely to complete in the order specified in the db2nodes.cfg file.

```
db2inst1@aries db2inst1]$ db2start

01-14-2005 14:42:26  1  0  SQL1063N  DB2START processing was successful.
01-14-2005 14:42:26  0  0  SQL1063N  DB2START processing was successful.
01-14-2005 14:42:26  2  0  SQL1063N  DB2START processing was successful.
01-14-2005 14:42:26  3  0  SQL1063N  DB2START processing was successful.
SQL1063N  DB2START processing was successful.
```

There may be times when a database administrator needs to be the only user attached to an instance to perform maintenance tasks. In these situations, use the **db2start** option **admin mode user** *userId* so only one user has full control of the instance. You can also do this from the Control Center by right-clicking on the desired instance in the Object Tree and choosing **Start Admin**.

5.3.9 Stopping a DB2 Instance

You can use the **db2stop** command to stop a DB2 instance that is currently running. Verify that the DB2INSTANCE environment variable is correctly set before issuing this command, as discussed in section 5.2.1, Environment Variables.

On Windows, since the DB2 instances are created as services, you can also stop the instances using the **NET STOP** command or stop the service from the Control Panel. To stop an instance from the Control Panel on Windows, right-click on the service and select **Stop** from the drop-down menu. Once the service is stopped the *Status* column will be blank, as the highlighted line shows in Figure 5.12.

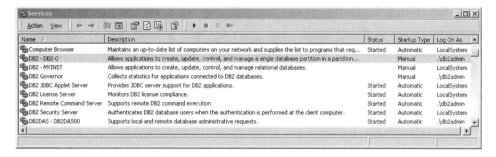

Figure 5.12   A stopped instance

You will not be able to stop the instance if there is a database that is active in the instance or if there are databases with one or more connections. You must first deactivate the database and/or reset the connections. In many cases you will have a large number of DB2 client machines running applications that connect to the database server, and you will not be able to go to each machine to close the application to terminate the connection. In this case you can use the **force** option with the **db2stop** command to force off all active connections and/or activations to stop the instance:

```
db2stop force
```

> **N O T E**   A **db2stop force** command has the same effect as issuing the **force applications all** command followed by the **db2stop** command. However, **db2stop force** prevents new connections from happening while the instance is being stopped. The **force applications** command is discussed in detail in Chapter 11, Understanding Concurrency and Locking.

In a multi-partitioned environment you only need to run the **db2stop** command once, and it will stop all of the partitions defined in the db2nodes.cfg file.

> **N O T E**   In many DB2 customer environments, the process of issuing a **db2stop** followed by a **db2start** command is called one or more of the following:
>
> • Recycling the instance
> • Bringing the instance down and up
> • Stopping and (re)starting the instance

5.3.10 Attaching to an Instance

To perform instance-level maintenance tasks, you first need to attach to the instance with the `attach` command. Some instance-level operations are

- Listing applications connected to your databases
- Forcing off applications
- Monitoring a database
- Updating the Database Manager Configuration parameters

Users often confuse attaching to an instance and connecting to a database. When in doubt as to which one to use, determine if the operation is to affect the instance or a particular database. For example, the `list applications` command lists all the applications connected to all the databases in your active instance. This is not an operation that you would perform at the database level, since you want to list all connections to all databases, so an attachment is what is required in this case. (Chapter 6, Configuring Client and Server Connectivity, discusses setting up database connections in detail. In that chapter we describe the **node directory**, which is used to encapsulate connectivity information, such as the hostname of a remote DB2 database server and the port number of the instance.)

> **N O T E**   Attachments are only applicable at the instance level; connections are only applicable at the database level.

When you attach to an instance, it can be a local instance or a remote one, and there will be corresponding entries for each in the node directory. A local instance resides on the same machine where you issue the `attach` command, while a remote instance resides on some other machine. Other than the active instance specified in the DB2INSTANCE variable, DB2 will look for connectivity information in the node directory for any other instance.

The syntax to attach to the active instance is:

```
attach to instance_name_as_indicated_in_DB2INSTANCE
```

For example:

```
attach to DB2
```

To attach to a local or remote instance that is not your active instance, use:

```
attach to node_name [user userId] [using password]
```

For example:

```
attach to mynode user peter using myudbpsw
```

where *mynode* is an entry in the node directory.

Attaching to the active instance (as specified in DB2INSTANCE) is normally done implicitly. However, there are special occasions where you do need to explicitly attach to the active instance, as you will see in following sections.

To detach from the current attached instance, issue the **detach** command:

```
attach to mynode
detach
```

5.3.11 Configuring an Instance

You can set DB2 configuration parameters at the instance level (also known as the database manager level) and at the database level. At the instance level, variables are stored in the Database Manager (DBM) Configuration file. Changes to these variables affect *all* databases associated to this instance. At the database level, variables are stored in the Database Configuration file. Changes to these variables only affect that specific database. In this section we discuss the DBM Configuration file in detail.

When you install DB2 and create an instance, the instance is assigned a default DBM configuration. You can view this configuration by running the **get dbm cfg** command. Figure 5.13 shows the output of this command on a Windows machine.

```
C:\Program Files\SQLLIB\BIN>db2 get dbm cfg


          Database Manager Configuration

     Node type = Database Server with local and remote clients

Database manager configuration release level                = 0x0a00

Maximum total of files open                  (MAXTOTFILOP) = 16000
CPU speed (millisec/instruction)                (CPUSPEED) = 1.113945e-006

Max number of concurrently active databases       (NUMDB) = 8
Data Links support                            (DATALINKS) = NO
Federated Database System Support             (FEDERATED) = NO
Transaction processor monitor name          (TP_MON_NAME) =

Default charge-back account              (DFT_ACCOUNT_STR) =

Java Development Kit installation path          (JDK_PATH) = C:\PROGRA~1\SQLLIB\ja
va\jdk

Diagnostic error capture level                (DIAGLEVEL) = 3
Notify Level                                 (NOTIFYLEVEL) = 3
Diagnostic data directory path                 (DIAGPATH) =
```

Figure 5.13   Contents of the DBM Configuration file *(continues)*

```
Default database monitor switches
  Buffer pool                          (DFT_MON_BUFPOOL) = OFF
  Lock                                    (DFT_MON_LOCK) = OFF
  Sort                                    (DFT_MON_SORT) = OFF
  Statement                               (DFT_MON_STMT) = OFF
  Table                                  (DFT_MON_TABLE) = OFF
  Timestamp                          (DFT_MON_TIMESTAMP) = ON
  Unit of work                             (DFT_MON_UOW) = OFF
Monitor health of instance and databases    (HEALTH_MON) = ON

SYSADM group name                        (SYSADM_GROUP) =
SYSCTRL group name                      (SYSCTRL_GROUP) =
SYSMAINT group name                    (SYSMAINT_GROUP) =
SYSMON group name                        (SYSMON_GROUP) =

Client Userid-Password Plugin           (CLNT_PW_PLUGIN) =
Client Kerberos Plugin                 (CLNT_KRB_PLUGIN) = IBMkrb5
Group Plugin                              (GROUP_PLUGIN) =
GSS Plugin for Local Authorization     (LOCAL_GSSPLUGIN) =
Server Plugin Mode                      (SRV_PLUGIN_MODE) = UNFENCED
Server List of GSS Plugins     (SRVCON_GSSPLUGIN_LIST) =
Server Userid-Password Plugin        (SRVCON_PW_PLUGIN) =
Server Connection Authentication        (SRVCON_AUTH) = NOT_SPECIFIED
Database manager authentication        (AUTHENTICATION) = SERVER
Cataloging allowed without authority   (CATALOG_NOAUTH) = NO
Trust all clients                      (TRUST_ALLCLNTS) = YES
Trusted client authentication          (TRUST_CLNTAUTH) = CLIENT
Bypass federated authentication           (FED_NOAUTH) = NO

Default database path                       (DFTDBPATH) = C:

Database monitor heap size (4KB)          (MON_HEAP_SZ) = 66
Java Virtual Machine heap size (4KB)     (JAVA_HEAP_SZ) = 512
Audit buffer size (4KB)                   (AUDIT_BUF_SZ) = 0
Size of instance shared memory (4KB)  (INSTANCE_MEMORY) = AUTOMATIC
Backup buffer default size (4KB)            (BACKBUFSZ) = 1024
Restore buffer default size (4KB)           (RESTBUFSZ) = 1024

Agent stack size                        (AGENT_STACK_SZ) = 16
Minimum committed private memory (4KB)    (MIN_PRIV_MEM) = 32
Private memory threshold (4KB)         (PRIV_MEM_THRESH) = 20000

Sort heap threshold (4KB)                   (SHEAPTHRES) = 10000

Directory cache support                      (DIR_CACHE) = YES

Application support layer heap size (4KB)    (ASLHEAPSZ) = 15
Max requester I/O block size (bytes)          (RQRIOBLK) = 32767
DOS requester I/O block size (bytes)      (DOS_RQRIOBLK) = 4096
Query heap size (4KB)                      (QUERY_HEAP_SZ) = 1000

Workload impact by throttled utilities(UTIL_IMPACT_LIM) = 10
```

Figure 5.13   Contents of the DBM Configuration file *(continues)*

```
Priority of agents                              (AGENTPRI) = SYSTEM
Max number of existing agents                  (MAXAGENTS) = 200
Agent pool size                            (NUM_POOLAGENTS) = 100(calculated)
Initial number of agents in pool           (NUM_INITAGENTS) = 0
Max number of coordinating agents        (MAX_COORDAGENTS) = MAXAGENTS
Max no. of concurrent coordinating agents  (MAXCAGENTS) = MAX_COORDAGENTS
Max number of client connections        (MAX_CONNECTIONS) = MAX_COORDAGENTS

Keep fenced process                            (KEEPFENCED) = YES
Number of pooled fenced processes            (FENCED_POOL) = MAX_COORDAGENTS
Initial number of fenced processes        (NUM_INITFENCED) = 0

Index re-creation time and redo index build  (INDEXREC) = RESTART

Transaction manager database name           (TM_DATABASE) = 1ST_CONN
Transaction resync interval (sec)      (RESYNC_INTERVAL) = 180

SPM name                                        (SPM_NAME) = RAULCHO1
SPM log size                            (SPM_LOG_FILE_SZ) = 256
SPM resync agent limit                  (SPM_MAX_RESYNC) = 20
SPM log path                              (SPM_LOG_PATH) =

NetBIOS Workstation name                          (NNAME) =

TCP/IP Service name                            (SVCENAME) =
Discovery mode                                 (DISCOVER) = SEARCH
Discover server instance                  (DISCOVER_INST) = ENABLE

Maximum query degree of parallelism    (MAX_QUERYDEGREE) = ANY
Enable intra-partition parallelism      (INTRA_PARALLEL) = NO

No. of int. communication buffers(4KB)(FCM_NUM_BUFFERS) = 1024
Number of FCM request blocks               (FCM_NUM_RQB) = AUTOMATIC
Number of FCM connection entries       (FCM_NUM_CONNECT) = AUTOMATIC
Number of FCM message anchors          (FCM_NUM_ANCHORS) = AUTOMATIC
```

Figure 5.13   Contents of the DBM Configuration file *(continued)*

Note that the *Node type* entry field at the top of the output identifies the type of instance. For example, in Figure 5.13 this field has the value *Database Server with local and remote clients*. This means it is a server instance. For a client instance the value of this field would be *Client*.

In this book you will learn some of the more important parameters for the DBM Configuration file. For a full treatment of all DBM Configuration parameters, refer to the *DB2 UDB Administration Guide: Performance*.

To update one or more parameters in the DBM Configuration file, issue the command:

```
update dbm cfg
      using parameter_name value parameter_name value ...
```

For example, to update the INTRA_PARALLEL DBM Configuration parameter, issue the command:

```
update dbm cfg using INTRA_PARALLEL YES
```

Issuing the **get dbm cfg** command after the **update dbm cfg** command shows the newly updated values. However, this does not mean that the change will take effect right away. Several parameters in the DBM Configuration file require a **db2stop** followed by a **db2start** for the new values to be used. For other parameters, the update is dynamic, so a **db2stop/db2start** is not required as the new value takes effect immediately. These parameters are called **configurable online parameters**. If you are updating a configuration parameter of a DB2 client instance, the new value takes effect the next time you restart the client application or if the client application is the CLP, after you issue the **terminate** command.

> **N O T E**   Configurable online parameters of the DBM Configuration file can be updated dynamically only if you first explicitly attach to the instance. This also applies to local instances. If you have not performed an attach, the parameter won't be changed until you perform a **db2stop/db2start**.

Refer to the file *ConfigurationParameters.pdf* included on the CD-ROM accompanying this book for a list of DBM Configuration parameters that are configurable online. The Control Center provides this information as well. Refer to section 5.3.12, Working with an Instance from the Control Center, for details.

To get the current, effective setting for each configuration parameter and the value of the parameter the next time the instance is stopped and restarted, use the **show detail** option of the **get dbm cfg** command. This option requires an instance attachment. If you run this command after changing the INTRA_PARALLEL configuration parameter as above, you will see that the current value is NO, but the next effective or delayed value is YES. The related output from the **get dbm cfg show detail** command would look like the following:

```
C:\Program Files\SQLLIB\BIN>db2 get dbm cfg show detail

Description                         Parameter       Current Value   Delayed Value
---------------------------------------------------------------------------------

...

Enable intra-partition parallelism    (INTRA_PARALLEL) = NO               YES
```

The **show detail** option is also helpful for determining the actual value of parameters listed as AUTOMATIC. For example, when you issue the **get dbm cfg** command while attached to an instance, you may see output as follows for the INSTANCE_MEMORY parameter:

```
C:\Program Files\SQLLIB\BIN>db2 get dbm cfg

...

Size of instance shared memory (4KB)  (INSTANCE_MEMORY) = AUTOMATIC
```

If you use the **show detail** option, the actual value is displayed:

```
C:\Program Files\SQLLIB\BIN>db2 get dbm cfg show detail

Description                              Parameter      Current Value    Delayed Value
--------------------------------------------------------------------------------------

...

Size of instance shared memory (4KB)  (INSTANCE_MEMORY) = AUTOMATIC(8405) AUTOMATIC(8405)
```

To reset all the DBM Configuration parameters to their default value, use the command **reset dbm cfg**.

5.3.12 Working with an Instance from the Control Center

The instance operations described in the previous sections can also be performed from the Control Center. Figure 5.14 shows the Control Center with the instance *MYINST* selected. When you

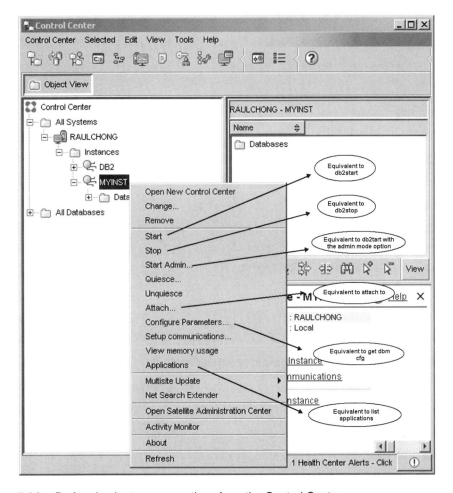

Figure 5.14   Performing instance operations from the Control Center

right-click on the instance, a menu with several options displays. Figure 5.14 highlights some of the menu items that map to the instance operations we have already described.

Figure 5.15 shows the DBM Configuration window that appears after selecting **Configure Parameters** from the menu shown in Figure 5.14. In Figure 5.15, the column *Pending Value Effective* indicates when the pending value for the parameter will take effect; for example, immediately or after the instance is restarted. The column *Dynamic* indicates whether the parameter is configurable online or not. The rest of the columns are self-explanatory.

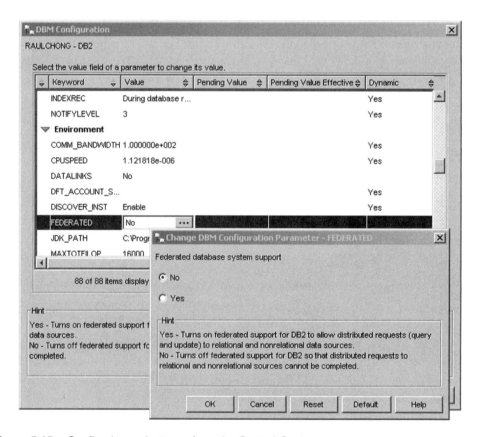

Figure 5.15   Configuring an instance from the Control Center

Figure 5.15 also illustrates how you can update a Database Manager Configuration parameter from the Control Center. For example, after selecting the parameter *FEDERATED* and clicking on the three dots button (...), a pop-up window displays that lists the possible values this parameter can accept. Choose the desired option and click *OK*.

5.3.13 The DB2 Commands at the Instance Level

Table 5.2 summarizes the most common DB2 commands used at the instance level.

Table 5.2   DB2 Instance-Level Commands

Command	Explanation
db2start	Starts an instance.
db2stop	Stops an instance.
db2icrt	Creates a new instance.
db2idrop	Drops an instance.
db2ilist	Lists all available instances in your system.
get dbm cfg	Displays the DBM Configuration file.
update dbm cfg	Updates the DBM Configuration file.
reset dbm cfg	Resets the DBM Configuration file to its default values.

5.4 THE DATABASE ADMINISTRATION SERVER

Prior to Version 8 there was another type of instance called the **Database Administration Server** (DAS) instance. There could only be one such instance per database server, and its main purpose was to allow for remote graphical administration of your database. In Version 7, if you installed the DB2 Administration Client (which comes with the graphical tools) on your Windows 2000 laptop and wanted to connect to a database server in Japan using graphical tools, the database server in Japan had to have this instance created and running.

With Version 8, this instance was converted into a background process, thereby hiding some of the required administration from the user. Nonetheless, you will still find commands that only apply to the DAS. On Linux and UNIX, a DAS user still needs to be created. The DB2 profile registry variable DB2ADMINSERVER contains the value of the DAS user. Normally, it is set to *DB2DAS00* on Windows and *dasusr1* on Linux/UNIX.

> **N O T E**   DB2 Administration Server and Database Administration Server are used interchangeably to refer to the DAS process.

5.4.1 The DAS Commands

Table 5.3 summarizes the most common commands for the DAS.

Table 5.3   DAS Commands

Command	Explanation
db2admin start	Starts the DAS.
db2admin stop	Stops the DAS.
dascrt	Creates the DAS in Linux and UNIX.
dasdrop	Drops the DAS in Linux and UNIX.
db2admin create	Creates the DAS in Windows.
db2admin drop	Drops the DAS in Windows.
get admin cfg	Displays the DAS admin configuration file.
update admin cfg	Updates the DAS admin configuration file.
reset admin cfg	Resets the DAS admin configuration file to its default values.

5.5 Configuring a Database

Database configuration and instance configuration are fairly similar. We will use the same format to describe database configuration as we used to discuss instance configuration earlier in this chapter. Database concepts are discussed in more detail in Chapter 7, Working with Database Objects.

A database is set up with a default configuration when you create it. You can view this configuration by running the **get db cfg for** *database_name* command. Figure 5.16 shows the output of this command on a Windows machine.

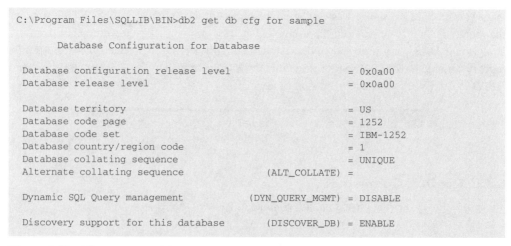

```
C:\Program Files\SQLLIB\BIN>db2 get db cfg for sample

      Database Configuration for Database

Database configuration release level                      = 0x0a00
Database release level                                    = 0x0a00

Database territory                                        = US
Database code page                                        = 1252
Database code set                                         = IBM-1252
Database country/region code                              = 1
Database collating sequence                               = UNIQUE
Alternate collating sequence            (ALT_COLLATE) =

Dynamic SQL Query management            (DYN_QUERY_MGMT) = DISABLE

Discovery support for this database     (DISCOVER_DB) = ENABLE
```

Figure 5.16   The contents of the database configuration file *(continues)*

```
Default query optimization class        (DFT_QUERYOPT) = 5
Degree of parallelism                     (DFT_DEGREE) = 1
Continue upon arithmetic exceptions  (DFT_SQLMATHWARN) = NO
Default refresh age                  (DFT_REFRESH_AGE) = 0
Default maintained table types for opt (DFT_MTTB_TYPES) = SYSTEM
Number of frequent values retained    (NUM_FREQVALUES) = 10
Number of quantiles retained           (NUM_QUANTILES) = 20

Backup pending                                         = NO

Database is consistent                                 = YES
Rollforward pending                                    = NO
Restore pending                                        = NO

Multi-page file allocation enabled                     = YES

Log retain for recovery status                         = NO
User exit for logging status                           = NO

Data Links Token Expiry Interval (sec)      (DL_EXPINT) = 60
Data Links Write Token Init Expiry Intvl(DL_WT_IEXPINT) = 60
Data Links Number of Copies            (DL_NUM_COPIES) = 1
Data Links Time after Drop (days)       (DL_TIME_DROP) = 1
Data Links Token in Uppercase              (DL_UPPER) = NO
Data Links Token Algorithm                 (DL_TOKEN) = MAC0

Database heap (4KB)                           (DBHEAP) = 600
Size of database shared memory (4KB) (DATABASE_MEMORY) = AUTOMATIC
Catalog cache size (4KB)            (CATALOGCACHE_SZ) = (MAXAPPLS*4)
Log buffer size (4KB)                        (LOGBUFSZ) = 8
Utilities heap size (4KB)              (UTIL_HEAP_SZ) = 5000
Buffer pool size (pages)                    (BUFFPAGE) = 250
Extended storage segments size (4KB)   (ESTORE_SEG_SZ) = 16000
Number of extended storage segments (NUM_ESTORE_SEGS) = 0
Max storage for lock list (4KB)             (LOCKLIST) = 50

Max size of appl. group mem set (4KB) (APPGROUP_MEM_SZ) = 30000
Percent of mem for appl. group heap  (GROUPHEAP_RATIO) = 70
Max appl. control heap size (4KB)      (APP_CTL_HEAP_SZ) = 128

Sort heap thres for shared sorts (4KB) (SHEAPTHRES_SHR) = (SHEAPTHRES)
Sort list heap (4KB)                        (SORTHEAP) = 256
SQL statement heap (4KB)                     (STMTHEAP) = 2048
Default application heap (4KB)             (APPLHEAPSZ) = 256
Package cache size (4KB)                   (PCKCACHESZ) = (MAXAPPLS*8)
Statistics heap size (4KB)              (STAT_HEAP_SZ) = 4384

Interval for checking deadlock (ms)        (DLCHKTIME) = 10000
Percent. of lock lists per application      (MAXLOCKS) = 22
Lock timeout (sec)                        (LOCKTIMEOUT) = -1

Changed pages threshold                 (CHNGPGS_THRESH) = 60
Number of asynchronous page cleaners  (NUM_IOCLEANERS) = 1
Number of I/O servers                   (NUM_IOSERVERS) = 3
```

Figure 5.16   The contents of the database configuration file *(continues)*

```
Index sort flag                              (INDEXSORT) = YES
Sequential detect flag                       (SEQDETECT) = YES
Default prefetch size (pages)          (DFT_PREFETCH_SZ) = AUTOMATIC

Track modified pages                          (TRACKMOD) = OFF

Default number of containers                            = 1
Default tablespace extentsize (pages)    (DFT_EXTENT_SZ) = 32

Max number of active applications             (MAXAPPLS) = AUTOMATIC
Average number of active applications        (AVG_APPLS) = 1
Max DB files open per application             (MAXFILOP) = 64

Log file size (4KB)                           (LOGFILSIZ) = 1000
Number of primary log files                  (LOGPRIMARY) = 3
Number of secondary log files                (LOGSECOND) = 2
Changed path to log files                    (NEWLOGPATH) =
Path to log files                                       = C:\DB2\NODE0000\SQL00
                                                          009\SQLOGDIR\
Overflow log path                        (OVERFLOWLOGPATH) =
Mirror log path                            (MIRRORLOGPATH) =
First active log file                                   =
Block log on disk full                    (BLK_LOG_DSK_FUL) = NO
Percent of max active log space by transaction(MAX_LOG) = 0
Num. of active log files for 1 active UOW(NUM_LOG_SPAN) = 0

Group commit count                            (MINCOMMIT) = 1
Percent log file reclaimed before soft chckpt (SOFTMAX) = 100
Log retain for recovery enabled              (LOGRETAIN) = OFF
User exit for logging enabled                  (USEREXIT) = OFF

HADR database role                                      = STANDARD
HADR local host name                     (HADR_LOCAL_HOST) =
HADR local service name                   (HADR_LOCAL_SVC) =
HADR remote host name                    (HADR_REMOTE_HOST) =
HADR remote service name                  (HADR_REMOTE_SVC) =
HADR instance name of remote server      (HADR_REMOTE_INST) =
HADR timeout value                          (HADR_TIMEOUT) = 120
HADR log write synchronization mode       (HADR_SYNCMODE) = NEARSYNC

First log archive method                    (LOGARCHMETH1) = OFF
Options for logarchmeth1                      (LOGARCHOPT1) =
Second log archive method                   (LOGARCHMETH2) = OFF
Options for logarchmeth2                      (LOGARCHOPT2) =
Failover log archive path                    (FAILARCHPATH) =
Number of log archive retries on error     (NUMARCHRETRY) = 5
Log archive retry Delay (secs)            (ARCHRETRYDELAY) = 20
Vendor options                                (VENDOROPT) =

Auto restart enabled                         (AUTORESTART) = ON
Index re-creation time and redo index build  (INDEXREC) = SYSTEM (ACCESS)
Log pages during index build              (LOGINDEXBUILD) = OFF
Default number of loadrec sessions        (DFT_LOADREC_SES) = 1
```

Figure 5.16   The contents of the database configuration file *(continues)*

```
Number of database backups to retain    (NUM_DB_BACKUPS) = 12
Recovery history retention (days)        (REC_HIS_RETENTN) = 366

TSM management class                     (TSM_MGMTCLASS) =
TSM node name                            (TSM_NODENAME) =
TSM owner                                (TSM_OWNER) =
TSM password                             (TSM_PASSWORD) =

Automatic maintenance                    (AUTO_MAINT) = OFF
  Automatic database backup              (AUTO_DB_BACKUP) = OFF
  Automatic table maintenance            (AUTO_TBL_MAINT) = OFF
    Automatic runstats                   (AUTO_RUNSTATS) = OFF
    Automatic statistics profiling       (AUTO_STATS_PROF) = OFF
      Automatic profile updates          (AUTO_PROF_UPD) = OFF
    Automatic reorganization             (AUTO_REORG) = OFF
```

Figure 5.16   The contents of the database configuration file *(continued)*

> **N O T E**   If you are connected to a database, issuing the command
> **get db cfg** displays the contents of database configuration file; you
> don't need to specify the database name as part of the command.

In this book you will learn some of the more important database configuration parameters. For a full treatment of all database configuration parameters, refer to the *DB2 UDB Administration Guide: Performance*.

To update one or more parameters in the database configuration file, issue the command:

```
update db cfg for database_name
     using parameter_name value  parameter_name value...
```

For example, to update the CHNGPGS_THRESH database configuration parameter in the *sample* database to a value of 20, issue the command:

```
update db cfg for sample using CHNGPGS_THRESH 20
```

Issuing the **get db cfg for database_name** command after the **update db cfg** command shows the newly updated values. However, this does not mean the change will take effect right away. Several parameters in the database configuration file require all connections to be removed before the changes take effect on the first new connection to the database. For other parameters, the update is dynamic, and the new value takes effect immediately after executing the command; these are called **configurable online parameters**.

> **N O T E**   Configurable online parameters of the database configura-
> tion file can be updated dynamically only if you first connect to the
> database. If a database connection has not been performed, the param-
> eter will not be changed immediately, but after all connections are
> removed.

Refer to the file *ConfigurationParameters.pdf* included on the CD-ROM accompanying this book for a list of database configuration parameters that are configurable online. The Control Center provides this information as well; refer to section 5.5.1, Configuring a Database from the Control Center, for details.

To get the current, effective setting for each configuration parameter along with the value of the parameter on the first new connection to the database after all connections are removed, use the **show detail** option of the **get db cfg** command. This option requires a database connection. If you run this command after changing the CHNGPGS_THRESH configuration parameter as above, you will see that the current value is 60, but the next effective or delayed value is 20. The related output from the **get db cfg show detail** command would look like the following:

```
C:\Program Files\SQLLIB\BIN>db2 get db cfg for sample show detail

Description                            Parameter       Current Value   Delayed Value
--------------------------------------------------------------------------------

...

Changed pages threshold               (CHNGPGS_THRESH) =     60               20
```

The **show detail** option is also helpful in determining the actual value of parameters listed as AUTOMATIC. For example, when you issue the **get db cfg** command while connected to a database, you may see output like the following for the MAXAPPLS parameter:

```
C:\Program Files\SQLLIB\BIN>db2 get db cfg

...

Max number of active applications       (MAXAPPLS) =    AUTOMATIC
```

If you use the **show detail** option, the actual value is displayed:

```
C:\Program Files\SQLLIB\BIN>db2 get db cfg show detail

Description                            Parameter       Current Value   Delayed Value
--------------------------------------------------------------------------------

...

Max number of active applications       (MAXAPPLS) =  AUTOMATIC(40)   AUTOMATIC(40)
```

To reset all the database configuration parameters to their default values, use the command **reset db cfg for** *database_name*.

5.5.1 Configuring a Database from the Control Center

You can also configure a database from the Control Center. Figure 5.17 shows the Control Center with the database *SAMPLE* selected. When you right-click on the database a menu with several options appears.

Although the Control Center's database menu has **Start** and **Stop** options, as shown in Figure 5.17, these are used to start and stop the instance where the selected database resides. There are

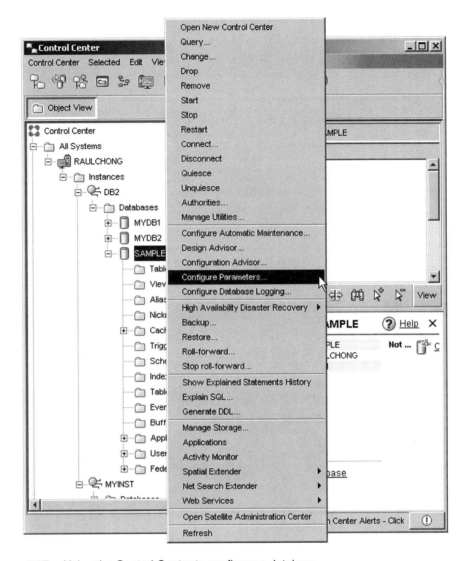

Figure 5.17   Using the Control Center to configure a database

no explicit commands to stop and start a database. To "stop" a database, simply ensure that all connections to the database are removed. You can do this with the **force applications** command or by disconnecting each application. The first connection to a database "starts" the database. The commands **activate database** and **deactivate database** are also related to these concepts, although they are mainly used for performance reasons.

The **activate database** command activates a database by allocating all the necessary database memory and services or processes required. The first connection to the database normally performs these operations; therefore, by using the **activate database** command before connecting, the first connection no longer has to pay the price of this extra overhead. The **deactivate database** command does the opposite; it stops all services or processes needed by the database and releases the memory. A database can be considered "started" when it is activated and "stopped" when it is deactivated.

> **NOTE** The **Restart** command option in Figure 5.17 maps to the **restart database** command, which you can use for recovery purposes when a database was left in an inconsistent state after a crash recovery. Don't use this command if you only want the new value of a database configuration parameter that is not dynamic to take effect. Instead, use the **force applications** command or ensure all applications disconnect from the database.

Figure 5.18 shows the Database Configuration window that appears after selecting **Configure Parameters** from the menu shown in Figure 5.17. In Figure 5.18 the column *Pending Value*

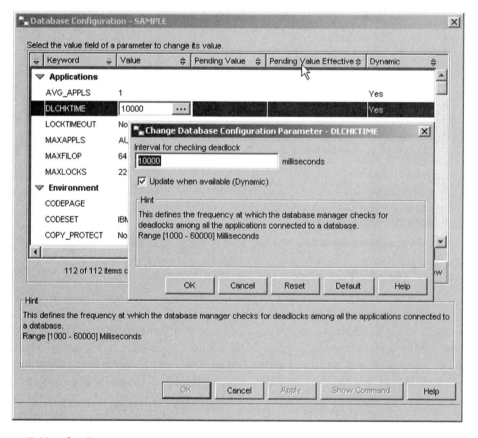

Figure 5.18   Configuring database parameters from the Control Center

Effective indicates when the pending value for the parameter will take effect, for example, immediately or after the database is "stopped" and "started". The column *Dynamic* indicates whether the parameter is configurable online. The rest of the columns are self-explanatory.

Figure 5.18 also illustrates how you can update a database configuration parameter from the Control Center. After selecting the parameter *DLCHKTIME* and clicking on the three dots button (...), a pop-up window appears displaying the values that this parameter can accept.

5.5.2 The DB2 Commands at the Database Level

Table 5.4 summarizes the most common commands used to configure a database. For more information about database concepts, refer to Chapter 7, Working with Database Objects.

> **NOTE**   If a DB2 registry variable, Database Manager Configuration parameter, or database configuration parameter accept only Boolean values, the values YES and ON and the values NO and OFF respectively are equivalent.

Table 5.4   The DB2 Database-Level Commands

Command	Explanation
get db cfg	Displays the database configuration file.
update db cfg	Updates the database configuration file.
reset db cfg	Resets the database configuration file to its default values.

5.6 INSTANCE AND DATABASE DESIGN CONSIDERATIONS

Now that you are familiar with the concepts of instances and how to configure instances and databases, you may be wondering about design issues. Is it better to have one instance or multiple instances per server machine? Is it better to have one database or multiple databases per instance?

You may want to have multiple instances per server machine for the following reasons.

- You want to separate your development and test environments but you cannot afford to have different servers.
- For security reasons, you want to have different instances. As you will see in Chapter 10, Implementing Security, you can grant SYSADM authority to an operating system group by assigning the name of this group to the SYSADM_GROUP Database Manager Configuration parameter. For example, if not all system administrators should have access to the *PAYROLL* database, you can put this database in its own instance and create an operating system group with only authorized user IDs, which you would then

assign to SYSADM_GROUP. The other instances would have another operating system group assigned to their own SYSADM_GROUP Database Manager Configuration parameter.

• You want to configure instances differently depending on your application. For example, as you will see in Chapter 16, Database Performance Considerations, the INTRA_PARALLEL Database Manager Configuration parameter should be set to NO when the workload is OLTP type, but set to YES when the workload is OLAP (or DSS) type. Because this is an instance-level parameter, all the databases inside the instance will use the same setting. Creating databases that will be used for either OLTP or OLAP in different instances will allow you to set INTRA_PARALLEL correctly for each case.

If none of the above applies to you, we recommend having one instance per server and one database per instance; this will guarantee that all resources are allocated to that one database and instance.

> **N O T E**
>
> • OLTP stands for online transaction processing. The OLTP type of workload implies short transactions performing simple SELECT, INSERT, UPDATE, and DELETE operations affecting a small number of rows.
> • OLAP stands for online analytical processing and DSS for decision support systems. OLAP and DSS have similar types of workload, and they imply complex SELECT statements, normally using several JOIN operations.

If you do decide to create multiple instances on a server, remember that an instance consumes some resources when started. Chapter 15, The DB2 Memory Model, discusses the memory allocated for instances. In general, an instance does not consume a great amount of resources; however, the databases inside the instances may consume a lot of memory depending, for example, on the size of their buffer pools. Keep in mind when you have many instances, each with many databases, that the memory used by all the databases and instances when they are active should be less than the physical memory of the machine; otherwise paging or swapping will occur, which will affect the performance of the entire system.

5.7 CASE STUDY

You have just returned from a DB2 training class and would like to practice what you have learned by changing some DB2 registry variables and configuration parameters. The system you are working with has one instance called *DB2* and two databases, *mydb* and *testdb*.

1. First, you save the contents of your configuration files by simply redirecting the output to files. This is just as a precaution in case you need to go back to your current configuration.

```
db2set -all > db2set.bk
db2 get dbm cfg > dbmcfg.bk
db2 get db cfg for mydb > dbcfg_mydb.bk
db2 get db cfg for testdb > dbcfg_testdb.bk
set > environmentVariables.bk
```

If you do need to go back to your current configuration, review the contents of these files and enter the appropriate commands to set your environment variables correctly (**set/export**), DBM Configuration file (**update dbm cfg**), database configuration file (**update db cfg**), and DB2 registry variables (**db2set**).

2. Then, you want to verify which instances have been created and which one is the current active one:

```
db2ilist
db2 get instance
```

The first command lists all instances in your server; in this case, there is only one instance, *DB2*. The second command shows you that the *DB2* instance is the current active instance.

3. Next, since you like to reuse CLP commands that you have typed before, you decide to increase the number of CLP commands that are kept as "history." You don't quite remember which DB2 registry variable has to be modified, so you issue the command:

```
db2set -lr
```

This lists all the DB2 registry variables you can set. You review the list and recognize the registry variable you need: DB2_CLP_HISTSIZE (discussed in Chapter 4, Using the DB2 Tools). You issue the command:

```
db2set DB2_CLP_HISTSIZE=50
```

This command sets the DB2_CLP_HISTSIZE registry variable only for the active instance because the **-i** option is the default.

4. You decide to make this change globally, so you issue:

```
db2set DB2_CLP_HISTSIZE=50    -g
```

You make sure that there are no spaces before and after the equal (=) sign to avoid getting an error.

5. You confirm that the registry variable is set by issuing the command:

```
db2set -all
```

You notice the same variable is set twice: once at the instance level (denoted by [i]), the other at the global level (denoted by [g]). You change your mind and decide to set this registry variable only for the current instance, not globally. You unset the registry variable as follows:

```
db2set DB2_CLP_HISTSIZE=    -g
```

As indicated in Table 5.1, to unset the value of a DB2 registry variable, leave a blank after the equal sign.

6. Next, you have to bring the instance down and then up by issuing the commands **db2stop** and **db2start** to ensure that the new registry variable value takes effect. Since you are planning to make other changes that may require an instance restart, you decide to wait until you finish all your changes.

After issuing the **get dbm cfg** command, you decide to make a small change to the SHEAPTHRESH parameter from 20000 to 20005. You will reverse the change afterwards, as you are only testing what you have learned about instance commands for now. You issue the command:

```
db2 update dbm cfg using SHEAPTHRES 20005
```

You want to see the current and delayed values for this parameter, so you issue the command:

```
db2 get dbm cfg show detail
```

7. Next, you want to make changes to your database configuration. You check your system with the **list applications** command. You know there are two databases in the instance, *mydb* and *testdb*. The output of the command shows that there are no connections to *mydb*, but *testdb* has 10 users connected to it. Also, other users are working heavily on the test machine, which is running other software. Since you don't want to interfere with their work, you don't want to connect to the *mydb* database as this would allocate memory for the different database resources. Nonetheless, you do realize that making changes to a Database Manager Configuration parameter does not require you to be connected to the database. After all, the database configuration is a binary file, so you are simply updating this file, and the database does not need to be active. You issue this command to increase the sort heap:

```
db2 update db cfg for mydb using SORTHEAP 1024
```

Since you are not connected to the database, you must specify the database name as part of the command. Given that the database is down, you don't really care whether the parameter SORTHEAP is configurable online or not. The next time there is a connection to the database, the new value will take effect. You do want to make sure the value has indeed been set to 1024, so you issue the command:

```
db2 get db cfg for mydb
```

8. Your boss is calling you, so you need to finish this exercise immediately. You write a note reminding yourself to revert the changes you didn't really want back to the way they were and then issue the **db2stop** and **db2start** commands once the other users in your system finish with their tests.

5.8 SUMMARY

This chapter discussed the DB2 environment and its environment variables and DB2 profile registry. It explained how to list the contents of environment variables and how to modify them either temporarily or permanently.

It also described how to manipulate the DB2 profile registry variables with the **db2set** command. The different levels of the DB2 profile registry were explained, as well as the priority that DB2 takes into consideration when the same variable is set at different levels.

There was a detailed explanation of instances, and it showed how an instance can be created, dropped, started, stopped, and configured. It also described the Database Administration Server (DAS), which is a background process that needs to be running at the database server to allow remote DB2 clients to graphically administer a database server. The chapter also discussed the similarity between configuring instance and database configuration parameters.

After reading this chapter you should have a solid background on how to work and manage instances as well as how to configure a database.

5.9 REVIEW QUESTIONS

1. Which environment variable determines the current active instance on your database server?
2. How can you set up your DB2 environment in Linux or UNIX?
3. Which command can you use to remove the DB2COMM registry variable from the DB2 Global-Level Profile Registry?
4. Which command can you use to list all the instances in your server?
5. What authority is required to create a DB2 instance on Linux or UNIX?
6. What authority is required to create a DB2 instance on Windows?
7. What command can be used to remove an unneeded instance from your server?
8. Does the **db2start** command need to be executed once per each database partition?
9. What can you do to gain exclusive access to an instance?
10. What is the difference between an attachment and a connection?
11. Which of the following commands will list all of the available registry variables in DB2?
    A. db2set –a
    B. db2set –all
    C. db2set –lr
    D. db2set -ltr

12. Which two of the following are not database configuration parameters?
    A. SHEAPTHRES
    B. SHEAPTHRES_SHR
    C. BUFFPAGE
    D. MAX_QUERYDEGREE
    E. MAXLOCKS

13. You have three databases: one for development, one for test, and one for production. To ensure that an error in an application in the development database will not affect the other databases, how would you configure these databases?
    A. Combine them into one database using different schemas
    B. Create all the databases in the same instance
    C. Put each database on a different drive/file system on the server
    D. Create each database in a different instance

14. Which of the following commands will show the current and delayed values for the Database Manager Configuration parameters?

A. get dbm cfg

B. get dbm cfg show detail

C. get dbm cfg show all

D. get complete dbm cfg

15. Which of the following commands updates the DAS configuration?

A. das update cfg

B. db2 update dbm cfg for das

C. db2admin update cfg

D. db2 update admin cfg

16. Which of the following commands changes the DAS configuration back to the default values?

A. das reset cfg

B. db2 reset dbm cfg for das

C. db2admin reset cfg

D. db2 reset admin cfg

17. Which of the following commands stops the DB2 instance even if there are active connections to databases in the instance?

A. db2 force applications all

B. db2 stop all applications

C. db2stop force

D. db2stop applications all

18. Which of the following commands/statements requires an attachment to a remote instance?

A. db2 list applications

B. db2 list db directory

C. db2 select * from employee

D. db2 create database mydb

19. Which of the following commands can be used to review the contents of the Database Configuration file for the database to which you are currently connected?

A. db2 list database configuration

B. db2 list db cfg

C. db2 get dbm cfg

D. db2 get db cfg

20. Which two of the following commands do not set the value of the INTRA_PARALLEL parameter to YES?

A. db2 update database manager configuration using INTRA_PARALLEL YES

B. db2 update dbm cfg using INTRA_PARALLEL 1

C. db2 update dbm cfg using INTRA_PARALLEL ON

D. db2 update database configuration using INTRA_PARALLEL YES

## CHAPTER 6

Configuring Client and Server Connectivity

This chapter describes different scenarios you can use to configure a DB2 client to connect to a DB2 server. The DB2 client can reside on the same machine as the DB2 server or it can be miles away on a different machine. In addition, a DB2 server can work as a DB2 client in some situations.

In this chapter you will learn about:

- The big picture of client and server connectivity
- The DB2 directories used for connectivity
- How to configure database connections manually using DB2 commands
- How to configure database connections using the Configuration Assistant graphical tool

6.1 CLIENT AND SERVER CONNECTIVITY: THE BIG PICTURE

Figure 6.1 illustrates a simplified overview of what is required to connect from a DB2 client to a DB2 server.

To connect to a **remote database** (a database that resides in a machine other than the client machine), follow this two-step process.

1. At the server, enable it to accept client connections by turning on listener processes.

   In Figure 6.1, the information required from the database servers is on the right side below the server machine. For example, if you are using the TCP/IP protocol, you need to set the DB2COMM registry variable to *tcpip* to start the DB2 TCP/IP listeners. In addition, you must specify the port that the databases of a given instance are listening to in the SVCENAME Database Manager Configuration parameter. This is the information you need to give to the client machine in step 2.

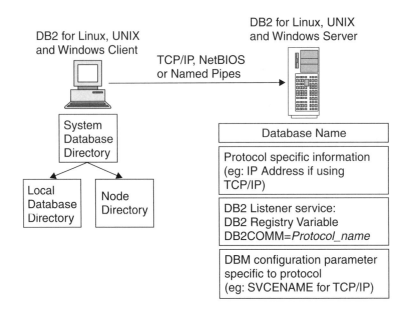

Figure 6.1   The big picture of client and server connectivity

2. At the client, make sure to enter the connection information (obtained from the first step) correctly into the system and node directories using the `catalog` command.

In Figure 6.1, on the left side below the DB2 client you can see the system database and node directories where you need to store the information obtained in step 1.

To connect to a **local database** (a database that resides in the same machine as the client machine), the `create database` command stores the required information in the system and local database directories automatically for you.

In the next sections you will also learn about the **Database Connection Services** (DCS) directory, which is required to connect to a DB2 server on the z/OS, OS/390, and iSeries platforms.

We first show you how to enter the information in the DB2 directories using DB2 commands. Once you are familiar with the commands, we show you how to configure client-server connectivity using the Configuration Assistant (CA), which populates these directories behind the scenes.

> **N O T E**   The Configuration Assistant and the Configuration Advisor (introduced in Chapter 5, Understanding the DB2 Environment, DB2 Instances, and Databases) are different tools. The Configuration Assistant is mainly used to set up client-server connectivity, while the Configuration Advisor is used exclusively to configure database manager and database configuration parameters.

6.2 THE DB2 DIRECTORIES

This section describes the DB2 directories and how they are related. Consider the following statement used to connect to the database with the alias *sample*:

```
CONNECT TO sample
```

Given only the database alias, how does DB2 know how to find the database *sample*? If *sample* resides on a remote server, how does the client know how to connect to the server?

All connect information is stored in the DB2 directories. Table 6.1 lists these directories and the corresponding commands to view, insert, and delete the contents. More information about the directories and commands is available in the next sections.

Table 6.1   The Commands to View, Insert, and Delete the Contents of the DB2 Directories

Directory Name	Command to View Contents	Command to Insert Contents	Command to Delete Contents
System database	`list db directory`	`catalog db` (for remote and local databases) or `create database` (for local databases only)	`uncatalog db` (for remote and local databases) or `drop database` (for local databases only)
Local database	`list db directory` `on path/drive`	`create database` (for local databases only)	`drop database` (for local databases only)
Node	`list node directory`	Depends on the protocol. For example, for TCP/IP use: `catalog TCPIP node`	`uncatalog node`
DCS	`list dcs directory`	`catalog DCS database`	`uncatalog DCS database`

Note that you cannot update an entry you entered with the **catalog** command. You have to delete the entry with the **uncatalog** command first, and then insert the new updated entry with the **catalog** command.

6.2.1 The DB2 Directories: An Analogy Using a Book

To understand how the DB2 directories work let's use an analogy. Above the dotted line in Figure 6.2 is the table of contents for a book called *The World*. This table of contents shows that the book is divided into several parts. If you jump to any of these parts, you will see a subset of the table of contents. The Resources section presents information about other books; with that information you can find a given book in a library or bookstore or on the Internet, and once you find the book, the process repeats itself where you first review the table of contents for that book and then look at its different parts.

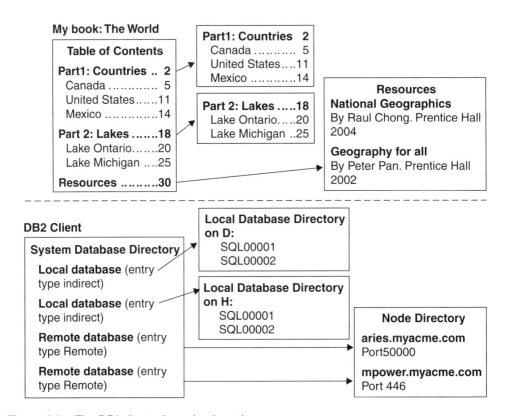

Figure 6.2   The DB2 directories: a book analogy

Similarly, with DB2 directories (shown below the dotted line), whenever you issue a **CONNECT TO** *database* statement, DB2 looks for the information in the **system database directory**, which is equivalent to the table of contents: it shows all the databases available for you to connect to from this machine. When an entry in this directory has the type *indirect*, it means the database is local (it resides on the current database server). To look for more information about this local database, you can review the **local database directory**, which is equivalent to the subset of the table of contents. When an entry in the system database directory is **remote**, it means that the database resides in a different system than the current one. Thus, you need to review the

node directory for information about how to access this remote server. This is similar to the Resources (or bibliography) section of a book, where information points to a different book with more information about a given topic.

The **Database Connection Services** (DCS) **directory** (not shown in Figure 6.2) contains extra information required when you connect to a host database server like DB2 for OS/390, z/OS and iSeries.

> **N O T E** In this chapter host database servers like DB2 for OS/390 and z/OS and DB2 for iSeries will only be used as database servers and not as clients. See Appendix E, Setting Up Database Connectivity for DB2 UDB for z/OS and DB2 UDB for iSeries, for the connectivity setup required for using host machines as clients.

6.2.2 The System Database Directory

As mentioned earlier, the system database directory is like a table of contents: it shows you all the databases you can connect to from your system. The system database directory is stored in a binary file with name *SQLDBDIR* and is in:

  DB2_install_directory\instance_name\sqldbdir   on Windows systems

  DB2_instance_home/sqllib/sqldbdir   on Linux/UNIX systems

You should not modify this file manually. To display the contents of the system database directory, use the `list db directory` command, as shown in Figure 6.3.

The system database directory shown in Figure 6.3 indicates that you can connect to three different databases from this system: *MYHOSTDB*, *MYRMTDB*, and *MYLOCDB*. Let's examine each of these database entries in detail starting from the bottom (Database 3 entry) to the top (Database 1 entry).

The relevant fields in Database 3 entry are

- Database alias = *MYLOCDB*. This indicates the alias you need to use in the **CONNECT** statement. It must be a unique name within the system database directory.
- Database name = *MYLOCDB*. This is the actual database name. For this particular entry it is the same as the alias name.
- Directory entry type = *Indirect*. An entry type of *Indirect* means that the database is local; that is, it resides on the same server where you are currently working.
- Database Drive = *H:\MYINST2*. From the previous field you know this database is local. This field tells where on the server this database is stored. Note that the example in Figure 6.3 is for a Windows system. For a Linux/UNIX system the field would be *Local database directory* instead of *Database Drive*.

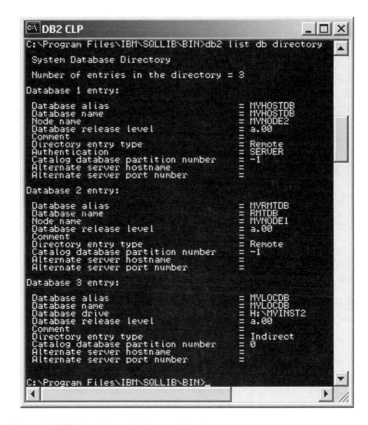

Figure 6.3   A sample DB2 system database directory

The relevant fields in Database 2 entry that have not been described yet are

- Directory entry type = *Remote*. An entry type of *Remote* means that the database resides on a different server than the one on which you are currently working.
- Node name = *MYNODE1*. From the previous field you know this database is remote. The node name field tells the name of the entry in the node directory where you can find the information about the server that stores the database and how to access it.

The relevant field in the Database 1 entry that has not been described earlier is

- Authentication = *SERVER*. This entry indicates that security is handled at the server system. Other options are discussed in Chapter 10, Implementing Security.

6.2.3 The Local Database Directory

The local database directory is also stored in a file called *SQLDBDIR*. However, this file is different from the *SQLDBDIR* file for the system database directory in that it resides on every *drive* (in Windows) or *path* (in Linux/UNIX) that contains a database. It contains information only for databases on that drive/path, and it is a subset of the system database directory. Use the `list db directory on` *`drive/path`* command to display the local database directory, as shown in Figure 6.4.

Figure 6.4   A sample DB2 local database directory

Figure 6.4 shows *MYLOCDB* is the only database stored in *H:\MYINST2*. Note that *MYLOCDB* also showed up in the system database directory in Figure 6.3, since the local database directory is a subset of the system database directory. On Windows, the **create database** command can only specify a drive, not a path, where a database can be created; therefore, the command **list db directory on H:** should return the same output as **list db directory on H:\MYINST2**. On Linux/UNIX, a path can be specified with the **create database** command; therefore, when using **the list db directory** command, specify the full path. Chapter 8, The DB2 Storage Model, explains the **create database** command in detail.

The relevant information in the entry of Figure 6.4 is:

- Database directory = *SQL00001*. This is the subdirectory where the database is physically stored in your server.

6.2.4 The Node Directory

The node directory stores information about how to communicate to a remote instance where a given database resides. It is stored in a file called *SQLNODIR* and is in:

   DB2_install_directory*instance_name*\sqlnodir   on Windows systems

   DB2_instance_home/sqllib/sqlnodir   on Linux/UNIX systems

One important field in the node directory is the communication protocol used to communicate with the server, as several other fields are displayed depending on this entry. For example, if the node directory contains a TCP/IP entry, then other fields provided are the IP address (or host name) of the server and the service name (or port number) of the instance where the database resides. Figure 6.5 shows an example of the contents of the node directory.

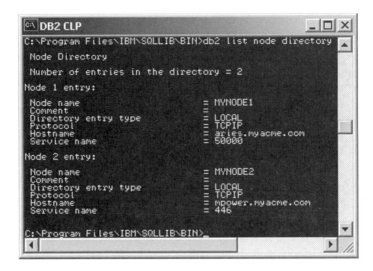

Figure 6.5   A sample DB2 node directory

There are two entries in Figure 6.5. We explain the first one in detail below; the second entry has a similar explanation, and thus will not be described.

Node 1 entry has these relevant fields:

- Node name = *MYNODE1*. This is the name of this node entry. It was chosen arbitrarily.
- Protocol = *TCPIP*. This is the communication protocol that is used to communicate with the remote system.
- Host name = *aries.myacme.com*. This is the host name of the remote database server. Alternatively, the IP address can be provided. This entry appears because it was cataloged as a TCP/IP node. If the entry is cataloged as a node using a different protocol, other items would be displayed.
- Service Name = *50000*. This is the TCP/IP port used by the instance in the remote server to listen for connections.

> **N O T E**   Since the node directory contains the information required to connect to an instance, it is not only used by the **CONNECT** statement but also by the **attach** command as described in Chapter 5, Understanding the DB2 Environment, DB2 Instances, and Databases.

6.2.5 The Database Connection Services Directory

The DCS directory is required only when connecting to a host server like DB2 for OS/390, z/OS, and iSeries. This directory is available only when the DB2 Connect software is installed. If you are running DB2 UDB Enterprise Server Edition (ESE), DB2 Connect support is built into the DB2 database product, so the DCS directory will also be available. Figure 6.6 shows the contents of a sample DCS directory.

Figure 6.6   A sample DCS directory

In Figure 6.6 the relevant fields are:

- Local database name = *MYHOSTDB*. This name must match the corresponding entry in the system database directory.
- Target database name = *HOSTPROD*. Depending on the host, this entry corresponds to the following:
  - For DB2 for OS/390 and z/OS: The location name of the DB2 subsystem
  - For DB2 for iSeries: The local RDB name

6.2.6 The Relationship Between the DB2 Directories

Now that you have a good understanding of the DB2 directories, let's see how all of them are related by using a few figures.

6.2.6.1 A Local Connection

Figure 6.7 illustrates the process of connecting to a local DB2 database. When a user issues the statement:

```
CONNECT TO mylocdb USER raul USING mypsw
```

DB2 follows these steps.

(1) Looks for the system database directory.

(2) Inside the system database directory, looks for the entry with a database alias of *MYLOCDB*.

(3) Determines the database name that corresponds to the database alias (in Figure 6.7 the database alias and name are the same).

(4) Determines if the database is local or remote by reviewing the *Directory entry type* field. In the figure, the entry type is *Indirect*, so the database is local.

(5) Since the database is local, DB2 reviews the *Database drive* field, which indicates the location of the local database directory. In Figure 6.7, it is *H:\MYINST2*.

(6) Looks for the local database directory.

(7) Inside the local database directory, DB2 looks for the entry with a database alias that matches the database name of *MYLOCDB*.

(8) Determines the physical location where the database resides by looking at the field *Database Directory*. In Figure 6.7, it is *SQL00001*.

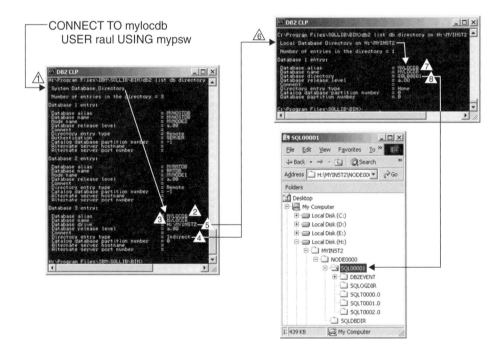

Figure 6.7   The local database connection process

6.2.6.2 A Remote Connection to a DB2 Server

Figure 6.8 illustrates the process of connecting to a remote DB2 database. When a user issues the statement:

```
CONNECT TO myrmtdb USER raulrmt USING myrmtpsw
```

DB2 follows these steps:

(1) Looks for the system database directory.

(2) Inside the system database directory, looks for the entry with a database alias of *MYRMTDB*.

(3) Determines the database name that corresponds to the database alias. In Figure 6.8 the database name is *RMTDB*. This information will later be used in step 8.

(4) Determines if the database is local or remote by reviewing the *Directory entry type* field. In the figure, the entry type is *Remote*, so the database is remote.

(5) Since the database is remote, DB2 reviews the *Node name* field, which indicates the entry name to look for in the node directory. In the figure, the node name is *MYNODE1*.

(6) Looks for the node directory.

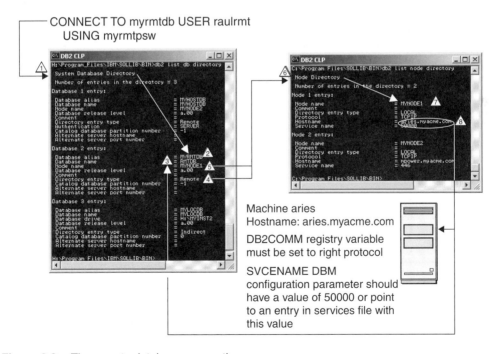

Figure 6.8 The remote database connection process

(7) Inside the node directory, looks for the entry with a node name of *MYNODE1*.

(8) Determines the physical location where the database resides. In this example, the TCP/IP protocol is used, so DB2 looks for the fields *Hostname* and *Service Name*. In Figure 6.8, their values are *aries.myacme.com* and *50000* respectively. With this information and the database name obtained in step 3, DB2 initiates the connection.

6.2.6.3 A Remote Connection to a Host DB2 Server

Figure 6.9 illustrates the process of connecting to a remote DB2 host server, which can be DB2 for z/OS, OS/390, or DB2 for iSeries. When a user issues the statement:

```
CONNECT TO myhostdb USER raulhost USING myhostpsw
```

DB2 follows these steps:

(1) Looks for the system database directory.

(2) Inside the system database directory, looks for the entry with a database alias of *MYHOSTDB*.

(3) Determines the database name that corresponds to the database alias. (in Figure 6.9 the database name are the same). This information will later be used in step 9.

(4) Determines if the database is local or remote by reviewing the *Directory entry type* field. In the figure, the entry type is *Remote*, so the database is remote.

(5) Since the database is remote, DB2 reviews the *Node name* field, which indicates the entry name to look for in the node directory. In the figure, the node name is *MYNODE2*.

(6) Looks for the node directory.

(7) Inside the node directory, DB2 looks for the entry with a node name of *MYNODE2*.

(8) Determines the physical location where the database resides. In this example, the TCP/IP protocol is used, therefore DB2 looks for the fields *Hostname* and *Service Name*. In Figure 6.9, their values are *mpower.myacme.com* and *446* respectively.

(9) DB2 detects that this is a host database server and thus, with the database name obtained in step 3, it accesses the DCS directory.

(10) Inside the DCS directory, DB2 looks for the entry with a local database name of *MYHOSTDB*.

(11) Determines the target database name that corresponds to *MYHOSTDB*. In this example it is *HOSTPROD*. With this information and the connectivity information obtained in step 8, DB2 initiates the connection.

CONNECT TO myhostdb USER raulhost
USING myhostpsw

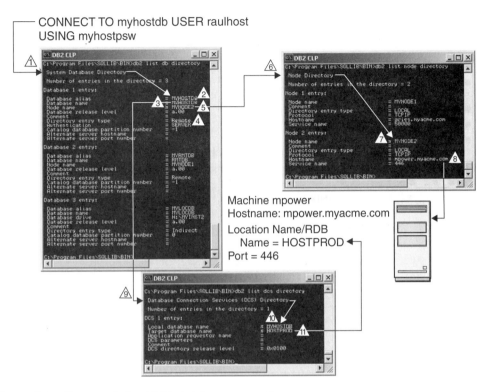

Figure 6.9   The remote host DB2 database connection process

6.3 SUPPORTED CONNECTIVITY SCENARIOS

In this section, we discuss the following four connectivity scenarios in detail.

- Scenario 1: Local connection from a DB2 client to a DB2 server
- Scenario 2: Remote connection from a DB2 client to a DB2 server
- Scenario 3: Remote connection from a DB2 client to a DB2 host server
- Scenario 4: Remote connection from a DB2 client to a DB2 host server through a DB2 Connect gateway

A DB2 host server can be DB2 for z/OS, OS/390, or iSeries.

You can configure a database connection by either:

- Cataloging the DB2 directories using DB2 commands manually
- Using the Configuration Assistant (CA) GUI tool

The Configuration Assistant is explained in section 6.4, Configuring Database Connections Using the Configuration Assistant.

It is useful to understand how to manually populate the DB2 directories using DB2 commands, so these scenarios focus on using the commands. Once you know how to do this, it will be a breeze to perform the configuration with the Configuration Assistant.

6.3.1 Scenario 1: Local Connection from a DB2 Client to a DB2 Server

Figure 6.10 illustrates a local connection.

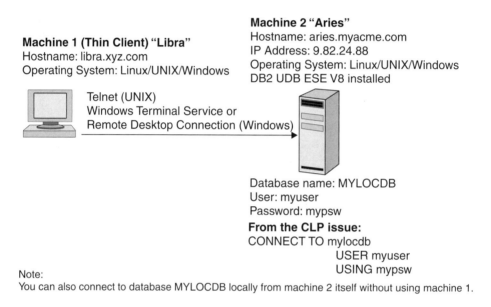

Machine 2 "Aries"
Hostname: aries.myacme.com
IP Address: 9.82.24.88
Operating System: Linux/UNIX/Windows
DB2 UDB ESE V8 installed

Machine 1 (Thin Client) "Libra"
Hostname: libra.xyz.com
Operating System: Linux/UNIX/Windows

Telnet (UNIX)
Windows Terminal Service or
Remote Desktop Connection (Windows)

Database name: MYLOCDB
User: myuser
Password: mypsw
From the CLP issue:
CONNECT TO mylocdb
                    USER myuser
                    USING mypsw

Note:
You can also connect to database MYLOCDB locally from machine 2 itself without using machine 1.

Figure 6.10   The process of connecting locally from a DB2 client to a DB2 Server

Even though Figure 6.10 shows two machines, Machine 1 and Machine 2, Machine 1 is used to connect to Machine 2 using operating system commands or utilities like the Windows Terminal Service or Remote Desktop Connection (on Windows) or telnet (on Linux/UNIX). Once you establish this connection, any command you issue from the keyboard at Machine 1 is equivalent to issuing the command locally at Machine 2. Under this setup, when the **connect to *database*** statement is issued from the keyboard at either Machine 1 or Machine 2, the connection is considered local.

In this configuration, the server must have one of the following installed:

- DB2 Personal Edition
- DB2 Workgroup Edition
- DB2 Express Edition
- DB2 Enterprise Server Edition

The database must exist in the server's system database directory with an entry type of *Indirect*.

When you create a database with the **create database** command, an entry is automatically created in the system database directory and the local database directory. You normally do not need to issue **catalog** commands for a local database. However, it is possible for a local database to get lost in the system database directory. For example, this can happen if someone issues the **uncatalog database** command to remove the database from the system database directory, or when the system database directory is reset when reinstalling DB2. In all cases, as long as the database was not dropped (either by the **drop database** command or using the Control Center), the database still physically exists on the system, and the entry in the system database directory is simply missing. To get the database back into the system database directory, use this command:

```
catalog db database_name [as database_alias] [on drive/path]
```

where:

drive (Windows)/**path** (UNIX) is the location where the database files are physically stored.

Once the database is cataloged, you can use it just like before.

> **N O T E**   If you drop an instance, the databases that belong to this instance are not dropped, because the databases reside on different directories from that of the instance. To recover these databases, all you need to do is to create a new instance with the same name as the one dropped and catalog the databases back using the **catalog db** command.

6.3.2 Scenario 2: Remote Connection from a DB2 Client to a DB2 Server

In most cases you do not have the authority to log on to the database server to perform a local database connection. Database servers are set up so that connections are performed through DB2 clients. In this scenario, DB2 client code is installed on a different machine from the database server machine. The **connect** statement is issued from the DB2 client machine. Figure 6.11 shows a connection from the machine *Libra* to a remote DB2 server that resides on *Aries*.

In this configuration, the machine Libra is considered a client to database server Aries. The client must have one of the following installed:

- DB2 Client (Runtime, Administration, or Application Development Client)
- DB2 Personal Edition
- DB2 Workgroup Edition
- DB2 Express Edition
- DB2 Enterprise Server Edition

The server must have one of the following installed:

- DB2 Workgroup Edition
- DB2 Express Edition
- DB2 Enterprise Server Edition

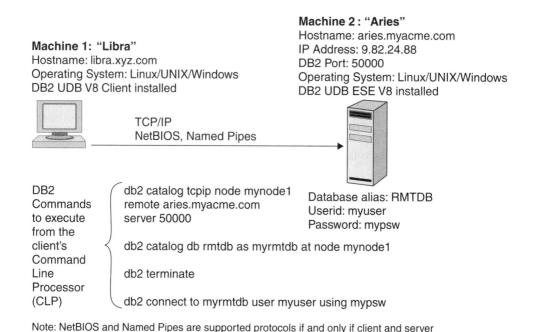

Figure 6.11   The process of connecting remotely from a DB2 client to a DB2 server

The supported communication protocols are

- TCP/IP
- NetBIOS   (only if both the client and server are Windows)
- Named Pipes   (only if both the client and server are Windows)

To configure the connection shown in Figure 6.11, you need to:

1. Enable the database server to accept client connections.
2. Catalog the node directory and the system database directory on the client.

The following sections describe these steps.

6.3.2.1 Enabling the Database Server to Accept Client Connections

Clients connect to the database server across the network using TCP/IP, NetBIOS (Windows only), or Named Pipes (Windows only). The server must have a process that is constantly up and running to receive these connect requests. We call this process a **listener** because it "listens" to any request that comes in from the network and tells the database manager to serve it.

6.3.2.1.1 TCP/IP connection

You need to perform the following steps on the database server to set up the listener if you are
using the TCP/IP communication protocol.

1. Update the services file to reserve a TCP/IP port for the DB2 instance.
   On Linux/UNIX, the services file is located in /etc/services.
   On Windows, the services file is located in C:\Windows\System32\drivers\etc\services.
   The entry in the services file must look like this:

   ```
   service_name      port_number/tcp
   ```

   where:

   service_name is an arbitrary name to associate with the port number.

   port_number is the TCP/IP port number you are going to reserve for this DB2
   instance.

   The port number must not already exist in the services file, and it must have a value of
   1024 or higher.

2. Update the SVCENAME parameter in the Database Manager Configuration file.
   Log on as the local administrator (Windows) or the instance owner (Linux/UNIX)
   and issue the following command from the Command Line Processor:

   ```
   update dbm cfg using svcename port_number/service_name
   ```

   You need to specify either the port number or the service name you defined in step 1.

3. Enable TCP/IP support for the instance. Issue the following command:

   ```
   db2set DB2COMM=TCPIP
   ```

4. Restart the instance to make the changes you made in the previous steps effective. Issue
   db2stop and **db2start**.

> **NOTE** If you are working with the default instance created and
> configured by the DB2 Setup Wizard, the services file, SVCENAME,
> and the DB2COMM parameters are already correctly configured.

6.3.2.1.2 NetBIOS or Named Pipes Connection

NetBIOS and Named Pipes are supported when the client and the server are on Windows platforms only. When NetBIOS or Named Pipes are used, you need to execute the following steps to
set up the server.

1. Make sure the server is available on the network.
   For NetBIOS, set NNAME in both the client and server's Database Manager Configuration file. NNAME identifies a workstation in a NetBIOS network, so it must be
   unique within the network. You do this by issuing the following command on both the
   client and the server:

   ```
   update dbm cfg using nname value
   ```

For example, if *server1* is the NetBIOS name of the server, issue

```
update dbm cfg using nname server1
```

2. Enable the instance for NetBIOS or Named Pipes support. Issue

```
db2set DB2COMM=NETBIOS
```

or

```
db2set DB2COMM=NPIPE
```

3. Restart the instance to make the changes effective.

6.3.2.2 Cataloging the Node Directory and Database Directory on the Client

After enabling the server to accept client connections, you need to tell the client how to connect to the server. You do this by cataloging the node directory and the system database directory at the client.

6.3.2.2.1 TCP/IP Connection

Use the information in Table 6.2 for completing the procedure in this section.

1. Catalog a TCP/IP node on the client:

```
catalog tcpip node    nodename
            remote hostname_or_IP_address_of_server
            server port_number_of_server
```

Table 6.2   TCP/IP Connectivity Worksheet

Parameter	Description	Sample Values
Host name or IP address	The host name or IP address of the remote server. If you are working on a DPF system, you can use any of the participating server's host names or IP addresses.	aries.myacme.com 9.82.24.88
Port number	The TCP/IP port number where the instance is listening for incoming connections on the server.	50000
Node name	An arbitrary name used to identify the remote server. It must be unique in the client's node directory.	mynode1
Database name	The database on the server. It is the database to which you want to connect.	RMTDB
Database alias (optional)	An alias for the database name. If specified, all connections must use this alias. If not specified, the database alias will be the same as the database name.	MYRMTDB

2. Catalog a database directory on the client:

```
catalog db database_name [as database_alias] at node nodename
```

3. Issue a **terminate** command to refresh the cache:

```
terminate
```

Table 6.3 demonstrates how to use these commands based on the example shown in Figure 6.11. The information in this table applies to Linux, UNIX, and Windows.

Table 6.3   Example of Configuring a Remote Connection to a DB2 Server Using TCP/IP

Information You Need to Obtain from Server Machine 2 (*Aries*) to Perform the Commands on Client Machine 1	Command to Run on Client Machine 1 (*Libra*)

Host name = aries.myacme.com
TCP/IP port in services file = 50000
	```db2 catalog tcpip node mynode1```
	``` remote aries.myacme.com```
	``` server 50000```

Database alias on Machine 2 = RMTDB
 	
Note: The database must exist in the system database directory of Machine 2. If the database alias and the database name are different, then the database alias should be used.
	```db2 catalog db rmtdb```
	``` as myrmtdb```
	``` at node mynode1```
	
	Note: *MYRMTDB* is an alias to the database *RMTDB*. It is optional; if specified, the alias is what you should use in the connect command. Otherwise, use the database name.

No information needed.	```db2 terminate``` Note: This command is needed to make the previous catalog commands effective.
A valid user ID and password that has **CONNECT** privileges to database RMTDB. This user ID will be used from Machine 1 to connect to RMTDB.	```db2 CONNECT TO myrmtdb``` ``` USER userid USING password```

After completing the two `catalog` commands in Table 6.3, the client machine's database directory and node directory will look like Figure 6.12.

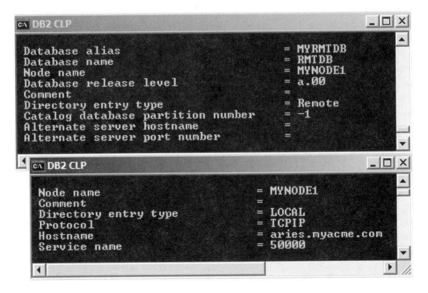

Figure 6.12   Sample client's system database directory and node directory for remote connection to a DB2 database

6.3.2.2.2 NetBIOS Connection

If you are using NetBIOS, use the information in Table 6.4 to catalog a NetBIOS node.

1. Issue the command:

```
catalog netbios node    nodename
                remote  nname_of_server
                adapter adapter_number
```

where:

nodename is an arbitrary name and it must be unique in the client's node directory.

2. Continue with step 2 in section 6.3.2.2.1, TCP/IP Connection, to finish cataloging the database.

Table 6.4   NetBIOS Connectivity Worksheet

Parameter	Description	Sample Value
NNAME of server	The NetBIOS name of the server workstation. You can get this from the server's Database Manager Configuration file using the **get dbm cfg** command.	server1
NNAME of client	The NetBIOS name of the client workstation. NNAME must be unique among all NetBIOS nodes in the network. You need to choose a name and update the client's Database Manager Configuration file using the **update dbm cfg** command.	client1
Adapter number	The client's logical adapter number used to connect to the DB2 server. To determine the adapter number: 1. From a command prompt, enter the **regedit** command to start the Registry Editor. 2. Locate the NetBIOS adapter assignments by expanding the *HKEY_LOCAL_MACHINE* folder and locating the *Software/Microsoft/Rpc/NetBIOS* folder. 3. Double-click on the entry that begins with *ncacn_nb_nbx*, where *x* can be 0, 1, 2... (usually you want to select the *nb0* adapter), to see the adapter number that is associated with the NetBIOS connection. Record the setting from the *Data value* field in the *Edit DWORD Value* window. Note: Ensure that both ends of the connection are using the same emulation.	2

6.3.2.2.3 Named Pipes Connection

If you are using Named Pipes as the communication protocol, use the worksheet in Table 6.5 to catalog an NPIPE node.

Table 6.5   Named Pipes Connectivity Worksheet

Parameter	Description	Sample Value
Computer name	The computer name of the server. On the server machine, click on **Start** > **Settings** > **Control Panel**. Double-click on the *Network* folder and select the *Identification* tab. Record the computer name.	db2server1
Instance name	The name of the DB2 instance on the server.	DB2

1. Issue the command:

   ```
   catalog npipe node    nodename
                  remote  computer_name_of_server
                  instance instance_name
   ```

   where:

   > *nodename* is an arbitrary name. It must be unique in the client's node directory.

2. Continue with step 2 in section 6.3.2.2.1, TCP/IP Connection, to finish cataloging the database.

6.3.3 Scenario 3: Remote Connection from a DB2 Client to a DB2 Host Server

Figure 6.13 illustrates the configuration used for this scenario. The machine *aries* is considered a client to the database server *mpower*.

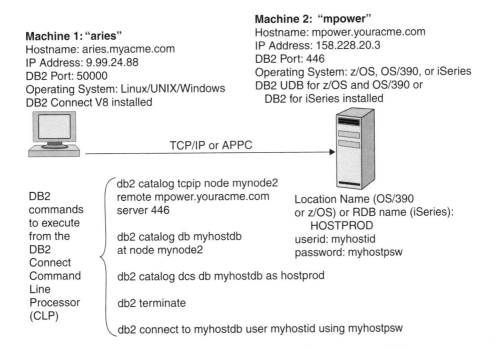

Figure 6.13   The process of connecting remotely from a DB2 client to a DB2 host server

The client must have one of the following installed:

- DB2 Connect Personal Edition
- DB2 Connect Enterprise Edition
- DB2 Enterprise Server Edition

The communication protocols supported are

- TCPIP
- APPC

Setting up a remote connection to a host DB2 database follows the same principle as setting up a connection to a DB2 for Linux, UNIX, and Windows database. You need to configure both the client and the server.

3. Enable the database server to accept client connections.
4. Catalog the node directory, system database directory, and DCS directory on the client.

6.3.3.1 Enabling the Database Server to Accept Client Connections

For DB2 for z/OS and OS/390, make sure that the distributed data facility (DDF) is running on the mainframe. DDF is the facility in DB2 for z/OS and OS/390 that allows for remote communication support. You can verify this by issuing the **-display ddf** command from the mainframe. To start DDF, issue the **-start ddf** command.

For DB2 for iSeries, make sure the distributed data management (DDM) is started. DDM is the facility in DB2 for iSeries that allows for remote communication support. To start DDM from the iSeries server or to verify that DDM is already started issue

```
STRTTCPSVR SERVER(*DDM)
```

The TCPIP port 446 is usually the default value. APPC can also be used instead of TCP/IP. Contact your host database administrator for specific connection information.

6.3.3.2 Cataloging the Node Directory, Database Directory, and DCS Directory on the Client

After you have enabled the server to accept client connections, you need to tell the client how to connect to the server. You do this by cataloging the node directory, system database directory, and DCS directory on the client.

6.3.3.2.1 TCP/IP Connection

Use the information in Table 6.6 for completing the procedure in this section.

1. Catalog a TCP/IP node on the client.

```
catalog tcpip node    nodename
                remote hostname_or_IP_address_of_server
                server port_number_of_server
```

Table 6.6 TCP/IP Connectivity Worksheet for DB2 Client to DB2 Host Connection

Parameter	Description	Sample Values
Host name or IP address	The host name or IP address of the remote server.	mpower.youracme.com 158.228.10.3
Port number	The TCP/IP port number on which DB2 is listening for incoming connections on the server.	446
Node name	This is an arbitrary name and is used to identify the remote server. It must be unique in the client's node directory.	mynode2
Target database name	The database on the host server. For DB2 for z/OS and OS/390 servers, this is the *Location name*. For DB2 for iSeries servers, this is the *RDB name*.	hostprod
Database name	An arbitrary name you would like to associate with the target database name.	myhostdb
Database alias (optional)	You can optionally specify a database alias for the database name. If specified, all connections must use this alias name; if not specified, the database alias will be the same as the database name.	myhostdb

2. Catalog a database directory on the client.

```
catalog db database_name [as database_alias] at node nodename
```

3. Catalog a DCS database directory on the client by issuing the following command from the client's command window:

```
catalog dcs db database_name as target_database_name
```

The **database_name** field must match the **database_name** in the **catalog db** command in step 2.

4. Issue the **terminate** command to refresh the cache.

```
terminate
```

Table 6.7 demonstrates how to use these commands based on the example shown in Figure 6.15.

After completing the three catalog commands in Table 6.7, the client machine's system database directory and node directory will look as shown in Figure 6.14.

Table 6.7 Example of Configuring a Remote Connection to DB2 for z/OS and OS/390 or DB2 for iSeries Database

Information You Need to Obtain from Host Server Machine 2 *(mpower)* to Perform the Commands on Client Machine 1 (*aries*)	Command to Run on Client Machine 1 (*aries*)
Host name of Machine 2 = mpower.youracme.com The TCP/IP port DB2 uses = 446	`db2 catalog tcpip node mynode2 remote mpower.youracme.com server 446`

(continues)

Table 6.7   Example of Configuring a Remote Connection to DB2 for z/OS and OS/390 or DB2 for iSeries Database *(Continued)*

Information You Need to Obtain from Host Server Machine 2 *(mpower)* to Perform the Commands on Client Machine 1 *(aries)*	Command to Run on Client Machine 1 *(aries)*

No information needed.	`db2 catalog db myhostdb`
	    `at node mynode2`
	
	Note: *myhostdb* is an arbitrary database name, but it must match the entry for the DCS directory below.

hostprod = The *Location name* if the server is DB2 for z/OS and OS/390 or *RDB name* if the server is DB2 for iSeries.	`db2 catalog dcs db myhostdb` `as hostprod`
No information needed.	`db2 terminate` Note: This command is needed to make the previous `catalog` commands effective.
A valid user ID and password that has connect privilege to the host database.	`db2 connect to myhostdb user` *`userid`* `using` *`password`*

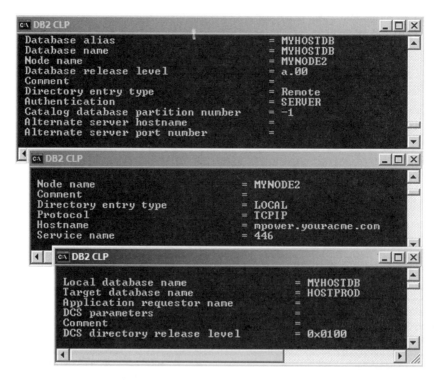

Figure 6.14   Sample client's system database directory, node directory, and DCS directory for remote connection to a DB2 host database

6.3.3.2.2 APPC Connection

If you use APPC instead of TCP/IP, you need to do more work on the client. In addition to cataloging the node, database, and DCS directories, you also need to configure the APPC software installed on the client. Table 6.8 lists the supported APPC software. Please refer to the APPC software manual for instructions on how to configure this software.

Table 6.8 Supported APPC Products

Platform	Software Needed to Support APPC Connection
Windows NT/2000	IBM Communications Server Version 6.1.1 or later IBM Personal Communications for Windows Version 6.0 with CSD 3 Microsoft SNA Server Version 3 with Service Pack 3 or later
Windows XP	IBM Personal Communications for Windows Version 6.5 with APAR IC23490
Windows Server 2003	APPC is not supported
AIX	IBM Communications Server for AIX Version 6.1 or later
HP-UX	SNAplus2 Link R6.11.00.00 SNAplus2 API R.6.11.00.00
Linux	APPC is not supported
Solaris	SNAP-IX for Solaris V7.02

After you have configured the APPC software, make sure the client can reach the host machine. This is similar to the *ping* test in TCP/IP. Then catalog the node, database, and DCS directories. You catalog the database and DCS directories the same way as TCP/IP (see section 6.3.3.2.1, TCP/IP Connection). However, the node directory is cataloged differently. Use the following command to catalog the node directory on the client:

```
catalog appc node    nodename
            remote   symbolic_destination_name
                     security security_type
```
where:

- *nodename* is an arbitrary name. It must be unique in the client's node directory.
- *symbolic_destination_name* can be found in the CPI-C Side Information profile. You should have created this during the APPC software configuration.
- *security_type* is SAME, SECURITY, or PROGRAM.

6.3.4 Scenario 4: Remote Connection from a DB2 Client to a DB2 Host Server via a DB2 Connect Gateway

Imagine you have 1,000 clients who need to connect to a host database. If you set up the connections using DB2 Connect Personal Edition, you will need to purchase and install DB2 Connect

Personal Edition on each of the 1,000 clients. This would be very costly. Wouldn't it be nice if you could only install DB2 Connect once on one machine, and use it as a gateway to service all connections from clients to the host database? Of course! For that scenario you need to use the DB2 Connect Enterprise Edition. Figure 6.15 illustrates this scenario.

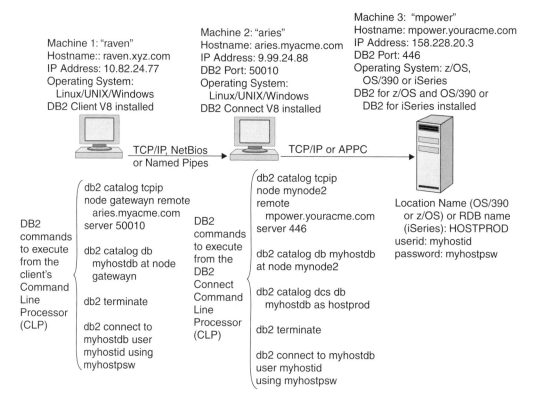

Figure 6.15   The process of connecting from a DB2 client to a DB2 server via a DB2 Connect gateway

In this configuration, Machine 1 is the client, Machine 2 is referred to as the DB2 Connect gateway, and Machine 3 is the host database server.

The DB2 Connect gateway is the only machine that needs to have DB2 Connect Enterprise Edition installed. Its task is to serve as a middleman between the clients and the host database server, since the clients do not have the ability to connect directly to the server. The gateway machine can serve hundreds of clients.

When configuring this type of connection, you can break the three-tier connection into two parts.

- Part one is the gateway-to-host server connection. This is identical to what we discussed in Scenario 3. Follow the same steps as in section 6.3.3, Scenario 3: Remote Connection from a DB2 Client to a DB2 Host Server, to configure the gateway. Make sure you can connect from the gateway to the host database before proceeding to the next step.

- Part two is the client-to-gateway connection. From the client's perspective, the gateway machine is the database server. (The client does not know anything about the host server mpower.) Thus, when cofiguring this part of the connection, treat the gateway as the server, and follow the same steps described in section 6.3.2, Scenario 2: Remote Connection from a DB2 Client to a DB2 Server.

6.3.5 Binding Utilities

After a client establishes a connection to a database server, it should be able to access the data in the database. However, if you issue the **import/export** commands or try to run a CLI/ODBC application, you will get SQL0805N "Package not found" error. This is because the client has not bound these utilities to the database server.

Utilities are database programs with embedded SQL; their packages must reside on the database server. Packages are version and FixPak level specific; therefore, a package created at the Version 8, FixPak 1 level cannot be used by a client running at Version 8, FixPak 2. If this client needs to use these utilities, it must create packages at its own DB2 level. (Refer to Chapter 7, Working with Database Objects, for a more detailed explanation of packages.)

To create all of these packages at once, run the following commands from a DB2 Administration Client or the Application Development Client's CLP window:

```
connect to database_alias user userid using password
bind @db2ubind.lst blocking all grant public
bind @db2cli.lst   blocking all grant public
```

If the database server is a host database, you must run one of the following commands on the DB2 Connect machine.

- If the host is DB2 for z/OS or OS/390:
  ```
  bind @ddcsmvs.lst blocking all grant public
  ```
- If the host is DB2 for iSeries:
  ```
  bind @ddcs400.lst blocking all grant public
  ```

You need to use the symbol @ when you specify a file that contains a list of bind files (with the .lst file extension), rather than a bind file (with the .bnd file extension) itself. The .lst files are in the *install_directory*\bnd directory on Windows and in the *instance_home*/sqllib/bnd directory on Linux/UNIX. Both contain a list of bind files the **bind** command will run against. A package is created for each of these bind files.

> **N O T E**   The DB2 Runtime Client does not include the required bind files, so you cannot run the **bind** command from a Runtime Client.

You must bind the utilities for each database you want to access. Binding only needs to be done once by a client. Once a package is successfully bound to the database, all DB2 clients of the same DB2 version and FixPak level can use it. If you have different versions and FixPaks of clients, you must bind the utilities for each client version and FixPak level.

> **NOTE** You must have BINDADD authority to create a new package in a database or BIND privilege if the package already exists.

6.4 Configuring Database Connections Using the Configuration Assistant

If you don't feel comfortable using DB2 commands, you can use the **Configuration Assistant** (**CA**), a graphical tool to configure connections on a client machine. The CA catalogs the DB2 directories for you.

The CA's **Add Database Wizard** offers three methods to configure a database connection from a client machine.

- **Search the network**: With this method, you do not need to know any communication-specific information about the database server, such as the TCP/IP port and database name. The CA will find that out for you using DB2's Discovery ability and will update the DB2 directories.
- **Use a profile**: A **profile** contains all the information necessary to create a connection between a client and a server. Using the information from a given profile, the CA will update the DB2 directories of the client to allow connections to the chosen database.
- **Manually configure a connection to a database**: You must know the specific connection information to the server, such as host name, port number, and database name. The CA will update the DB2 directories based on the information you provide.

The following sections discuss each of these methods in more detail.

> **NOTE** You can only use the Configuration Assistant to configure connections *from* a client *to* a server. You still need to enable the server to accept client connections *manually* before you start using the CA to configure the client.

6.4.1 Configuring a Connection Using DB2 Discovery in the Configuration Assistant

You can perform Discovery in one of two ways.

- The **search discovery** method searches the network for any DB2 servers accessible by clients. You do not need to know the name of the server. The CA returns a list of valid servers and their database information. Use this method only in a small network where there are not many hubs, otherwise the search process may take a long time to complete.

- The **known discovery** method requires you to provide the server name you want to access, and the CA returns the instance and database information on that server.

Table 6.9 shows the parameters that control DB2 Discovery at the server and the files where they are located.

Table 6.9 The Parameters That Control Discovery at the Server

Configuration File	Parameter Name	Possible Values	Explanation
DAS configuration file	DISCOVER	SEARCH	The default value. Both search and known discovery can be used.
		KNOWN	Only known discovery can be used.
		DISABLE	Discovery method can't be used for instances.
DBM configuration file	DISCOVER _INST	ENABLE	The default value. The instance can be discovered.
		DISABLE	The instance can't be discovered.
Database configuration file	DISCOVER_DB	ENABLE	The default value. The database can be discovered.
		DISABLE	The database can't be discovered.

Table 6.10 shows the parameter that controls DB2 Discovery at the client.

Table 6.10 The Parameter That Controls Discovery at the Client

Configuration File	Parameter Name	Possible Values	Explanation
DBM configuration file	DISCOVER	SEARCH	The default value. The client can issue search and known discovery requests
		KNOWN	The client can only issue known discovery requests.
		DISABLE	Discovery is disabled at the client.

By default all the instances and databases of a database server are visible to all clients using the CA. If you have security concerns, you can control the level of visibility by modifying the values of these parameters. For example, if you set DISCOVER_ INST=DISABLE at the instance level, then the instance and all its databases will not be visible by clients who try to discover them using the CA.

Figure 6.16 shows an example of a database server with two instances and different values for the parameters affecting DB2 discovery.

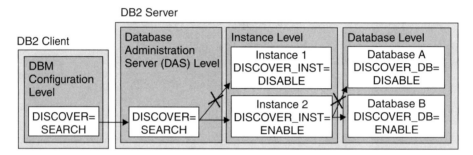

Figure 6.16   Discovery hierarchy

In Figure 6.16, the client can use the CA to see the database server because DISCOVER is set to SEARCH in the server's DAS. The client can see instance 2 but not instance 1. In instance 2, the client can see database B but not A.

The DAS on the server also needs to have the parameter DISCOVER_COMM set to TCP/IP, which is the only protocol the discovery method supports.

> **N O T E**   The DAS on each DB2 server you want to locate using Discovery must be configured and running.

The procedure to add a database connection using the discovery method in the CA is:

1. Open the CA from the **IBM DB2** menu or enter **db2ca** from a command line. Figure 6.17 shows the CA interface.
2. The databases that are already cataloged on the client are displayed in the CA window. To add more connections, click **Selected** and choose **Add Database Using Wizard**. You will see the Add Database Wizard, shown in Figure 6.18.
3. Choose *Search the network* to use the DB2 Discovery methods. This displays the window shown in Figure 6.19. The systems the client currently knows are displayed in the *Known systems* folder. *SYLVIA2* is the only known system to this client. If the database server you want to connect to is already in the Known systems folder, expand the tree to look for it. If the database server is not listed, you need to add it to the list.

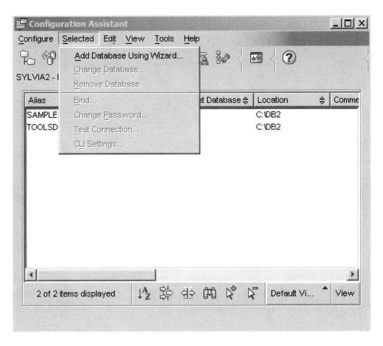

Figure 6.17   The Configuration Assistant

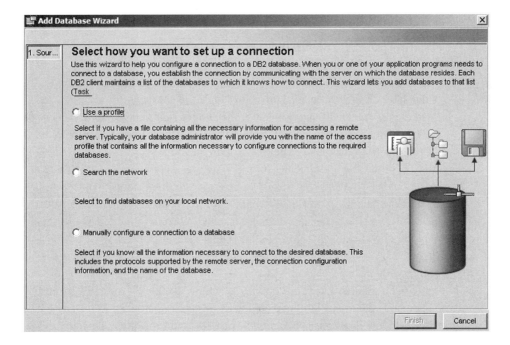

Figure 6.18   Add Database Wizard—Configuration methods

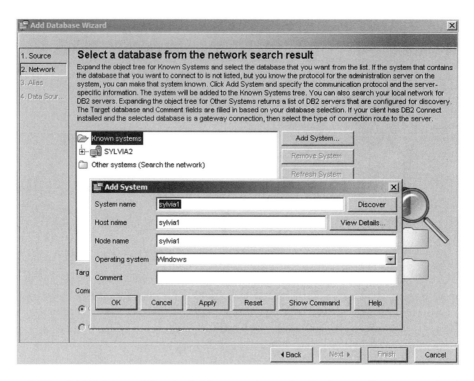

Figure 6.19   Add Database Wizard—Adding a system using the known discovery method

4. You have two choices to add the new system.
    *   To use the *search discovery* method, double-click on the *Other systems (Search the network)* folder. The CA will then search for and display all database servers that have Discovery enabled on the system.
    *   To use the *known discovery* method, click on the *Add System* button. This displays the *Add System* window (see Figure 6.19). Enter the information as required. The Node Name and Comment fields are optional.
5. Figure 6.20 shows the search result for the system name you entered. In this example, the system name is *SYLVIA1*. Expand the tree to see all databases visible on this system. Select the database you want to connect to. If you do not want to specify an alias for the database and register this database as an ODBC data source, you can finish the configuration by clicking the *Finish* button. Otherwise, click *Next*.
6. In Figure 6.21 you can specify a database alias. This is the name you will use during all connect requests. Click *Finish* or *Next*.
7. In Figure 6.22, you have the choice to register this database as an ODBC data source. When you click the *Finish* button to complete the configuration, an Add Database Confirmation window displays. You can click *Close* to return to the CA main window or *Test Connection* to verify the connection to the database.

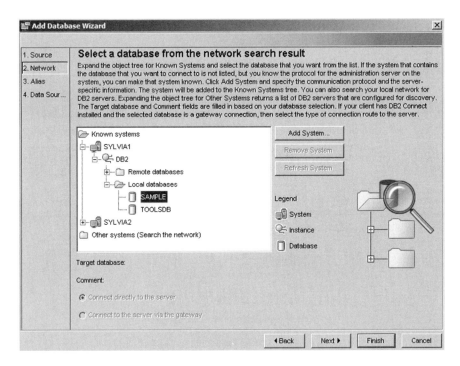

Figure 6.20   Add Database Wizard—Network search result

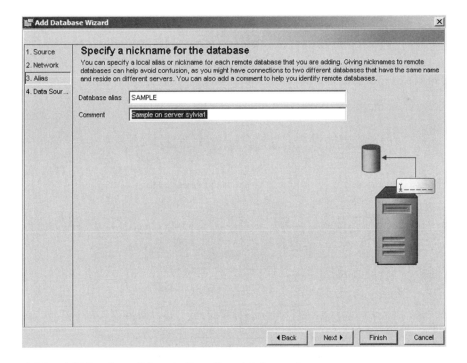

Figure 6.21   Add Database Wizard—Specify a database alias

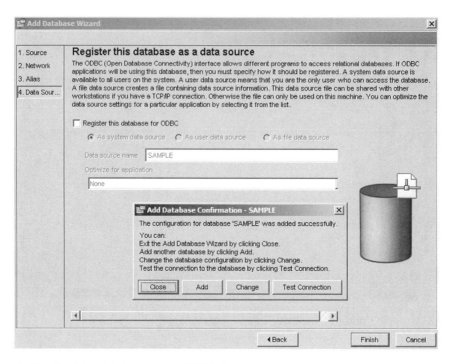

Figure 6.22   Register database as an ODBC data source

Figure 6.23 shows the window displayed if you choose to test the connection. The user ID must be valid on the database server.

Figure 6.24 shows the window after testing a successful connection.

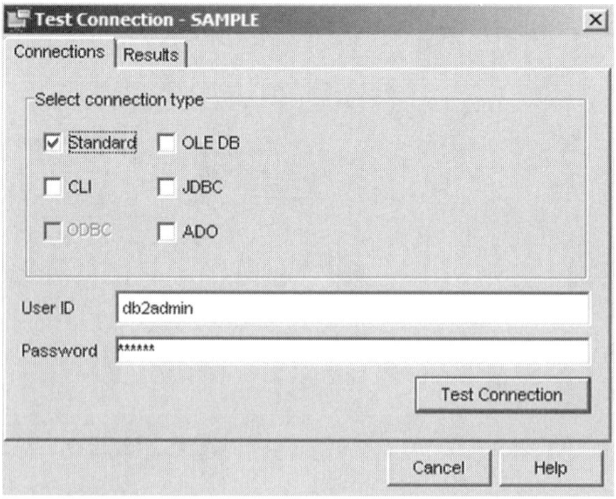

Figure 6.23   Test connection to the new system

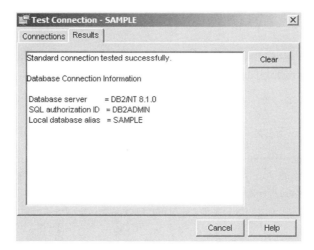

Figure 6.24   Test connection result window

The CA automatically updates the node directory and database directory, as shown in Figure 6.25. Note that the node name is an arbitrary name chosen by the CA.

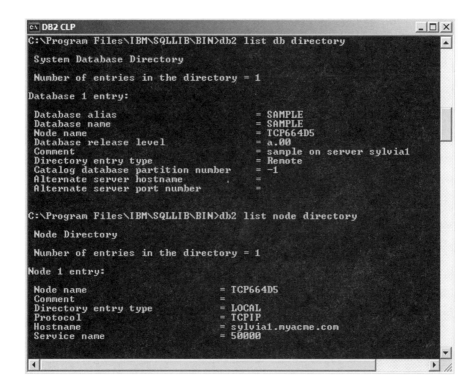

Figure 6.25   Updated node directory and database directory

6.4.2 Configuring a Connection Using Access Profiles in the Configuration Assistant

An **access profile** is a file that contains all the information necessary to create a connection between a client and a server. This process automatically catalogs the DB2 directories on the client. Use access profiles if you have many clients that need to be configured to connect to the same DB2 servers.

You can obtain an access profile either from a configured client or from the server itself.

- If you have a client that has been configured to connect to DB2 servers, use this client's CA to export its configuration to the access profile file. You can then transfer this file to other clients and configure them using this information.
- You can use the server's CA to export an access profile that contains information about all the instances that have DISCOVER_INST=ENABLE in the Database Manager Configuration file and all databases that have DISCOVER_DB=ENABLE in the database configuration file. You can then transfer this access profile to clients and configure them using the information in this file.

6.4.2.1 Using the Configuration Assistant to Export an Access Profile

1. In the Configuration Assistant, choose **Configure** > **Export Profile**. (You can also do this by using the **db2cfexp** command.) Figure 6.26 shows the three Export Profile options.

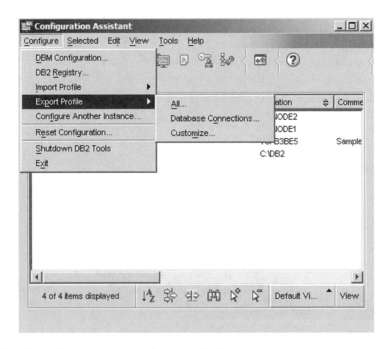

Figure 6.26   Exporting an access profile using the CA

- **All** creates a profile that contains all of the databases cataloged on the system. In addition, the profile includes specific information about the system, such as the DB2 registry variables and Database Manager Configuration.
- **Database Connections** creates a profile that contains only the database catalog information.
- **Customize** lets you select specific databases that are cataloged on the system.

2. In this example, let's select **Customize**. This displays the *Customize Export Profile* window (see Figure 6.27).

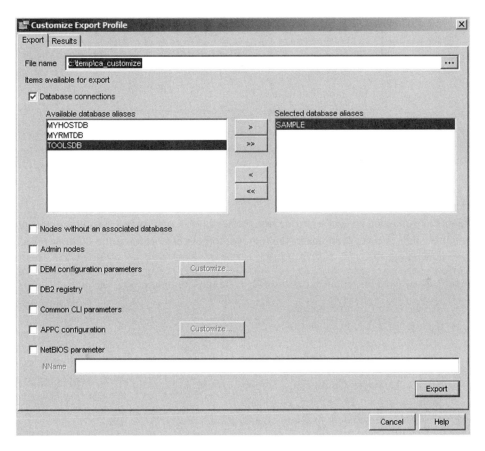

Figure 6.27   The Customize Export Profile window

3. From the *Available database aliases* list, choose the database(s) for which you would like to export the connection information. Then click the > button to transfer it to the *Selected database aliases* list.
4. Enter a file name for the access profile.

5. If you want to export specific information about the system, such as DBM Configuration parameters or the DB2 registry, you can do so by checking the boxes beside each option.
6. Click the *Export* button. Figure 6.28 shows the export result. If the operation is successful, an access profile file is created in the specified directory.

Figure 6.28   Export access profile result

6.4.2.2 Using the Configuration Assistant to Import an Access Profile

After you have obtained an access profile from either a client or a server, you can use this profile to configure other clients. You transfer the file over to the client you want to configure and start the CA on the client.

There are two ways to import an access profile using the Configuration Assistant.

- Use the CA's Import function
- Use the CA's Add Database Wizard

6.4.2.2.1 Importing an Access Profile Using the CA's Import Profile Function

1. In the CA, choose **Configure > Import Profile** as shown in Figure 6.29 (You can also do this using the **db2cfimp** command.)
    There are two options when importing a profile.
    - **All** imports all of the configuration information from a given profile.
    - **Customize** lets you select the information you would like to import.
2. If you choose **Customize**, the window shown in Figure 6.30 is displayed.
3. Enter the name of the access profile you would like to import and click the *Load* button.
    This loads the information in the profile into the *Items available for import* section of the window. You can choose the database(s) you want from the *Available database aliases* list and transfer it to the *Selected database aliases* list.

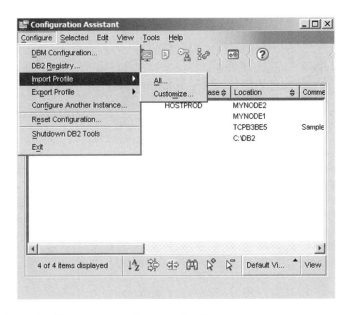

Figure 6.29   Importing the access profile using the CA

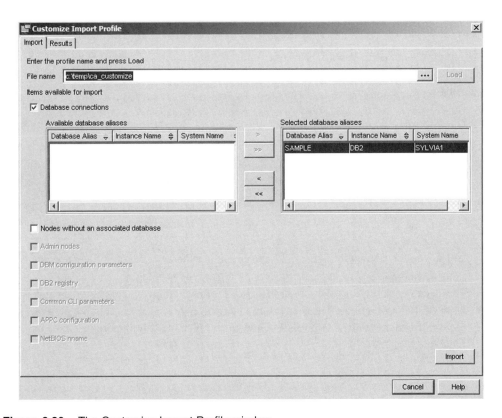

Figure 6.30   The Customize Import Profile window

4. If the profile contains information such as DBM configuration parameters, the DB2 registry, or CLI parameters, the corresponding checkboxes will be available. You can click the checkbox for each to import that information as well. In Figure 6.30 they are grayed out because they are not contained in the access profile.

5. Click the *Import* button and the window shown in Figure 6.31 appears.

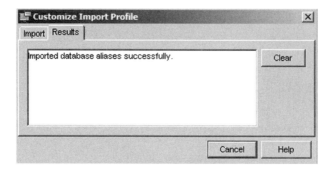

Figure 6.31   Import access profile result

If the import is successful, you now have the ability to connect to the database(s) you have chosen. The client's node directory and system database directory have been updated to include this new database.

6.4.2.2.2 Importing an Access Profile Using the CA's Add Database Wizard

You can also import the information in an access profile using the Configuration Assistant's Add Database Wizard. However, when using this method you can only add one database at a time. If you want to add multiple databases, using the Import function discussed in the previous section is a better choice.

1. From the *Select how you want to set up a connection* window (shown in Figure 6.18), select *Use a profile*.

2. The window shown in Figure 6.32 appears. Enter the access profile file name and click the *Load* button. This loads the information from the profile into the window.

3. You can click on *Next* to configure an alias for the database and register the database as an ODBC data source. These steps are identical to those discussed in the previous section. If you don't click *Next*, click *Finish* to complete the configuration.

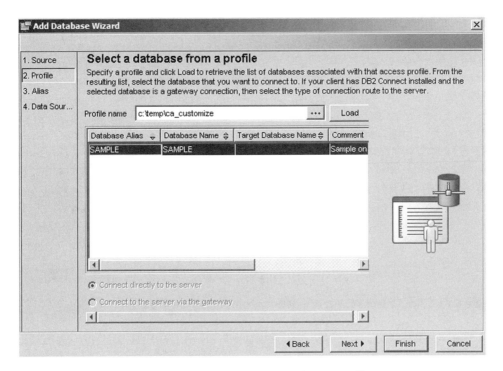

Figure 6.32   Add Database Wizard—Select a database from a profile

6.4.3 Configuring a Connection Manually Using the Configuration Assistant

You can also manually configure a connection in the Configuration Assistant. Using this method, you must know the specific server connection information, such as host name, port number, and database name. The CA will update the DB2 directories based on the information you provide.

1. In the CA, choose **Selected** > **Add Database Using Wizard**. Choose *Manually configure a connection to a database* (see Figure 6.18) and click *Next*. The window shown in Figure 6.33 appears.
2. Select the protocol you will use to connect to the database. Also, if the database resides on a host system, check the corresponding box. Click *Next*.
3. Enter the host name or TCP/IP address of the server and the service name or port number that the DB2 instance is using on the server, as shown in Figure 6.34. If you are using a different communication protocol, refer to Table 6.11 for the required communication information. Click *Next*.
4. Enter the database name, as shown in Figure 6.35. The database name in this entry corresponds to the database alias on the server. If you want, complete the optional *Database alias* and *Comment* fields. The alias is what you will use in the **CONNECT** statement. Click *Next*.

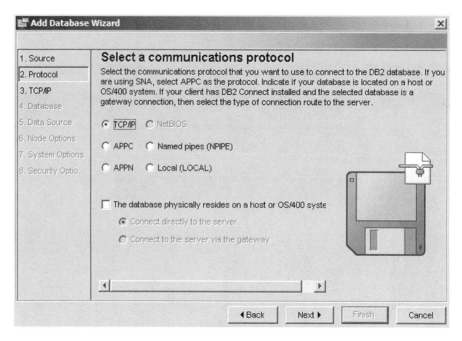

Figure 6.33   Add Database Wizard—Select a communications protocol

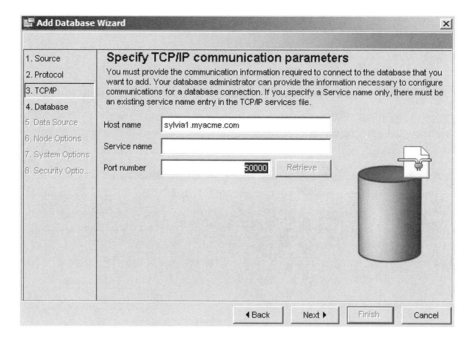

Figure 6.34   Add Database Wizard—Specify TCP/IP communications parameters

Table 6.11   Information Required in the Add Database Wizard for the Communication Protocol

Communication Protocol	Information Required
NetBIOS	Server workstation name and adapter number
Named Pipes	Server computer name and instance name
APPC	Server symbolic destination name

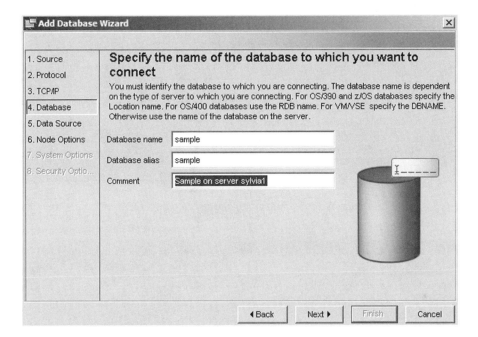

Figure 6.35   Add Database Wizard—Specify database name

5. Once you have completed the screen shown in Figure 6.36, you can choose to either continue through the next screens or you can click *Finish*. If you continue to any of the subsequent screens, you can click *Finish* at any time.

6. In the screen shown in Figure 6.37, specify the operating system and instance name on the database server. Since this information affects the behavior of the Control Center, it is important that you fill them in. Click *Next*.

7. In Figure 6.38, enter the system name and host name. The system name is the name you want to use for the database server. If you click on the *View Details* button, the CA will retrieve the TCP/IP name and address information for the server. Click *Next*.

8. In Figure 6.39, choose a security option for this connection and then click *Finish*. The CA will automatically update DB2 directories.

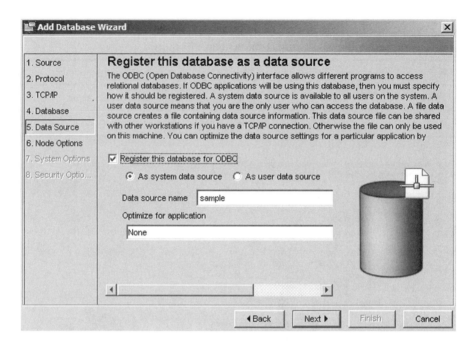

Figure 6.36   Add Database Wizard—Register this database as a ODBC data source

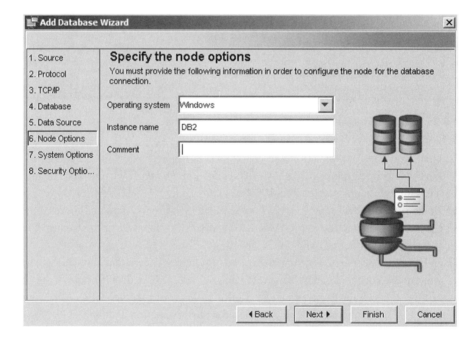

Figure 6.37   Add Database Wizard—Specify the node options

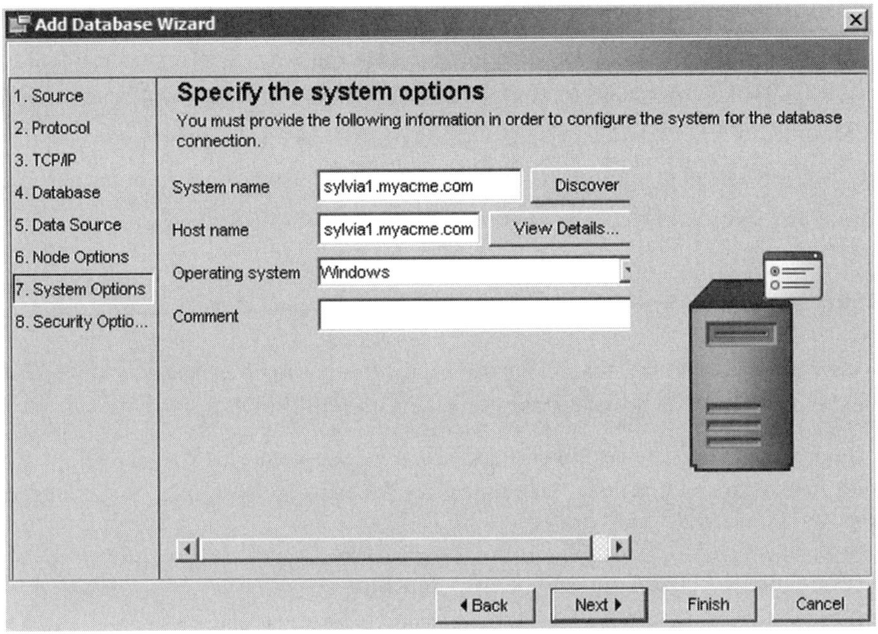

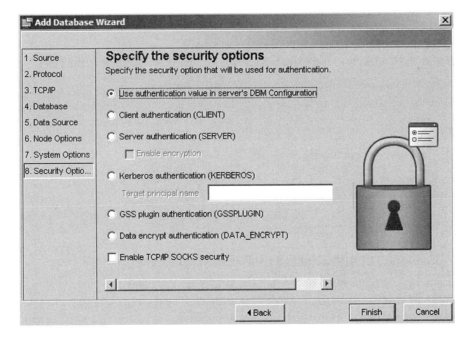

Figure 6.38   Add Database Wizard—Specify the system options

Figure 6.39   Add Database Wizard—Specify the security options

6.5 CASE STUDY

You have just installed DB2 Connect Enterprise Edition on an AIX machine. You will use this machine as a DB2 Connect gateway for DB2 clients connecting to your company's DB2 for z/OS server.

You are given the following information by the database administrator (DBA) of the host database:

```
Hostname          = jupiter.myacme.com
Port Number       = 446
Location Name     = OS390L1
User ID           = user1
Password          = userpwd
```

For security reasons, the DB2 for z/OS location name is not to be exposed to the DB2 clients. The clients will refer to the host database using the name DB2PROD.

When you installed DB2 Connect, an instance *db2inst1* was created. Now you will perform the following steps to set up this three-tier connection. All steps are performed while logged on as *db2inst1*.

Step 1: Configure the DB2 Connect Gateway Machine

Use the information given by the DB2 for z/OS database administrator to catalog the node directory, system database directory, and the DCS directory on the DB2 Connect gateway:

```
catalog tcpip node node1 remote jupiter.myacme.com server 446
catalog db db2prod at node node1
catalog dcs db db2prod as os390l1
terminate
```

Step 2: Test the Connection from the DB2 Connect Gateway Machine to the Host

Use the following DB2 command to connect to the host database:

```
CONNECT TO db2prod USER user1 USING userpwd
```

If the connection fails, the problem could be that:

- The user ID or password is incorrect.
- There is a network problem.
- The host server is not set up properly to accept client connections.

As the problem is likely to be on the host side, contact your host's DBA first to investigate the problem before moving on to step 3.

Step 3: Enable the TCP/IP Listener on the Gateway Machine

To make this gateway machine capable of accepting client connections, you need to enable the TCP/IP listener for the *db2inst1* instance. If you created the *db2inst1* instance using the DB2 Setup Wizard during product installation, you do not need to perform this step because it has already been done for you. However, since you created *db2inst1* manually using the **db2icrt** command, you need to perform the following steps to enable the TCP/IP listener.

1. Manually add the following entry in the etc/services file:

```
db2conn1 50000/tcp #DB2 connection port for db2inst1
```

2. Execute the following DB2 commands:

```
update dbm cfg using svcename db2conn1
db2set DB2COMM=TCPIP
db2stop
db2start
```

Step 4: Configure a DB2 Client to Connect to the Host via the Gateway

The DB2 client will connect to the host database via the DB2 Connect gateway. On the client, perform the following commands to catalog the client's node directory and database directory to connect to the gateway. The host name of the gateway is *mercury.myacme.com*.

```
catalog tcpip node node1 remote mercury.myacme.com server 50000
catalog db db2prod at node node1
terminate
```

To connect to the host from the client, execute:

```
CONNECT TO db2prod USER user1 USING userpwd
```

If the connection is successful, proceed to the next step to configure other clients.

Step 5: Configure the Rest of the Clients Using a Client Profile

You need to configure 100 more DB2 clients. You could perform step 4 on all 100 clients, or you can export the catalog information on the client you have just configured and use this profile to configure other clients. Of course, the second option is the faster way.

Since the client is an AIX client without X-Windows installed, you cannot export the client profile using the Configuration Assistant. Therefore, you decide to use the **db2cfexp** and **db2cfimp** commands instead.

On the client that has been configured in step 4, export its catalog information into an access profile *accessprofile* under the /tmp directory:

```
db2cfexp /tmp/accessprofile TEMPLATE
```

FTP the *accessprofile* file to the other clients, and on each of them execute:

```
db2cfimp accessprofile
```

6.6 SUMMARY

In this chapter you learned the setup required to connect from a DB2 client to a DB2 server. Four supported connection scenarios were discussed in detail:

- Local connection from a DB2 client to a DB2 server
- Remote connection from a DB2 client to a DB2 server
- Remote connection from a DB2 client to a DB2 host server
- Remote connection from a DB2 client to a DB2 host server via a DB2 Connect gateway

A local connection occurs when a DB2 client and a DB2 server reside on the same server. A connection from a DB2 client to a DB2 server requires that at least the DB2 Runtime Client be installed on the client machine. On the server machine, at least DB2 Workgroup Edition is required. A connection from a DB2 client to a DB2 host server requires that at least the DB2 Connect Personal Edition software be installed on the client machine. The supported host servers are DB2 for z/OS and OS/390 and DB2 for iSeries.

TCP/IP is the supported communication protocol for all of the above connections. NetBIOS and Named Pipes are supported if both the client and the server are on Windows, and APPC is supported for outbound connection to DB2 host servers.

Connectivity information is stored in four main directories: the system database directory, the local database directory, the node directory, and the DCS directory.

The system database directory contains the names and aliases of both remote and local databases. The local database directory contains the names and aliases of databases that exist locally on a particular drive (on Windows) or path (on Linux/UNIX). The information about how to reach a remote server is stored in the client's node directory. For a TCP/IP connection, the remote server's host name or IP address and the DB2 port number are stored. To connect to a database residing on a host server, a DCS directory is also required. An entry in the DCS directory contains the actual database name known to the host server.

There are two methods you can use to configure client-server connections:

- Catalog the node directory, database directory, and DCS directory manually
- Use the Configuration Assistant for automatic configuration

If you use the CA, you can use any of the three CA methods:

- Access profiles
- Search the network
- Manual configuration

After configuring the connections, you need to bind database utilities or else the client will not be able to use any of the database utilities such as import or export. Run the **bind** command on the *db2ubind.lst* file to bind database utilities. If the client is going to run CLI/ODBC applications, run the **bind** command on the *db2cli.lst* file as well to create CLI packages on the server.

If the server is DB2 for z/OS or OS/390, use the *ddcsmvs.lst* file in the **bind** command. If the server is DB2 for iSeries, use the *ddcs400.lst* file.

The binding of utilities must be done for each database you want to access. Once a package is successfully bound to the database, all DB2 clients of the same type and DB2 level can use it.

6.7 REVIEW QUESTIONS

1. Which DB2 directory contains information about all the databases you can connect to from a DB2 client machine?

2. Which command is used to review the contents of the local database directory located in drive H: on a Windows machine?

3. If the system database directory contains an entry with a type of *indirect*, what does this say about the entry?

4. If the SVCENAME database manager parameter has a value of db2_cDB2, which port is being used?

5. Which communication protocols are supported when connecting from a DB2 Connect gateway to a DB2 for z/OS server?

6. Why is DB2 Connect Enterprise Edition the recommended DB2 Connect product to use to support 1,000 clients connecting to a DB2 for iSeries server?

7. Which command can you use to remove an incorrect entry from the DCS directory?

8. Which command can you use to remove an incorrect entry from the node directory?

9. Which command can you use to remove an incorrect entry from the system database directory?

10. In which case would "Search the network" not be an appropriate choice to set up connectivity to your databases?

11. Given the following command:

    ```
    catalog tcpip node srv2 remote server2 server db2port
    ```
    which of the following DB2 directories will be updated?

    A. DCS directory
    B. System database directory
    C. Local database directory
    D. Node directory

12. Which of the following products will not make use of the DCS directory?

    A. DB2 Connect Personal Edition
    B. DB2 Connect Enterprise Edition
    C. DB2 Personal Edition
    D. DB2 Enterprise Server Edition

13. The following entry appears in the Windows services file of the DB2 client machine:

    ```
    db2c_DB2      60000
    ```
    while the SVCENAME value for the DB2 instance at the server is 50005. Which of the following commands is the correct one to use?

    A. `catalog tcpip node mynode remote aries server 60000`
    B. `catalog tcpip node mynode remote aries server 50005`
    C. `catalog tcpip node mynode remote aries server db2c_DB2`
    D. `catalog tcpip node mynode remote aries server 50000`

14. Which of the following commands inserts an entry in the system database directory?

    A. `catalog system database directory mydb at node mynode`

    B. `insert into system db value (mydb)`

    C. `create database mydb on F:`

    D. `catalog dcs db mydb`

15. Which of the following commands is required to enable a DB2 server for TCPIP connectivity? (Choose all that apply.)

    A. `update dbm cfg using SVCENAME 50000`

    B. `db2set DB2COMM=TCPIP`

    C. `connect to sample`

    D. `ping myhost`

16. Which of the following is not a supported method from the DB2 Configuration Assistant?

    A. Manually configure a connection to a database

    B. Search the network

    C. Use a Profile

    D. Unknown discovery

17. Which of the following commands is required to prevent the use of the Discover method for a database server from any DB2 client?

    A. `update admin cfg using DISCOVER disable` (at the server machine)

    B. `update dbm cfg using DISCOVER disable` (at the server machine)

    C. `update admin cfg using DISCOVER disable` (at the client machine)

    D. `update dbm cfg using DISCOVER disable` (at the client machine)

18. Which of the following commands is required to prevent the use of the Discover method only for database mydb while connected to that database?

    A. `update admin cfg using DISCOVER disable`

    B. `update dbm cfg using DISCOVER disable`

    C. `update dbm cfg using DISCOVER_INST disable`

    D. `update db cfg using DISCOVER_DB disable`

19. Which of the following commands removes an entry from the local database directory?

    A. `uncatalog local database directory mydb at node mynode`

    B. `delete from local db where value = 'mydb'`

    C. `drop database mydb`

    D. `uncatalog dcs db mydb`

20. The command `get dbm cfg | grep DISCOVER` returns two lines in my Linux server:

```
Discovery mode                  (DISCOVER) = SEARCH
Discover server instance   (DISCOVER_INST) = ENABLE
```

Which command prevents this server from using the Discover method against other server machines?

    A. `db2 update dbm cfg using DISCOVER_INST disable`

    B. `db2 update dbm cfg using DISCOVER disable`

    C. `db2 update dbm cfg using DISCOVER known`

    D. `db2 update dbm cfg using DISCOVER_INST known`

## CHAPTER 7

Working with Database Objects

In this chapter we discuss the various objects that may exist in your database, such as tables, indexes, views, sequence objects, and stored procedures. We also describe the different data types supported by DB2. This chapter is closely related to Chapter 8, The DB2 Storage Model, where the implementation and manipulation of several of these objects is explained, and to Chapter 9, Leveraging the Power of SQL, which explains how to work with these database objects using the SQL language.

In this chapter you will learn about:

- The big picture of the DB2 database objects
- The definitions of databases, database partitions, partition groups, buffer pools, and table spaces
- The DB2 data types
- How to work with tables, indexes, views, and schemas
- The definition of application-related objects like packages, triggers, user-defined functions, stored procedures, and sequences

7.1 DB2 DATABASE OBJECTS: THE BIG PICTURE

A database is a collection of database objects, and you can create it in one or more database partitions. A **database partition**, as its name implies, is part of a database. We discuss these concepts in more detail in the next sections; for now, we introduce you to the DB2 database objects. Figure 7.1 illustrates these objects in a database created in a single-partition environment (database partition 0). The database objects are described next.

- A **partition group** is a logical object representing a collection of database partitions. In a single-partition environment, partition groups are not relevant; however, in multi-partition

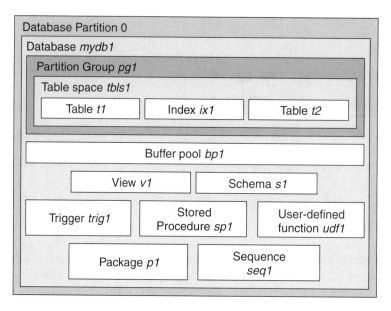

Figure 7.1   An overview of the DB2 database objects

environments, a partition group facilitates the work of a database administrator, as he is
able to perform database operations on several partitions at a time. Partition groups can
contain one or more table spaces. In Figure 7.1, partition group *pg1* contains table
space *tbls1*.

- **Table spaces** are logical objects that associate tables and indexes to the physical
  devices where these objects are stored, as well as to the physical memory where the
  data in these objects is cached. Tables and indexes must be created inside a table space
  as illustrated in Figure 7.1, where tables *t1* and *t2* and index *ix1* are all created inside
  table space *tbls1*.
- **Tables** consist of rows and columns, like spreadsheets. Data can be inserted, deleted,
  and updated within a table. Figure 7.1 has two tables, *t1* and *t2*.
- **Indexes** are an ordered set of keys each pointing to a row in a table. They improve the
  performance when looking for specific rows. Indexes can also be used to guarantee the
  uniqueness of rows. In Figure 7.1, index *ix1* is associated to table *t1*.
- A **buffer pool** is an area in physical memory that caches the database information most
  recently used. Without buffer pools, every single piece of data has to be retrieved from
  disk, which is very slow. Buffer pools are associated to tables and indexes through a
  table space. In Figure 7.1, table space *tbls1* is associated to buffer pool *bp1*, therefore
  tables *t1* and *t2* and index *ix1* use buffer pool *bp1*.
- A **view** is an alternate way of representing data that exists in one or more tables. A view
  can include some or all of the columns from one or more tables. It can also be based on
  other views. In Figure 7.1, view *v1* is based on table *t1*.

- Every object in the database is created with a two-part name separated by a dot:

  `schema_name.object_name`

  The first part of this two-part name is the schema name. A **schema** is an object that provides a logical grouping of other database objects. A schema can be owned by an individual who can control access to the objects within it. Schemas can be implicitly or explicitly specified when accessing an object.
- A **trigger** is an object that contains application logic that is triggered by specific actions like an update to a table. For example, in Figure 7.1, a trigger can be created so that after table *t1* is updated, table *t2* is also updated with some other information.
- A **stored procedure** is an object used to move application logic to your database. By keeping part of the application logic in the database, there are performance improvements as the amount of network traffic between the application and the database is considerably reduced.
- **User-defined functions** (UDFs) allow database users to extend the SQL language by creating functions that can be used anywhere a DB2 built-in function is used. Similar to stored procedures, application logic can be moved to the database by using UDFs.
- A **package** is an object containing the compiled version of your SQL queries as well as the access path that the DB2 optimizer, the brain of DB2, has chosen to retrieve the data for those queries.
- A **sequence** object allows the generation of unique numbers in sequence. These numbers can be used across the database as a unique identifier for tables or for applications.

To create, modify, or delete database objects, you use the Data Definition Language (DDL) consisting of the following SQL statements:

- **CREATE**
- **DECLARE**
- **ALTER**
- **DROP**

The following objects can be created and dropped using the **CREATE** and **DROP** statements, respectively:

- Tables
- Indexes
- Schemas
- Views
- User-defined functions
- User-defined types
- Buffer pools
- Table spaces
- Stored procedures
- Triggers

- Servers (for federated databases)
- Wrappers (for federated databases)
- Nicknames (for federated databases)
- Sequences

You use the **DECLARE** statement to create temporary tables, and the **ALTER** statement to change one or more characteristics of an existing database object. You can alter most, but not all, of the database objects created with the **CREATE** statement.

The **CREATE**, **DECLARE**, **ALTER**, and **DROP** statements are used throughout this chapter.

7.2 DATABASES

A **database** is a collection of information organized into interrelated objects such as table spaces, partition groups, and tables. Each database is an independent unit containing its own system information, temporary space, transaction logs, and configuration files, as illustrated in Figure 7.2.

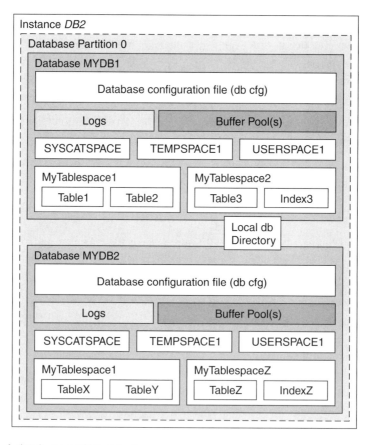

Figure 7.2   A database and its objects

Figure 7.2 shows two databases, *MYDB1* and *MYDB2*, inside instance *DB2* in a single-partition environment (Database Partition 0). The box showing *Database Partition 0* is included for completeness; in a single-partition environment you can ignore this box. Since databases are independent units, object names from different databases can be the same. For example, the name of the table space *MyTablespace1* is repeated in both databases in the figure.

Figure 7.2 also shows three table spaces that DB2 creates by default when you create a database: SYSCATSPACE, TEMPSPACE1, and USERSPACE1. These table spaces are described in section 7.4, Table Spaces.

In this chapter we only discuss database objects. Configuration files are discussed in Chapter 5, Understanding the DB2 Environment, DB2 Instances, and Databases. The local database directory is discussed in Chapter 6, Configuring Client and Server Connectivity. Logs are discussed in Chapter 13, Developing Database Backup and Recovery Solutions.

To create a database, use the **CREATE DATABASE** command (Chapter 8, The DB2 Storage Model, discusses this command in detail). To perform operations against database objects, you first need to connect to the database using the **CONNECT** statement (see Chapter 6, Configuring Client and Server Connectivity).

7.2.1 Database Partitions

You can create a single-partition or a multi-partition database, depending on your needs.

In a multi-partition environment, a **database partition** (or simply **partition**) is an independent part of a database containing its own data, indexes, configuration files, and transaction logs. Database functions are also distributed between all the database partitions. This provides for unlimited scalability.

Multiple database partitions can reside on one physical server; these are sometimes referred to as **logical partitions** sharing the resources of the machine. Database partitions can also reside on different physical servers. The collection of all of these partitions corresponds to one database.

Multi-partition database support uses the database partitioning feature of DB2 UDB Enterprise Server Edition (ESE), which comes built-in with the product but requires the purchase of a separate license.

Figure 7.3 shows two databases, *MYDB1* and *MYDB2*, in a multi-partition environment with three database partitions.

As mentioned in Chapter 2, DB2 at a Glance: The Big Picture, an instance associates the DB2 binary code to databases. Database partitions, on the other hand, are used to split your database into different parts. Therefore, an instance in a multi-partition environment associates the DB2 binary code to the different database partitions. Figure 7.3 shows this association.

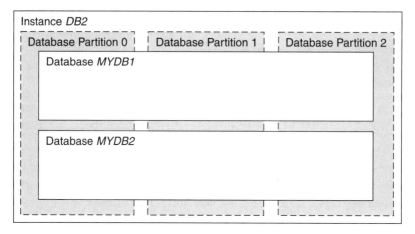

Figure 7.3   Database partitions

7.2.2 The Database Node Configuration File (db2nodes.cfg)

In a multi-partition environment you define the database partitions that are part of your database by entering the appropriate information in the database node configuration file, db2nodes.cfg.

On Linux and UNIX platforms, the db2nodes.cfg file can contain up to five columns, as shown in Table 7.1.

Table 7.1   Columns of the db2nodes.cfg Configuration File for Linux and UNIX

	Partition Number	Hostname	Logical Port	Netname	Resourcesetname
Is the Column Required?	Yes.	Yes.	Sometimes.	Sometimes.	Optional.
Description	DB2 uses this column to identify the partition.	The TCP/IP host name of the server where the partition is created.	This column must be used if you want to create more than one partition on the same server. It specifies the logical port for the partition within the server and must be unique within a server.	Supports a host that has more than one active TCP/IP interface, each with its own host name. It is required if you are using a high speed interconnect for interpartition communication or if the resourcesetname column is used	It specifies the operating system resource that the partition should be started in.

On Windows there is also another column, Computername, which contains the computer name for the machine on which a partition resides. Table 7.2 shows the order of the columns on Windows systems and whether they are required.

Table 7.2   Columns of the db2nodes.cfg Configuration File for Windows

	Partition Number	Hostname	Computername	Logical Port	Netname	Resourcesetname
Is the Column Required?	Yes.	Yes.	Yes.	Sometimes.	Sometimes.	Optional.

When you create an instance in DB2 ESE, a default db2nodes.cfg file is created with one row. On Linux and UNIX the default file has three columns and looks like the following:

```
0     mypenguin     0
```

On Windows the default file has four columns and looks like the following:

```
0     myserver     myserver     0
```

The db2nodes.cfg file is located

- Under the sqllib directory for the instance owner on Linux and UNIX
- Under the SQLLIB*Instance_name* directory on Windows

There is only one db2nodes.cfg file per instance, and all the databases you create under this instance will be partitioned at CREATE DATABASE time based on the contents of this file. To create multiple partitions, edit the db2nodes.cfg file and add an entry for each database partition. For example, assume you have an eight-way SMP server (a server with eight CPUs) running Linux as shown in Figure 7.4.

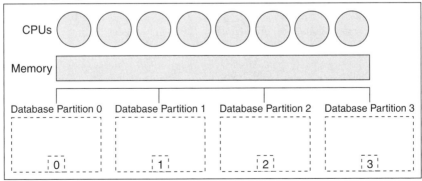

Figure 7.4   An eight-way SMP Linux server with four database partitions

You need to edit the db2nodes.cfg file to make it look like the following:

```
0     mypenguin    0
1     mypenguin    1
2     mypenguin    2
3     mypenguin    3
```

In another scenario, assume you are installing DB2 on a cluster of eight two-way SMP Linux servers, and you want to create one partition on each server as illustrated in Figure 7.5 (not all servers are shown).

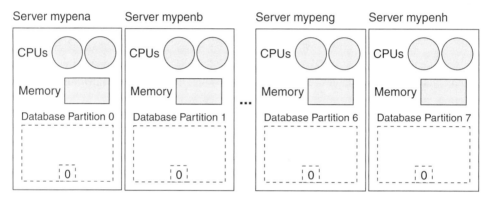

Figure 7.5 A cluster of eight two-way SMP Linux servers with eight partitions in total

You need to edit the db2nodes.cfg file to make it look like the following:

```
0     mypena    0
1     mypenb    0
2     mypenc    0
3     mypend    0
4     mypene    0
5     mypenf    0
6     mypeng    0
7     mypenh    0
```

In yet another scenario, assume you are installing DB2 on a cluster of four UNIX servers with four CPUs each and you want to create two partitions on each server as shown in Figure 7.6.

You need to edit the db2nodes.cfg file to make it look like the following:

```
0     myuxa    0
1     myuxa    1
2     myuxb    0
3     myuxb    1
4     myuxc    0
5     myuxc    1
6     myuxd    0
7     myuxd    1
```

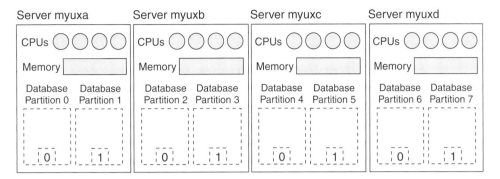

Figure 7.6 A cluster of four four-way SMP UNIX servers with eight database partitions in total

On Linux and UNIX you can edit the db2nodes.cfg file with any ASCII editor. On Windows, you cannot edit the db2nodes.cfg file directly; instead, use the **db2ncrt** and **db2ndrop** commands to add and drop database partitions, respectively.

You can also use the **db2start** command to add and/or remove a database partition from the DB2 instance and the db2nodes.cfg file as follows.

- Use the **db2start** command with the **add dbpartitionnum** option to add a partition to the database and insert an entry for the partition into the db2nodes.cfg file.
- Use the **db2start** command with the **drop dbpartitionnum** option to remove a partition from the database and delete its entry from the db2nodes.cfg file.

You can also use the **add dbpartitionnum** command to add a partition to the database even if the partition already has an entry in the db2nodes.cfg file. The **drop dbpartitionnum** command will remove the specified partition from the database but will not remove its entry from the instance's db2nodes.cfg file.

7.3 PARTITION GROUPS

A database **partition group** is a set of one or more database partitions. By grouping database partitions, you can perform database operations at the partition group level rather than individually on each partition. This allows for database administration flexibility. For example, let's say you want to create a buffer pool with the same definition in three partitions. If you first create a partition group *pgall* that consists of the three partitions, you can associate the buffer pool *bp1* you are about to create with this partition group. This lets you use the same buffer pool definition on each partition.

Partition groups also allow you to associate table spaces to database partitions. For example, if you would like table space *tbls1* to use only database partitions 1 and 2, you can create a partition group *pg12* with these two partitions, and then associate the table space *tbls1* to *pg12*.

Figure 7.7 illustrates the objects discussed in the preceding examples.

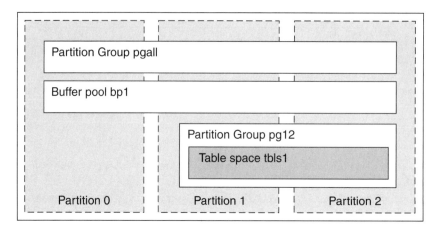

Figure 7.7   Partition groups

In Figure 7.7 the buffer pool definition is repeated across all the partitions. If you create the buffer pool with 20,000 4K pages, each partition will allocate 20,000 4K pages. Note that the 20,000 4K pages are *not* split across all three partitions as the figure may suggest.

To create a partition group, use the **CREATE DATABASE PARTITION GROUP** statement. Refer to Chapter 8, The DB2 Storage Model, for more details.

When you create a database, three partition groups are created by default.

- **IBMCATGROUP** is the partition group where the DB2 catalog table space (SYSCATSPACE) resides. It consists of only one partition, the one where the **CREATE DATABASE** command is issued.
- **IBMTEMPGROUP** is the partition group where the system temporary table space (TEMPSPACE1) resides. It spans all partitions.
- **IBMDEFAULTGROUP** is the partition group where the user table space (USERSPACE1) resides. It spans all partitions.

These default partition groups are discussed in detail in Chapter 8, The DB2 Storage Model.

7.4 TABLE SPACES

A **table space** is a logical object of your database. It is used to associate your logical tables and indexes to your physical devices (containers) and physical memory (buffer pools). All tables and indexes must reside inside a table space.

7.4.1 Table Space Classification

Table spaces can be classified based on how the table space is managed and on what type of data they contain.

Based on how the table space is managed, a table space can be one of the following types.

- **System-managed space (SMS)**: This type of table space is managed by the operating system and requires minimal administration. This is the default table space type.
- **Database-managed space (DMS)**: This type of table space is managed by the DB2 database manager, and it requires some administration.

SMS and DMS table spaces are discussed in detail in Chapter 8, The DB2 Storage Model.

Based on the type of data it contains, a table space can be one of the following types.

- **Regular**: Use this type of table space to store any kind of data except temporary data. This is the default type.
- **Large**: Use this type of table space to store LONG VARCHAR, LONG VARGRAPHIC, or LOB data (see section 7.7.1.2, String Data Types) as well as index data. This table space is supported only with DMS table spaces.
- **Temporary**: Use this type of table space to hold temporary data. In turn, temporary table spaces can be further classified as two types.

  - **System**: These table spaces hold temporary data required by the database manager to perform operations such as sorts or joins, which require extra space for processing a result set.
  - **User**: These table spaces hold temporary data from tables created with the **DECLARE GLOBAL TEMPORARY TABLE** statement. This type of table is explained in section 7.8.11, Temporary Tables.

> **N O T E** System temporary table spaces and user temporary table spaces are commonly confused. Remember that system temporary table spaces are used by DB2, while user temporary table spaces are used by users when they declare global temporary tables.

> **N O T E** Indexes can be stored in either regular or large table spaces.

To create a table space, use the **CREATE TABLESPACE** statement. A table space can be created with any of these page sizes: 4K, 8K, 16K, and 32K. A corresponding buffer pool of the same page size must exist prior to issuing this statement. Refer to Chapter 8, The DB2 Storage Model, for details.

7.4.2 Default Table Spaces

When a database is first created, the following table spaces are created by default.

- **SYSCATSPACE** contains the DB2 system catalog tables and views. This set of tables and views contains system information about all the objects in the database.

- **TEMPSPACE1** is used for system temporary data when DB2 needs temporary tables to process large sort or join operations.
- **USERSPACE1** is the table space where most tables are created by default if a table space name has not been explicitly indicated in the **CREATE TABLE** statement. Section 7.8.3, User Tables, describes in detail the rules followed when a table space is implicitly assigned to a table.

7.5 BUFFER POOLS

The database **buffer pool** is a piece of real memory used by DB2 to temporarily store (cache) regular data and index pages when they are read from disk to be scanned or modified. The buffer pool improves the performance of the database because the pages can be accessed much more quickly from memory than from disk.

When you create a database, a default buffer pool, IBMDEFAULTBP, is automatically created. This buffer pool is associated with the default table spaces SYSCATSPACE, TEMPSPACE1, and USERSPACE1, and you cannot drop it.

To create a buffer pool, use the **CREATE BUFFERPOOL** statement. This statement allows you to indicate, among other things, how large the buffer pool will be and which page size it will use. Refer to Chapter 8, The DB2 Storage Model, for details.

7.6 SCHEMAS

A **schema** is a database object used to logically group other database objects. Every database object name has two parts:

```
schema_name.object_name
```

This two-part name (also known as the fully qualified name) must be unique within the database. Here are some examples:

```
db2admin.tab1
mary.idx1
sales.tblspace1
```

When you create an object, it is always created within a schema, even if you do not explicitly specify the schema name. When you do not specify the schema name, DB2 uses the **authorization ID** (the ID used to connect to the database) as the object's schema. If you connect to a database as *peter* and in a query specify a table simply as *tab1*, DB2 will interpret this as *peter.tab1*.

> **NOTE**   A schema does *not* need to map to a user ID. Any user with the appropriate authorization can create a schema. For example, assuming user *peter* has the correct authorizations, he can create the schema *foo*, where *foo* does not map to anything at all.

To create the schema *user1*, use the **CREATE SCHEMA** statement as follows:

```
CREATE SCHEMA user1
```

Or, if you are connected to the database as *user1*, when you create the first new object using this connection without explicitly typing the schema name, DB2 will automatically create the schema *user1* and then the object. This assumes you have the appropriate authorization, in this case, the IMPLICIT_SCHEMA privilege. The following statement creates the schema *user1*, followed by the table *table1*.

```
CREATE TABLE table1 (mycol int)
```

If you are connected to the database as *user1*, you can also create objects under a different schema. In this case, explicitly indicate the schema name, for example:

```
CREATE TABLE newuser.table1 (mycol int)
```

This statement creates a table called *table1* in schema *newuser*. If the schema doesn't already exist, it is created. Although running both of these **CREATE TABLE** statements results in two tables in the database called *table1*, they are different tables because one is in schema *user1*, and the other is in schema *newuser*.

> **N O T E**   Creating schemas implicitly or explicitly requires the user to have the appropriate authorizations or privileges. Refer to Chapter 10, Implementing Security, for more details.

When you access a database object, you can omit the schema name. Let's say you are connected to the database as *user1*, and you issue the following statement:

```
SELECT * FROM table1
```

This statement references table *user1.table1*.

If the table you want to access is *newuser.table1*, you must explicitly include the schema name:

```
SELECT * FROM newuser.table1
```

You cannot alter a schema, but you can drop it (as long as no objects exist within the schema) and recreate it with the new definition. Use the **DROP SCHEMA** statement to drop a schema:

```
DROP SCHEMA newuser RESTRICT
```

You must specify the **RESTRICT** keyword; it is part of the **DROP SCHEMA** syntax and serves as a reminder that you cannot drop a schema unless it is unused.

7.7 DATA TYPES

Before continuing with our discussion of database objects, you need to understand the data types supported by DB2. A **data type** indicates what type of data can be saved in a column or variable and how large it can be. DB2 data types are either:

- Built-in data types
- User-defined types (UDTs)

7.7.1 DB2 Built-in Data Types

DB2 provides several built-in data types, which can be classified into the following categories:

- Numeric
- String
- Datetime
- Datalink

Figure 7.8 summarizes the built-in data types supported in DB2.

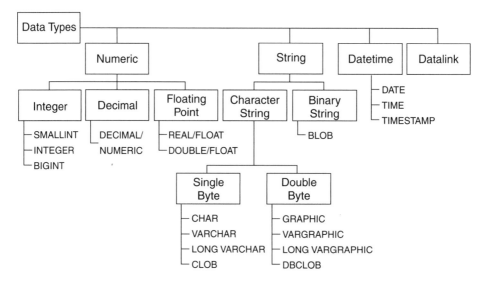

Figure 7.8   The DB2 built-in data types

7.7.1.1 Numeric Data Types

The numeric data types include the following:

- Small integer (SMALLINT)
- Integer (INT or INTEGER)
- Big integer (BIGINT)
- DECIMAL/NUMERIC

- REAL/FLOAT
- DOUBLE/FLOAT

A SMALLINT uses the least amount of storage in the database for each value. The data value range for a SMALLINT is –32768 to 32767. The precision for a SMALLINT is 5 digits to the left of the decimal. Each SMALLINT column value uses 2 bytes of database storage.

An INTEGER uses twice as much storage as a SMALLINT but has a greater range of possible values. The data value range for an INTEGER data type is –2,147,483,648 to 2,147,483,647. The precision for an INTEGER is 10 digits to the left of the decimal. Each INTEGER column value uses 4 bytes of database storage.

The BIGINT data type is available for supporting 64-bit integers. The value range for BIGINT is –9,223,372,036,854,775,808 to 9,223,372,036,854,775,807. Since platforms include native support for 64-bit integers, processing large numbers with BIGINT is more efficient than processing with DECIMAL and more precise than using DOUBLE or REAL. Each BIGINT column value uses 8 bytes of database storage.

The SMALLINT, INTEGER, and BIGINT data types do not allow any digits to the right of the decimal.

A DECIMAL or NUMERIC data type is used for numbers with fractional and whole parts. The DECIMAL data is stored in a packed format. You must provide the precision and scale when using a DECIMAL data type. The **precision** is the total number of digits (ranging from 1 to 31 digits), and the **scale** is the number of digits in the fractional part of the number.

> **N O T E** If you do not explicitly specify the precision and scale, DB2 will use a default value of DECIMAL(5,0), that is, a precision of 5 digits and a scale of 0 digits.

A REAL or FLOAT data type is an approximation of a number. The approximation requires 32 bits or 4 bytes of storage. To specify a single-precision number using the REAL data type, you must define its length between 1 and 24 (especially if you use the FLOAT data type, as it can represent both single- and double-precision numbers and is determined by the integer value specified).

A DOUBLE or FLOAT data type is also an approximation of a number. The approximation requires 64 bits or 8 bytes of storage. To specify a double-precision number using the FLOAT data type, you must define its length between 25 and 53.

7.7.1.2 String Data Types

You can define string or character columns as either fixed length or variable length. The character string data types include the following:

- Character (CHAR)
- Variable character (VARCHAR)

- Long variable character (LONG VARCHAR)
- Character large object (CLOB)
- GRAPHIC
- VARGRAPHIC
- LONG VARGRAPHIC
- Double-byte character large object (DBCLOB)

A CHAR column is stored as a fixed-length field in the database; if the string you enter is shorter than the defined length of the column, the string will be padded with blanks. This wastes space within the database if you tend to store strings that are a lot shorter than the length of the column. A fixed-length character column can have a maximum length of 254 characters. If no length is specified, DB2 will use the default length of 1 character.

A VARCHAR column stores only the characters entered for the string, and its maximum size closely corresponds to the page size for the table. For example, for a table created in a table space with a 32K page size, the maximum length of a VARCHAR string is 32,672 characters.

A LONG VARCHAR column also stores only the characters entered for the string, but it does not store them in the data object with the other columns. LONG VARCHAR is a special data type stored in a separate long object. The maximum length of a LONG VARCHAR string is 32,700 characters.

> **N O T E**   You can use the FOR BIT DATA clause of CHAR, VAR-
> CHAR, and LONG VARCHAR data types to indicate the data will be
> stored as a sequence of bytes. The clause can be used for non-tradi-
> tional data like video and audio. Code page conversions do not occur
> because data is compared bit by bit.

GRAPHIC data types use 2 bytes of storage to represent a single character. There are three types:

- GRAPHIC: fixed length with a maximum of 127 characters
- VARGRAPHIC: varying length with a maximum of 16,336 characters
- LONG VARGRAPHIC: varying length with a maximum of 16,350 characters

> **N O T E**   The LONG VARCHAR and LONG VARGRAPHIC data
> types are deprecated, meaning that they are still supported but are no
> longer enhanced. These data types are not manipulated in the buffer
> pool but are accessed directly from disk, a direct input/output (I/O)
> operation, so using them may impact performance. Instead, use the
> VARCHAR or VARGRAPHIC data types, respectively, because their
> maximum lengths are very close to those of the LONG data types, but
> VARCHAR and VARGRAPHIC provide better performance.

When a VARCHAR data type's maximum size of 32,672 bytes is not enough to hold your data, use large objects. Large objects can store data greater than 32K up to 2GB in size. They are typically used to store information such as a long XML document, an audio file, or a picture.

Three kinds of LOB data types are provided with DB2:

- Binary large object (BLOB)
- Single-byte character large object (CLOB)
- Double-byte character large object (DBCLOB)

BLOBs store variable-length data in binary format and are ideal for storing video or audio information in your database. This data type has some restrictions; for example, you cannot sort by this type of column.

CLOBs store large amounts of variable-length single-byte character set (SBCS) or multi-byte character set (MBCS) character strings, for example, large amounts of text such as white papers or long documents.

DBCLOBs store large amounts of variable-length double-byte character set (DBCS) character strings, such as large amounts of text in Chinese.

Similar to LONG VARCHAR and LONG VARGRAPHIC data types, LOBs are accessed directly from disk without going through the buffer pool, so using LOBs is slower than using other data types. In addition, because changes to a database are logged in transaction log files, these files might get filled quickly when modifying a LOB column. To prevent this from happening, the **CREATE TABLE** statement has the **NOT LOGGED** option for LOB columns. For LOB columns defined as more than 1GB in size, **NOT LOGGED** is required.

The **CREATE TABLE** statement also has the **COMPACT** option for LOBs to allocate just the necessary disk space. However, if you perform an update to the LOB column that would increase the size of the LOB, DB2 would need to allocate more space at that time, which incurs a performance penalty. Note that this option does not compress the LOBs.

> **NOTE**   Do not use LOBs to store data less than 32K in size. Instead, use VARCHAR or VARCHAR FOR BIT DATA, which can hold a maximum of 32,672 bytes. This will help with database performance.

7.7.1.3 Datetime Data Types

Date and time data types are special character data types used to store date and/or time values in specific formats. DB2 supports three datetime data types: DATE, TIME, and TIMESTAMP.

- The DATE type stores a date value (month, day, and year) in the format MM-DD-YYYY or MM/DD/YYYY.
- The TIME type stores a time value (hour, minute, and second) in the format HH:MM:SS or HH.MM.SS.

  • The TIMESTAMP type combines the DATE and TIME types but also stores the time
    down to the nanosecond in the format MM-DD-YYYY-HH.MM.SS.NNNNNN.

7.7.1.4 Datalink Data Types

Datalinks allow relational databases to work with file systems. By using a DATALINK column, you
can point to files and take advantage of the power of relational database features like referential
integrity. Refer to the *DB2 UDB SQL Reference* manual for more information about datalinks.

7.7.2 User-Defined Types

User-defined types (UDTs) allow database users to create or extend the use of data types to their
own needs. UDTs can be classified as DISTINCT, STRUCTURE, or REFERENCE. This section discusses only DISTINCT types. Please refer to the *DB2 UDB SQL Reference* manual for
the other kinds of UDTs.

A DISTINCT UDT can enforce business rules and prevent data from being used improperly.
UDTs are built on top of existing DB2 built-in data types.

To create a UDT, use the **CREATE DISTINCT TYPE** statement:

```
CREATE DISTINCT TYPE type_name AS built-in_datatype WITH COMPARISONS
```

The **WITH COMPARISONS** clause is required for all data types, except BLOB, CLOB,
DBCLOB, LONG VARCHAR, LONG VARGRAPHIC, and DATALINK data types. This clause
causes DB2 to create system-generated SQL functions to perform casting between the types;
these are known as **casting functions**.

For example, let's say you create two UDTs, *celsius* and *fahrenheit*:

```
CREATE DISTINCT TYPE  celsius   AS integer WITH COMPARISONS
CREATE DISTINCT TYPE fahrenheit AS integer WITH COMPARISONS
```

The first statement creates a casting function named *celsius*, and the second statement creates a
casting function named *fahrenheit*.

Now, let's say you create a table using the newly created UDTs:

```
CREATE TABLE temperature
      (country         varchar(100),
       average_temp_c  celsius,
       average_temp_f  fahrenheit
      )
```

Table *temperature* keeps track of the average temperature of each country in the world in both
Celsius and Fahrenheit. If you would like to know which countries have an average temperature
higher than 35 degrees Celsius, you can issue this query:

```
SELECT country FROM temperature WHERE average_temp_c > 35
```

Would this query work? At first, you may think it will, but remember that *average_temp_c* has data
type *celsius*, while 35 is an INTEGER. Even though *celsius* was created based on the INTEGER

built-in data type, this comparison cannot be performed as is. To resolve this problem, use the casting function generated with the creation of the *celsius* UDT as shown below:

```
SELECT country FROM temperature WHERE average_temp_c > celsius(35)
```

UDTs enforce business rules by preventing illegitimate operations. For example, the following query will not work:

```
SELECT country FROM temperature WHERE average_temp_c = average_temp_f
```

Because column *average_temp_c* and *average_temp_f* are of different data types, this query will result in an error. If UDTs had not been created and the INTEGER built-in data type had been used instead for both columns, the query would have worked—but what meaning in real life would that have?

To drop a UDT, use the statement **DROP DISTINCT TYPE *type_name***. This will also drop the casting functions associated to the UDT.

7.7.3 Choosing the Proper Data Type

It is important to choose the proper data type because this affects performance and disk space. To choose the correct data type, you need to understand how your data will be used and its possible values. Table 7.3 summarizes what you should consider.

Table 7.3   Choosing the Proper Data Types

Question	Data Type
Is your data variable in length, with a maximum length of fewer than 10 characters?	CHAR
Is your data variable in length, with a minimum length of 10 characters?	VARCHAR
Is your data fixed in length?	CHAR
Is your data going to be used in sort operations?	CHAR, VARCHAR, DECIMAL, INTEGER
Is your data going to be used in arithmetic operations?	DECIMAL, REAL, DOUBLE, BIGINT, INTEGER, SMALLINT
Does your data require decimals?	DECIMAL, REAL, DOUBLE, FLOAT
Do you need to store very small amounts of non-traditional data like audio or video?	CHAR FOR BIT DATA, VARCHAR FOR BIT DATA, LONG VARCHAR FOR BIT DATA
Do you need to store non-traditional data like audio or video, or data larger than a character string can store?	CLOB, BLOB, DBCLOB

(continues)

Table 7.3   Choosing the Proper Data Types *(Continued)*

Question	Data Type
Does the data contain timestamp information?	TIMESTAMP
Does the data contain time information?	TIME
Does the data contain date information?	DATE
Do you need a data type to enforce your business rules that has a specific meaning (beyond DB2 built-in data types)?	User-defined type
Will you manage files from your database?	DATALINK

> **N O T E**   For the first two rows of Table 7.3 we chose CHAR versus VARCHAR depending on the length of the data. If the maximum length is fewer than 10 characters, we suggest using a CHAR data type; otherwise, we recommend VARCHAR. Normally for small variable-length columns, a CHAR column provides better performance. We chose the value of 10 characters based on our experience, but it may vary depending on your data.

7.8 TABLES

A **table** is an unordered set of records, consisting of rows and columns. Each column has a defined data type, and each row represents an entry in the table. Figure 7.9 shows an example of a table with *n* rows and *m* columns. The *sales_person* column with a VARCHAR data type is the first column in the table, followed by the *region* column with a CHAR data type. The *year* column is the *m*th column in the table and has an INTEGER data type.

	Column 1 sales_person VARCHAR(20)	Column 2 region CHAR(10)		Column *m* year INTEGER
Row1 →	Mary	South		2002
Row 2 →	John	North		2002
Row 3 →	Sam	North	•••	2000
		•••		
Row *N* →	John	South		2001

Figure 7.9   An example of a table

7.8.1 Table Classification

Tables in DB2 can be classified as illustrated in Figure 7.10. You will learn more about each of these tables in the next sections.

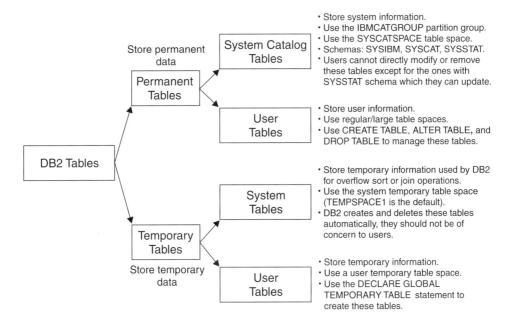

Figure 7.10 Classification of tables in DB2

7.8.2 System Catalog Tables

DB2 automatically creates system catalog tables when a database is created. They always reside in the SYSCATSPACE table space. System catalog tables contain information about all the database objects in the database. For example, when you create a table space, its information will be loaded into one or more system catalog tables. When this table space is referenced during a later operation, DB2 checks the corresponding system catalog tables to see whether the table space exists and whether the operation is allowed. Without the system catalog tables, DB2 will not be able to function.

Some of the information contained in system catalog tables includes the following:

- Definitions of all database objects
- Column data types of tables and views
- Defined constraints
- Object privileges
- Object dependencies

System catalog tables or views use the SYSIBM, SYSCAT, or SYSSTAT schemas.

- The **SYSIBM schema** is used for the base system catalog tables.
- The **SYSCAT schema** is used for views defined on the system catalog tables. DB2 users should normally query the SYSCAT views rather than the SYSIBM tables for information.
- The **SYSSTAT schema** is used for views containing information about database statistics and is also based on the system catalog tables.

Although you cannot update the tables and views residing under the SYSIBM and SYSCAT schemas, you can update the views under the SYSSTAT schema. Updating these views can sometimes influence the DB2 optimizer to choose a specific access path.

Refer to Appendix D, Using the DB2 System Catalog Tables, for details about the system catalog tables.

7.8.3 User Tables

User tables are used to store a user's data. A user can create, alter, drop, and manipulate user tables.

To create a user table, use the **CREATE TABLE** statement. You can specify the following:

- The name of the table
- The columns of the table and their data types
- The table spaces where you want the table, index, and long objects to be stored within the database
- The constraints you want DB2 to build and maintain on the table, such as referential constraints and unique constraints

The following example illustrates the creation of the table *myemployees* with four columns.

```
CREATE TABLE myemployees (
        empID    INT           NOT NULL PRIMARY KEY,
        empname  VARCHAR(30)   NOT NULL,
        mngrID   INT           NOT NULL,
        history  CLOB)
```

In which table space would the table *myemployees* be created? In cases where a table space is not specified, as in this example, follow the flow chart shown in Figure 7.11 to determine what table space would be used.

This next example uses the same **CREATE TABLE** situation, but it indicates the table spaces to be used for the table data, index, and long objects.

```
CREATE TABLE myemployees (
          empID    INT           NOT NULL PRIMARY KEY,
          empname  VARCHAR(30)   NOT NULL,
          mngrID   INT           NOT NULL,
          history  CLOB)
          IN datadms
      INDEX IN indexdms
      LONG  IN largedms
```

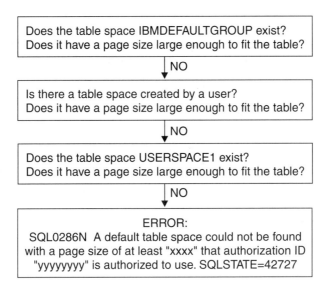

Figure 7.11 Guidelines for determining how the default table space is chosen for a table

Use the **IN** clause to specify the table space where the table data will reside. Use the **INDEX IN** clause to specify where all indexes for the table will reside. Use the **LONG IN** clause to indicate where the LOB, LONG VARCHAR, or LONG VARGRAPHIC objects will reside.

> **N O T E** If different table spaces are used for the table, index, and long data, all of these table spaces must be DMS. In addition, the table space where the long data is to be stored must be defined as a *large* table space.

> **N O T E** Prior to Version 8, *large* table spaces were known as *long* table spaces. Though the syntax of the **CREATE TABLESPACE** statement uses the **LARGE** clause, the syntax of the **CREATE TABLE** statement still uses **LONG**.

Figure 7.12 shows the command used to create the table *myemployees* and also the corresponding table space commands to create the required table spaces. Note that the third statement creates a large table space.

You can also create a table based on the definition of another table, for example:

```
CREATE TABLE clone LIKE myemployees
```

```
DB2 CLP                                                               _ □ ×
CREATE TABLESPACE datadms MANAGED BY DATABASE USING (FILE 'C:\DATADMS\DATADMSFIL
E'   1000)
DB20000I  The SQL command completed successfully.

CREATE TABLESPACE indexdms MANAGED BY DATABASE USING (FILE 'C:\INDEXDMS\INDEXDMS
FILE' 1000)
DB20000I  The SQL command completed successfully.

CREATE LARGE TABLESPACE largedms MANAGED BY DATABASE USING (FILE 'C:\LARGEDMS\LA
RGEDMSFILE' 1000)
DB20000I  The SQL command completed successfully.

CREATE TABLE myemployees ( empID    INT              NOT NULL PRIMARY KEY, em
pname  VARCHAR(30)     NOT NULL, mngrID  INT          NOT NULL, history  CLOB)
 IN datadms INDEX IN indexdms LONG  IN largedms
DB20000I  The SQL command completed successfully.

C:\Program Files\IBM\SQLLIB\BIN>
```

Figure 7.12   Creating a table where table, index, and long data are stored in different DMS table spaces

The table *clone* will have the same definition as the table *myemployees*, however, other objects like constraints, indexes, or triggers associated to the table are not copied. Table data is not copied either.

Another alternative is to create the table structure based on the result of a query, as shown next:

```
CREATE TABLE clone2 AS (SELECT * FROM myemployees) DEFINITION ONLY
```

The **DEFINITION ONLY** clause is required so that only the structure of the table is copied; otherwise, you would be creating a materialized query table (MQT), which is described in section 7.8.10, Materialized Query Tables and Summary Tables.

Once you have created a table, you cannot change the column names or data types; however, you are allowed to increase the length of VARCHAR columns or add new columns to the end of the table. You can do this with the **ALTER TABLE** statement. For example, to add the column *address* to the table *myemployees*, use this statement:

```
ALTER TABLE myemployees ADD COLUMN address CHAR(45)
```

You cannot remove a column from a table using the **ALTER TABLE** statement. If you want to remove a column from a table, you have two choices:

- Use a view to hide the column you want removed. (Views are discussed in section 7.11.)
- Drop the table and recreate it.

To drop a table and all its contents, use the **DROP TABLE** statement, for example:

```
DROP TABLE myemployees
```

7.8.4 Default Values

In the **CREATE TABLE** statement, you can use the **DEFAULT** clause for a given column to provide a default value for the column. This means that when you use an **INSERT** statement to insert a row that does not provide a value for the column, the default value specified in the **DEFAULT** clause will be used. For example, let's say you create the table *company* with this statement:

```
CREATE TABLE company (
       companyID        INTEGER,
       companyName      VARCHAR(30),
       city             VARCHAR(20) DEFAULT 'TORONTO'
       )
```

Inserting a record with either of the following two statements provides the same result.

```
(1)    INSERT INTO company  (companyID, companyName,  city)
                    VALUES (   111   , 'cityOne' , DEFAULT)
(2)    INSERT INTO company  (companyID, companyName)
                    VALUES (   111,       'cityOne' )
```

The following row would be inserted.

```
COMPANYID   COMPANYNAME                      CITY
----------- ------------------------------   --------------------
        111 cityOne                          TORONTO
```

In the first **INSERT** statement, the **DEFAULT** keyword is used. In the second **INSERT** statement, the third column (*city*) is not included in the statement. In both cases, this means that the default value as defined in the table is inserted for that column.

What about the table columns that do not have a **DEFAULT** clause? What is inserted when test columns are omitted from the **INSERT** statement? In such scenarios, DB2 will insert a NULL, assuming the column accepts NULL values. If the column does not accept NULL values, you will receive an error. (We describe NULLs in the next section.) For example, the result of this statement:

```
       INSERT INTO company  (city)
              VALUES ('ATLANTA')
```

is:

```
COMPANYID   COMPANYNAME                      CITY
----------- ------------------------------   --------------------
        - -                                  ATLANTA
```

The dash (-) represents a NULL value.

The columns of a table can also be defined with the **DEFAULT** keyword just by itself. In such a scenario, DB2 will use default values depending on the data type of the column. Typically, DB2 chooses a zero for numeric data types and a blank for character strings. For example, let's recreate the table *company* as follows:

```
CREATE TABLE company (
       companyID        INTEGER     DEFAULT,
       companyName      VARCHAR(30) DEFAULT,
       city             VARCHAR(20) DEFAULT 'TORONTO'
       )
```

Issuing the following statement:

```
INSERT INTO company  (city)
            VALUES (DEFAULT)
```

returns:

```
COMPANYID   COMPANYNAME                         CITY
----------- ----------------------------- ------------
          0                                       TORONTO
```

This example shows that because the columns *companyID* and *companyName* are both defined with the **DEFAULT** clause just by itself, DB2 chose a default value of zero for column *companyID*, which is an INTEGER, and a blank for column *companyName*, which is a VARCHAR.

7.8.5 Using NULL Values

NULL values represent an unknown state. For example, let's review the contents of the table *student*, which contains NULL values.

```
NAME                  MARK
--------------------- -----------
Peter                         100
Mary                           60
John                            -
Raul                           80
Tom                             -
```

John and Tom were sick the day of the exam, therefore the teacher put NULL values for their marks. This is different than giving them a mark of zero. If you issue this statement:

```
SELECT avg(mark) as average FROM student
```

The result is:

```
AVERAGE
-----------
         80
```

Note that the average was calculated as follows: (100 + 60 + 80) / 3. The total number of students considered in the calculation was three, not five, because NULL values were not taken into consideration in the calculation.

Your business requirements dictate when NULL values are allowed in your columns. Let's review another example to illustrate when using **NOT NULL** is appropriate. The following statement creates a table that stores a company phone directory.

```
CREATE TABLE telephoneDirectory (
    empID     CHAR(3)       NOT NULL PRIMARY KEY,
    phone_no  VARCHAR(15)   NOT NULL,
    deptname  VARCHAR(20)   NOT NULL DEFAULT 'Marketing',
    position  VARCHAR(30)   DEFAULT 'Clerk'
)
```

In the example, let's assume the business requirements indicate that the column *empID* must uniquely identify a row. Thus, *empID* should be created as NOT NULL so that NULL values are not accepted; otherwise, several rows may have NULLs, which would not make the rows unique.

Next, the column *phone_no* is also defined as NOT NULL per the business requirements. If the purpose of this table is to store telephone numbers, it's understandable that this column does not accept NULLs.

The third column, *deptname*, is defined as NOT NULL with a **DEFAULT** value of Marketing. This means that a NULL value is not accepted, and when the column is omitted in an **INSERT** statement, the default value of Marketing is used. For example, if you issue this statement:

```
INSERT INTO telephoneDirectory (empID, phone_no)
                  VALUES ('111', '905-123-4567')
```

The result is:

```
EMPID PHONE_NO        DEPTNAME             POSITION
----- --------------- -------------------- -----------------------
111   905-123-4567    Marketing            Clerk
```

The fourth column, *position*, allows NULL values and has a default value of Clerk. This case was explained in section 7.8.4, Default Values. The NOT NULL DEFAULT *value* clause works the same as the DEFAULT *value* clause only that NULL values are not allowed.

7.8.6 Identity Columns

An **identity column** is a numeric column in a table that automatically generates a unique numeric value in sequence for each row inserted. A unique identifier is often used in applications to identify a specific row. Unlike sequence objects, which we discuss in section 7.16, Sequences, identity columns are bound to the table they are defined on. There can be only one identity column per table. DB2 can generate the identity column values in two ways.

- Generated always: The values are always generated by DB2. Applications are not allowed to provide an explicit value.
- Generated by default: The values can be explicitly provided by an application; if no value is given, DB2 generates one. In this case, however, DB2 cannot guarantee the uniqueness of the value generated.

To create an identity column, use the **CREATE TABLE** statement with the **GENERATED** clause and make sure it contains the **IDENTITY** keyword because **GENERATED** can also be used to generate other values automatically that are not identity columns. Here is an example.

```
CREATE TABLE product (
      productno   INTEGER GENERATED ALWAYS AS
                        IDENTITY (START WITH 200 INCREMENT BY 1),
      description VARCHAR(50) )
```

The column *productno* is an INTEGER defined as an identity column that is always generated. The value generated will start from 200, and it will be incremented by 1. Let's perform a few **INSERT** statements and see the results obtained.

```
INSERT INTO product VALUES (DEFAULT,'banana');        --->inserts 200,banana
INSERT INTO product (description) VALUES ('apple');   --->inserts 201,apple
INSERT INTO product VALUES (300,'pear');              --->error SQL0798N
COMMIT;

INSERT INTO product (description) VALUES ('orange');  --->inserts 202,orange
ROLLBACK;

INSERT INTO product (description) VALUES ('plum');    --->inserts 203,plum
COMMIT;
```

The following query shows the final result.

```
SELECT * FROM product;

PRODUCTNO    DESCRIPTION
-----------  ------------
        200  banana
        201  apple
        203  plum
```

The first two **INSERT** statements show that two identity column values were generated: 200 and 201. The third **INSERT** statement returns an error because you cannot explicitly insert a value for an identity column generated as **ALWAYS**. After the third **INSERT** statement, we issue a **COMMIT** to guarantee these rows are stored in the database. The fourth **INSERT** statement causes another identity column value, 202, to be generated; however, we issue a **ROLLBACK** statement right after, so this row is not stored in the database. Note that the final **INSERT** statement, which inserts the product plum, generates a value of 203, not 202. (**COMMIT** and **ROLLBACK** statements are explained in more detail in Chapter 13, Developing Database Backup and Recovery Solutions.)

> **N O T E**   An identity column value is generated only once. Once the value has been generated, even if a **ROLLBACK** statement is performed, it will not be generated again.

Now let's review another example, this time creating the same table *product* with the **GENERATED BY DEFAULT** clause.

```
CREATE TABLE product (
       productno   INTEGER GENERATED BY DEFAULT AS
                           IDENTITY (START WITH 200 INCREMENT BY 1),
       description VARCHAR(50) )
```

Next, we insert a few rows.

```
INSERT INTO product VALUES (DEFAULT,'banana');        --->inserts 200,banana
INSERT INTO product (description) VALUES ('apple');   --->inserts 201,apple
INSERT INTO product VALUES (300,'pear');              --->inserts 300,pear
INSERT INTO product VALUES (201,'orange');            --->inserts 201,orange
COMMIT;
INSERT INTO product (description) VALUES ('papaya');  --->inserts 202,papaya
ROLLBACK;
INSERT INTO product (description) VALUES ('plum');    --->inserts 203,plum
COMMIT;
```

The following query shows the final result.

```
SELECT * FROM product

PRODUCTNO   DESCRIPTION
----------- ---------------------
        200 banana
        201 apple
        300 pear
        201 orange
        203 plum
```

The first two **INSERT** statements show that two identity column values were generated: 200 and 201. For the third and fourth **INSERT** statements, we explicitly provided the values 300 and 201, respectively, for the identity column. Note that DB2 did not return an error as in the previous example because we defined the identity column as **GENERATED BY DEFAULT**. After the fourth **INSERT** statement, we issue a **COMMIT** to guarantee these rows are stored in the database. The fifth **INSERT** statement causes another identity column value, 202, to be generated; however, we issue a **ROLLBACK** statement right after, so this row is not stored in the database. Note that the final **INSERT** statement, which inserts the product plum, generates a value of 203, not 202.

The following final example illustrates a **GENERATED** value, which is not an identity column. The example uses **GENERATED ALWAYS**, but you can also use **GENERATED BY DEFAULT**.

```
CREATE TABLE income (
  empno     INTEGER,
  salary    INTEGER,
  taxRate   DECIMAL(5,2),
  netSalary DECIMAL(7,2) GENERATED ALWAYS AS (salary * (1 - taxRate))
)
```

If you insert the following row:

```
INSERT INTO income (empno, salary, taxRate) VALUES (111, 50000, 0.3)
```

The result is:

```
EMPNO        SALARY      TAXRATE NETSALARY
----------- ----------- ------- ---------
        111       50000    0.30  35000.00
```

DB2 generates the value of the last column *NETSALARY* based on the *SALARY* and *TAXRATE* columns.

7.8.7 Constraints

Constraints allow you to create rules for the data in your tables. You can define four types of constraints on a table.

- A **unique** constraint ensures that no duplicate key values can be entered in the table.
- A **referential** constraint ensures that a value in one table must have a corresponding entry in a related table.
- A **check** constraint ensures that the values you enter into the column are within the rules specified when the table was defined.
- An **informational** constraint allows you to enforce or not enforce a constraint.

These constraints are discussed further in the following sections.

7.8.7.1 Unique Constraints

A unique constraint indicates that the values for a given column must all be unique. A unique constraint is defined in the **CREATE TABLE** or **ALTER TABLE** statements using the **UNIQUE** clause or the **PRIMARY KEY** clause. A primary key, as you will see in the next section, is also a unique constraint.

All the columns that make up a unique constraint must be defined as NOT NULL. For the following example, the column *empID* must be defined as NOT NULL because it is the primary key. The column *deptID* must also be defined as NOT NULL because it is a unique constraint.

```
CREATE TABLE employ (
      empID   INT        NOT NULL PRIMARY KEY,
      name    CHAR(30)   ,
      deptID  INT        NOT NULL UNIQUE
      )
```

Now, let's perform a few **INSERT** statements in sequence.

```
INSERT INTO employ VALUES (111, 'Peter', 999)   ---> inserts 111, Peter, 999
INSERT INTO employ VALUES (111, 'Peter', 123)   ---> SQL0803N error, duplicate primary key 111
INSERT INTO employ VALUES (789, 'Peter', 999)   ---> SQL0803N error, duplicate unique key 999
```

This example illustrates that an error (SQL0803N) occurs if the value you attempt to insert for a unique or primary key column is not unique (it already exists in the table).

Unique constraints are implemented using unique indexes. When a **CREATE TABLE** statement has the **UNIQUE** or **PRIMARY KEY** keywords, DB2 automatically creates a corresponding unique index. The name of this system-generated index starts with "SQL" followed by a time-stamp. For the example just shown, two unique indexes were generated with these names:

```
SQL040422135806320
SQL040422135806460
```

Both indexes were created on April 22, 2004, at 1:58 p.m.

Though you would normally not refer to an index name directly in an application, a good index name may be helpful when analyzing an **explain** output. An explain output, as you will see in Chapter 16, Database Performance Considerations, displays the access path DB2 chooses to access your data for a given query. Therefore, rather than letting DB2 generate system names for your indexes, we recommend using the **ALTER TABLE** statement in the case of primary key columns and the **CONSTRAINT** clause to explicitly give names to the indexes. For example, let's rewrite the **CREATE TABLE** statement used in the previous example as follows:

```
CREATE TABLE employ (
      empID    INT       NOT NULL,
      name     CHAR(30)  ,
      deptID   INT       NOT NULL CONSTRAINT unique_dept_const UNIQUE
      )

ALTER TABLE employ ADD CONSTRAINT employ_pk PRIMARY KEY (empID)
```

In this example, we removed the **PRIMARY KEY** clause of the **CREATE TABLE** statement and added an **ALTER TABLE** statement. The **ALTER TABLE** statement allowed us to put in a name for the constraint (*employ_pk*), which also becomes the name of the corresponding unique index.

Instead of the **ALTER TABLE** statement, you can also use the following two statements with the same result:

```
CREATE UNIQUE INDEX employ_pk ON employ (empID)
ALTER TABLE employ ADD PRIMARY KEY (empID)
```

In this case, the **CREATE UNIQUE** statement explicitly creates the unique index and specifies the desired name for the index. Next, the **ALTER TABLE** statement indicates that the same column used for the unique index is also used as the primary key. After executing the **ALTER TABLE** statement, you will receive this warning message:

```
SQL0598W  Existing index "EMPLOY_PK" is used as the index for the
primary key or a unique key. SQLSTATE=01550
```

This warning is acceptable because this is in fact what is desired.

In the previous **CREATE TABLE** statement, we also added a unique constraint using the clause **CONSTRAINT unique_dept_const UNIQUE**. With this clause, DB2 generates a corresponding unique index with the name *unique_dept_const*.

You can also use the **ALTER TABLE** statement to add a unique constraint, as shown in this example:

```
ALTER TABLE employ ADD CONSTRAINT unique_dept_const UNIQUE (deptID)
```

7.8.7.2 Referential Constraints

Referential constraints are used to support **referential integrity**. Referential integrity allows your database to manage relationships between tables.

7.8.7.2.1 Using Primary, Unique, and Foreign Keys to Establish Referential Integrity

Referential integrity can be better explained with examples. Assume you have two tables, as illustrated in Figure 7.13.

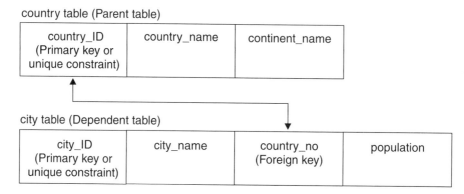

Figure 7.13   Referential integrity between two tables

The figure shows the tables *country* and *city,* where *country* is the parent table containing information about all the countries in the world, and *city* is the dependent table containing information about a particular city for a given country. Note that the column *country_ID* and the column *country_no* are used to establish a relationship between the two tables.

The *country_ID* column is a primary key column. A primary key consists of one or more columns; it is a special case of a unique constraint. While there can be many unique constraints in a table, there can be only one primary key. A primary key is used to establish a referential integrity relationship with another table.

The *country_no* column, known as the foreign key column, will reference the primary key column of the parent table. Because of this relationship, the *country_no* column cannot have a value that does not exist in the *country_ID* column. The data type for this column must be compatible with the primary key column of the parent table. For the example illustrated in Figure 7.13, if the parent key column is defined as type INTEGER, the foreign key column can be defined as type DECIMAL because it is a numeric data type for which conversion is allowed; however, it cannot be defined as type CHAR. Other than this restriction, the foreign key can be treated like any other column. It can use the **NOT NULL**, **UNIQUE**, and even **PRIMARY KEY** clauses.

To establish the referential integrity relationship between the two tables, let's look at the corresponding **CREATE TABLE** statements for both tables.

```
CREATE TABLE country (
        country_ID      INT            NOT NULL PRIMARY KEY,
        country_Name    VARCHAR(30)    NOT NULL,
        continent_Name  CHAR(15)
        )

CREATE TABLE city (
        city_ID         INT            NOT NULL PRIMARY KEY,
        city_name       VARCHAR(30)    NOT NULL,
        country_no      INT            REFERENCES country,
        population      INT
        )
```

Note that the **CREATE TABLE** statement for the *city* table includes the **REFERENCES** clause and that it does not need to specify any column of the parent table *country*. DB2 will automatically look for the primary key column of the parent table to establish the relationship.

What if there is no primary key column for the parent table but a unique constraint instead? What if the parent table contains more than one unique constraint? In such cases, use the **REFERENCES** clause followed by the correct column name(s). For example, let's say we actually created the *country* table in Figure 7.13 with no primary key but two unique constraints, as follows.

```
CREATE TABLE country (
        country_ID      INT            NOT NULL UNIQUE,
        country_Name    VARCHAR(30)    NOT NULL,
        continent_Name  CHAR(15)       NOT NULL UNIQUE
        )
```

To establish referential integrity using the column *country_ID*, this column must be specified in the **CREATE TABLE** statement for the *city* table, as shown below.

```
CREATE TABLE city (
        city_ID         INT            NOT NULL PRIMARY KEY,
        city_name       VARCHAR(30)    NOT NULL,
        country_no      INT            REFERENCES country(country_ID),
        population      INT
        )
```

> **N O T E** A unique constraint on a column that has been defined as NOT NULL can also be referenced by a foreign key clause because a primary key is basically the same as a unique constraint.

You can also use the **ALTER TABLE** statement to add a foreign key, for example:

```
ALTER TABLE city
        ADD FOREIGN KEY (country_no) REFERENCES country (country_ID)
```

This statement would add to the table *city* the foreign key using column *country_no*, which would reference column *country_ID* in table *country*.

> **NOTE**   Using primary keys, unique keys, and foreign keys is one method to implement referential integrity. Another method is to use triggers. By using triggers, you can code your own logic that may differ from the rules described in this section. Triggers are discussed in section 7.13.

7.8.7.2.2 Referential Integrity Implications on SQL Operations

The enforcement of referential integrity has implications on **INSERT**, **UPDATE**, and **DELETE** operations, which must follow certain rules. To explain these rules, let's look at the following example using Figure 7.14.

country table (Parent table)

country_ID (Primary key or unique constraint)	country_name	continent_name
1	Canada	North America

city table (Dependent table)

city_ID (Primary key or unique constraint)	city_name	country_no (Foreign key)	population
11	Toronto	1	8,000,000
22	Montreal	1	6,000,000
33	Calgary	1	5,000,000

district table (Dependent table)

district_ID (Primary key or unique constraint)	district_name	city_no (Foreign key)	registrations
111	North York	11	300
222	Markham	11	900

Figure 7.14   An example to illustrate SQL operations under referential integrity

We used the first two tables, *country* and *city*, in previous examples. In this particular example, we have inserted a few records in each of these tables. A new table, *district*, which is dependent on table *city*, is also illustrated. Here is the **CREATE TABLE** statement for the table *district*.

```
CREATE TABLE district (
        district_ID     INT          NOT NULL PRIMARY KEY,
        district_name   VARCHAR(30)  NOT NULL,
        city_no         INT          REFERENCES city,
        registrations   INT
        )
```

The following cases are examined.

Inserting to a Parent Table

What would happen if the following record were inserted in table *country*?

```
INSERT INTO country  VALUES (2,'Spain',4)
```

Because *country* is the parent table at the top of Figure 7.14, any value can be inserted into this table without a need to worry about the dependent tables.

Inserting to a Dependent Table

What would happen if the following record were inserted in table *city*?

```
INSERT INTO city     VALUES (44,'Vancouver',3,4000000)
```

Table *city* is dependent on table *country* based on column *country_no* (the third column in the *city* table). This **INSERT** statement is trying to insert a record with a value of 3 for the *country_no* column. From Figure 7.14 you can see this value is not present in table *country*; therefore, this record cannot be inserted and an error would be returned.

Deleting a Row from the Parent Table

What would happen if the following record were deleted from table *country*?

```
DELETE FROM country WHERE country_name = 'Canada'
```

This **DELETE** statement would fail with an error SQL0532N because there are related dependent rows. This is the default behavior, also called the **NO ACTION** delete rule.

You can specify **DELETE** rules in the **CREATE TABLE** statement of the dependent table. In addition to **NO ACTION**, you can use the following rules.

- **RESTRICT**: The behavior is exactly the same as the **NO ACTION** rule. The difference is when this constraint is enforced. For more details, refer to the *DB2 UDB SQL Reference* manual.
- **CASCADE**: All the dependent rows will be deleted when the parent table row is deleted.
- **SET NULL**: All the dependent rows will have the value of the foreign key column set to NULL, if NULLs are allowed; otherwise, an error is returned. All the other columns remain unchanged.

For example, let's say we actually created the table *city* as follows.

```
CREATE TABLE city (
        city_ID         INT              NOT NULL PRIMARY KEY,
        city_name       VARCHAR(30)      NOT NULL,
        country_no      INT              REFERENCES country(country_ID)
                                         ON DELETE CASCADE,
        population      INT
        )
```

Note that we added the clause **ON DELETE CASCADE** to the foreign key column *country_no*.

If we execute the following statement again, will it work this time?

```
DELETE FROM country WHERE country_name = 'Canada'
```

The answer is no. Though we defined the **CASCADE** rule correctly in the *city* table, we did not define it in the *district* table. All dependent tables need to be defined using **CASCADE** if you want all the dependent rows to be deleted. In this example, if we had defined the *district* table correctly, all the rows of all the tables would have been deleted.

Deleting a Row from a Dependent Table

You can delete a row from a dependent table with no implications unless the dependent table is the parent table of another table.

Updating a Row from the Parent Table

You cannot update the primary key of the parent table. To ensure you don't duplicate an existing value, DB2 does not allow this operation.

Updating a Row from a Dependent Table

You can update the foreign key of a dependent table only if the new value already exists in the parent table and the foreign key is defined as **NOT NULL**. This is the default behavior, which corresponds to the **NO ACTION** update rule.

For example, issuing this statement:

```
UPDATE city SET country_no = 7 WHERE city_name = 'Montreal'
```

would return error SQL0530N, which indicates the value of 7 does not exist in the parent table.

The other **UPDATE** rule possible is **RESTRICT**, which behaves similarly to the **NO ACTION** rule. The difference is when the rule enforcement takes place. For details about this rule, please review the *DB2 UDB SQL Reference* manual.

You can specify **UPDATE** rules on the **CREATE TABLE** statement of a dependent table. For example, we could have created the *city* table as follows (on top of the **DELETE** rules of the previous example).

```
CREATE TABLE city (
        city_ID         INT              NOT NULL PRIMARY KEY,
        city_name       VARCHAR(30)      NOT NULL,
```

```
        country_no      INT              REFERENCES country(country_ID)
                                         ON DELETE CASCADE
                                         ON UPDATE RESTRICT,

        population      INT
)
```

7.8.7.3 Check Constraints

Check constraints are used to enforce data integrity at the table level. Once the check constraint is defined, every **INSERT** or **UPDATE** operation must satisfy the constraint; otherwise, you will receive an error. For example, let's create the table *student*.

```
CREATE TABLE student (
        student_ID      INT              NOT NULL PRIMARY KEY,
        name            VARCHAR(30)      NOT NULL,
        sex             CHAR(1)          NOT NULL
        CONSTRAINT sex_check_const CHECK (sex in ('M ', 'F '))
        )
```

This table has the check constraint *sex_check_const* defined which verifies that the column *sex* has the values of M or F. Now let's attempt the following statement.

```
INSERT INTO student VALUES (1, 'Tom', 'Z')
```

We will receive an error SQL0545N because the value Z does not satisfy the check constraint.

You can also add a check constraint with the **ALTER TABLE** statement, as shown here.

```
ALTER TABLE student
     ADD CONSTRAINT sex_check_const CHECK (sex in ('M ', 'F '))
```

If you are adding a check constraint with the **ALTER TABLE** statement to a table that already has data, DB2 will check the entire table to make sure the existing data satisfies the check constraint. If it doesn't, the **ALTER TABLE** statement will fail with error SQL0544N.

If you do not want DB2 to check the table when a check constraint is added, you can use the **SET INTEGRITY** statement. This statement turns off check constraint and referential constraint checking. For example, let's say we create the *student* table without a check constraint and insert some rows that will later be invalid for the check constraint.

```
CREATE TABLE student (
        student_ID      INT              NOT NULL PRIMARY KEY,
        name            VARCHAR(30)      NOT NULL,
        sex             CHAR(1)          NOT NULL
        )

INSERT INTO student VALUES (1, 'Tom',  'Z')
INSERT INTO student VALUES (2, 'Mary', 'A')
```

Now we attempt to add the following check constraint.

```
ALTER TABLE student
     ADD CONSTRAINT sex_check_const CHECK (sex in ('M ', 'F '))
```

You receive error SQL0544N, as indicated earlier. Thus, use the **SET INTEGRITY** command to turn off constraint checking so that you can add the constraint.

```
SET INTEGRITY FOR student OFF
```

At this point, the *student* table is put in CHECK PENDING state, a state that allows only a few operations on the table, like **ALTER TABLE**. Other operations such as **SELECT**, **INSERT**, **UPDATE**, and **DELETE** are disallowed.

After turning off constraint checking, you can repeat the **ALTER TABLE** statement, which this time should be successful. Use the **SET INTEGRITY** statement again to turn constraint checking on as follows:

```
SET INTEGRITY FOR student CHECK IMMEDIATE UNCHECKED
```

The **IMMEDIATE UNCHECKED** option turns on check constraints again but does not check the existing table data. Alternatively, you can also issue:

```
SET INTEGRITY FOR student IMMEDIATE CHECKED
```

In this case, the **IMMEDIATE CHECKED** option turns on check constraints again and also checks the existing table data. If a violation is encountered, the table will remain in CHECK PENDING state. The **SET INTEGRITY** statement has an option to move the violating records to an exception table.

```
SET INTEGRITY FOR student IMMEDIATE CHECKED
    FOR EXCEPTION IN student USE my_exception_table
```

The name of the exception table in this example is *my_exception_table*. This table must exist with at least the same columns as the original source table, in this case, the *student* table. After this **SET INTEGRITY** statement is executed, the violating rows would be moved to the exception table, and the CHECK PENDING status would be removed. For more details about the **SET INTEGRITY** statement, refer to the *DB2 UDB SQL Reference* manual.

7.8.7.4 Informational Constraints

Prior to Version 8.1, DB2 always enforced constraints once you defined them. Though you can turn constraint checking off with the **SET INTEGRITY** statement, this is mainly used to perform table alterations to add new constraints to existing tables, as you saw in the previous section. Using the **SET INTEGRITY** statement puts your table in CHECK PENDING status, which prevents you from performing many operations on your table.

What if your application already performs constraint checking, and thus there is no need for DB2 to check the data again? For example, large applications such as SAP, PeopleSoft, and Siebel are written to check the constraints before they insert the data into DB2. In this case, defining the constraint in DB2 would cause extra overhead if DB2 is also enforcing the rule and revalidating the constraint. However, if you do not define these constraints, the DB2 optimizer cannot use them to its advantage in choosing the most optimal access plans. (Chapter 16, Database Performance Considerations, explains the DB2 optimizer in more detail.)

With Version 8.1, informational constraints were introduced. Informational constraints allow you to spccify whether or not DB2 should enforce the constraint and whether or not it can be used by the optimizer to choose the best access plan for the application statements.

The default operation when you create a constraint is that it is always enforced and can be used by the optimizer. You can change this default behavior by using informational constraints, which are implemented by using the following clauses of the **CREATE TABLE** statement.

- **ENFORCED**: This is the default option. Use this clause if you want DB2 to check the constraints for every operation on the table.
- **NOT ENFORCED**: Use this clause if you do not want DB2 to check the constraints for every operation on the table.
- **ENABLE QUERY OPTIMIZATION**: Use this clause so that DB2 can use the knowledge of the constraint when building the plan for accessing the table or referenced tables.
- **DISABLE QUERY OPTIMIZATION**: Use this clause if you want the DB2 optimizer to ignore the constraints defined on your table.

The following example illustrates how informational constraints work.

```
CREATE TABLE student (
        student_ID      INT             NOT NULL PRIMARY KEY,
        name            VARCHAR(30)     NOT NULL,
        sex             CHAR(1)         NOT NULL
        CONSTRAINT sex_check_const CHECK (sex in ('M ', 'F '))
        NOT ENFORCED
        ENABLE QUERY OPTIMIZATION
        )
```

Note that the constraint for table *student* will not be enforced, but the constraint is used for query optimization. Now let's perform the following statements.

```
(1)  INSERT INTO student VALUES (5, 'John', 'T')
(2)  SELECT * FROM student WHERE sex = 'T'
```

The first statement executes successfully—a T can be inserted for the *sex* column because the constraint *sex_check_const* is not enforced.

The second statement returns zero records because query optimization is enabled. Therefore, the optimizer does not scan the table but checks the constraints defined for the *sex* column in the DB2 catalog tables and assumes it has only values of M or F, quickly returning a result of zero records. Of course, this result is incorrect. If you want to obtain the correct result, disable query optimization. You can do this with the **ALTER TABLE** statement:

```
ALTER TABLE student
     ALTER CHECK sex_check_const DISABLE QUERY OPTIMIZATION
```

If you perform the second statement again, this time you should get one record.

```
SELECT * FROM student WHERE sex = 'T'

STUDENT_ID  NAME                               SEX
----------- ---------------------------------- ---
          5 John                               T
```

> **N O T E**   After issuing the **ALTER TABLE** statement to enable or
> disable query optimization, make sure to issue a **terminate** com-
> mand if working from the CLP so the change will take effect.

> **N O T E**   Use informational constraints only if you are certain the
> data to be inserted or updated has been correctly checked by your
> application. Normally you want to use the options **NOT ENFORCED**
> and **ENABLE QUERY OPTIMIZATION** together because you want
> DB2 to reduce overhead by not performing constraint checking, but
> having the DB2 optimizer take into account the constraint definition.

7.8.8 Not Logged Initially Tables

The **NOT LOGGED INITIALLY** clause of the **CREATE TABLE** statement allows you to create a
table that will not be logged when an **INSERT**, **UPDATE**, **DELETE**, **CREATE INDEX**, **ALTER
TABLE**, or **DROP INDEX** operation is performed in the same unit of work in which the **CREATE
TABLE** statement was issued. For example, let's say you execute the following statements in a
script.

```
CREATE TABLE products (
       productID    INT,
       product_Name VARCHAR(30)
       )
       NOT LOGGED INITIALLY;

INSERT INTO products VALUES (1,'door');
INSERT INTO products VALUES (2,'window');
...
INSERT INTO products VALUES (999999,'telephone');

COMMIT;

INSERT INTO products VALUES (1000000,'television');
UPDATE products SET product_name = 'radio' where productID = 3456;

ALTER TABLE products ACTIVATE NOT LOGGED INITIALLY

INSERT INTO products VALUES (1000001,'desk');
INSERT INTO products VALUES (1000002,'table');
...
INSERT INTO products VALUES (1999999,'chair');

COMMIT;
```

Any operation from the **CREATE TABLE** statement until the first **COMMIT** is not logged. Once
the **COMMIT** is issued, any subsequent operation is logged. For this example, the **INSERT** and
UPDATE statements after the first **COMMIT** are logged.

After creating the table as **NOT LOGGED INITIALLY**, if you would like to turn off logging temporarily again, you can use the **ALTER TABLE** statement with the **ACTIVATE NOT LOGGED INITIALLY** clause, as shown in the example. Any operations between the **ALTER TABLE** and the second **COMMIT** are not logged.

> **N O T E**   You can use the statement **ALTER TABLE** *table_name*
> **ACTIVATE NOT LOGGED INITIALLY** only for tables that were
> originally created with the **NOT LOGGED INITALLY** clause.

You can also use the **WITH EMPTY TABLE** clause as part of the **ALTER TABLE** *table_name* **ACTIVATE NOT LOGGED INITIALLY** statement to remove all the data of the table. This method is faster than using a **DELETE FROM** *table_name* statement. For example, to remove all the rows of the table *products*, issue:

```
ALTER TABLE products ACTIVATE NOT LOGGED INITIALLY WITH EMPTY TABLE
```

7.8.9 Table Compression

You can compress tables to a certain extent by using the **VALUE COMPRESSION** clause of the **CREATE TABLE** statement. This clause tells DB2 that it can use a different internal format for the table rows so they occupy less space. In a sense, this clause turns on compression for the table; however, you need to specify another clause, **COMPRESS SYSTEM DEFAULT**, for each column that you want to compress. Only the columns whose values are normally NULL or the system default value of 0 can be compressed. Also, the data type must not be DATE, TIME, or TIMESTAMP. If the data type is a varying-length string, this clause is ignored. Here's an example:

```
CREATE TABLE company (
     company_ID    INTEGER    NOT NULL PRIMARY KEY,
     name          CHAR(10),
     address       VARCHAR(30)          COMPRESS SYSTEM DEFAULT,
     no_employees  INTEGER    NOT NULL COMPRESS SYSTEM DEFAULT
     )
       VALUE COMPRESSION
```

The column *address* would be ignored since it's a VARCHAR column, and the column *no_employees* would be compressed. Table compression saves space especially for tables used in data warehousing applications where many rows contain NULLs or the system default value of 0. However, **UPDATE** operations may be impacted when changing to a different value than the default of 0 because the compressed value would first have to be expanded and then updated.

For an existing table containing data, you can enable table compression using the **ALTER TABLE** statement, as shown in this example.

```
ALTER TABLE city ACTIVATE VALUE COMPRESSION

ALTER TABLE city
     ALTER COLUMN population COMPRESS SYSTEM DEFAULT
```

In this example, we enable compression by using the first statement, and then we specify which column to compress by using the second statement. In addition, if the table *city* were populated, the **REORG** utility would have to be executed on the table for the compression to take effect on the existing rows. Chapter 12, Maintaining Data, discusses the **REORG** utility in more detail.

7.8.10 Materialized Query Tables and Summary Tables

Materialized query tables (MQTs) allow users to create tables with data based on the results of a query. The DB2 optimizer can later use these tables to determine whether a query can best be served by accessing an MQT instead of the base tables. Here is an example of an MQT:

```
CREATE SUMMARY TABLE my_summary
          AS  (SELECT  city_name, population
                  FROM country A, city B
                  WHERE  A.country_id = B.country_no)
          DATA INITIALLY DEFERRED
          REFRESH DEFERRED
```

The **SUMMARY** keyword is optional. The **DATA INITIALLY DEFERRED** clause indicates that DB2 will not immediately populate the *my_summary* MQT table after creation, but following the **REFRESH TABLE** statement:

```
REFRESH TABLE my_summary
```

The **REFRESH DEFERRED** clause in the **CREATE SUMMARY TABLE** statement indicates that the data in the table is refreshed only when you explicitly issue a **REFRESH TABLE** statement. Alternatively, you can create the MQT with the **REFRESH IMMEDIATE** clause, which means DB2 immediately refreshes the data when the base tables are changed.

DB2 checks the registry variable *CURRENT REFRESH AGE* to determine whether or not the MQT contains up-to-date information. This registry can have a value from 0 up to 99999999999999 (9,999 years, 99 months, 99 days, 99 hours, 99 minutes, and 99 seconds), which indicates the maximum duration the DB2 optimizer can wait since the last **REFRESH TABLE** statement was issued on an MQT to consider MQT tables in its calculations. For example, if an MQT were refreshed today, and the *CURRENT REFRESH AGE* has a value of 5 days, the DB2 optimizer can consider the MQT for its calculations for the next 5 days. If the value of this register is 0, only the tables created with the **REFRESH IMMEDIATE** clause can be used for optimization.

Prior to Version 8, MQTs were known as automatic summary tables (ASTs). With Version 8, ASTs are considered a special case of MQTs whose fullselect contains a **GROUP BY** clause summarizing data from the tables referenced in the fullselect.

7.8.11 Temporary Tables

Temporary tables can be classified as system or user tables. DB2 manages system temporary tables in the system temporary table space. DB2 creates and drops these tables automatically. Since users don't have control over system temporary tables, we don't discuss them any further in this section.

You create user temporary tables inside a user temporary table space. For example, the following statement creates a user temporary table space called *usrtmp4k*.

```
CREATE USER TEMPORARY TABLESPACE usrtmp4k
     MANAGED BY SYSTEM USING ('C:\usrtmp')
```

User temporary tables, referred to as temporary tables from here on, store temporary data, that is, data that will be destroyed after a session or when a connection ends. Temporary tables are typically used in situations where you need to compute a large result set from an operation, and you need to store the result set temporarily to continue with further processing.

Though transaction logging is allowed with temporary tables, most users don't need to log temporary data. In fact, not having transaction logging for this type of table improves performance.

Temporary tables exist only for one connection; therefore, there are no concurrency or locking issues.

To create a temporary table, use the **DECLARE** statement. Here's an example.

```
DECLARE GLOBAL TEMPORARY TABLE temp_table1 (col1 int, col2 int)
   ON COMMIT PRESERVE ROWS
   NOT LOGGED
   IN  usrtmp4k
```

Table *temp_table1* is created in *usrtmp4k*, the user temporary table space we created earlier.

DB2 uses the schema *session* for all temporary tables regardless of the user ID connected to the database. After you create a temporary table, you can access it just like any regular table. The following statement inserts a row into table *temp_table1*.

```
INSERT INTO session.temp_table1 (1,2)
```

The following statement selects all the rows in table *temp_table1*:

```
SELECT * FROM session.temp_table1
```

You can drop and alter temporary tables, but you cannot create views or triggers against them. Indexes are allowed.

> **NOTE** When working with temporary tables, make sure to explicitly specify the schema *session*. If you work with objects without specifying the schema, DB2 defaults to the authorization ID or connection ID.

7.9 INDEXES

Indexes are database objects that are built based on one or more columns of a table. They are used for two main reasons:

- To improve query performance because they can access the data faster with direct access to rows based on their key values
- To guarantee uniqueness when defined as unique

7.9.1 Working with Indexes

To create an index, use the **CREATE INDEX** statement. This statement requires at a minimum:

- The name of the index
- The name of the associated table
- The columns that make up the index (also known as index keys)

In addition, you can specify the following:

- Whether the index is unique (enforce uniqueness for the key values) or non-unique (allow duplicates)
- Which order DB2 should use to build and maintain the key values: ascending (**ASC**, the default) or descending (**DESC**) order
- Whether bi-directional scans of the index are allowed (**ALLOW REVERSE SCANS**)
- Whether to create **INCLUDE** columns that are not part of the index key but are columns often retrieved by your queries

For example, let's consider the following statement.

```
CREATE UNIQUE INDEX company_ix
      ON company (company_ID ASC, name DESC)
      INCLUDE (no_employees)
      ALLOW REVERSE SCANS
```

This statement creates a unique index *company_ix*. This index is associated to the table *company* based on the column *company_ID* in ascending order and *name* in descending order. Bi-directional scans are allowed because we specified **ALLOW REVERSE SCANS**. If this is not specified and the index needs to be traversed in opposite direction, the index cannot be used; a sort will be required. In addition, an **INCLUDE** column *no_employees* was added to the index definition. This column does not belong to the index key, that is, the index will not be built and maintained taking this column into consideration. Instead, an **INCLUDE** column is useful for performance reasons. Assuming the users of table *company* often retrieve the *no_employees* column, without the **INCLUDE** column, DB2 would first have to access the index page and then the data page. Rather than performing two access operations, why not add the desired column in the index?

> **N O T E**   **INCLUDE** columns in an index can improve performance at the cost of having a larger index. The effect of adding an **INCLUDE** column versus including the column as part of the index key is the same; however, the maintenance cost of updating **INCLUDE** columns is less than that of updating key columns.

Now let's consider another example that shows how an index looks. The following statement was used to create a table containing the sales records of a company.

```
CREATE TABLE sales (
      sales_person      VARCHAR(30)    NOT NULL,
      region            CHAR(5)        NOT NULL,
```

```
number_of_sales   INT           NOT NULL,
year              INT
)
```

Figure 7.15 illustrates the contents of this table.

sales_person	region	number_of_ sales	year
Mary	South	10	2002
John	North	9	2000
Sam	North	8	2000
Mary	East	12	2001
John	West	13	2001
Sam	South	12	2001
Mary	West	15	2002
Sam	South	15	2002
Mary	East	12	2002
John	West	12	2000
Sam	North	14	2001
John	South	21	2002

Figure 7.15   The *sales* table

Let's define an index on the *sales_person* column of the *sales* table using the following **CREATE INDEX** statement.

```
CREATE INDEX index1 ON sales (sales_person)
```

When DB2 builds the index *index1*, it creates pointers to the data pages of each record in the table. Each record is identified by a record ID (RID). An index on the *sales_person* column is shown in Figure 7.16.

Rows are stored on physical disks, and disks are divided into extents. An **extent** contains a fixed number of pages. We will talk about pages and extents in detail in Chapter 8, The DB2 Storage Model. For now, we will treat extents as portions of the disk.

Let's say you issue the following query:

```
SELECT * FROM sales WHERE sales_person = 'Sam'
```

For this query, DB2 would use index *index1,* and as you can see from Figure 7.16, it would follow the pointers to extents 1, 2, 4, and 5; all of these extents have a data page with a record where the salesperson is Sam. An index gives you a direct access to the records you are looking for. Without an index, DB2 may scan all the data pages in all the extents for the table. This operation is known as a **table scan,** and for very large tables, it can be a very expensive operation.

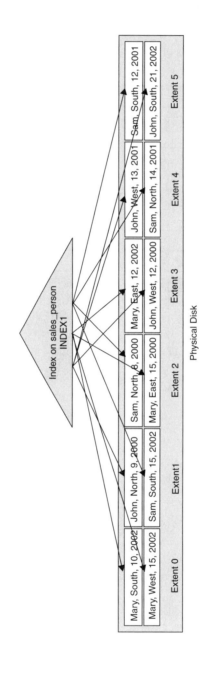

Figure 7.16   An index defined on the *sales_person* column

Once an index has been created, it cannot be modified. To add or remove a key column from the index, you must drop and recreate the index. To drop an index, use the **DROP INDEX** statement. For example:

```
DROP INDEX index1
```

> **N O T E**   An index automatically created by the database manager when a primary key or unique constraint was defined cannot be dropped with the **DROP INDEX** statement. To drop these indexes, use the **ALTER TABLE** statement with the **DROP PRIMARY KEY** or **DROP UNIQUE** *constraint_name* clauses, respectively.

Indexes can improve query performance considerably; however, the more indexes you define on a table, the more the cost incurred when updating the table because the indexes will also need to be updated. The larger you define the size of an index (based on the number of key columns and their columns sizes), the more the cost to update the index. Choose your indexes wisely.

The Index Advisor, part of the Design Advisor tool, can recommend indexes for you based on a specific query or a set of queries. You can launch the Design Advisor from the Control Center by choosing a given database, right-clicking on it, and choosing Design Advisor. You can also invoke the Index Advisor directly from the command line by using the **db2advis** command.

7.9.2 Clustering Indexes

In the example in section 7.9.1, Working with Indexes, you saw that index *index1* (based on the *sales_person* column) improved query performance over table scans. However, because the data pages for the corresponding records were spread across different extents, several I/O requests to the disk were required. Would it not be more efficient to keep all of the desired data pages clustered together on the same extent?

You can achieve this by using a clustering index. A **clustering index** is created so that the index pages physically map to the data pages. That is, all the records that have the same index key are physically close together. Figure 7.17 illustrates how *index1* works when created as a clustering index using the **CLUSTER** clause as follows.

```
CREATE INDEX index1 ON sales (sales_person) CLUSTER
```

In the figure, when you issue this query:

```
SELECT * FROM sales WHERE sales_person = 'Sam'
```

DB2 would still use index *index1* but it requires less I/O access to the disk because the desired data pages are clustered together on extents 4 and 5.

> **N O T E**   There can be only one clustering index per table.

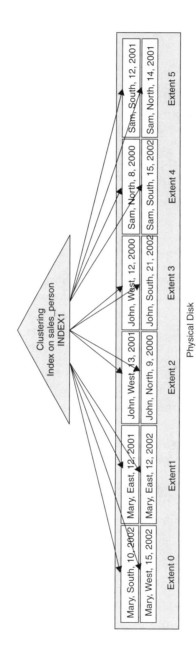

Figure 7.17 A clustering index on the *sales_person* column

290

7.10 MULTIDIMENSIONAL CLUSTERING TABLES AND BLOCK INDEXES

Multidimensional clustering (MDC), as its name implies, allows for clustering of the physical data pages in multiple dimensions. For example, using the *sales* table illustrated previously in Figure 7.15, you can cluster the data based on two dimensions: *sales_person* and *year* columns. This method of clustering has several benefits over clustering indexes.

- With MDC, the data pages are physically clustered by several dimensions simultaneously. With clustering indexes, only one cluster index is allowed per table; the other indexes in the table are unclustered.
- MDC guarantees clustering over time even though frequent **INSERT** operations are performed. Thus, less maintenance and overhead is required. With clustering indexes, this is not the case. As data pages are filled up, a clustered **INSERT** operation may encounter that the row to insert does not fit the right page to maintain the clustering of the data. In such cases, the row may end up on a page that is not close to the other related rows. Clustering indexes require an administrator to perform periodic table reorganizations to recluster the table and set up pages with additional free space to accommodate future clustered **INSERT** requests.
- MDC uses **block indexes**, indexes that point to an entire block of pages. These are smaller indexes than regular and clustering indexes, which point to a single record.

> **N O T E**   MDC is primarily intended for data warehousing environments; however, it can also work in online transaction processing (OLTP) environments.

7.10.1 MDC Tables

Let's redefine our *sales* table as an MDC table, using dimensions *sales_person* and *year*.

```
CREATE TABLE sales (
      sales_person      VARCHAR(30)   NOT NULL,
      region            CHAR(5)       NOT NULL,
      number_of_sales   INT           NOT NULL,
      year              INT
      )
ORGANIZE BY DIMENSIONS (sales_person, year)
```

DB2 places records that have the same *sales_person* and *year* values in physical locations that are close together as they are inserted into the table. These locations are called **blocks**. A block can be treated as an extent. The size of an extent can be defined in the **CREATE TABLESPACE** statement. The minimum size for a block is two pages, like extents.

Figure 7.18 illustrates the contents of the *sales* table using the new MDC definition. For simplicity, in this example a block can hold only two records.

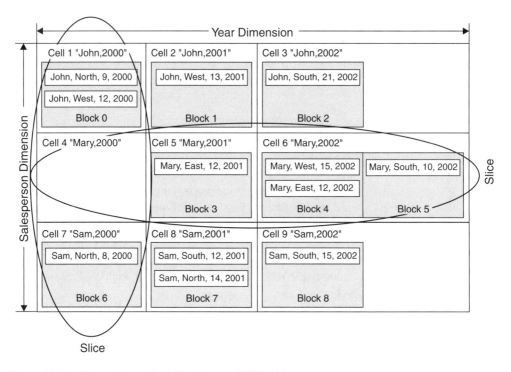

Figure 7.18   The *sales* table defined as an MDC table

The figure shows this MDC table is physically organized such that records having the same *year* and s*ales_person* values are grouped together into separate blocks. For example, all records in block 0 have s*ales_person* = John and *year* = 2000. All records in block 4 have *sales_person* = Mary and *year* = 2002.

When a block is filled, DB2 will allocate a new block or reuse an old block for the new records inserted. In Figure 7.18, block 4 was filled, and thus block 5 had to be created.

Blocks that have the same dimension values are grouped into **cells**. Each cell represents a unique combination of the dimension values. If there are X different values for *sales_person*, and Y different values for y*ear*, there are X*Y number of cells. In Figure 7.18, you see the table *sales* has three values for dimension *sales_person*, namely, John, Mary, and Sam. It also has three values for dimension *year*, namely, 2000, 2001, and 2002. Therefore, nine cells are illustrated, one for each combination.

A cell contains only the necessary blocks to store the records that have the dimension values of that cell. If there are no records (as in the case of cell 4 in Figure 7.18), no blocks will be allocated.

In Figure 7.18, we also illustrate the concept of a slice. A **slice** consists of all the cells that belong to a specific value of a dimension. Figure 7.18 highlights two out of six slices, one for dimension *year* with a value of 2000 and the other for dimension *sales_person* with a value of Mary.

7.10.2 Block Indexes

Block indexes are pointers to a block, not a single record. A block index points to the beginning of each block, which has a unique block ID (BID). MDC tables use only block indexes. Figure 7.19 shows a comparison between a regular index and a block index.

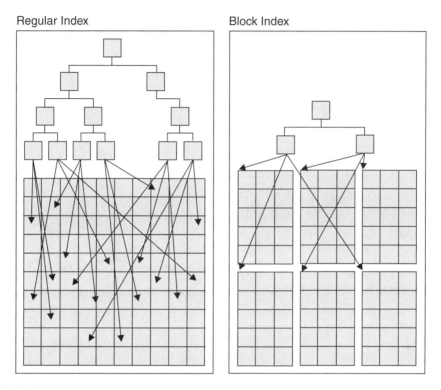

Figure 7.19   A regular index versus a block index

A block index has the following advantages over a regular index.

- Block indexes are significantly smaller than regular indexes because they point to a block rather than a record. The reduced size makes index scans much faster.
- Less maintenance overhead is associated with block indexes. They only need to be updated when adding the first record to a block and removing the last record from a block.
- Prefetching is done in blocks, thus the amount of I/O is reduced.

An MDC table defined with even a single dimension can benefit from block indexes and can be a viable alternative to a regular table using a clustering index.

When an MDC table is created, a **dimension block index** is created for each specified dimension. For our *sales* table, two dimension block indexes are created, one for the *sales_person* dimension and one for the *year* dimension, as illustrated in Figure 7.20.

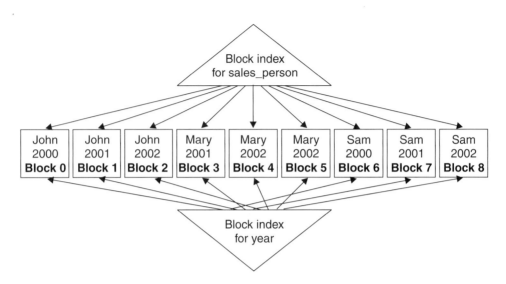

Figure 7.20   Block indexes for *sales_person* and *year*

A query requesting records that have *sales_person* = John can use the *sales_person* block index to quickly access all three blocks (block 0, 1, and 2) that satisfy this criteria. Another query can use the *year* block index to independently access all blocks that have *year* = 2002 (blocks 2, 4, 5, and 8).

In addition to the dimension block indexes, a **composite block index** is also created during MDC table creation. A composite block index contains all columns across all dimensions and is used to maintain the clustering of data over **INSERT** and **UPDATE** activity. If a single dimension block index already contains all the dimension key columns, a composite block index is not created.

7.10.3 The Block Map

A **block map** is an array containing an entry for each block of an MDC table. The entry indicates whether or not a block is in use. Each block has a unique identifier (BID) and also an **IN_USE** status bit. When a **DELETE** operation removes the last record in a block, DB2 frees the block by changing its **IN_USE** status bit and removing its BID from all block indexes. When new records are inserted and they can no longer fit into existing blocks, DB2 first scans for free blocks, looking for ones without the **IN_USE** bit set. If a free block is found, DB2 reuses it, updates its **IN_USE** bit, and adds its BID to block indexes.

Reusing free blocks greatly reduces fragmentation and in turn minimizes the need to reorganize the MDC table even though pages within the blocks may be fragmented.

7.10.4 Choosing Dimensions for MDC Tables

Choosing the right dimensions for an MDC table is crucial for obtaining the maximum advantages MDC can provide. You should consider the following:

- Choose columns with the lowest cardinality.

    One of the advantages of using block indexes is that they point to a block rather than a record; therefore, there are fewer pointers to traverse. If each block contains only one record, the block index essentially becomes a regular index. You should try to minimize the number of blocks by increasing the number of records they can contain. You can achieve this by choosing columns with the lowest cardinality, that is, the lowest number of distinct values. For example, a column like *region*, with possible values of North, South, East, and West, is a good choice. A column like *employee_id*, which uniquely identifies each employee of a company that has 100,000 employees, is definitely a bad choice.

- Choose the correct block size (extent size).

    MDC tables allocate space in blocks. The entire block is allocated even if only one record is inserted. For example, if your block can hold 100 pages, and on average only 10 records are inserted per block (assuming only one record can fit in a page), then 90% of the space is wasted. Thus, make sure you choose the correct block size.

- Choose the right number of dimensions.

    The higher the number of dimensions, the more possible combinations you can have, and therefore the higher the number of possible cells. If there are many cells, each cell will likely contain only a few records, and if that is the case, the block size needs to be set to a small number.

> **N O T E** The Design Advisor tool can make recommendations on what dimensions to choose for a given table.

7.11 VIEWS

A **view** is a virtual table derived from one or more tables or other views. It is virtual because it does not contain any data, but a definition of a table based on the result of a **SELECT** statement. Figure 7.21 illustrates view *view1* derived from table *table1*.

A view does not need to contain all the columns of the base table. Its columns do not need to have the same names as the base table, either. This is illustrated in Figure 7.21, where the view

View1

ID	Name
001	John
002	Mary
003	Sam
004	Julie

Table1

Employee_ID	Name	Salary	Deptno
001	John	60000	101
002	Mary	60000	101
003	Sam	65000	111
004	Julie	70000	112

Figure 7.21 A view derived from a table

consists of only two columns, and the first column of the view has a different name than the corresponding column in the base table. This is particularly useful for hiding confidential information from users.

You can create a view using the **CREATE VIEW** statement. For example, to create the view *view1* shown in Figure 7.21, issue this statement.

```
CREATE VIEW view1 (id, name)
      AS SELECT employee_id, name FROM table1
```

To display the contents of *view1*, use the following statement.

```
SELECT * FROM view1
```

You can also create views based on multiple tables. Figure 7.22 shows a view created from two tables.

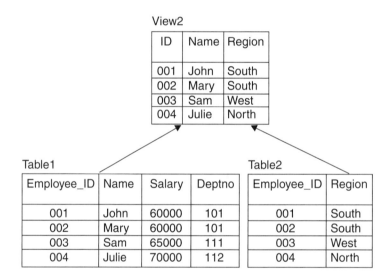

Figure 7.22   A view derived from two tables

Here is the corresponding **CREATE VIEW** statement for Figure 7.22.

```
CREATE VIEW view2 (id, name, region)
AS SELECT table1.employee_id, table1.name, table2.region
     FROM table1,table2
   WHERE table1.employee_id = table2.employee_id
```

With this statement we have combined the information of *table1* and *table2* into *view2*, while limiting access to the salary information.

When you create a view, its definition is stored in the system catalog table SYSCAT.VIEWS. This table contains information about each view such as its name, schema, whether or not it is read-only, and the SQL statement used to create the view. For example, in Figure 7.23 we show part of the information for views *view1* and *view2* in SYSCAT.VIEWS.

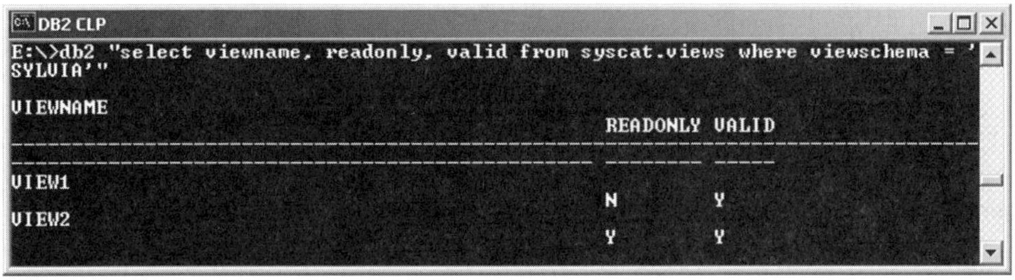

Figure 7.23 View definitions stored in the SYSCAT.VIEWS table

When a view is referenced in a query, DB2 reads and executes the view definition from the SYSCAT.VIEWS table, pulls the data from the base table, and presents it to the users.

To remove a view, use the **DROP VIEW** statement. For example, to remove the view *view1* use:

```
DROP VIEW view1
```

If any of the base tables or views is dropped, the views that are dependent on them will be marked invalid and the value in the VALID column shown in Figure 7.23 will be set to X instead of Y. When this happens, you will not be able to use these views. This is true even if you have recreated the base table or view afterward.

7.11.1 View Classification

Views are classified by the operations they allow. There are four classes of views:

- Deleteable views
- Updatable views
- Insertable views
- Read-only views

In the SYSCAT.VIEWS catalog table, when the value of the column READ-ONLY is Y, this indicates that the view is read-only; otherwise, it is either a deleteable, updatable, or insertable view. Figure 7.23 shows *view2* is a read-only view, but *view1* is not.

Figure 7.24 illustrates the relationship between the different types of views. The views are discussed further in the next sections.

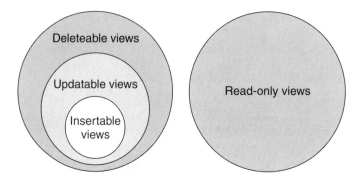

Figure 7.24   View classifications and relationships

7.11.1.1 Deleteable Views

A **deleteable view** allows you to execute the **DELETE** statement against it. All of the following must be true.

- Each **FROM** clause of the outer fullselect identifies only one base table (with no **OUTER** clause), a deleteable view (with no **OUTER** clause), a deleteable nested table expression, or a deleteable common table expression (cannot identify a NICKNAME used with federated support).
- The outer fullselect does not include a **VALUES** clause.
- The outer fullselect does not include a **GROUP BY** clause or a **HAVING** clause.
- The outer fullselect does not include column functions in the **SELECT** list.
- The outer fullselect does not include **SET** operations (**UNION**, **EXCEPT**, or **INTERSECT**), with the exception of **UNION ALL**.
- The base tables in the operands of a **UNION ALL** must not be the same table, and each operand must be deleteable.
- The select list of the outer fullselect does not include **DISTINCT**.

For further detail, refer to the *DB2 UDB SQL Reference* manual. In our previous example, *view1* is a deleteable view. However, *view2* is not because it does not follow the first rule. In *view2*'s definition, the **SELECT** statement contains two base tables in the **FROM** clause.

7.11.1.2 Updatable Views

An **updatable view** is a special case of a deleteable view. A view is updatable when at least one of its columns is updatable. All of the following must be true.

- The view is deleteable.
- The column resolves to a column of a base table (not using a dereference operation), and the **READ ONLY** option is not specified

- All the corresponding columns of the operands of a **UNION ALL** have exactly matching data types (including length or precision and scale) and matching default values if the fullselect of the view includes a **UNION ALL**.

In our previous example, *view1* is an updatable view. However, *view2* is not because it is not deleteable.

You can update *view1* using the **UPDATE** statement, and the changes will be applied to its base table. For example, the following statement changes the value of column *employee_id* to 100 for records with the *name* value of Mary in *table1*.

```
UPDATE view1 SET id='100' WHERE name = 'Mary';
```

7.11.1.3 Insertable Views

An **insertable view** allows you to execute the **INSERT** statement against it. A view is insertable when all of its columns are updatable. For example, *view1* fits this rule. The following statement will insert a row into *table1*, which is the base table of *view1*.

```
INSERT INTO view1 VALUES ('200', 'Ben');
```

Figure 7.25 displays the contents of *table1* after executing the **INSERT** statement on *view1*. Note that the *salary* and *deptno* columns for Ben contain NULL values because these two columns are not contained in *view1*.

Figure 7.25   Contents of *table1* after inserting a row into *view1*

If *table1* were defined such that NULL values were not allowed in one of the *salary* or *deptno* columns, the **INSERT** statement would fail, and *view1* would not be an insertable view.

7.11.1.4 Read-Only Views

A **read-only view** is not deleteable. In Figure 7.22, shown earlier, *view2* is a read-only view. Its read-only property is also stored in the SYSCAT.VIEWS table, which is shown in Figure 7.23.

N O T E Even if a view is read-only, **INSERT**, **UPDATE**, and **DELETE** operations are still possible by using an **INSTEAD OF** trigger. For more information, see section 7.13, Triggers.

7.11.2 Using the WITH CHECK OPTION

You can define a view to selectively display a subset of rows of its base table by using the **WHERE** clause in the **CREATE VIEW** statement. To ensure that all the **INSERT** and **UPDATE** operations conform to the criteria specified in the **WHERE** clause of the view, you can use the **WITH CHECK OPTION** clause. For example, let's create the view *view3* derived from table *table1* (see Figure 7.22) as follows.

```
CREATE VIEW view3 (id, name,deptno)
      AS SELECT employee_id, name, deptno
          FROM table1
          WHERE deptno = 101
      WITH CHECK OPTION
```

If you issue a **SELECT * FROM view3** statement, you will obtain the following result:

```
ID  NAME                 DEPTNO
--- -------------------- -----------
001 John                    101
002 Mary                    101
```

Only two rows are retrieved because these are the only rows that satisfy the **WHERE** clause. What happens if you issue the following statement?

```
INSERT INTO view3 VALUES ('007','Shawn',201)
```

This statement fails because 201 does not conform to the criteria of the **WHERE** clause used in the **CREATE VIEW** definition, which is enforced because of **WITH CHECK OPTION**. If *view3* had not been defined with this clause, the **INSERT** statement would have succeeded.

7.11.3 Nested Views

Nested views are ones based on other views, for example:

```
CREATE VIEW view4
      AS SELECT * FROM view3
```

In this example, *view4* has been created based on *view3*, which was used in earlier examples. The **WITH CHECK OPTION** clause specified in *view3* is still in effect for *view4*; therefore, the following **INSERT** statement fails for the same reason it fails when inserting into *view3*.

```
INSERT INTO view4 VALUES ('007','Shawn',201)
```

When a view is defined with the **WITH CHECK OPTION** clause, the search condition is propagated through all the views that depend on it.

7.12 PACKAGES

A **package** is a database object consisting of executable SQL, including the access path the DB2 optimizer will take to perform the SQL operation.

To explain how a package works, let's review Figure 7.26, which illustrates the preparation of a C application program with embedded SQL.

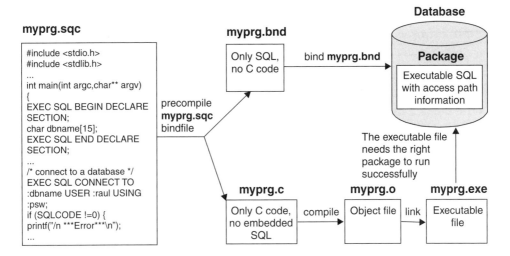

Figure 7.26   How a package is obtained

In the figure, the C program myprg.sqc contains embedded SQL. Issuing the **precompile** command (also known as the **prep** command) with the **bindfile** option generates two files, the myprg.bnd bind file containing only SQL information and the myprg.c file containing only C code.

The bind file will be compiled using the **bind** command to obtain a package that is stored in the database. To issue the **bind** command, a connection to the database must exist.

The myprg.c file will be compiled and linked like any regular C program. The resulting executable file myprg.exe has to be in sync with the package stored in the database to successfully execute.

7.13 TRIGGERS

A **trigger** is a database object associated to a table or a view that contains some application logic, which is executed automatically upon an **INSERT**, **UPDATE**, or **DELETE** operation on the table or view. For example, you can use a trigger:

- To validate the input in an **INSERT** statement
- To compare the new value of a row being updated to an old value
- To insert logging information to another table for audit trail purposes when a row is deleted

Triggers can be classified as **BEFORE**, **AFTER**, or **INSTEAD OF** triggers.

BEFORE triggers are activated before any table data is affected by the triggering SQL statement. For example, if you are inserting a row into a table, the **BEFORE** trigger is activated first, before the **INSERT** is completed.

AFTER triggers are activated after the triggering SQL statement has successfully completed. For example, if a **DELETE** operation on table *A* completed successfully, an **AFTER** trigger could be invoked to perform an **INSERT** on table *B*.

INSTEAD OF triggers are used to perform **INSERT**, **UPDATE**, or **DELETE** operations on views where these operations are otherwise not allowed. Though read-only views cannot be modified, the underlying tables can; thus, by using an **INSTEAD OF** trigger, you can make sure that logic is triggered when the view is affected, but the action is performed on the tables themselves.

To create a trigger, use the **CREATE TRIGGER** statement as demonstrated here.

```
CREATE TRIGGER default_time
      NO CASCADE BEFORE INSERT ON schedule
      REFERENCING NEW AS n
      FOR EACH ROW
      MODE DB2SQL
      WHEN (n.start_time IS NULL)
            SET n.start_time = '12:00'
```

This example shows a **BEFORE** trigger that is activated when an **INSERT** statement is performed on table *schedule*. If the row being inserted has a value of NULL for column *start_time*, the code will assign a value of 12:00 and then continue with the **INSERT** operation. The **REFERENCING NEW** clause simply indicates a way to identify the new value of a column.

Here is another example, this time for an **AFTER** trigger.

```
CREATE TRIGGER audit_qty
      AFTER UPDATE OF quantity ON inventory
      REFERENCING OLD AS o NEW AS n
      FOR EACH ROW
      MODE DB2SQL
      INSERT INTO sold
         VALUES (n.product_ID, n.daysold, o.quantity - n.quantity)
```

This **AFTER** trigger can be used in the following scenario. Let's say you administer a convenience store. You would like to know how many items of each product are sold per day; therefore, you perform a count every night and update your database with the new count. With the help of this **AFTER** trigger, you can easily query the *sold* table, which is automatically updated when you update the column *quantity* of table *inventory*. The number of items sold for the day is obtained by substracting the old quantity value minus the new quantity value.

Next we show an example of an **INSTEAD OF** trigger.

```
CREATE TRIGGER update_view2
      INSTEAD OF UPDATE
      ON view2
```

```
REFERENCING OLD AS o NEW AS n
FOR EACH ROW
MODE DB2SQL
BEGIN ATOMIC
   UPDATE table2
   SET region = n.region
   WHERE region = o.region;
END
```

This example demonstrates how a read-only view can still be updated by using **INSTEAD OF** triggers. In the example, the trigger updates the *region* column of table *table2* when the view *view2* (a read-only view) is updated.

7.14 STORED PROCEDURES

Stored procedures are programs whose executable binaries reside at the database server. They serve as subroutines to calling applications, and they normally wrap multiple SQL statements with flow logic. Figure 7.27 depicts a situation in which stored procedures are useful.

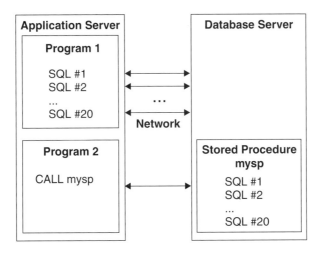

Figure 7.27   Reducing network traffic by using stored procedures

In the figure, *Program 1* and stored procedure *mysp* execute the same set of SQL statements. *Program 1*, however, does not perform as well as *Program 2* because of the extra overhead of sending each SQL statement through the network and waiting for its return. On the other hand, *Program 2* only needs to call the stored procedure *mysp* once and then wait for its return. Because *mysp* performs all the SQL statements within the database server, there is minimal network overhead.

Besides improving response time for applications running on a different server than the database server, stored procedures also provide a central location to store database application logic. This allows for a single place to maintain your code.

You can write stored procedures in several languages, such as C, Java, and SQL PL. SQL PL procedures are the most popular ones because they are easy to learn, provide very good performance, and are very compatible across the DB2 platforms, including DB2 for z/OS and DB2 for iSeries.

To create a stored procedure in the database, use the **CREATE PROCEDURE** statement. Stored procedures that do not use the SQL PL language are known as **external procedures**. For this type of procedure, the **CREATE PROCEDURE** statement simply registers the procedure to DB2. The executable code is normally kept under the sqllib\function\routine subdirectory.

In the case of SQL PL stored procedures, the source code is included with the **CREATE PROCE-DURE** statement. Moreover, executing the **CREATE PROCEDURE** statement will compile the code, bind the SQL statements, and create the necessary packages.

V8.2

> **N O T E**   Prior to Version 8.2, a C/C++ compiler was required to create SQL PL stored procedures because these procedures were first converted to the C language. Version 8.2 does not require this compiler. DB2's engine performs the preparation/compilation of the stored procedure without any other requirement.

The following is an example of an SQL PL stored procedure created in the database *sample* (which is provided with DB2).

```
CREATE PROCEDURE CSMMGR.NEW_SALARY (IN  p_empno    CHAR(6),
                                    OUT p_empName VARCHAR(30) )
         LANGUAGE SQL
-------------------------------------------------------------------
-- SQL Stored Procedure used to update the salary of an employee
-------------------------------------------------------------------
P1: BEGIN
  DECLARE v_firstName VARCHAR(12);
  DECLARE v_lastName  VARCHAR(15);

  UPDATE employee SET salary = salary * 1.05
       WHERE empno = p_empno;

  SELECT lastname, firstnme INTO v_lastName, v_firstName
    FROM employee WHERE empno = p_empno;

  SET p_empName = v_lastName || ', ' || v_firstName;
END P1
```

In this example, the procedure name is *CSMMGR.NEW_SALARY*. This procedure takes an input parameter *p_empno* and an output parameter *p_empName*. The procedure will increase by 5% the value in the *salary* column of table *employee* for the employee with employee number *p_empno*. It will then return the name of the employee who received the increase in the format *lastname, firstname*. Figure 7.28 shows the Development Center tool used to develop the procedure. At the bottom of the figure, you can see the result of its execution.

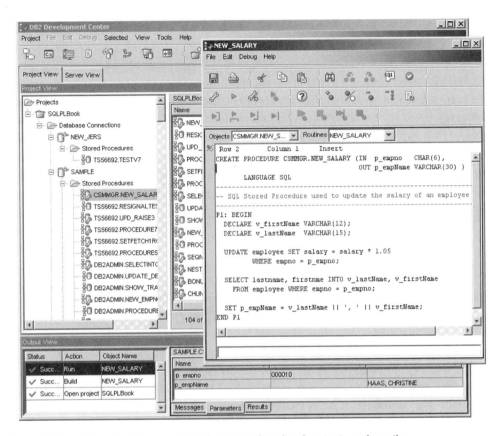

Figure 7.28 Using the Development Center tool to develop, test, and run the *CSMMGR.NEW_SALARY* stored procedure

> **NOTE** We recommend using the Development Center tool to develop, debug, and test your SQL PL stored procedures. From the tool you can also drop and alter procedures.

> **V8.2**
>
> **NOTE** We recommend the book *DB2 SQL PL: Essential Guide for DB2 UDB on Linux, UNIX, Windows, i5/OS, and z/OS* by Zamil Janmohamed, Clara Liu, Drew Bradstock, Raul Chong, Michael Gao, Fraser McArthur, and Paul Yip for a detailed explanation of the SQL PL language.

To change the properties of your stored procedures, you can use the **ALTER PROCEDURE** statement. To drop a store procedure, use the **DROP PROCEDURE** statement.

Stored procedures are also classified as fenced or unfenced. A **fenced stored procedure** runs in a different address space than the DB2 engine. This guarantees that a failure from the procedure will not corrupt the DB2 engine itself. In Linux and UNIX, a fenced user needs to be created to work with fenced stored procedures. Refer to Chapter 5, Understanding the DB2 Environment, DB2 Instances, and Databases, for details.

An **unfenced stored procedure** runs in the same address space as the DB2 engine. In terms of performance, unfenced stored procedures run faster than fenced ones; however, there is a risk that unfenced procedures may corrupt DB2 information, so you should make sure to test these procedures thoroughly.

> **NOTE** SQL PL stored procedures can run only unfenced.

7.15 User-Defined Functions

DB2 provides built-in functions that allow you to manipulate your data within an SQL statement. For example, the **year** function can retrieve the year of a timestamp column, as shown here.

```
db2 select year(current timestamp) from sysibm.sysdummy1

1
-----------
       2005
```

In addition to built-in functions, DB2 allows you to create your own functions. These **user-defined functions** (UDFs) allow you to simplify database application development by moving some of the logic to the database. A UDF takes zero to many input parameters and returns a value, a row or a table. To create a UDF, use the **CREATE FUNCTION** statement.

UDFs can be classified as follows.

- **Sourced functions**: These functions are created on top of DB2 built-in functions. Here's an example.

  ```
  CREATE FUNCTION trim (p_var1 VARCHAR(50))
      RETURNS VARCHAR(50)
      RETURN RTRIM(LTRIM(p_var1))
  ```

  In this example, **RTRIM** is a DB2 built-in function that removes all the blanks at the end of a string. **LTRIM** is a DB2 built-in function that removes all the blanks at the beginning of a string. The UDF **trim** is created to remove blanks at the beginning and the end of a string by using these two built-in functions. To test the function, you can use the **VALUES** statement as follows:

  ```
  VALUES (trim('     hello     '))
  ```

  which returns:

  ```
  1
  ------------------------------------------------
  hello
  ```

- **SQL functions**: These functions are written in SQL PL language. They can return a scalar value, a single row, or a table of data. The following code shows an example of an SQL UDF returning a scalar value: the rounded salary of an employee.

```
CREATE FUNCTION csmmgr.salary_round(p_empno CHAR(6))
    RETURNS INTEGER
    LANGUAGE SQL
F1: BEGIN ATOMIC
    DECLARE v_salary INTEGER;
    SET v_salary = (SELECT ceiling(salary) FROM employee
                    WHERE empno = p_empno);
    RETURN v_salary;
END
```

This function takes an employee number as input and returns the salary rounded to the highest integer value. SQL functions can be developed by using the Development Center, as illustrated in Figure 7.29.

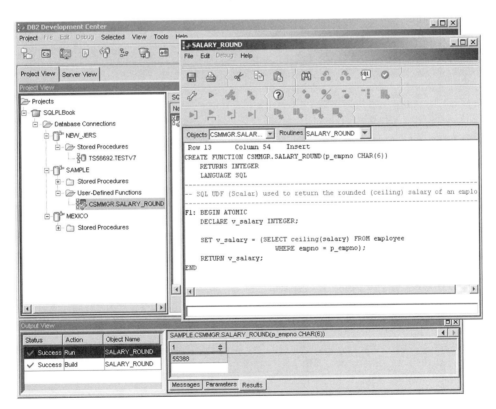

Figure 7.29 Using the Development Center tool to develop, test, and run the `csmmgr.salary_round` user-defined function

- **External functions**: These functions are defined in the database with references to object code libraries that are written in C, Java, or OLE. Consider this example.

```
CREATE FUNCTION csmmgr.db2killapp(INT)
      RETURNS INT
      EXTERNAL NAME 'db2killapplib!db2killapp'
      LANGUAGE C
      PARAMETER STYLE SQL
      NOT FENCED
      RETURNS NULL ON NULL INPUT
      NOT DETERMINISTIC
      NO SQL
      NO EXTERNAL ACTION
```

This statement registers the UDF **csmmgr.db2killapp** to DB2. It is an external function written in C. The C executable code is stored in the *db2killapplib* library, which is stored under the sqllib\function subdirectory.

7.16 SEQUENCES

A **sequence** is a database object that allows automatic generation of values. Unlike identity columns, this object does not depend on any table—the same sequence object can be used across the database.

To create a sequence, use the **CREATE SEQUENCE** statement as demonstrated here.

```
CREATE SEQUENCE myseq AS INTEGER
      START WITH 1 INCREMENT BY 1
      NO MAXVALUE
      NO CYCLE
      CACHE 5
```

This statement creates the sequence *myseq*, which is of type INTEGER. The sequence starts with a value of 1 and then increases by 1 each time it's invoked for the next value.

The **NO MAXVALUE** clause indicates there is no explicit maximum value in which the sequence will stop; therefore, it will be bound by the limit of the data type, in this case, INTEGER.

The **NO CYCLE** clause indicates the sequence will not start over from the beginning once the limit is reached.

CACHE 5 indicates five sequence numbers will be cached in memory, and the sixth number in the sequence would be stored in a catalog table. Sequence numbers are cached in memory for performance reasons; otherwise, DB2 needs to access the catalog tables constantly to retrieve the next value in line. What would happen if your computer crashed and the following numbers were in the cache: 5, 6, 7, 8, and 9? These numbers would be lost, and the next time DB2 needed to retrieve a number, it would obtain the number from the catalog tables. In this example, 10 is the next number to be generated. If you are using the sequence number to generate unique identifiers, which must be in sequence with no gaps allowed, this would not work for you. The solution would be to use the **NO CACHE** clause to guarantee sequentially generated numbers with no gaps, but you will pay a performance cost.

For the sequence value, you can use any exact numeric data type with a scale of zero, including SMALLINT, INTEGER, BIGINT, and DECIMAL. In addition, any user-defined distinct type based on these data types can hold sequence values.

> **N O T E**   The options supported for sequence objects are the same as the ones for identity columns.

Table 7.4 shows other statements you can use with sequences.

Table 7.4   Other Statements Used with Sequences

Statement	Explanation
`ALTER SEQUENCE`	Alters the characteristics of a sequence, like the increment value
`DROP SEQUENCE`	Drops the sequence
`NEXTVAL FOR` *sequence_name* or `NEXT VALUE FOR` *sequence_name*	Retrieves the next value generated in the sequence
`PREVVAL FOR` *sequence_name* or `PREVIOUS VALUE FOR` *sequence_name*	Retrieves the previous value generated in the sequence

7.17 CASE STUDY

You have been given the task to create several DB2 database objects for a proof-of-concept exercise on a single-partition environment. You start by creating the database *testdb* on your Windows server's E: drive as follows:

```
CREATE DATABASE testdb ON E:
```

This command takes a few minutes to complete as it creates several default database objects, including the default table spaces (SYSCATSPACE, TEMPSPACE1, and USERSPACE1) and the default buffer pool (IBMDEFAULTBP). Because this is just a test database, you decide to use the USERSPACE1 default table space for your user tables and the default buffer pool.

After the database is created, before you can create any object, you need to connect to the database; thus you perform this operation:

```
CONNECT TO testdb
```

Given that this is a single-partition environment, you don't bother about creating partition groups. Therefore, you start with the creation of your tables. The requirements for this proof-of-concept exercise indicate that you need to create a table for the departments in your organization. Every department must have a department ID, which must be unique within the organization. Every department must also have a name and a manager ID. Because all three of these columns are required, you need to define them as NOT NULL. To ensure that the department ID is unique, you have two options: create a unique index or define the column as the primary key for the table. You decide to create a primary key because you want to define relationships between the department ID in this table and other tables later.

Therefore, you create the table as follows.

```
CREATE TABLE dept (
      deptID    INT        NOT NULL PRIMARY KEY,
      deptname  CHAR(30)   NOT NULL,
      mngrID    INT        NOT NULL)
```

You also could have created the table in two steps as follows.

```
CREATE TABLE dept (
      deptID    INT        NOT NULL,
      deptname  CHAR(30)   NOT NULL,
      mngrID    INT        NOT NULL)
```

```
ALTER TABLE dept ADD PRIMARY KEY (deptID)
```

Next, because your applications tend to scan the table looking for department names on a regular basis, you create an index on the *deptname* column in the *dept* table as follows.

```
CREATE INDEX deptnmx ON dept (deptname)
```

Next, you create the table of employees for your organization. Every employee has an employee ID, first and last names, and a salary. In addition, every employee belongs to a department. You issue the following statement to create the *emp* table.

```
CREATE TABLE emp (
      empID   INT              NOT NULL PRIMARY KEY,
      fname   CHAR(30)         NOT NULL,
      lname   CHAR(30)         NOT NULL,
      deptID  INT              NOT NULL,
      salary  DECIMAL (12,2)
      )
```

Because your applications scan the table looking for employees' names on a regular basis, you also create an index on the first and last name columns in the table as follows.

```
CREATE INDEX empnmx ON emp (lname, fname)
```

The employee and department tables are related: the department table is the parent table, and the employee table is the dependent table; therefore, any department ID in the employee table must exist in the department table. To establish this relationship, you create a referential constraint as follows.

```
ALTER TABLE emp ADD FOREIGN KEY (deptID) REFERENCES dept
```

Alternatively, you could have set up the same referential constraint by using a unique constraint in the dept table instead of the primary key as follows.

```
CREATE TABLE dept (
       deptID    INT        NOT NULL,
       deptname  CHAR(30)   NOT NULL,
       mngrID    INT        NOT NULL
       )
```

```
ALTER TABLE dept ADD CONSTRAINT deptun UNIQUE (deptID)
ALTER TABLE emp  ADD FOREIGN KEY (deptID) REFERENCES dept (deptID)
```

This is important because you may want to have more than one referential constraint for the same base table, and this allows you to reference different keys in the parent table.

There is also a requirement to enforce a rule that no employee can have a salary greater than $100,000.00; therefore, you create a check constraint as follows.

```
ALTER TABLE emp ADD CONSTRAINT salary CHECK (salary <= 100000.00)
```

After the table successfully completes, you test the **CHECK** constraint with the following statement.

```
INSERT INTO emp VALUES (123, 'Sam ', 'Johnson ', 345, 100005)
```

This **INSERT** statement fails as expected with this message.

```
SQL0545N  The requested operation is not allowed because a row does not satisfy the
check constraint "MYSCHEMA.EMP.SALARY". SQLSTATE=23513
```

You know your applications already perform the salary check constraint before the data is entered into DB2, so you wonder if you can remove this constraint in DB2. However, when you ask your manager, he says the problem with that approach is that DB2 would not know that those rules exist and may therefore need to do extra checks that could cause inefficient access. To overcome this, you create informational constraints so that the DB2 optimizer knows about the rules when building the optimal access plan, but DB2 does not enforce the rules when the data is being manipulated. Therefore, you change the constraint you created earlier.

First you drop the constraint.

```
ALTER TABLE emp DROP CONSTRAINT salary
```

Then you recreate it again as follows.

```
ALTER TABLE emp ADD CONSTRAINT salary
     CHECK (salary < 100000.00)
     NOT ENFORCED ENABLE QUERY OPTIMIZATION
```

You save all of these commands in a script file. Next, because several developers in your company will use this *testdb* database to test different things, you decide to create the objects again, but this time using a different schema. Because you have SYSADM authority, you can issue the following commands.

```
CREATE SCHEMA developer1
SET CURRENT SCHEMA developer1
```

You then execute the script file, which creates all the objects again, but in a different schema.

And that's it for your proof-of-concept exercise!

7.18 SUMMARY

This chapter discussed the concept of databases, database partitions, and the DB2 database objects. Among the DB2 database objects, it explained how to work with partition groups, table spaces, buffer pools, tables, views, indexes, schemas, stored procedures, and so on. Some of these objects are further explained in Chapter 8, The DB2 Storage Model.

The chapter also discussed the DB2 data types (DB2 built-in and user-defined types), which are used as ways to define the columns of a table or as parameters to stored procedures and functions.

There was a detailed explanation about table objects because there are many topics associated with tables, such as constraints, referential integrity, the use of NULLs, identity columns, and table compression.

It also described indexes and the different clauses of the **CREATE INDEX** statement such as **INCLUDE** and **ALLOW REVERSE SCANS**. More complex subjects, such as multidimensional clustering (MDC) tables, were also discussed. MDC tables allow for greater flexibility to cluster your data by several dimensions.

Views and their classification (deleteable, updatable, insertable, and read-only) were also explored.

The chapter also introduced application-related objects such as packages, triggers, stored procedures, user-defined functions, and sequences. Although this is not a DB2 application development book, this chapter provided you with the foundation to understand these objects.

Referring to the figures presented in the chapter should help you remember all the concepts introduced.

7.19 REVIEW QUESTIONS

1. Consider the following instructions/commands/statements:

```
Login to your Linux server as user JDOE
su db2inst1 (switch user to db2inst1)
CONNECT TO sample USER foo USING bar
SELECT * FROM t1
```

Which table will you select data from?

A. JDOE.t1

B. db2inst1.t1

C. foo.t1

D. bar.t1

2. Which of the following is not created when you create a database?
   A. IBMDEFAULTBP
   B. IBMDEFAULTSPACE
   C. IBMDEFAULTGROUP
   D. SYSCATSPACE
   E. IBMTEMPGROUP
3. Which of the following objects will ensure rows are assigned a unique value across multiple tables?
   A. Identity column
   B. Unique index
   C. Sequence
   D. Row ID
4. Which of the following commands will delete all rows from the table *t1* without logging?
   A. Truncate table
   B. Delete * from t1 no log
   C. Alter table t1 activate not logged initially with truncate
   D. Alter table t1 activate not logged initially with empty table
5. To ensure that a column can contain only the values T or F, which option should you choose?
   A. Create a unique index on the column.
   B. Create a check constraint on the column.
   C. Specify the column as NOT NULL.
   D. Create a view on the table.
6. When deleting a row from a table that has a primary key defined, which of the following options on a foreign key clause will delete all rows with the same value in the foreign key table?
   A. Restrict
   B. Cascade
   C. Drop
   D. Set NULL
7. Which two of the following can be referenced by a foreign key constraint?
   A. Unique index
   B. Unique constraint
   C. Check constraint
   D. Primary key
   E. Identity column
8. Given the table created as follows:

```
CREATE TABLE product (
        productno    INTEGER GENERATED ALWAYS AS
                             IDENTITY (START WITH 0 INCREMENT BY 5),
        description VARCHAR(50) )
```

And these statements:

```
INSERT INTO product VALUES (DEFAULT,'banana')
INSERT INTO product (description) VALUES ('apple')
INSERT INTO product VALUES (300,'pear');
```

How many rows will be in the table?

A. 0

B. 1

C. 2

D. 3

9. Consider the following statement.

```
CREATE TABLE wqwq (c1 DECIMAL)
```

What will the precision and scale be for column $c1$?

A. Precision = 15, scale = 0

B. Precision = 15, scale =15

C. Precision = 5, scale = 0

D. Precision = 5, scale = 10

10. Which of the following is not a supported type of trigger?

A. INBETWEEN

B. AFTER

C. INSTEAD OF

D. BEFORE

11. Which of the following does not belong to a database?

A. Schema

B. Logs

C. Registry variables

D. System catalogs

12. Consider the following statement.

```
CREATE TABLE foo (c1 INT NOT NULL PRIMARY KEY, c2 INT)
```

How many database objects are created?

A. 1

B. 2

C. 3

D. 4

13. Consider the following db2nodes.cfg file.

```
0 mysrv1 0
1 mysrv1 1
2 mysrv2 0
3 mysrv2 1
```

How many servers are the partitions running on?

A. 1

B. 2

C. 3

D. 4

14. Which of the following objects cannot be created in a large table space?

    A. Data
    A. Index
    A. LONG VARCHAR
    A. LOB

15. To create the table space *ts1* successfully in the database *sample*, place the following steps in the correct order.

    ```
    1. CREATE TABLESPACE ts1 PAGESIZE 16K BUFFERPOOL bp1
    2. CONNECT TO sample
    3. CREATE BUFFERPOOL bp1 SIZE 100000 PAGESIZE 16K
    ```

    A. 1, 2, 3
    B. 3, 2, 1
    C. 2, 1, 3
    D. 2, 3, 1

16. Which of the following objects' definitions can be altered by using the **ALTER** statement?

    A. Table
    B. View
    C. Index
    D. Schema

17. A package contains which of the following? (Choose all that apply.)

    A. Executable SQL statements
    B. The access path that the DB2 optimizer chooses to retrieve the data
    C. A collection of stored procedures and functions
    D. A list of bind files

18. Tables with the same name can be created within the same database by creating them in which of the following?

    A. Different partitions
    B. Different partition groups
    C. Different table spaces
    D. Different schemas

19. Which of the following can be used to obtain the next value of the sequence *seq1*? (Choose all that apply.)

    A. seq1.nextValue
    B. NEXTVAL FOR seq1
    C. NEXT VALUE FOR seq1
    D. seq1.next

20. Which of the following statements is true?

    A. A user temporary table space is created with the **create temporary table** statement.
    B. The creation of a user temporary table space will fail if no system temporary table space is available.

C. A user temporary table is created in TEMPSPACE1.

D. A user temporary table space is needed so that declared global temporary tables can be declared.

## CHAPTER 8

The DB2 Storage Model

T his chapter describes how DB2 stores its objects on disk and introduces the concepts of table spaces, pages, and extents. It discusses how you can create and modify these objects on your database server so that your system will perform as optimally as possible and so that you do not run out of space when working with the database.

In this chapter you will learn about:

- DB2's storage model
- Database creation and structure
- Partition groups
- Table spaces
- Containers
- Extents
- Pages
- Buffer pools

8.1 THE DB2 STORAGE MODEL: THE BIG PICTURE

This section provides an overview of the DB2 storage model. In Figure 8.1 you can see the interaction between the different database objects as they relate to the DB2 storage model. This figure presents a combination of physical and logical views of the primary database objects.

Figure 8.1 illustrates a user retrieving some data from the table *t2*. From this user's perspective, the information he needs is stored in a table, and how and where it is stored on disk is irrelevant. When this user issues the SQL statement:

```
SELECT ProdId FROM t2 WHERE ProdName = 'Plum'
```

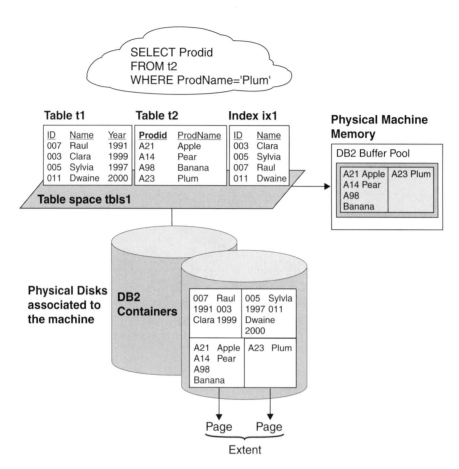

Figure 8.1   A view of the DB2 database objects

the column from the specified rows in the table is retrieved by DB2 and returned to the user. Behind the scenes, DB2 may need to read a number of pages of data from one or more physical disks or from memory to provide this information to the user.

DB2 stores table and index data on **pages**, which are the smallest unit of storage in a DB2 database. Figure 8.1 shows four pages for the table *t2*, and each page contains one or more rows from the tables *t1* and *t2* and one or more key values for the index *ix1* on table *t1*.

When DB2 processes SQL statements, it must scan the data and/or index pages. DB2 only scans these pages in the buffer pools. If the page is already in a buffer pool due to the processing of other SQL statements, DB2 can process the request immediately. If the page is not in the buffer pool, DB2 must read it from disk and place it in the buffer pool, as shown on the right side of Figure 8.1.

Rather than reading one page at a time, DB2 can group pages together into **extents** and read multiple pages with each I/O request. In Figure 8.1 you can see that pages are grouped together in extents of two pages. You can also see that the tables and indexes are stored in table spaces. Table spaces are a logical layer only and do not physically exist. **Containers** are the physical storage for the table spaces.

To optimize performance, DB2 lets you specify the table spaces in which you want your tables and indexes stored. You can also associate buffer pools with specific table spaces so that you can optimize the placement of tables and indexes within memory.

8.2 DATABASES: LOGICAL AND PHYSICAL STORAGE OF YOUR DATA

This section discusses how DB2 logically and physically creates databases.

8.2.1 Creating a Database

As mentioned in Chapter 2, DB2 at a Glance: The Big Picture, you used the **CREATE DATA-BASE** command to create a database. The basic syntax of the command is

```
CREATE DATABASE database name ON drive/path
```

The database name:

- Can be a maximum of eight characters long
- Cannot contain all numbers
- Cannot start with a number
- Cannot contain spaces
- Cannot already have been used within the same DB2 instance

DB2 creates the database on the drive or path specified by the DFTDBPATH Database Manager Configuration parameter. On Windows this will be a drive, and on Linux and UNIX this will be the path to a file system. By default, the DFTDBPATH configuration parameter is the drive where DB2 is installed on Windows. On Linux and UNIX it is the instance owner's home directory. When you do specify the drive or the path for the database, keep the following in mind.

- It cannot be a LAN drive, an NFS mounted file system, or a General Parallel File System (GPFS).
- The file system or drive cannot be a read-only device.
- The instance owner must have write permission on the drive or file system.
- There must be sufficient space available on the drive or file system to hold at least the system catalogs.

In addition, in the **CREATE DATABASE** command you can optionally specify

- The database partition number for the catalog table space (multi-partition environments).
- The definition of the temporary and default user table spaces if you do not want to use the default locations.

- The code set and territory allow you to specify the character set that you want DB2 to use to store your data and return result sets.
- The collating sequence lets you specify how DB2 should sort data when you create indexes or use the **SORT** or **ORDER BY** clauses in select statements.
- Whether you want to automatically configure the instance for the specified workload.

When a database is created using the default syntax of the **CREATE DATABASE** command, several objects are created.

- The partition group IBMCATGROUP, which contains
    - The table space SYSCATSPACE (catalog table space), which contains the DB2 catalog tables and views
- The partition group IBMTEMPGROUP, which contains
    - The table space TEMPSPACE1 (system temporary table space)
- The partition group IBMDEFAULTGROUP, which contains
    - The table space USERSPACE1 (user table space)
- The buffer pool IBMDEFAULTBP
- A database configuration file

Figure 8.2 below shows these default objects that are created when you create a database.

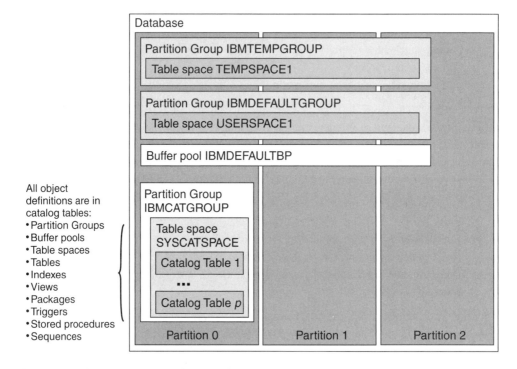

Figure 8.2   A database with default database objects created

When you create a database you can specify different locations and table space types for the temporary and user table spaces.

```
CREATE DATABASE sales ON /data
    TEMPORARY TABLESPACE MANAGED BY SYSTEM USING ('/temp')
    USER TABLESPACE MANAGED BY SYSTEM USING ('/userspc')
```

The example above lets the catalog table space default to a directory under the database path (/data). You are also specifying to use SMS table spaces for the user and temporary table space, but that the temporary table space will use the file system /temp, and the user table space will use the file system /userspc.

You can also create the user table space as a DMS table space:

```
create database sales on /data
    temporary tablespace managed by system using ('/temp')
    user tablespace managed by database using (file '/userspc/cont1' 40M)
```

SMS and DMS table spaces are discussed in detail in section 8.4, Table Spaces.

The **CREATE DATABASE** command in a multi-partition environment automatically takes the contents of the database partition configuration file (db2nodes.cfg) into consideration. The partition where you issue the **CREATE DATABASE** command becomes the catalog partition for the database, and the system catalog tables for this database will be created on that partition. If you do not explicitly connect to a database partition or server, the database will be created with the system catalogs on the first partition in the db2nodes.cfg file.

8.2.2 The Default Database Structure

When you create a database using default values, DB2 automatically creates a set of directories that correspond to the objects it creates by default. Figure 8.3 shows the default directory structure that is created.

In Figure 8.3, NODE0000 represents the partition number of the database. In a multi-partition environment, there will be one NODE*xxxx* directory per partition, where *xxxx* matches the partition number specified in the first column of the db2nodes.cfg file.

SQL00001 represents the directory where the first database created resides. This is a unique directory name. If you create another database on the same server in the same instance using the default drive/path, DB2 creates a directory SQL00002 for this database. Subsequent databases created in the same manner are each stored in similar directories. Note that if you drop a database and later create a new database on the same drive or path, DB2 will reuse the directory name from the database that was dropped.

In Figure 8.3 you can see that underneath the SQL*xxxxx* directory, DB2 also creates a number of additional subdirectories. Table 8.1 explains DB2's usage of each of these directories.

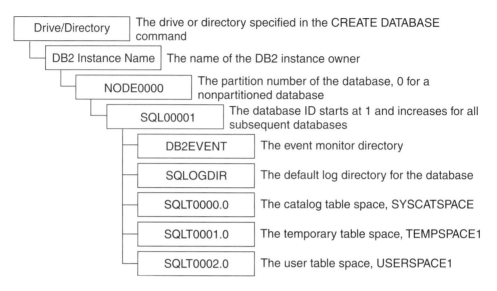

Figure 8.3   The default database structure

Table 8.1   Description of the Subdirectories of SQL*xxxxx*

Directory Name	Description
DB2EVENT	The event monitor output directory.
SQLLOGDIR	The default directory for the transaction logs.
SQLT0000.0	The directory for table space SYSCATSPACE (the catalog table space).
SQLT0001.0	The directory for table space TEMPSPACE1 (the system temporary table space).
SQLT0002.0	The directory for table space USERSPACE1 (the default user table space).

8.2.3 Database Creation Examples

In this section we provide two examples of how to create a database. The first example is for a single-partition environment, and the second example is for a multi-partition environment.

8.2.3.1 Creating a Database in a Single-Partition Environment

Let's say you are working on a single-partition DB2 environment running on a Windows server and the DB2 instance name you created is *myinst*. If you issue the command:

```
CREATE DATABASE sales ON E:
```

several directories will be created on the E: drive as shown in Figure 8.4.

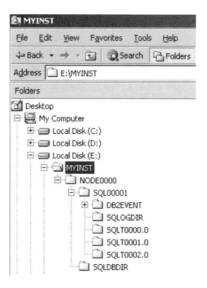

Figure 8.4   Directories created when a database is created

Continuing with the example, you can create two additional databases, *test* and *prod,* using the following commands:

```
CREATE DATABASE test ON E:
CREATE DATABASE prod ON E:
```

Figure 8.5 shows the additional directories these commands create. Table 8.2 shows the database name and the directory that DB2 used when the database was created.

Using the **LIST DB DIRECTORY ON *drive/path*** lets you map the SQL*xxxxx* directory to the actual database name. In this case if you issue the command:

```
LIST DB DIRECTORY ON E:
```

you would get the output shown in Figure 8.6.

If you drop one of these databases, its SQL*xxxxx* directory will be deleted as well. If you create a new database at a later time, this directory name will be reused. For example, if you drop the database *test*, the directory SQL00002 will be deleted. If you then create a new database called *QA*, the directory SQL00002 will be recreated and used for the QA database.

8.2.3.2 Creating a Database in a Multi-Partition Environment

Let's say you are working on a DB2 multi-partition environment running on a single SMP Linux server with the following db2nodes.cfg file:

```
0    mylinx1    0
1    mylinx1    1
2    mylinx1    2
```

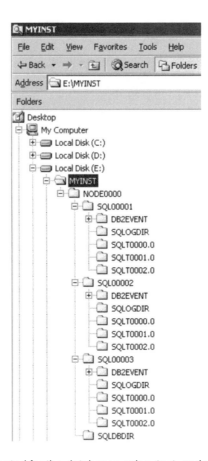

Figure 8.5   Directories created for the databases sales, test, and prod

Table 8.2   The Databases and Their Directories

Database Name	Directory Name
Sales	SQL00001
Test	SQL00002
Prod	SQL00003

If you log in as the instance owner *db2inst1* on this server and create a database with this command:

```
create database sales on /data
```

the directory structure shown in Figure 8.7 will be created.

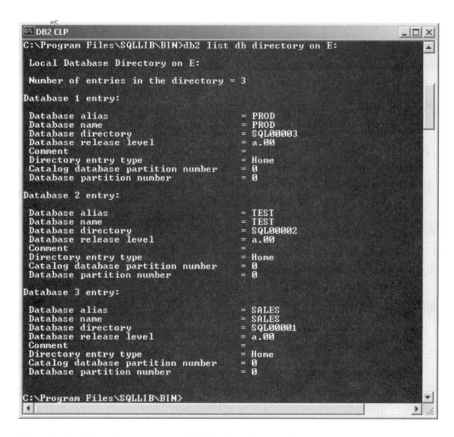

Figure 8.6   Output from the command list db directory on E:

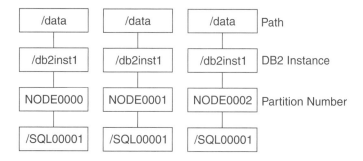

Figure 8.7   Directory structure for a three-partition database

As Figure 8.7 illustrates, there are three NODE*xxxx* directories, one for each database partition. The NODE*xxxx* directory is named based on the database instance's expanded four-digit partition number designated in the first column in the db2nodes.cfg file. Since the partition numbers used in the db2nodes.cfg file are 0, 1, and 2, these directories are NODE0000, NODE0001, and NODE0002.

8.2.4 Listing Databases

When you create a database with the **CREATE DATABASE** command, entries in the system database directory and local database directory are automatically entered. To list the system database directory contents, issue the command:

```
list db directory
```

To list the local database directory contents, issue the command:

```
list db directory on drive/path
```

Chapter 6, Configuring Client and Server Connectivity, discusses the system and local database directories in detail.

8.2.5 Dropping Databases

If you no longer need the data in a database, you can drop or (remove) the database from the system using the **DROP DATABASE** command. This command removes the database from the local and system database directories and deletes all table spaces, tables, logs, and directory structure supporting the database. After dropping a database, the space is immediately available for reuse.

For example, if you run the command:

```
DROP DATABASE sales
```

the entries in the system and local database directories for this database are removed, and the database's SQL*xxxxx* directory is also removed. The local database directory (SQLDBDIR) is *not* removed when you drop a database, because there may be other databases in the same path or on the same drive.

> **N O T E**   Removing a database is only supported using the **DROP DATABASE** command. Manually deleting the SQL*xxxxx* directory for the database is not supported, because it leaves the database entries in both the local and system database directories.

8.2.6 The Sample Database

DB2 contains a program to create a sample database that can be used for testing, or for learning purposes when you first start working with DB2. To create this database the instance must be started, and then you can run the program **db2sampl**. This creates a new database called *sample*, and the database will contain some tables with a few rows of data in each.

Use the command's **-k** option if you would like the *sample* database to be created with primary keys. In addition, you can specify the path if you would like this database to be created in a different location. For example, the command

```
db2sampl /data -k
```

creates the *sample* database in the */data* path, and the tables in the database have primary keys associated with them.

8.3 DATABASE PARTITION GROUPS

In a multi-partition environment, a database partition is an independent subset of a database that contains its own data, indexes, configuration files, and transaction logs. A partition group is a logical grouping of one or more database partitions that lets you control the placement of table spaces and buffer pools within the database partitions.

8.3.1 Database Partition Group Classifications

Partition groups are classified based on the number of database partitions they contain.

- Single-partition partition groups contain only one database partition.
- Multi-partition partition groups contain more than one database partition.

Figure 8.8 shows four database partition groups.

- *pgall* is a multi-partition partition group that spreads across all the database partitions.
- *pg01* is a multi-partition partition group that spreads across partitions 0 and 1.
- *pg12* is a multi-partition partition group that spreads across partitions 1 and 2.
- *pg1* is a single-partition partition group that resides on database partition 1.

> **NOTE** Database partitions can belong to more than one partition group. For example, in Figure 8.8 database partition 1 is part of all four partition groups.

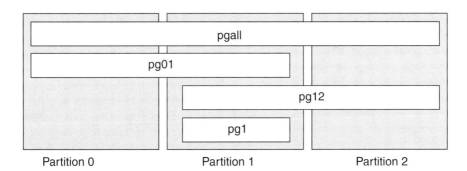

| | | |
| Partition 0 | Partition 1 | Partition 2 |

Figure 8.8   Single- and multipartition partition groups

8.3.2 Default Partition Groups

When you create a database, DB2 automatically creates three partition groups within that database. Table 8.3 describes these partition groups.

Table 8.3   Default Partition Groups

Partition Group Name	Description
IBMDEFAULTGROUP	By default, this partition group contains all database partitions that you have defined in the db2nodes.cfg file.
	This is the default partition group for any tables that you create.
	You can alter this partition group to either add or remove database partitions.
	This partition group cannot be dropped.
IBMTEMPGROUP	This partition group spans all database partitions that you have defined in the db2nodes.cfg file.
	This partition group is where all temporary tables created during database processing are placed.
	This partition group cannot be dropped.
IBMCATGROUP	This partition group only exists on the database's catalog partition. The catalog partition is the partition where you executed the CREATE DATABASE command.
	This is the partition where the system catalog tables are created.
	This partition group cannot be altered to either add or remove database partitions.
	This partition group cannot be dropped.

> **N O T E**   If you create a user temporary table space, you must create it in the IBMDEFAULTGROUP or any other partition group that you have created. DB2 does not allow you to create a user temporary table in the IBMTEMPGROUP. (User temporary table spaces are used for declared global temporary tables, which are described in Chapter 7, Working with Database Objects.)

8.3.3 Creating Database Partition Groups

You create a database partition group with the statement **CREATE DATABASE PARTITION GROUP**. The statement also records the partition group definition in the database system catalog tables.

The following commands show how to create the partition groups you see in Figure 8.8. For this example assume that the db2nodes.cfg file contains the following entries for the database partitions numbered 0, 1, and 2:

```
0    mylinx1    0
1    mylinx1    1
2    mylinx1    2
```

Starting with *pgall*, there are two ways to create this partition group using the **CREATE DATA-BASE PARTITION GROUP** statement:

```
create database partition group pgall on dbpartitionnums (0,1,2)
```

or

```
create database partition group pgall on all dbpartitionnums
```

You would create the other partition groups in Figure 8.8 as follows:

```
create database partition group pg01 on dbpartitionnums (0,1)
create database partition group pg12 on dbpartitionnums (1,2)
create database partition group pg1  on dbpartitionnums (1)
```

8.3.4 Modifying a Database Partition Group

You can modify a partition group with the **ALTER DATABASE PARTITION GROUP** statement. This statement changes the definition of an existing partition group by adding or removing partitions. If you want to add a new partition to the partition group, that partition must already be defined in the db2nodes.cfg file.

Continuing with the example from the previous section, you can add a new database partition to the instance by editing the db2nodes.cfg file and adding a fourth line:

```
0    mylinx1    0
1    mylinx1    1
2    mylinx1    2
3    mylinx1    3
```

If you now want to alter the partition group *pgall* to add partition number 3, issue this statement:

```
alter database partition group pgall add dbpartitionnum (3)
```

Notice that partition number 1 in this example is one part of all partitions groups. To reduce some of the load on that partition you can remove it from partition group *pgall*, as follows:

```
alter database partition group pgall drop dbpartitionnum (1)
```

8.3.5 Listing Database Partition Groups

You can list all partition groups in your database with the **LIST DATABASE PARTITION GROUP** statement. This lists all the partition groups that are defined in the database, regardless of which database partition you are currently connected to. The following is the output of this statement for the example we have been discussing.

```
DATABASE PARTITION GROUP
---------------------------------------------
IBMCATGROUP
IBMDEFAULTGROUP
```

```
PGALL
PG01
PG1
PG12
```

To see which partitions are included in each partition group, use the **SHOW DETAIL** option with the **LIST DATABASE PARTITION GROUP** statement. This option provides additional information, including:

- PMAP_ID: The partitioning map associated with the partition group.
- DATABASE PARTITION NUMBER: The database partition number as defined in the db2nodes.cfg file.
- IN_USE: The status of the database partition.

The output of this command contains three columns, and one row for each database partition that is part of the partition group, with the exception of the IBMTEMGROUP.

```
DATABASE PARTITION
GROUP                 DATABASE PARTITION NUMBER    IN_USE
------------------    -------------------          -------
IBMCATGROUP           0                            Y
IBMDEFAULTGROUP       0                            Y
IBMDEFAULTGROUP       1                            Y
IBMDEFAULTGROUP       2                            Y
IBMDEFAULTGROUP       3                            Y
PGALL                 0                            Y
PGALL                 1                            Y
PGALL                 2                            Y
PGALL                 3                            Y
PG01                  2                            Y
PG01                  3                            Y
PG12                  2                            Y
PG12                  3                            Y
PG1                   2                            Y
```

> **NOTE** This information is also available in the system catalog table SYSCAT.NODEGROUPDEF.

8.3.6 Dropping a Database Partition Group

While a partition group does not consume any system resources, if a partition group is not being used, you can drop it using the **DROP DATABASE PARTITION GROUP** statement. If you wanted to drop the partition group *pg12* from our example, use the statement:

```
DROP DATABASE PARTITION GROUP pg12
```

8.4 TABLE SPACES

As discussed in Chapter 7, Working with Database Objects, a table space is a logical, not physical, database object. You cannot point to anything on disk or your server and say "This is my table space." In DB2, all tables and indexes must be created in table spaces. Therefore, it is important to understand how to create and change table spaces.

A table space is a collection of one or more underlying physical storage devices known as **containers**. This allows you complete control over the placement of the containers on the disks, devices, and file systems available on your server.

There are two types of table spaces depending on how the physical space is allocated: system managed space (SMS) and database managed space (DMS). SMS table spaces store data in operating system files, and space for tables is allocated on-demand. In DMS table spaces, the database manager controls the storage space. You provide a list of devices or files and their size to belong to a table space when the DMS table space is defined, and DB2 then allocates the defined amount of space.

Before we can continue discussing table spaces, it is important to explain how a table space's containers work and how data is striped across the containers in a table space, based on extents.

8.4.1 Containers

When you create a table space, you define the container(s) for the table space to define the physical storage of the table space. How you define the container depends on the type of table space that you are creating. For SMS table spaces, a container can only be a directory. For DMS table spaces, a container can either be a file or a logical device or drive name.

When you create a table space, you have to define at least one container. A table space can have a number of containers associated with it, but once it has been defined, a container can belong to one and only one table space. Figure 8.9 illustrates this.

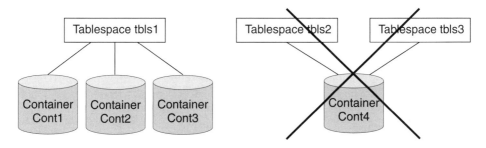

Figure 8.9   One table space can contain multiple containers, but a container can be associated to only one table space

8.4.2 Pages

DB2 stores table and index data on a **page**, which is the smallest unit of storage in a DB2 database. DB2 creates and manages the pages in the table space automatically, but you can control the page size for your table spaces. If you do not explicitly specify the page size when you create the table space, DB2 will use the default size of 4K. DB2 supports four different page sizes: 4K, 8K, 16K, and 32K.

It is important to note that a row within a table cannot span pages (i.e., the entire row must fit on a single page). The page size for the table must be large enough to hold all of the columns in the table. For example, if a table is created as follows:

```
CREATE TABLE mytable (lastname   CHAR(100),
                      firstname  CHAR(100),
                      address    CHAR(4000)
                     )
```

the total space required to store a row is the sum of the column sizes, and this exceeds the size of a 4K page. Therefore, this table must be created in a table space with a page size is of at least 8K.

Tables are described in detail in Chapter 7, Working with Database Objects.

> **N O T E**   Once you have created a table space with a given page size, you cannot alter the page size. The only option is to drop and recreate the table space using a different page size.

8.4.3 Extents

An **extent** is a collection of consecutive pages in a table space. For performance reasons, DB2 reads and writes extents of pages rather than single pages to optimize I/O. An extent can only contain pages for one object. For example, DB2 will not allow one page within an extent to belong to table A and another one to index A or table B.

If you are familiar with RAID (redundant array of inexpensive disks) or striped file systems, you understand the concept of **striping**—where data is written to the various underlying disks in pieces. DB2 does the same basic operation within its table spaces. When you create a table space with more than one container, DB2 writes the data to the containers in a round-robin fashion. DB2 fills an extent in one container, then fills an extent in the next container, and so on until it has written an extent in all of the containers in the table space. DB2 will then fill the second extent in each of the containers, and so on.

For example, if you create a table space with four containers, and create a table in that table space, as you add data to the table, the data will be striped across the table space containers as follows: The first extent of pages for the table is placed in the first container (i.e., Container 0). Next, extent number one is written to Container 1, extent number two is written to Container 2, and extent number three is written to Container 3. At this point there is one extent in each of the four containers, so DB2 will start striping the data back at the first extent again. Therefore, extent number four will be written to Container 0, extent number five will be written to Container 1, and so on as more data is added to the table. Figure 8.10 illustrates this.

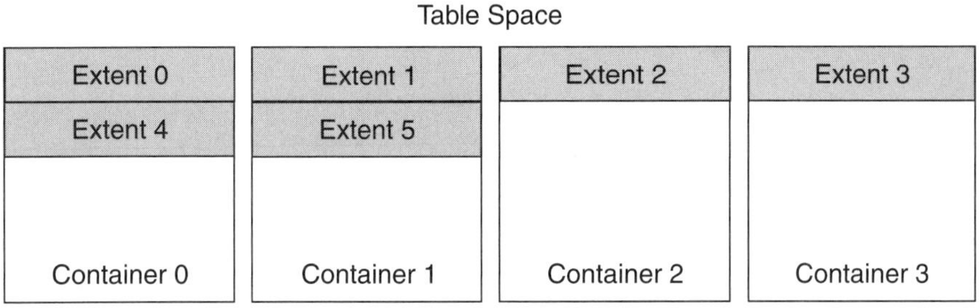

Table Space

Extent 0	Extent 1	Extent 2	Extent 3
Extent 4	Extent 5		
Container 0	Container 1	Container 2	Container 3

Figure 8.10   Table spaces, containers, and extents

> **N O T E**   The first extent (Extent 0) for each object can start in any of the defined containers. Not all objects start in Container 0.

You can control the extent size when you create a table space with the **EXTENTSIZE** clause of the **CREATE TABLESPACE** statement. If you do not explicitly specify the extent size when you create the table space, DB2 uses the default extent size based on the database configuration parameter DFT_EXTENT_SZ.

> **N O T E**   Once you have created a table space with a given extent size, you cannot alter the extent size. The only option is to drop and recreate the table space to use a different extent size.

8.4.4 Creating Table Spaces

You create a table space is with the **CREATE TABLESPACE** statement. Figure 8.11 shows a simplified version of the syntax diagram for this statement.

```
                 .-REGULAR---------------.
>>-CREATE--+-----------------------+---------------------------->
           +-LARGE-----------------+
           | .-SYSTEM-.            |
           '-+--------+---TEMPORARY-'
             '-USER---'
```

Figure 8.11   The CREATE TABLESPACE statement *(continues)*

```
>--TABLESPACE--tablespace-name----------------------------------->

>--+------------------------------------------------------------+-->
   |        .-DATABASE PARTITION GROUP-.                         |
   '-IN--+-------------------------+--db-partition-group-name-'

     .-PAGESIZE--4096-----------.
>--+----------------------------+--------------------------------->
   '-PAGESIZE--integer--+---+-'
                        '-K-'

>--MANAGED BY--+-SYSTEM--| system-containers |-----+------------>
               '-DATABASE--| database-containers |-'

>--+--------------------------------+--------------------------->
   '-EXTENTSIZE--+-number-of-pages-+-'
                 '-integer--+-K-+--'
                            '-M-'

>--+---------------------------------+-------------------------->
   '-PREFETCHSIZE--+-number-of-pages-+-'
                   '-integer--+-K-+--'
                              +-M-+
                              '-G-'

>--+--------------------------------+--------------------------->
   '-BUFFERPOOL--bufferpool-name-'

     .-OVERHEAD--12.67------------------.
>--+----------------------------------+------------------------->
   '-OVERHEAD--number-of-milliseconds-'

     .-FILE SYSTEM CACHING----.
>--+------------------------+----------------------------------->
   '-NO FILE SYSTEM CACHING-'

     .-TRANSFERRATE--0.18------------------.
>--+-------------------------------------+---------------------->
   '-TRANSFERRATE--number-of-milliseconds-'

>--+--------------------------------+-------------------------->< 
   '-DROPPED TABLE RECOVERY--+-ON--+-'
                             '-OFF-'
```

Figure 8.11   The CREATE TABLESPACE statement *(continued)*

To summarize, when you create a table space you must define the following.

- To indicate the type of data that the table space will store, include one of these keywords:
  - REGULAR (the default)
  - LARGE
  - TEMPORARY

- To indicate the type of table space based on how it is managed use:
  - MANAGED BY SYSTEM for SMS table spaces
  - MANAGED BY DATABASE for DMS table spaces
- To indicate the page size to use for all tables and indexes in the table space use:
  - PAGESIZE *integer* (4K is the default)
- To indicate the extent size for the table space use:
  - EXTENTSIZE *number of pages* (the default is determined by the database configuration file parameter DFT_EXTENT_SZ)
- To indicate the name of the buffer pool associated to this table space use:
  - BUFFERPOOL *buffer pool name.* This buffer pool must exist before you create the table and must have the same page size as you specify for the table space. By default, the table space will be associated with the IBMDEFAULTBP buffer pool. You can change this when you create the table space since the page size of the table space must match the page size of the associated buffer pool. If you are using a multi-partitioned database, you also need to tell DB2 in which partition group to create the table space.

In addition, you can optionally specify the following table space characteristics:

- The I/O characteristics of the table spaces and its containers:
  - The overhead, which is the same as the seek time for the disks. The default is 12.67 milliseconds. If you have one kind of disk, then you can usually find this value on the disks or from the manufacturer. If you have a mixture of disks in the table space, you need to calculate the average overhead, seek time, and latency for the disks.
  - The transfer rate for the disks specifies the amount of time (in milliseconds) required for the I/O subsystem to read one page from disk into memory. As with the overhead, if you are using a mixture of disk types, calculate an average value for this parameter.
- The prefetch size for the table space, which indicates the number of pages fetched ahead of time to improve performance. DB2 uses the database configuration file parameter DFT_PREFTECH_SZ if you do not specify this value.
- The database partition group where the table space will be created
- Allow dropped table recovery. If you accidentally drop a table and this option is enabled, you can specify the RECOVER TABLE ON option when you are rolling forward so that the table will not be deleted and you can recover the table's data. This option can only be specified for a REGULAR table space.

By default, the table space will be associated with the IBMDEFAULTBP buffer pool. You can change this when you create the table space since the page size of the table space must match the page size of the associated buffer pool. If you are using a multi-partitioned database, you also need to tell DB2 in which partition group to create the table space.

8.4.5 Container Tags

When you create a table space, DB2 puts a special marker in all of the table space containers to identify the container. This marker is called the **container tag**, and in an SMS table space it is a file named SQLTAG.NAM. In a DMS table space the first extent of each container contains the container tag. This tag identifies the container, its table space, and the database it belongs to. The tag ensures that DB2 will not reuse a device, file, or directory if it is already assigned as a container for another table space.

In previous versions of DB2 the container tag for DMS containers was stored in a single page at the beginning of the container to minimize the space requirements (aka a one-page container tag). Large Storage Area Networks (SANs) and disk arrays using RAID technology have become more popular, and many databases are being created on RAID-protected disks. If DB2 uses a one-page container tag, the beginning and end of the extents in the table space cannot be made to line up with the beginning and end of a stripe on the underlying disks. This causes suboptimal I/O performance since each database I/O operation needs to access more than one disk.

To force DB2 to create the tag on a single page, the registry variable DB2_USE_PAGE_CONTAINER_TAG must be set to ON before creating the table space:

```
db2set DB2_USE_PAGE_CONTAINER_TAG=ON
```

> **NOTE** For databases migrated from Version 7 with page-sized container tags, the tag size will not change regardless of the registry variable setting. DB2 will work fine in this case. A restore will respect the type of the containers and the size of the container tag in the backup image, whereas a redirected restore will respect the registry variable.

8.4.6 SMS Table Spaces

System-managed space (SMS) table spaces use the file system manager to manage the tables and indexes stored within the table space. The only type of container allowed for an SMS table space is a directory, which you specify in the **CREATE TABLESPACE** statement. When you create tables and indexes, DB2 creates a file for every object within the table space inside the directory containers.

Since you cannot add containers to an SMS table space using the **ALTER TABLESPACE** statement, it is very important for you to create the table space on a file system with enough space.

> **NOTE** Although you cannot normally add containers to an SMS table space directly, you can increase the size of the existing file system containers using operating system commands. You can add a container to an SMS table space on a partition where there are no existing containers for the table space using the SYSTEM CONTAINER clause. You can also add a container indirectly, by backing up the database and performing a redirected restore.

8.4.6.1 Creating SMS Table Spaces

You need to use the **CREATE TABLESPACE** statement with the **MANAGED BY SYSTEM** clause to create an SMS table space. You also specify the path for the containers for the table space. For example, the following statement creates an SMS table space *space1* using one directory container *'c:\space1'*:

```
CREATE TABLESPACE space1
   MANAGED BY SYSTEM USING ('c:\space1')
```

Note that the path is included with the **USING** keyword. You can specify this as an absolute or a relative path. The above example uses an absolute path (it completely specifies the location of the directory). This is the same example, but using a relative path:

```
CREATE TABLESPACE space1
   MANAGED BY SYSTEM USING ('space1')
```

A relative path is relative to the database directory (i.e., the SQL*xxxxx* directory) where the database is created. The following statement creates the following directory assuming the active instance is *DB2*, and there is only one database created on the C: drive on Windows:

```
C:\DB2\NODE0000\SQL00001\SPACE1
```

For the instance *db2inst1* with only one database created on /mydata file system on Linux or UNIX, the above command creates the directory:

```
/mydata/db2inst1/NODE0000/SQL00001/space1
```

> **N O T E** If the directory you specify does not exist, DB2 will create it. If the directory does exist, it cannot contain any files or subdirectories

You can create more than one container for the table space as follows:

```
create tablespace space1
managed by system using
('c:\space1',  'd:\space1')
```

or

```
create tablespace space1
managed by system using
('/data1/space1', '/data1/space2')
```

> **N O T E** In the preceding examples you created the containers on the same drive and file system. In practice you should not do this, as this is not an optimal configuration and could cause I/O contention.

If you create a table in an SMS table space, DB2 creates a file for each object, and stores the information for the object in that file. Whenever you create a table it is assigned an object ID. Each of the files that is created for an object associated with the same table will be assigned the same object ID by DB2 if the table is in an SMS table space. This object ID is then used in the file name for the objects in an SMS table space.

If you look inside an SMS table space, you will see several files named SQL*xxxxx*.DAT, SQL*xxxxx*.INX, SQL*xxxxx*.LB, SQL*xxxxx*.LBA, and SQL*xxxxx*.LF. Let's take a look at the catalog table space directory (SQLT0000.0) for the *sales* database you created earlier on Windows. Figure 8.12 provides a partial view of this directory.

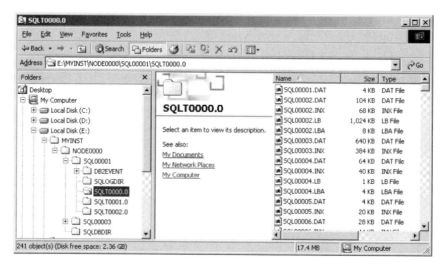

Figure 8.12   The contents of an SMS table space directory

Table 8.4 describes the files based on the file extension.

If the table space has more than one container, DB2 creates the same files in all of the table space's containers.

Table 8.4   The Files Inside an SMS Tablespace Directory Container

Filename Extension	Contents of the File
.DAT	Data objects for the table.
.INX	Normal RID index objects for the table.
.BKM	Block indexes available for multidimensional clustering (MDC) tables.
.LF	Long varchar columns for the table.
.LB	LOB columns for the table. Every .LB file has a .LBA file associated with it.
.LBA	The placement of the LOBs within the .LB file.

8.4.7 DMS Table Spaces

DB2 manages the storage and retrieval of database objects from within the table space with **database-managed space** (**DMS**) table spaces. When you create a DMS table space, the only type of containers that can be specified are files, logical drives, or logical devices (raw devices). With DMS table spaces, when you create tables and indexes DB2 places the pages for these objects in the table space and keeps track of where things are located.

8.4.7.1 Creating DMS Table Spaces

To create a DMS table space, specify **MANAGED BY DATABASE** with the **CREATE TABLESPACE** statement. You then specify the path for the containers as follows:

```
CREATE TABLESPACE tablespace_name
    MANAGED BY DATABASE USING
        (FILE 'file_name' size)
```

or

```
CREATE TABLESPACE tablespace_name
    MANAGED BY DATABASE USING
        (DEVICE 'device_name' size)
```

> **NOTE** If the file already exists, DB2 checks to make sure it is not used as a container for another tablespace. If it is not already used, DB2 will use the file.
>
> If you are using a logical drive or raw logical device, you must first create the drive or device using operating system commands.

8.4.7.1.1 Using Device Containers

If you are building a table space on Linux or UNIX and want to use a raw device, you must first create a logical volume using the tools provided by your operating system. If you are using Windows, create a disk partition that can be used as the container, but you need to remember *not* to format the partition to create a file system.

It is important to note the size of these volumes or partitions, so that when you are creating the table space and assigning the containers to the devices you do not waste space. Since the volume/partition cannot be used for any other purpose, you might as well size the container to use the whole device/partition.

> **NOTE** You can extend or resize the container later to use up the free space if you do leave some space on the logical volumes/disk partitions.

When you create the table space, you can specify the size of the containers in either:

- Number of pages based on the page size for the table space (the default)
- Actual size in KB, MB, or GB

The following are two examples of creating DMS table spaces with device containers.

```
CREATE TABLESPACE ts1 MANAGED BY DATABASE USING
    (DEVICE '/dev/rmydisk1' 20000)

CREATE TABLESPACE ts2 MANAGED BY DATABASE USING
    (DEVICE '\\.\G:' 200MB)
```

8.4.7.1.2 Using File Containers

As with SMS containers, when you specify the name for a file container, you can use either a relative file name or the absolute file name. When you issue the **CREATE TABLESPACE** statement you specify the container name(s) and size(s). If the file exists, DB2 checks to see if the file is the right size and if it is used for any other purpose. If it is the right size and not used for another purpose, DB2 will use the file. If it is not the right size but is not used for any other purpose, DB2 will either expand or shrink the file to make it the right size. If the file does not exist, DB2 will create it with the size that you specfied.

In the same manner as with device containers, you can specify the size of the containers in either:

- Number of pages based on the page size for the table space (the default)
- Actual size in KB, MB, or GB

The following are two examples of creating DMS table spaces with file containers.

```
CREATE TABLESPACE ts1 MANAGED BY DATABASE USING
    (file '/myfile1' 2GB)

CREATE TABLESPACE ts2 MANAGED BY DATABASE USING
    (file 'C:\dbfiles\ts2' 20000)
```

8.4.8 Table Space Considerations in a Multi-Partition Environment

When you create table spaces in a multi-partition database, the table space may be defined on more than one of the database partitions. As discussed earlier, the partition group that you specify for the table space determines on which partitions the table space will be created.

If you are using a cluster of Linux servers with one database partition on each server, and each server has its own set of physical disks, this process is a lot less confusing. However, given the popularity of SAN storage and Network Attached Storage (NAS), and the growing use of large UNIX-based SMP servers, there are many times where the database partitions will be sharing the same underlying disks. In this case it is very important that you take the time to determine a naming convention for your table spaces and containers.

You can specify the container name on each database partition using the ON DBPARTITIONNUM parameter:

```
CREATE TABLESPACE ts2 MANAGED BY DATABASE
     USING (FILE '/dbfiles/ts2c1p0' 2GB) ON DBPARTITIONNUM (0)
     USING (FILE '/dbfiles/ts2c1p1' 2GB) ON DBPARTITIONNUM (1)
     USING (FILE '/dbfiles/ts2c1p2' 2GB) ON DBPARTITIONNUM (2)
     USING (FILE '/dbfiles/ts2c1p3' 2GB) ON DBPARTITIONNUM (3)
```

DB2 also lets you use an expression to automatically add the partition number into the container name so the container names will be unique across the database. This partition expression can be used anywhere within the name of the container and must be preceded by a space. The expression is **$N** and can be used as follows:

```
CREATE TABLESPACE ts2 MANAGED BY DATABASE
     USING (FILE '/dbfiles/ts2c1p $N' 2GB)
```

For the same four-partition database as above, it would create the containers:

> /dbfiles/ts2c1p0 on partition 0
> /dbfiles/ts2c1p1 on partition 1
> /dbfiles/ts2c1p2 on partition 2
> /dbfiles/ts2c1p3 on partition 3

You can also use this expression if the table space has more than one container:

```
CREATE TABLESPACE ts2 MANAGED BY DATABASE
     USING (FILE '/dbfiles/ts2c1p $N' 2GB,
     FILE '/dbfiles/ts2c2p $N' 2GB)
```

For the same four-partition database as above, it would create the containers:

> /dbfiles/ts2c1p0 on partition 0
> /dbfiles/ts2c2p0 on partition 0
> /dbfiles/ts2c1p1 on partition 1
> /dbfiles/ts2c2p1 on partition 1
> /dbfiles/ts2c1p2 on partition 2
> /dbfiles/ts2c2p2 on partition 2
> /dbfiles/ts2c1p3 on partition 3
> /dbfiles/ts2c2p3 on partition 3

8.4.9 Listing Table Spaces

You can get a list of all of the table spaces in your database using the **LIST TABLESPACES** command. This command lists every table space in the database to which you are currently connected, as well as the following information:

- The table space ID (the internal ID that DB2 uses for the table space)
- The table space name
- The table space storage type (DMS or SMS)

- The table space contents (Regular (any data), Large, or Temporary)
- The state of the table space

Figure 8.13 shows an example of the output of the **LIST TABLESPACES** command.

```
                Tablespaces for Current Database

Tablespace ID                    = 0
Name                             = SYSCATSPACE
Type                             = System managed space
Contents                         = Any data
State                            = 0x0000
   Detailed explanation:
     Normal

Tablespace ID                    = 1
Name                             = TEMPSPACE1
Type                             = System managed space
Contents                         = System Temporary data
State                            = 0x0000
   Detailed explanation:
     Normal

Tablespace ID                    = 2
Name                             = USERSPACE1
Type                             = System managed space
Contents                         = Any data
State                            = 0x0000
   Detailed explanation:
     Normal
```

Figure 8.13   Output from the command LIST TABLESPACES

You can get more information about the table space by specifying the **SHOW DETAIL** option. This provides the following additional information about the table space.

- The total number of pages
- The number of usable pages
- The number of used pages
- The number of free pages
- The table space high-water mark (in pages)
- The page size (in bytes)
- The extent size (in bytes)
- The prefetch size (in pages)
- The number of containers in the table space

Figure 8.14 shows an example of the output of the **LIST TABLESPACES SHOW DETAIL** command for the USERSPACE1 table space.

```
Tablespace ID                    = 2
  Name                           = USERSPACE1
  Type                           = Database managed space
  Contents                       = Any data
  State                          = 0x0000
    Detailed explanation:
      Normal
  Total pages                    = 100000
  Useable pages                  = 999968
  Used pages                     = 5740
  Free pages                     = Not applicable
  High water mark (pages)        = Not applicable
  Page size (bytes)              = 4096
  Extent size (pages)            = 32
  Prefetch size (pages)          = 16
  Number of containers           = 1
```

Figure 8.14   Output from the LIST TABLESPACES SHOW DETAIL command

You can use this extra information to examine how full your table spaces are, so you can take action if the table space is getting close to being full.

> **NOTE** For SMS table spaces, the information does *not* indicate how full the table space is since DB2 is not aware of the size of the file system. The Health Monitor, which is part of DB2 in Version 8, does examine the file system size when it looks at the percentage of free space for the table space, so you can use this to make sure your table space is not filling the file system.

You can also get information about the table spaces in a database using the **GET SNAPSHOT FOR TABLESPACES** command. This command provides the following information:

- The table space ID (the internal ID that DB2 uses for the table space)
- The table space storage type (DMS or SMS)
- The table space contents (Regular (any data), Large, or Temporary)
- The page size for the table space
- The extent size for the table space
- The prefetch size for the table space
- The current buffer pool used by the table space
- The buffer pool used at the next database startup
- The table space state
- The size (in pages)
- The number of usable pages
- The number of used pages
- The number of pending free pages

- The number of free pages
- The table space high-water mark
- An indicator of whether rebalancing is occurring (rebalancing is discussed in section 8.4.10.2, Shrinking a Table Space)
- The minimum point in time for roll forward recovery
- The number of table space quiescers
- The number of containers
- Container information such as
  - The container name
  - The container ID
  - The container type
  - The total pages in the container
  - The number of usable pages in the container
  - The stripe set number
  - An indicator of whether the container is accessible
- The table space map for DMS table spaces

Figure 8.15 shows an example of the output of the **GET SNAPSHOT FOR TABLESPACES** command for an SMS table space; Figure 8.16 shows the output for a DMS table space.

```
        Tablespace Snapshot

First database connect timestamp        = 01-07-2005 15:26:42.235201
Last reset timestamp                    =
Snapshot timestamp                      = 01-07-2005 15:47:20.522435
Database name                           = W
Database path                           = C:\DB2\NODE0000\SQL00001\
Input database alias                    = W
Number of accessed tablespaces          = 3

Tablespace name                         = SYSCATSPACE
Tablespace ID                           = 0
Tablespace Type                         = System managed space
Tablespace Content Type                 = Any data
Tablespace Page size (bytes)            = 4096
Tablespace Extent size (pages)          = 32
Tablespace Prefetch size (pages)        = 16
Buffer pool ID currently in use         = 1
Buffer pool ID next startup             = 1
Tablespace State                        = 0x'00000000'
Detailed explanation:
    Normal
  Total number of pages                 = 0
  Number of usable pages                = 0
Number of used pages                  = 0
Minimum Recovery Time                 =
Number of quiescers                   = 0
Number of containers                  = 1
```

Figure 8.15 Output from the command GET SNAPSHOT FOR TABLESPACES for an SMS table space *(continues)*

```
Container Name                              = C:\DB2\NODE0000\SQL00004\SQLT0000.0

Container ID                                = 0
Container Type                              = Path
Total Pages in Container                    = 0
Usable Pages in Container                   = 0
Stripe Set                                  = 0
Container is accessible                     = Yes
```

Figure 8.15   Output from the command GET SNAPSHOT FOR TABLESPACES for an SMS table space *(continued)*

```
Tablespace name                             = TS1
Tablespace ID                               = 3
Tablespace Type                             = Database managed space
Tablespace Content Type                     = Any data
Tablespace Page size (bytes)                = 4096
Tablespace Extent size (pages)              = 32
Tablespace Prefetch size (pages)            = 16
Buffer pool ID currently in use             = 1
Buffer pool ID next startup                 = 1
Tablespace State                            = 0x'00000000'
 Detailed explanation:
   Normal
Total number of pages                       = 5000
Number of usable pages                      = 4960
Number of used pages                        = 160
Number of pending free pages                = 0
Number of free pages                        = 4800
High water mark (pages)                     = 160
Rebalancer Mode                             = No Rebalancing
Minimum Recovery Time                       =
Number of quiescers                         = 0
Number of containers                        = 1
Container Name                              = d:\ts1
    Container ID                            = 0
    Container Type                          = File (extent sized tag)
    Total Pages in Container                = 5000
    Usable Pages in Container               = 4960
    Stripe Set                              = 0
    Container is accessible                 = Yes

 Table space map:
  Range  Stripe Stripe  Max        Max   Start  End   Adj. Containers
  Number Set    Offset  Extent     Page  Stripe Stripe
  [   0] [   0]      0     154      4959      0    154   0    1 (0)
```

Figure 8.16   Output from the command GET SNAPSHOT FOR TABLESPACES for a DMS table space

Table 8.5 summarizes the differences between SMS and DMS table spaces. As you can see, both table space types stripe the extents in a round-robin fashion between the containers. SMS tables spaces grow and shrink as data is added or deleted, while DMS table spaces are preallocated when the table space is created. Both types of table spaces provide very good performance.

Table 8.5   Comparing SMS and DMS Characteristics

Characteristic	SMS	DMS
Striping	Yes.	Yes.
Object management	Operating system using unique file names.	DB2.
Space allocation	Grows/shrinks on demand.	Preallocated.
Ease of administration	Easy.	Average.
Performance	Very Good.	Best. Can achieve up to 5 to 10 percent advantage with raw containers. Index, LOBs, and data for a single table can be spread across table spaces.

8.4.10 Altering a Table Space

You can change the size and other characteristics—such as the prefetch size, overhead, and transfer rate—of both SMS and DMS tables spaces in your databases using the **ALTER TABLESPACE** statement. You can also change buffer pool assigments and bring an offline table space back online. The storage characteristics can only be modified for DMS table spaces.

To change the I/O characteristics for your table spaces, you must first connect to the database, then use the **ALTER TABLESPACE** statement with the parameter you want to change. For example:

```
ALTER TABLESPACE    ts2     PREFETCHSIZE 128
ALTER TABLESPACE    ts1     OVERHEAD     10
ALTER TABLESPACE    mytspc  TRANSFERRATE 100
```

8.4.10.1 Enlarging a Table Space

You can change the amount of space available for your DMS table spaces by adding containers to the table space or by increasing the size of the current containers in the table space.

> **N O T E**   You cannot add or remove containers from SMS table spaces. However, you can add a container to an SMS table space on a partition where there are no existing containers for the table space using the **SYSTEM CONTAINER** clause.

To add a new container to an existing table space, use the **ADD** clause of the **ALTER TABLESPACE** statement. If you do not explicitly tell DB2 at which offset within the table space (aka stripe set) to add the container, DB2 will choose the stripe set based on the size of the existing containers and the new container(s). When you run the **ALTER TABLESPACE** command, DB2 may need to asynchronously rebalance the data in the table space so that it is balanced across the containers evenly. If you do not want DB2 to rebalance the data, which can affect the performance of your system, you can specify the **BEGIN NEW STRIPE SET** clause; this essentially adds the container to the bottom of the table space for use as new data is added.

Let's look at some examples of adding containers to table spaces using the following table space:

```
CREATE TABLESPACE myts MANAGED BY DATABASE USING
    (FILE 'cont0' 50,
    FILE 'cont1' 50,
    FILE 'cont2' 30)
    EXTENTSIZE 10
```

Since each container has a tag that consumes a full extent, there will be a total of four, four, and two extents of available space in the containers respectively, as Figure 8.17 shows logically.

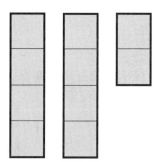

Figure 8.17   Table space with three containers

> **N O T E**   The following examples show containers of different sizes within a table space for the purposes of illustration. For performance reasons it is recommended that containers within a table space are the same size.

If you add a container that is at least large enough to go from the top to the end of the table space, the container will be added at the top of the table space and will then extend stripe zero to the end of the existing table space as follows:

```
ALTER TABLESPACE myts ADD (FILE 'cont3' 60)
```

Figure 8.18 shows the effect of this statement.

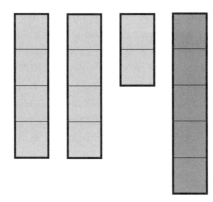

Figure 8.18   Adding a larger container

If you add a new container that is not large enough to go from the top to the bottom of the table space, that is, it is not as large as the largest container, it will be added such that its last extent lines up with the end of the table space, as follows:

```
ALTER TABLESPACE myts ADD (FILE 'cont3' 40)
```

Figure 8.19 shows the effect of this statement.

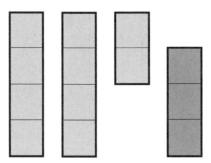

Figure 8.19   Adding a smaller container

If you add multiple containers at the same time, DB2 applies the rules about where to add the container to each container individually, in the order they are added in the **ALTER TABLESPACE** statement. You can add two containers with five and three extents of available space as follows:

```
ALTER TABLESPACE myts ADD (FILE 'cont3a' 60, FILE 'cont3b' 40)
```

Figure 8.20 shows the effect of this statement.

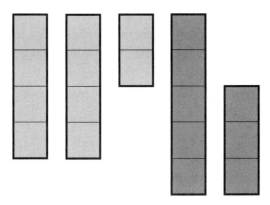

Figure 8.20 Adding two containers of different sizes

If you specify the **BEGIN NEW STRIPE SET** clause when adding a container, the container will be added to the end of the table space. This avoids any rebalance, as the new container will only be used as new data is added to the table space. The statement to use is

```
ALTER TABLESPACE myts ADD (FILE 'cont3' 60) BEGIN NEW STRIPE SET
```

and the effect of the statement is shown in Figure 8.21.

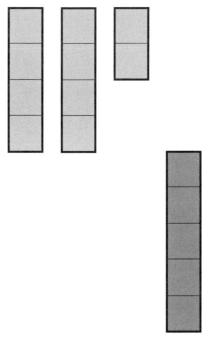

Figure 8.21 Adding a container with a new stripe set

To make the containers in an existing table space bigger, you can either extend them or resize them. The **EXTEND** option increases the container by the size specified, while the **RESIZE** option changes the size of the container to the size specified. You can also use the **RESIZE** option to increase or reduce the size of a container.

Let's continue using the same table space as given earlier to illustrate these options. To recap, the table space was created as follows:

```
CREATE TABLESPACE myts MANAGED BY DATABASE USING
    (FILE 'cont0' 50,
    FILE 'cont1' 50,
    FILE 'cont2' 30)
    EXTENTSIZE 10
```

To increase the size of the third container (that is, *cont2*) to 50 pages like the other containers, you can use either of the following commands:

```
ALTER TABLESPACE myts
    EXTEND (FILE 'cont2' 20)
```

or

```
ALTER TABLESPACE myts
    RESIZE (FILE 'cont2' 50)
```

To increase the size of all the containers to 100 pages, you can use one of the following commands:

```
ALTER TABLESPACE myts
    EXTEND (FILE 'cont0' 50,  FILE 'cont1' 50,  FILE 'cont2' 70)
```

or

```
ALTER TABLESPACE myts
    RESIZE   (FILE 'cont0' 100,
        FILE 'cont1' 100,
        FILE 'cont2' 100)
```

or

```
ALTER TABLESPACE myts
    RESIZE (all containers 100)
```

To increase the size of all of the containers by 100 pages, you can use the command:

```
ALTER TABLESPACE myts
    EXTEND  (all containers 100)
```

8.4.10.2 Shrinking a Table Space

If you find that you have a lot of free space in some of your table spaces, you may be able to free up that space for use by other table spaces or for other file systems on your server. You can reduce the amount of space available for your DMS table spaces by dropping or removing containers from the table space or by reducing the size of the current containers in the table space.

DB2 will not let you remove a container or shrink the existing container(s) if the result would not leave enough space in the table space to hold all of the existing data stored in the table space. Also, DB2 will not **REORG** the data and indexes in the table space to remove free space from within the pages.

8.4.10.2.1 The Table Space High-Water Mark

You also cannot reduce the number of table space containers or shrink the existing containers so that the table space would be smaller than its high-water mark. The **high-water mark** is the first page after the highest page number that has been allocated within the table space. This is not always going to be the same as the number of used pages, because you may have inserted some data, established the table space high-water mark, then deleted some data. The table space will then show these pages where the data was deleted are available for use, but the high-water mark will not be moved down. Figure 8.22 illustrates the concept of the table space high-water mark. Consider the following:

- The table space has 1,000 usable pages and its extent size is 100. Therefore, there will be ten extents in the tablespace.
- By default, Extents 0, 1, and 2 will be used for the table space overhead.
- If you create a table named *org*, Extent 3 will be allocated for its object map, and Extent 4 will be allocated for its table object.
- If you create a table named *dept*, Extent 5 will be allocated for its object map, and Extent 6 will be allocated for its table object.

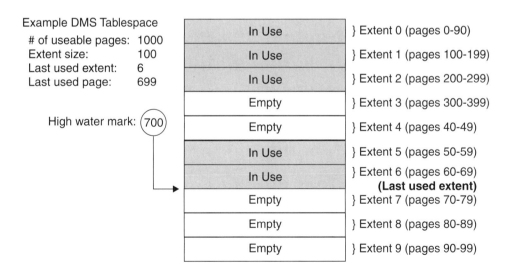

Figure 8.22   The table space high-water mark

- If you drop the table *org*, Extents 3 and 4 will be freed up for reuse by other data and/or objects. There will be four extents in use, which means that the total number of pages used by the tables would be 400.
- The highest allocated page number in this tablespace is 699, which means that the high-water mark is 700 (699 + 1).

DB2 will not allow you to drop a container or reduce the size of the containers if you are attempting to remove more extents from the table space than are above the table space high water mark. In this example, there are three extents above the high water mark, so you can reduce the table space by a maximum of three extents.

Let's step through some other examples. For these, assume that the high-water mark is not an issue and that there is enough free space available in the table space to allow the operation to complete successfully.

Assume that you have a table space created with the following command:

```
CREATE TABLESPACE myts MANAGED BY DATABASE USING
    (FILE 'cont0' 250,
    FILE 'cont1' 300,
    FILE 'cont2' 200)
    EXTENTSIZE 10
```

To decrease the size of the third container (*cont2*) to be only 150 pages, you can use either of the following commands:

```
ALTER TABLESPACE myts
    RESIZE (FILE 'cont2' 150)
```

or

```
ALTER TABLESPACE myts
    REDUCE (FILE 'cont2' 50)
```

To remove the third container (*cont2*) from the table space, you can use the command:

```
ALTER TABLESPACE myts
    DROP (FILE 'cont2')
```

To decrease the size of the first and second containers to make them both 200 pages, you can use either of the following methods:

```
ALTER TABLESPACE myts
    RESIZE (FILE 'cont0' 200)
```

plus

```
ALTER TABLESPACE myts
    RESIZE (FILE 'cont1' 200)
```

or

```
ALTER TABLESPACE myts
    RESIZE (FILE 'cont0' 200, file 'cont1' 200)
```

It is better to call the **ALTER TABLESPACE** statement once and specify both of the containers that you want to change rather than doing this in two steps. If you do this in two steps like in the first example, DB2 needs to complete a rebalance of the data after the first **ALTER TABLESPACE** command, and another one after the second **ALTER TABLESPACE** command. If you do this with one **ALTER TABLESPACE** command, DB2 only needs to rebalance the data once, saving time and causing less impact on the system.

When you alter a table space to either add or remove space, the table space may need to be rebalanced. In Version 8, the table space snapshot has been enhanced to include information about any table space rebalancing that may be occurring. If a rebalance is occurring, the rebalancer mode field will be either forward (starting from page zero and working down through the table space), or reverse (starting at the end of the table space and working up through the table space). The snapshot will also show when the rebalance was started and how many extents in the table space still need to be moved as part of the rebalance process. The following is part of the table space snapshot that shows this information.

```
High water mark (pages)                  = 21771
Rebalancer Mode                          = Reverse
    Start Time                           = 01-16-2004 11:02:33.000000
    Restart Time                         = 01-16-2004 11:02:33.000000
    Number of extents processed          = 1102
    Number of extents remaining          = 484
    Last extent moved                    = 1160
```

8.4.10.3 Dropping a Table Space

While an SMS table space will not consume any space unless there are objects (i.e., tables and indexes) in the table space, a DMS table space will continue to hold all of its allocated space. If you create a table space and find that you did not create any objects in the table space, it is good practice to drop the table space.

Dropping a table space can also be a very fast and efficient method for dropping tables. If you drop a table space and there are tables in the table space, then DB2 will drop the tables as well, as long as there are no objects for the tables in other table spaces (i.e., the data object for the table is in one table space while the index object is in another table space). When you drop a table space this way, DB2 does not log all of the row and page deletions as it does for a drop table operation; therefore, this can be a much more efficient method to drop a table, especially if you have only that table defined in the table space.

To drop a table space you use the **DROP TABLESPACE** statement:

```
DROP TABLESPACE myts
```

This removes all entries for the table space from the system catalogs as well as its entries in the table spaces file, and it drops all objects defined wholly within the table space.

8.5 BUFFER POOLS

The database buffer pools are the area where all of the work in a database really happens. All regular data and index keys are read, scanned, updated, inserted, and deleted within the database buffer pools.

The database buffer pool area is a piece of real memory that is used by DB2 to temporarily store (cache) the regular data and index pages when they are read from disk to be scanned or modified. The buffer pool area improves the performance of the database, since the pages can be accessed much more quickly from memory than from disk.

When you connect to a database, the database buffer pools (along with the lock list, database heap, and so on) are allocated in memory. When you (and anyone else using the database) disconnect all applications from the database, this memory is freed back to the operating system.

If your applications frequently connect to and disconnect from the database, you should consider activating the database (using the **ACTIVATE DATABASE** command) so that the buffer pools and all database-related memory remain allocated. This eliminates the overhead of allocating all of this memory each time an application connects to the database. When you then want to "close" the database, use the **DEACTIVATE DATABASE** command.

8.5.1 Creating Buffer Pools

When you create a database, DB2 creates a default buffer pool named IBMDEFAULTBP. On Linux and Windows the default buffer pool is 250 pages or 1MB, while on UNIX the default buffer pool is 1,000 pages or 4MB. You cannot drop the default buffer pool, but you can change its size using the **ALTER BUFFERPOOL** statement.

You can also create additional buffer pools if your data and workloads can benefit from isolating the different database objects into their own separate work areas. You can use the **CREATE BUFFERPOOL** statement to create a new buffer pool and can specify the following information with this statement:

- The name of the buffer pool. This name cannot already be used within the database and cannot begin with the characters SYS or IBM.
- Whether to create the buffer pool immediately or wait until the database is stopped and restarted.
  - If you tell DB2 to create the buffer pool immediately but there is not enough memory available, DB2 will instead create it deferred.
  - The default option is immediate.
- The database partition group on which to create the buffer pool. If you do not specify a database partition group, the buffer pool will be created on all partitions.
- The page size used for the buffer pool. The default page size is 4K or 4096 bytes.
- The size of the buffer pool, specified in the number of pages.
  - In a partitioned database, this will be the default size for all database partitions where the buffer pool exists.

- The **EXCEPT ON DBPARTITIONNUMS** clause allows the buffer pool to have different sizes on the different database partitions.
- The number of pages to be created in the block-based area of the buffer pool. This area cannot be more than 98 percent of the total buffer pool size. Specifying a value of 0 will disable block I/O for the buffer pool.
- The number of pages within a given block in the block-based area of the buffer pool. The block size must be between 2 and 256 pages; the default value is 32 pages.
- Whether buffer pool victim pages can be copied to extended storage, a secondary cache between the buffer pools, and disk. Extended storage is more efficient than retrieving data from disk but less efficient than retrieving data from the buffer pool, so this is not applicable to 64-bit environments.

> **N O T E** The page size and buffer pool name cannot be altered once it has been defined for a buffer pool.

Enabling block-based I/O by setting NUMBLOCKPAGES to a value greater than zero can help performance for applications that perform a lot of sequential prefetching.

> **N O T E** NUMBLOCKPAGES does not need to be set to allow prefetching to occur.

The following are a couple limitations that you need to be aware of.

- You cannot specify both a block-based area in the buffer pool and tell it to use extended storage.
- You cannot specify a block-based area in the buffer pool if the buffer pool is set up to support Address Windowing Extensions (AWE) on Windows. If you tell the buffer pool to use both AWE support and block-based I/O, then block-based I/O support will be disabled automatically.

To examine buffer pools in more detail, let's look at a few examples. Consider a database that is used for an online Web-based ordering application. Performance is fine most of the time, but once a week management runs some reports that cause the system to slow down. In examining the reports you notice that they are large, multiple joins that create a large temporary table. To isolate the creation of the temporary table from overwhelming the buffer pool, you can create a 10,000-page buffer pool dedicated to the temporary table space as follows:

```
CREATE BUFFERPOOL tempbp SIZE 10000
```

You then need to tell the table space to use the buffer pool:

```
ALTER TABLESPACE tempspace1 BUFFERPOOL tempbp
```

As mentioned earlier, the default page size for a database is 4K. If you want to create a table that is more than 4005 bytes, you need to create a table space with a larger page size. But before you can create this table space, you need to create a buffer pool with the same page size. For this example, assume that a 16K page size is best for this table.

```
CREATE BUFFERPOOL bp16k SIZE 100000 PAGESIZE 16K
```

You can then create the table space as follows:

```
CREATE TABLESPACE tspc16k PAGESIZE 16K BUFFERPOOL bp16k
```

If you know that this table will be scanned a lot and that it would benefit from sequential prefetch, you could set aside a portion of the buffer pool for block-based I/O as follows:

```
CREATE BUFFERPOOL bp16k
    SIZE 100000
    PAGESIZE 16K
    NUMBLOCKPAGES 24000
    BLOCKSIZE 256
```

If you specify a block size that is larger than 98 percent of the buffer pool size, you will get the following error.

```
SQL20150N The number of block pages for a buffer pool is too large for the size of the
buffer pool. SQLSTATE=54052
```

> **N O T E** If you are using block-based I/O, you should ensure that the block size you set is set based on the table space's extent size.

If you are creating a buffer pool in a multi-partition database, and the table space you are creating the buffer pool for is in a database partition group that is not defined on all database partitions, you can specify in which partition group the buffer pool will be created:

```
CREATE BUFFERPOOL bp16k
    SIZE 100000
    PAGESIZE 16K
    NUMBLOCKPAGES 24000
    BLOCKSIZE 256
    DATABASEPARTITIONGROUP pg16k
```

If you are creating a buffer pool in a multi-partition database and you want the buffer pool to be sized larger on some database partitions, you can specify these partitions and their sizes as follows:

```
CREATE BUFFERPOOL bp16k
    SIZE 100000
    PAGESIZE 16K
    NUMBLOCKPAGES 24000
    BLOCKSIZE 256
    EXCEPT ON DBPARTITIONNUMS 1,2,3 SIZE 200000
```

In this case you can also use the commands:

```
CREATE BUFFERPOOL bp16k
    SIZE 100000
    PAGESIZE 16K
    NUMBLOCKPAGES 24000
    BLOCKSIZE 256
    EXCEPT ON DBPARTITIONNUMS 1 TO 3 SIZE 200000
```

or

```
CREATE BUFFERPOOL bp16k
    SIZE 100000
    PAGESIZE 16K
    NUMBLOCKPAGES 24000
    BLOCKSIZE 256
    EXCEPT ON DBPARTITIONNUM 1 SIZE 200000
    EXCEPT ON DBPARTITIONNUM 2 SIZE 200000
    EXCEPT ON DBPARTITIONNUM 3 SIZE 200000
```

8.5.2 Maximizing Buffer Pool Size on Windows

When working with Windows 2000, the total addressable memory can be up to 64GB. Therefore, the maximum buffer pool sizes that can be created on Windows equals 64GB minus the memory used by the operating system and other DB2 memory allocations, assuming that the server is dedicated to DB2. The support for large memory addressing on Windows is provided by AWE. Through AWE, Windows 2000 Advanced Server provides support for up to 8GB of memory addressing, while the Windows 2000 Data Center Server provides support for up to 64GB of memory.

For the complete details on how to use AWE with DB2, refer to Chapter 15, The DB2 Memory Model.

8.5.3 Altering Buffer Pools

You can change some of the attributes of a buffer pool using the **ALTER BUFFERPOOL** statement. DB2 allows you to change the following:

- Size
- Database partition group
- Block-based area
- Block size
- Enabling or disabling extended storage

Given a buffer pool created with the statement:

```
CREATE BUFFERPOOL bp16k
    SIZE 100000
    PAGESIZE 16K
    NUMBLOCKPAGES 24000
    BLOCKSIZE 256
    DATABASEPARTITIONGROUP PG16K
```

to make the buffer pool twice as large, you would use the statement:

```
ALTER BUFFERPOOL bp16k
    SIZE 200000
```

Notice that since you did not want to change the block-based area size or the block size, you did not specify these options in the **ALTER BUFFERPOOL** statement.

To make the size of the block-based area 32,000 pages instead of 24,000 pages, you would use the statement:

```
ALTER BUFFERPOOL bp16k
    NUMBLOCKPAGES 32000
```

To allocate this buffer pool also on the partitions in the database partition group *pg1234*, use the statement:

```
ALTER BUFFERPOOL bp16k
    DATABASEPARTITIONGROUP pg1234
```

8.5.4 Dropping Buffer Pools

You will not be able to drop any buffer pools that are associated with a table space. Before you can drop the buffer pool you will need to associate the table space with a different buffer pool using the **ALTER TABLESPACE** statement.

Once there are no longer any table spaces associated with the buffer pool, you can drop the buffer pool using the **DROP BUFFERPOOL** statement. This will release the memory back to the operating system for use by other DB2-related buffers and heaps, or for other application memory requests.

To drop the buffer pool BP16K, use the statement:

```
DROP BUFFERPOOL bp16k
```

8.6 CASE STUDY

Let's start by creating a database named *mydb* on your Windows server's C: drive as follows:

```
CREATE DATABASE mydb ON c:
```

Your server was configured with four physical hard drives that are dedicated to your database, so you want to create a new table space that will use these drives. Since DMS table spaces are more flexible, you have decided to use DMS file containers for the table space. Once you have formatted the four drives using the operating system tools and given them the labels G, H, I, and J drives, you are ready to create the table space.

First you need to connect to the database:

```
CONNECT TO mydb
```

You can then create the table space:

```
CREATE TABLESPACE myts MANAGED BY DATABASE USING
    (FILE 'g:\ts1' 50000,
    FILE 'h:\ts1' 50000,
    FILE 'i:\ts1' 50000,
    FILE 'j:\ts1' 50000)
```

To optimize access to data in this table space you can add a new buffer pool, and then assign the *myts* table space to use the buffer pool:

```
CREATE BUFFERPOOL mytsbp SIZE 50000
ALTER TABLESPACE myts BUFFERPOOL mytsbp
```

You have a table with a large number of columns that will not fit the default 4K page, so you will need to create a new table space with a larger page size. However, before you can create the table space you must first create a buffer pool with the page size you intend to use for the table space:

```
CREATE BUFFERPOOL my16kbp SIZE 50000 PAGESIZE 16K
CREATE TABLESPACE myts16k
    PAGESIZE 16k
    MANAGED BY DATABASE USING
    (FILE 'g:\ts16k' 50000,
    FILE 'h:\ts16k' 50000,
    FILE 'i:\ts16k' 50000,
    FILE 'j:\ts16k' 50000)
    BUFFERPOOL my16kbp
```

To create the table you need to specify the 16K page size table space:

```
CREATE TABLE foo
    (c1 VARCHAR(2500),
     c2 VARCHAR(2500)
    ) IN myts16K
```

You execute the command

```
CREATE TABLE foo2
    (c1 VARCHAR(250),
     c2 VARCHAR(250)
    )
```

and DB2 puts the table in the first user-created table space, *myts*. You can verify this by querying the SYSCAT.TABLES catalog table:

```
SELECT tabname, tbspace FROM syscat.tables
    WHERE tabname='FOO2'
```

You want to create another table and store any indexes defined on the table in a different table space, so you must specify the data and index table spaces when you create the table. You first need to create the index table space.

```
CREATE TABLESPACE INXts16k
    PAGESIZE 16K
    MANAGED BY DATABASE USING
    (FILE 'g:\INX16k' 500,
```

```
FILE 'h:\INX16k' 500,
FILE 'i:\INX16k' 500,
FILE 'j:\INX16k' 500)
BUFFERPOOL my16kbp
```

You can then create the table and specify that the data will be stored in the table space *myts16k*, and the index in the table space will be *INXts16k*.

```
CREATE TABLE staff
    (empid INT,
    fname VARCHAR(30),
    lname VARCHAR(30),
    deptid INT
    )
    IN myts16K
    INDEX IN INXts16K
```

When you now create any indexes on the staff table, they will be placed in the *INXts16K* table space.

```
CREATE INDEX staffx ON staff (empid)
```

As you can see above, the index table space only has 2,000 pages of space defined. Since you anticipate having a large number of rows in this table, you enlarge the table space:

```
ALTER TABLESPACE INXts16k EXTEND (ALL CONTAINERS 40000)
```

8.7 SUMMARY

In this chapter you learned about the DB2 storage model, a topic that is closely related to the database objects discussed in Chapter 7, Working with Database Objects. This chapter described databases and the various components that are part of databases. Table spaces and containers define the logical and physical storage of your tables and indexes, while partition groups are used to give you control over where your table spaces will be stored in a multi-partition database.

As data is inserted into your tables, pages are also written to the table's data and index objects. When the table space has multiple containers, DB2 will fill these on a round-robin basis among the extents, filling an extent at a time. When you then access your data, it must first be read into the database's buffer pool(s) to be scanned and read. You can assign table spaces to specific buffer pools, and give these buffer pools different sizes to optimize your performance.

8.8 REVIEW QUESTIONS

1. What is the largest number of partitions supported by DB2?
2. What is the name of the buffer pool created automatically by DB2 in every database?
3. For the table created as:

```
CREATE TABLE mytable (col1   VARCHAR(100),
                      Col2   int,
                      Col3   VARCHAR(9000)
                      )
```

what is the minimum page size required?

4. What type of object is stored in the DB2 file *SQL00018.DAT*?
5. What command can be used to determine the amount of free space in a table space?
6. Which type of table space is preallocated when it is created?
7. Which type of table space can grow and shrink as tables grow and shrink within it?
8. When can a user-defined table space not be dropped?
9. What is the main reason for creating a block-based area in your buffer pool?
10. Which command can be used to determine if a rebalance is occurring due to the addition or removal of a container in the table space?
11. Which of the following page sizes is not supported by DB2?
    A. 2K
    B. 4K
    C. 8K
    D. 16K
    E. 32K
12. If a database has 12 table spaces all using an 8K page size, what is the minimum number of buffer pools that must exist in the database?
    A. 1
    B. 2
    C. 8
    D. 12
13. Given the following db2nodes.cfg file:

```
0 mysrv1 0
1 mysrv1 1
2 mysrv2 0
3 mysrv2 1
```

    what is the largest table that can exist in a database created in this instance?
    A. 64GB
    B. 256GB
    C. 1TB
    D. 2TB
14. Given the following db2nodes.cfg file for the instance *inst1*:

```
0 mysrv1 0
1 mysrv1 1
2 mysrv2 0
3 mysrv2 1
```

    and the command **create database foo on /data**, what directories will be created under the /data directory?
    A. NODE0002 and NODE0003
    B. NODE0000 and NODE0001
    C. DB2
    D. inst1

15. Given the following db2nodes.cfg file for the instance *inst1*:

```
0 mysrv1 0
1 mysrv1 1
2 mysrv2 0
3 mysrv2 1
```

and the command **create database foo on /data**, what directories will be created under the /data/inst1 directory on server *mysrv2*?

A. NODE0002 and NODE0003

B. NODE0000 and NODE0001

C. NODE0002

D. NODE0000, NODE0001, NODE0002, and NODE0003

16. Given a newly created nonpartitioned instance on Windows named *DB2* and the command **create database foo on C:**, how many directories will be created under the subdirectory C:\DB2\NODE0000\SQL00001?

A. 1

B. 2

C. 3

D. 4

E. 5

17. Given the following sequence of events:

1. Create database *sample* on C:.

2. Create database *sales* on C:.

3. Create database *test* on C:.

4. **drop db sales**

5. **create db my_sales**

what subdirectory will the database *my_sales* be located in?

A. SQL00001

B. SQL00002

C. SQL00003

D. SQL00004

18. Given the following db2nodes.cfg file for the instance *inst1*:

```
0 mysrv1 0
1 mysrv1 1
2 mysrv2 0
3 mysrv2 1
```

and the following sequence of commands:

```
telnet myserv2
create database foo on /data
```

which of the following is the catalog partition for the database *foo*?

A. Partition 0

B. Partition 1

C. Partition 2

D. Partition 3

19. To create the table space *TS1* successfully in the database *sample*, place the following steps in the correct order:

    1. `CREATE TABLESPACE ts1 PAGESIZE 16K BUFFERPOOL bp1`

    2. `CONNECT TO sample`

    3. `CREATE BUFFERPOOL bp1 SIZE 100000 PAGESIZE 16K`

  A. 1, 2, 3

  B. 3, 2, 1

  C. 2, 1, 3

  D. 2, 3, 1

20. Given a database with six partitions, which of the following statements will create a buffer pool with a size of 100MB on partitions 1, 2, 3, 4, and 5, and a size of 150MB on partition 0?

  A. `CREATE BUFFERPOOL BP1`

      `SIZE 100MB on all DBPARTITIONNUMS`

      `except DBPARTITIONNUM 0 size 150MB`

  B. `CREATE BUFFERPOOL BP1`

      `SIZE 100MB on DBPARTITIONNUMS 1,2,3,4,5`

      `150MB on DBPARTITIONNUM 0`

  C. `CREATE BUFFERPOOL BP1`

      `SIZE 150MB`

      `except on DBPARTITIONNUMS 1,2,3,4,5 size 100MB`

  D. `CREATE BUFFERPOOL BP1`

      `SIZE 100MB on DBPARTITIONNUMS 1,2,3,4,5`

      `SIZE 150MB on DBPARTITIONNUM 0`

## CHAPTER 9

Leveraging the Power of SQL

Structured Query Language (SQL) lets users access and manipulate data in relational database management systems. Now that you have learned about the fundamentals of DB2, this chapter shows you how to leverage the power of SQL to obtain and update data that is stored in DB2 databases. The examples provided in this chapter use the *sample* database. Chapter 8, The DB2 Storage Model, describes the *sample* database in more detail.

In this chapter you will learn about:

- The **SELECT** SQL statement to query data
- The **INSERT**, **UPDATE**, and **DELETE** SQL statements to modify data
- Recursive SQL statements
- Select query data that just got inserted, updated, or deleted in the same SQL statement
- The **MERGE** SQL statement to combine insert, update, or delete operations in one statement

> **NOTE** If you are following the examples in this chapter using the Command Line Processor (CLP), the Command Window, or the Command Editor, these tools have autocommit enabled by default, so the changes you make will be stored permanently on disk. Refer to Chapter 4, Using the DB2 Tools, for more information.

9.1 QUERYING DB2 DATA

You use the **SELECT** statement to query tables or views from a database. At a minimum, the statement contains a **SELECT** clause and a **FROM** clause. The following are two examples of a

SELECT statement. This first example uses the wildcard symbol (*) to indicate that all columns from the *employee* table are selected:

```
SELECT * FROM employee;
```

In this example, the column names are specified in the **SELECT** statement:

```
SELECT empno, firstnme, lastname FROM employee;
```

9.1.1 Derived Columns

When data is retrieved from a table using the **SELECT** clause, you can derive new columns based on other columns. Figure 9.1 illustrates this: the column *totalpay* is derived by adding the *salary* and *comm* columns.

```
SELECT empno, firstnme, lastname, (salary + comm) AS totalpay
  FROM employee

EMPNO  FIRSTNME     LASTNAME         TOTALPAY
------ ------------ ---------------- ------------
000010 CHRISTINE    HAAS                 4320.00
000020 MICHAEL      THOMPSON            44550.00
000030 SALLY        KWAN                41310.00
000050 JOHN         GEYER               43389.00
000060 IRVING       STERN               34830.00
. . .
```

Figure 9.1   Example of a derived column

9.1.2 The SELECT COUNT Statement

The **SELECT COUNT** statement lets you get a row count of the result set. For example, the SQL statement in Figure 9.2 returns the number of rows in the *sales* table whose *region* column has the value *Quebec*. In this case, there are 12 records that match this criteria.

```
SELECT COUNT(*)
  FROM sales
 WHERE region = 'Quebec'

1
-----------
         12
  1 record(s) selected.
```

Figure 9.2   Example of a SELECT COUNT statement

9.1.3 The **SELECT DISTINCT** Statement

To eliminate duplicate rows in a result set, use the **DISTINCT** keyword in the **SELECT** statement. The SQL statement in Figure 9.3 selects the distinct values of the *region* column from the *sales* table.

```
SELECT DISTINCT region FROM sales

REGION
---------------
Manitoba
Ontario-North
Ontario-South
Quebec
   4 record(s) selected.
```

Figure 9.3   Example of a SELECT DISTINCT statement

You can also use the **DISTINCT** keyword with the **SELECT COUNT** statement. For example, the SQL statement in Figure 9.4 returns the number of distinct regions in the *sales* table.

```
SELECT COUNT (DISTINCT region) FROM sales

1
-----------
          4

  1 record(s) selected.
```

Figure 9.4   Example of a SELECT COUNT DISTINCT statement

The output shows that there are four distinct regions in the *sales* table. This value agrees with the **SELECT DISTINCT region FROM sales** result obtained in Figure 9.3.

9.1.4 DB2 Special Registers

DB2 **special registers** are memory registers that allow DB2 to provide information to an application about its environment. They can be referenced in SQL statements. The most commonly used special registers are listed in Table 9.1. For a complete list of DB2 special registers, refer to the *DB2 UDB SQL Reference Guide*.

To display the value of a special register, use the following statement:

```
VALUES special_register
```

Table 9.1   DB2 Special Registers

DB2 Special Registers	Descriptions
CURRENT DATE	A date based on the time-of-day clock at the database server. If this register is referenced more than once in a single statement, the value returned will be the same for all references.
CURRENT ISOLATION	Identifies the isolation level for any dynamic SQL statements issued within the current session.
CURRENT LOCK TIMEOUT	Specifies the number of seconds that an application will wait to obtain a lock.
CURRENT PACKAGE PATH	Identifies the path to be used when resolving references to packages.
CURRENT PATH	Identifies the SQL path used to resolve procedure, functions, and data type references for dynamically prepared SQL statements. The value of this special register is a list of one or more schema names.
CURRENT SCHEMA	Identifies the schema name used to qualify unqualified database objects in dynamic SQL statements. The default value is the authorization ID of the current user. This special register can be modified using the **SET CURRENT SCHEMA** statement.
CURRENT TIME	A time based on the time-of-day clock at the database server. If this register is referenced more than once in a single statement, the value returned will be the same for all references.
CURRENT TIMESTAMP	A timestamp based on the time-of-day clock at the database server. If this register is referenced more than once in a single statement, the value returned will be the same for all references.
SESSION_USER	Specifies the authorization ID to be used for the current session. This is the same as the USER special register.
SYSTEM_USER	Specifies the authorization ID of the user who connected to the database.
USER	Specifies the runtime authorization ID used to connect to the database.

For example, to display the value of the CURRENT TIMESTAMP special register, issue:

```
VALUES CURRENT TIMESTAMP
```

SQL also supports expressions using DB2 special registers. Figure 9.5 uses the CURRENT DATE register to derive the *retiredate* column.

Some of the special registers are updatable. For example, to change the value of the CURRENT ISOLATION special register to RR (Repeatable Read), issue:

```
SET CURRENT ISOLATION RR
```

```
SELECT empno, firstnme, lastname
     , (salary + comm) AS totalpay
     , CURRENT DATE AS retiredate
  FROM employee

EMPNO  FIRSTNME      LASTNAME          TOTALPAY      RETIREDATE
------ ------------  ----------------  ------------  ----------
000010 CHRISTINE     HAAS                 4320.00 04/01/2005
000020 MICHAEL       THOMPSON            44550.00 04/01/2005
000030 SALLY         KWAN                41310.00 04/01/2005
000050 JOHN          GEYER               43389.00 04/01/2005
000060 IRVING        STERN               34830.00 04/01/2005
. . .
```

Figure 9.5 Example of using DB2 special registers in a SELECT statement

9.1.5 Scalar and Column Functions

Invoking a function against the column values is also very useful. Consider the following example where you want to obtain the name of the day for each employee's hire date. You can use the **DAYNAME** built-in function supplied by DB2 as shown in Figure 9.6.

```
SELECT empno, firstnme, lastname
     , (salary + comm) AS totalpay
     , DAYNAME(hiredate) AS dayname
  FROM employee

EMPNO  FIRSTNME      LASTNAME          TOTALPAY      DAYNAME
------ ------------  ----------------  ------------  ------------
000010 CHRISTINE     HAAS                 4320.00 Friday
000020 MICHAEL       THOMPSON            44550.00 Wednesday
000030 SALLY         KWAN                41310.00 Saturday
000050 JOHN          GEYER               43389.00 Wednesday
000060 IRVING        STERN               34830.00 Friday
. . .
```

Figure 9.6 Example of a scalar function

The function **DAYNAME** used in Figure 9.6 is called a scalar function. A **scalar function** takes input values and returns a single value. Another type of function, called a **column function**, operates on the values of an entire column. The example in Figure 9.7 shows how to calculate the average values of the *salary* column.

The **AVG** column function, which is a built-in function, calculates the average of all the salary values in the employee table. Notice that the **DECIMAL** function is also used; this casts the average result to a decimal representation with a precision of 9, and scale of 2.

```
SELECT DECIMAL( AVG(salary), 9, 2 ) AS avgsalary
  FROM employee

AVGSALARY
-----------
  25658.28
  1 record(s) selected.
```

Figure 9.7   Example of a column function

9.1.6 The CAST Expression

There are many occasions where a value with a given data type needs to be cast to a different data type. For example, when manipulating data using the **DATE** and **TIMESTAMP** data types, **TIMESTAMP** might need to be cast to **DATE**. Figure 9.8 illustrates such an example.

```
SELECT CURRENT TIMESTAMP, CAST(CURRENT TIMESTAMP AS DATE)
  FROM SYSIBM.SYSDUMMY1

1                                2
-------------------------- ----------
2005-04-01-17.00.24.637001 04/01/2005

  1 record(s) selected.
```

Figure 9.8   Example of a CAST expression

9.1.7 The WHERE clause

For better performance, you should always write your SQL statements so that only the required data is returned. One way to achieve this is to limit the number of columns to be retrieved by explicitly specifying the column names in the **SELECT** statement (as illustrated in previous examples). The other way is to limit the number of rows to be retrieved using the **WHERE** clause. Figure 9.9 illustrates an example of a **SELECT** statement that returns employees who are managers with a salary greater than $1,000.

```
SELECT empno, firstnme, lastname
  FROM employee
  WHERE salary > 1000
    AND job = 'MANAGER'

EMPNO  FIRSTNME      LASTNAME
------ ------------- ----------------
000020 MICHAEL       THOMPSON
000030 SALLY         KWAN
```

Figure 9.9   Example of a WHERE clause *(continues)*

```
000050 JOHN          GEYER
000060 IRVING        STERN
000070 EVA           PULASKI
000090 EILEEN        HENDERSON
000100 THEODORE      SPENSER
   7 record(s) selected.
```

Figure 9.9   Example of a WHERE clause *(continued)*

9.1.8 Using FETCH FIRST *n* ROWS ONLY

Sometimes you may want to obtain just the first few rows from the result set. Use the **FETCH FIRST *n* ROWS ONLY** clause of the **SELECT** statement to accomplish this. For example, to limit only three rows to be returned from the example illustrated in Figure 9.9, use the statement shown in Figure 9.10.

```
SELECT empno, firstnme, lastname
  FROM employee
 WHERE workdept > 'A0'
   AND job = 'MANAGER'
 FETCH FIRST 3 ROWS ONLY

EMPNO  FIRSTNME     LASTNAME
------ ------------ ---------------
000020 MICHAEL      THOMPSON
000030 SALLY        KWAN
000050 JOHN         GEYER
   3 record(s) selected.
```

Figure 9.10   Example of FETCH FIRST *n* ROWS ONLY

9.1.9 The LIKE Predicate

The **LIKE** predicate lets you search for patterns in character string columns. For example, the SQL statement in Figure 9.11 returns all the rows for employees whose last name starts with the letter M in the *employee* table.

```
SELECT empno, firstnme, lastname FROM employee
 WHERE lastname LIKE 'M%' OR workdept LIKE 'D2_'

EMPNO  FIRSTNME     LASTNAME         WORKDEPT
------ ------------ ---------------- --------
000230 JAMES        JEFFERSON        D21
000260 SYBIL        JOHNSON          D21

   2 record(s) selected.
```

Figure 9.11   Example of a LIKE predicate

In SQL, the percent sign (%) is a wildcard character that represents zero or more characters. It can be used any place in the search string, and as many times as you need it.

The other wildcard character used with the **LIKE** predicate is the underline character (_). This character represents one and only one character. In Figure 9.11, it matches items in *workdept* that have strings exactly three characters long, with the first two characters of *D2*.

9.1.10 The BETWEEN Predicate

The **BETWEEN** predicate lets you search for all the rows whose value falls between the values it indicates. For example, the SQL statement in Figure 9.12 returns all the rows from the employee table whose salary is between $40,000 and $50,000.

```
SELECT firstnme, lastname, salary FROM employee
WHERE salary BETWEEN 40000 AND 50000

FIRSTNME      LASTNAME           SALARY
------------  ----------------   ----------
MICHAEL       THOMPSON             41250.00
JOHN          GEYER                40175.00
VINCENZO      LUCCHESSI            46500.00
   3 record(s) selected.
```

Figure 9.12   Example of a BETWEEN predicate

9.1.11 The IN Predicate

The **IN** predicate lets you search rows based on a set of values. The SQL statement in Figure 9.13 returns all the rows from the *sales* table whose value in the *sales_date* column is either *12/31/1995* or *03/29/1996*.

```
SELECT * FROM sales
WHERE sales_date IN ('12/31/1995', '03/29/1996')

SALES_DATE SALES_PERSON      REGION            SALES
---------- ----------------  ----------------  ----------
12/31/1995 LUCCHESSI         Ontario-South           1
12/31/1995 LEE               Ontario-South           3
12/31/1995 LEE               Quebec                  1
12/31/1995 LEE               Manitoba                2
12/31/1995 GOUNOT            Quebec                  1
03/29/1996 LUCCHESSI         Ontario-South           3
03/29/1996 LUCCHESSI         Quebec                  1
03/29/1996 LEE               Ontario-South           2
03/29/1996 LEE               Ontario-North           2
03/29/1996 LEE               Quebec                  3
03/29/1996 LEE               Manitoba                5
```

Figure 9.13   Example of an IN predicate *(continues)*

```
03/29/1996  GOUNOT            Ontario-South          3
03/29/1996  GOUNOT            Quebec                 1
03/29/1996  GOUNOT            Manitoba               7

   14 record(s) selected.
```

Figure 9.13   Example of an IN predicate *(continued)*

9.1.12 The ORDER BY Clause

SQL does not return the results retrieved in a particular order; the order of a result may be different each time when the same **SELECT** statement is executed. To sort the result set, use the **ORDER BY** clause as shown in Figure 9.14.

```
SELECT empno, firstnme, lastname
  FROM employee
 WHERE job='MANAGER'
 ORDER BY lastname

EMPNO  FIRSTNME     LASTNAME
------ ------------ ----------------
000050 JOHN         GEYER
000090 EILEEN       HENDERSON
000030 SALLY        KWAN
000070 EVA          PULASKI
000100 THEODORE     SPENSER
000060 IRVING       STERN
000020 MICHAEL      THOMPSON

   7 record(s) selected.
```

Figure 9.14   Example of an ORDER BY clause

Note that you must specify the column names in the **ORDER BY** clause; column numbers are not allowed.

9.1.13 The GROUP BY...HAVING Clause

When you need to group multiple rows into a single row based on one or more columns, the **GROUP BY** clause comes in handy. Figure 9.15 shows an example that sums up the salary of all the employees in each department. The **HAVING** clause specifies which of the combined rows are to be retrieved. In the statement in Figure 9.15, only department names starting with *E* are retrieved.

```
SELECT workdept, SUM(salary) AS total_salary
  FROM employee
 GROUP BY workdept
HAVING workdept LIKE 'E%'
```

Figure 9.15   Example of GROUP BY and HAVING clauses *(continues)*

```
WORKDEPT TOTAL_SALARY
-------- --------------------------------
E01                               40175.00
E11                              104990.00
E21                               95310.00

  3 record(s) selected.
```

Figure 9.15   Example of GROUP BY and HAVING clauses *(continued)*

9.1.14 Joins

Sometimes information that you want to retrieve does not reside in a single table. You can join two or more tables in a **SELECT** statement. Consider the example in Figure 9.16.

```
SELECT empno, firstnme, lastname, deptname
  FROM employee, department
 WHERE workdept = deptno
   AND admrdept='A00'

EMPNO  FIRSTNME      LASTNAME         DEPTNAME                         MGRNO
------ ------------  ---------------  -----------------------------    -----
000010 CHRISTINE     HAAS             SPIFFY COMPUTER SERVICE DIV.     00010
000110 VINCENZO      LUCCHESSI        SPIFFY COMPUTER SERVICE DIV.     00010
000120 SEAN          O'CONNELL        SPIFFY COMPUTER SERVICE DIV.     00010
000020 MICHAEL       THOMPSON         PLANNING                         00020
000030 SALLY         KWAN             INFORMATION CENTER               00030
000130 DOLORES       QUINTANA         INFORMATION CENTER               00030
000140 HEATHER       NICHOLLS         INFORMATION CENTER               00030
000050 JOHN          GEYER            SUPPORT SERVICES                 00050

  8 record(s) selected.
```

Figure 9.16   Example of an INNER join

The example in Figure 9.16 retrieves a list of employees, their department names, and manager's employee numbers whose administrative department is *A00*. Since the *employee* table only stores the department number of the employees but not the department names, you need to join the *employee* table with the *department* table. Note that the two tables are joined in the **FROM** clause. Records with matching department numbers (*workdept = deptno*) are retrieved.

This type of join is called an **inner join**; it results in matched rows that are present in both joined tables. The **INNER JOIN** keywords can be omitted as demonstrated in Figure 9.16. However, if you choose to explicitly use the **INNER JOIN** syntax, the **SELECT** statement in Figure 9.16 can be rewritten as the following:

```
SELECT empno, firstnme, lastname, deptname
  FROM employee INNER JOIN department
```

```
    ON workdept = deptno
 WHERE admrdept='A00'
```

Note that **INNER JOIN** is used in the **FROM** clause. The **ON** keyword specifies the join predicates and categorizes rows as either joined or not-joined. This is different from the **WHERE**
clause, which is used to filter rows.

There are three other types of joins: **LEFT OUTER JOIN**, **RIGHT OUTER JOIN**, and **FULL
OUTER JOIN**. Outer joins are useful when you want to include rows that are present in the left
table, right table, or both tables, in addition to the rows returned from the implied inner join. A
table specified on the left side of the **OUTER JOIN** operator is considered the left table, and the
table specified on the right side of the **OUTER JOIN** operator is considered the right table.

A left outer join includes rows from the left table that were missing from the inner join. A right
outer join includes rows from the right table that were missing from the inner join. A full outer
join includes rows from both the left and right tables that were missing from the inner join. Figures 9.17, 9.18, and 9.19 demonstrate information to be retrieved and an example of each join.

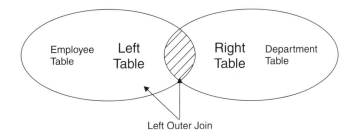

```
SELECT empno, firstnme, lastname, deptname
   FROM employee LEFT OUTER JOIN department
       ON workdept = deptno
```

Figure 9.17   Example of a LEFT OUTER join

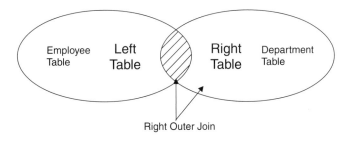

```
SELECT empno, firstnme, lastname, deptname
   FROM employee RIGHT OUTER JOIN department
       ON workdept = deptno
```

Figure 9.18   Example of a RIGHT OUTER join

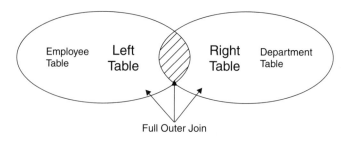

Full Outer Join

```
SELECT empno, firstnme, lastname, deptname
  FROM employee FULL OUTER JOIN department
    ON workdept = deptno
```

Figure 9.19   Example of a FULL OUTER join

9.1.15 Working with NULLs

A NULL in DB2 represents an unknown value. The following is an example of how to check if a value is NULL:

```
SELECT empno FROM employee WHERE midinit IS NULL
```

When working with NULL values, the **COALESCE** function comes in very handy: It checks whether the input is NULL. The value of the input is returned if it is not NULL, otherwise it returns the value provided in the second expression of the **COALESCE** function. Refer to Figure 9.20 for an example that returns 0 if *comm* is NULL.

```
SELECT id, name, COALESCE(comm, 0) AS comm
  FROM staff
 FETCH FIRST 6 ROWS ONLY

ID     NAME      COMM
------ --------- ---------------
    10 Sanders          0.00
    20 Pernal         612.45
    30 Marenghi         0.00
    40 O'Brien        846.55
    50 Hanes            0.00
    60 Quigley        650.25

  6 record(s) selected.
```

Figure 9.20   Example of the COALESCE function

9.1.16 The CASE Expression

When you want to perform a particular operation depending on the evaluation of a value, you can use a **CASE** expression to simplify your code. The example in Figure 9.21 introduces this expression.

```
SELECT firstnme, lastname,
  CASE
    WHEN salary < 10000 THEN 'Need a raise'
    WHEN salary > 10000 AND salary < 20000 THEN 'Fair pay'
    ELSE 'Overpaid'
  END AS comment
FROM employee


FIRSTNME       LASTNAME          COMMENT
------------   ---------------   ------------
CHRISTINE      HAAS              Need a raise
MICHAEL        THOMPSON          Overpaid
SALLY          KWAN              Overpaid
JOHN           GEYER             Overpaid
IRVING         STERN             Overpaid
WILLIAM        JONES             Fair pay

  6 record(s) selected.
```

Figure 9.21   Example of a CASE expression

In Figure 9.21, the values of the *salary* column are evaluated. If the value is less than $10,000, the string *Need a raise* is returned. If the value is between $10,000 and $20,000, *Fair pay* is returned. For all other values, *Overpaid* is returned.

9.1.17 Adding a Row Number to the Result Set

Recall that the **FETCH FIRST *n* ROWS ONLY** clause lets you return only the first *n* rows. What if you want to return row 30 or more? The **ROWNUMBER** and **OVER** functions solve this problem. Figure 9.22 shows a column derived with sequential row numbers generated by **ROWNUMBER() OVER()**.

```
SELECT ROWNUMBER() OVER() AS rowid, firstnme, lastname FROM employee

ROWID                   FIRSTNME       LASTNAME
--------------------    ------------   ---------------
                   1    CHRISTINE      HAAS
                   2    MICHAEL        THOMPSON
                   3    SALLY          KWAN
                   4    JOHN           GEYER
                   5    IRVING         STERN
                   6    EVA            PULASKI
                   7    EILEEN         HENDERSON
                   8    THEODORE       SPENSER
                   9    VINCENZO       LUCCHESSI
                  10    SEAN           O'CONNELL
                  11    DOLORES        QUINTANA
                  12    HEATHER        NICHOLLS
                  13    BRUCE          ADAMSON
```

Figure 9.22   Example 1: Using ROWNUMBER() OVER() *(continues)*

```
                    14 ELIZABETH     PIANKA
                    15 MASATOSHI     YOSHIMURA
                    16 MARILYN       SCOUTTEN
                    17 JAMES         WALKER
                    18 DAVID         BROWN
                    19 WILLIAM       JONES
                    20 JENNIFER      LUTZ
                    21 JAMES         JEFFERSON
                    22 SALVATORE     MARINO
                    23 DANIEL        SMITH
                    24 SYBIL         JOHNSON
                    25 MARIA         PEREZ
                    26 ETHEL         SCHNEIDER
                    27 JOHN          PARKER
                    28 PHILIP        SMITH
                    29 MAUDE         SETRIGHT
                    30 RAMLAL        MEHTA
                    31 WING          LEE
                    32 JASON         GOUNOT

  32 record(s) selected.
```

Figure 9.22   Example 1: Using ROWNUMBER() OVER() *(continued)*

To return rows higher than 30, use the **ROWNUMBER() OVER()** expression to the **FROM** clause. Figure 9.23 shows this trick.

```
SELECT rowid, firstnme, lastname
FROM ( SELECT ROWNUMBER() OVER() AS rowid, firstnme, lastname
         FROM employee) AS temp
WHERE rowid > 30

ROWID                  FIRSTNME      LASTNAME
-------------------- ------------  ----------------
                  31 WING          LEE
                  32 JASON         GOUNOT

  2 record(s) selected.
```

Figure 9.23   Example 2: Using ROWNUMBER() OVER()

You can also sort the result set before numbering the rows, as shown in Figure 9.24.

```
SELECT rowid, firstnme, lastname
FROM ( SELECT ROWNUMBER() OVER( ORDER BY salary, comm ) AS rowid,
            firstnme, lastname
         FROM employee) AS temp
WHERE rowid > 30
```

Figure 9.24   Example 3: Using ROWNUMBER() OVER() *(continues)*

```
ROWID                   FIRSTNME    LASTNAME
-------------------- ------------ ---------------
               31 MICHAEL        THOMPSON
               32 VINCENZO       LUCCHESSI

  2 record(s) selected.
```

Figure 9.24 Example 3: Using ROWNUMBER() OVER() *(continued)*

9.2 MODIFYING DB2 DATA

You modify DB2 data using the **INSERT**, **UPDATE**, and **DELETE** statements. Most of the clauses and functions described in the previous section also work with these statements. We will use some examples to explain their basic usages.

You can specify all the column values in the **INSERT** statement like this:

```
INSERT INTO employee
VALUES ( '000998', 'SMITH', 'A', 'JOHN',  NULL, NULL, NULL, NULL, 18,
        'M', NULL, NULL, NULL, NULL ) ;
```

Alternatively, you can explicitly specify the column list for which values will be provided in the **INSERT** statement:

```
INSERT INTO employee (empno, firstnme, midinit, lastname, edlevel)
VALUES ( '000999', 'SMITH', 'A', 'JOHN', 18 );
```

You can also insert multiple rows in one **INSERT** statement:

```
INSERT INTO employee (empno, firstnme, midinit, lastname, edlevel)
VALUES ( '000999', 'SMITH', 'A', 'JOHN', 18 )
    , ( '000998', 'LOPEZ', 'M', 'JEN' , 18 )
    , ( '000997', 'FRASER', 'B', 'MARC', 28 );
```

A multi-row insert is achieved with values obtained from a **SELECT** statement:

```
INSERT INTO employee_temp ( SELECT * FROM employee );
```

It is fairly straightforward to update one or more rows in a table by simply assigning the new values in the **SET** clause:

```
UPDATE employee SET salary = salary * 1.5, comm = 0
 WHERE empno='000999';
```

This next **UPDATE** statement obtains the department number from the *department* table. Note that the DB2 special register **CURRENT DATE** is used as the value to the hire date.

```
UPDATE employee
   SET (hiredate, workdept) = (SELECT CURRENT DATE, deptno
                                  FROM department
                                 WHERE deptname='PLANNING')
 WHERE empno='000999';
```

The **DELETE** statement is used to delete rows from a table. To remove all rows from the *employee* table, use the following statement:

```
DELETE FROM employee;
```

To remove only certain rows, use the **WHERE** clause to filter the rows:

```
DELETE FROM employee WHERE workdept IS NULL;
```

To remove rows with a row number greater than 100, use the **ROWNUMBER()OVER()** functions like this:

```
DELETE FROM
  (SELECT ROWNUMBER() OVER(ORDER BY empno) AS rowid
    FROM employee)
WHERE rowid > 100
```

9.3 SELECTING FROM UPDATE, DELETE, AND INSERT

While the **INSERT**, **UPDATE**, and **DELETE** statements change data in the specified tables, they only return a message indicating whether the statement completed successfully. If the statement completed successfully, you need to issue a separate SQL statement to find out what changed. In the next example, to determine which rows are to be deleted, you first issue a **SELECT** statement to capture the rows you will delete on the following **DELETE** statement. Both statements have the same **WHERE** condition to filter the same rows.

```
SELECT empno, firstnme, lastname FROM employee WHERE workdept = 'A00';
DELETE FROM employee WHERE workdept = 'A00';
```

Rather than issuing two separate statements, they can be optimized to use just one SQL statement like this:

```
SELECT empno, firstnme, lastname
FROM OLD TABLE (DELETE FROM employee WHERE workdept = 'A00');
```

Whenever a table is inserted, updated, or deleted, DB2 maintains one or more internal temporal tables known as **transition tables**. You specify the transition tables with the **NEW TABLE** and **OLDTABLE** clauses. Depending on the SQL operation, different transition tables are available. Refer to Table 9.2 for a summary of their availability.

Table 9.2   Availability of Transition Tables Depending on the SQL Statement Issued

SQL Statement	NEW TABLE	OLD TABLE
INSERT	Yes	No
UPDATE	Yes	Yes
DELETE	No	Yes

To demonstrate a **SELECT** from **UPDATE**, consider the following example in which you want to increase the salary of all the employees in department A00. Using **OLD TABLE** lets you perform the update as well as return the new salaries.

```
SELECT salary
   FROM OLD TABLE (UPDATE employee
                       SET salary = salary * 1.1
                     WHERE workdept = 'A00')
```

Similarly, if you want to retrieve the new salary, you can use **NEW TABLE** instead:

```
SELECT salary
   FROM NEW TABLE (UPDATE employee
                       SET salary = salary * 1.1
                     WHERE workdept = 'A00')
```

SELECT from **INSERT** works just like the preceding example:

```
SELECT salary
   FROM NEW TABLE (INSERT INTO employee
                       (empno, firstnme, midinit, lastname, edlevel)
                     VALUES ( '000999', 'SMITH', 'A', 'JOHN', 18 ))
```

You cannot retrieve both the new and old salary values by using **NEW TABLE** and **OLD TABLE** alone. To do this, use the **INCLUDE** clause.

```
SELECT salary as new_salary, old_salary
   FROM NEW TABLE ( UPDATE employee INCLUDE (old_salary DECIMAL(9,2))
                       SET salary    = salary * 1.10,
                           old_salary = salary
                     WHERE workdept = 'A00')
```

The **INCLUDE** clause in the nested **UPDATE** statement creates a new column that can be selected from the outer **SELECT** statement. You can see that the *old_salary* gets the old salary value while the table column salary is increased by 10%.

Finally, you should also know about the **FINAL TABLE** clause. When executing an **INSERT**, **UPDATE**, or **DELETE** statement, there may still be **AFTER** triggers or referential constraints that result in further modification of data in the target table. Using **FINAL TABLE** can prevent these types of changes.

For instance, assume that an **AFTER** trigger is defined to delete all rows from the *employee* table when an employee's salary is updated. If **FINAL TABLE** is used, the **UPDATE** statement will fail. This protects you from any unforeseen side-effects not visible to the application.

For example, an error is received if the following SQL statement is issued:

```
SELECT salary
   FROM FINAL TABLE (UPDATE employee
                       SET salary = salary * 1.1
                     WHERE workdept = 'A00')
SQL0989N  AFTER trigger "AUDIT_TRIG" attempted to modify a row in table
"EMPLOYEE" that was modified by an SQL data change statement within a FROM clause.
SQLSTATE=560C3
```

9.4 THE MERGE STATEMENT

A **MERGE** statement combines an **INSERT** statement with an **UPDATE** or **DELETE** statement. For example, if a row in table *T1* also exists in table *T2*, the existing row in *T2* should be updated. If a row in *T1* does not exist in *T2*, it should be inserted into *T2*. A new and efficient way to code this logic can be implemented with one statement: the **MERGE** statement. Figure 9.25 shows this **MERGE** statement.

```
MERGE INTO T2 as target
    USING (SELECT ... FROM T1) AS source
        ON target.id=source.id
    WHEN NOT MATCHED THEN
        INSERT INTO T2 ...
    WHEN MATCHED THEN
        UPDATE T2 SET ...
```

Figure 9.25   Example of a MERGE statement

Figure 9.26 illustrates the syntax of a **MERGE** statement. The **MERGE** statement has a lot of intricate details; see the *DB2 UDB SQL Reference* manual for more examples and additional information.

```
>>-MERGE INTO--+-table-name-------+---------------------------->
               +-view-name--------+
               '-(--fullselect--)-'

>--+------------------------+--USING--table-reference---------->
   '-| correlation-clause |-'

>--ON--search-condition---------------------------------------->

   .-----------------------------------------------------------.
   V                                                           |
>----WHEN--| matching-condition |--THEN--+-| modification-operation |+>
                                         '-signal-statement---------'

   .-ELSE IGNORE-.
>--+-------------+---------------------------------------------><
```

Figure 9.26   Syntax of the MERGE statement

N O T E   Refer to Chapter 1, Introduction to DB2 UDB, for a description of the DB2 syntax diagram conventions.

9.5 RECURSIVE SQL

Recursive SQL is a powerful way to query hierarchies of data. Organizational structures, bills-of-material, product classifications, and document hierarchies are all examples of hierarchical data. Let's use an example to demonstrate how a recursive SQL statement is written.

Assume that there is a table called *children* with definition and date as shown in Figure 9.27.

```
CREATE TABLE children ( person_id INTEGER
               , name      VARCHAR(50)
               , age       INTEGER
               , gender    CHAR(1)
               , parent_id INTEGER )
PERSON_ID   NAME      AGE          GENDER PARENT_ID
----------- --------  -----------  ----- -----------
          1 Apple            10 F          10
          2 Zoe              11 F           3
          3 John             30 M          13
          4 Mary             25 F          24
          5 Peter            14 M           4
          6 Jenny            13 F           4
         24 Robert           60 M          30

  7 record(s) selected.
```

Figure 9.27   Sample data in the children table

To retrieve the ancestors of *Jenny*, you would use the recursive query shown in Figure 9.28.

```
WITH temptab (person_id, name, parent_id) AS        (1)
     (SELECT person_id, name, parent_id            (2)
        FROM children
       WHERE name = 'Jenny'

     UNION ALL                                      (3)

     SELECT c.person_id, c.name, c.parent_id       (4)
       FROM children c, temptab super
      WHERE c.person_id = super.parent_id

) SELECT * FROM temptab                             (5)
```

Figure 9.28   A recursive SQL example

A **common table expression** (CTE) temporarily stores data as the query execution progresses. In Figure 9.28, the CTE is called *temptab* and it is created with the **WITH** clause at line (1). The definition of the CTE is specified at lines (2), (3), and (4) inside the parenthesis.

Line (2) obtains the initial result set which contains the record with the name 'Jenny'. Then, the recursion takes place by joining each row in *temptab* with its parents (4). The result of one execution of this recursion is added to *temptab* via **UNION ALL** at line (3).

The final query (5) extracts the *person_id*, *name*, and *parent_id* out of the *temptab* CTE.

The recursive SQL will return Jenny's parents and their parents, similar to Figure 9.29.

```
PERSON_ID   NAME                             PARENT_ID
----------- -------------------------------- -----------
SQL0347W  The recursive common table expression "DB2ADMIN.TEMPTAB" may contain an
infinite loop.  SQLSTATE=01605

        6 Jenny                            4
        4 Mary                            24
       24 Robert                          30

   3 record(s) selected with 1 warning messages printed.
```

Figure 9.29   Result of a recursive SQL

Notice that a warning message is also returned indicating that the CTE may contain an infinite loop. To avoid an infinite loop, you can specify the maximum number of recursive levels in the query, as shown in Figure 9.30.

```
WITH temptab (person_id, name, parent_id, level) AS
     (SELECT person_id, name, parent_id, 1
        FROM children
       WHERE name = 'Jenny'

     UNION ALL

     SELECT c.person_id, c.name, c.parent_id, super.level + 1
       FROM children c, temptab super
      WHERE c.person_id = super.parent_id
        AND level < 5

) SELECT * FROM temptab
```

Figure 9.30   A recursive SQL example with a maximum number of recursive levels

9.6 THE UNION, INTERSECT, AND EXCEPT OPERATORS

UNION, **INTERSECT**, and **EXCEPT** are operators that can be used to obtain the union, intersection, and difference between *fullselect*, *subselect*, or *values-clause*. Figure 9.31 shows the syntax diagram of the **UNION**, **INTERSECT**, and **EXCEPT** operators.

```
>>-+-subselect---------+------------------------------------------>
   +-(fullselect)------+
   '-| values-clause |-'


     .----------------------------------------------.
     V                                              |
>----+-----------------------------------------+-+-+------------->
       '-+-UNION---------+--+-subselect---------+-'
         +-UNION ALL-----+  +-(fullselect)------+
         +-EXCEPT--------+  '-| values-clause |-'
         +-EXCEPT ALL----+
         +-INTERSECT-----+
         '-INTERSECT ALL-'


>--+-----------------+--+-------------------+----------------->< 
   '-order-by-clause-'  '-fetch-first-clause-'
```

Figure 9.31   Syntax diagram of the UNION, INTERSECT, and EXCEPT operators

9.6.1 The **UNION** and **UNION ALL** Operators

A **UNION** operation combines two sets of columns and removes duplicate rows. Specifying **UNION ALL** gives the same result as the **UNION** operation, but it also includes the duplicate rows. Consider the two result tables, R1 and R2, in Figure 9.32.

```
R1                    R2
------------          -----------
Apple                 Apple
Apple                 Apple
Apple                 Banana
Banana                Banana
Banana                Banana
Cranberry             Cranberry
Cranberry             Mango
Cranberry
Orange
```

Figure 9.32   R1 and R2 result tables

Figure 9.33 shows the results of the **UNION** and **UNION ALL** operations on the two tables illustrated in Figure 9.32. As you can see, the **UNION** operator removes duplicates.

```
SELECT R1 FROM R1 UNION SELECT R2 FROM R2 ORDER BY 1

R1 UNION R2
------------------
Apple
```

Figure 9.33   Examples of UNION and UNION ALL *(continues)*

```
Banana
Cranberry
Mango
Orange

SELECT R1 FROM R1 UNION ALL SELECT R2 FROM R2 ORDER BY 1


R1 UNION ALL R2
-----------------------
Apple
Apple
Apple
Apple
Apple
Banana
Banana
Banana
Banana
Banana
Cranberry
Cranberry
Cranberry
Cranberry
Mango
Orange
```

Figure 9.33   Examples of UNION and UNION ALL *(continued)*

9.6.2 The INTERSECT and INTERSECT ALL Operators

An **INTERSECT** operation retrieves the matching set of distinct values from two columns; **INTERSECT ALL** returns the set of matching rows. The examples in Figure 9.34 use tables R1 and R2 from Figure 9.32.

```
SELECT R1 FROM R1 INTERSECT SELECT R2 FROM R2 ORDER BY 1

R1 INTERSECT R2
------------------
Apple
Banana
Cranberry


SELECT R1 FROM R1 INTERSECT ALL SELECT R2 FROM R2 ORDER BY 1

R1 INTERSECT ALL R2
-----------------------:
Apple
Apple
Banana
Banana
Cranberry
```

Figure 9.34   Examples of INTERSECT and INTERSECT ALL

9.6.3 The EXCEPT and EXCEPT ALL Operators

An **EXCEPT** operation retrieves the set of distinct values that exist in the first table but not in the second table. **EXCEPT ALL** returns the set of rows that exist only in the first table. The examples in Figure 9.35 use tables R1 and R2 from Figure 9.32.

```
SELECT R1 FROM R1 INTERSECT SELECT R2 FROM R2 ORDER BY 1

R1 INTERSECT R2
-------------------
Mango

SELECT R1 FROM R1 INTERSECT ALL SELECT R2 FROM R2 ORDER BY 1

R1 INTERSECT ALL R2
------------------------
Apple
Cranberry
Cranberry
Mango
```

Figure 9.35   Examples of EXCEPT and EXCEPT ALL

> **N O T E**   The file *Command_and_SQL_Examples.pdf* on the CD-ROM accompanying this book lists all of the SQL statements and DB2 commands with examples.

9.7 CASE STUDY

Let's review some of the SQL statements you have learned in this chapter. This section gives scenarios and then shows the commands and resulting output.

1. Return a result of *deptno*, *admrdept*, and a derived *comment* column from the *department* table where *deptname* contains *CENTER*. Order the result with the first column of the result set.

```
SELECT deptno
     , admrdept
     , 'it is a center' AS comment
  FROM department
 WHERE deptname
  LIKE '%CENTER%'
 ORDER BY 1

DEPTNO ADMRDEPT COMMENT
------ -------- --------------
C01    A00      it is a center
D01    A00      it is a center

  2 record(s) selected.
```

2. Return the *name* and *id* of staffs whose year of service is NOT NULL. Order the result by *years* and *id*. Fetch only the first five rows of the result.

```
SELECT years
     , name
     , id
  FROM staff
 WHERE years IS NOT NULL
ORDER BY years DESC, id DESC
FETCH FIRST 5 ROWS ONLY

YEARS  NAME       ID
------ --------- ------
    13 Graham       310
    12 Jones        260
    10 Quill        290
    10 Lu           210
    10 Hanes         50

 5 record(s) selected.
```

3. Return a list of employees who do not work as a SALESREP in the OPERATIONS department.

```
SELECT a.empno, a.lastname, b.deptno AS dept
  FROM employee a, department b
 WHERE a.workdept = b.deptno
   AND a.job       <> 'SALESREP'
   AND b.deptname = 'OPERATIONS'

EMPNO  LASTNAME         DEPT
------ --------------- ----
000090 HENDERSON        E11
000280 SCHNEIDER        E11
000290 PARKER           E11
000300 SMITH            E11
000310 SETRIGHT         E11

 5 record(s) selected.
```

4. Insert multiple rows into the *emp_act* table.

```
INSERT INTO emp_act VALUES
    ('200000' ,'ABC' ,10 ,NULL ,'2003-10-22',CURRENT DATE)
   ,('200000' ,'DEF' ,10 ,1.4  ,NULL        ,DATE (CURRENT TIMESTAMP))
   ,('200000' ,'IJK' ,10 ,1.4  ,'2003-10-22', DEFAULT)

DB20000I  The SQL command completed successfully.
```

5. Insert the result of a query into the *emp_act* table.

```
INSERT INTO emp_act
    SELECT LTRIM(CHAR(id + 600000))
         , SUBSTR(UCASE(name),1,6)
         , 180
         , 100
         , CURRENT DATE
         , CURRENT DATE + 100 DAYS
      FROM staff

DB20000I  The SQL command completed successfully.
```

6. Update multiple rows in the *emp_act* table using a result of a query.

```
UPDATE emp_act
   SET ( actno
       , emstdate
       , projno ) = ( SELECT MAX(salary)
                           , CURRENT DATE + 2 DAYS
                           , MIN(CHAR(id))
                        FROM staff
                       WHERE id <> 33 )
   WHERE empno LIKE '600%';
```

```
DB20000I  The SQL command completed successfully.
```

7. Delete records from the *emp_act* table where *emstdate* is greater than 01/01/2004.

```
DELETE FROM emp_act WHERE emstdate > '01/01/2004'
```

```
DB20000I  The SQL command completed successfully.
```

8. Query records just inserted.

```
SELECT * FROM NEW TABLE (
    INSERT INTO emp_act VALUES
        ('200000' ,'ABC' ,10 ,NULL ,'2003-10-22',CURRENT DATE)
       ,('200000' ,'DEF' ,10 ,1.4  ,NULL, DATE (CURRENT TIMESTAMP))
       ,('200000' ,'IJK' ,10 ,1.4  ,'2003-10-22', DEFAULT)
     )
```

```
EMPNO  PROJNO ACTNO  EMPTIME EMSTDATE   EMENDATE
------ ------ ------ ------- ---------- ----------
200000 abc       10       - 10/22/2003 04/23/2004
200000 DEF       10    1.40 -          04/23/2004
200000 IJK       10    1.40 10/22/2003 -

  3 record(s) selected.
```

9. Query records just deleted.

```
SELECT * FROM OLD TABLE (
    DELETE FROM emp_act WHERE emstdate > '01/01/2003' )
```

```
EMPNO  PROJNO ACTNO  EMPTIME EMSTDATE   EMENDATE
------ ------ ------ ------- ---------- ----------
200000 abc       10       - 10/22/2003 04/23/2004
200000 abc       10       - 10/22/2003 04/23/2004
20000  IJK       10    1.40 10/22/2003 -

  3 record(s) selected.
```

10. Query records just inserted in the order they were inserted.

```
SELECT empno
     , projno
     , actno
     , row#
  FROM FINAL TABLE
       ( INSERT INTO emp_act (empno, projno, actno)
             INCLUDE ( row# SMALLINT )
              VALUES ('300000', 'XXX', 999, 1)
                  , ('300000', 'YYY', 999, 2) )
  ORDER BY row#
```

```
EMPNO   PROJNO ACTNO  ROW#
------  ------ ------ ------
300000 XXX        999    1
300000 YYY        999    2

    2 record(s) selected.
```

9.8 SUMMARY

This chapter shows the power of SQL statements to manipulate the database data, including the **SELECT, INSERT, UPDATE**, and **DELETE** statements. In the SQL statements, you can use the DB2 special registers to obtain information about the environment such as the current date and current user connected to the database.

Besides the basic SQL statements to manipulate data, you can also use column and scalar functions, cast expressions, **WHERE** clauses, **ORDER BY** clauses, **GROUP BY** clauses, **FETCH FIRST** *n* **ROWS ONLY** options, and many other features to customize the result that you want to obtain.

It is very common that data requested is from more than one table. Inner and outer joins are used to combine data from two or more tables in a **SELECT** statement.

SQL enhancement returns selective data from data being deleted, updated, or inserted in a single SQL statement because it provides a simplified and optimized way to write SQLs. For example, rather than issuing two separate statements to query data you are going to delete and then perform the delete, DB2 lets you combine the two operations in a single statement. It definitely simplifies the application code as well as improves performance in most cases.

The **MERGE** statement is one of the SQL enhancements introduced in DB2 Version 8. It combines an **INSERT** with an **UPDATE** or **DELETE** statement.

9.9 REVIEW QUESTIONS

1. Given the following *employee* table:

```
empno      firstnme     lastname        salary
---------------------------------------------
000010    Peter        Smith          38752.00
000020    Christine    Haas           52234.00
000030    John         Geyer          38250.00
000040    Irving       Poon           40175.00
000050    Eva          Pulaski        36170.00
```

How many rows are returned from the following SQL statement?

```
SELECT empno
  FROM employee
 WHERE lastname LIKE 'P%'
   AND salary > 38500
```

A. 1

B. 2

C. 3

D. 4

E. 5

2. Given the following table *t1*:

```
id     job     bonus
--------------------------
1      Mgr      -
2      Sales    10
3      Mgr      -
4      DBA      15
```

Which of the following SQL statement will retrieve the rows that have unknown values in the *bonus* column?

A. SELECT * FROM t1 WHERE bonus = NULL

B. SELECT * FROM t1 WHERE bonus = ''

C. SELECT * FROM t1 WHERE bonus = '' OR bonus = 'NULL'

D. SELECT * FROM t1 WHERE bonus IS NULL

E. SELECT * FROM t1 WHERE bonus = '' OR bonus = ""

3. Given the following table *t1*:

```
id     job     bonus
--------------------------
1      Mgr      -
2      Sales    10
3      Mgr      -
4      DBA      15
```

Which of the following describes the result if this statement is executed in DB2 V8.1 FixPak 6?

```
SELECT id, job FROM OLD TABLE (DELETE FROM t1 WHERE bonus IS NULL)
```

A. The statement will fail because a SELECT statement cannot contain a DELETE statement.

B. The statement will succeed if no row is found for the DELETE statement.

C. The statement will succeed and return the number of rows deleted with the DELETE statement.

D. The statement will succeed and return the number of rows left in *t1* after the DELETE statement is executed.

4. Given the following tables:

```
Student_classA
   NAME          AGE
--------------------------
   Mary           30
   Peter          35
   John           45
   Lilian         38
   Raymond        26
   Lilian         24
   Peter          38
   Peter          40
Student_classB
   NAME          AGE
--------------------------
```

```
Paul        26
Peter       35
Peter       29
Christ      32
Raymond     26
Lilian      24
```

If the following SQL statement is executed, how many rows will be returned?

```
SELECT name FROM student_classA
INTERSECT
SELECT name FROM student_classB
```

A. 1

B. 2

C. 3

D. 4

E. 5

5. If you are working on a UNIX system and you want to select all rows from the *org* table, which of the following commands must be used?

   A. db2 select * from org

   B. db2 select(*) from org

   C. db2 "select * from org"

   D. db2 "select(*) from org"

6. Which of the following statements will return only 30 rows from the *employee* table?

   A. SELECT FIRST 30 ROWS FROM employee

   B. SELECT * FROM employee READ FIRST 30 ROWS ONLY

   C. SELECT * FROM employee OPTIMIZE FOR 30 ROWS

   D. SELECT * FROM employee FETCH FIRST 30 ROWS ONLY

7. Which of the following is a valid wildcard character in a LIKE clause of a SELECT statement?

   A. %

   B. _

   C. *

   D. @

8. Given the following **CREATE TABLE** statement:

```
CREATE TABLE employee
( id   INTEGER NOT NULL
, name VARCHAR(50)
, dept VARCHAR(10) NOT NULL DEFAULT 'A00'
, PRIMARY KEY (id) )
```

Which two of the following statements will execute successfully?

   A. INSERT INTO employee VALUES (NULL, NULL, 'A00')

   B. INSERT INTO employee (name, dept) VALUES ('Peter', DEFAULT)

   C. INSERT INTO employee (id, name) VALUES (1234, 'Peter')

   D. INSERT INTO employee (id) VALUES (1234)

9. Given the following table:

```
CREATE TABLE employee
( id    INTEGER NOT NULL
, name VARCHAR(50)
, dept VARCHAR(10) NOT NULL DEFAULT 'A00'
, PRIMARY KEY (id) )
```

If the following **SELECT** statement is executed, which of the following describes the order of the rows in the result returned?

```
SELECT id FROM employee
```

  A. The rows are not sorted in any particular order.
  B. The rows are sorted by *id* in ascending order.
  C. The rows are sorted by *id* in descending order.
  D. The rows are ordered based on the sequence of when the data were inserted into the table.

10. Given the following table, *newborn*:

```
baby_name        birth_date          doctor_name
-------------------------------------------------
JEREMY           05/22/2005          REICHER
KATHY            03/03/2005          WONG
CHLOE            01/23/2005          RICCI
WESLEY           10/24/2004          ATKINSON
FIONA            12/25/2004          JOHNSON
```

Which of the statements returns the list of baby names and their doctors who were born five days ago?

  A. SELECT baby_name, doctor_name
       FROM newborn
       WHERE birth_date = DAYADD(TODAY, 5)
  B. SELECT baby_name, doctor_name
       FROM newborn
       WHERE birth_date = CURRENT DATE – 5 DAYS
  C. SELECT baby_name, doctor_name
       FROM newborn
       WHERE birth_date < TODAY – 5 DAYS
  D. SELECT baby_name, doctor_name
       FROM newborn
       WHERE birth_date = DAYADD(CURRENT DATE, 5)

11. Given a table created using the statement:

```
CREATE TABLE foo (c1 INT, c2 INT, c3 INT)
```

To retrieve only the columns c1 and c3 from the table, which of the following statements should be used?

  A. SELECT * FROM foo
  B. SELECT c1,c3 FROM foo
  C. SELECT 1,3 FROM foo
  D. SELECT columns 1 and 3 FROM foo

12. To insert the current date into the column named *dt* in the table *foo*, which of the following statements should be used?

    A. INSERT INTO foo (dt) VALUES date

    B. INSERT INTO foo (dt) VALUES current date

    C. INSERT INTO foo (dt) VALUES (date)

    D. INSERT INTO foo (dt) VALUES (currentdate)

13. Which of the following statements deletes all the rows from the table?

    A. DELETE FROM foo

    B. DELETE * FROM foo

    C. DELETE (SELECT * FROM foo)

    D. DELETE ALL FROM foo

14. Given the following tables:

```
Table T                 Table S

col 1     col2          col 1     col2
-------   ------        -------   ------
2         Raul          2         Susan
4         Mary          5         Clara
8         Tom           6         Jenny
9         Glenn         9         Luisa
```

How many rows will the following MERGE statement return?

```
MERGE INTO t USING s
     ON    t.col1 = s.col1
     WHEN MATCHED THEN
      UPDATE SET t.col2 = s.col2
     WHEN NOT MATCHED THEN
         INSERT VALUES (s.col1, s.col2)
```

    A. 0

    B. 2

    C. 4

    D. 6

    E. 8

15. Given the same tables as in question 14, how many rows will the following statement return?

```
SELECT * FROM t INNER JOIN s ON s.col1 = t.col1
```

    A. 0

    B. 1

    C. 2

    D. 3

    E. 4

16. Given the same tables as in question 14, how many rows will the following statement return?

```
SELECT * FROM t FULL OUTER JOIN s ON s.col1 = t.col1
```

     A. 0

     B. 2

     C. 4

     D. 6

     E. 8

17. Given the same tables as in question 14, how many rows will the following statement return?

```
SELECT * FROM t LEFT OUTER JOIN s ON s.col1 = t.col1
```

     A. 0

     B. 2

     C. 4

     D. 6

     E. 8

18. Given the same tables as in question 14, how many rows will the following statement return?

```
SELECT * FROM t RIGHT OUTER JOIN s ON s.col1 = t.col1
```

     A. 0

     B. 2

     C. 4

     D. 6

     E. 8

19. Assuming the table *employee* has 32 records, how many rows will the following statement return?

```
SELECT empno, salary
   FROM FINAL TABLE (INSERT INTO employee
               (empno, firstnme, midinit, lastname, edlevel)
               VALUES ('000999', 'SMITH', 'A', 'JOHN', 18 ),
                      ('001000', 'JOHNSON', 'A', 'TOM', 22 )
               )
```

     A. 0

     B. 2

     C. 32

     D. 34

     E. 36

20. Assuming the table *employee* has 10 records, how many records will there be in total after executing the following statement?

```
SELECT salary
   FROM NEW TABLE (INSERT INTO employee
                   (empno, firstnme, midinit, lastname, edlevel)
                   VALUES ('000999 ', 'SMITH ', 'A ', 'JOHN ', 18 ),
                          ('001000 ', 'JOHNSON ', 'A ', 'TOM ', 22 ) )
```

A. 0

B. 2

C. 4

D. 10

E. 12

## CHAPTER 10

Implementing Security

A ll tasks and concepts presented in the previous chapters assumed you had the administrative rights to set up client and server connectivity, execute SQL statements, create database objects, and so on. In the real world, administrative rights are typically given only to selected individuals. In addition, the ability for users to access data must be controlled to comply with business requirements. DB2 uses a few constituents to support various security schemes. This chapter discusses each of the security components and provides examples.

In this chapter you will learn about:

- The big picture of the DB2 security model
- Different authentication methods that DB2 supports
- Authentication methods using customized loadable libraries
- How to enable data encryption
- Database operations you can perform with the various administrative authorities
- Controlling access to database objects
- Obtaining the authorities and privileges information from the metadata
- Considerations for Windows domain users

10.1 DB2 SECURITY MODEL: THE BIG PICTURE

The DB2 security model consists of three major components: authentication, administrative authorization, and database object security (also known as database object privileges). Figure 10.1 illustrates these components.

A combination of external security services and internal DB2 authorization mechanisms handle DB2 security. As shown in Figure 10.1, a user goes through the authentication process before

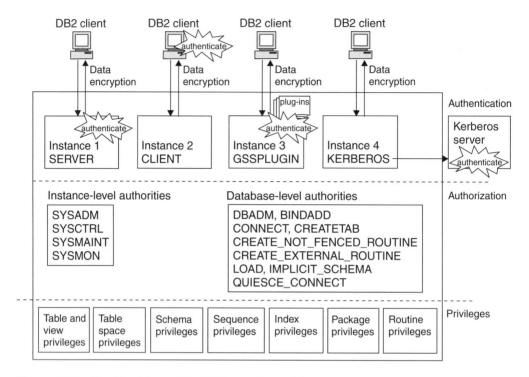

Figure 10.1   The big picture of the DB2 security model

connecting to the database. Once the user ID and password have been successfully verified, an internal DB2 process takes over and makes sure that the user is authorized to perform the requested operations. This is represented by the Authorization and Privileges components in Figure 10.1.

10.2 AUTHENTICATION

Authentication is the process of validating a supplied user ID and password against a security facility. This authentication occurs when you try to connect to a database or attach to an instance. The security facility is external to DB2; user IDs and passwords are not stored in a DB2 server. Authentication can occur at any of the following:

- At a DB2 server (Figure 10.1, Instance 1)
- At a DB2 client (Figure 10.1, Instance 2)
- Using a customized loadable library via Generic Security Service (GSS) (Figure 10.1, Instance 3)
- At a Kerberos security service (Figure 10.1, Instance 4)

The authentication process also determines which operating system groups the user belongs to. Group membership lookup is essential because it lets users inherit certain authorities or privileges through groups.

The following sections describe how to configure the authentication type by using configuration parameters at the DB2 server and at the client respectively. The combination of the client and server authentication configuration determines where and how the authentication will take place (the authentication method).

10.2.1 Configuring the Authentication Type at a DB2 Server

To configure the authentication type at a DB2 server, you use the Database Manager (DBM) Configuration parameter AUTHENTICATION. If you are not already familiar with DBM Configuration parameters, refer to Chapter 5, Understanding the DB2 Environment, DB2 Instances, and Databases. For completeness, we are including the command here to display the current DBM parameter settings:

```
get dbm cfg
```

From the output, locate the following line where the authentication type is specified:

```
Database manager authentication          (AUTHENTICATION) = SERVER
```

SERVER is the default authentication type of an instance. Figure 10.2 shows this authentication type.

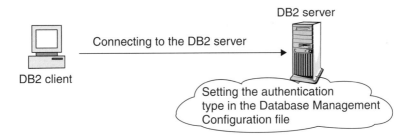

Figure 10.2   Configuring the authentication type at a DB2 server

To change the value to the KERBEROS authentication type, for example, use this DB2 command:

```
update dbm cfg using authentication KERBEROS
```

Alternatively, you can use the Control Center to make this change. Chapter 4, Using the DB2 Tools, describes the Control Center in detail.

Table 10.1 summarizes the values the AUTHENTICATION parameter accepts.

Table 10.1   Description of the Authentication Types

Authentication Type	Description
SERVER	Authenticates users at the DB2 server. This is the default value.
SERVER_ENCRYPT	Authenticates users at the DB2 server. When the user ID and password are sent to the server, they are both encrypted.
KERBEROS	Authenticates users at a Kerberos server.
KRB_SERVER_ENCRYPT	Authenticates users at a Kerberos server if both the DB2 server and client support Kerberos security service. Use SERVER_ENCRYPT instead if the client does not support Kerberos security service.
GSSPLUGIN	Authenticates users using an external GSS Application Programming Interface (GSSAPI)-based security mechanism.
GSS_SERVER_ENCRYPT	Authenticates users using an external GSSAPI-based security mechanism if both the DB2 server and client support GSS. Use SERVER_ENCRYPT instead if the client does not support GSS.
CLIENT	Authenticates users at the DB2 client depending on the settings of two other configuration parameters: TRUST_CLNTAUTH and TRUST_ALLCLNTS.

The output of the **get dbm cfg** command includes another authentication-related parameter, called server connection authentication (SRVCON_AUTH):

```
Server Connection Authentication          (SRVCON_AUTH) = NOT_SPECIFIED
```

This parameter sets the authentication type at the DB2 server for incoming database connections. Note that only database connections evaluate the value of this parameter. Explicit instance attachment and operations that require implicit instance attachment still use AUTHENTICATION to resolve the authentication type.

These examples show how to implicitly attach to an instance:

```
update dbm cfg
create database SAMPLE
```

By default, SRVCON_AUTH has a value of NOT_SPECIFIED. In this case, the value of AUTHENTICATION is used instead.

10.2.2 Configuring the Authentication Type at a DB2 Client

When a client is configured to connect to a database, you need to catalog the node and the database. The **catalog database** command has an option called AUTHENTICATION that allows you to indicate the authentication type to be used when connecting to the specified database from a DB2 client as shown in Figure 10.3.

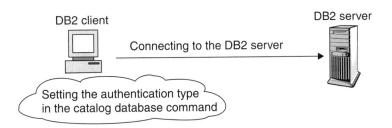

Figure 10.3   Configuring the authentication type at a DB2 client

Figure 10.4 illustrates the syntax of the **catalog database** command.

```
>>-CATALOG---+-DATABASE-+---database-name--+-----------+---------->
             '-DB-------'                   '-AS--alias-'

>--+------------------+------------------------------------------>
   +-ON--+-path--+-----+
   |     '-drive-'     |
   '-AT NODE--nodename-'

>--+----------------------------------------------------------+-->
   '-AUTHENTICATION--+-SERVER------------------------------+-'
                     +-CLIENT------------------------------+
                     +-SERVER_ENCRYPT----------------------+
                     +-KERBEROS TARGET PRINCIPAL--principalname-+
                     +-SQL_AUTHENTICATION_DATAENC----------+
                     +-SQL_AUTHENTICATION_DATAENC_CMP------+
                     '-GSSPLUGIN---------------------------'

>--+-------------------------+-----------------------------------><
   '-WITH--"comment-string"-'
```

Figure 10.4   Syntax of the CATALOG DATABASE command

The authentication type SERVER is the default. To change this setting, explicitly specify the AUTHENTICATION keyword along with one of the supported values shown in Table 10.2. The following is an example of using GSSPLUGIN authentication.

```
catalog db sample at node dbsrv authentication gssplugin
```

Table 10.2 Authentication Types Supported at DB2 Clients

Supported Authentication Values	Description
SERVER	Authenticates users at the DB2 server where the database resides. This is the default value.
SERVER_ENCRYPT	Authenticates users at the DB2 server where the database resides. When the user ID and password are sent to the server, they are both encrypted.
KERBEROS	Authenticates users at a Kerberos server.
TARGET PRINCIPAL *principalname*	Fully qualify the Kerberos principal name for the target server.
	For UNIX and Linux systems, use a name like:
	• name/instance@REALM
	For Windows 2000, *principalname* is the logon account of the DB2 server service, which may look like one of the following:
	• userid@DOMAIN • userid@xxx.xxx.xxx.com • domain\userid
SQL_AUTHENTICATION_DATAENC	Authenticates users at the DB2 server. In addition, data encryption must be used for the connections.
SQL_AUTHENTICATION_DATAENC_CMP	Authenticates users at the DB2 server. In addition, data encryption must be used. If the client or server does not support data encryption, use SERVER_ENCRYPT instead.
GSSPLUGIN	Authenticates users with an external GSSAPI-based security mechanism.
CLIENT	Authenticates users at the DB2 client depending on the settings of two other configuration parameters: TRUST_CLNTAUTH and TRUST_ALLCLNTS

10.2.3 Authenticating Users at the DB2 Server

As mentioned earlier, authenticating a user and the associated password at the DB2 server is the default behavior. The DBM configuration parameter at the server and the authentication option in the database directory entry are both set to SERVER. DB2 does not maintain any user and password information. This implies that the user ID and password pair must be defined in the security facility built in the operating system of the server. Figure 10.5 demonstrates a few scenarios of server authentication.

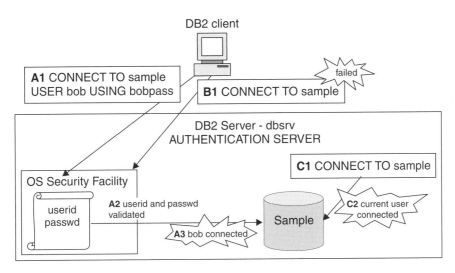

Figure 10.5   Example of SERVER authentication

> **N O T E**   As long as the database server authentication type is set to
> SERVER, authentication will always take place at the server.

In Scenario A, A1 issues a **CONNECT** statement to connect to the SAMPLE database that is
remotely located in the *dbsrv* DB2 server. The user ID *bob* and the password *bobpass* are also
provided. This pair of information is validated by the DB2 server security facility at A2. Once
validated, *bob* is connected to SAMPLE in A3 provided that he has the appropriate CONNECT
privilege (privileges are discussed later in this chapter).

Scenario B uses the same environment except that no user ID and password are provided in the
CONNECT statement. When a remote database connection is requested, it is mandatory to supply
a user ID and password. Therefore, the **CONNECT** statement specified in B1 fails.

 Scenarios A and B are both remote requests. It is also very common to make local database connections from the DB2 server itself. Scenario C demonstrates such a request. Since you must
have already logged into the server console with a valid user ID and password, it is not necessary
to supply a user ID and password in the **CONNECT** statement at C1. If you choose to connect to
the database with a different user ID, then you need to issue the **CONNECT** statement with the
user ID and password you wish as shown in A1.

The SERVER_ENCRYPT authentication type behaves exactly the same as SERVER authentication except that both the user ID and password are encrypted.

10.2.4 Authenticating Users with the Kerberos Security Service

Kerberos is a network authentication protocol that employs secret-key cryptography to provide strong authentication for client/server applications. By using an encrypted key, Kerberos makes single sign-on to a remote DB2 server possible. Refer to Figure 10.6 to see how Kerberos authentication works with DB2.

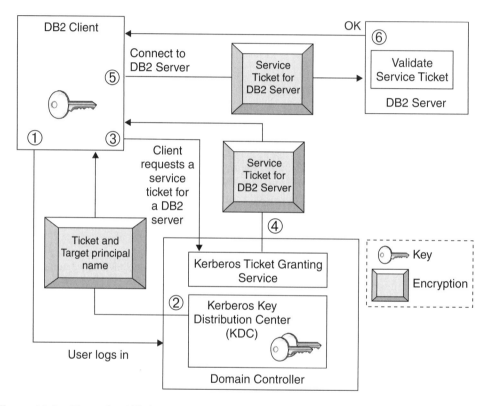

Figure 10.6   Example of Kerberos authentication

In Figure 10.6:

(1) A user logs in to the Kerberos system.

(2) The Kerberos key distribution center generates a ticket and target principal name.

(3) The DB2 client requests a service ticket for a DB2 server.

(4) The Kerberos Key Distribution Center (KDC) grants a service ticket for the DB2 server.

(5) The DB2 client connects to the DB2 server using the service ticket.

(6) The DB2 server validates the service ticket and accepts the DB2 client connection request.

> **N O T E** Prior to DB2 Version 8.2, Kerberos only supported Windows 2000 platforms. With Version 8.2, Kerberos extended support to the Linux and UNIX platforms too.

The AUTHENTICATION type KERBEROS allows Kerberos-enabled clients to be authenticated at the Kerberos server. Although Kerberos is gaining popularity, there will be clients that do not have Kerberos support enabled. To accommodate these clients and at the same time ensure all clients are able to connect securely, you can set the authentication type at the DB2 server as KRB_SERVER_ENCRYPT. This option allows all Kerberos-enabled clients to be authenticated with Kerberos security service, while other clients use SERVER_ENCRYPT authentication instead.

Table 10.3 summarizes the resolved authentication types based on different client and server authentication settings related to Kerberos.

Table 10.3 Summary of Kerberos-Related Client/Server Authentication Types

Client Specification	Server Specification	Client/Server Resolution
KERBEROS	KRB_SERVER_ENCRYPT	KERBEROS
Any other setting	KRB_SERVER_ENCRYPT	SERVER_ENCRYPT

V8.2 10.2.5 Authenticating Users with Generic Security Service Plug-ins

With DB2 Version 8.2, you can write authentication mechanisms to implement your own security model. These authentication modules follow the Generic Security Service Application Programming Interface (GSSAPI) standard as documented in the Internet's Requests for Comments (RFC) (see www.rfc-editor.org/rfc.html).

To employ the authentication plug-in, set the AUTHENTICATION type to GSSPLUGIN or GSS_SERVER_ENCRYPT so that the specified library modules are loaded at instance start time. DB2 clients then load an appropriate plug-in based on the security mechanism negotiated with the server during **CONNECT** or **attach**. You use the LOCAL_GSSPLUGIN Database Manager Configuration parameter to specify the name of the plug-in and must include the library name when using GSSPLUGIN or GSS_SERVER_ENCRYPT. Figure 10.7 illustrates an example of GSS.

When clients do not support the GSSPLUGIN security mechanism, you can use the GSS_SERVER_ENCRYPT authentication type, which allows those clients to establish database connections with behavior equivalent to SERVER_ENCRYPT.

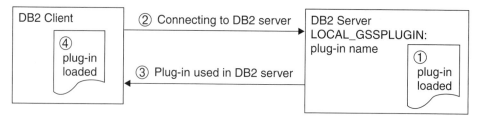

Figure 10.7   Example of GSS authentication

The DB2 Version 8.2 authentication scheme requires plug-ins to manage the following:

- Group membership
- Authentication at the client
- Authentication at the server

If you do not specify the loadable libraries, DB2-supplied plug-ins are used instead. A few Database Manager Configuration parameters are introduced to support authentication plug-ins, and they are listed in Table 10.4. Table 10.4 lists the new Database Manager Configuration parameters that support authentication plug-ins.

V8.2   **Table 10.4**   Database Manager Parameters for Authentication Plug-ins

Database Manager Parameter	Description
GROUP_PLUGIN	The name of the group management plug-in library.
CLNT_PW_PLUGIN	The name of the client-side password authentication plug-in. The functions in the named plug-in will also be used for local instance-level actions if the AUTHENTICATION parameter is set to SERVER, CLIENT, SERVER_ENCRYPT, DATAENC, or DATAENC_COMP.
CLNT_KRB_PLUGIN	The name of the client-side Kerberos plug-in. This plug-in will also be used for local instance-level actions, that is, when the AUTHENTICATION parameter is set to KERBEROS or KRB_SERVER_ENCRYPT.
SRVCON_PW_PLUGIN	The name of the server-side password authentication module.
SRVCON_GSSPLUGIN_LIST	The list of names of all GSSAPI plug-ins separated by commas. The number of plug-ins supported by the server is unlimited; however, the maximum length of the list of plug-in names is 256 characters, and each plug-in name must be fewer than 32 characters. This list should be stated with the most preferred plug-in first.

(continues)

V8.2 **Table 10.4** Database Manager Parameters for Authentication Plug-ins *(Continued)*

Database Manager Parameter	Description
SRV_PLUGIN_MODE	Indicates if the plug-in is to be run in fenced or unfenced mode. (**Fenced** means that the plug-ins run in a different address space from the DB2 system controller process and **unfenced** means executing the plug-ins in the same address space.) It is recommended to run user-defined modules in fenced mode to protect the system controller.

Since this is an instance-level parameter, it applies to all plug-ins within the same instance.

The default value is FENCED. |

DB2 provides sample plug-ins so you can develop your own plug-ins more easily. You must place the library files in the designated directory where DB2 looks for:

- Client-side user authentication plug-ins in the directory
  $DFTDBPATH/security/client-plugins (for Linux/UNIX)
  $DFTDBPATH\security\client-plugins (for Windows)
- Server-side user authentication plug-ins in the directory
  $DFTDBPATH/security/server-plugins (for Linux/UNIX)
  $DFTDBPATH\security\server-plugins (for Windows)
- Group plug-ins in the directory
  $DFTDBPATH/security/group-plugins (for Linux/UNIX)
  $DFTDBPATH\security\group-plugins (for Windows)

You specify the name of the plug-in as a Database Manager Configuration parameter. Use the full name of the library file, but do not include the file extension or the path. For example, to configure the group plug-in, issue:

```
update dbm cfg using group_plugin mygrplib
```

10.2.6 Authenticating Users at the DB2 Clients

When you want to allow DB2 clients to perform their own authentication, set the server authentication type to CLIENT. This setting does not mean that client authentication applies to every client; qualified clients are determined by two other DBM Configuration parameters—TRUST_ALLCLNTS and TRUST_CLNTAUTH.

TRUST_ALLCLNTS (as you can tell from the name) specifies whether DB2 is going to trust all clients. DB2 categorizes clients into these types:

- **Untrusted** clients do not have a reliable security facility, such as Windows 98, Windows ME, and Classic Mac OS.
- **Trusted** clients have reliable security facilities like Windows 2000, AIX, z/OS, and Linux.

- **Distributed Relational Database Architecture** (DRDA) clients are on host legacy systems with reliable security facilities, including DB2 for z/OS, DB2 for iSeries, and DB2 for VM and VSE.

> **N O T E**   Even though all DB2 Version 8 clients use the DRDA database communication protocol to communicate with DB2 servers, only clients running on mainframe legacy systems are considered as DRDA clients for historical and backward compatibility reasons.

TRUST_ALLCLNTS accepts any of the values summarized in Table 10.5.

Table 10.5   Values Allowed for TRUST_ALLCLNTS

TRUST_ALLCLNTS value	Description
YES	Trusts all clients. This is the default setting. Authentication will take place at the client. See the exception mentioned in the TRUST_CLNTAUTH discussion.
NO	Trust only clients with reliable security facilities (i.e., trusted clients). Untrusted clients must provide user ID and password for authentication to take place at the server.
DRDAONLY	Trusts only clients that are running on iSeries, zSeries, VM, and VSE platforms. All other clients must provide user IDs and passwords.

You can specify a more granular security scheme with TRUST_ALLCLNTS. For example, you can let trusted clients perform authentication on their own and, at the same time, force untrusted clients to be authenticated at the server.

Consider a scenario in which you log into a Windows 2000 machine as *localuser* and connect to the remote database without specifying a user ID and password. *localuser* will be the connected authorization ID at the database. What if you want to connect to the database with a different user ID, for example, *poweruser,* who has the authority to perform a database backup? To allow such behavior, use TRUST_CLNTAUTH to specify where authentication will take place if a user ID and password are supplied in a **CONNECT** statement or **attach** command. Table 10.6 presents the values for TRUST_CLNTAUTH.

Table 10.6   Values Allowed for TRUST_CLNTAUTH

TRUST_CLNTAUTH Value	Description
CLIENT	Authentication is performed at the client; user ID and password are not required.
SERVER	Authentication is done at the server only if the user ID and password are supplied.

DB2 evaluates TRUST_ALLCLNTS and TRUST_CLNTAUTH only if you set AUTHENTICA-TION to CLIENT on the DB2 server. Figures 10.8, 10.9, 10.10, and 10.11 illustrate how to use these parameters.

In Figure 10.8, TRUST_ALLCLNTS is set to YES, so all clients are considered trusted and can perform their own authentication.

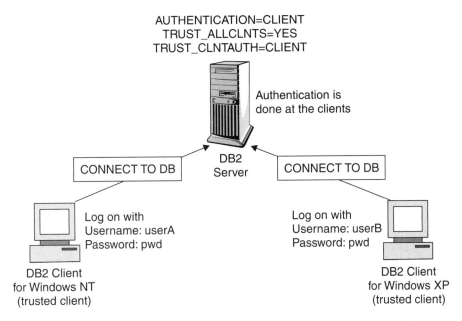

Figure 10.8   Example 1: TRUST_ALLCLNTS and TRUST_CLNTAUTH

In Figure 10.9, TRUST_ALLCLNTS is set to NO, so only trusted clients perform their own authentication. Authentication for untrusted clients is done at the server.

In Figure 10.10, TRUST_CLNAUTH is set to SERVER. When user ID and password are specified in the **CONNECT** statement, authentication is performed at the server.

In Figure 10.11, TRUST_CLNTAUTH is set to SERVER and both clients provide user ID and password in the **CONNECT** statement. Hence, authentication is performed at the server for both clients.

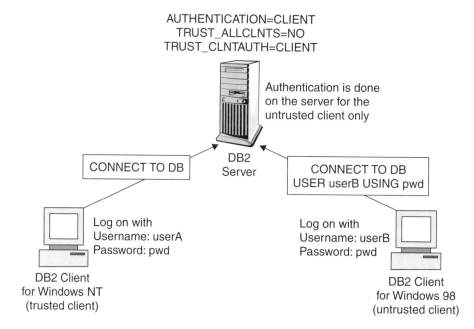

Figure 10.9   Example 2: TRUST_ALLCLNTS and TRUST_CLNTAUTH

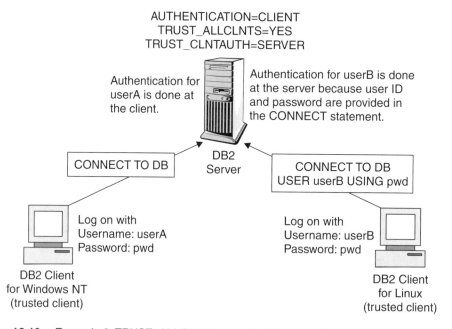

Figure 10.10   Example 3: TRUST_ALLCLNTS and TRUST_CLNTAUTH

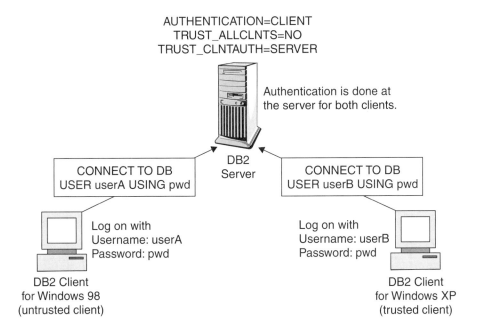

Figure 10.11 Example 4: TRUST_ALLCLNTS and TRUST_CLNTAUTH

V8.2 10.3 DATA ENCRYPTION

In the discussion of the SERVER_ENCRYPT authentication type we mentioned that the user ID and password supplied in the **CONNECT** statement are encrypted to protect from eavesdropping. DB2 Version 8.2 is further enhanced to also provide encryption of data as it travels over the network. DB2 is compliant with the Federal Information Processing Standard 140-2 (FIPS 140-2). You can now encrypt and decrypt user data using encryption mechanisms.

To use data encryption both the DB2 client and server must support it. The authentication value SQL_AUTHENTICATION_DATAENC in the **catalog database** command enforces SERVER authentication and also enables data encryption for that connection. If a product does not support data encryption, the SQL_AUTHENTICATION_DATAENC_CMP authentication type becomes very helpful. It lets these clients connect as SERVER_ENCRYPT, which means the data is not encrypted but that the user ID and the password are.

10.4 ADMINISTRATIVE AUTHORITIES

Once the user is successfully authenticated, DB2 checks to see if the user has the proper authority for the requested operations, such as performing database manager maintenance operations and managing database objects. Figure 10.12 shows the authorities supported in DB2 and Table 10.7 describes each of them.

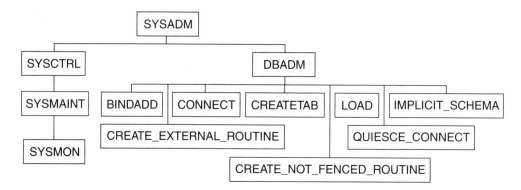

Figure 10.12   DB2 administrative authority levels

Table 10.7   Descriptions of DB2 Administrative Authority Levels

DB2 Administrative Authority	Description
SYSADM	These users have the highest authority level and full privileges for managing the instance. They also have access to all data in the underlying databases.
SYSCTRL	These users have certain privileges in managing the instance, its databases, and database objects. They can create new databases, but do not have access to the data. For example, they cannot issue statements such as `DELETE FROM employee` or `SELECT * FROM employee`.
SYSMAINT	Similar to SYSCTRL, SYSMAINT users have certain privileges in managing the instance, its databases, and database objects. However, they cannot create new databases and do not have access to the data. For example, these users cannot issue statements such as `DELETE FROM employee` or `SELECT * FROM employee`.
SYSMON	These users can turn snapshot monitor switches on, collect snapshot data, and access other database system monitor data. No other task can be performed unless the required authority or privileges are granted to the same user by other means.
DBADM	Database-level authority that allows users to perform administrative tasks on the specified database. Note that they also have full data access to the database

(continues)

Table 10.7 Descriptions of DB2 Administrative Authority Levels *(Continued)*

DB2 Administrative Authority	Description
LOAD	These users can only run the load utility against the specified database. Before the user can load data into a table, he or she must also have the privilege to INSERT and/or DELETE on the target table. (Database object privileges are discussed in more detail in the next section.)
CONNECT	Grants users access the database. Without the CONNECT authority, a user cannot connect to the database even though he or she is successfully authenticated by the security facility.
BINDADD	Allows users to create new packages in the database.
CREATETAB	Allows users to create new tables in the database.
CREATE_NOT_FENCED_ROUTINE	Allows users to create nonfenced routines such as user-defined functions and stored procedures. When a nonfenced routine is invoked, it executes in the database manager's process rather than in its own address space.
IMPLICIT_SCHEMA	Allows users to create a schema implicitly via database object creation. For example, if *bob* wants to create a table *jeff.sales* and the schema *jeff* does not already exist, *bob* needs to hold the IMPLICIT_SCHEMA authority for this database.
QUIESCE_CONNECT	Allows users to access the database while it is quiesced. When a database is quiesced, only users with SYSADM, DBADM, and QUIESCE_CONNECT authorities can connect to the database and perform administrative tasks.
CREATE_EXTERNAL_ROUTINE	Allows users to create routines written in external languages such as C, Java, and OLE.

To give you a better idea of what the system and DBADM authorities can and cannot do, Table 10.8 summarizes some common functions and the authorities required to perform them. For functions that are not listed here, refer to the DB2 manuals. The manuals clearly list the authorities and privileges needed to execute commands and SQL statements.

Table 10.8 Summary of DB2 Administrative Authorities

Function	SYSADM	SYSCTRL	SYSMAINT	SYSMON	DBADM
Update Database Manager Configuration parameters	YES	NO	NO	NO	NO

(continues)

Table 10.8   Summary of DB2 Administrative Authorities *(Continued)*

Function	SYSADM	SYSCTRL	SYSMAINT	SYSMON	DBADM
Grant/revoke DBADM authority	YES	NO	NO	NO	NO
Establish/change SYSCTRL authority	YES	NO	NO	NO	NO
Establish/change SYSMAINT authority	YES	NO	NO	NO	NO
Force users off the database	YES	YES	NO	NO	NO
Create/drop databases	YES	YES	NO	NO	NO
Restore to new database	YES	YES	NO	NO	NO
Update database configuration parameters	YES	YES	YES	NO	NO
Back up databases/table spaces	YES	YES	YES	NO	NO
Restore to existing database	YES	YES	YES	NO	NO
Perform roll forward recovery	YES	YES	YES	NO	NO
Start/stop instances	YES	YES	YES	NO	NO
Restore table spaces	YES	YES	YES	NO	NO
Run traces	YES	YES	YES	NO	NO
Obtain monitor snapshots	YES	YES	YES	YES	NO
Query table space states	YES	YES	YES	NO	YES
Prune log history files	YES	YES	YES	NO	YES
Quiesce table spaces	YES	YES	YES	NO	YES
Quiesce databases	YES	NO	NO	NO	YES
Quiesce instances	YES	YES	NO	NO	NO
Load tables	YES	NO	NO	NO	YES

(continues)

Table 10.8   Summary of DB2 Administrative Authorities *(Continued)*

Function	SYSADM	SYSCTRL	SYSMAINT	SYSMON	DBADM
Set/unset check pending status	YES	NO	NO	NO	YES
Create/drop event monitors	YES	NO	NO	NO	YES

10.4.1 Managing Administrative Authorities

Now that you understand the roles of different authorities in DB2, it's time to show you how to "give" a user or a group of users an authority. The verb *give* is used because a user receives the system and database authorities through different commands and statements.

Recall that SYSADM, SYSCTRL, SYSMAINT, and SYSMON are system authorities for an instance. You set these with the Database Manager Configuration parameters by assigning a user group defined in the operating system or security facility to the associated parameters. The following are the entries for the configuration parameters:

```
SYSADM group name      (SYSADM_GROUP) =
SYSCTRL group name     (SYSCTRL_GROUP) =
SYSMAINT group name    (SYSMAINT_GROUP) =
SYSMON group name      (SYSMON_GROUP) =
```

On Windows, the parameters are set to NULL, which implies that members of the Windows Administrators group own all the system authorities. On Linux and UNIX systems, the primary group of the instance owner is the default value for all the SYS*_GROUP.

To set any of the system groups, you use the **update dbm** command. For example, if *admgrp* and *maintgrp* are valid groups, the following command configures the SYSADM_GROUP and SYSMAINT_GROUP:

```
update dbm cfg using sysadm_group admgrp sysmaint_group maintgrp
```

This command does not validate the existence of the group. It is your responsibility to enter a valid group name. To reset them to the default value of NULL, specify:

```
update dbm cfg using sysadm_group NULL
```

> **NOTE**   Resetting DBM and DB configuration parameters to the default value, you must use NULL in uppercase. DB2 treats the lowercase *null* as an input value.

Since the SYS*_GROUP parameters are not configurable online, you need to stop and restart the instance for the changes to take effect.

You grant and revoke database authorities with the **GRANT** and **REVOKE** statements to a user or group of users. Figures 10.13 and 10.14 show the syntax of these statements, and Figure 10.15 illustrates how to use them.

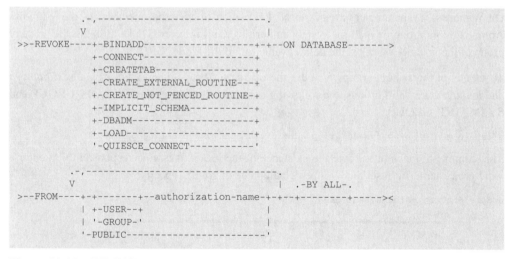

```
          .-,-----------------------------.
          V                               |
>>-GRANT----+-BINDADD--------------------+-+--ON DATABASE-------->
            +-CONNECT-------------------+
            +-CREATETAB-----------------+
            +-CREATE_EXTERNAL_ROUTINE---+
            +-CREATE_NOT_FENCED_ROUTINE-+
            +-IMPLICIT_SCHEMA-----------+
            +-DBADM---------------------+
            +-LOAD---------------------+
            '-QUIESCE_CONNECT----------'


          .-,-----------------------------.
          V                               |
>--TO----+-+-------+--authorization-name-+-+------------------->><
         | +-USER--+                      |
         | '-GROUP-'                      |
         '-PUBLIC----------------------'
```

Figure 10.13   GRANT statement for database authorities

```
          .-,-----------------------------.
          V                               |
>>-REVOKE----+-BINDADD--------------------+-+--ON DATABASE------->
             +-CONNECT-------------------+
             +-CREATETAB-----------------+
             +-CREATE_EXTERNAL_ROUTINE---+
             +-CREATE_NOT_FENCED_ROUTINE-+
             +-IMPLICIT_SCHEMA-----------+
             +-DBADM---------------------+
             +-LOAD---------------------+
             '-QUIESCE_CONNECT----------'


          .-,-------------------------------.
          V                                 |   .-BY ALL-.
>--FROM----+-+-------+--authorization-name-+-+--+--------+----->><
           | +-USER--+                      |
           | '-GROUP-'                      |
           '-PUBLIC-----------------------'
```

Figure 10.14   REVOKE statement for database authorities

```
CONNECT TO sample;
GRANT IMPLICIT_SCHEMA, CREATETAB ON DATABASE TO USER john;
GRANT LOAD ON DATABASE TO GROUP loadgrp, USER john;
GRANT BINDADD ON DATABASE TO PUBLIC;

REVOKE LOAD ON DATABASE FROM GROUP loadgrp;
REVOKE CREATETAB ON DATABASE FROM PUBLIC;
```

Figure 10.15   Examples of granting and revoking database authorities

You must first connect to the target database before you specify one or more authorities you want to grant or revoke. The keywords USER and GROUP are optional for both **GRANT** and **REVOKE** statements. However, on Linux and UNIX, if you have a user ID and group name defined with the same name, you must specify **USER** or **GROUP** explicitly; otherwise you will receive an error message.

Notice that the last example of Figure 10.15 uses the keyword PUBLIC is used. PUBLIC is not the name of a group defined in the operating system or in the external security facility; it is a special group to which everyone belongs. PUBLIC by default receives a few database authorities and/or database object privileges depending on the type of operations performed. Refer to the next section for more information about implicit privileges.

The **REVOKE** statement uses the BY ALL option as its default. This means that this command revokes each named authority (as well as privileges—that will be discussed later in this chapter) from all named users and/or groups who were explicitly granted those authorities (and privileges). However, there is no cascade effect to also revoke authorities (and privileges) that were implicitly granted. Stay tuned for the implicit privileges discussion in the following section.

10.5 DATABASE OBJECT PRIVILEGES

Controlling access to database objects is as important as authenticating users and managing administrative authorities. Privileges give users the right to access each individual database object in a specific way. Privileges can be granted explicitly and implicitly. The following sections list all the supported privileges for each database object and discuss implicit privileges.

If you are not familiar with any database objects discussed in the following sections, see Chapter 7, Working with Database Objects.

10.5.1 Schema Privileges

There are three schema privileges:

- CREATEIN allows users to create objects within the schema.
- ALTERIN allows users to alter objects within the schema.
- DROPIN allows users to drop objects within the schema.

For example, you can specify the **GRANT** and **REVOKE** statements against a given schema, as shown in the syntax diagrams in Figures 10.16 and 10.17.

```
            .-,------------.
            V              |
>>-GRANT----+-ALTERIN--+-+--ON SCHEMA--schema-name-------------->
            +-CREATEIN-+
            '-DROPIN---'

      .-,--------------------------------.
      V                                  |
>--TO----+-+-------+--authorization-name-+-+-------------------->
         | +-USER--+                       |
         | '-GROUP-'                       |
         '-PUBLIC----------------------'

>--+------------------+------------------------------------------><
   '-WITH GRANT OPTION-'
```

Figure 10.16   GRANT syntax diagram for schema privileges

```
            .-,------------.
            V              |
>>-REVOKE----+-ALTERIN--+-+--ON SCHEMA--schema-name-------------->
             +-CREATEIN-+
             '-DROPIN---'

      .-,-----------------------------------.
      V                                     |  .-BY ALL-.
>--FROM----+-+-------+--authorization-name-+-+---+--------+-----><
           | +-USER--+                       |
           | '-GROUP-'                       |
           '-PUBLIC----------------------'
```

Figure 10.17   REVOKE syntax diagram for schema privileges

Previously we introduced the IMPLICIT_SCHEMA database authority, which allows the grantee to create a schema via the creation of database objects. You can also create a new schema explicitly using the **CREATE SCHEMA** statement, for example:

```
CONNECT TO sample USER dbowner;
CREATE SCHEMA dev AUTHORIZATION devuser;
```

The **CREATE SCHEMA** statement requires that user *dbowner* has the SYSADM or DBADM authorities on database *SAMPLE*. This creates a schema called *dev* where *devuser* is the schema owner.

You can also create a schema and database objects within that schema in one SQL statement. Figure 10.18 demonstrates a straightforward example. You simply fully qualify the object name with the schema. For example, in Figure 10.18, the table *dairyprod* and index *prodindx* are created in the schema of *grocery*. Schema *grocery* will be automatically created if it does not already exist.

```
CREATE TABLE grocery.dairyprod
    ( prodno SMALLINT NOT NULL
    , desc VARCHAR(100)
    , qty INTEGER );

CREATE INDEX grocery.prodindx ON grocery.dairyprod (prodno);
```

Figure 10.18   Example of CREATE SCHEMA and DDL in one statement

Before moving to the next database object privilege, you may be wondering about the WITH GRANT OPTION in the **GRANT** statement in Figure 10.16. This option allows the named authorized user to grant the named privileges to other users. It also applies to all other database object privileges (except for indexes).

10.5.2 Table Space Privileges

Tables and table spaces are logical objects, as discussed in Chapter 7, Working with Database Objects. Tables are logically stored in table spaces, and table spaces are associated to physical storage devices. You need some USE privileges to be able to define tables in a table space. Figures 10.19 and 10.20 show the **GRANT** and **REVOKE** syntax diagrams with the USE privilege available for a specific table space. When a table space is created, its USE privilege is granted to PUBLIC by default. If you want to restrict usage of the table space, you should revoke the USE privilege from PUBLIC and grant it to selected users or groups individually.

```
>>-GRANT--USE---OF TABLESPACE--tablespace-name--TO--------------->

     .-,-------------------------------.
     V                                 |
>----+-+-------+--authorization-name-+-+----------------------->
       | +-USER--+                    |
       | '-GROUP-'                    |
       '-PUBLIC----------------------'

>--+------------------+------------------------------------------><
   '-WITH GRANT OPTION-'
```

Figure 10.19   GRANT syntax diagram for table space privileges

```
>>-REVOKE USE OF TABLESPACE--tablespace-name--FROM--------------->

     .-,------------------------------.
     V                                |   .-BY ALL-.
>----+-+-------+--authorization-name-+-+---+--------+---------->< 
       | +-USER--+                    |
       | '-GROUP-'                    |
       '-PUBLIC----------------------'
```

Figure 10.20   REVOKE syntax diagram for table space privileges

The following examples show how to grant and revoke the table space privileges.

```
GRANT USE OF TABLESPACE userspace1 TO USER db2admin;
REVOKE USE OF TABLESPACE userspace1 FROM PUBLIC;
```

10.5.3 Table and View Privileges

There are additional privileges for tables and views. Table 10.9 describes these privileges.

Table 10.9   Summary of Table and View Privileges

Table and View Privileges	Descriptions
CONTROL	Provides users with all privileges for a table or view as well as the ability to grant those privileges (except CONTROL) to others.
ALTER	Allows users to alter a table or view.
DELETE	Allows users to delete records from a table or view.
INSERT	Allows users to insert an entry into a table or view.
REFERENCES	Allows users to create and drop a foreign key, specifying the table as the parent in a relationship.
SELECT	Allows users to retrieve data from a table or view.
UPDATE	Allows users to update entries in a table or view. This privilege can also limit users to update specific columns only.
ALL PRIVILEGES	Grants all the above privileges except CONTROL on a table or view.

Figures 10.21 and 10.22 show the **GRANT** and **REVOKE** syntax diagrams for table and view privileges respectively.

```
                  .-PRIVILEGES-.
>>-GRANT--+-ALL--+------------+-----------------------------+----->
          |  .-,-----------------------------------------.  |
          |  V                                           |  |
          '---+-ALTER----------------------------------+-+-'
              +-CONTROL--------------------------------+
              +-DELETE---------------------------------+
              +-INDEX----------------------------------+
              +-INSERT---------------------------------+
              +-REFERENCES--+-----------------------+-+
              |             |       .-,----------.  | |
              |             |       V            |  | |
              |             '-(----column-name-+--)-' |
              +-SELECT---------------------------------+
                  .-PRIVILEGES-.
```

Figure 10.21   GRANT syntax diagram for table and view privileges *(continues)*

```
>>-GRANT--+-ALL--+------------+--------------------------+----->
          |  .-,-------------------------------------.  |
          |  V                                       |  |
          '---+-ALTER----------------------------+-+-'
              +-CONTROL---------------------------+
              +-DELETE----------------------------+
              +-INDEX-----------------------------+
              +-INSERT----------------------------+
              +-REFERENCES--+--------------------+-+
              |             |    .-,----------.  | |
              |             |    V           |   | |
              |             '-(----column-name-+--)-'  | |
              +-SELECT----------------------------+
              '-UPDATE--+----------------------+-----'
                        |    .-,-----------.   |
                        |    V            |    |
                        '-(----column-name-+--)-'


         .-TABLE-.
>--ON--+-------+--+-table-name-----+-------------------------->
                  +-view-name------+
                  '-nickname-------'


         .-,-------------------------------.
         V                                 |
>--TO----+-+-------+--authorization-name-+-+------------------->
         | +-USER--+                     |
         | '-GROUP-'                     |
         '-PUBLIC-----------------------'


>--+------------------+-------------------------------------->< 
   '-WITH GRANT OPTION-'
```

Figure 10.21   GRANT syntax diagram for table and view privileges *(continued)*

```
                    .-PRIVILEGES-.        .-TABLE-.
>>-REVOKE--+-ALL--+------------+-+--ON--+-------+--------------->
           |  .-,--------------.  |
           |  V              |    |
           '---+-ALTER------+-+--'
               +-CONTROL----+
               +-DELETE-----+
               +-INDEX------+
               +-INSERT-----+
               +-REFERENCES-+
               +-SELECT-----+
               '-UPDATE-----'

>--+-table-name-+------------------------------------------->
   +-view-name--+
   '-nickname---'
```

Figure 10.22   REVOKE syntax diagram for table and view privileges *(continues)*

```
        .-,----------------------------------.
        V                                    |    .-BY ALL-.
>--FROM----+-+--------+--authorization-name-+-+--+--------+----->< 
           | +-USER--+                        |
           | '-GROUP-'                         |
           '-PUBLIC-----------------------'
```

Figure 10.22   REVOKE syntax diagram for table and view privileges *(continued)*

The following examples show how to grant and revoke some table and view privileges.

```
GRANT ALL PRIVILEGES ON TABLE employee TO USER db2admin WITH GRANT OPTION;
GRANT UPDATE ON TABLE employee (salary, comm) TO GROUP db2users;
REVOKE CONTROL ON TABLE employee FROM PUBLIC;
```

You probably noticed that the above **GRANT** and **REVOKE** statements also apply to **nicknames** (database objects that represent remote tables and views residing in different databases). The remote databases can be databases in the DB2 family or non-DB2 databases. This feature is known as **federated database support** and was briefly discussed in Chapter 2, DB2 at a Glance: The Big Picture.

10.5.4 Index Privileges

Privileges for managing indexes is fairly straightforward: you can only drop an index after it is created. To change an index key, for example, you need to drop the index and recreate it. The CONTROL privilege allows the grantee to drop the index. Figures 10.23 and 10.24 list **GRANT** and **REVOKE** statements with index privileges.

```
>>-GRANT--CONTROL--ON INDEX--index-name------------------------>

        .-,----------------------------------.
        V                                    |
>--TO----+-+--------+--authorization-name-+-+--------------------><
         | +-USER--+                         |
         | '-GROUP-'                          |
         '-PUBLIC-----------------------'
```

Figure 10.23   GRANT syntax diagram for index privileges

```
>>-REVOKE CONTROL ON INDEX--index-name------------------------->

        .-,----------------------------------.
        V                                    |    .-BY ALL-.
>--FROM----+-+--------+--authorization-name-+-+--+--------+----->< 
           | +-USER--+                        |
           | '-GROUP-'                         |
           '-PUBLIC-----------------------'
```

Figure 10.24   REVOKE syntax diagram for index privileges

The following examples show how to grant and revoke index privileges.

```
GRANT CONTROL ON INDEX empind TO USER db2admin;
REVOKE CONTROL ON INDEX empind FROM db2admin;
```

10.5.5 Package Privileges

A **package** is a database object that contains the data access plan of how SQL statements will be executed. A package needs to be bound to a database before its associated program can execute it. The following are the privileges you use to manage packages.

- BIND allows users to rebind an existing package.
- EXECUTE allows users to execute a package.
- CONTROL provides users the ability to rebind, drop, or execute a package as well as the ability to grant these privileges (except CONTROL) to others.

Figures 10.25 and 10.26 show the **GRANT** and **REVOKE** statements for package privileges respectively.

```
                 .-,----------------.
                 V                  |
>>-GRANT----+-BIND---------+-+------------------------------------>
            +-CONTROL------+
            '-EXECUTE------'

>--ON--PACKAGE-------+--------------+--package-id--------------->
                     '-schema-name.-'

          .-,--------------------------------.
          V                                  |
>--TO----+-+-------+--authorization-name-+-+--------------------->
         | +-USER--+                       |
         | '-GROUP-'                       |
         '-PUBLIC-----------------------'

>--+------------------+-------------------------------------------><
   '-WITH GRANT OPTION-'
```

Figure 10.25   GRANT syntax diagram for package privileges

```
              .-,----------------.
              V                  |
>>-REVOKE----+-BIND---------+-+----------------------------------->
             +-CONTROL------+
             '-EXECUTE------'

>--ON--PACKAGE-------+--------------+--package-id--------------->
                     '-schema-name.-'
```

Figure 10.26   REVOKE syntax diagram for package privileges *(continues)*

```
          .-,---------------------------------.
          V                                   |   .-BY ALL-.
>--FROM----+-+-------+--authorization-name-+-+--+--------+----->< 
            | +-USER--+                      |
            | '-GROUP-'                      |
            '-PUBLIC----------------------'
```

Figure 10.26   REVOKE syntax diagram for package privileges *(continued)*

The following examples show how to grant and revoke package privileges:

```
GRANT EXECUTE, BIND ON PACKAGE emppack1 TO GROUP db2grp WITH GRANT OPTION;
REVOKE BIND ON PACKAGE emppack1 FROM USER db2dev;
```

10.5.6 Routine Privileges

To be able to use a routine, a user must be granted with its associated EXECUTE privilege. As illustrated in Figures 10.27, and 10.28, EXECUTE is the only routine privilege, but it applies to all types of routines: functions, methods, and stored procedures.

```
>>-GRANT EXECUTE ON--+-| function-designator |----------+------->
                     +-FUNCTION--+---------+--*---------+
                     |           '-schema.-'            |
                     +-| method-designator |------------+
                     +-METHOD * FOR--+-type-name------+-+
                     |               '-+---------+--*-' |
                     |                 '-schema.-'      |
                     +-| procedure-designator |---------+
                     '-PROCEDURE--+---------+--*--------'
                                  '-schema.-'

       .-,-------------------------------.
       V                                 |
>--TO----+-+-------+--authorization-name-+-+------------------->
         | +-USER--+                     |
         | '-GROUP-'                     |
         '-PUBLIC----------------------'

>--+-----------------+--------------------------------------->< 
   '-WITH GRANT OPTION-'
```

Figure 10.27   GRANT syntax diagram for routine privileges

The following examples show how to grant and revoke routine privileges:

```
GRANT EXECUTE ON PROCEDURE salary_increase TO USER db2admin WITH GRANT OPTION;
REVOKE EXECUTE ON PROCEDURE salary_increase FROM USER db2admin;
```

```
>>-REVOKE EXECUTE ON--+-| function-designator |----------+------>
                      +-FUNCTION--+---------+--*--------+
                      |            '-schema.-'          |
                      +-| method-designator |-----------+
                      +-METHOD * FOR--+-type-name------+-+
                      |               '-+---------+--*-' |
                      |                 '-schema.-'      |
                      +-| procedure-designator |---------+
                      '-PROCEDURE--+---------+--*--------'
                                   '-schema.-'

         .-,---------------------------------.
         V                                   |
>--FROM----+-+-------+--authorization-name-+-+----------------->
           | +-USER--+                      |
           | '-GROUP-'                      |
           '-PUBLIC----------------------'

   .-BY ALL-.
>---+--------+--RESTRICT----------------------------------------><
```

Figure 10.28   REVOKE syntax diagram for routine privileges

10.5.7 Sequence Privileges

A **sequence object** generates sequential numeric values. By default, the group PUBLIC can use any sequence object unless they are controlled by the USAGE privilege, as shown in Figure 10.29. You can restrict usage of certain sequence object by revoking USAGE from PUBLIC.

There may also be cases where you want to change the sequence object definition, such as the minimum, maximum, and incremental values. You probably want to limit the ability to alter a sequence object to only a few users. Use the ALTER privilege (shown in Figures 10.29 and 10.30) to do that. RESTRICT is the default behavior that prevents the sequence from being dropped if dependencies exist.

```
        .-,---------.
        V           |
>>-GRANT----+-USAGE-+-+--ON SEQUENCE--sequence-name------------->
            '-ALTER-'

      .-,---------------------------------.
      V                                   |
>--TO----+-+-------+--authorization-name-+-+------------------->
         | +-USER--+                      |
         | '-GROUP-'                      |
         '-PUBLIC----------------------'

>--+---------------------------+-------------------------------><
   '-WITH GRANT OPTION-'
```

Figure 10.29   GRANT syntax diagram for sequence privileges

```
              .-,---------.
              V           |
>>-REVOKE----+-ALTER-+-+---ON SEQUENCE--sequence-name------------>
             '-USAGE-'


        .-,-------------------------------.
        V                                 |    .-RESTRICT-.
>--FROM----+-+-------+---authorization-name-+-+---+----------+---><
           | +-USER--+                     |
           | '-GROUP-'                     |
           '-PUBLIC-----------------------'
```

Figure 10.30   REVOKE syntax diagram for sequence privileges

The following examples show how to grant and revoke sequence privileges.

```
GRANT USAGE, ALTER ON SEQUENCE empseq TO USER d2admin WITH GRANT OPTION;
REVOKE ALTER ON SEQUENCE empseq FROM db2admin RESTRICT;
```

10.5.8 Implicit Privileges

As discussed previously, DB2 privileges usually are granted explicitly with **GRANT** statements. In some cases users may also obtain privileges implicitly or indirectly by performing certain operations. You should pay attention to these privileges and determine whether they are valid per the security policies in your company.

- A user who is granted DBADM authority is also implicitly granted BINDADD, CONNECT, CREATETAB, CREATE_NOT_FENCED, and IMPLICIT_SCHEMA privileges.
- When a user creates a database, the following authorities and privileges are also granted implicitly:
  - DBADM authority is granted to the database creator.
  - CONNECT, CREATETAB, BINADD, and IMPLICIT_SCHEMA privileges are granted to PUBLIC.
  - USE OF TABLESPACE privilege on the table space USERSPACE1 is granted to PUBLIC.
  - BIND and EXECUTE privileges on each successfully bound utility are granted to PUBLIC.
  - EXECUTE privileges WITH GRANT OPTION on all functions in the SYSFUN schema is granted to PUBLIC.
- A user who creates a table, view, index, schema, or package automatically receives CONTROL privilege on the database object he or she creates.

If a program is coded with static SQL statements, packages that contain data access plans are generated and bound to the database at compile time. When a user executes the package, explicit privileges for database objects referenced in the statements are not required. The user only needs

EXECUTE privilege on the package to execute the statements. However, this does not mean that the user has direct access to the underlying database objects.

Consider the example illustrated in Figure 10.31. A package *dev.pkg1* containing **UPDATE**, **SELECT**, and **INSERT** statements are bound to the database. A user who only has EXECUTE privilege on *dev.pkg1* can only manipulate table *t1* through the package. He cannot issue **SELECT**, **UPDATE**, and **INSERT** statements directly to *t1*.

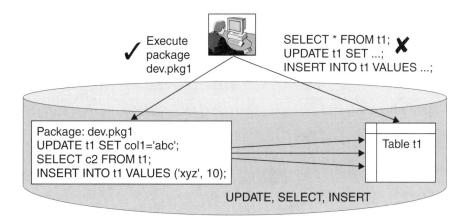

Figure 10.31   Example of controlling database object access via packages

As mentioned earlier in this chapter, when a privilege is revoked, there is no cascade effect to also revoke the implicit privileges. For example, if user *bob* is granted DBADM authority, he also implicitly receives the privileges BINDADD, CONNECT, CREATETAB, CREATE_NOT_FENCED, and IMPLICIT_SCHEMA. Assuming, for some reason, DBADM is revoked from *bob* with this statement:

```
REVOKE dbadm FROM USER bob
```

bob no longer has DBADM authority, but he still has BINDADD, CONNECT, CREATETAB, CREATE_NOT_FENCED, and IMPLICIT_SCHEMA authorities. Each of them must be explicitly revoked if you want to remove all authorities from *bob*.

10.6 AUTHORITY AND PRIVILEGE METADATA

Up to this point we have introduced different authorities and privileges. Now we will show you where all these security information is stored and how to easily retrieve it.

Just like most of the information about a database, authorities and privileges metadata is stored in the catalog tables and views listed in Table 10.10. For a complete list of all DB2 catalog tables and descriptions, refer to Appendix D, Using the DB2 System Catalog Tables, or the *DB2 UDB SQL Reference* manual.

Table 10.10   System Catalog Views Containing Authority and Privilege Metadata

Catalog View	Description
SYSCAT.COLAUTH	Stores column privileges for each grantee. Column privileges are granted through table and view privileges. The two privilege types are Update and Reference.
SYSCAT.DBAUTH	Stores database authorities for each grantee.
SYSCAT.INDEXAUTH	Stores index privileges for each grantee.
SYSCAT.PACKAGEAUTH	Stores package privileges for each grantee.
SYSCAT.PASSTHRUAUTH	Stores information about authorizations to query data sources in pass-through sessions. Pass-through sessions (not discussed in this book) are used in federated database environments.
SYSCAT.ROUTINEAUTH	Stores routine privileges for each grantee.
SYSCAT.SCHEMAAUTH	Stores schema privileges for each grantee.
SYSCAT.SEQUENCEAUTH	Stores sequence privileges for each grantee.
SYSCAT.TABAUTH	Stores table privileges for each grantee.
SYSCAT.TBSPACEAUTH	Stores table space privileges for each grantee.

While querying the catalog views give you everything (and sometimes more than) you want to know, the following are a few commands and tools you will find handy.

From the DB2 CLP, you can obtain the authorities of users connected to the database in the current session with this command:

```
get authorizations
```

The command extracts and formats information stored in SYSCAT.DBAUTH. It lists the database authorities for the users. In addition to showing the authorities directly granted to the current user, it also shows implicit authorities inherited. Figure 10.32 shows the output of this command.

You can also retrieve the same result from the DB2 Control Center. Right-click on the database you want to know about and then select **Authorities** (see Figure 10.33). This displays the Database Authorities window (see Figure 10.34), where you can manage database-level authorities for existing and new users and groups.

> **N O T E**   Recall that user IDs and user groups are defined outside of DB2 (e.g., the operating system of the DB2 server). The user IDs and user groups shown in the Control Center refer to existing users and groups at the external security facility level. To add an existing user to the Control Center, use the *Add User* button.

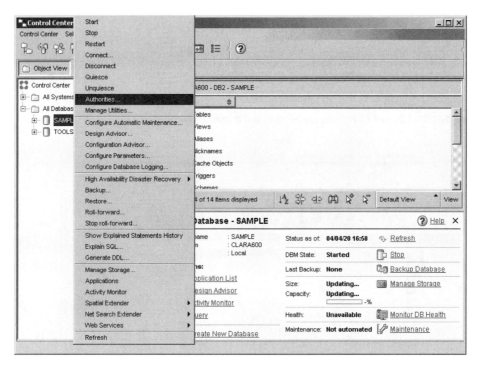

Figure 10.32 Obtaining database authorities from the Control Center

```
Administrative Authorizations for Current User
 Direct SYSADM authority                      = NO
 Direct SYSCTRL authority                     = NO
 Direct SYSMAINT authority                    = NO
 Direct DBADM authority                       = YES
 Direct CREATETAB authority                   = YES
 Direct BINDADD authority                     = YES
 Direct CONNECT authority                     = YES
 Direct CREATE_NOT_FENC authority             = YES
 Direct IMPLICIT_SCHEMA authority             = YES
 Direct LOAD authority                        = YES
 Direct QUIESCE_CONNECT authority             = YES
 Direct CREATE_EXTERNAL_ROUTINE authority     = YES

 Indirect SYSADM authority                    = YES
 Indirect SYSCTRL authority                   = NO
 Indirect SYSMAINT authority                  = NO
 Indirect DBADM authority                     = NO
 Indirect CREATETAB authority                 = YES
 Indirect BINDADD authority                   = YES
```

Figure 10.33 Output of the get authorizations command *(continued)*

```
Indirect CONNECT authority                  = YES
Indirect CREATE_NOT_FENC authority          = NO
Indirect IMPLICIT_SCHEMA authority          = YES
Indirect LOAD authority                     = NO
Indirect QUIESCE_CONNECT authority          = NO
Indirect CREATE_EXTERNAL_ROUTINE authority  = NO
```

Figure 10.33   Output of the get authorizations command *(continued)*

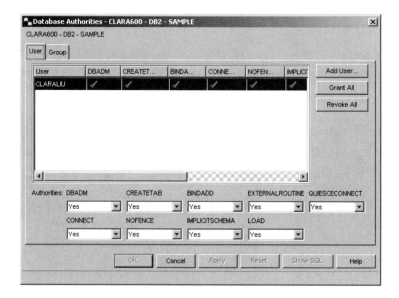

Figure 10.34   Managing database authorities from the Control Center

To manage privileges for each individual database object, right-click on the target object from the Control Center and select **Privileges** (see Figure 10.35).

Using the window shown in Figure 10.36, you can manage the privileges associated to the object. For example, you can grant or revoke particular privileges of a table for a particular user or for all users.

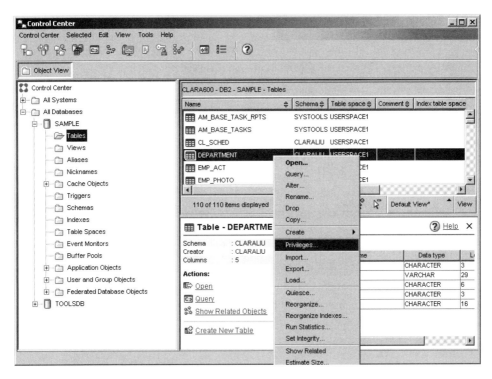

Figure 10.35 Managing database object privileges from the Control Center

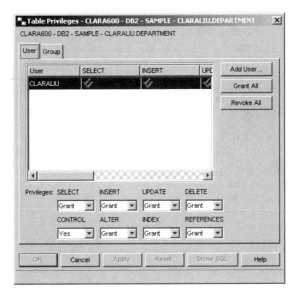

Figure 10.36 Managing database table privileges from the Control Center

10.7 WINDOWS DOMAIN CONSIDERATIONS

In almost all production environments, database administrators group users together and grant certain privileges or database authorities to those groups. As you can imagine, this is more efficient than maintaining privileges for each individual user. Given that DB2 does not maintain any user and group authentication information, it is important to understand how the groups are being looked up for the users. Windows domain environments in particular have different types of user groups that warrant some discussion.

10.7.1 Windows Global Groups and Local Groups

For example, a DB2 server is defined on the Windows domain MMDOM, and within the domain, a domain controller is a server that maintains a master database of all the domain users' credentials. It is also used to authenticate domain logons. In Figure 10.37 you can see that a user ID *db2admin* is a member of global group MMDBA in the domain MMDOM. To use global groups, you must include them inside a local group on the DB2 server. When DB2 enumerates all the groups that a person is a member of, it also lists the local groups the user is a member of indirectly. Permission to access the database and/or object must be granted to this local group.

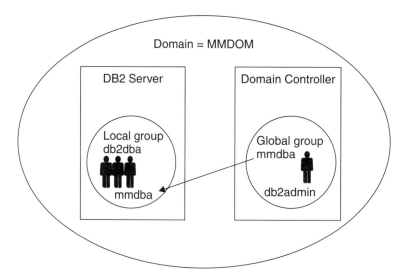

Figure 10.37 Support of global groups in DB2

Figure 10.38 shows a second scenario, where the same user ID, *db2admin*, is also defined locally at the DB2 server and is a member of a local group called DB2DBA.

A user connects to the database as *db2admin* and tries to drop a table. Which group do you want DB2 to enumerate for *db2admin*? It is important for DB2 to enumerate the right group because

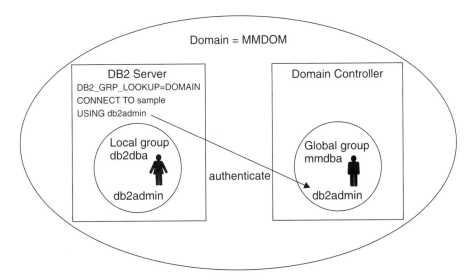

Figure 10.38 Support of LOCAL or DOMAIN group lookup

local group DB2DBA might only hold SELECT privileges on the table, whereas the global group MMDBA has SYSADM authority.

The first option is to include the Windows domain with the user ID during authentication, such as in the **CONNECT** statement or the **attach** command. The fully qualified DB2 authentication ID can be as long as 30 characters. This makes group lookup on Windows more deterministic.

V8.2 `CONNECT TO sample USER mmdba/db2admin USING password`

Note that the fully qualified authentication ID also works in **GRANT** and **REVOKE** statements. For example:

`GRANT SELECT ON TABLE employee TO USER mmdba/db2admin`

Alternatively, use the DB2 registry variable DB2_GRP_LOOKUP to tell DB2 where to validate user accounts and perform group member lookup. Set the variable to LOCAL to force DB2 to always enumerate groups and validate user accounts locally on the DB2 server. Set the variable to DOMAIN to force DB2 to always enumerate groups and validate user accounts on the Windows domain to which the user account belongs. For example:

`db2set DB2_GRP_LOOKUP = DOMAIN`

V8.2 **10.7.2 Access Tokens**

If a user wants to log onto his or her laptop as a domain user in a disconnected environment, Windows supports this via cached credentials. When a credential is cached, information kept from the last logon is referenced if the machine cannot contact the domain controller. DB2 supports this behavior by using an access token.

An access token is created after a user has successfully logged on to the system. The token is an object that describes the security context of a process or thread. The information in an access token includes the identity, all of the groups the user belongs to, and privileges of the user account associated with the process or thread.

You can also use the DB2_GRP_LOOKUP registry variable to enable access token support. Besides LOCAL and DOMAIN, there are three other valid values: TOKEN, TOKENLOCAL, and TOKENDOMAIN. These values can be used with LOCAL or DOMAIN to determine where to look up groups if an access token is not available. Table 10.11 highlights the behavior of these values.

Table 10.11   DB2_GRP_LOOKUP Registry Variable Settings

DB2_GRP_LOOKUP Setting	Description
TOKEN	Enables access token support to look up all groups that the user belongs to at the location where the user account is defined.
LOCAL, TOKENLOCAL	Enables access token support to look up local groups or to fallback to use LOCAL group lookup if an access token is not available.
DOMAIN, TOKENDOMAIN	Enables access token support to look up domain groups or to fallback to DOMAIN group lookup if an access token is not available.

10.8 CASE STUDY

Assume that you have just created a database (SAMPLE) in a DB2 instance (DB2) for application testing. Before the testers can access the database, you need to make sure they have all the necessary privileges and authorities to perform requested database operations.

First of all, you want to enforce that all client authentications are validated at the server. To retrieve the current authentication setting, issue the following command:

```
get dbm cfg
```

The result indicates that user IDs and passwords will be authenticated at the DB2 server:

```
Database manager authentication      (AUTHENTICATION) = SERVER
```

Recently, a company-wide alert announced that encryption should be used wherever possible to prevent eavesdropping. To do this, you can update the database manager authentication to SERVER_ENCRYPT so that both user IDs and passwords are encrypted.

You decide to update the authentication type using the **update dbm cfg** command:

```
update dbm cfg using authentication server_encrypt
```

You then stop and restart the DB2 instance.

Besides encrypting user IDs and passwords, data requested from and returned to the database can also be encrypted. You configure this at each DB2 client using the following command:

```
catalog db sample at node dbsrv authentication sql_authentication_dataenc_cmp
```

Besides configuring the DB2 clients and server to perform secured authentication and data encryption, data access must be restricted to authorized users only. As you can see from the result of the **get dbm cfg** command, the system groups all default to NULL (i.e., users who have system administrative or root privileges).

To make sure only the assigned users can perform DB2 administrative tasks, you set the system groups to the appropriate groups:

```
update dbm cfg using sysadm grpadmin sysctrl grpctrl
    sysmaint grpmaint sysmon grpmon
```

Cynthia, who is a member of the *grpadmin* group, connects to the SAMPLE database and issues the following statements:

```
CREATE TABLE topsecret_table
    ( empno          CHAR(6)
    , name           VARCHAR(50)
    , perf_grade     CHAR(1)
    , salary_inc_pct INTEGER);

INSERT INTO topsecret_table
    VALUES ('000010', 'Bill', 'F', 0)
        , ('000020', 'John', 'A', 80)
        , ('000030', 'Kathy','C', 20);
```

The *topsecret_table* was successfully created and populated because *Cynthia* is a member of the SYSADM group who can perform any operation on the instance and its associated databases.

Bill found out that he will be getting an *F* grade in his performance review and will not get any salary increase. Being a member of the *grpmaint* group, he thinks he has the authority to update the records in the *topsecret_table* table. Therefore, he connects to the SAMPLE database and issues the following statement:

```
UPDATE topsecret_table
   SET perf_grade = 'A', salary_inc_pct = 100
 WHERE empno = '000010'
```

The update was not successful. The following error was received:

```
SQL0551N  "DB2USER" does not have the privilege to perform operation "UPDATE" on
object "DB2ADMIN.EMPLOYEE".  SQLSTATE=42501
```

This works as expected because users who have just the SYSCTRL, SYSMAINT, or SYSMON authority do not have the ability to retrieve or modify data. They only have the authority to perform system maintenance or monitor tasks.

By default, four privileges are granted to PUBLIC when a database is created. You should lock down the database by revoking privileges that are implicitly granted:

```
REVOKE CONNECT, CREATETAB, BINADD, IMPLICIT_SCHEMA
    ON DATABASE FROM PUBLIC
```

Then, grant privileges to users which they only need.

```
GRANT SELECT, UPDATE, DELETE, INDEX ON TABLE employee TO USER john
```

10.9 SUMMARY

This chapter introduced the DB2 security model. To connect to a DB2 database, user and password authentication is performed outside of DB2 using the security facility provided by the operating system of the DB2 server, by Kerberos, or through customized security plug-ins. Security plug-ins are loadable library modules that implement security mechanisms to be used for user authentication.

Setting the authentication type at the DB2 server and client determines where authentication will take place. At the DB2 server, authentication type is defined in the Database Manager Configuration file. DB2 clients specify an authentication type for each database it connects to when the database is being cataloged.

Once a user is successfully authenticated, the user must have appropriate database authorities and/or privileges before he or she can perform database tasks and operations. Database authorities are required for a user to perform database administration tasks such as database creation or database backup.

Database privileges for various types of database objects are granted and revoked through the **GRANT** and **REVOKE** statements.

There are special considerations for a DB2 server on Windows configured in a Windows domain, for example, for local or global group lookup. DB2 lets you use the registry variable DB2_GRP_LOOKUP to identify where the user is being enumerated for group resolution.

10.10 REVIEW QUESTIONS

1. Where does DB2 store information about the users who can access DB2?
2. Besides performing user ID and password authentication at the DB2 server or DB2 client, what other authentication mechanisms does DB2 support?
3. When does a user need the BINDADD privilege on a database?
4. If *bob* is connected to a database and wants to create a table *foo* in the *ts1* table space, what privileges must he have to run the following statement?
    ```
    CREATE TABLE mary.foo (c1 INT, c2 INT) IN ts1
    ```
5. A user ID *bob* that is a member of group *dba* is defined on the DB2 server. Why would the following fail to give SYSCTRL authority to user *bob*?
    ```
    update dbm cfg using sysctrl bob
    ```

6. In a Windows environment where a DB2 server is defined inside a domain called *dom-prod*, user ID *db2admin* is only defined in the domain controller as a member of the global group *glbgrp*. If you want to log on to the DB2 server as the domain user *dom-prod\db2admin* and perform tasks such as creating a new database, what are the three key steps you have to take?

7. You want to authenticate users at the clients. What are the three types of clients that the parameter TRUST_ALLCLNTS evaluates?

8. You have just created a database. Other than the members of the SYSADM group, you want to allow only *bob* to create new tables in the database. What DCL command do you have to issue?

9. *Mary* wrote an embedded SQL program with static SQL statements. A package is created and bound to the database. What privilege does *bob* need to use the package?

10. Given the following Database Manager Configuration parameters on your DB2 instance running on the Linux Server DBL1:

```
Database manager authentication      (AUTHENTICATION) = CLIENT
Trust all clients                    (TRUST_ALLCLNTS) = NO
Trusted client authentication        (TRUST_CLNTAUTH) = CLIENT
```

If you are connecting to the database from a Windows ME client, where will authentication take place?

11. If you are connecting to a DB2 database on a UNIX server named DBX1 from a Linux client named DBL1, where will the user ID be authenticated by default?
   A. DBL1
   B. DBX1

12. If you have configured DB2 with the authentication set to SERVER_ENCRYPT, which of the following describes what is encrypted?
   A. Data
   B. Data and user IDs
   C. User IDs and passwords
   D. Data, user IDs, and passwords

13. Given the following Database Manager Configuration parameters on your DB2 instance running on the Linux Server DBL1:

```
Database manager authentication      (AUTHENTICATION) = CLIENT
Trust all clients                    (TRUST_ALLCLNTS) = YES
   Trusted client authentication        (TRUST_CLNTAUTH) = CLIENT
```

If you are connecting to the database from a Windows ME client, where will authentication take place?
   A. The client
   B. The server

14. Which two of the following DB2 authorities can select data from tables?
   A. SYSADM
   B. SYSCTRL
   C. SYSMAINT

D. DBADM

E. SYSMON

15. Which of the following can be encrypted with DB2?

    A. User IDs

    B. Passwords

    C. All data

    D. User IDs, passwords, and data

16. Which of the following groups can create and drop event monitors?

    A. SYSADM

    B. SYSMON

    C. SYSCTRL

    D. SYSMAINT

17. Which of the following authorities cannot take a DB2 trace?

    A. SYSADM

    B. SYSMON

    C. SYSCTRL

    D. SYSMAINT

18. Given the following:

    • User1 grants CREATEIN privilege on the schema *foo* to Fred with grant option

    • Joe grants CREATEIN privilege on the schema *foo* to Barney with grant option

    • User1 revokes CREATEIN privilege on the schema *foo* from Fred.

    • Barney grants CREATEIN privilege on the schema *foo* to Wilma.

    • Wilma grants CREATEIN privilege on the schema *foo* to Betty.

    Which of the following still have CREATEIN privilege on the schema *foo*?

    A. Barney

    B. Barney and Wilma

    C. Barney, Wilma, and Betty

    D. No one

19. Given the table space *tsp1* that is created with default options, which of the following sets of commands will ensure only the group *grp1* can use the table space?

    A. GRANT USE OF TABLESPACE tsp1 TO grp1

    B. GRANT USER OF TABLESPACE tsp1 TO grp1 WITH GRANT OPTION

    C. REVOKE USE OF TABLESPACE FROM ALL

    D. GRANT USE OF TABLESPACE tsp1 TO GRP1

    E. REVOKE USE OF TABLESPACE FROM PUBLIC

    F. GRANT USE OF TABLESPACE tsp1 TO GRP1

20. If a DBA wants to find out whether user *bob* has CREATETAB privileges, which of the following system catalog tables should the DBA query?

    A. SYSCAT.TABAUTH

    B. SYSCAT.TABLES

    C. SYSCAT.DBAUTH

    D. SYSCAT.SCHEMAAUTH

Understanding Concurrency and Locking

You need to establish some rules and locking mechanisms to guarantee data integrity in case more than one user tries to update the same row of data in a multi-user database environment. DB2 uses four isolation levels to support different levels of concurrency. Each isolation level is implemented by slightly different locking behavior. In this chapter we will look at their differences and some examples on how they can be used in the application. As a database administrator or an application developer it is very helpful to know troubleshooting skills to identify locking problems, and this chapter covers DB2 monitoring tools to do this.

In this chapter you will learn about:

- The big picture of the DB2 locking mechanism
- Different concurrency scenarios
- The DB2 isolation levels
- How DB2 isolation levels affect locking
- Troubleshooting tools that come with DB2 to identify locking problems
- Avoiding locking problems

11.1 DB2 Locking and Concurrency: The Big Picture

Figure 11.1 provides an overview of the DB2 locking mechanism using isolation levels. Isolation levels can be configured by various methods. Depending on the isolation level specified, DB2 performs database locking differently. The following sections discuss these in more detail.

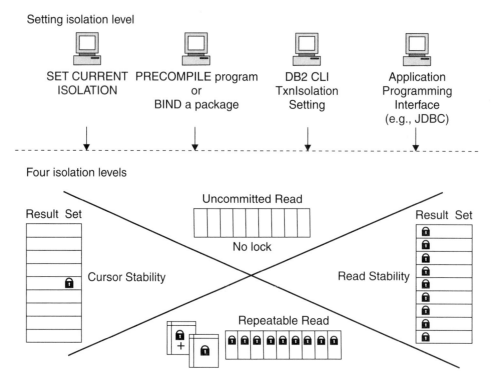

Figure 11.1   Overview of locking and concurrency

11.2 CONCURRENCY AND LOCKING SCENARIOS

Like many other database systems, DB2 provides support for concurrent data access. While the database is being accessed and manipulated by multiple users, it is important to keep data integrity by using database locking. Before getting into detailed discussions of DB2 locking, you should first understand various concurrent data access scenarios you may encounter and how each DB2 isolation level can prevent these scenarios from occurring or allow these scenarios to occur.

11.2.1 Lost Updates

Assume there is an airline reservation system with multiple agents answering calls for seat reservations. A table called *reservations* is defined to store flight numbers, seat assignments, and passenger names. Each seat on every flight is represented by a single row of data. Figure 11.2 shows the *reservations* table.

Suppose customer Harry wants to reserve a seat on Flight 512 and calls the reservation center. An agent, Sam, receives the call and finds the only seat available, 4A, for Harry. While Harry is confirming the itinerary with his wife, Sam maintains the searched result on screen. At this time, agent Mary helps another customer, Billy, to fulfill his request. Mary also finds 4A, the last seat on Flight 512.

Flight	Seat	Passenger Name
512	1C	John Smith
512	1D	Arnold Page
512	23A	Tim Chan
512	13B	Bernard Reid
512	4A	–

Figure 11.2   Sample content of the reservations table

Eventually, Harry decides to confirm the seat and Sam assigns seat 4A to Harry. However, Mary does not see Harry's update and she assigns the same seat to Billy. Both seat assignments are successful, but guess who gets the seat? If the list of seats is retrieved again, you will see that the second update overwrites the first one (see Figure 11.3). Hence, Sam loses the seat assignment and Harry will not be able to get on the plane as he expects.

Flight	Seat	Passenger Name
512	1C	John Smith
512	1D	Arnold Page
512	23A	Tim Chan
512	13B	Bernard Reid
512	4A	Billy Bee

Figure 11.3   Sample content of the updated reservations table

This example demonstrates that if there is no mechanism in place to maintain the accuracy of data, it is possible to lose updates without knowing it or until the customers find out for themselves.

By default, DB2 acquires a lock on every record that the agent is updating. This default behavior cannot be changed. With this type of lock, no other agent can update the same row of data. If this reservation system is implemented in DB2, this scenario of lost update will never occur. When Sam is updating the record, all other read operations (except uncommitted read) and write operations to the same row of data will wait until Sam's transaction is completed. Once Sam has committed the change, Mary will see the new seat assignment in her next data retrieval, so Billy will not be assigned to the seat.

Two terms are introduced here that warrant some discussion. A **transaction** (also known as a **unit of work**) is a sequence of SQL statements that the database manager treats as a whole. Any reading from or writing to the database is performed in a transaction. At the end of a transaction, the application can `COMMIT` or `ROLLBACK` the changes. Once you issue a `COMMIT` operation, changes are written to the database. A `ROLLBACK` operation causes the changes within the transaction to be rolled back. Transactions are discussed in more detail in Chapter 13, Developing Backup and Recovery Solutions.

11.2.2 Uncommitted Reads

Using the same flight reservation example, assume Sam is updating a row to assign a seat. Since DB2 locks the row by default, no other agent can read or update the same record. Meanwhile, the manager wants to run a report to determine how many passengers are scheduled to fly on Flight 512. Because of the default locking behavior, the manager's request has to wait until Sam's update is completed. However, if the manager's application is implemented to read uncommitted data, the manager can run the report without waiting for Sam to complete his transaction. This type of read is called an **uncommitted read** or a **dirty read**. However, changes Sam makes are not guaranteed to be written to the database. Therefore, if he decides to roll back the changes, the manager will get a different result when running the report again.

Whether an uncommitted read is allowed or avoided is based on the application design. As you can imagine, performance of applications with the ability to read uncommitted data is better because there is no need to acquire and wait for locks. However, you must understand that the data retrieved is *not* committed data, which means that the data may not be the same the next time you query it.

11.2.3 Nonrepeatable Reads

Suppose Harry asks Sam to find an aisle seat on Flight 512. Sam issues a query and retrieves a list of available seats on the flight. Figure 11.4 shows such a list where – (the NULL value) in the Passenger Name column means the seat is not assigned.

Flight	Seat	Passenger Name
512	5B	–
512	6E	–
512	8C	–
512	13E	–
512	15E	–

Figure 11.4   Available seats on Flight 512

In this aircraft model, only C and D seats are aisle seats. There is only one aisle seat available on this flight, seat 8C. Before Sam reserves seat 8C for Harry, no lock is acquired on this row highlighted in Figure 11.4. At this time, Mary has assigned and committed the same aisle seat to another customer, Billy. When Sam is ready and tries to assign Seat 8C to Harry, the update fails because the seat is no longer available. If the same query is issued, Figure 11.5 shows that seat 8C is no longer available.

Flight	Seat	Passenger Name
512	5B	–
512	6E	–
512	13E	–
512	15E	–

Figure 11.5   Updated available seats on Flight 512

This is an example of a **nonrepeatable read** scenario for which a different result set is returned with the same query within the same transaction. To avoid this situation, all the rows returned from the result set, shown in Figure 11.4, should be locked. This way, no other user can update the rows currently being read until the transaction is completed. However, concurrency will be decreased because of the extra locks being held.

11.2.4 Phantom Reads

A **phantom read** is very similar to a nonrepeatable read: while rows currently read are not updatable or removable by another user, new rows *can* be inserted into the tables that fall under the query criteria.

The flight reservation application is designed in a way that all rows in a result set are locked. Due to the demand of this particular flight, the airline decides to upgrade the aircraft to a larger one so that more passengers can be served. Since more seats are added to the flight, the same query used before to obtain available seat will now return extra rows. If the aircraft upgrade is made in the middle of another query transaction, the next execution of the same query will result in extra phantom rows. Depending on the situation, reading phantom rows may work with the application. To avoid this behavior, extra locking is required.

11.3 DB2 ISOLATION LEVELS

DB2 provides four isolation levels to control locking behavior. From the lowest isolation level to the highest these are

- Uncommitted read

- Cursor stability
- Read stability
- Repeatable read

These isolation levels use different locking strategies, so you can choose the level of data protection depending on the application design.

11.3.1 Uncommitted Reads

An **uncommitted read** (UR) is the lowest isolation level but provides the highest concurrency to the database applications. When you configure an application to perform uncommitted reads, the application will not acquire any row lock to read data. However, a nonrestrictive table lock is required (see Section 11.5, DB2 Locking, for more information). Since no row locks are acquired, there is no conflict with any read or write operations undergoing on the same data. With this isolation level, uncommitted reads, nonrepeatable reads, and phantom reads can still occur.

Figure 11.6 shows an example of two applications accessing the same row. Assume that App A locks row 2 for an update operation. No other application can make changes to row 2. The only concurrent operation that can be issued against row 2 is an uncommitted read as illustrated by App B.

No lock is acquired for read operations for applications configured with the UR isolation level. For any update, insert, or delete operation, an application with UR will still hold locks until the transaction is committed or rolled back. App C in Figure 11.6 illustrates this.

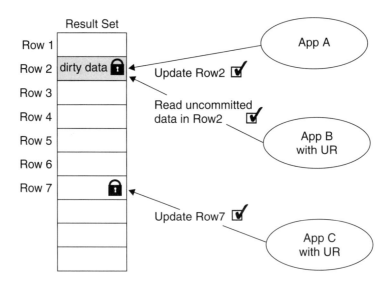

Figure 11.6   Concurrent data access with the uncommitted read isolation level

11.3.2 Cursor Stability

Cursor stability (CS) is the default DB2 isolation level. This isolation level works well with most applications because it uses a certain degree of locking to protect data, and at the same time it also provides a high level of concurrency. As the name of this isolation level implies, it uses a mechanism to provide a stable read where the cursor is positioned. DB2 will only lock the row where the cursor is pointing.

A cursor can be viewed as a pointer to one row in a set of rows (also called a **result set**). You need to OPEN the cursor so that it is positioned just before the first row of the result set. To move the cursor to the next row, you execute a FETCH operation. As a best practice, you should CLOSE the cursor when it is no longer required.

When a cursor is opened, no lock is acquired until the application fetches the first row of the result set. In the same unit of work, if the application fetches the second row, DB2 will release the previous row lock and acquire a lock on the second row. In Figure 11.7, App A with a CS isolation level fetches row 2. This application will only lock the row it is reading: row 2. When App D tries to alter that particular row, it has to wait.

In Figure 11.7 App B holds a lock on row 7 for read (fetching). At the same time, App C obtains a share lock and can still read the same row. Therefore, with isolation level CS, concurrent reads are still possible.

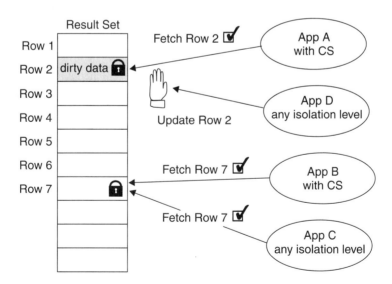

Figure 11.7   Concurrent read with two applications in cursor stability isolation level

Using isolation level CS, nonrepeatable read and phantom read scenarios can still occur; however, the uncommitted read scenario is not possible.

Now you understand that a row lock is released when the application with CS reads the next row. But what happens if the application makes changes to a row while it is being read? Figure 11.8 illustrates this scenario.

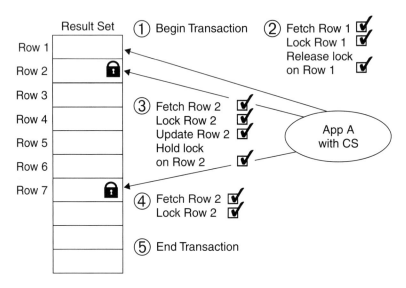

Figure 11.8   Reading and updating data with cursor stability isolation level

(1) App A uses CS isolation level and starts a transaction.

(2) App A locks row 1 for read. App A releases the lock on row 1 when it fetches row 2.

(3) Row 2 is locked. During the read, the App A decides to update the row. The lock will be held until the current transaction is completed (5).

(4) App A fetches row 7 and acquires a lock. At this point App A holds two locks: one for read and one for update.

(5) The current transaction is completed and all locks will be released.

11.3.3 Read Stability

Read stability (RS) is another isolation level DB2 uses to protect data. Unlike CS, RS not only locks the current row that is being fetched, it also applies the appropriate locks to all rows that are in the result set. This ensures that within the same transaction, rows that have been previously read by a cursor cannot be altered by other applications.

Figure 11.9 shows that all the rows in the result set are locked even when the cursor is only processing a particular row. No wait is necessary if more than one application reads the same set of rows concurrently. However, any update operation will have to wait until the reads are completed.

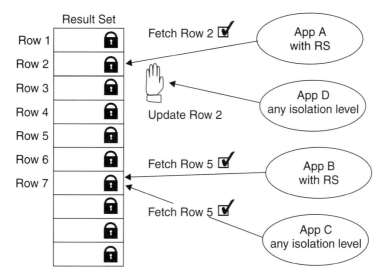

Figure 11.9 The read stability isolation level

RS causes DB2 to perform more locking than the UR or CS isolation levels. With RS, the uncommitted read and nonrepeatable read scenarios cannot occur; however, phantom reads can still happen.

Similar to the other isolation levels, if an application with RS updates a row, a lock will be held until the transaction is completed.

11.3.4 Repeatable Reads

Repeatable (RR) read is the highest isolation level. It also gives you the lowest concurrency. Similar to RS, applications with RR forces DB2 to lock all the rows in the result set as well as rows that are used to build the result set. A query that involves a two-table join is issued and DB2 decides to perform table scans on both tables to obtain the result. This isolation level locks all the rows in the two tables. If a row is read by the application using RR, no other application can alter it until the transaction is completed. This ensures that your result set is consistent throughout the duration of the unit of work. One consideration is that due to the additional locking, it can greatly reduce concurrency.

In Figure 11.10, you can see that behavior for applications A, B, C, and D is the same as RS. However, if App E tries to update a row in table T1 that is not in the result set, it has to wait until the lock is released.

With repeatable read isolation level, none of the locking scenarios can occur. Applications with RR can only read committed data and perform repeatable read.

Table 11.1 summarizes the four isolation levels and locking scenarios that may occur.

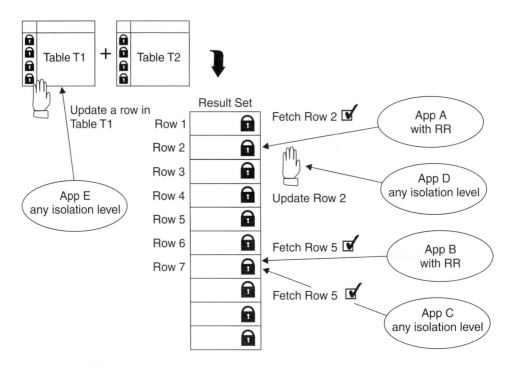

Figure 11.10   The repeatable read isolation level

Table 11.1   Four Isolation Levels and Locking Scenarios

Locking Scenarios	Uncommitted Read	Cursor Stability	Read Stability	Repeatable Read
Lost update	No	No	No	No
Uncommitted read	Yes	No	No	No
Nonrepeatable read	Yes	Yes	No	No
Phantom read	Yes	Yes	Yes	No

11.4 CHANGING ISOLATION LEVELS

The isolation level is not bound to a database. Each application can use a different isolation level so that a different locking mechanism can be applied. Isolation levels can be set at different levels:

- Session level
- Application level
- Statement level

The following sections describe each of these levels.

11.4.1 Using the DB2 Command Window

The current isolation level is stored in a DB2 special register called CURRENT ISOLATION. The special register is a value with two characters (data type of CHAR(2)) of the current isolation level for any dynamic SQL statements issued within the current session.

To obtain the current isolation level value, connect to the database and issue either of these statements:

```
VALUES CURRENT ISOLATION
SELECT CURRENT ISOLATION FROM sysibm.sysdummy1
```

The following are the possible values:

- UR (uncommitted read)
- CS (cursor stability)
- RS (read stability)
- RR (repeatable read)
- Blank (means that the default isolation level is used)

To change the isolation level, use the **SET CURRENT ISOLATION** statement. Figure 11.11 shows the syntax diagram for this statement.

```
         .-CURRENT-.                    .-=-.
 >>-SET--+---------+--ISOLATION--+---+--+-UR----+--------------><
                                        +-CS----+
                                        +-RR----+
                                        +-RS----+
                                        '-RESET-'
```

Figure 11.11 Syntax diagram for the SET CURRENT ISOLATION command

Figure 11.12 demonstrates a few examples of how to set and obtain the current isolation level.

It is important to understand that changes to the DB2 special register affects the current session. Subsequent dynamic SQL statements executed in this session will use this isolation level. The

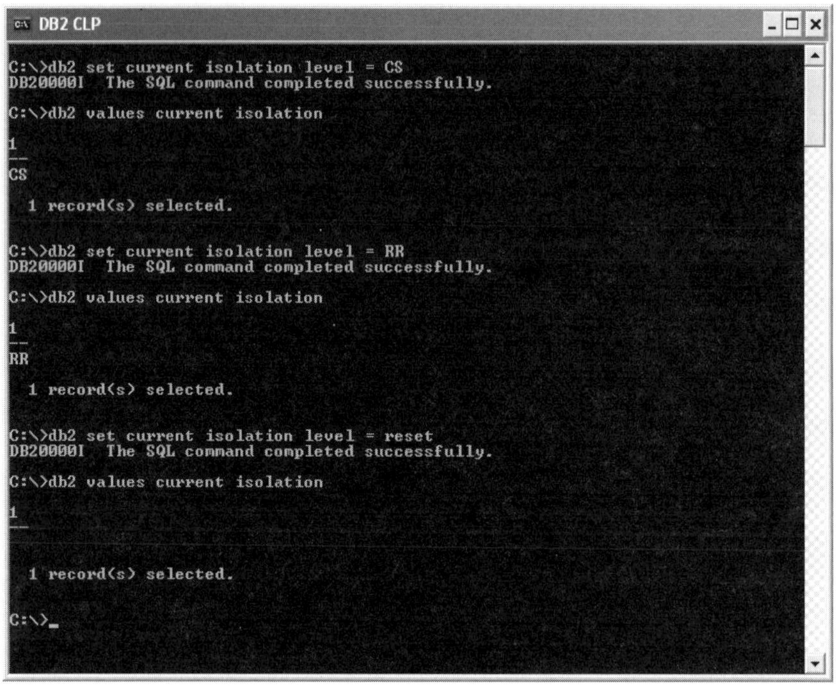

Figure 11.12   Examples of the SET CURRENT ISOLATION LEVEL command

change only applies for dynamic SQL statements. For static SQL statements or packages, you can control the isolation level through the DB2 `bind` command discussed in the next section.

11.4.2 Using the DB2 PRECOMPILE and BIND Commands

To execute an SQL statement, it must be compiled in an executable form that DB2 understands. This executable form of the statement is known as the **data access plan**. Data access plans are stored in database objects called **packages**.

Data access plans for dynamic SQL statements are created at execution time. DB2 uses the most current database statistics, configuration parameters, and DB2 special register settings (such as CURRENT ISOLATION) to evaluate and generate the most optimal plan.

When an application with static SQL statements is precompiled, the prepared statements are stored in a bind file generated by the DB2 precompiler. To create the database access plan from the bind file, you need to invoke the bind utility. The utility takes the bind file as input, creates a package that contains the data access plan, and binds it to the database.

Both the DB2 `precompile` and `bind` commands let you specify some characteristics of how the package should be executed, like the query optimization level, use of row blocking, and the

isolation level. For example, if you want to precompile or bind a package using a nondefault isolation level, use:

```
precompile appfile.sqc isolation RR
```

or

```
bind bindfilename.bnd isolation RR
```

where *appfile.sqc* is an embedded C program containing static SQL, and *bindfilename.bnd* is a
bind file containing SQL in internal format that is to be bound into a package.

Once the package is bound, you can use the system catalog tables or DB2 Control Center to find
out the isolation level specified.

Using the system catalog tables, you can issue the following query:

```
SELECT pkgschema, pkgname, isolation FROM syscat.packages
```

Using the DB2 Control Center, navigate to the folders **Instance** > **Database** > **Application Objects** >
Packages. You should see the isolation level column on the right panel, as shown in Figure
11.13. For example, the package highlighted in Figure 11.13 was bound with isolation level CS.

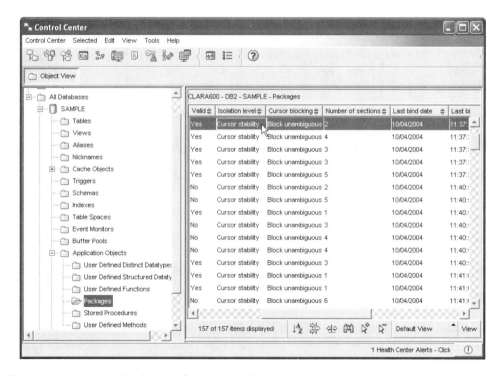

Figure 11.13   Using the Control Center to retrieve the isolation level of packages

11.4.3 Using the DB2 Call Level Interface

The DB2 call level interface (CLI) is the IBM callable SQL interface to DB2 database servers. It is a C/C++ application programming interface (API) for database access. If your application is using the DB2 CLI API, you can also set the isolation level with the CLI setting.

At the DB2 client, launch the Configuration Assistant. Right-click on the database you want to set the isolation level for, and select **CLI Settings** (see Figure 11.14).

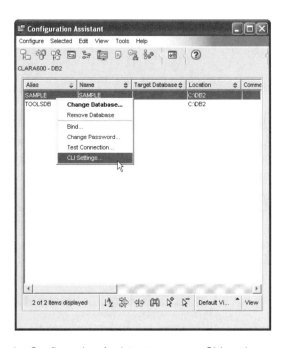

Figure 11.14   Using the Configuration Assistant to access CLI settings

Switch to the *Settings* tab and click *Add*. This displays the *Add CLI Parameter* window as shown in Figure 11.15. Under the list of CLI keywords, select *TxnIsolation* and choose the desired isolation level. Note that the CLI settings apply to a database. This means that every application connecting to the database through this DB2 client will use the isolation level specified.

If the Configuration Assistant is not available at the client, you can also update the DB2 CLI initialization file (db2cli.ini) directly. The file is located at the DB2 install directory. Insert *TxnIsolation* under the database name you wish and enter the isolation level you want to use. Each isolation level is identified by a number (see Table 11.2). The following example shows how to set the isolation for the SAMPLE database to repeatable read.

```
[SAMPLE]
DBALIAS=SAMPLE
TXNIsolation=8
```

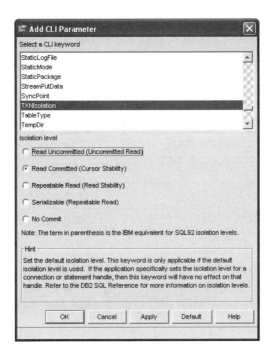

Figure 11.15   Setting the isolation level from the DB2 Configuration Assistant

Table 11.2   DB2 CLI Values for the Isolation Levels

	Uncommitted Read	Cursor Stability	Read Stability	Repeatable Read
TXNIsolation Value	1	2	4	8

11.4.4 Using the Application Programming Interface

In addition to the CLI, DB2 provides various types of programming interfaces that your application can use. The Java Common Client for DB2 is one example. Most APIs such as Java Database Connectivity (JDBC) provide an option to specify the isolation level. A code snippet from a JDBC program is listed in Figure 11.16. For other APIs, check with the associated programming documentations.

```
Class.forName("com.ibm.db2.jcc.DB2Driver");
Connection con=null;
con = DriverManager.getConnection (jdbc:db2:sample,username,password);
con.setTransactionIsolation(TRANSACTION_READ_UNCOMMITTED);
```

Figure 11.16   Snippet of a JDBC program to specify an isolation level

The names of the isolation levels used in APIs are usually different from those used in DB2. JDBC and DB2 isolation level mappings are listed in Table 11.3. For other APIs, refer to the documentation.

Table 11.3 Comparable JDBC and DB2 Isolation Levels

JDBC	DB2
TRANSACTION_READ_UNCOMMITTED	Uncommitted read
TRANSACTION_READ_COMMITTED	Cursor stability
TRANSACTION_REPEATABLE_READ	Read stability
TRANSACTION_SERIALIZABLE	Repeatable read

11.4.5 Working with Statement Level Isolation Level

So far, you have seen that isolation level can be set for a connection. To provide more granular concurrency control, DB2 has the ability to specify isolation level at the statement level.

Suppose an application has started a transaction with CS isolation level. To increase concurrency of a particular statement, you want the statement to be executed with RR isolation level. To do so, use the isolation clause **WITH RR**:

```
UPDATE employee SET salary = 10000 WHERE empno='000010' WITH RR
```

Similarly, you can apply the **WITH** clause to the **INSERT**, **DELETE**, and **SELECT** statements. The same clause in the **SELECT** statement has an extra option for the RR and RS isolation level. Figure 11.17 shows the syntax diagram of the **SELECT** statement's isolation clause.

```
>>-+-------------------------------------------+--------------------->< 
   '-WITH--+-RR--+---------------------+-+-' 
           |     '-lock-request-clause-' | 
           +-RS--+---------------------+-+ 
           |     '-lock-request-clause-' | 
           +-CS--------------------------+ 
           '-UR--------------------------' 
lock-request-clause: 

>>-USE AND KEEP--+-UPDATE----+---LOCKS---------------------------->< 
                 '-EXCLUSIVE-' 
```

Figure 11.17 Syntax diagram of the SELECT statement's isolation clause

The `lock-request-clause` is optional and specifies the type of lock that DB2 will acquire and hold. The owner of an UPDATE lock can update the row being locked. Concurrent processes can only read the data in the locked object but cannot update it. EXCLUSIVE lock, on the other hand, is a more restrictive type of lock. It does not allow concurrent processes to acquire any lock on the data.

A **SELECT** statement with the isolation clause will look similar to the following:

```
SELECT empno, lastname, firstnme
  FROM employee
 WHERE deptno='A01'
  WITH RR USE AND KEEP EXCLUSIVE LOCKS
```

11.5 DB2 LOCKING

DB2 uses various levels of locking to provide concurrent data access and at the same time protect the data. Depending on the operations requested, the database manager can acquire locks on databases, buffer pools, table spaces, tables, table blocks, and table rows. Locks are acquired implicitly by DB2 according to the semantics defined by the isolation level.

11.5.1 Lock Attributes

During normal data manipulation processing, DB2 uses row-level locking by default. You can override this rule to acquire table-level locking instead. The **ALTER TABLE** statement with the **LOCKSIZE** option forces DB2 to place a table lock whenever the table is accessed. The statement will look like this:

```
ALTER TABLE employee LOCKSIZE TABLE
```

This setting is retained until you execute:

```
ALTER TABLE employee LOCKSIZE ROW
```

The only objects that you can explicitly lock are databases, tables, and table spaces. To explicitly lock a database, use the **CONNECT** statement with the appropriate lock mode. For example:

```
CONNECT TO sample IN EXCLUSIVE MODE
```

This causes an exclusive lock to be applied to the database. It prevents concurrent application from executing any operations at the database. This lock mode is useful when exclusive administrative tasks must be performed. You can also connect to the database in SHARE MODE, which allows other concurrent connections to the database but prevents other users from connecting in exclusive mode.

> **N O T E**   When you need to perform exclusive administrative tasks at the instance, rather than the database level, use the **start database manager admin mode** command as explained in Chapter 5, Understanding the DB2 Environment, DB2 Instances, and Databases.

Table spaces of a particular table can be quiesced. **Quiesing** a table space is like locking a table space so that administrative tasks (e.g., a load operation) can be performed. With the different quiesce modes, shown in Figure 11.18, DB2 obtains different types of locks for the table and its associated table space(s). The syntax diagram of the **quiesce tablespaces for table** command is presented in Figure 11.18.

```
>>-QUIESCE TABLESPACES FOR TABLE--+-tablename--------+---------->
                                  '-schema.tablename-'

>--+-SHARE-----------+------------------------------------------><
   +-INTENT TO UPDATE-+
   +-EXCLUSIVE--------+
   '-RESET-----------'
```

Figure 11.18   Syntax diagram of the quiesce tablespaces for table command

If you have quiesced the table spaces with a restrictive mode, access to tables within those tablespaces are not allowed. For example, this command:

`quiesce tablespaces for table employee exclusive`

puts superexclusives lock on the table space where table *employee* is stored, and on the table *employee*. The state of the table space changes to QUIESCED EXCLUSIVE. No other access to the table spaces is allowed. This means that access to another table that is stored in the same table space is not allowed. You will receive the following error.

`SQL0290N Table space access is not allowed SQLSTATE=55039`

To unquiesce the table space, issue the same **quiesce tablespaces for table** command but with the **reset** option.

You can also lock a table explicitly with the **LOCK TABLE** statement. Similarly, different lock modes are available as shown in Figure 11.19. The **LOCK TABLE** statement locks the specified table until the transaction is completed.

```
>>-LOCK TABLE--+-table-name-+--IN--+-SHARE-----+--MODE---------><
               '-nickname---'      '-EXCLUSIVE-'
```

Figure 11.19   Syntax diagram of the LOCK TABLE statement

Each lockable object can be locked in a different mode; this represents the type of access allowed for the lock owner. They also control the type of access permitted for concurrent users of the locked object.

11.5.1.1 Table-Level Lock Modes

Table and row locks are the most commonly used types of locks. Figure 11.20 shows the table-level lock modes. The table lock modes IN, IS, IX, and SIX are used to support row-level locking. An application requires an IN lock on the table before it can perform an uncommitted read. The IS, IX, and SIX locks permit row-level locking while preventing more exclusive locks on the table by other applications.

The other table lock modes—S, U, X, and Z—are strict table locking and do not use row-level locking. For example, if an application holds an X lock on a table, the lock owner can read or update any data in the table but cannot obtain a row lock. Refer to Table 11.4 for a summary of all table lock modes.

Table Lock Mode	Description
IN	Intent None
IS	Intent Share
IX	Intent eXclusive
SIX	Share with Intent eXclusive
S	Share
U	Update
X	eXclusive
Z	Superexclusive

(IN, IS, IX, SIX — Row locking also used)

(S, U, X, Z — Strict table locking)

Figure 11.20   Table Lock Mode Compatibility Chart

11.5.1.2 Row Lock Modes

Row lock modes require support of some kind of table lock. The minimum table locks DB2 must acquire before obtaining a row lock are listed in Figure 11.21. For example, an application can lock a row in Share mode if it also holds an IS lock on the table.

Besides table and row locks, there are other types of objects DB2 locks. Table 11.4 presents a summary of lockable objects and lock modes. *Y* means that the lock mode applies to that type of object; a dash means that it does not apply.

> **N O T E**   If you use multidimensional clustering (MDC) tables, you can impose table block locks.

Row Lock Mode	Description	Minimum Table Lock Required
S	**S**hare	IS
U	**U**pdate	IX
X	e**X**clusive	IX
W	**W**eak Exclusive	IX
NS	**N**ext Key **S**hare	IS
NW	**N**ext Key **W**eak Exclusive	IX

Figure 11.21   Row Lock Mode Compatibility Chart

Table 11.4   Lock Modes Summary

Lock Mode	Buffer Pool	Table Space	Table Block	Table	Row	Description
IN (Intent None)	–	Y	Y	Y	–	The lock owner can read any data in the object, including uncommitted data, but cannot update any of it. Other concurrent applications can read or update the table.
IS (Intent Share)	–	Y	Y	Y	–	The lock owner can read data in the locked object but cannot update its data. Other applications can read or update the object.
NS (Next Key Share)	–	–	–	–	Y	The lock owner and all concurrent applications can read, but not update, the locked row. This lock is acquired on rows of a table where the isolation level of the application is either RS or CS. NS lock mode is not used for next-key locking. It is used instead of S mode during CS and RS scans to minimize the impact of next-key locking on these scans.
S (Share)	–	–	Y	Y	Y	The lock owner and all concurrent applications can read but not update the locked data.

(continues)

Table 11.4   Lock Modes Summary *(Continued)*

Lock Mode	Buffer Pool	Table Space	Table Block	Table	Row	Description
IX (**I**ntent e**X**clusive)	–	Y	Y	Y	–	The lock owner and concurrent applications can read and update data. Other concurrent applications can both read and update the table.
SIX (**S**hare with **I**ntent e**X**clusive)	–	–	Y	Y	–	The lock owner can read and update data. Other concurrent applications can read the table.
U (**U**pdate)	–	–	Y	Y	Y	The lock owner can update data. Other units of work can read the data in the locked object but cannot update it.
NW (**N**ext Key **W**eak Exclusive)	–	–	–	–	Y	When a row is inserted into an index, an NW lock is acquired on the next row. The lock owner can read but not update the locked row. This lock mode is similar to an X lock, except that it is also compatible with W and NS locks.
X (e**X**clusive)	Y	–	Y	Y	Y	The lock owner can both read and update data in the locked object. Only uncommitted read applications can access the locked object.
W (**W**eak Exclusive)	–	–	–	–	Y	This lock is acquired on the row when a row is inserted into a table. The lock owner can change the locked row. This lock is used during insertion into a unique index to determine if a duplicate value is found. This lock is similar to an X lock except that it is compatible with the NW lock. Only uncommitted read applications can access the locked row.
Z (**S**uper Exclusive)	–	Y	–	Y	–	This lock is acquired on a table in certain conditions, such as when the table is altered or dropped, an index on the table is created or dropped, and for some types of table reorganization. No other concurrent application can read or update the table.

Figures 11.22 and 11.23 (from the DB2 manual *Administration Guide: Performance*) present lock mode compatibility charts for table and row locks respectively. *NO* means the requesting application must wait for the lock to be released and *YES* means the lock can be granted.

Mode of Lock for App A \ Mode of Lock for App B	IN	IS	S	IX	SIX	U	X	Z
IN	YES	YES	YES	YES	YES	YES	YES	NO
IS	YES	YES	YES	YES	YES	YES	NO	NO
IX	(YES)	(YES)	NO	(YES)	NO	NO	NO	NO
S	YES	YES	YES	NO	NO	YES	NO	NO
SIX	YES	YES	NO	NO	NO	NO	NO	NO
U	YES	YES	YES	NO	NO	NO	NO	NO
X	YES	NO	NO	NO	NO	NO	NO	NO
Z	NO	NO	NO	NO	NO	NO	NO	NO

Figure 11.22   Table lock mode compatibility chart

Mode of Lock for App A \ Mode of Lock for App B	S	U	X	W	NS	NW
S	YES	YES	NO	NO	YES	NO
U	(YES)	NO	NO	NO	(YES)	NO
X	NO	NO	NO	NO	NO	NO
W	NO	NO	NO	NO	NO	YES
NS	YES	YES	NO	NO	YES	YES
NW	NO	NO	NO	YES	YES	NO

Figure 11.23   Row lock mode compatibility chart

Let's use an example to demonstrate how to use the charts. Assume that application A is holding an IX lock on a table. Looking at the compatibility chart in Figure 11.22, you can see that another application can only lock the same table in IN, IS, or IX mode as highlighted with the circles in the figure.

If application B requests an IS lock at the table level and tries to read some rows in the table, use the row lock chart in Figure 11.23 to determine the compatibility of concurrent data access. As long as application A holds locks that are compatible with the lock mode application B is requesting, both applications can work concurrently with each other. For example, if application A is holding a U lock on a row, application B can only obtain an S or NS lock (refer to compatibility values circled in Figure 11.23). Otherwise, application B must wait for application A to complete its transaction.

11.5.2 Lock Waits

A discussion of DB2 locking mechanisms is not really complete if lock wait and deadlock scenarios are not covered. As the number of concurrent applications increases, the possibility of running into situations with incompatible locks is relatively higher. In the examples used to describe the behavior of the different isolation levels, you saw how an application might have to wait for a lock. This is known as **lock wait**. Deadlocks are discussed in the next section.

It is generally not possible to totally avoid lock wait as concurrency increases. After all, DB2 relies on the locking mechanism to keep data integrity. However, you should minimize lock waits and each wait length as much as possible. They put a hold on processing the statements, hence, they affect performance.

Note that you should minimize lock waits and the duration of each wait. You can use the database configuration parameter called LOCKTIMEOUT to define how long an application is going to wait for a lock. By default, LOCKTIMEOUT is set to -1, which stands for infinite wait. We recommended setting it to a finite number that works well with your application and business requirement.

If an application reaches the LOCKTIMEOUT value, it receives the following message:

```
SQL0911N The current transaction has been rolled back because of a deadlock or
timeout.  Reason code "68".
```

Reason code 68 indicates the transaction is rolled back due to a lock timeout. LOCKTIMEOUT applies to any application connecting to the database. In some cases, you may want to set the timeout duration for a given application rather than providing the same value for all applications. You can directly control how long an individual application will wait for a lock using the **set current lock timeout** command. This command overrides the LOCKTIMEOUT parameter and stores the new value in the DB2 special register CURRENT LOCK TIMEOUT. This would be useful, for example, in a system where there is a mixed workload of long-running reports as well as update batch jobs. Figure 11.24 gives the syntax of the command.

```
        .-CURRENT-.                  .-=-.
>>-SET--+---------+--LOCK TIMEOUT--+---+------------------------->

>--+-WAIT------------------------+------------------------------><
   +-NOT WAIT------------------+
   +-NULL----------------------+
   | .-WAIT-.                  |
   +-+------+--integer-constant-+
   '-host-variable-------------'
```

V8.2 **Figure 11.24**   Syntax diagram of the set current lock timeout command

You can set the lock timeout period to the following.

- WAIT specifies that the application will wait infinitely for a lock.
- NOT WAIT specifies that the application will not wait for locks that cannot be obtained.
- NULL specifies that the application will use the value of the LOCKTIMEOUT database configuration parameter as the duration to wait for locks.
- WAIT *integer_constant* specifies an integer value of how long the application will wait for a lock. The value -1 will have the same behavior as WAIT (without an integer value). A value of 0 is equivalent to specifying NOT WAIT.

To validate the value of the CURRENT LOCK TIMEOUT special register, you can use the **VALUES** statement:

```
VALUES CURRENT LOCK TIMEOUT
```

11.5.3 Deadlocks

There is another undesirable lock scenario to avoid: deadlock. **Deadlock** is a situation when two applications are waiting for locks that the other is holding. Consider the situation in Figure 11.25.

(1) App A starts a transaction and updates the record where *empno* = 100. The record is locked by App A with an X lock.

(2) App B starts a transaction and updates the record where *empno* = 105. The record is locked by App B with an X lock.

(3 and 4) In the same transaction as (1), App A queries the table and scans for *empno* = 106. Assume that DB2 chooses to use a table scan to read each *empno* and see if it is 106. To perform a read, App A needs an S lock on every row. An S lock cannot be obtained for *empno* = 105 because the row is locked by App B with an incompatible lock, X.

(5 and 6) Similarly, App B is executing the same program to search for *empno* = 101. Assume that it also has to scan all the rows. App B will stop and wait for *empno* = 100 that is being locked by App A.

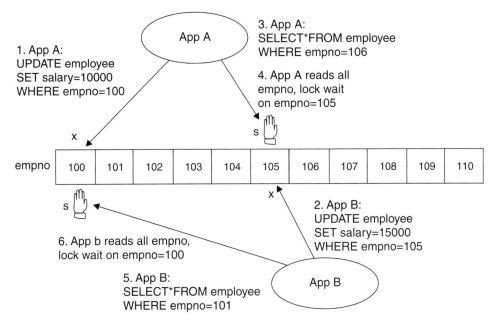

Figure 11.25   Example of a deadlock situation

Apps A and B in this example now encounter a deadlock situation. DB2 has a deadlock detector running around the clock to identify any deadlock. Once one is detected, it will randomly pick a victim and roll back its transaction. By rolling back, all the locks that particular application is holding will be released. This allows the other application that is involved in the deadlock to complete its processing.

The application that is rolled back will receive the message:

```
SQL0911N The current transaction has been rolled back because of a deadlock or
timeout.  Reason code "2".
```

Reason code 2 means that the transaction is rolled back due to a deadlock. The failed user application is then responsible to report the error and retry the transaction if necessary. The deadlock detector is activated periodically as determined by the DLCHKTIME database configuration parameter. The default value for this parameter is 10,000 milliseconds (10 seconds).

To avoid deadlocks or any unnecessary lock waits, you need to understand your application. Design the application and tune the database in a way that the application will only read the data it requires. Figure 11.25 shows an example of two applications manipulating data on different rows. Why would it still encounter a deadlock? The key to this problem is that DB2 scans every *empno* value to see if the row qualifies the queries. If only a portion of the values are scanned, the applications may not run into a deadlock. This can be achieved by creating proper indexes and maintaining current database statistics so DB2 can choose a more efficient data access plan.

A deadlock may still occur even with proper indexing and database maintenance. In that case, you can make use of a new feature lock deferral, which is discussed next.

11.5.4 Lock Deferral

You can enable lock deferral for CS or RS isolation level scans with the DB2_EVALUNCOMMITTED registry variable. DB2 evaluates the row before trying to lock it. To enable this feature issue the command:

```
db2set DB2_EVALUNCOMMITTED=YES
```

To disable it issue:

```
db2set DB2_EVALUNCOMMITTED=
```

Figure 11.26 shows that lock deferral no longer requires App A to put an S lock on *empno* = 105. App A can then read the *empno* = 106 row. Similar logic applies to App B.

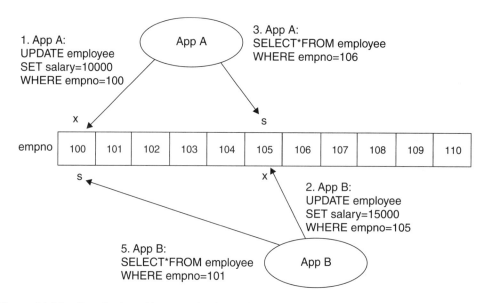

Figure 11.26   Deadlock problem resolved with EVALUNCOMMITTED enabled

11.5.5 Lock Escalation

When DB2 acquires a lock on an object, it allocates memory for each lock from the database shared memory area called the *locklist*. A tunable database configuration parameter by the same name lets you indicate the maximum storage allowed for locks in each database. To resize the locklist, update the LOCKLIST parameter with a new value in units of 4K.

Regardless of the type of lock, each lock uses about 36 bytes of memory on 32-bit DB2 instances and 56 bytes of memory on 64-bit DB2 instances. As the number of locks being held by all applications connected to the database increases, it is possible that the locklist will get full. When this happens, DB2 attempts to free memory by allocating a table lock and releasing the row locks. This internal operation is called **lock escalation**.

Lock escalation degrades performance because it can significantly reduce database concurrency. When you monitor your database, you should ideally see very few to no escalations. It is important to tune the LOCKLIST parameter appropriately so that lock escalations are avoided.

The MAXLOCKS database configuration parameter also has a direct effect on lock escalation. MAXLOCKS defines the percentage of the total locklist permitted to be allocated to a single application. Proper configuration of MAXLOCKS prevents any one application from using up all the memory available in the locklist. When the amount of locks an application holds reaches the MAXLOCKS percentage, DB2 escalates the row locks of the particular application to a table lock. The table with the most row locks is escalated first. Lock escalation continues until the percentage of the locklist held is below the value of MAXLOCKS.

The database manager determines which locks to escalate by looking through the locklist for the application and finding the table with the most row locks. If after replacing these with a single table lock, the MAXLOCKS value is no longer exceeded, lock escalation will stop. If not, escalation continues until the percentage of the locklist held is below the value of MAXLOCKS. The MAXLOCKS parameter multiplied by the MAXAPPLS parameter cannot be less than 100.

As the number of row locks being held increases, the chance of locking escalations occurring also increases. Take this into consideration when choosing isolation levels. For example, the RR isolation level locks all the rows in the result set as well as the rows referenced to build the result set. With this isolation level you should choose an appropriate value for your MAXLOCKS and LOCKLIST parameters.

11.6 DIAGNOSING LOCK PROBLEMS

We have discussed how isolation levels affect the DB2 locking strategy. The various lock modes allow DB2 to provide diversified concurrent scenarios. For many applications the locking mechanism works transparently, but for others issues such as lock waits, deadlocks, and lock escalations can occur.

DB2 has a comprehensive set of tools that you can use to obtain information about locking. In the following sections we will look at some of the tools that are available and how they can be used to troubleshoot locking problems.

11.6.1 Using the list applications Command

The `list applications` command issued with the `show detail` clause shows the status of each application. Use this command as the first diagnostic step if you suspect a lock wait condition exists. You can also use the Control Center to get similar information. From the object tree right-click on the desired instance name and choose **Applications**. Note, however, that not all the columns from the `list applications show detail` command are reported by the Control Center.

Figure 11.27 shows the output of the `list applications show detail` command. The output is over 240 bytes wide; to understand locking behavior, focus on the output columns listed in Table 11.5.

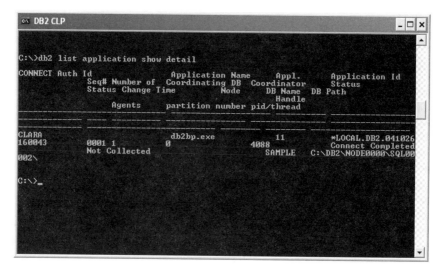

Figure 11.27   Output of the list applications show detail command

Table 11.5   Output Columns of the list applications show detail Command

Output Column	Description
Status	A value of *Lock-wait* means the application is blocked by a lock held by a different application. Don't be confused by a value of *UOW Waiting*, which means that the application (unit of work) is in progress and not blocked by a lock. It is simply not doing any work at the moment.
Status Change Time	This is of particular interest for an application with *Lock-wait* status. The value shows when the lock wait began. Note that the UOW monitor switch must be on for the status change time to be reported.
Appl. Handle	The handle is a unique ID for an active application. Being able to identify the application handle is important when it is holding locks that are causing contention problems. You can use the application handle in the **FORCE APPLICATION** command to terminate its current transaction.

11.6.2 Using the force application Command

You can use the `force application` command in conjunction with the `list applications` command to resolve concurrency problems. A typical scenario occurs when user *Bob* issues a query that does not COMMIT. He then goes for a one-hour coffee break, leaving other users unable to continue their work because Bob's query is holding several locks on the same objects. In this scenario, a DBA can issue a `list applications` command to identify that the connection is from Bob by looking at the *Appl. Handle* column, as shown in Figure 11.28.

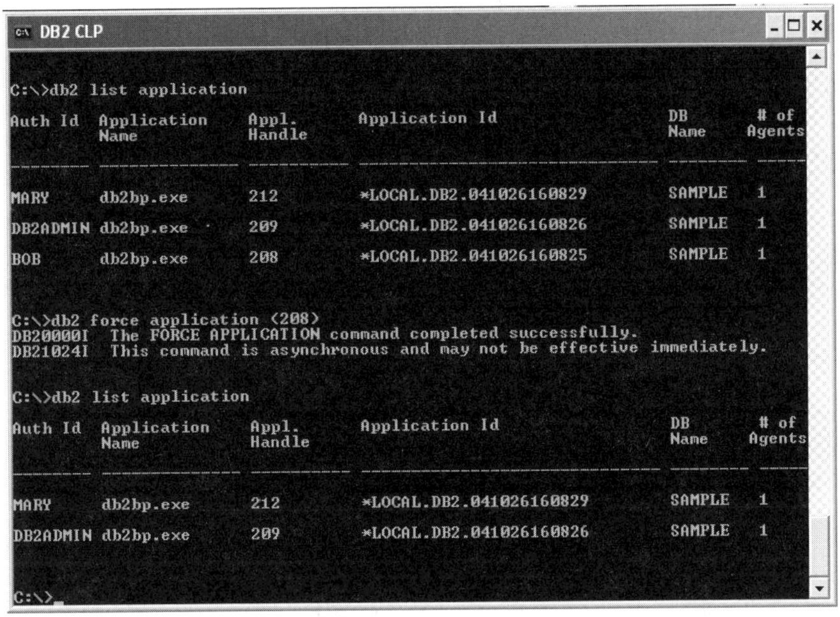

Figure 11.28 The force application command

Figure 11.28 shows there are three connections to the *SAMPLE* database. Next, the DBA identifies user BOB whose connection has the application handle of 208, and issues the command:

```
force application (208)
```

The command executes asynchronously, meaning that it will not wait for the connection to be terminated to return. After a few seconds, when he issues the `list applications` command again, he sees that Bob's connection has been removed, allowing the other connections to continue their work.

To force several connections in one command use the syntax:

```
force application (Appl. Handle, Appl. Handle, ... )
```

There may be situations when you need to force all the connections against all the databases in the instance. In such situations use the **all** option of the `force application` command:

```
force application all
```

> **N O T E** The `force application` command does not prevent other users from connecting to a database..
>
> The `force application` command always preserves database integrity, so only users who are idling or executing interruptible database operations can be terminated.

11.6.3 Using the Snapshot Monitor

You can use the **Snapshot Monitor** to capture information about a database and any connected applications at a specific time. Snapshot monitoring provides the majority of the useful information for dealing with lock issues. Before you can obtain snapshot information in full extent, you must turn on the monitor switches. See section 16.7, Snapshot Monitoring, for a detailed discussion on setting monitor switches and capturing information. In this section we focus on the relevant commands required to continue with our lock diagnostic discussion.

Turn on all the monitor switches with this command:

```
update monitor switches using bufferpool on lock on sort on
    statement on table on timestamp on uow on
```

To get a database snapshot, issue:

```
get snapshot for all on database_name
```

From the output of this command you obtain the following snapshot monitoring components in sequence. Snapshots that are most relevant to locking are have an asterisk (*) after them.

- Database snapshot*
- Buffer pool snapshot
- Dynamic SQL snapshot
- Application snapshot*
- Table space snapshot
- Database lock snapshot*
- Table snapshot

The database snapshot part of the result contains a good summary of the locking information for the specified database. Figure 11.29 shows only the pertinent lines to locking from a sample database snapshot output.

If you want to "zoom" into each application and understand the types of locks they are holding, examine the application snapshots. Figure 11.30 shows the most important subset of information for an application in a lock wait situation.

```
Database Snapshot
. . . .

Locks held currently = 8
Lock waits = 0
Time database waited on locks (ms) = 315704
Lock list memory in use (Bytes) = 1692
Deadlocks detected = 0
Lock escalations = 0
Exclusive lock escalations = 0
Agents currently waiting on locks = 1
Lock Timeouts = 0
```

Figure 11.29 Database snapshot with lock-related information

```
Application Snapshot

Application handle                        = 14                              (1)
Application status                        = Lock-wait
Status change time                        = 08-15-2004 14:30:36.907312
Snapshot timestamp                        = 08-15-2004 14:30:43.414574
Time application waited on locks (ms)      = 6507                            (2)
Total time UOW waited on locks (ms)       = 6507
UOW start timestamp                       = 08-15-2004 14:30:36.889356
Statement start timestamp                 = 08-15-2004 14:30:36.890986
Dynamic SQL statement text:
select * from org                                                           (3)


ID of agent holding lock                  = 13
Application ID holding lock               = *LOCAL.DB2.011905182946
Lock name                                 = 0x020002000000000000000000054
Lock attributes                           = 0x00000000
Release flags                             = 0x00000001
Lock object type                          = Table
Lock mode                                 = Exclusive Lock (X)             (4)
Lock mode requested                       = Intention Share Lock (IS)      (5)
Name of tablespace holding lock           = USERSPACE1
Schema of table holding lock              = WILKINS
Name of table holding lock                = ORG
Lock wait start timestamp                 = 08-15-2004 14:30:36.907318
```

Figure 11.30 Application snapshot with lock-related information

In Figure 11.30:

(1) You can see that application handle 14 is in a lock-wait state.

(2) It has been waiting for 6,507 milliseconds for locks.

(3, 5) It is currently executing a SELECT statement and requesting for an Intent Share (IS) lock on a table.

(4) However, application handle 13 holds an exclusive (X) lock on the same table.

To further investigate on the problem, you can use the **`list application`** command and see what application handle 13 is doing and check its application snapshot for more information.

Like the application snapshot, the database lock snapshot has a section for each connected application (see Figure 11.31).

```
                Database Lock Snapshot

Database name                        = SAMPLE
Database path                        = C:\DB2\NODE0000\SQL00002\
Input database alias                 = SAMPLE
Locks held                           = 3
Applications currently connected     = 1
Agents currently waiting on locks    = 0
Snapshot timestamp                   = 03-04-2004 13:39:06.465057

Application handle                   = 18
Application ID                       = *LOCAL.DB2.01D3C4183155
Sequence number                      = 0007
Application name                     = db2bp.exe
CONNECT Authorization ID             = CLARALIU
Application status                   = UOW Waiting
Status change time                   = Not Collected
Application code page                = 1252
Locks held                           = 3
Total wait time (ms)                 = 0

List Of Locks
  Lock Name                          = 0x02000500040000000000000052
  Lock Attributes                    = 0x00000020
  Release Flags                      = 0x40000000
  Lock Count                         = 1
  Hold Count                         = 0
  Lock Object Name                   = 4
  Object Type                        = Row
  Tablespace Name                    = USERSPACE1
  Table Schema                       = CLARALIU
  Table Name                         = EMPLOYEE
  Mode                               = X

  Lock Name                          = 0x94928D848F9F949E7B89505241
  Lock Attributes                    = 0x00000000
  Release Flags                      = 0x40000000
  Lock Count                         = 1
  Hold Count                         = 0
  Lock Object Name                   = 0
  Object Type                        = Internal P Lock
  Mode                               = S

  Lock Name                          = 0x02000500000000000000000054
  Lock Attributes                    = 0x00000000
  Release Flags                      = 0x40000000
```

Figure 11.31   Database lock snapshot *(continues)*

```
Lock Count                    = 1
Hold Count                    = 0
Lock Object Name              = 5
Object Type                   = Table
Tablespace Name               = USERSPACE1
Table Schema                  = CLARALIU
Table Name                    = EMPLOYEE
Mode                          = IX
```

Figure 11.31   Database lock snapshot *(continued)*

The snapshot in Figure 11.31 shows that application handle 18 is holding 3 locks. One of them is an exclusive (X) lock on a row in the employee table, another lock is an internal P lock, and the last one is an Intent Exclusive (IX) lock on the table employee. (Internal P locks are internal locks managed by DB2; there is nothing you can do about them.)

11.6.4 Using Snapshot Table Functions

You can also invoke SQL functions to produce locking information displayed in a table format. The function **SNAPSHOT_LOCK** produces one row for each lock held, and **SNAPSHOT_LOCKWAIT** produces one row for each lock wait condition. Each row contains the same data that is provided in the snapshot monitoring output discussed in the previous section.

To invoke these snapshot table functions, use:

```
SELECT * FROM TABLE ( SNAPSHOT_LOCK ('sample', 0) ) AS s
SELECT * FROM TABLE ( SNAPSHOT_LOCKWAIT ('sample', 0) ) AS s
```

The first argument of the snapshot function specifies the database you want to monitor and the second argument is the database partition number.

11.6.5 Using the Event Monitor

You can use a DB2 Event Monitor to obtain performance information on events as they occur on the server, such as statement or transaction completion and deadlock resolution. For DB2 locking issues, the Event Monitor is particularly useful for collecting deadlock information. Snapshots can provide counts on the number of deadlocks that are occurring. However, you need to obtain application details before the deadlock is detected and rolled back by the deadlock detector. The only way to guarantee that you get detailed information on each deadlock is to create and activate an Event Monitor for deadlocks with details. Chapter 4, Using the DB2 Tools, and Chapter 16, Database Performance Considerations, also discuss Event Monitors.

Figure 11.32 shows how to create a deadlock Event Monitor from the Control Center. To display the Create Event Monitor window, right-click on the Event Monitors folder under database you want to monitor, and then click on **Create**. In the Create Event Monitor window, specify the name of the Event Monitor. Under *Event Types*, select *Deadlocks* and also check the *With details* option. Then click *OK*.

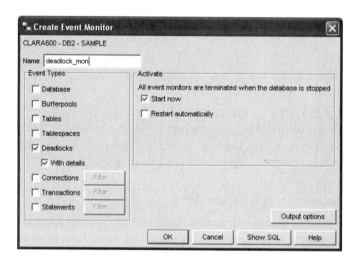

Figure 11.32   Creating a deadlock Event Monitor

After clicking *OK*, the new Event Monitor is created and started.

If a deadlock occurs, the DB2 deadlock detector identifies the two applications involved and rolls back one of the transactions. From the Control Center, right-click on the Event Monitor you just created and choose *Stop Event Monitoring* (see Figure 11.33). Next, from the Control Center right-click again on the Event Monitor you just created and choose *Analyze Event Monitor Records*. This displays the Event Analyzer window, (see Figure 11.34).

From the Event Analyzer window, select the *Deadlocked Connection* as shown in Figure 11.34.

At this point you will see the connections that were involved in the deadlock. You can then drill down to the Data Elements on any connection for more information as shown in Figure 11.35.

In the Data Elements window (see Figure 11.36), you will see the statements that are involved and the locks the application is holding. For example, from Figure 11.36 you can tell that five locks were held on the *employee* table when the statement **SELECT * FROM employee** was executing.

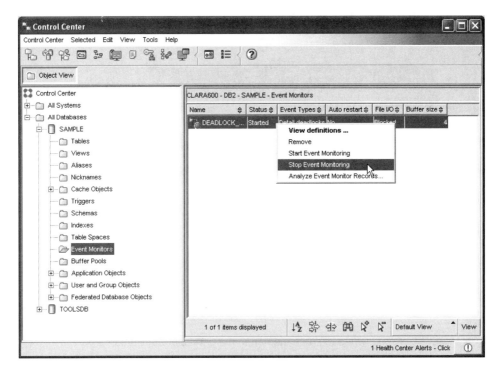

Figure 11.33　Stopping event monitoring and analyzing Event Monitor records

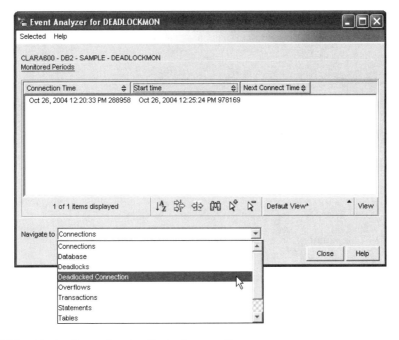

Figure 11.34　Navigating to the deadlocked connection

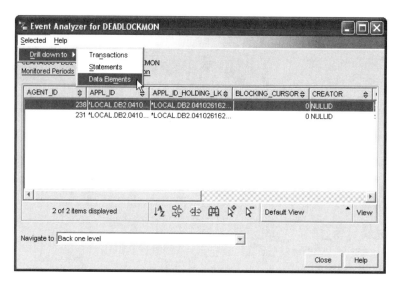

Figure 11.35   Drilling down to the data elements of a particular application

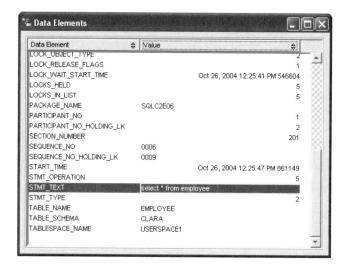

Figure 11.36   Data elements in an application

11.6.6 Using the Activity Monitor

Chapter 4, Using the DB2 Tools, introduced the activity monitor. We limit our discussion in this chapter to locking-related topics.

Set up the Activity Monitor by selecting the database you want to monitor as illustrated in Figure 11.37.

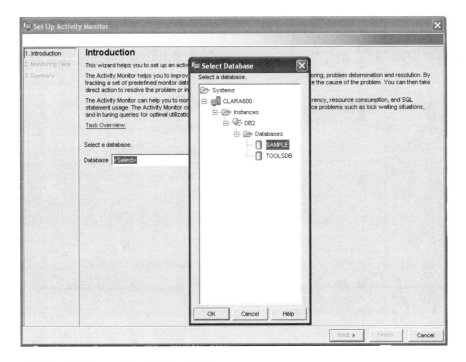

Figure 11.37 Setting up the Activity Monitor

Select or create a monitoring task. There are few system-defined monitoring tasks. One of them is to capture locking information, which is highlighted in Figure 11.38. You can also create a new monitoring task by clicking the *New* button.

You can see In Figure 11.39 that you can choose to monitor all or selected applications. Click *Finish* to complete the Activity Monitor setup.

As applications are connected to the database, the activity and status of each will be listed under *Report data* (see Figure 11.40).

To zoom into a particular application and examine its associated lock chains, right-click on the application handle number and choose **Show Lock Chains** (see Figure 11.41).

You will get a pictorial view of the locks being held by the application in the Lock Chain dialog,. Click on the *Legend* button to find out what each icon means (see Figure 11.42).

You can also see the lock details for each node by selecting *Show Lock Details* as shown in Figure 11.43.

You can use the similar information (shown in Figure 11.44) for detailed locking analysis.

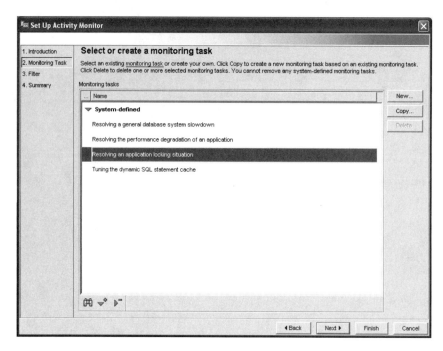

Figure 11.38 Selecting or creating a monitoring task

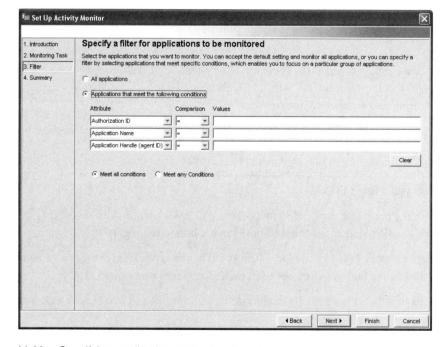

Figure 11.39 Specifying applications to be monitored

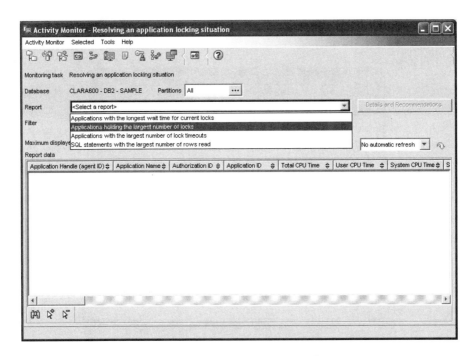

Figure 11.40 Selecting the type of information to be reported

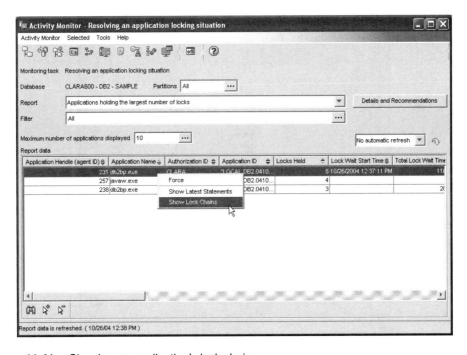

Figure 11.41 Showing an application's lock chains

477

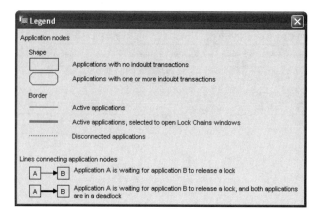

Figure 11.42   The application lock chain legend

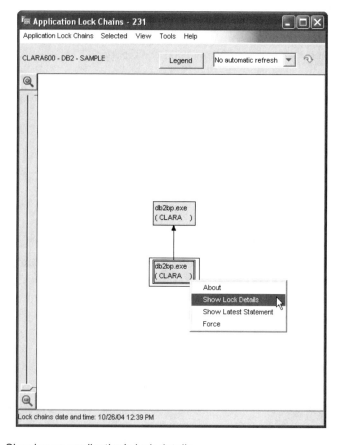

Figure 11.43   Showing an application's lock details

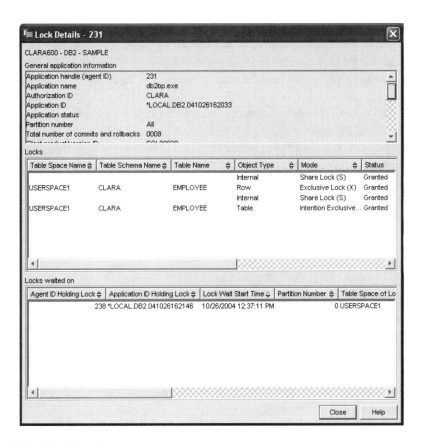

Figure 11.44 Lock details

11.6.7 Using the Health Center

The Health Center is a graphical tool used to analyze and improve the health of DB2. It provides four indicators in the Application Concurrency category: lock escalation rate, lock list utilization, percentage of applications waiting on locks, and deadlock rate. You can set warning and alarm levels for the indicators, enable the indicators, and define an action to be taken when the thresholds are reached, such as taking a snapshot in the Health Center. The Health Center is discussed in more detail in Chapter 4, Using the DB2 Tools.

11.7 TECHNIQUES TO AVOID LOCKING

It is good to know how to diagnose locking problems, but it is even better to know how to prevent them. Avoiding locking problems requires a good application design. The following is a list of items you should consider when developing your applications. For a detailed explanation of these and other techniques, refer to the *DB2 UDB Administration Guide*.

- Choose the appropriate isolation level: UR, CS, RS, or RR. As discussed earlier, UR allows for the most concurrency and the least number of locks required, while RR allows for the least concurrency and the most number of locks required. For example, if your application is used for estimation purposes and the exact value of columns is not needed, isolation UR should be used. Choosing the right isolation level guarantees that DB2 takes the right amount of locks that your application requires.
- Issue **COMMIT** statements as frequently as the application logic allows. Issuing a **COMMIT** incurs I/O costs because data is flushed to disk, but it releases locks allowing for more concurrency. Issue **COMMIT** statements even for read-only applications, since S locks are taken (unless using UR Isolation).
- Specify the **FOR FETCH ONLY** clause in the **SELECT** statement. This clause prevents exclusive locks from being taken. The **FOR READ ONLY** clause is equivalent.
- Perform **INSERT**, **UPDATE**, and **DELETE** statements at the end of a unit of work if possible. These operations require exclusive locks, and they are kept until the end of the UOW (commit/roll back). Putting these statements at the end of a UOW allows for maximum concurrency
- Avoid lock escalations impacting concurrency by tuning the LOCKLIST and MAXLOCKS database configuration parameters.
- When declaring cursors, be specific about their use. If the cursor is to be used only for reads, include the **FOR READ ONLY** clause in the declaration; if the cursor is to be used for updates, include the **FOR UPDATE** clause. In addition, you can specify the columns to be updated in the **FOR UPDATE** clause. For example:

```
DECLARE mycur1 CURSOR FOR
    SELECT * FROM employee WHERE salary > 10000
    FOR UPDATE OF firstnme, lastname
```

By explicitly declaring the use of the cursor, DB2 will choose the correct locks.

11.8 CASE STUDY

On a Monday morning, a developer calls you and requests assistance to resolve a deadlock problem. You find that two identical applications are being executed concurrently and receive this SQL0911 error:

```
SQL0911N The current transaction has been rolled back because of a deadlock or
timeout.  Reason code "2".
```

Reason code *2* indicates that a deadlock was encountered and the transaction was rolled back. Few tools are available to diagnose deadlock problems and you choose to use the deadlock Event Monitor.

Data from the deadlock Event Monitor shows that:

- Application A updated a row in the *employee* table.
- At the same time, application B updated another row in the *employee* table as well.

- Before both applications commited their updates, they queried the *employee* table again for some additional information.

This caused a deadlock like the one in Figure 11.25. To resolve the locking problem, you enable lock deferral with:

```
db2set DB2_EVALUNCOMMITTED=YES
```

That same day, an application is promoted from the Development environment to the Test environment. The application is a reservation system that is expected to handle requests from at most 200 users concurrently. On the very first run of the application, there are many locking issues, so you are asked to review the application design. Using monitoring information like snapshots (discussed in Chapter 16, Database Performance Considerations), you first note that there is an incredible number of lock escalations. You review the LOCKLIST and MAXLOCKS parameters and decide to increase LOCKLIST by 50 percent. A second run of the application performs a lot better, and the snapshots for this run show there are no longer lock escalation problems, but still there are locking issues.

Next, you review the SQL issued by the application using the snapshots. All the cursors defined in the application are ambiguous; that is, they have not been defined with a **FOR READ ONLY** or **FOR UPDATE** clause, so DB2 may not be choosing the correct locking. You also note that the transactions are very long; in other words, **COMMIT** statements are not issued frequently enough. You voice these concerns to the application developers, who decide to stop the testing while they implement your suggestions.

11.9 SUMMARY

In this chapter you learned about locking scenarios that you may encounter when a database is concurrently manipulated. Some scenarios might be desirable, but some are not. To control the behavior of how DB2 handles concurrent database access, use the different isolation levels.

There are four types of isolation levels: uncommitted read, cursor stability (the default), repeatable read, and read stability. The behavior of DB2 locking and lock attributes are controlled by the isolation level specified for the database. When an application is holding many locks that have exceeded its quota (through the setting of MAXLOCKS), lock escalation may occur. Lock escalation should be minimized as much as possible because it significantly reduces the concurrency of the database.

There are command line tools as well as graphical tools that can help you identify and solve locking problems, and you can implement techniques when developing your applications to avoid locking.

11.10 REVIEW QUESTIONS

1. A batch operation is encountering lock escalations. If it is the only application running when the lock escalation occurs, which database configuration parameter can be used to reduce the lock escalations?

2. Sam issues a **SELECT** statement that returns the following result set of three rows:

```
Name           Seat
---------------
Liu            1A
Chong          14F
Snow           3B
```

Without committing or rolling back the current transaction, he issues the same **SELECT** statement again. The following is returned:

```
Name           Seat
---------------
-              1A
Chong          14F
Qi             3B
```

Why is that?

3. What database objects can a DB2 user explicitly lock using a DB2 command or statement?

4. If an application holds a U lock on a row, what lock must another application request to access this row concurrently?

5. What does error SQL0911N with reason code *68* mean?

6. What does error SQL0911N with reason code *2* mean?

7. A user complained about poor performance. With the DB2 Snapshot Monitor you obtained the following information:

```
Locks held currently = 855
Lock waits = 1123
Time database waited on locks (ms) = 3157040000
Lock list memory in use (Bytes) = 16920
Deadlocks detected = 0
Lock escalations = 103
Exclusive lock escalations = 0
Agents currently waiting on locks = 38
Lock Timeouts = 2232
```

How would you troubleshoot the high number of lock escalations?

8. What tools that come with DB2 can assist you in diagnosing lock problems?

9. The following is captured by the Snapshot Monitor. What does it tell you?

```
Application Snapshot

Application handle                      = 14
Application status                      = Lock-wait
Status change time                      = 08-15-2004 14:30:36.907312
Snapshot timestamp                      = 08-15-2004 14:30:43.414574
Time application waited on locks (ms)   = 6507
Total time UOW waited on locks (ms)     = 6507
UOW start timestamp                     = 08-15-2004 14:30:36.889356
Statement start timestamp               = 08-15-2004 14:30:36.890986
```

```
Dynamic SQL statement text:
select * from org

ID of agent holding lock              = 13
Application ID holding lock           = *LOCAL.DB2.011905182946
Lock name                             = 0x0200020000000000000000000054
Lock attributes                       = 0x00000000
Release flags                         = 0x00000001
Lock object type                      = Table
Lock mode                             = Exclusive Lock (X)
Lock mode requested                   = Intention Share Lock (IS)
Name of tablespace holding lock       = USERSPACE1
Schema of table holding lock          = WILKINS
Name of table holding lock            = ORG
Lock wait start timestamp             = 08-15-2004 14:30:36.907318
```

10. Bob was connected to the *sample* database. He turned auto-commit OFF and issued the following statement:

    `UPDATE employee SET salary = salary * 1.5 WHERE empno='000010'`

    A database administrator, Mike, who had just joined the company was monitoring the system. He noticed that Bob had acquired a table lock on the *employee* table. Since Bob did not commit or roll back the transaction, no one can access the table (except for UR applications).

    Mike asked Bob to commit or roll back the transaction. That released the locks and business went on as usual. Then another user, Mary, issued the following statement:

    `SELECT name, salary FROM employee WHERE empno = '000020'`

    Mary also had auto-commit turned OFF and didn't commit or rollback the transaction. Once again, the *employee* table was locked.

    Mike is concerned about these two locking incidents, Could you assist him with what might be the cause?

11. Which of the following is not a DB2 isolation level?

    A. Uncommitted read

    B. Cursor stability

    C. Cursor with hold

    D. Repeatable read

12. On which of the following objects does DB2 not obtain locks?

    A. Row

    B. Page

    C. Table

    D. Table space

13. Which of the following is the default isolation level in DB2?

    A. Uncommitted read

    B. Cursor stability

    C. Read stability

    D. Repeatable read

14. Which of the following isolation levels typically causes the most locks to be obtained?
    A. Uncommitted read
    B. Cursor stability
    C. Read stability
    D. Repeatable read

15. Which of the following isolation levels does not obtain row level locks?
    A. Uncommitted read
    B. Cursor stability
    C. Read stability
    D. Repeatable read

16. Which of the following isolation levels lets you see data that has been updated by other applications before it is committed?
    A. Uncommitted read
    B. Cursor stability
    C. Read stability
    D. Repeatable read

17. Given a transaction that issues the same SQL statement twice. Which of the following isolation levels will allow new rows to be returned in the result set, but will not allow rows to be removed from the result set?
    A. Uncommitted read
    B. Cursor stability
    C. Read stability
    D. Repeatable read

18. If the current session has an isolation level of CS, which of the following will change the isolation level to UR for the current statement?
    A. Select * from foo use UR
    B. Select * from foo with UR
    C. Select * from foo isolation UR
    D. Select * from foo UR

19. Using the `alter table` statement, which two of the following can you change the locksize to?
    A. Column
    B. Page
    C. Row
    D. Index
    E. Table

20. To specify that your application should return immediately rather than wait for a lock, which of the following commands must be used?
    A. Set lock timeout = nowait
    B. Set lock timeout = not wait
    C. Set lock timeout = NULL
    D. Set lock nowait

## CHAPTER 12

Maintaining Data

Moving data from one database server to another is a very common task in a production environment and in almost every phase of the development cycle. For example, a developer may want to export data from a production database and load it into her tables for testing. In a production environment, a database administrator may want to export a few tables from production to a test database server to investigate a performance problem.

DB2 provides a number of utilities so that you can accomplish these tasks very easily. We will introduce each utility and discuss different options supported.

In this chapter you will learn about:

- The big picture of the DB2 data movement utilities
- Different file formats used to move data
- The EXPORT utility
- The IMPORT utility
- The LOAD utility
- The DB2MOVE utility
- The DB2RELOCATEDB utility
- How to generate the Data Definition Language for a database
- The different data maintenance utilities

12.1 DB2 DATA MOVEMENT UTILITIES: THE BIG PICTURE

Figure 12.1 presents the big picture of the DB2 data movement utilities. The utilities provide a way to move data from one database to another. The source and target databases can be the same instance, in different instances on the same server, on different servers on the same platform, or

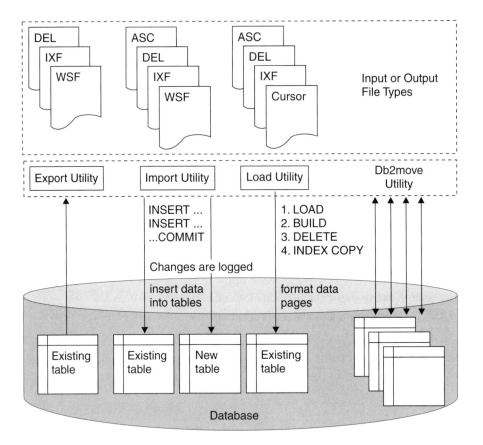

Figure 12.1   DB2 data movement utilities

on different platforms entirely. For example, you can move data stored in DB2 on z/OS to a data-base defined in DB2 on a Linux server. Data movement within DB2 is very efficient and flexible.

Figure 12.1 shows that all data movement utilities use a file either for input or output. The file can be of types DEL, IXF, ASC, WSF, and Cursor.

To extract data from a table in a database, you use the export utility. The import and load utilities insert data from the input files into a specified table. **db2move** is a batch version of the data movement utilities; it can export, import, or load multiple tables with just one command. Each utility is discussed in more detail in the sections that follow.

12.2 Data Movement File Formats

Before learning about moving data between DB2 databases and/or other data sources, it is important to first understand the file formats that the data movement utilities use. You can choose from five different file formats:

- Delimited ASCII (DEL)
- Non-delimited ASCII (ASC)
- PC version of Integrated Exchange Format (PC/IXF)
- Worksheet format (WSF)
- Cursor

12.2.1 Delimited ASCII (DEL) Format

As the name implies, this file format contains a stream of ASCII characters that are separated by row and column delimiters. Comma (,) is the default column delimiter and the carriage return is the default row delimiter. For character strings, DB2 uses double quotes (" ") as the string delimiter. For example, a DEL file will look similar to Figure 12.2. Note that all the string data is surrounded by a pair of double quotes and each column value is separated by a comma.

12.2.2 Non-Delimited ASCII (ASC) Format

The ASC file format is also known as **fixed length ASCII file format** because each column length in the file has the same length as defined for the corresponding column definition in the table. For example, variable-length character column definitions in a table are padded with blanks in an ASC file and represented using their maximum length. Figure 12.3 shows the same data as in Figure 12.2 but in ASC format.

12.2.3 PC Version of IXF (PC/IXF) Format

PC/IXF (or simply IXF) files cannot be edited with a normal text editor. It uses the IXF data interchange architecture, which is a generic relational database exchange format that lets you move data among DB2 databases. PC/IXF can only be used for moving data between DB2 databases because it is an IBM proprietary format. In addition to data, the file also contains the data types and structure of the table. Therefore it can be used to first create the table in the target database and then import data.

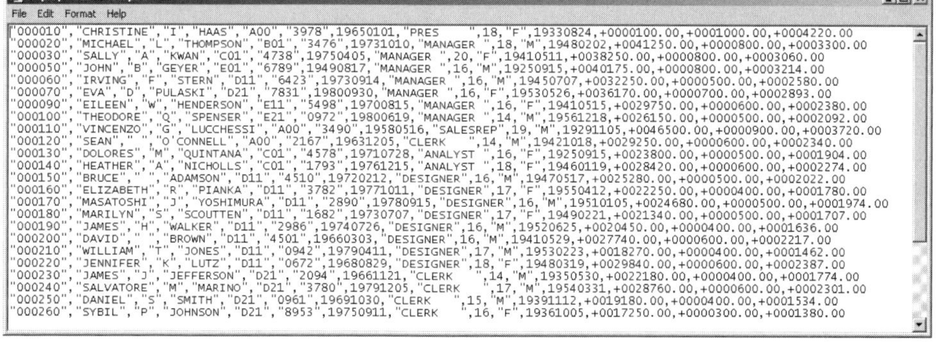
employee.del - Notepad
File Edit Format Help

```
"000010","CHRISTINE","I","HAAS","A00","3978",19650101,"PRES    ",18,"F",19330824,+0000100.00,+0001000.00,+0004220.00
"000020","MICHAEL","L","THOMPSON","B01","3476",19731010,"MANAGER ",18,"M",19480202,+0041250.00,+0000800.00,+0003300.00
"000030","SALLY","A","KWAN","C01","4738",19750405,"MANAGER ",20,"F",19410511,+0038250.00,+0000800.00,+0003060.00
"000050","JOHN","B","GEYER","E01","6789",19490817,"MANAGER ",16,"M",19250915,+0040175.00,+0000800.00,+0003214.00
"000060","IRVING","F","STERN","D11","6423",19730914,"MANAGER ",16,"M",19450707,+0032250.00,+0000500.00,+0002580.00
"000070","EVA","D","PULASKI","D21","7831",19800930,"MANAGER ",16,"F",19530526,+0036170.00,+0000700.00,+0002893.00
"000090","EILEEN","W","HENDERSON","E11","5498",19700815,"MANAGER ",16,"F",19410515,+0029750.00,+0000600.00,+0002380.00
"000100","THEODORE","Q","SPENSER","E21","0972",19800619,"MANAGER ",14,"M",19561218,+0026150.00,+0000500.00,+0002092.00
"000110","VINCENZO","G","LUCCHESSI","A00","3490",19580516,"SALESREP",19,"M",19291105,+0046500.00,+0000900.00,+0003720.00
"000120","SEAN"," ","O'CONNELL","A00","2167",19631205,"CLERK   ",14,"M",19421018,+0029250.00,+0000600.00,+0002340.00
"000130","DOLORES","M","QUINTANA","C01","4578",19710728,"ANALYST ",16,"F",19250915,+0023800.00,+0000500.00,+0001904.00
"000140","HEATHER","A","NICHOLLS","C01","1793",19761215,"ANALYST ",18,"F",19460119,+0028420.00,+0000600.00,+0002274.00
"000150","BRUCE"," ","ADAMSON","D11","4510",19720212,"DESIGNER",16,"M",19470517,+0025280.00,+0000500.00,+0002022.00
"000160","ELIZABETH","R","PIANKA","D11","3782",19771011,"DESIGNER",17,"F",19550412,+0022250.00,+0000400.00,+0001780.00
"000170","MASATOSHI","J","YOSHIMURA","D11","2890",19780915,"DESIGNER",16,"M",19510105,+0024680.00,+0000500.00,+0001974.00
"000180","MARILYN","S","SCOUTTEN","D11","1682",19730707,"DESIGNER",17,"F",19490221,+0021340.00,+0000500.00,+0001707.00
"000190","JAMES","H","WALKER","D11","2986",19740726,"DESIGNER",16,"M",19520625,+0020450.00,+0000400.00,+0001636.00
"000200","DAVID"," ","BROWN","D11","4501",19660303,"DESIGNER",16,"M",19410529,+0027740.00,+0000600.00,+0002217.00
"000210","WILLIAM","T","JONES","D11","0942",19790411,"DESIGNER",17,"M",19530223,+0018270.00,+0000400.00,+0001462.00
"000220","JENNIFER","K","LUTZ","D11","0672",19680829,"DESIGNER",18,"F",19480319,+0029840.00,+0000600.00,+0002387.00
"000230","JAMES","J","JEFFERSON","D21","2094",19661121,"CLERK   ",14,"M",19350530,+0022180.00,+0000400.00,+0001774.00
"000240","SALVATORE","M","MARINO","D21","3780",19791205,"CLERK   ",17,"M",19540331,+0028760.00,+0000600.00,+0002301.00
"000250","DANIEL","S","SMITH","D21","0961",19691030,"CLERK   ",15,"M",19391112,+0019180.00,+0000400.00,+0001534.00
"000260","SYBIL","P","JOHNSON","D21","8953",19750911,"CLERK   ",16,"F",19361005,+0017250.00,+0000300.00,+0001380.00
```

Figure 12.2 Sample DEL file

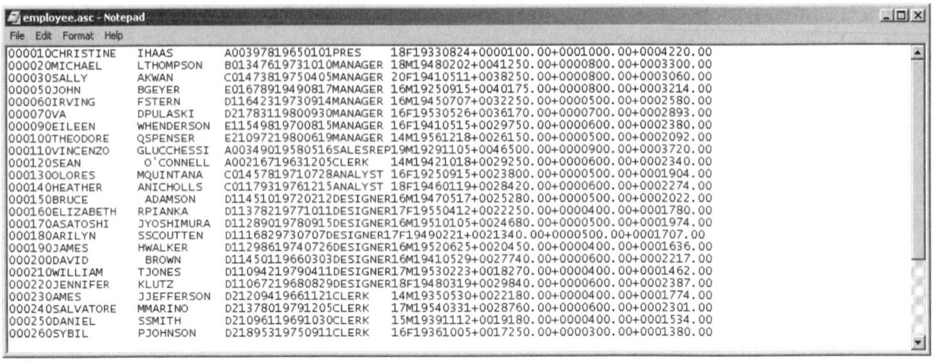

```
000010CHRISTINE    IHAAS       A00397819650101PRES     18F19330824+0000100.00+0001000.00+0004220.00
000020MICHAEL      LTHOMPSON   B01347619731010MANAGER 18M19480202+0041250.00+0000800.00+0003300.00
000030SALLY        AKWAN       C01473819750405MANAGER 20F19410511+0038250.00+0000800.00+0003060.00
000050JOHN         BGEYER      E01678919490817MANAGER 16M19250915+0040175.00+0000800.00+0003214.00
000060IRVING       FSTERN      D11642319730914MANAGER 16M19450707+0032250.00+0000500.00+0002580.00
000070VA           DPULASKI    D21783119800930MANAGER 16F19530526+0036170.00+0000700.00+0002893.00
000090EILEEN       WHENDERSON  E11549819700815MANAGER 16F19410515+0029750.00+0000600.00+0002380.00
000100THEODORE     QSPENSER    E21097219800619MANAGER 14M19561218+0026150.00+0000500.00+0002092.00
000110VINCENZO     GLUCCHESSI  A00349019580516SALESREP19M19291105+0046500.00+0000900.00+0003720.00
000120SEAN          O'CONNELL  A00216719631205CLERK   14M19421018+0029250.00+0000600.00+0002340.00
000130OLORES       MQUINTANA   C01457819710728ANALYST 16F19250915+0023800.00+0000500.00+0001904.00
000140HEATHER      ANICHOLLS   C01179319761215ANALYST 18F19460119+0028420.00+0000600.00+0002274.00
000150BRUCE         ADAMSON    D11451019720212DESIGNER16M19470517+0025280.00+0000500.00+0002022.00
000160ELIZABETH    RPIANKA     D11378219771011DESIGNER17F19550412+0022250.00+0000400.00+0001780.00
000170ASATOSHI     JYOSHIMURA  D11289019780915DESIGNER16M19510105+0024680.00+0000500.00+0001974.00
000180ARILYN       SSCOUTTEN   D1116829730707DESIGNER17F19490221+0021340.00+0000500.00+0001707.00
000190JAMES        HWALKER     D11298619740726DESIGNER16M19520625+0020450.00+0000400.00+0001636.00
000200DAVID         BROWN      D11450119660303DESIGNER16M19410529+0027740.00+0000600.00+0002217.00
000210WILLIAM      TJONES      D11094219790411DESIGNER17M19530223+0018270.00+0000400.00+0001462.00
000220JENNIFER     KLUTZ       D11067219680829DESIGNER18F19480319+0029840.00+0000600.00+0002387.00
000230AMES         JJEFFERSON  D21209419661121CLERK   14M19350530+0022180.00+0000400.00+0001774.00
000240SALVATORE    MMARINO     D21378019791205CLERK   17M19540331+0028760.00+0000600.00+0002301.00
000250DANIEL       SSMITH      D21096119691030CLERK   15M19391112+0019180.00+0000400.00+0001534.00
000260SYBIL        PJOHNSON    D21895319750911CLERK   16F19361005+0017250.00+0000300.00+0001380.00
```

Figure 12.3 Sample ASC file

12.2.4 WSF Format

WSF files are Lotus 1-2-3 and Symphony worksheets that the database manager supports. Any file names with these extensions are accepted: WKS, WK1, WRK, WR1, and WJ2. WSF files are mainly used for moving data between DB2 and these worksheets.

12.2.5 Cursor

The cursor format lets you load data into a table using a cursor. The cursor must be declared against an SQL query first before it can be referenced in the `load` command. You can only use the cursor file format with the load utility. Section 12.5.2.2, Loading from a CURSOR, shows how to use this format.

12.3 THE DB2 EXPORT UTILITY

The export utility extracts data from a table into a file. Figure 12.4 shows the syntax diagram of the `export` command.

As you can see, the command supports many different options. Let's start with a simple export command and discuss how to use the options to customize the command. The following example of the `export` command exports all the rows in the *employee* table to the file *empdata.ixf* in IXF format.

```
export to empdata.ixf of ixf select * from employee
```

All the keywords in this command are mandatory, that is, you have to provide the output file name, specify the file format, and the `SELECT` statement that will retrieve the rows to be exported. The exported file can be in a format of DEL, IXF, or WSF.

Using the optional `messages` clause you can specify a file name where warning and error messages of the export operation are logged. If no message file accompanies the `messages` clause, the messages are written to standard output. Though optional, we highly recommend you use this clause so that all the messages generated by the utility are saved.

```
>>-EXPORT TO--filename--OF--filetype--------------------------->

>--+-----------------------+--+--------------------------+--------->
   |           .-,--------. | |           .-,--------. |
   |           V          | | |           V          | |
   '-LOBS TO----lob-path-+-'  '-LOBFILE----filename-+-'

>--+---------------------------------+------------------------->
   |                 .-------------. |
   |                 V             | |
   '-MODIFIED BY----filetype-mod-+-'

>--+------------------------------+------------------------->
   |               .-,----------. |
   |               V            | |
   '-METHOD N--(----column-name-+--)-'

>--+------------------------+------------------------------>
   '-MESSAGES--message-file-'

>--+-select-statement------------------------------------------+-><
   '-HIERARCHY--+-STARTING--sub-table-name-+---+--------------+-'
               '-| traversal-order-list |-'  '-where-clause-'

traversal-order-list:

      .-,--------------.
      V                |
|--(----sub-table-name-+--)------------ ----------------------|
```

Figure 12.4   Syntax diagram of the export command

The **export** command also supports **SELECT** statements with join. Thus, if you want to export data from two tables, they can be joined as shown in the following example:

```
export to deptmgr.del of del messages deptmgr.out
   select deptno, deptname, firstnme, lastname, salary
     from employee, department
   where empno = mgrno
```

The above example joins the *employee* and *department* tables to obtain information for each department manager. If the command is successfully executed, the number of rows exported is returned :

```
Number of rows exported: 8
```

When the command finishes successfully with no warning or error message, the message file *deptmgr.out* will only include entries that indicate the beginning and end of the utility execution:

```
SQL3104N  The Export utility is beginning to export data to file "c:\deptmgr.del".

SQL3105N  The Export utility has finished exporting "8" rows.
```

12.3.1 File Type Modifiers Supported in the Export Utility

The export utility exports data to a file using default file formats. For example, as mentioned earlier, if you are exporting a table to a file in DEL format, the default column delimiter is a comma,
and the default string delimiter is the double quote. What happens if the table data to be exported
contains these delimiters as part of the data? The file exported may contain data that can be con-
fused as a delimiter, making it impossible for an import or load operation to work correctly. To
customize the export file format to use different delimiters, use the **modified by** clause. The
following sections introduce some of the most common file type modifiers. For a complete list
of the modifier options, see the *DB2 UDB Data Movement Utilities Guide and Reference*.

12.3.1.1 Changing the Column Delimiter

To use a different column delimiter other than the comma, specify the **coldel** file type modifier in the **modified by** clause. The following example specifies to use a semicolon as the column modifier. Note that there is no space between the keyword **coldel** and the semicolon.

```
export to deptmgr.del of del
  modified by coldel;
  messages deptmgr.out
  select deptno, deptname, firstnme, lastname, salary
    from employee, department
  where empno = mgrno
```

12.3.1.2 Changing the Character Delimiter

You can enclose character strings with a different delimiter by using the keyword **chardel**.
Continuing with the previous example, the character delimiter used here is a pair of single quote.

```
export to deptmgr.del of del
  modified by coldel; chardel''
  messages deptmgr.out
  select deptno, deptname, firstnme, lastname, salary
    from employee, department
  where empno = mgrno
```

12.3.1.3 Changing the Date Format

You can also export data in a specific date format you prefer by using the **timestampformat**
modifier.

```
export to deptmgr.del of del
  modified by coldel; chardel'' timestampformat="yyyy.mm.dd hh:mm"
  messages deptmgr.out
  select deptno, deptname, firstnme, lastname, salary
    from employee, department
  where empno = mgrno
```

12.3.1.4 Changing the Code Page

In many cases, the code page of the target database server is not the same as the source server. To
ensure data is handled correctly in the target server, you should pay attention to the code page of

the exported data. By default, data exported is in the same code page as the application for which the **export** command is invoked. With the export utility, you can use the **codepage** modifier to convert character data from the application.

```
export to deptmgr.del of del
  modified by coldel; chardel'' timestampformat="yyyy.mm.dd hh:mm"
            codepage=1208
  messages deptmgr.out
  select deptno, deptname, firstnme, lastname, salary
    from employee, department
   where empno = mgrno
```

Note that this modifier cannot be used with the **lobinsfile** modifier, which is discussed in the next section.

12.3.2 Exporting Large Objects

DB2 supports the following types of large objects: character large objects (CLOBs), binary large objects (BLOBs), and double-byte character large objects (DBCLOBs). LOB values can be as large as 2GB for CLOBs and BLOBs and 1GB for DBCLOBs. Due to these sizes, the export utility by default extracts only the first 32KB of data of the LOB values in the export file. To extract the entire LOB, you must use the **lobsinfile** modifier. All the LOB values for a particular LOB column are stored in a single file that is separate from the regular export data file. The export data file, however, contains a LOB location specifier (LLS) to link the regular data for the row with the LOB data of this row. Since all LOB values are stored in one file, the LLS string indicates the starting position (offset) where the associated LOB data can be found and the length of the LOB. The format of the LLS is

filename.ext.nnn.mmm

where:

- *filename.ext* is the name of the file that contains the LOB.
- *nnn* is the offset (measured in bytes) of the LOB within the file.
- *mmm* is the length (measured in bytes) of the LOB.

For example, the following **export** command generates three files. One file is the message file, *mgrresume.out*. Another file, *mgrresume.del*, is the data file, which contains all data columns for the rows except the LOB data. The third file, *resume.001*, is the file containing the LOB values for all rows.

```
export to mgrresume.del of del
  messages mgrresume.out
  lobs to c:\lobs
  lobfile resume modified by lobsinfine
    select deptno, deptname, firstnme, lastname, resume
      from employee a, emp_resume b
     where a.empno = b.empno
```

Note that the output file *mgrresume.del* contains the LLS instead of the LOB data. Figure 12.5 illustrates the contents of *mgrresume.del*. Notice that in the third column the LLS value is *resume.001.0.1313*, which means that the LOB of this record is stored in file *resume.001*. It begins at an offset of 0 bytes, then follows by the size of the LOB (1313 bytes). The following LLS entry shows the LOB data for the next row is also stored in file *resume.001.0.1313* starting at offset 1313 and with a length of 1817 bytes. The next entry would start at offset 3130 (1313 + 1817). If the indicated size in the LLS is 0, the LOB is considered to have a length of 0. If the length is -1, the LOB is considered to be NULL and the offset and file name are ignored.

```
mgrresume.del - Notepad
File  Edit  Format  Help
"DOLORES","QUINTANA","resume.001.0.1313/"
"DOLORES","QUINTANA","resume.001.1313.1817/"
"HEATHER","NICHOLLS","resume.001.3130.1316/"
"HEATHER","NICHOLLS","resume.001.4446.1878/"
"BRUCE","ADAMSON","resume.001.6324.1363/"
"BRUCE","ADAMSON","resume.001.7687.1923/"
"JAMES","WALKER","resume.001.9610.1292/"
"JAMES","WALKER","resume.001.10902.1852/"
```

Figure 12.5   A sample export data file with LOB location specifier (LLS)

12.3.3 Specifying Column Names

The **method n** (column names) option is useful when a column is derived from one or more columns. For example, if you use the following **SELECT** statement in the **export** command:

```
SELECT empno, firstnme, lastname, salary * 1.3
  FROM employee
 WHERE workdept='A00'
```

the following shows what the output of the **SELECT** statement would be. Notice that the last column in the select list is a derived column that does not have a column name.

```
EMPNO   FIRSTNME      LASTNAME          4
------  ------------  ----------------  -------------
000010  CHRISTINE     HAAS                   130.000
000110  VINCENZO      LUCCHESSI         60450.000
000120  SEAN          O'CONNELL         38025.000
```

The import utility (which is discussed in more detail in section 12.4, The DB2 import Utility) can be executed with a **create** option that lets you create the target table if it does not already exist before data is imported. The input file must also contain the definition of the table. If you were to import the above result with the **create** option, the newly created table would have the fourth column named *4*. Rather than using a number, you can provide a more descriptive name using the **AS** clause in the **SELECT** statement:

```
export to newsalary.ixf of ixf
  messages newsalary.out
  select empno, firstnme, lastname, salary * 1.3 as new_salary
    from employee
   where workdept='A00'
```

Alternatively, use the **method n** option to explicitly specify all the column names. This option is only supported when the export file format is IXF or WSF.

```
export to newsalary.ixf of ixf
  messages newsalary.out
  method n ('EMPLOYEENO', 'FIRSTNAME', 'LASTNAME', 'NEWSALARY')
  select empno, firstnme, lastname, salary * 1.3
    from employee
   where workdept='A00'
```

With the **method n** clause and the specified columns, the resulting file will contain the new column names:

```
EMPLOYEENO FIRSTNAME    LASTNAME         NEWSALARY
---------- ------------ ---------------- -------------
000010     CHRISTINE    HAAS                   130.000
000110     VINCENZO     LUCCHESSI            60450.000
000120     SEAN         O'CONNELL           38025.000
```

12.3.4 Authorities Required to Perform an Export

There is no special authorization requirement to perform an export. Any authenticated user is able to execute the **export** command. However, the user must be able to access the data of the table being exported. Therefore, the user must hold SYSADM, DBADM, CONTROL, or SELECT privileges on each table or view referenced in the **SELECT** statement of the command.

12.3.5 Exporting a Table Using the Control Center

You can also perform an export from the Control Center. In the Control Center right-click on the table you want to export and select the **Export** option as shown in Figure 12.6.

This displays the Export Table dialog (see Figure 12.7). You can specify all the options discussed earlier in this chapter in this dialog, such as the output file, message file, file format, and the **SELECT** statement.

To specify the column names and LOB options, switch to the *Columns* tab (illustrated in Figure 12.8).

The last tab, *Schedule*, lets you run the export now or schedule it to run at some other time (see Figure 12.9).

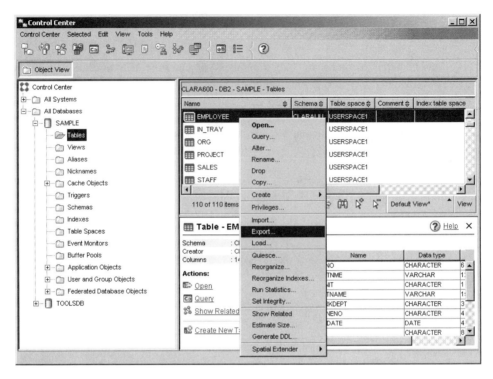

Figure 12.6   Exporting data from the Control Center

Figure 12.7   The Export Table dialog

Figure 12.8 Specifying column names and LOB options for the export operation

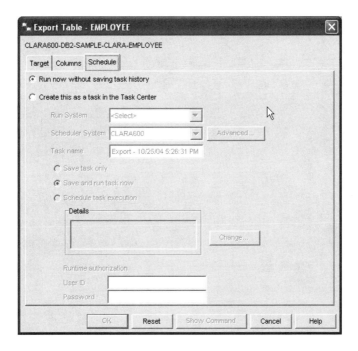

Figure 12.9 Specifying when to run the export

12.4 THE DB2 IMPORT UTILITY

The import utility inserts data from an input file into a table or a view. The utility performs inserts as if it was executing **INSERT** statements. Just like normal insert operations, DB2 validates the data and checks against the table definitions, constraints (such as referential integrity and check constraints), and index definitions. Triggers with satisfying conditions are also activated.

The utility supports options and import modes that let you customize its behavior. The syntax diagram of the **import** command is very long; Figure 12.10 shows only a portion of it. Please refer to the *DB2 Command Reference* for the complete syntax diagram.

```
>>-IMPORT FROM--filename--OF--filetype------------------------->

>--+-------------------------+----------------------------------->
   |            .-,--------. |
   |            V          | |
   '-LOBS FROM----lob-path-+-'


>--+--------------------------+---------------------------------->
   |             .--------------. |
   |             V              | |
   '-MODIFIED BY----filetype-mod-+-'

   .-ALLOW NO ACCESS----.
>--+--------------------+--+-------------------------+-------->
   '-ALLOW WRITE ACCESS-'  '-COMMITCOUNT--+-n---------+-'
                                          '-AUTOMATIC-'

>--+--------------------+--+--------------+--------------------->
   '-+-RESTARTCOUNT-+--n-'  '-ROWCOUNT--n-'
     '-SKIPCOUNT----'

>--+-----------------+--+-----------+---------------------------->
   '-WARNINGCOUNT--n-'  '-NOTIMEOUT-'

>--+-----------------------------+------------------------------->
   '-MESSAGES--message-file-'

>--+-+-INSERT---------+--INTO--+-table-name--+-----------------+-+------+-->
   | +-INSERT_UPDATE--+        |             |.-,-------------. | |    |
   | +-REPLACE--------+        |             |  V             | | |    |
   | '-REPLACE_CREATE-'        |             '-(-insert-column-+-)-' |    |
   '-CREATE--INTO--+-table-name+------------| tblspace-specs |----'

tblspace-specs:

|--+-----------------------------------------------------------------+--|
   '-IN--tablespace-name--+---------------------+--+--------------------+-'
                          '-INDEX IN—tspace-name-'  '-LONG IN--tspace-name-'
```

Figure 12.10   Simplified syntax diagram of the import command

Although the syntax diagram may seem complex, it is quite easy to understand and follow. Let's start with a simple **import** command and discuss the mandatory options. To a certain degree, the **import** command is structured much like the **export** command: you have to specify the input file name, format of the file, and the target table name. For example:

```
import from employee.ixf of ixf
  messages employee.out
  insert into employee
```

This command takes the file *employee.ixf,* which is in IXF format, as the input and inserts data into the *employee* table. The import utility supports input files in ASC, DEL, IXF, and WSF formats. We also recommend you to specify the optional clause **messages** to save the errors and warning messages and the import status. In section 12.4.4, Restarting a Failed Import, you will see that the message file can be used to identify where to restart an import operation.

12.4.1 Import Mode

The previous example uses **insert** to indicate that new data is to be appended to the existing *employee* table. Table 12.1 lists the modes supported by the import utility.

Table 12.1   Import Modes

Mode	Description
INSERT	Adds the imported data to the table without changing the existing table data. The target table must already exist.
INSERT_UPDATE	Adds the imported data to the target table or updates existing rows with matching primary keys. The target table must already exist with primary keys.
CREATE	Creates the table, index definitions, and row contents. The input file must use the IXF format because this is the only format that stores table and index definitions.
REPLACE	Deletes all existing data from the table and inserts the imported data. The table definition and index definitions are not changed.
REPLACE_CREATE	If the table exists, this option behaves like the **replace** option. If the table does not exist, this option behaves like the **create** option, which creates the table and index definitions and then inserts the row contents. This option requires the input file to be in IXF format.

Figures 12.11, 12.12, and 12.13 demonstrate some of the import modes and other options.

In Figure 12.11, the input data of specific columns are selected from the DEL input file and imported into the *empsalary* table. The **warningcount** option indicates that the utility will stop after 10 warnings are received.

```
import from employee.del of del
  messages empsalary.out
  warningcount 10
  replace into empsalary (salary, bonus, comm)
```

Figure 12.11   Example 1: import command

In Figure 12.12, the **import** command deletes all the rows in the table (if table *newemployee* exists) and inserts the row contents. If the *newemployee* table does not exist, the command creates the table with definitions stored in the IXF input file and inserts the row contents. In addition to specifying the columns you want to import as demonstrated in Figure 12.11, you can also limit the number of rows to be imported using the **rowcount** option. In Figure 12.12, the number of rows to import is limited to the first 1000 rows.

```
import from employee.ixf of ixf
  messages employee.out
  rowcount 1000
  replace_create into newemployee
```

Figure 12.12   Example 2: import command

If the **create** option is used as in Figure 12.13, you can also specify which table space the new table is going to be created in. The **in** clause tells DB2 to store the table data in a particular table space, and the **index in** clauses indicates where the index is to be stored.

```
import from employee.ixf of ixf
  messages newemployee.out
  create into newemployee in datats index in indexts
```

Figure 12.13   Example 3: import command

12.4.2 Allow Concurrent Write Access

While the import utility is adding new rows to the table, the table by default is locked exclusively to block any read/write activities from other applications. This is the behavior of the **allow no access** option. Alternatively, you can specify **allow write access** in the command to allow concurrent read/write access to the target table. A less restrictive lock is acquired at the beginning of the import operation.

Both the **allow write access** and **allow no access** options require some type of table lock. It is possible that the utility will be placed in lock-wait state and eventually will be terminated due to a lock timeout. You can specify the **notimeout** option so that the utility will not time out while waiting for locks. This option supersedes the LOCKTIMEOUT database configuration parameter.

12.4.3 Regular Commits During an Import

The import utility inserts data into a table through normal insert operations. Therefore, changes made during the import are logged, and they are committed to the database upon successful completion of the import operation. By default, an import, behaves like a non-atomic compound statement for which more than one insert is grouped into a transaction. If any insert fails, the rest of the inserts will still be committed to the database. Atomic and non-atomic compound statements are discussed in detail in Chapter 9, Leveraging the Power of SQL.

If you were to import a few million rows into a table, you would need to make sure there was enough log space to hold the insertions because they are treated as one transaction. However, sometimes it is not feasible to allocate large log space just for the import. You can specify the **commitcount** *n* option to force a commit after every *n* records are imported. With **commit-count automatic**, the utility will commit automatically at an appropriate time to avoid running out of active log space and avoid lock escalation.

Figure 12.14 shows the messages captured during the following **import** command. Note that a COMMIT is issued every 1,000 rows. The message file also serves as a very good progress indicator, because you can access this file while the utility is running.

```
import from employee.ixf of ixf
  commitcount 1000
  messages newemployee.out
  create into newemployee in datats index in indexts
```

Figure 12.14 Importing with intermediate commits

12.4.4 Restarting a Failed Import

If you have import failures due to invalid input, for example, you can use the message file generated from an **import** command that uses the **commitcount** and **messages** options to identify which record failed. Then you could issue the same **import** command with **restartcount** *n* or **skipcount** *n* to start the import from record *n*+1. This is a very handy method to restart a failed import. Here is an example:

```
import from employee.ixf of ixf
  commitcount 1000
  skipcount 550
  messages newemployee.out
  create into newemployee in datats index in indexts
```

12.4.5 File Type Modifiers Supported in the Import Utility

The import utility also has the **modified by** clause to allow customization. Some modifiers supported in the export utility also apply to the import utility. Refer to the *DB2 Data Movement Utilities Guide and Reference* for a complete listing specific to the import utility. The following sections describe some of the more useful modifiers.

12.4.5.1 Handling Target Tables with Generated and Identity Columns

Tables with generated columns or identity columns are defined in a way that column values will be automatically generated when records are inserted into the tables. Since import operations perform inserts in the background, new values will be generated at the target server. Therefore, you need to decide whether values stored in the source input file should be used or if new values should be generated. The import utility supports a few file type modifiers to take care of that.

The file modifier **generatedignore** forces the import utility to ignore data for all generated columns presented in the data file. The utility generates the values of those columns. The file modifier **identityignore** behaves the same way as **generatedignore**.

You can use the **generatemissing** modifier to inform the import utility that the input data file contains no data for the generated columns (not even NULLs), and the import utility will therefore generate a value for each row. This behavior also applies to **identitymissing** modifier.

12.4.6 Importing Large Objects

If you are exporting LOB data in separate files (as described in Section 12.3.2, Exporting Large Objects), you need to tell the import utility the location and name of the files. Consider the following **import** command.

```
import from mgrresume.ixf of ixf
   lobs from c:\lobs1, c:\lobs2, c:\lobs3
   modified by lobsinfile
   commitcount 1000
   messages mgrresume.out
   create into newemployee in datats index in indexts long in lobts
```

This command takes *mgrresume.del* as the input file. With the **lobsinfile** modifier, the utility searches the paths specified in the **lobs from** clause for the LOB location specifier (LLS). Recall that each LOB data has a LLS that represents the location of a LOB in a file stored in the LOB file path.

Notice that an additional clause, **long in lobts**, is added to the **create into** option. It indicates that all LOB data will be created and stored in *lobts* table space. If this clause is omitted, LOB data will be stored in the same table space with the other data. Typically, we recommend that you use DMS table space and keep regular data, LOB data, and indexes in different table spaces.

12.4.7 Selecting Columns to Import

There are three ways to select particular columns you want to import. **method 1** uses the starting and ending position (in bytes) for all columns to be imported. This method only supports ASC files. For example:

```
import from employee.asc of asc
    messages employee.out
    method l (1 5, 6 14, 24 30)
    insert into employee
```

This command imports three selected columns of data into the *employee* table: bytes 1 to 5 from the first column, bytes 6 to 14 from the second column, and bytes 24 to 30 from the third column.

The other two methods specify the names of the columns (**method n**) or the field numbers of the input data (**method p**). **method n** is only valid for IXF files and **method p** can be used with IXF or DEL files. The following shows an example of an **import** command with **method n** and **method p** clauses.

```
import from employee.ixf of ixf
    messages employee.out
    method n (empno, firstnme, lastname)
    insert into employee (empno, firstnme, lastname)

import from employee.ixf of ixf
    messages employee.out
    method p (1, 2, 4)
    insert into employee (empno, firstnme, lastname)
```

12.4.8 Authorities Required to Perform an Import

Depending on the options you have chosen for the import, specific authorization and privileges are required. Since SYSADM and DBADM hold the highest authority for an instance and a database respectively, both of them can issue **import** commands with all of the options discussed above. For users who do not have SYSADM and DBADM privileges, refer to Table 12.2 for the privileges required to perform each import option. If you are not already familiar with DB2 security, refer to Chapter 10, Implementing Security.

Table 12.2 Privileges Required for Different Import Scenarios

Import Scenario	Privileges Required
Import to an existing table with the **insert** option	CONTROL privilege on each participating table or view or INSERT and SELECT privileges on each participating table or view.

(continues)

Table 12.2 Privileges Required for Different Import Scenarios *(Continued)*

Import Scenario	Privileges Required
Import to an existing table using the `insert_update` option	CONTROL privilege on the table or view or INSERT, SELECT, UPDATE, and DELETE privileges on each participating table or view.
Import to an existing table using the `replace` or `replace_create` option	CONTROL privilege on the table or view or INSERT, SELECT, and DELETE privileges on the table or view.
Import to a new table using the `create` or `replace_create` option	CREATETAB authority on the database and USE privilege on the table space and IMPLICIT_SCHEMA authority on the database, if the implicit or explicit schema name of the table does not exist or CREATIN privilege on the schema, if the schema name of the table refers to an existing schema.
Import to a hierarchy that does not already exist using the `CREATE` option *or* the `REPLACE_CREATE` option. This import scenario requires one of the authorities listed on the right.	CREATETAB authority on the database and USE privilege on the table space and: IMPLICIT_SCHEMA authority on the database, if the schema name of the table does not exist or CREATEIN privilege on the schema, if the schema of the table exists or CONTROL privilege on every subtable in the hierarchy if the `replace_create` option on the entire hierarchy is used

12.4.9 Importing a Table Using the Control Center

You can invoke the import utility from the Control Center by right-clicking on the target table and selecting **Import**. This displays the Import table dialog (shown in Figure 12.15).

12.5 THE DB2 LOAD UTILITY

The load utility is another tool you can use to insert data into a table. Note that you cannot run the load tool against a view; the target must be a table that already exists. The major difference between a load and an import is that a load is much faster. Unlike the import tool, data is not written to the database using normal insert operations. Instead, the load utility reads the input

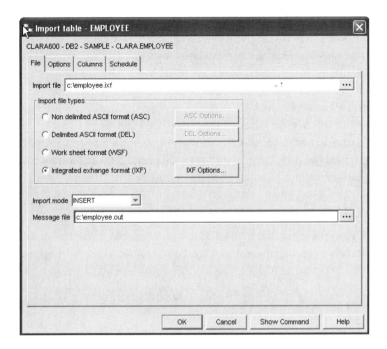

Figure 12.15   Invoking the import utility from the Control Center

data, formats data pages, and writes directly to the database. Database changes are not logged and constraint validations are not performed during a load operation.

12.5.1 The Load Process

Basically, a complete load process consists of four phases.

1. During the **load phase**, the load utility scans the input file for any invalid data rows that do not comply with the table definition; for example, if a table column is defined as INTEGER but the input data is stored as "abcd". Invalid data will not be loaded into the table. The rejected rows and warnings will be written to a dump file specified by the `dumpfile` modifier. Valid data is then written into the table. At the same time, table statistics (if the `statistics` option was specified) and index keys are also collected. If the `savecount` option is specified in the `load` command, points of consistency are recorded in the message file. Consistency points are established by the load utility. They are very useful when it comes to restarting the load operation. You can restart the load from the last successful consistency point.

2. During the **build phase**, indexes are produced based on the index keys collected during the load phase. The index keys are sorted during the load phase, and index statistics are collected (if the `statistic` option was specified).

504   **Chapter 12 • Maintaining Data**

3. In the **load phase**, the utility only rejects rows that do not comply with the column definitions. Rows that violated any unique constraint will be deleted in the delete phase. Note that only unique constraint violated rows are deleted. Other constraints are not checked during this phase or during any load phase. You have to manually check it after the load operation is complete. Refer to Section 12.5.7, Validating Data Against Constraints, for more information.

4. During the **index copy phase**, index data is copied from a system temporary table space to the original table space. This will only occur if a system temporary table space was specified for index creation during a load operation with the **read access** option specified (see section 12.5.2.5, Locking Considerations During a Load).

12.5.2 The LOAD Command

The load utility is so powerful that its command can be executed with many different options. Figure 12.16 presents a simplified version of the **load** command syntax diagram.

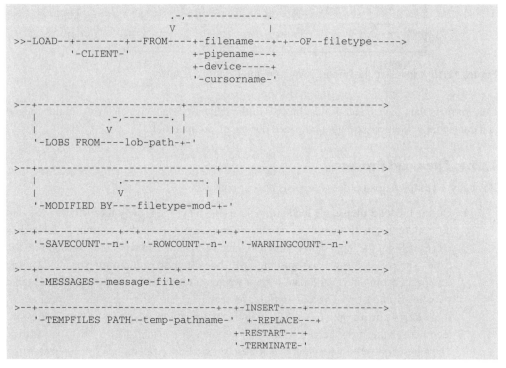

Figure 12.16   Simplified syntax diagram of the load command *(continues)*

```
>--INTO--table-name--+--------------------------+---------------->
                     |      .-,-------------.    |
                     |      V               |    |
                     '-(----insert-column-+--)-'

>--+--------------------------+--------------------------------->
   '-FOR EXCEPTION--table-name-'

>--+--------------------------------+------------------------->
   '-STATISTICS--+-USE PROFILE-+-'
                 '-NO----------'

>--+---------------------------------------------------------------+-->
   |    .-NO-------------------------------------------------.     |
   +-COPY--+-YES--+-USE TSM--+--------------------------+--------+-+-+
   '-NONRECOVERABLE-------------------------------------------------'

>--+------------------+--+------------------------------+----------->
   '-WITHOUT PROMPTING-'  '-DATA BUFFER--buffer-size-'

>--+--------------------------+--+------------------------+--------->
   '-SORT BUFFER--buffer-size-'  '-CPU_PARALLELISM--n-'

>--+---------------------+----------------------------------->
   '-DISK_PARALLELISM--n-'

>--+------------------------------+------------------------->
   '-INDEXING MODE--+-AUTOSELECT--+-'
                    +-REBUILD-----+
                    +-INCREMENTAL-+
                    '-DEFERRED----'

   .-ALLOW NO ACCESS----------------------------.
>--+--------------------------------------------+-------------->
   '-ALLOW READ ACCESS--+--------------------+-'
                        '-USE--tablespace-name-'

>--+--------------------------------------+------------------->
   '-CHECK PENDING CASCADE--+-IMMEDIATE-+-'
                            '-DEFERRED--'

>--+------------------+------------------------------------->
   '-LOCK WITH FORCE-'
```

Figure 12.16   Simplified syntax diagram of the load command *(continued)*

As you can see, there are many options available to customize your load operation. The following examples illustrate how to use some of them.

12.5.2.1 The MESSAGES, SAVECOUNT, and WARNINGCOUNT Options

In Figure 12.17, data in a DEL input file is loaded into a list of columns in table *stock*. The **messages** option is used to record warnings and errors encountered during the load operation. This particular load will stop when the threshold of warnings (in this case, 10) is encountered. You can check the output file for warnings and errors.

The **savecount** option establishes consistency points after every 1,000 rows are loaded. Because a message is issued at each consistency point, ensure that the **savecount** value is sufficiently high to minimize performance impact.

```
load from stock.del of del
   savecount 1000
   warningcount 10
   messages stock.out
   insert into stock(itemid, itemdesc, cost, inventory)
```

Figure 12.17   Example 1: load command

Consistency points are established during the load phase. You can use these to restart a failed or terminated load operation. By specifying the same **load** command but replacing **insert** with the **restart** option, the load operation will automatically continue from the last consistency point.

To terminate a load, issue the same **load** command but use the **terminate** option in place of **insert**. For example:

```
load from stock.del of del
   savecount 1000
   warningcount 10
   messages stock.out
   terminate
```

12.5.2.2 Loading from a CURSOR

The load utility supports four file formats: IXF, DEL, ASC, and CURSOR (described in Section 12.2, Data Movement File Formats). When using the CURSOR file type as demonstrated in Figure 12.18, the cursor must be already declared but does not need to be opened. The entire result of the query associated with the specified cursor will be processed by the load utility. You must also ensure that the column types of the SQL query are compatible with the corresponding column types in the target table.

```
declare cur1 cursor as select * from oldstock;
load from cur1 of cursor
   messages curstock.out
   insert into stock
```

Figure 12.18   Example 2: load command

12.5.2.3 MODIFIED BY dumpfile and Exception Table

As mentioned earlier, the load process goes through four phases. During the load phase, data that does not comply with the column definition will not be loaded. Rejected records can be saved in a dump file by using the **modified by** *dumpfile* modifier. If *dumpfile* is not specified, rejected records will not be saved. Since the load utility will not stop unless it reaches the warning threshold if one is specified, it is not easy to identify the rejected records. Hence, it is always a good practice to use the modifier and validate the message file after a load is completed. Figure 12.19 shows how to use **modified by** *dumpfile*.

```
load from stock.ixf of ixf
  modified by dumpfile=stockdump.dmp
  messages stock.out
  replace into stock
  for exception stockexp
```

Figure 12.19   Example 3: load command

Assume that the input file *stock.ixf* contains the data in Table 12.3.

Table 12.3   Data Stored in the Input File *stock.ixf*

itemid	itemdesc	inventory
10	~~~	1
20	~~~	–
30	~~~	3
30	~~~	4
40	~~~	X
50	~~~	6
50	~~~	7
80	~~~	8

The target table *stock* is defined with three columns using this **CREATE TABLE** statement:

```
CREATE TABLE stock
        ( itemid    INTEGER NOT NULL
        , itemdesc  VARCHAR(100)
        , inventory INTEGER NOT NULL
        , PRIMARY KEY (itemid) )
```

Notice that the second and fifth records in *stock.ixf* do not comply with the NOT NULL and numeric definitions. If the `load` command shown in Figure 12.19 is executed, a dump file (*stockdump.dmp*) will be created to save rows that are not loaded due to incompatible data type and the nullability attribute. Table 12.4 shows that the dump file *stockdump.dmp* contains the rows not loaded.

Table 12.4   Rows Not Loaded But Stored in the Dump File *stockdump.dmp*

itemid	itemdesc	inventory
20	~~~	–
40	~~~	X

Recall that in the third phase the load process deletes rows that violate any unique constraint defined in the target table. You can save the deleted rows in a table called an **exception table** using the `for exception` option. If an exception table is not specified, the rows will be discarded.

You need to create an exception table manually before you can use it. The table should have the same number of columns, column types, and nullability attributes as the target table to be loaded. You can create such a table with this command:

```
CREATE TABLE stockexp LIKE stock
```

To log when and why rows are rejected, you can add two other optional columns to the end of the exception table. The first column is defined as a TIMESTAMP data type to record when the record was deleted. The second column is defined as CLOB (32K) or larger and tracks the constraint names that the data violates. To add columns to the table, use the **ALTER TABLE** statement:

```
ALTER TABLE stockexp
  ADD COLUMN load_ts TIMESTAMP
  ADD COLUMN load_msg CLOB(32k)
```

Like the *dumpfile* modifier, it is a good practice to also use the exception table, especially if unique violations are possible. The exception table illustrated in Table 12.5 contains rows that violated the unique constraints.

Table 12.5   Exception Table *stockexp*

itemid	itemdesc	inventory
30	~~~	4
50	~~~	7

Figure 12.20 shows the big picture of the concepts of *dumpfile* and the exception table.

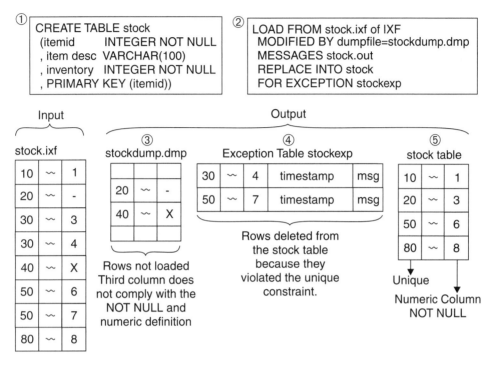

Figure 12.20   Loading data with dumpfile and an exception table

(1) Create the target table *stock*.

(2) Issue the **load** command with **modified by *dumpfile***, **messages**, and **for exception** options.

(3) Rows that do not comply with the table definition (NOT NULL and numeric column) are recorded in the *stockdump.dmp* file.

(4) Rows that violated the unique constraint are deleted from the *stock* table and inserted into the exception table.

(5) Four rows are successfully loaded into the *stock* table.

12.5.2.4 Loading from a Client

In all the examples you have seen so far, the load commands are executed from the database server and the input files are located on the database server. You may sometimes want to invoke a load operation from a remote client as well as using a file that resides at the client. To do so, specify the **client** keyword in the command as demonstrated in Figure 12.21.

```
load client from stock.ixf of ixf
  modified by dumpfile=stockdump.dmp
  rowcount 5000
  messages stock.out
  tempfiles path c:\loadtemp
  replace into stock
  for exception stockexcept
  lock with force
```

Figure 12.21   Example 4: load command

You cannot load a CURSOR file type from a client. The *dumpfile* and *lobsinfile* modifiers (discussed in the following sections) refer to files on the server even when the command includes the `client` keyword.

> **N O T E**   Use the **load client** command when the input file resides on the client from which you are issuing the command. Use the *dumpfile, tempfile,* and *lobsinfile* modifiers for files located on the DB2 server.

The `rowcount` option works exactly the same as the one supported by the import utility. You can control the number of rows to be loaded with this option.

During the load process, the utility uses temporary files. By default, it allocates temporary files from the directory where the `load` command was issued. To explicitly specify a path for this purpose, use the `tempfiles` option as shown in Figure 12.21.Notice that the example also uses the `replace` mode, which replaces the old data in the target table with the new data.

12.5.2.5 Locking Considerations During a Load

The utility acquires various locks during the load process. If you choose to give the load operation a higher priority then other concurrent applications, you can specify the `lock with force` option (in Figure 12.21) to immediately terminate other applications that are holding conflicting locks so that the load utility does not have to wait for locks.

By default, no other application can access the target table that is being loaded. The utility locks the target table for exclusive access until the load completes. You can set this default behavior with the `allow no access` option. This is the only valid option for `load replace`.

You can increase concurrency by locking the target table in share mode and allowing read access. In Figure 12.22, the `allow read access` option is enabled, which lets readers access data that existed before the load. New data will not be available until the load has completed.

```
load from stock.ixf of ixf
  modified by dumpfile=stockdump.dmp
  messages stock.out
  replace into stock
  for exception stockexcept
  allow read access
  indexing mode incremental
```

Figure 12.22 Example 5: load command

12.5.2.6 The INDEXING MODE Option

The last option in Figure 12.22, `indexing mode`, indicates whether the load utility is to rebuild indexes or to extend them incrementally. This is done in the build phase. You can use the options in Table 12.6.

Table 12.6 INDEXING MODE Options for the load Command

INDEXING MODE option	Description
REBUILD	Forces all indexes to be rebuilt.
INCREMENTAL	Extends indexes with new data.
AUTOSELECT (default)	The load utility will automatically choose between REBUILD or INCREMENTAL mode.
DEFERRED	Indexes will not be rebuilt but will be marked as needing a refresh. An index will be rebuilt when it is first accessed or when the database is restarted.

12.5.3 File Type Modifiers Supported in the Load Utility

The file type modifiers supported in the load utility are as comprehensive as those supported in the export and import utilities. The following section discusses a few of the modifiers. Refer to the *DB2 Data Movement Utilities Guide and Reference* for a complete list of load utility modifiers.

12.5.3.1 Leaving Free Space in Data and Index Pages

When you insert data into a table with the insert, import, or load operations, DB2 tries to fit as much of the data into the data and index pages as possible. Consider pages tightly packed as shown in Figure 12.23.

When a certain record is updated with data larger than the original size, new data might not be able to fit into the original data page. DB2 will then search for the next free page to store the updated record. The updated record is referenced from the original page by a **pointer**. When a request comes in to retrieve the record, DB2 first locates the original data page and then searches for the new data page as referenced by the pointer. This is called **page overflow** (see Figure 12.24).

Figure 12.23   A tightly packed data or index page

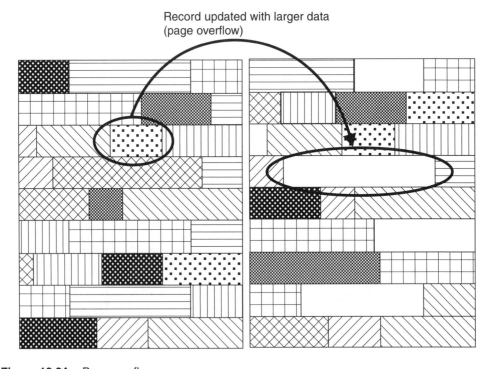

Figure 12.24   Page overflow

The higher the number of page overflows, the more time DB2 will spend finding the data or index page. Hence, you want to avoid page overflows as much as possible to improve performance.

To minimize page overflows, you can customize the table definition so that certain free space is reserved so that the pages are not tightly packed. The **CREATE TABLE**, **ALTER TABLE**, and **CREATE INDEX** statements have options for leaving free space in data and/or index pages. The `load` command also has options to override the default set for the target table. You can specify this using the file type modifiers: `indexfreespace`, `pagefreespace`, and `totalfreespace`.

Modifiers `pagefreespace=x` and `indexfreespace=x` can be used to specify the percentage of each data and/or index page that is to be left as free space. For example, Figure 12.25 illustrates leaving 20 percent of free space on each data and index page.

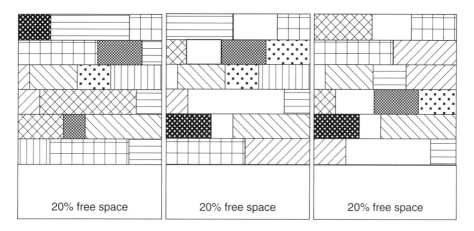

Figure 12.25 Leaving free space for the pagefreespace and indexfreespace file modifiers

The modifier `totalfreespace=x` specifies the percentage of the total pages in the table that is to be appended to the end of the table as free space. For example, if x = 20, and the table has 100 data pages after the data has been loaded, 20 additional empty pages will be appended. The total number of data pages for the table will be 120 (see Figure 12.26).

12.5.4 Loading Large Objects

The load utility uses the same option and modifier as the import utility to specify the path where LOBs are stored. For example, the following command lists the directories where LOBs are stored with the **lobs from** option.

```
load from stock.ixf of ixf
  lobs from c:\lobs1, c:\lobs2, c:\lobs3
  modified by dumpfile=stockdump.dmp lobsinfile
  messages stock.out
  replace into stock
  for exception stockexcept
```

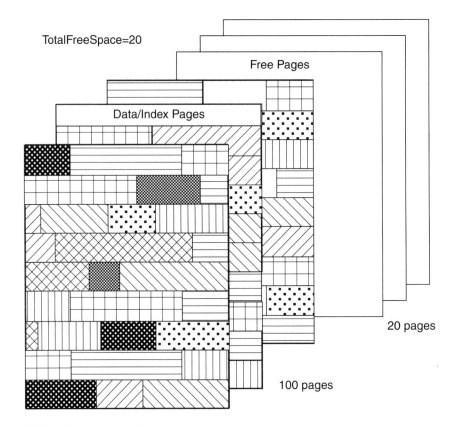

Figure 12.26   Using the totalfreespace file modifier

12.5.5 Collecting Statistics

During the load phase of the process, the load utility also collects table statistics if you specify `statistics`. You can either collect statistics using the statistic profile with **the statistics use profile** option, or specify not to collect statistics with the **statistics no** option. A **statistic profile** is a set of options that specify which statistics are to be collected, such as table, index, or distribution statistics.

If you choose not to collect statistics during the load, you should always update the statistics at the earliest convenient time. When large amounts of new data are inserted into a table, you should update the statistics to reflect the changes so that the optimizer can determine the most optimal access plan.

12.5.6 The COPY YES/NO and NONRECOVERABLE Options

Recall that changes made to the target tables during the load are not logged. This is one of the characteristics of the load utility that improves performance. However, it also takes away the ability to perform roll forward recovery for the load operation. DB2 puts the table space where the target table resides in backup pending state when the load operation begins. After the load completes, you must back up the table space or database. This ensures that the table space can be restored to the point where logging is resumed if you ever need to restore the table space restore. This is the behavior of the load option **copy no**. You can also specify **copy yes** if archival logging is enabled. With **copy yes**, a copy of the loaded data will be saved and the table space will not be in backup pending state upon load completion. However, this negatively impacts the performance of the load. Table space status related to load operation will be discussed later in this chapter.

When you cannot afford to have a window to perform a table space backup after the load is complete but you also need the load to complete as fast as possible, neither **copy yes** nor **copy no** is a good solution. You may want to consider using the option **nonrecoverable** if the target table can be recreated and data can be reloaded.

The **nonrecoverable** option specifies that the target table is marked as nonrecoverable until the associated table space is backed up. In case of failure, such as disk or database failure, the table space needs to be restored and rolled back. The roll forward utility marks the data being loaded as *invalid* and skips the subsequent transactions for the target table. After the roll forward operation is completed, the target table is not accessible and it can only be dropped. Note that other tables in the same table space are not affected by this option.

12.5.7 Validating Data Against Constraints

The load utility checks for invalid data and unique constraints during the load process. However, other constraints such as referential integrity and check constraints are not validated. DB2 therefore puts target tables defined with these constraints in check pending state. This forces you to manually validate the data before the tables are available for further processing.

The **set integrity** command gives you the ability to do just that. The command can be as simple as the following, which immediately validates data against the constraints for table *stock*.

```
set integrity for stock immediate checked
```

There are many other options; refer to the *DB2 UDB Command Reference* for the complete syntax of the command.

12.5.8 Performance Considerations

You can further speed up the load performance by taking advantage of the extra hardware resources you might have on the machine. Table 12.7 lists options and modifiers you can use.

Table 12.7   Modifiers That Improve Load Performance

Performance-Related Modifiers	Description
DATA BUFFER	Specifies the number of 4KB pages to use as buffered space for transferring data within the load utility.
SORT BUFFER	Specifies the amount of memory used to sort index keys during the load operation.
CPU_PARALLELISM	Specifies the number of processes that the load utility will spawn for parsing, converting, and formatting records during the load operation.
DISK_PARALLELISM	Specifies the number of processes that the load utility will spawn for writing data to the table space containers.
FASTPARSE	Reduces syntax checking on input data. Note that this modifier may not detect invalid data.
ANYORDER	Specifies that preserving source data order is not required.

12.5.9 Authorities Required to Perform a Load

To perform a load, you must have SYSADM, DBADM, or LOAD authority. With the LOAD authority, you also need specific privileges on the target tables depending on the mode used in the `load` command. For example, you need INSERT privileges on the table when the load utility is invoked in INSERT mode. If you use REPLACE mode, you need INSERT and DELETE privileges on the target table.

Note that you also need appropriate access to the exception table if one is specified. In addition, when using the `copy yes` option, you need SYSADM, SYSCTRL, or SYSMAINT authority because a backup is performed during the load operation.

12.5.10 Loading a Table Using the Control Center

The Control Center provides a graphical tool to invoke a load operation. Right-click on the target table and select **Load** to start the Load Wizard (Figure 12.27). The Load Wizard walks you through the process of loading a table.

12.5.11 Monitoring a Load Operation

During the phases of a load, the target table and its associated table spaces are in different states. By checking the state of the table and table space, you can tell which phase the load operation is currently in. Before introducing the tools to obtain this information, let's first discuss the different table and table space states.

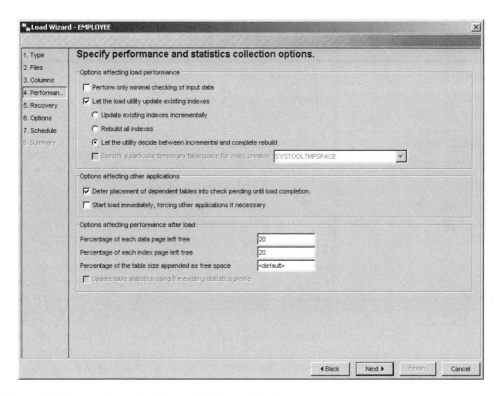

Figure 12.27   Loading a table from the Control Center

12.5.11.1 Table States

Table 12.8 lists the states in which Tables can be placed by the database manager. You can control some of these; others are caused by the load utility.

Table 12.8   Table States

Table State	Description
Normal	The table is in normal state.
Check pending	Table is placed in check pending because it has constraints that have not yet been verified. When the load operation begins, it places tables with constraints (foreign key constraint and check constraint) in this state.
Load in progress	Load is in progress on this table.

(continues)

Table 12.8 Table States *(Continued)*

Table State	Description
Load pending	A load operation has been activated on this table. However, it was aborted before data could be committed. Issue the `load` command with the `terminate`, `restart`, or `replace` option to bring the table out of this state.
Read access only	The table data is available for read access queries. Load operations using the `allow read access` option placed the table in this state.
Unavailable	The table is unavailable. You can drop or restore it from a backup. Rolling forward through a non-ecoverable load operation will place a table in this state.
Not load restartable	When information required for a load restart operation is unreliable, the table will be placed in this state. This prevents a load restart operation from taking place. For example, a table is placed in this state when a roll forward operation is started after a failed load operation that has not been successfully restarted or terminated.
Type-1 indexes	Type-1 indexes are used in DB2 prior to Version 8. Tables currently using type-1 indexes can be converted to type-2 indexes using the REORG utility with CONVERT option. Type-2 indexes provide significant locking enhancements. They are also required to perform some online maintenance tasks, such as REORG.
Unknown	The table state cannot be determined.

12.5.11.2 Table Space States

Table 12.9 lists the states in which table spaces can be placed by the database manager.

Table 12.9 Table Space States

Table State	Description
Normal	The table space is in normal state.
Quiesced: SHARE	The table space has been quiesced in SHARED mode.
Quiesced: UPDATE	The table space has been quiesced in UPDATE mode.
Quiesced: EXCLUSIVE	The table space has been quiesced in EXCLUSIVE mode.
Load pending	A table space is put in this state if a load operation has been active on one of its associated tables but has been aborted before data could be committed.

(continues)

Table 12.9   Table Space States *(Continued)*

Table State	Description
Delete pending	A table space is put in this state if one of its associated tables is undergoing the delete phase of a load operation but has been aborted or failed.
Backup pending	A table space is put in this state after a Point In Time roll forward operation, or after a load operation with the `no copy` option. You must back up the table space before using it. If it is not backed up, then you cannot update the table space, and only read-only operations are allowed.
Roll forward in progress	A table space is put in this state when a roll forward operation on that table space is in progress. Once the roll forward operation completes successfully, the table space is no longer in roll forward-in-progress state. The table space can also be taken out of this state if the roll forward operation is cancelled.
Roll forward pending	A table space is put in this state after it is restored or following an I/O error. After it is restored, the table space can be rolled forward to the end of the logs or to a Point In Time. Following an I/O error, the table space must be rolled forward to the end of the logs.
Restore pending	A table space is put in this state if a roll forward operation on that table space is cancelled, or if a roll forward operation on that table space encounters an unrecoverable error, in which case the table space must be restored and rolled forward again.
Load in progress	A table space is put in this state if it is associated with a load operation. The load in progress state is removed when the load operation is completed or aborted.
Reorg in progress	An REORG operation is in progress on one of the tables associated to the table space.
Backup in progress	A backup is in progress on the table space.
Storage must be defined	For DB2 database manager internal use only.
Restore in progress	A restore is in progress on the table space.
Offline and not accessible	DB2 failed to access or use one or more containers associated to the table space, so the table space is placed offline. To take the table space out of this state, repair the containers.

12.5.11.3 Load Querying

DB2 has two utilities that you can use to obtain the table state. Figure 12.28 presents the syntax diagram of one of them, the **load query** command.

```
>>-LOAD QUERY--TABLE--table-name--+------------------------+---->
                                  '-TO--local-message-file-'

>--+-------------+--+----------+------------------------------><
   +-NOSUMMARY---+  '-SHOWDELTA-'
   '-SUMMARYONLY-'
```

Figure 12.28   Syntax diagram of the load query command

You can specify the following command to check the status of the load operation:

`load query table stock to c:/stockstatus.out`

The output file *stockstatus.out* might look similar to Figure 12.29.

```
SQL3501W  The table space(s) in which the table resides will not be placed in backup
pending state since forward recovery is disabled for the database.

SQL3109N  The utility is beginning to load data from file "stock.del"

SQL3500W  The utility is beginning the "LOAD" phase at time "03-21-2002
11:31:16.597045".

SQL3519W  Begin Load Consistency Point. Input record count = "0".

SQL3520W  Load Consistency Point was successful.

SQL3519W  Begin Load Consistency Point. Input record count = "104416".

SQL3520W  Load Consistency Point was successful.

SQL3519W  Begin Load Consistency Point. Input record count = "205757".

SQL3520W  Load Consistency Point was successful.

SQL3532I  The Load utility is currently in the "LOAD" phase.


Number of rows read         = 205757
Number of rows skipped      = 0
Number of rows loaded       = 205757
Number of rows rejected     = 0
Number of rows deleted      = 0
Number of rows committed    = 123432
Number of warnings          = 0

Tablestate:
  Load in Progress
```

Figure 12.29   Sample output of a load query command

12.5.11.4 The LIST UTILITIES Command

The `list utilities` command displays the list of active utilities on the instance. Use the `show detail` option to also display detailed progress information. Figure 12.30 illustrates sample output.

```
list utilities show detail

ID                                 = 1
Type                               = LOAD
Database Name                      = SAMPLE
Partition Number                   = 0
Description                        = OFFLINE LOAD Unknown file type AUTOMATIC INDEXING
INSERT COPY NO
Start Time                         = 03/15/2004 00:41:08.767650
Progress Monitoring:
    Phase Number                   = 1
        Description                = SETUP
        Total Work                 = 0 bytes
        Completed Work             = 0 bytes
        Start Time                 = 03/15/2004 00:41:08.786501
    Phase Number [Current]         = 2
        Description                = LOAD
        Total Work                 = 11447 rows
        Completed Work             = 5481 rows
        Start Time                 = 03/15/2004 00:41:09.436920
```

Figure 12.30 Output of the list utilities command

The report generated in Figure 12.30 indicates that a load was performed on the database *sample* and includes a brief description of the operation. *Progress Monitoring* tells you the current phase of the load and the number of rows already loaded and to be loaded.

The table space in which the load target table resides will be placed in backup pending state if **COPY NO** (the default) option is specified. The utility places the table space in this state at the beginning of the load operation. The table spaces stays in backup pending mode even when the load is complete until you perform a database or table space level backup.

Figure 12.31 shows how to retrieve the table space status.

```
list tablespaces show detail

Tablespace ID                      = 2
  Name                             = USERSPACE1
  Type                             = System managed space
  Contents                         = Any data
```

Figure 12.31 Retrieving the table space status *(continues)*

```
   State                             = 0x0000
     Detailed explanation:
       Backup pending
   Total pages                       = 527
   Useable pages                     = 527
   Used pages                        = 527
   Free pages                        = Not applicable
   High water mark (pages)           = Not applicable
   Page size (bytes)                 = 4096
   Extent size (pages)               = 32
   Prefetch size (pages)             = 16
   Number of containers              = 1
```

Figure 12.31   Retrieving the table space status *(continued)*

12.6 THE DB2MOVE UTILITY

You can only operate the export, import, and load utilities on one table at a time. To move a large number of tables between DB2 databases, use the **db2move** utility. Based on the action you request, the utility calls the DB2 export, import, and load application programming interfaces (APIs) accordingly. Refer to Figure 12.32 for options supported by **db2move**.

```
                          .---------------------------.
                          V                           |
>>-db2move--dbname--action----+-----------------------+-+------><
                              +--tc--table-creators---+
                              +--tn--table-names------+
                              +--sn--schema-names-----+
                              +--ts--tablespace-names-+
                              +--tf--filename---------+
                              +--io--import-option----+
                              +--lo--load-option------+
                              +--l--lobpaths----------+
                              +--u--userid------------+
                              +--p--password----------+
                              '--aw------------------'
```

Figure 12.32   Syntax diagram of the db2move command

The **db2move** command can also be used without any options. This example exports all tables in the *sample* database:

```
db2move sample export
```

To import tables with schema *dbaadmin* and schemas that start with *dbauser*, you can specify the **-tc** option and provide a list of schema names; the command also accepts the wildcard (*).

```
db2move sample import -tc dbaadmin,dbauser*
```

You can also specify the replace mode and *lobpath*:

```
db2move sample load -lo replace -l c:\lobpath1,c:\lobpath2
```

There is no specific authorization prerequisite to invoke this utility. However, the user ID must have the correct authorization and/or privileges for the associated utility (export, import, and load) to take action.

12.7 THE DB2RELOCATEDB UTILITY

The **db2relocatedb** utility renames a database and relocates a database or part of a database you specify in the configuration file. This tool makes the necessary changes to the DB2 instance and database files.

You can alter the following properties of a database using the **db2relocatedb** utility:

- The database name
- The instance it belongs to
- The database directory
- The database partition number
- The log directory (if it does not reside in the database directory)
- The location of table space containers (if they do not reside in the database directory)

The syntax for the db2relocatedb command is

```
db2relocatedb -f configuration_file_name
```

The format of the configuration file is

```
DB_NAME=oldName,newName
DB_PATH=oldPath,newPath
INSTANCE=oldInst,newInst
NODENUM=nodeNumber
LOG_DIR=oldDirPath,newDirPath
CONT_PATH=oldContPath1,newContPath1
CONT_PATH=oldContPath2,newContPath2
...
```

If the *sample* database belongs to instance db2inst1 and was created under /data, to rename the *sample* database to *sample1*, edit a configuration file as follows and run the **db2relocatedb** command using this file:

```
DB_NAME=SAMPLE,SAMPLE1
DB_PATH=/data
INSTANCE=db2inst1
```

To move the *sample* database from the instance *db2inst1* on path /data to instance *db2inst2* on the same path, do the following:

- Move all the files in /data/db2inst1 to /data/db2inst2

- Edit a configuration file as follows and run **db2relocatedb** using this file:

```
DB_NAME=SAMPLE
DB_PATH=/data
INSTANCE=db2inst1, dn2inst2
```

If the *sample* database belongs to instance *db2inst1*, was created under /data, and has a SMS table space container /home/db2inst1/ts1 must be moved to /home/db2inst1/ts/ts1, do the following:

- Copy all the files in /home/db2inst1/ts1 to /home/db2inst1/ts/ts1.
- Edit a configuration file and run **db2relocatedb** using this file:

```
DB_NAME=SAMPLE
DB_PATH=/data
INSTANCE=db2inst1
CONT_PATH=/home/db2inst1/ts1,/home/db2inst1/ts/ts1
```

Refer to the file *Command_and_SQL_Examples.pdf* included with the CD-ROM accompanying this book for more examples on how to use **db2relocatedb**.

12.8 GENERATING DATA DEFINITION LANGUAGE

So far this chapter has introduced tools and utilities that you can use to extract data and table definitions using export. In cases when you just want to extract the definition of a table, the **db2look** command comes very handy.

db2look extracts the Data Definition Language (DDL) of database objects. Besides that, the tool can also generate the following:

- UPDATE statistics statements
- Authorization statements such as GRANT statements (also known as the Data Control Language (DCL)
- **update** commands for the following Database Manager Configuration parameters:
    - cpuspeed
    - intra_parallel
    - comm_bandwidth
    - nodetype
    - federated
    - fed_noauth
- **update** commands for the following database configuration parameters:
    - locklist
    - dft_degree
    - maxlocks
    - avg_appls
    - stmtheap
    - dft_queryopt

- The **db2set** command for the following DB2 registry variables:

    - DB2_PRED_FACTORIZE
    - DB2_CORRELATED_PREDICATES
    - DB2_LIKE_VARCHAR
    - DB2_SORT_AFTER_TQ
    - DB2_HASH_JOIN
    - DB2_ORDERED_NLJN
    - DB2_NEW_CORR_SQ_FF
    - DB2_PART_INNER_JOIN
    - DB2_INTERESTING_KEYS

The syntax diagram for the **db2look** command in Figure 12.33 shows all the supported options.

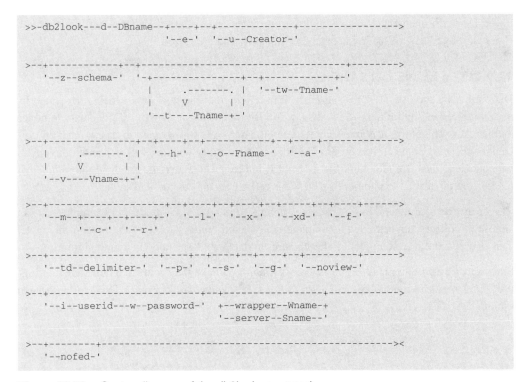

```
>>-db2look---d--DBname--+----+--+-------------+---------------->
                        '--e-'  '--u--Creator-'

>--+---------------+--+------------------------------------+-------->
   '--z--schema-'  '-+--------------+--+----------+-'
                     |  .-------.  |  '--tw--Tname-'
                     |  V        | |
                     '--t----Tname-+-'

>--+-----------------+--+----+--+----------+--+----+------------->
   |   .-------.  |  '--h-'  '--o--Fname-'  '--a-'
   |   V        | |
   '--v----Vname-+-'

>--+------------------+--+----+--+----+--+-----+--+----+------->
   '--m--+----+--+----+-'  '--l-'  '--x-'  '--xd-'  '--f-'
         '--c-'  '--r-'

>--+-----------------+--+----+--+----+--+----+--+----------+------->
   '--td--delimiter-'  '--p-'  '--s-'  '--g-'  '--noview-'

>--+---------------------------+--+-----------------+----------->
   '--i--userid---w--password-'  +--wrapper--Wname-+
                                 '--server--Sname--'

>--+--------+----------------------------------------------->< 
   '--nofed-'
```

Figure 12.33   Syntax diagram of the db2look command

Refer to the *DB2 Command Reference Manual* for more information about each option. The following examples demonstrate how the command can be used.

- In the *sample* database, the command generates the DDL of objects created by *db2admin* under the schema *prod*. It also generates authorization statements. The output file *db2look.sql* captures this result. .

  ```
  db2look -d sample -u db2admin -z prod -e -x -o db2look.sql
  ```

- In the *sample* database, the command extracts the DDL from the *staff*, *department*, and *employee* tables, and generates UPDATE statements used to replicate statistics of the tables and the associated **runstats** commands.

  ```
  db2look -d sample -t staff department employee -m -r
  ```

- In the *sample* database, the command generates the DDL for all the database objects including the authorization statements, and stores the result in *db2look.sql*.

  ```
  db2look -d sample -xd -o db2look.sql
  ```

12.9 DB2 MAINTENANCE UTILITIES

Performing maintenance activities on your databases is essential to ensure that they are optimized for performance and recoverability. In this section, we introduce a few utilities that you should use regularly to ensure the database is healthy and optimized.

12.9.1 The RUNSTATS Utility

DB2 utilizes a sophisticated cost-based optimizer to determine how data is being accessed. Its decisions are heavily influenced by statistical information about the size of the database tables and indexes. Therefore, it is important to keep the database statistics up to date so that an efficient data access plan can be chosen. The RUNSTATS utility updates statistics about the physical characteristics of a table and the associated indexes. Characteristics include the number of records (cardinality), the number of pages, the average record length, and so on.

 The **runstats** command has been greatly enhanced in DB2 Version 8.2. For example, you can choose to collect statistics for the complete table or only on a sample of the rows in the table. This is very helpful for completing the statistics update on a large table in a limited time.

Since **runstats** command supports many different options, the syntax diagram shown in Figure 12.34 is not a complete one. Refer to the *DB2 Command Reference* for details on each option.

```
>>-RUNSTATS--ON TABLE--table name--+-USE PROFILE------------+--->
                                   '-| Statistics Options |-'

>--+---------------------------------------+------------------->< 
   '-UTIL_IMPACT_PRIORITY--+----------+-'
                           '-priority-'
```

Figure 12.34   Partial syntax diagram of the runstats command

The following examples illustrate how to use this command.

- This command collects statistics on the table *db2user.employee* while letting readers and writers access the table while the statistics are being calculated.

  ```
  runstats on table db2user.employee allow write access
  ```

- This command collects statistics on the table *db2user.employee*, as well as on the columns *empid* and *empname* with distribution statistics. While the command is running, the table is only available for read-only requests.

  ```
  runstats on table db2user.employee with distribution
      on columns ( empid, empname ) allow read access
  ```

- The following command collects statistics on the table *db2user.employee* and detailed statistics on all its indexes.

  ```
  runstats on table db2user.employee and detailed indexes all
  ```

- This command collects statistics on the table *db2user.employee* with distribution statistics on only 30 percent of the rows.

  ```
  runstats on table db2user.employee with distribution
      tablesmple bernoulli(30)
  ```

12.9.2 The REORG and REORGCHK Utilities

As data is inserted, deleted, and updated in the database, the data might not be physically placed in a sequential order, which means that DB2 must perform additional read operations to access data. This usually requires more disk I/O operations, and we all know such operations are costly. To minimize I/O operations, you should consider physically reorganizing the table to the index so that related data are located close to each other.

An index is said to have a **high cluster ratio** when the data with equal or near key values is physically stored close together. The higher the cluster ratio, the better rows are ordered in index key sequence. Figure 12.35 shows the difference between indexes with high and low cluster ratio.

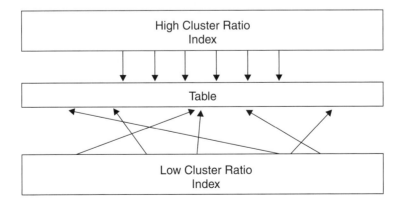

Figure 12.35   Indexes with high and low cluster ratio

An index's cluster ratio is part of the database statistics. You will learn in Chapter 16, Database Performance Considerations, that keeping database statistics is very important when it comes to performance. REORGCHK is a data maintenance utility that has an option to retrieve current database statistics or update the database statistics. It generates a report on the statistics with indicators identifying tables and indexes that should be reorganized (or defragmented). Using the statistics formulae, **reorgchk** marks the tables or indexes with asterisks (*) if there is a need to REORG. Figure 12.36 shows the syntax diagram of the **reorgchk** command.

```
               .-UPDATE STATISTICS--.
>>-REORGCHK--+--------------------+----------------------------->
               '-CURRENT STATISTICS-'

   .-ON TABLE USER----------------.
>--+-----------------------------+-----------------------------><
   '-ON--+-SCHEMA--schema-name---+-'
         |            .-USER-------. |
         '-TABLE--+-SYSTEM-----+-'
                  +-ALL--------+
                  '-table-name-'
```

Figure 12.36   Syntax diagram of the reorgchk command

For example, the following command generates a report of the current statistics on all tables that are owned by the runtime authorization ID:

```
reorgchk current statistics on table user
```

This command updates the statistics and generates a report on all the tables created under the schema *smith*:

```
reorgchk update statistics on schema smith
```

Figure 12.37 shows a sample output of a **reorgchk** command. You can see that the report contains table and index statistics. Every table and index defined in the database is listed. If statistics are not collected for the table or index, a dash (–) is displayed.

To reorganize tables or indexes, use the REORG utility. It reorganizes data for a table and/or index. Although data is physically rearranged, DB2 provides the option of performing this online or offline. By default, offline REORG lets other users read the table. You can restrict table access by specifying the **allow no access** option. Online REORG (also called **inplace REORG**) does not support read or write access to the table. Since data pages are rearranged, concurrent applications have to wait for REORG to complete with the current pages. You can easily stop, pause, or resume the process with the appropriate options. Figure 12.38 illustrates the syntax diagram of the **reorg** command.

```
Table statistics:

F1: 100 * OVERFLOW / CARD < 5
F2: 100 * (Effective Space Utilization of Data Pages) > 68
F3: 100 * (Required Pages / Total Pages) > 80

SCHEMA      NAME                CARD   OV   NP   FP   TSIZE   F1  F2   F3 REORG
--------------------------------------------------------------------------------
SYSIBM      SYSATTRIBUTES        -    -    -    -      -     -   -    - ---
SYSIBM      SYSBUFFERPOOLNODES   -    -    -    -      -     -   -    - ---
SYSIBM      SYSBUFFERPOOLS       1    0    1    1     52     0   - 100 ---
SYSIBM      SYSCHECKS            -    -    -    -      -     -   -    - ---
SYSIBM      SYSCODEPROPERTIES    -    -    -    -      -     -   -    - ---
SYSIBM      SYSCOLAUTH           -    -    -    -      -     -   -    - ---


Index statistics:

F4: CLUSTERRATIO or normalized CLUSTERFACTOR > 80
F5: 100*(KEYS*(ISIZE+9)+(CARD-KEYS)*5) / ((NLEAF-NUM_EMPTY_LEAFS)*INDEXPAGESIZE) > 50
F6: (100-PCTFREE)*((INDEXPAGESIZE-96)/(ISIZE+12))**(NLEVELS-2)*(INDEXPAGESIZE-96)/
(KEYS*(ISIZE+9)+(CARD-KEYS)*5) < 100
F7: 100 * (NUMRIDS DELETED / (NUMRIDS DELETED + CARD)) < 20
F8: 100 * (NUM EMPTY LEAFS / NLEAF) < 20

SCHEMA      NAME              CARD  LEAF ELEAF LVLS ISIZE NDEL KEYS  F4  F5 F6 F7 F8 REORG
------------------------------------------------------------------------------------------
Table: SYSIBM.SYSATTRIBUTES
SYSIBM      IBM83              -     -    -    -     -     -    -    -   -  -  -  - -----
SYSIBM      IBM84              -     -    -    -     -     -    -    -   -  -  -  - -----
SYSIBM      IBM85              -     -    -    -     -     -    -    -   -  -  -  - -----
Table: SYSIBM.SYSBUFFERPOOLNODES
SYSIBM      IBM69              -     -    -    -     -     -    -    -   -  -  -  - -----
Table: SYSIBM.SYSBUFFERPOOLS
SYSIBM      IBM67              1     1    0    1    22     0    1  100  -  -  0  0 -----
SYSIBM      IBM68              1     1    0    1    10     0    1  100  -  -  0  0 -----
Table: SYSIBM.SYSCHECKS
SYSIBM      IBM37              -     -    -    -     -     -    -    -   -  -  -  - -----
```

Figure 12.37   Sample output of the reorgchk command

```
>>-REORG------------------------------------------------------->

>--+-TABLE--table-name--| Table Clause |-----------------+------>
   '-INDEXES ALL FOR TABLE--table-name--| Index Clause |-'


>--+--------------------------------------+------------------------><
   '-| Database Partition Clause |-'


Table Clause:

|--+-----------------+-----------------------------------------------------------> 
   '-INDEX--index-name-'
        .-ALLOW READ ACCESS-.
>--+-+---------------------+--+---------------+--+------------+--+-------------+-+--|
   | '-ALLOW NO ACCESS---'  '-USE--tbspace-'   '-INDEXSCAN-'  '-LONGLOBDATA-' |
   |           .-ALLOW WRITE ACCESS-.                          .-START--.     |
   '-INPLACE--+-+-----------------------+--+------------------+--+--------------+-+---'
              | '-ALLOW READ ACCESS--'   '-NOTRUNCATE TABLE-'  '-RESUME-' |
              '-+-STOP--+--------------------------------------------------'
                '-PAUSE-'
```

Figure 12.38   Syntax diagram of the reorg command *(continues)*

```
Index Clause:

   .-ALLOW READ ACCESS--.
|--+--------------------+--+--------------------------+----------|
   +-ALLOW NO ACCESS----+  |                  .-ALL---. |
   '-ALLOW WRITE ACCESS-'  +-CLEANUP ONLY--+-------+-+
                           |               '-PAGES-' |
                           '-CONVERT----------------'
```

Figure 12.38   Syntax diagram of the reorg command *(continued)*

The following command reorganizes table *db2user.employee* and its index *db2user.idxemp*. The operation lets others perform writes to the same table.

```
reorg table db2user.employee index db2user.idxemp inplace allow write access
```

To pause a REORG operation, issue the command with the same options but specify the **pause** option:

```
reorg table db2user.employee index db2user.idxemp inplace pause
```

> **NOTE** The REORG utility rearranges the data physically but does not update the database statistics. Therefore, it is important to always execute a RUNSTATS upon completion of a REORG.

12.9.3 The REBIND Utility and the FLUSH PACKAGE CACHE Command

Before a database application program or any SQL statement can be executed, DB2 precompiles it and produces a package. A **package** is a database object that contains compiled SQL statements used in the application source file. DB2 uses the packages to access data referenced in the SQL statements. How does the DB2 optimizer choose the data access plan for these packages? It relies on database statistics at the time the packages are created.

For static SQL statements, packages are created and bound to the database at compile time. If statistics are updated to reflect the physical database characteristics, existing packages should also be updated. The REBIND utility lets you recreate a package so that the current database statistics can be used. The command is very simple:

```
rebind package package_name
```

When you execute dynamic SQL statements, they are not known until the application is run. They are precompiled at runtime and stored in the package cache. If statistics are updated, you can flush the cache so that dynamic SQL statements are compiled again to pick up the updated statistics. Use the command:

```
flush package cache dynamic
```

12.9.4 Database Maintenance Process

You have just learned about a few database maintenance utilities: RUNSTATS, REORG, REORGCHK, REBIND, and FLUSH PACKAGE. Figure 12.39 summarizes the maintenance process that you should perform regularly against your database.

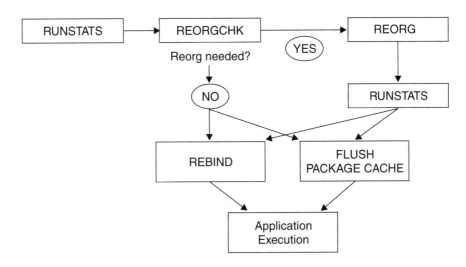

Figure 12.39 Database maintenance process

12.10 CASE STUDY

Assume your company wants to deploy a new accounting application very soon, but the finance department director has demanded a more thorough testing. The only test machine that is available for testing has DB2 for Windows installed. However, you need to obtain data from a DB2 for AIX database server. Since the source and target platforms are different and not every table and views are required for testing, you choose to use data movement utilities to move data to the Windows server.

First, you connect to the source server and then export the required tables with this command:

```
export to newsalary.ixf of ixf
  messages newsalary.out
  select empno, firstnme, lastname, salary * 1.3 as new_salary
    from employee
  where workdept='A00'
```

You find out that the accounting application needs all of the 100 tables under the schema *acct*. To save the time and effort of typing the **export** command for each of the 100 tables, you choose to use the **db2move** command.

```
db2move proddb export -sn acct
```

Because the output files are in IXF format, you can create the tables and import data directly to the target database using the import utility.

```
import from newsalary.ixf of ixf
  messages newsalary.out
  create into newsalary in datats index in indexts
```

Not that a new table called *newsalary* is created in the *datats* table space and that its indexes are stored in the *indexts* table space.

After the first few successful completions of the import operation, you realize that you cannot finish all the imports within the estimated time. The import utility performs insert statements behind the scenes, and thus activates constraint checking, logging, and triggers. The load utility, on the other hand, goes behind the DB2 engine and loads the data directly to the pages. You can choose to perform logging as well as performing only primary and unique key checks. Thus, for the sake of performance, you decide to change the plan and use the load utility instead.

To capture all rows that violated unique constraints of the target table, you create an exception table with this statement:

```
CREATE TABLE salaryexp
( empno CHAR(6), firstnme VARCHAR(12), lastname VARCHAR(15)
, new_salary DECIMAL(9,2), load_ts TIMESTAMP, load_msg CLOB(2K))
```

Since you are not that familiar with the syntax of the **load** command, you decide to use the Control Center to invoke the load utility. Each graphical tool has a *Show Command* button. You click on this button because you want to store the **load** command generated in a script so you can use it in the future. You obtain the following command, which you can issue later:

```
load from newsalary.ixf of ixf
  modified by dumpfile=salarydump.dmp
  rowcount 5000
  messages salary.out
  tempfiles path c:\loadtemp
  create into salary
  for exception salaryexp
```

After the load is completed successfully, the table is not accessible (by default) due to table space backup pending. Therefore, you need to perform a table space or database backup (see section 13.4, Performing Database and Table Space Backups).

If the table has any constraints defined such as referential integrity and check constraint, you need to validate the data integrity with the following command:

```
set integrity for newsalary immediate checked
```

The target tables should be ready and accessible for testing.

12.11 SUMMARY

In this chapter you were introduced to the different data movement utilities that come with DB2. The utilities support the following file formats: DEL, ASC, IXF, WSF, and CURSOR.

The Export utility extracts data from a table or view into a file. Only a few options are available in the **export** command. However, at a minimum, you should specify the output file name (where exported data is stored), its file format, the message file name, and a **SELECT** statement.

The import utility, on the other hand, inserts data into a specified table or view from a file. You can choose to import to an existing or new table (or view). By default, DB2 only issues one COMMIT at the very end of the import operation. In case of failure during the import, all the changes will be rolled back, and you need to restart the import from the beginning. Alternatively, you can use options such as **commitcount**, **restartcount**, and **skipcount** to enable the ability of restarting an import.

The load utility is another method to insert data into a specified table or view and is much faster. The utility formats the data pages while bypassing DB2 buffering and logging. The utility is composed of four phases: load, build, delete, and index copy. You can check the load message file or the status of the table or use the **load query** command to monitor the load operation.

The **db2move** utility can be used to move more than one table using just one command. The utility lets you specify the action: export, import, or load. This utility comes in very handy when many tables need to be moved.

The RUNSTATS, REORG, and REORGCHK utilities are very important data maintenance utilities that should be performed regularly to ensure that the most optimal data access plans are used.

12.12 REVIEW QUESTIONS

1. Which data movement utility supports the CURSOR input file type?
2. What other privileges are needed to load a table if the person already has LOAD authority?
3. Bob creates the *stock* table:

```
CREATE TABLE stock ( id        INTEGER NOT NULL
                  , name      VARCHAR(10)
                  , bandlevel INTEGER NOT NULL
                  , PRIMARY KEY (id) )
```

He then loads the table with this **load** command:

```
load from stock.del of del
modified by dumpfile=stockdump.dmp
messages stock.out
replace into stock
for exception stockexp
```

The input file *stock.del* looks like this:

```
10, "AAA", 30
20, "BBB", -
30, "CCC", 3
30, "DDD", 4
40, "EEE", x
```

After the **load** command is executed, which rows will be stored in the *stockdmp.dmp* file?

4. With the same target table definition, **load** command, and input file as in question 3,, which rows will be stored in the *stockexp* exception table?

5. A table is created with the following statement:

```
CREATE TABLE employee
    ( id    SMALLINT NOT NULL
    , name VARCHAR(10)
    , job  CHAR(5) CHECK (job IN ('Sales', 'Mgr', 'Clerk') )
    , PRIMARY KEY (id))
```

If this **load** command is issued, what state would the *employee* table be in?

```
load from emp2.del of del insert into emp2
```

6. A table is created with the following statement:

```
CREATE TABLE employee
    ( id    SMALLINT NOT NULL
    , name VARCHAR(10)
    , job  CHAR(5) CHECK (job IN ('Sales', 'Mgr', 'Clerk') )
    , PRIMARY KEY (id))
```

If this **import** command is issued, what state would the *employee* table be in?

```
import from emp2.del of del insert into emp2
```

7. What will this command do?

```
db2look -d department -a -e -m -x -f -o db2look.sql
```

8. Bob just completed a load operation to insert 300,000 rows of data into various tables. He performed a **RUNSTATS** to update the database statistics so that the DB2 optimizer knows about the new data. However, when the user logs in and runs the application, the performance is not acceptable. The application is mainly coded in static SQL and SQL stored procedures. What can Bob do to improve performance?

9. Bob tries to execute the following command:

```
import from largeinputfile.ixf of ixf
    messages import.out
    create into newtable in datats index in indexts
```

However, he receives log full errors. What can he do to solve this problem?

10. What is the prerequisite for a table to be imported with the **insert_update** option?

11. Which of the following tools will read data from an ASCII file and add them to a table?

    A. insert

    B. merge

    C. load

    D. export

    E. import

12. Which of the following tools will read data from an ASCII file and add them to a view?

    A. insert

    B. merge

    C. load

    D. export

    E. import

13. Which of the following formats is not supported by the import utility?

    A. IXF

    B. DEL

    C. ASC

    D. XLS

14. You want to import the following rows of data in the file *foo.txt* into the table *foo*:

```
"Hello"|"World"
"Goodbye"|"Cruel World"
```

Which of the following commands must you run?

    A. Import from foo.txt of txt insert into foo

    B. Import from foo.txt of del insert into foo

    C. Import from foo.txt of pipedel insert into foo

    D. Import from foo.txt of del modified by coldell insert into foo

15. Which of the following tools cannot act on a view?

    A. Export

    B. Import

    C. Load

16. Which of the following tools, commands, or statements can be used to rename a database?

    A. Rename database

    B. db2relocatedb

    C. db2move

    D. db2renamedb

17. Which of the following tools can capture statistics on the data it adds to the table?

    A. Export

    B. Import

    C. Load

18. Which of the following are true?

    A. The load utility locks the whole table space for the table being loaded.

    B. The load utility locks the whole table being loaded.

    C. The load utility by default locks only the existing data in the table until the load completes.

    D. The load utility allows read access to all data that existed in the table before the load was run.

19. Which of the following tools can create a new table as well as populating the table?

    A. Load

    B. Import

    C. Export

    D. db2look

20. Given a table is defined with PCTFREE = –1, which of the following tools will not leave free space in a table for subsequent inserts?

    A. Load

    B. Import

    C. Reorg

CHAPTER **13**

Developing Database Backup and Recovery Solutions

A power failure may hit your database system while it is busy processing. A user may accidentally drop a very important table that you really need. How can you recover the table that has been dropped? What can you do to ensure that the data in the database remains consistent even when processing has been interrupted by a power failure? DB2's backup and recovery methods are designed to help you in those situations.

In this chapter you will learn about:

- The concept of transaction logging and the various logging methods
- How to perform backup operations
- How to perform restore operations
- How to perform roll forward operations
- How to inspect your databases for corruptions
- What split mirroring is
- What High Availability Disaster Recovery (HADR) is and how to set it up

13.1 DATABASE RECOVERY CONCEPTS

Database recovery is how DB2 makes your database consistent in the event of a failure. A database is "consistent" when all committed transactions have been applied to the database and any uncommitted transactions that might have been performed have been rolled back.

13.1.1 Recovery Scenarios

To minimize the loss of your data, you need to have a recovery strategy, ensure that it works, and constantly practice it. The following are some recovery scenarios you should consider.

- System outage: A power failure, hardware failure, or software failure can cause your database to be in an inconsistent state.
- Transaction failure: Users may inadvertently corrupt your database by modifying it with incorrect data or delete useful data.
- Media failure: If your disk drive becomes unusable, you may lose all or part of your data.
- Disaster: The facility where your system is located may be damaged by fire, flooding, or other catastrophe.

13.1.2 Recovery Strategies

To plan your recovery strategy, ask yourself:

- Can the data be loaded from another source?
- How much data can we afford to lose?
- How much time can we spend recovering the database?
- What storage resources are available for storing backups and log files?

13.1.3 Unit of Work (Transactions)

A **unit of work** (UOW), also known as a **transaction**, consists of one or more SQL statements that end with a **COMMIT** or **ROLLBACK** statement. All of the statements inside this UOW are treated as a unit, which ensures data consistency. A typical example to explain this concept is that of a customer trying to transfer $100 from his savings account to his checking account. The UOW in this case would include all three of the following:

```
DELETE 100 dollars from SAVINGS  account
INSERT 100 dollars  to  CHECKING account
COMMIT
```

If these statements are not treated as a unit and a hardware failure occurs after the **DELETE** and before the **INSERT**, then this person loses $100! Since the statements are treated as a unit, this will never happen because DB2 knows that the unit did not complete as a **COMMIT** was not issued. When the system is restarted after the failure, DB2 will **ROLLBACK** the statements, meaning it will bring the database back to the state prior to beginning of the transaction.

> **N O T E**   An analogy for understanding the **COMMIT** statement is to compare it to the *Save* button in word processing software. When you click this button, you expect your text document to be saved. Changes made after you save the document are lost if your server crashes, but what was saved will remain on disk. Similarly, when you issue a **COMMIT** statement, changes made to the database are saved. If your server crashes, anything that was committed can be recovered, and anything that was not will be lost.

13.1.4 Types of Recovery

There are three types of recovery in DB2:

- Crash recovery
- Version recovery
- Roll forward recovery

Each of these types of recovery is discussed in detail in the next sections.

13.1.4.1 Crash Recovery

Crash recovery protects a database from being left in an inconsistent state following an abnormal termination. An example of an abnormal termination is a power failure. Using the banking example, if a power failure occurs prior to the **COMMIT** statement, the next time DB2 is restarted and the database accessed, DB2 will **ROLLBACK** the **INSERT** statement, followed by the **DELETE** statement. Note that statements are rolled back in reverse order, not in the order they were originally executed. This ensures that the data is consistent, and that the person still has the $100 in his savings account.

By default, DB2 automatically initiates crash recovery when a database is accessed for the first time following an abnormal termination. You can disable the automatic crash recovery by setting the database configuration parameter AUTOSTART to OFF. If you do that, you will need to perform crash recovery manually using the **RESTART DATABASE** command. If you do not restart the database manually in the event of a system crash, you will receive the following error when you try to connect to the database:

```
SQL1015N The database must be restarted because the previous session did not conclude
normally.
```

13.1.4.2 Version Recovery

Version recovery allows for the restoration of a previous version of a database using a backup image created with the **BACKUP** command. The restored database will be in exactly the same state it was in when the **BACKUP** command was executed. If further activity was performed against the database after this backup was taken, those updates are lost. For example, assume you back up a database and then create two tables, *table1* and *table2*. If you restore the database using the backup image, your restored database will not contain the two new tables.

13.1.4.3 Roll Forward Recovery

Roll forward recovery extends version recovery by using full database backups in conjunction with log files. A backup must be restored first as a baseline, and then logs are applied on top of this backup image. Therefore, changes you made *after* you backed up the database can be applied to the restored database. Using the previous example, with roll forward recovery you have three choices to restore your database:

- You can restore the database using only the backup image. This is identical to version recovery. In this case, the restored database will not contain *table1* and *table2*.
- You can restore the database using the backup image, and then roll forward the logs to the point when *table1* was created. In this case, the restored database will contain *table1* but not *table2*.
- You can restore the database using the backup image, and then roll forward the logs all the way to the end of the logs. In this case, the restored database will contain both *table1* and *table2*.

By default, crash recovery and version recovery are enabled. You will learn how to enable roll forward recovery in Section 13.2.4, Logging Methods.

13.2 DB2 Transaction Logs

DB2 uses transaction logs to record all changes to your database so that they can be either reapplied or rolled back in the event of problems.

13.2.1 Understanding the DB2 Transaction Logs

The ability to perform both crash recovery and roll forward recovery is provided by the database transaction logs. **Transaction logs** keep track of changes made to database objects and data. During the recovery process, DB2 examines these logs and decides which changes to redo or undo.

Logs can be stored in files or in raw devices. In this chapter, we use files in our examples for simplicity. To ensure data integrity, DB2 uses a "write-ahead logging" mechanism to write to the logs before writing (externalizing) the database changes to disk. To illustrate this process, assume a user issues the following statements:

```
UPDATE t1 SET year = 2000 WHERE ID = '007'
UPDATE t1 SET year = 2001 WHERE ID = '011'
COMMIT
UPDATE t1 SET year = 2004 WHERE ID = '003'
```

Table *t1* and its index *ix1* are shown in the logical view of Figure 13.1.

As each statement is executed, the following takes place (the figure uses the first UPDATE statement for illustration purposes).

- The DB2 optimizer parses the query and determines that using index *ix1* is the fastest way to retrieve the desired data. An index page access followed by a data page access is required.
- The statement and access plan information is stored in the package cache (1).
- The extent containing the desired index page (2) is brought from disk to the buffer pool (3). The index points to a record in the data page, and thus the extent containing the pertinent data page (4) is also brought from disk to the buffer pool (5).

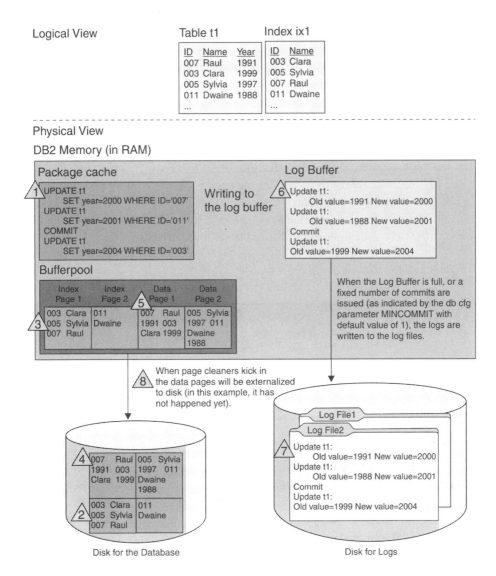

Figure 13.1   Concept of transaction logging

- The **UPDATE** operation takes place in the buffer pool.
- The **UPDATE** operation is recorded in the log buffer. The old and new values are kept in case the operation needs to be reverted (6).

DB2 checks to see if the log buffer is full or if MINCOMMIT commits have been performed. If any of these occurred, the information in the log buffers is written to the log files in the disk for the logs (7).

> **N O T E**   The MINCOMMIT database configuration parameter indicates the minimum number of **COMMIT** commands required before writing from the log buffer to the disks for the logs.

The log files can contain committed or uncommitted data. When a crash recovery happens, DB2 will undo any statement that was not committed, and will redo any statements that were committed.

Note too that the information that was changed in the buffer pool and that was written to the log files has not yet been saved in the disks for the database. This will eventually happen when "page cleaner" processes are run to "clean" the modified pages in the buffer pool and write them to disk (8). This is not done immediately after the statement is executed for performance reasons. DB2 is already storing the information in the log files on disk, so there is no need to perform another I/O right away to store the changed pages to the database disk.

When data is committed and saved in the disk for the database, the data is considered to be **externalized**.

> **N O T E**   We discuss the DB2 optimizer and page cleaners in detail in Chapter 16, Database Performance Considerations.

13.2.2 Primary and Secondary Log Files

The *Disk for Logs* in Figure 13.1 is known as the **active log directory** or **log space**. Its location is specified in the database configuration parameter *Path to log files*.

The size of the log space is controlled by three database configuration parameters.

- The **LOGPRIMARY** parameter specifies the number of primary log files that are allocated in the active log directory. Primary log files are allocated during the first database connect or during database activation by the **ACTIVATE DATABASE** command.
- The **LOGSECOND** parameter controls the maximum number of secondary log files that can be allocated in the active log directory. Secondary log files are allocated dynamically one at a time as needed, when there are no more primary logs available for transaction processing.
- The **LOGFILSIZ** parameter controls the size of the log files. This value is specified as a number of 4KB pages.

For example, let's say you have the following values in your database configuration:

```
Log file size (4KB)           (LOGFILSIZ)  = 250
Number of primary log files   (LOGPRIMARY) = 3
Number of secondary log files (LOGSECOND)  = 2
Path to log files                          = C:\mylogs\
```

Since each file is 1MB (250 x 4KB), and there are a total of 5 log files (3 primary logs and 2 secondary logs), the log space is 5MB.

NOTE The maximum log space you can configure is 256GB.

In this example, as soon as the first connection to the database is established, 3 primary log files of 250 4KB-pages each are allocated. If you change directories to C:\mylogs, you will see the three files:

```
2004-03-10 06:06p 1,032,192 S0000000.LOG
2004-03-10 06:06p 1,032,192 S0000001.LOG
2004-03-10 06:06p 1,032,192 S0000002.LOG
3 File(s) 3,096,576 bytes
```

Now, let's say you decide to perform the following transaction, which inserts a million records into a table:

```
INSERT INTO TABLE1 VALUES(1);
INSERT INTO TABLE1 VALUES(2);
...
INSERT INTO TABLE1 VALUES(1000000);
COMMIT;
```

DB2 will fill up the first log file, continue with the second log file, and then the third log file. After it fills up the third log file, there are no more primary logs available (remember that LOGPRIMARY is set to 3, so a maximum of three primary logs can exist at any time). At this point DB2 will dynamically allocate a secondary log file. Once the first secondary log file is filled up, DB2 will allocate another secondary log file, and this process will continue until the maximum number of secondary log files, indicated by the database configuration parameter LOGSECOND, is reached. In this example the maximum is two.

At the point when the maximum number of secondary log files is reached, if DB2 still needs more space to complete the transaction, a **log full** condition occurs. This means there is no more room in the log space to complete the transaction. The first transaction causing this log full condition will be rolled back. (Section 13.2.4, Logging Methods, discusses how DB2 tries to reuse the old logs first, if possible, before creating a new one. DB2 uses an algorithm that reduces the chances of encountering a log full condition.)

Log full is a very undesirable condition: Not only all the work performed up to this point is lost, but roll back may take a long period of time. For this reason, it is important to ensure that you allocate enough log space to accommodate your workload.

Generally, you do not want to allocate a huge number of PRIMARY logs, because they are allocated when a database is activated. If you specify a large number, DB2 will spend a lot of time creating these files; thus your first connection will take a long time. Moreover, if your transaction workload is generally small throughout the day, all that log space will be wasted. Instead, you may specify enough LOGSECOND log files to handle a spike in your workload (e.g., a heavier workload with long transactions at the end of a month).

Another undesirable condition is the **log disk full** condition. Unlike a log full condition, where DB2 runs out of logging space because the maximum numbers of primary and secondary log files have been reached, a log disk full condition occurs when the file system that hosts the active log directory is physically full, meaning no more log files can be created, even though the maximum numbers of primary and secondary log files may not have been reached. This condition could be caused by the file system being too small or the active log directory becoming filled by too many inactive (aka archive) log files. (You will learn what inactive logs are in the next section.)

By default, a transaction that receives a disk full error will fail and will be rolled back, just as in the case of a log full condition. However, you can change this behavior by setting the database configuration parameter BLK_LOG_DSK_FUL to YES. Setting this parameter to YES causes applications to block or wait instead of rolling back when DB2 encounters a disk full error when writing log files. While the applications are waiting (or blocked), DB2 attempts to create the log file every five minutes until it succeeds. After each attempt, DB2 writes a message to the administration notification log. The way to confirm that your application is blocked because of a log disk full condition is to monitor the administration notification log.

> **N O T E**   The administration notification log is discussed in Chapter 17, Diagnosing Problems.

Until the log file is successfully created, any user application that attempts to update table data will not be able to commit transactions. Read-only queries may not be directly affected; however, if a query needs to access data that is locked by an update request or a data page that is fixed in the buffer pool by the updating application, read-only queries will also appear to hang.

Once you have determined that the hang is caused by a disk full error, you can resolve the situation by moving inactive log files to another file system or by increasing the size of the file system so that hanging applications can complete.

13.2.3 States of Logs

The state of a log is determined by whether the transactions it contains are committed and whether the transactions have been externalized to disk. There are three states of logs: active, online archive, and offline archive.

13.2.3.1 Active Logs

A log is considered **active** if one of the following applies:

- It contains transactions that have not yet been committed or rolled back.
- It contains transactions that have been committed but whose changes have not yet been written to the database disk (externalized).

In Figure 13.1, log file 2 is an active log because it contains a transaction that has not been committed (the last **UPDATE** statement). Log file 2 also contains a transaction that has been committed but has not been externalized to disk (the first two **UPDATE** statements).

Imagine that at this point a power failure strikes and everything in the log buffer and the buffer pool is wiped out. The only place where you can find a record of these transactions is in the log files. When the database is restarted, it will go through crash recovery. DB2 will first open log file 2 and read its contents. DB2 will redo the transactions that have a `commit` or `rollback`, and undo the transactions that do not. Using the example in Figure 13.1, DB2 will redo the first two `UPDATE` statements, but undo the last `UPDATE` statement.

Active log files are necessary for crash recovery. If you lose the active logs, crash recovery will fail and the database will be inaccessible.

Active logs typically reside in the active log path. If you have enabled infinite logging, archived log files may need to be retrieved from the archive site. (Infinite logging is covered in section 13.2.4, Logging Methods.)

13.2.3.2 Online Archive Logs

Online archive logs are files that contain only committed, externalized transactions. In other words, they are logs that are no longer active, and therefore no longer needed for crash recovery.

Online archive logs reside in the active log directory as well. This is why they are called "online." The term *online archive logs* may sound complicated, but all it means is that inactive logs reside in the active log directory.

Although these logs are no longer needed for crash recovery, they are retained for roll forward recovery. You will see why in section 13.2.4, Logging Methods.

13.2.3.3 Offline Archive Logs

A file system has limited space. If all the online archive logs stay in the active log directory, this directory will soon be filled up, causing a disk full condition. Therefore, the online archive logs should be moved out of the active log directory as soon as possible. You can do this manually, or DB2 can invoke a program to do this for you. Once this has been done, these logs become **offline archive logs**. They are called "offline" because they reside outside of the active log directory.

Like the online archive logs, offline archive logs are also retained for roll forward recovery.

13.2.4 Logging Methods

DB2 supports three logging methods: circular logging, archival logging, and infinite active logging.

13.2.4.1 Circular Logging

Circular logging is the default logging mode for DB2. As the name suggests, in this method the logs are reused in a circular mode. For example, if you have three primary logs, DB2 uses them in this order: Log #1, Log #2, Log #3, Log #1, Log #2....

Note that in the above sequence Log #1 and Log #2 are reused. When a log file is reused, its contents are completely overwritten. Therefore, a log can be reused if and only if the transactions it contains have already been committed and externalized to the database disk. In other works, the log must not be an active log. This ensures DB2 will have the necessary logs for crash recovery when needed.

Figure 13.2 shows how circular logging works.

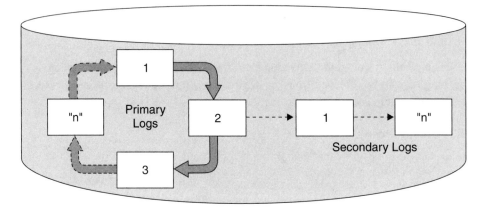

Figure 13.2   Circular logging

During database activation, DB2 creates LOGPRIMARY number of logs. If LOGPRIMARY is 3, during transactions, DB2 fills up the first log file, continues with the second log file, and then the third log file. After it finishes with the third log file, DB2 cannot allocate a new primary log because the maximum number of primary logs is three. DB2 then checks if log #1 has become inactive. If it has, then DB2 reuses log #1. If it has not, then DB2 allocates a secondary log. When another log is needed, DB2 checks to see if any of the primary logs can be reused and repeats the same process until the maximum specified in LOGSECOND is reached, at which point the log full condition occurs.

With this logging method, DB2 reuses or overwrites logs that are no longer active. Although ability to recover from a crash is assured, you cannot reapply the transactions that were in these logs, because they have been overwritten. Therefore, circular logging only supports crash recovery, not roll forward recovery.

13.2.4.2 Archival Logging

Archival logging keeps the logs even after they contain committed and externalized data. To enable this mode, you have to change the LOGARCHMETH1 database configuration parameter to ON. We will discuss the possible values to which this parameter can be set later in this section.

With archival logging, roll forward recovery is supported. The contents of inactive logs are saved rather than overwritten; therefore, they can be reapplied during roll forward recovery.

Depending on the value set in LOGARCHMETH1, you can have it saved to various locations. When the log is needed during roll forward recovery, DB2 retrieves it from that location and restores it into the active log directory.

With archival logging, if you have three primary logs in a database, DB2 uses them in this order: Use Log #1, use Log #2, use Log #3, archive Log #1, create and use Log #4, archive Log #2, create and use Log #5.... Notice that the log number increases as new logs are required. Unlike circular logging where log numbers stay the same, only the log content is overwritten.

Figure 13.3 shows how archival logging works.

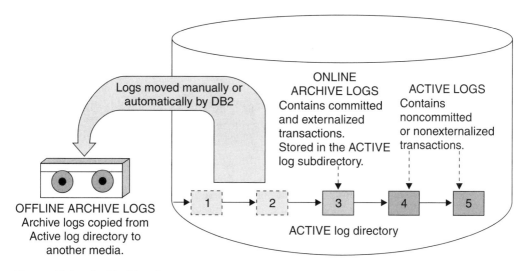

Figure 13.3   Archival logging

How DB2 archives and retrieves a log file depends on the value set in the LOGARCHMETH1 database parameter. The possible values are OFF, LOGRETAIN, USEREXIT, TSM, and VENDOR.

V8.2

- LOGARCHMETH1 = OFF
    This is the default. When set to OFF, archival logging is disabled and circular logging is used.
- LOGARCHMETH1 = LOGRETAIN
    Let's use the example in Figure 13.3 to demonstrate how LOGRETAIN works. DB2 starts with three primary logs: log #1, log #2, and log #3. When DB2 fills up all these three logs, it checks if log #1 has become inactive. If it has, DB2 creates log #4 as a primary log. The set of primary logs then becomes log #2, log #3, and log #4. If log #1 is still active, DB2 creates log #4 as secondary log. When a new log is needed, DB2 checks if log #2 has become inactive. If it has, DB2 creates log #5 as a primary log. If not, it creates log #5 as a secondary log. The process is repeated until LOGSECOND is reached, at which point the log full condition occurs.

Note with LOGRETAIN, inactive log files are never overwritten. In Figure 13.3, even though log #1 and log #2 have already become inactive, they still remain in the active log directory. (At this point, they are online archive logs.) You have to manually move them to a different location or the active log directory will soon be filled up by these logs. However, you should never delete these logs without making a copy of them somewhere, because they may be needed for roll forward recovery. After logs #1 and #2 have been moved to another location, they become offline archive logs.

- LOGARCHMETH1 = USEREXIT

    With LOGARCHMETH1 set to USEREXIT, the archive and retrieval of the logs are performed automatically by a user-supplied user exit program called **db2uext2**.

    The user exit program archives a log file to a different location as soon as it becomes full, even if it is still active. Archiving a log file simply means making a copy of it somewhere; the log itself still remains in the active log directory. If the log is still active, DB2 will not reuse it. If the log is inactive, when a new log is required, DB2 will rename it and reuse it.

    Once again, let's use the example in Figure 13.3 to explain how the USEREXIT works. DB2 starts with three primary logs: log#1, log #2, and log #3. As soon as these logs are full, DB2 calls the user exit program to archive them. When DB2 needs a new log, it checks to see if log #1 is active. If log #1 is still active, DB2 creates secondary log #4. If log #1 is inactive, DB2 renames log #1 to log #4 and reuses it (instead of creating a new log #4). This helps to eliminate the overhead of creating a new file. There is no loss of data in reusing a log that has been archived, because its copy can always be retrieved when needed.

    When logs are needed during recovery, DB2 calls the user exit program to retrieve the necessary logs. Because everything is handled by the user exit program, you should not manipulate the log files manually. Doing so may potentially interfere with the user exit program.

- LOGARCHMETH1 = DISK:*directory*

    With this setting archival logging uses a similar algorithm as in USEREXIT. The only difference is instead of calling the user exit program, DB2 will automatically archive the logs from the active log directory to the specified *directory*. During recovery, DB2 will automatically retrieve these logs back to the active log directory.

- LOGARCHMETH1 = TSM:[management class name]

    With this setting archival logging uses a similar algorithm as in USEREXIT. The only difference is that the logs will be archived on the local Tivoli Storage Manger (TSM) server. The management class name parameter is optional. If not specified, the default management class is used.

- LOGARCHMETH1 = VENDOR:*library*

    With this setting archival logging uses a similar algorithm as in USEREXIT. The only difference is that logs are archived using the specified vendor library.

- LOGARCHMETH2

    This optional parameter specifies the secondary archive log method. It can be set using the same values as for LOGARCHMETH1. If set, logs will be archived to both this destination and the destination specified by the LOGARCHMETH1 parameter.

> **NOTE** LOGARCHMETH1 and LOGARCHMETH2 are new database configuration parameters introduced in DB2 Version 8.2. They replace the LOGRETAIN and USEREXIT parameters, which are still supported for backward compatibility. If you update the USEREXIT or LOGRETAIN parameters, LOGARCHMETH1 will automatically be updated and vice versa. However, if you are using either USEREXIT or LOGRETAIN, LOGARCHMETH2 must be set to OFF.

In addition to LOGARCHMETH1 and LOGARCHMETH2, a number of other logging-related database parameters are also introduced in DB2 Version 8.2. Table 13.1 lists them.

Table 13.1 New Logging-Related Database Configuration Parameters in DB2 Version 8.2

New DB CFG Parameters	Description
FAILARCHPATH	Failover archive path. Specifies a third target to archive log files if the primary and secondary archival paths fail. The media must be disk. It is a temporary storage area for the log files until the primary path(s) becomes available again, at which time the log files will be moved from this directory to the primary archive path(s). By moving the log files to this temporary location, log directory full situations might be avoided.
NUMARCHRETRY	Specifies the number of retries attempted on primary target(s) before archiving to FAILARCHPATH. The default is 5.
ARCHRETRYDELAY	Specifies the number of seconds between retry attempts. The default is 20 seconds.
LOGARCHOPT1 and LOGARCHOPT2	Specifies a string that is passed on to the TSM server or vendor APIs. For TSM, this field is used to allow the database to retrieve logs that were generated on a different TSM node or by a different TSM user. The string must be provided in the following format: `"-fromnode=nodename -fromowner=ownername"` where *nodename* is the name of the TSM node that originally archived the log files, and *ownername* is the name of the TSM user who originally archived the log files. Each log archive options field corresponds to one of the log archive methods: LOGARCHOPT1 is used with LOGARCHMETH1, and LOGARCHOPT2 is used with LOGARCHMETH2.

13.2.4.3 Infinite Active Logging

Infinite active logging is actually a spin-off of archival logging. With circular logging and archival logging, log space can potentially be filled with active logs. If you have a long-running transaction and do not want to run out of log space in the log path, you can use infinite active logging.

To enable infinite active logging:

- Set the LOGSECOND database configuration parameter to -1.
- Archive logging must be enabled with one of the automatic archival methods; that is, LOGARCHMETH1 must be set to one of USEREXIT, DISK, TSM, or VENDOR.

When archival logging is enabled, a log is archived as soon as it becomes full. DB2 leaves the log in the log directory until it becomes inactive and then renames the file for reuse. With infinite logging, DB2 still archives the log as soon as it is full, but it does not wait for it to become inactive before it renames the file for reuse. This guarantees that the active log directory will never fill up, because any logs can be reused once they are filled. Note that the use of infinite active logging can prolong crash recovery times as active logs may need to be retrieved from the archive site.

13.2.5 Handling the DB2 Transaction Logs

DB2 logs are crucial for roll forward recovery. A missing or corrupted log will cause roll forward recovery to fail and can potentially render the database unusable. Therefore, we recommend that you do not handle any logs manually.

If it becomes necessary for some reason to handle the logs manually, exercise extra care. Never remove log files based solely on their timestamps. Understanding how logs are timestamped may save you from losing active logs and creating a potential disaster.

When primary logs are created at database activation, they are *all* given a timestamp based on the activation time. These timestamps do not change until DB2 writes transaction updates to the logs, one log file at a time. These logs are kept in the active log directory, even though they may be empty. For example, if LOGPRIMARY is set to 20, then 20 log files will be created at timestamp A. Suppose transactions begin and write to logs 1 through 10 at timestamps greater than A. At this point in time, you still have 20 logs in the active log directory. Logs 1 through 10 will have timestamps greater than A. Logs 11 through 20 will have timestamps at exactly A. Assume that these logs (logs 1 to 10) span multiple days of work. In this scenario, it is possible to think that logs 11 to 20 are older logs, because of their older timestamps, and can be removed. In fact, these logs are still active logs. If you remove them, and DB2 requires those logs (e.g., the next log required would be log 11), the database will crash and be marked as corrupted. The only way to recover is to restore from a recent backup. Therefore, we highly recommend that you let DB2 handle the logs automatically.

To determine which log files are active and which ones are not, look at the value of the *First active log file* parameter in the database configuration. All the logs prior to the value are inactive; all the log files starting at the value are active—therefore, you should not touch them.

For example, if the first active log file is S0000005.LOG, then logs 1, 2, 3, and 4 are inactive. All the logs starting at log 5 are active.

13.2.6 Userexit

We have mentioned user exit several times in this chapter. But what exactly is a user exit?

A **user exit** is a program written in the C language that handles the archival and retrieval of DB2 logs automatically when called by DB2.

DB2 provides two sample user exit programs: db2uext2.cdisk and db2uext2.ctsm. You can customize them and use them in your environment. They are found in:

- *DB2_install_dir*\SQLLIB\samples\c on Windows
- *DB2_instance_home*/sqllib/samples/c on Linux/UNIX

The db2uext2.cdisk program archives logs to a local disk on the database server. The db2uext2.ctsm program archives logs to Tivoli Storage Manager (TSM).

Instructions on how to use them are included in these sample programs. You need a C compiler to compile the programs; the resulting executable is called db2uext2. It must be installed in:

- *DB2_install_dir*\SQLLIB\bin directory on Windows
- *DB2_instance_home*/sqllib/adm directory on Linux/UNIX

To enable it, set the database configuration parameter LOGARCHMETH1 to USEREXIT.

Prior to Version 8.2, a user exit was the only way users could "ask" DB2 to automatically archive and retrieve logs. Users had to archive and retrieve the logs manually using LOGRETAIN, or not use archival logging at all. In Version 8.2, you can specify how you want the logs to be archived and retrieved by setting the LOGARCHMETH1 parameter. For example, LOGARCHMETH1 = DISK replaces the db2uext2.cdisk program, and LOGARCHMETH1=TSM replaces the db2uext2.ctsm program.

There is no need to use user exit anymore, but for compatibility reasons user exit support is still available in Version 8.2.

13.3 RECOVERY TERMINOLOGY

Depending on the type of backups that you take, there are different methods that you can use to recover your database in the event of an error. In addition, the configuration you choose for your database will determine whether you can use the database logs to reapply transactions that might otherwise be lost if you need to restore your database from a backup.

13.3.1 Logging Methods Versus Recovery Methods

Circular logging supports only crash and version recovery. Archival logging supports all types of recovery: crash, version, and roll forward.

13.3.2 Recoverable Versus Nonrecoverable Databases

Recoverable databases can be recovered using crash or roll forward recovery, and as discussed before, archival logging is required to support roll forward recovery . Nonrecoverable databases do not support roll forward recovery and use only circular logging. Table 13.2 shows which logging and recovery methods work together.

Table 13.2   Summary of Logging and Recovery Methods

Logging Method	Supports Crash Recovery	Supports Version Recovery	Supports Roll Forward Recovery	Recoverable Database
Circular Logging (LOGARCHMETH1 = OFF)	Yes	Yes	No	No
Archival Logging (LOGARCHMETH1 = LOGRETAIN, USEREXIT, DISK, TSM, or VENDOR)	Yes	Yes	Yes	Yes

13.4 PERFORMING DATABASE AND TABLE SPACE BACKUPS

There are two different granularities that you can choose for your backups, and you have two different options for how the backup can be performed. You can choose to back up the entire database or one or more table spaces from within the database. You can also choose whether you want the backup to be taken online, meaning regular database access is permitted while the backup is taken, or offline, meaning that no database access is permitted while the backup is take. All four of these options can be combined to give you a very flexible recovery mechanism for your databases.

13.4.1 Online Access Versus Offline Access

In the following sections we use the terms "online" and "offline" quite often. An **online** operation (backup, restore, or roll forward) allows other applications or processes to connect to the database, as well as read and modify data while the operation is running. An **offline** operation does *not* allow other applications or processes access to the database and its objects while the operation is being performed.

13.4.2 Database Backup

A **database backup** is a complete copy of your database objects. Besides the data, a backup copy contains information about the table spaces, containers, the database configuration file, the log control file, and the recovery history file. Note that a backup does *not* store the Database Manager Configuration file or the values of registry variables. Only the database configuration file is backed up.

You must have SYSADM, SYSCTRL, or SYSMAINT authority to perform a backup.

The following is the syntax for the **BACKUP DATABASE** command:

```
BACKUP DATABASE database_alias [USER username [USING password]]
[TABLESPACE (tblspace-name [{,tblspace-name} ... ])] [ONLINE]
[INCREMENTAL [DELTA]] [USE {(TSM | XBSA) OPTIONS ("option string" | @ filename)]}
[OPEN num-sess SESSIONS]] |
TO dir/dev [{,dir/dev} ... ] | LOAD lib-name OPTIONS ("option string" | @ filename)]
[OPEN num-sess SESSIONS]]
[WITH num-buff BUFFERS] [BUFFER buffer-size] [PARALLELISM n]
[COMPRESS [COMPRLIB name [EXCLUDE]] [COMPROPTS string]]
[UTIL_IMPACT_PRIORITY priority] [EXCLUDE LOGS| INCLUDE LOGS]
[WITHOUT PROMPTING]
```

- To perform an offline backup of the sample database and store the backup copy in the directory d:\mybackups, use the following syntax for Windows:

```
BACKUP DATABASE sample
TO d:\mybackups
```

- To perform an offline backup of the sample database and store the backup copy in two separate directories, use the following syntax for Linux/UNIX:

```
BACKUP DATABASE sample              (1)
TO /db2backup/dir1, /db2backup/dir2  (2)
WITH 4 BUFFERS                       (3)
BUFFER 4096                          (4)
PARALLELISM 2                        (5)
```

where:

(1) Indicates the name (or alias) of the database to back up.

(2) Specifies the location(s) where you want to store the backup file. DB2 will write to both locations in parallel.

(3) Indicates how many buffers from memory can be used during the backup operation. Using more than one buffer can improve performance.

(4) Indicates the size of each buffer in 4KB pages.

(5) Specifies how many media reader and writer processes or threads are used to take the backup.

If not specified, DB2 automatically chooses optimal values for the number of buffers, the buffer size, and the parallelism settings. The values will be based on the amount of utility heap memory available, the number of processors available, and the database configuration. The objective is to minimize the time it takes to complete a backup operation.

There is no keyword **OFFLINE** in the syntax, as this is the default mode.

• If you have a 24x7 database, shutting down the database is not an option. To perform backups to ensure the database's recoverability, you can perform online backups instead. You must specify the keyword **ONLINE** in the **BACKUP DATABASE** command:

```
BACKUP DATABASE sample
ONLINE
TO /dev/rdir1, /dev/rdir2
```

Since there are users accessing the database while it is being backed up, it is likely that some of the changes made by these users will not be stored in the backup. A transaction may be in the middle of processing when the backup was taken. This means the backup image contains a database in an inconsistent state.

If this online backup is used to restore a database, as soon as the restore operation finishes, DB2 places the database in roll forward pending state. A roll forward operation must be performed to bring the database back to a consistent state before you can use it. If you have set LOGARCHMETH1 to USEREXIT, DISK, TSM, or VENDOR, DB2 automatically retrieves the logs into the active log directory. Otherwise, if LOGRETAIN was set, you must retrieve the log files manually before rolling forward the database. To perform the roll forward, all logs that were active at the time of the backup must be in the active log directory.

> **NOTE**   Archival logging must be enabled to perform online backups.

V8.2 Version 8.2 has a new option in the **BACKUP DATABASE** utility called **INCLUDE LOGS**. When you specify this, the logs will be backed up along with the database during an online backup operation. This ensures that if the archived logs are not available, the backup will still be restored to a minimum Point In Time (PIT) using the logs that are included in the backup image. If you want to restore to a later PIT, additional log files may be required.

For example, to take an online backup of the SAMPLE database along with the logs, using the destination directory /dev/rdir1, issue:

```
BACKUP DATABASE sample
ONLINE
TO /dev/rdir1 INCLUDE LOGS
```

13.4.3 Table Space Backup

In a database where only some of your table spaces change considerably, you may opt not to back up the entire database but only specific table spaces. To perform a table space backup you can use the following syntax:

```
BACKUP DATABASE sample
TABLESPACE (syscatspace, userspace1, userspace2)
ONLINE
TO /db2tbsp/backup1, /db2tbsp/backup2
```

The keyword TABLESPACE indicates this is a table space backup, not a full database backup. You can also see from the example that you can include as many table spaces as desired in the backup. Temporary table spaces cannot be backed up using a table space-level backup.

You will usually back up related table spaces together. For example, if using DMS table spaces where one table space is used for the table data, another one for the indexes, and another one for LOBs, you should back up all of these table spaces at the same time so that you have consistent information. This is also true for table spaces containing tables defined with referential constraints between them.

13.4.4 Incremental Backups

As database sizes continue to expand, the time and hardware resources required to back up and recover these databases also grows substantially. Full database and table space backups are not always the best approach when dealing with large databases, because the storage requirements for multiple copies of such databases are enormous.

To address this issue, DB2 provides incremental backup and recovery. An **incremental backup** is a backup image that contains only pages that have been updated since the previous backup was taken. In addition to updated data and index pages, each incremental backup image also contains all of the initial database metadata (such as database configuration, table space definitions, database history, and so on) that is normally stored in full backup images.

There are two kinds of incremental backups.

- In incremental **cumulative** backups, DB2 backs up all of the data that has changed since the last full database backup.
- In delta backups.DB2 backs up only the data that has changed since the last successful full, cumulative, or delta backup.

Figure 13.4 illustrates these concepts.

For incremental backups, if there was a crash after the incremental backup on Friday, you would restore the first Sunday full backup, followed by the incremental backup taken on Friday.

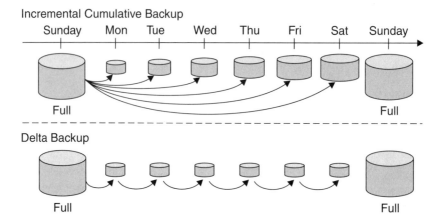

Figure 13.4   Incremental and delta backups

For delta backups, if there was a crash after the delta backup on Friday, you would restore the first Sunday full backup, followed by each of the delta backups taken from Monday until Friday inclusive.

To enable incremental and delta backups, the TRACKMOD database parameter must be set to YES. This allows the database manager to track database modifications so that the **backup database** utility can detect which subsets of the database pages must be examined by an incremental backup and potentially included in the backup image. After setting this parameter to YES, you must take a full database backup to have a baseline against which incremental backups can be taken.

For example, to perform a cumulative incremental backup on the SAMPLE database to destination directory /dev/rdir1, issue:

```
BACKUP DB sample
INCREMENTAL TO /dev/rdir1
```

To perform a delta backup on the SAMPLE database to destination directory /dev/rdir1, issue:

```
BACKUP DB sample
INCREMENTAL DELTA TO /dev/rdir1
```

13.4.5 Performing Backups with the Control Center

You can use the Backup Wizard to perform backups. From the Control Center, expand your database folder, right-click on the database name you wish to back up and select **Backup**. The database Backup Wizard appears. Figure 13.5 shows that you can choose to perform either a database-level backup or a table space-level backup. From here, the Backup Wizard will guide you through backup command options.

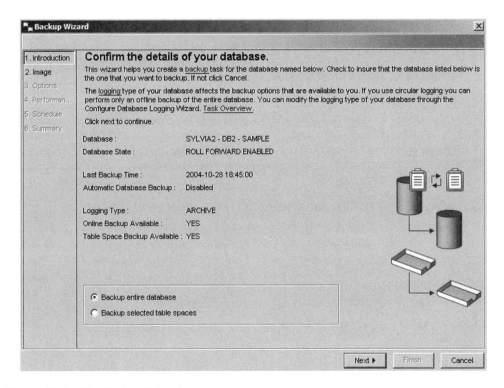

Figure 13.5   The Backup Wizard

13.4.6 The Backup Files

The backup images are stored as files. The name of a backup file contains the following parts:

- Database alias
- Type of backup (0=Full database, 3=Table space, 4=Copy from LOAD)
- Instance name
- Database partition (always NODE0000 for a single-partition database)
- Catalog partition number (always CATN0000 for a single-partition database)
- Timestamp of the backup
- The image sequence number

The exact naming convention varies slightly by platform. In Figure 13.6, you can see that on Windows systems the file that actually contains the backup image is 131259.001.

When DB2 backs up a database on Windows, it creates a hierarchy of directories. For example, the command

```
BACKUP DATABASE sample to D:\temp
```

produces the directories and backup image shown in Figure 13.7.

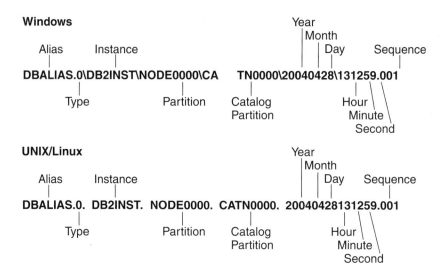

Figure 13.6   Backup file name hierarchy

Figure 13.7   Backup file hierarchy on Windows

When performing a restore, you specify the directory that was specified in the **BACKUP DATA-BASE** command, not the subdirectory where the backup image actually resides.

On Linux and UNIX systems, DB2 does not create additional directories. The backup image can be found in the directory specified in the **BACKUP DATABASE** command, or the current directory where the command is issued.

13.5 DATABASE AND TABLE SPACE RECOVERY USING THE RESTORE DATABASE COMMAND

You can restore the backup image obtained by the **BACKUP DATABASE** command using the **RESTORE DATABASE** command. You can choose to recover the entire database or just the individual table space(s).

13.5.1 Database Recovery

You can restore a database backup image into a new or existing database. You need SYSADM, SYSCTRL, or SYSMAINT authority to restore into an existing database, and SYSADM or SYSCTRL authority restore to a new database.

This syntax of the **RESTORE** command is:

```
RESTORE DATABASE source-database_alias { restore_options | CONTINUE | ABORT }
```

You can use one or more of the following for **restore_options**:

```
[USER username [USING password]] [{TABLESPACE [ONLINE] |
TABLESPACE (tblspace-name [ {,tblspace-name} ... ]) [ONLINE] |
HISTORY FILE [ONLINE] | COMPRESSION LIBRARY [ONLINE] | LOGS [ONLINE] }] [INCREMENTAL
[AUTOMATIC | ABORT]]
[{USE {(TSM | XBSA) [OPTIONS ("option string" | @ filename)]}
[OPEN num-sess SESSIONS] |
FROM dir/dev [ {,dir/dev} ... ] | LOAD shared-lib [OPTIONS ("option string" | @
filename)]
[OPEN num-sess SESSIONS]}] [TAKEN AT date-time] [TO target-directory]
[INTO target-database_alias] [LOGTARGET directory]
[NEWLOGPATH directory][WITH num-buff BUFFERS] [BUFFER buffer-size]
[DLREPORT file-name] [REPLACE EXISTING] [REPLACE HISTORY FILE] [REDIRECT] [PARALLELISM
n] [COMPRLIB name] [COMPROPTS string]
[WITHOUT ROLLING FORWARD] [WITHOUT DATALINK]
[WITHOUT PROMPTING][LOGTARGET]
```

To perform a restore of the sample database, use this syntax:

```
RESTORE DATABASE sample       (1)
FROM C:\DBBACKUP              (2)
TAKEN AT 20040428131259       (3)
WITHOUT ROLLING FORWARD       (4)
WITHOUT PROMPTING             (5)
```

(1) Indicates the name of the database image to restore.

(2) Specifies the location where the input backup image is located.

(3) If there is more than one backup image in the directory, this option identifies the specific backup based on the timestamp, which is part of the backup file name or directory structure.

(4) If a database has archival logging enabled, a restore operation puts the database in roll forward pending state, regardless of whether the backup was online or offline. If restoring from an offline backup, you can choose not to roll forward. This option tells DB2 not to place the database in roll forward pending state. When restoring from an online backup, the "without rolling forward" option cannot be used, as you must roll forward to at least the time that the backup completed.

(5) Specifies that the restore is to be performed unattended. Action that normally requires user intervention will return an error message. When using a removable media device, such as tape or diskette, you will be prompted when the device ends even if this option is specified.

Note that there is no keyword **OFFLINE** in the syntax, as this is the default mode. In fact, for the **RESTORE** utility, this is the only mode allowed for databases.

V8.2 In section 13.4.2, Database Backup, we mentioned that in Version 8.2 a new option, **INCLUDE LOGS** in the **BACKUP DATABASE** command, allows you to back up the logs needed for roll forward recovery. If you specified this option, you need to provide a location to restore the log files with the **LOGTARGET** option. Or you can choose to only restore the log files without restoring the backup image.

For example, on Windows, to restore the SAMPLE database from a backup image residing in the C:\DBBACKUP directory and restore the log files to C:\DB2\NODE0000\SQL00001\SQLOGDIR directory, issue:

```
RESTORE DATABASE sample
FROM C:\DBBACKUP
LOGTARGET C:\DB2\NODE0000\SQL00001\SQLOGDIR
```

To restore just the logs, issue:

```
RESTORE DATABASE sample
LOGS FROM C:\DBBACKUP
LOGTARGET C:\DB2\NODE0000\SQL00001\SQLOGDIR
```

13.5.2 Table Space Recovery

You can restore table spaces either from a full database backup or from a table space backup. Table space recovery requires some careful planning, as it is easy to make mistakes that can put your data into an inconsistent state.

The following is an example of a table space restore:

```
RESTORE DATABASE sample                    (1)
TABLESPACE ( mytblspace1 )                 (2)
ONLINE                                     (3)
FROM /db2tbsp/backup1, /db2tbsp/backup2    (4)
```

where:

(1) Indicates the name of the database image to restore.

(2) Indicates that this is a table space restore, and specifies the name of the table space(s) to restore.

(3) Indicates this is an online restore. Note that for user table spaces, both online and offline restores are allowed. As mentioned earlier, only offline restores are allowed for databases.

(4) Specifies the location where the input backup file is located.

13.5.3 Table Space Recovery Considerations

After a table space is restored, it is *always* placed in roll forward pending state. To make the table space accessible, the table space must be rolled forward to at least a minimum Point In Time. This minimum PIT ensures that the table space and logs are consistent with the system catalogs.

For example:

1. Say at time t1 you took a full database backup that included table space *mytbls1*.
2. At time t2 you created table *myTable* in the table space *mytbls1*. This set the minimum PIT for recovery of the table space mytbs1 to t2.
3. At time t3 you decided to restore only table space mytbls1 from the full database backup taken at t1.
4. After the restore is complete, table space mytbls1 will be placed in a roll forward pending state. If you were allowed to roll forward to a point prior to the minimum PIT, table space mytbls1 will not contain the table myTable, but the system catalog would say that the table does exist in mytbls1. To avoid inconsistencies like this, DB2 forces you to roll forward at least to the minimum PIT when you restore a table space.

A minimum PIT is updated when DDL statements are run against the table space or against tables in the table space. To determine the minimum PIT of recovery for a table space you can do either of the following:

- Execute the `LIST TABLESPACES SHOW DETAIL` command
- Obtain a table space snapshot: `GET SNAPSHOT FOR TABLESPACE ON dbname`.

In offline mode, the system catalog table space (SYSCATSPACE) must be rolled forward to the end of logs. We discuss more about the `ROLLFORWARD` command in the next section.

13.5.4 Performing RESTOREs with the Control Center

You can use the Restore Data Wizard to perform restores. In the Control Center, expand your database folder, right-click on the database name you want to restore, and select **Restore**. The Restore Data Wizard is launched.

Figure 13.8 shows that you have the options to restore to an existing database, a new database, or only the history file. The Restore Data Wizard guides you through the restore command options. (We will discuss the history file in section 13.7, Recovering a Dropped Table.)

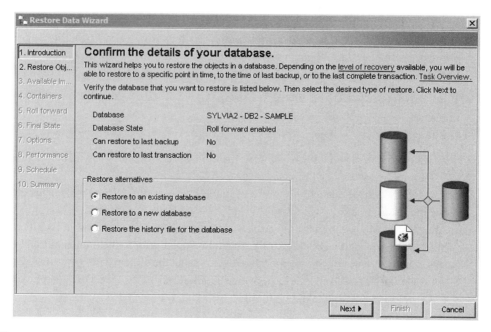

Figure 13.8   The Restore Data Wizard

13.5.5 Redirected Restore

We mentioned earlier that a backup file includes information about the table spaces and containers. For example, let's say one of the table spaces, TS2, has a file container */database/ts2/cont1*. This information is stored in the backup image. When you restore this backup image to a different server, DB2 will try to create exactly the same container. If the directory /database does not exist, DB2 will try to create it. But most likely this will fail because DB2 does not have the proper authority.

In this case, a regular restore will not work. However, a **redirected restore** solves this problem. During a redirected restore, you can specify new paths for the table space containers, and data will be restored to the new containers.

To change the container definitions during a redirected restore, you need to obtain the current container definitions on the source database. Use the `LIST TABLESPACES` command to list all the table spaces including their table space IDs, and then use the `LIST TABLESPACE CONTAINERS FOR tablespace ID` command to obtain the container definition for each table space. Once you have this information, you can proceed with the redirected restore operation.

A redirected restore is performed in three steps:

> **1.** Start the restore operation, but pause it so that you can change the table space definitions. To do this, include the `REDIRECT` keyword as part of the `RESTORE` command. The following shows an example of the command and output:

```
RESTORE DATABASE DB2CERT FROM C:\DBBACKUP
INTO NEWDB REDIRECT

SQL1277N Restore has detected that one or more table space containers are
inaccessible, or has set their state to 'storage must be defined'.
DB20000I The RESTORE DATABASE command completed successfully.
```

2. Specify the container definition for any table space you want to change.

```
SET TABLESPACE CONTAINERS FOR 0 USING (FILE "d:\newdb\cat0.dat" 5000)
SET TABLESPACE CONTAINERS FOR 1 USING (FILE "d:\newdb\cat1.dat" 5000)
...
SET TABLESPACE CONTAINERS FOR n USING (PATH "d:\newdb2")
```

In this example, *n* represents an ID of one of the table spaces in the backup. When using redirected restore, you cannot change the type of the table space from DMS to SMS or vice versa. The types must stay the same.

3. Restore the data itself into the new containers by including the keyword **CONTINUE**:

```
RESTORE DATABASE DB2CERT CONTINUE
```

You can also use redirected restore to add containers to SMS table spaces. As discussed in Chapter 7, Working with Database Objects, SMS table spaces cannot be altered to add a container. Redirected restore provides a workaround to this limitation by redefining the containers.

13.6 DATABASE AND TABLE SPACE ROLL FORWARD

If you have to restore your database or a table space in one of your databases, you will lose any changes made since the backup was taken unless you have log retain enabled and use the **ROLLFORWARD** command to replay the logs for your database.

13.6.1 Database Roll Forward

If a backup operation is performed online, then there are still users connecting to the database and they may be in the middle of a transaction. Therefore, an online backup contains the backup image of a database that is in an inconsistent state. After restoring the backup image into a database, the database is immediately placed in a roll forward pending state. You must run the **ROLLFORWARD DATABASE** command to bring the database back to a normal state.

If you performed an offline backup but your database is configured to use archival logging, then the database is also placed in a roll forward pending state following a restore. In this case, you do not need to use the **ROLLFORWARD** command because an offline backup implies that the database is already in a consistent state. To avoid this, use the **WITHOUT ROLLING FORWARD** option in the **RESTORE DATABASE** command. You need SYSADM, SYSCTRL, or SYSMAINT authority to perform the **ROLLFORWARD** command.

During a roll forward, the transactions in the log files are applied. You can apply all the changes in the log files, that is, roll forward to the end of logs, or you can roll forward to a Point In Time. This means DB2 will traverse the logs and redo or undo all database operations recorded in the logs up to the specified PIT. However, you must roll forward the database to at least the minimum recovery time. This is the earliest point in time to which a database must be rolled forward to ensure database consistency. If you attempt to roll forward but fail to do so, you will receive the following error message:

```
SQL1275N The stoptime passed to roll-forward must be greater than or equal to
"timestamp", because database "dbname" on node(s) "0" contains information later than
the specified time.
```

The *timestamp* given in the error message is the minimum PIT to which you must roll forward the database.

Though we will not cover the **QUIESCE** command in this chapter, it is worth mentioning that you can use this command during regular database operations to create consistency points. You can always perform a point in time recovery to any of these points and be assured your database will be consistent. (See section 11.5.1 Lock Attributes, for more information about the **QUIESCE** command.)

During roll forward processing, DB2 does the following:

1. Looks for one log file at a time in the active log directory.
2. If found, reapplies transactions from the log file.
3. If the log file is not found in the active log directory, DB2 searches for the logs in the OVERFLOWLOGPATH, if specified in the **ROLLFORWARD DATABASE** command.

If DB2 does not find the log file in the active log directory, and you did not specify the **OVER-FLOWLOGPATH**, then the logs have to be retrieved from their archive location. The method used is determined by the LOGARCHMETH1 database configuration parameter. If it is set to LOGRETAIN, then you have to retrieve the logs manually. If it is set to USEREXIT, then the user exit program **db2uext2** is called to retrieve the log file. If it is set to DISK, TSM, or VENDOR, then DB2 automatically retrieves the log file from the respective archive locations.

Once the log is found in the active log directory or the **OVERFLOWLOGPATH** option, DB2 reapplies the transactions it contains and then goes to retrieve the next file it needs.

The syntax of the **ROLLFORWARD** command is:

```
ROLLFORWARD DATABASE database_alias [USER username [USING password]]
[TO {isotime [ON ALL DBPARTITIONNUMS] [USING LOCAL TIME] | END OF LOGS
[On-DbPartitionNum-Clause]}] [AND {COMPLETE | STOP}] |
{COMPLETE | STOP | CANCEL | QUERY STATUS [USING LOCAL TIME]}
[On-DbPartitionNum-Clause] [TABLESPACE ONLINE | TABLESPACE (tblspace-name
[ {,tblspace-name} ... ]) [ONLINE]] [OVERFLOW LOG PATH (log-directory
[{,log-directory ON DBPARTITIONNUM db-partition-number} ... ])] [NORETRIEVE]
[RECOVER DROPPED TABLE dropped-table-id TO export-directory]
```

You can use one or more of the following options for *On_DbPartitionNum_Clause*:

```
ON {{DBPARTITIONNUM | DBPARTITIONNUMS} (db-partition-number
[TO db-partition-number] , ... ) | ALL DBPARTITIONNUMS [EXCEPT
{DBPARTITIONNUM | DBPARTITIONNUMS} (db-partition-number
[TO db-partition-number] , ...)]}
```

To perform a roll forward of the *sample* database you can use any of the following statements:

```
ROLLFORWARD DATABASE sample TO END OF LOGS AND COMPLETE    (1)
ROLLFORWARD DATABASE sample TO timestamp AND COMPLETE      (2)
ROLLFORWARD DATABASE sample TO timestamp
USING LOCAL TIME AND COMPLETE                              (3)
```

Example (1) rolls forward to the end of the logs, which means that all archived and active logs are traversed. At the end DB2 completes the roll forward operation and brings the database from rollforward pending state to a usable state.

Example (2) rolls forward to the specified Point In Time. The timestamp used is in UTC (Universal Coordinated Time), which can be calculated as follows:

> Local time—value in the CURRENT_TIMEZONE special register

For example, to look at the value of the CURRENT_TIMEZONE special register, connect to the database and issue the following SQL statement:

```
db2 "VALUES (CURRENT_TIMEZONE)"
```

If the local time is 2004-05-29-14.42.38.000000, and **CURRENT_TIMEZONE** is -5, then the corresponding UTC time is 2004-05-29-19.42.38.000000.

Example (3) is similar to example (2), but the timestamp can be expressed using local time.

Note that there is no keyword **OFFLINE** in the syntax, as this is the default mode. In fact, for the **ROLLFORWARD** command, this is the only mode allowed.

13.6.2 Table Space Roll Forward

You can perform table space roll forwards either online or offline, except for the system catalog table space (SYSCATSPACE) which can only be rolled forward offline. The following is an example of a table space ROLLFORWARD:

```
ROLLFORWARD DATABASE sample
TO END OF LOGS AND COMPLETE
TABLESPACE ( userspace1 ) ONLINE
```

The options in this example have already been explained in section 13.6.1, Database Roll Forward. The only difference is the **TABLESPACE** option, which specifies the table space to be rolled forward.

13.6.3 Table Space Roll Forward Considerations

If the registry variable DB2_COLLECT_TS_REC_INFO is enabled, only the log files required to recover the table space are processed. The **ROLLFORWARD** command will skip over log files that are not required, which may speed recovery time.

You can use the **QUERY STATUS** option of the **ROLLFORWARD** command to list the log files that DB2 has rolled forward, the next archive log file required, and the timestamp of the last committed transaction since roll forward processing began. For example:

```
ROLLFORWARD DATABASE sample QUERY STATUS USING LOCAL TIME
```

After a table space Point In Time roll forward operation completes, the table space is placed into backup pending state. A backup of the table space or database must be taken because all updates made to it between the PIT that the table space was recovered to and the current time have been lost.

13.6.4 Performing ROLLFORWARDs with the Control Center

You can use the Rollforward Wizard to perform a roll forward. In the Control Center, expand your database folder, right-click on the database name you want to roll forward, and select **Rollforward** from the menu. Alternatively, you can click on the database name and then select **Rollforward** from the **Selected** pull-down menu. The database must be in roll forward pending state to invoke the Rollforward Wizard. Figure 13.9 shows that you can choose to roll forward to the end of logs or to a PIT. The Rollforward Wizard guides you through the roll forward command options.

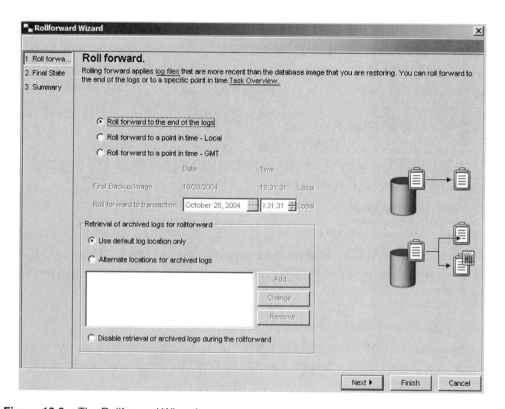

Figure 13.9   The Rollforward Wizard

13.7 RECOVERING A DROPPED TABLE

You may accidentally drop a table that has data you still need. To recover such a table, you can perform a database restore operation, followed by a database roll forward operation to a Point In Time before the table was dropped. However, all of the changes you made after the table was dropped are lost. Moreover, this process may be time-consuming if the database is large, and your data will be unavailable during recovery.

DB2 offers a dropped table recovery feature that makes recovering a dropped table easier. This feature lets you recover your dropped table data using table space-level restore and roll forward operations. This is faster than database-level recovery, and your database remains available to users.

For a dropped table to be recoverable, the table space in which the table resides must have the **DROPPED TABLE RECOVERY** option turned on. By default, dropped table recovery is enabled for newly created data table spaces. To alter this feature, use the **ALTER TABLESPACE** statement. To determine if a table space is enabled for dropped table recovery, you can query the **DROP_RECOVERY** column in the SYSCAT.TABLESPACES catalog table.

```
SELECT TBSPACE, DROP_RECOVERY FROM SYSCAT.TABLESPACES
```

> **N O T E** The DROPPED TABLE RECOVERY option is limited to regular table spaces only, and does not apply to temporary table spaces and table spaces containing LOBs and LONG VARCHARs

To recover a dropped table, perform the following steps.

1. Identify the dropped table by invoking the **LIST HISTORY** command with the **DROPPED TABLE** option. This command displays the dropped table ID in the Backup ID column and shows the DDL statement to recreate the table.
   ```
   LIST HISTORY DROPPED TABLE ALL FOR dbname
   ```
2. Restore a database-level or table space-level backup image taken before the table was dropped.
   ```
   RESTORE DB dbname TABLESPACE (tablespace_name) ONLINE
   ```
3. Create an export directory to which files containing the table data are to be written. In a partitioned database environment, this directory must either be accessible to all database partitions or exist on each partition.
4. Roll forward to a Point In Time after the table was dropped using the **RECOVER DROPPED TABLE** option on the **ROLLFORWARD DATABASE** command. Alternatively, roll forward to the end of the logs, so that updates to other tables in the table space or database are not lost.
   ```
   ROLLFORWARD DB dbname
   TO END OF LOGS TABLESPACE ONLINE
   RECOVER DROPPED TABLE dropped_table_id
   TO export_directory
   ```

If successful, subdirectories under this export directory are created automatically by each database partition. These subdirectories are named NODE*nnnn*, where *nnnn* represents the database partition number. Data files containing the dropped table data as it existed on each database partition are exported to a lower subdirectory called *data*. For example:

```
\export_directory\NODE0000\data
```

The *data* file is a delimited file.

5. Recreate the table using the **CREATE TABLE** statement from the recovery history file, obtained in step 1.

6. Import the table data that was exported during the roll forward operation into the table.

```
IMPORT FROM data OF DEL INSERT INTO table
```

> **NOTE** The DB2 Recovery Expert is a multiplatform tool that you can use to easily recover a dropped table and its dependent objects, including indexes, authorizations, DDL, and data. See the Resources section for more information about this tool.

13.8 THE RECOVERY HISTORY FILE

DB2 keeps tracks of all the backup, restore, and roll forward operations performed in a file called db2rhist.asc, also known as the **recovery history file**. There is a recovery history file for each database, and it is stored in the directory where the database resides. The file is automatically updated when any of the following events occurs:

- A database or table space is backed up
- A database or table space is restored
- A database or table space is rolled forward
- A table space is created
- A table space is altered
- A table space is quiesced
- A table space is renamed
- A table space is dropped
- A table is loaded
- A table is dropped
- A table is reorganized

To see the entries in the recovery history file, use the **LIST HISTORY** command. For example, to list all the backup operations performed on the SAMPLE database, issue

```
LIST HISTORY BACKUP ALL FOR sample
```

The output looks like this:

```
Op Obj Timestamp+Sequence Type Dev Earliest Log Current Log  Backup ID
-- --- ------------------ ---- --- ------------ ------------ ---------
 B  D  20050529122918001   D    D  S0000007.LOG S0000007.LOG
```

```
----------------------------------------------------------------
Contains 3 tablespace(s):

00001 SYSCATSPACE
00002 USERSPACE1
00003 SYSTOOLSPACE
----------------------------------------------------------------
   Comment: DB2 BACKUP SAMPLE OFFLINE
Start Time: 20050529122918
  End Time: 20050529122939
    Status: A
----------------------------------------------------------------
 EID: 21 Location: d:\temp\SAMPLE.0\DB2\NODE0000\CATN0000\20050529
```

For each backup operation performed, an entry like the one shown above is entered in the history file. The following list shows the information recorded and includes the corresponding information from the preceding output.

- The time of the operation: 20050529122918001
- The command used: DB2 BACKUP SAMPLE OFFLINE
- The table spaces that were backed up: SYSCATSPACE, USERSPACE1, and SYSTOOLSPACE
- The location of the backup image: d:\temp\SAMPLE.0\DB2\NODE0000\CATN0000\20050529

If an error occurred during the operation, the error will be recorded as well.

With the recovery history file, you can easily track all the backup operations, restore operations, and more.

V8.2 13.9 DATABASE RECOVERY USING THE **RECOVER DATABASE** COMMAND

DB2 Version 8.2 introduces a very simple new **RECOVER DATABASE** command that combines the **RESTORE** and **ROLLFORWARD** command operations into one step. The **RECOVER DATABASE** command automatically determines which backup image to use by referring to the information in the Recovery History file. For example:

- To recover the SAMPLE database from the best available backup image and rollforward to end of logs, use:

  ```
  RECOVER DB sample
  ```
- To recover the SAMPLE database to the Point In Time 2004-05-21-13.50.00 (note that the PIT is specified in local time, not UTC time), issue:

  ```
  RECOVER DB sample TO 2004-05-21-13.50.00
  ```
- To recover the SAMPLE database to an old PIT that is no longer contained in the current history file, you need to provide a saved history file from this time period:

  ```
  RECOVER DB sample
     TO 1999-12-31-04:00:00
     USING HISTORY FILE (/home/user/old1999files/db2rhist.asc)
  ```

13.10 HIGH AVAILABILITY THROUGH ONLINE SPLIT MIRRORING AND SUSPENDED I/O SUPPORT

Although the online backup method provides the ability to take a database backup without having to bring down the database, for a large database this process, and the process of restoring from the backup, could be time-consuming.

DB2's split mirroring and suspended I/O support solve this problem. With split mirroring, you can take a disk mirror image of the current database using your operating system's utility and put this mirror image into a new database. This process has the following advantages over the traditional DB2 backup method:

- It eliminates backup operation overhead from the primary server.
- It is a faster way to set up a new database using the mirror image. No DB2 restore operation is necessary.

13.10.1 Split Mirroring Key Concepts

Splitting a mirror means creating an "instantaneous" copy of the primary database by writing the data to a hard disk. When required, this disk copy can be used to clone a new, but identical database.

The method you choose to split the mirror is not within the control of DB2. You could take a file system copy of the database directory if you wish. However, we strongly recommend that you use any intelligent storage devices, such as the IBM Enterprise Storage Server (ESS), known as "Shark," and the EMC Symmetrix 3330. Using the FlashCopy technology, the ESS can establish near-instantaneous copies of the data entirely within itself. The instant split feature of EMC TimeFinder software on Symmetrix is also capable of splitting the mirror in a similar manner.

A split mirror of a database includes the entire contents of the database directory, all the table space containers, and the local database directory. The active log directory may or may not be included, depending on how you want to clone your database, which will be discussed later.

When splitting the mirror, it is important to ensure that there are no page writes occurring on the source database. DB2's **suspended I/O** support allows online splitting mirroring without shutting down the database. While the database is in write-suspended mode, all of its table spaces are placed in SUSPEND_WRITE state. All operations continue to function normally. However, some transactions may have to wait if they require disk I/O. These transactions will proceed normally once the write operations on the database are resumed. Use the following commands to suspend and resume write operations on a database.

To suspend write operations:

```
SET WRITE SUSPEND FOR DATABASE
```

To resume write operations:

```
SET WRITE RESUME FOR DATABASE
```

Because the split mirror was taken while the database was in write-suspend mode, it is not usable right away. You must use the **db2inidb** command to initialize the split mirror database to a functional state. The syntax for the db2inidb command is:

```
db2inidb database_alias
as snapshot | standby | mirror
[relocate using config_file]
```

You can choose to initialize the split mirror database in three different ways.

- **Snapshot** uses the split mirror to clone a database.
- **Standby** uses the split mirror to create a standby database.
- **Mirror** uses the split mirror as a backup image of the primary database.

If you use the Snapshot or the Standby option, by default, the split mirror database cannot exist on the same system as the primary database, because it must have the same directory structure and use the same instance name as the primary database. (You cannot share the same database directory between two databases.) If the mirrored database must exist on the same system as the primary database, you can use the **db2relocatedb** utility or the **RELOCATE USING** option of the **db2inidb** command to accomplish this. This restriction does not apply to the Mirror option (you will see why in section 13.10. 4, Creating a Backup Image of the Primary Database Using the db2inidb Mirror Option.).

13.10.2 Cloning a Database Using the db2inidb Snapshot Option

When you clone a database using the **db2inidb** command and the **snapshot** option, the split mirror database goes through a crash recovery during the initialization. After the crash recovery is completed, the database is usable. It cannot roll forward any log files from the source database.

Follow these steps to create a clone database using the **db2inidb snapshot** option.

1. Suspend I/O on the source database by issuing:
   ```
   CONNECT TO source-database
   SET WRITE SUSPEND FOR DATABASE
   ```
2. Split the mirror. This process differs from vendor to vendor. Please consult the storage vendor documentation applicable to your device on how to create a split mirror. Regardless of the variations on the split mirror process, all of the following must be split at the same time:
   - The entire contents of the database directory
   - All the table space containers
   - The local database directory
   - The active log directory, if it does not reside on the database directory
3. You can resume I/O on the source database by issuing the following command (note that you must use the same connection session from step 1 when issuing this command):
   ```
   SET WRITE RESUME FOR DATABASE
   ```

4. Make the split mirror accessible.

    A. On the target server, create the same DB2 instance as it is on the primary server.

    B. Restore all the items obtained from step 2 to exactly the same paths as they are on the primary server.

    C. Run the following command to catalog the database on the target server:

```
CATALOG DATABASE database-name as database_alias on path
```

    where **database_alias** must match the database alias of the primary database, and **path** must match the database path of the primary database (use the **LIST DB DIRECTORY** command to display the database path).

5. Initialize the split mirror database to be a clone database.

    A. Start the instance on the target server using the **db2start** command.

    B. Initialize the split mirror database using the snapshot option:

```
db2inidb database_alias as snapshot
```

This **db2inidb** command initiates a crash recovery, which rolls back all uncommitted transactions at the time of split mirroring, thereby making the database consistent. It is essential to have all the log files from the source that were active at the time of the split. The active log directory must not contain any log file that is not a part of the split mirror. After the completion of the crash recovery, the database is available for operation.

13.10.3 Creating a Standby Database Using the db2inidb Standby Option

When you create a database using the **standby** option, no crash recovery takes place. The split mirror database will be placed in a roll forward pending state following the initialization process. The log files of the source database must be applied on the target database before it is usable.

To create a standby database using the **db2inidb standby** option, follow these steps.

1. Suspend I/O on the source database.

```
SET WRITE SUSPEND FOR DATABASE
```

2. Split the mirror.

    Use the appropriate method to split mirror from the primary database:

- The entire contents of the database directory
- All the table space containers
- The local database directory

    You do *not* need to split the active log directory in this scenario.

3. Resume I/O on the source database.

```
SET WRITE RESUME FOR DATABASE
```

4. Make the split mirror accessible.

    Follow the same steps in the snapshot scenario to make the split mirror accessible. If the active log directory of the primary database does not reside in the database directory, then you must manually create this on the target server. (This is because the active log directory is not included in the split mirror in this scenario.)

5. Initialize the spilt mirror database as a standby database.

The following command initializes the database and puts it in a rollforward pending state, so logs from the source database can be applied.

```
db2inidb database_alias as standby
```

6. Roll forward the logs obtained from the source database.

Copy all the logs currently in the active log directory of the source database to the active log directory of the target database. Issue the following command to roll forward the logs:

```
ROLLFORWARD DB database_alias TO END OF LOGS AND COMPLETE
```

After the roll forward process is completed, the database is ready for use.

13.10.4 Creating a Backup Image of the Primary Database Using the db2inidb Mirror Option

You can use the **mirror** option of the **db2inidb** command to create a quick mirror file backup of a primary database. The split mirror can be used to restore the primary database if needed. This procedure can be used instead of performing the backup and restore database operations on the primary database.

The following are the steps to create a backup image of the source database using the db2inidb mirror option.

1. Suspend I/O on the source database.

```
SET WRITE SUSPEND FOR DATABASE
```

2. Split the mirror. Use the appropriate method to split mirror from the primary database:

- The entire contents of the database directory
- All the table space containers
- The local database directory

You do *not* need to split the active log directory in this scenario.

3. Resume I/O on the source database.

```
SET WRITE RESUME FOR DATABASE
```

4. Restore the primary database using the split mirror image. There is no "target" database in this scenario. The intent of this scenario is to use the mirror copy to recover the primary database when needed.

A. Stop the instance using the **db2stop** command.

B. Copy the data files of the split mirror database over the original database.

C. Start the instance using the **db2start** command.

D. Issue the following command to initialize the split mirror database. This replaces the source database with the split mirror image and places it into a rollforward pending state, so logs can be reapplied.

```
db2inidb database_alias as mirror
```

E. Roll forward the database to end of logs. After the roll forward process is completed, the database is ready for use.

```
ROLLFORWARD DB database_alias TO END OF LOGS AND COMPLETE
```

13.10.5 Split Mirroring in Partitioned Environments

In a partitioned database environment, you must suspend the I/O on each partition during the split mirror process, but the I/O must be resumed on each partition afterwards. The same applies to the **db2inidb** tool, which must be run on each mirrored partition to initialize the database.

Because each partition is treated independently, the partitions can be suspended independently of one another. That means you do not need to issue a **db2_all** to suspend I/O on all of the partitions. The recommended way is to suspend the partitions individually. In this case, you must suspend the catalog partition last, because an attempt to suspend I/O on any of the non-catalog nodes requires a connection to the catalog partition for authorization. If the catalog partition is suspended, then the connection attempt may hang.

The **db2inidb** tool does not require any connections to the database. Therefore, you can run the tool independently on each split mirror, or you can use **db2_all** to run it on all partitions simultaneously. The only requirement is for the database manager to be started.

For example, to suspend writes on a database with three partitions, 0, 1, 2, with partition 0 being the catalog partition, issue:

```
export DB2NODE=1
db2 terminate
db2 connect to database_alias
db2 set write suspend for database

export DB2NODE=2
db2 terminate
db2 connect to database_alias
db2 set write suspend for database

export DB2NODE=0
db2 terminate
db2 connect to database_alias
db2 set write suspend for database
```

To run **db2inidb** on all partitions simultaneously, issue:

```
db2_all "db2inidb database_alias as standby|snapshot|mirror"
```

V8.2 13.11 HIGH AVAILABILITY DISASTER RECOVERY

High Availability Disaster Recovery (HADR) uses log record shipping to keep a standby database in synch with your primary database. Then if that primary server fails, your applications can automatically switch their processing to the secondary server with absolutely no data loss.

13.11.1 Overview of HADR

DB2 **High Availability Disaster Recovery** (HADR) is a database replication feature that provides a high-availability and disaster recovery solution for complete as well as partial site failures. HADR is available as part of DB2 Enterprise Server Edition, and as an additional cost option on DB2 Workgroup Server Edition and DB2 Express Edition. In an HADR environment you will have two database servers, the primary and secondary.

The primary server is where the source database is stored and accessed (see Figure 13.10). As transactions are processed on the source database server, database log records are automatically shipped to the secondary server. The secondary server has a database that is cloned from the source database, typically by backing up the database and restoring it. When HADR is started, log records are captured on the primary database and sent to the secondary database. Once received they are replayed on the secondary database. Through continuous replay of the log records, the secondary database keeps an in-synch replica of the primary database and acts as a standby database.

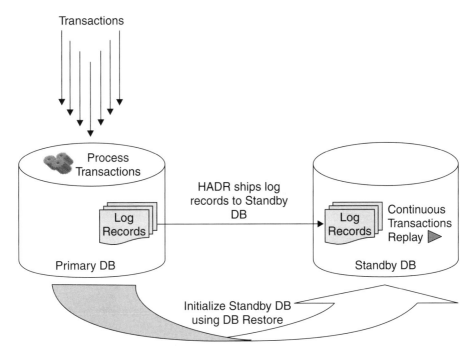

Figure 13.10   Overview of HADR

When a failure occurs on the primary database, the standby database takes over the transactional workload and becomes the new primary database (see Figure 13.11). If the failed server later becomes available again, it can be resynchronized to catch up with the new primary database and the transactions that have been performed. At this time the former primary database now becomes the new standby database (see Figure 13.12).

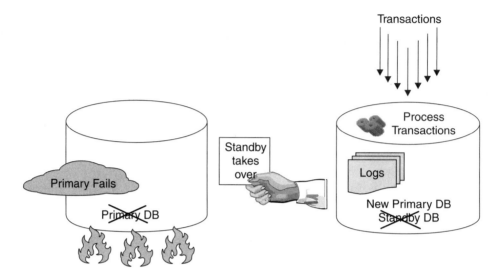

Figure 13.11   Standby database taking over primary database role

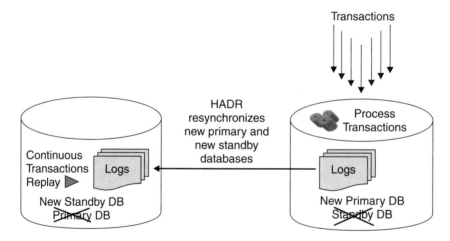

Figure 13.12   New standby database resynchronizes and catches up with the new primary DB

13.11.2 Overview of HADR Setup

Now that you understand how HADR works, let's take a closer look at the steps for setting up HADR.

13.11.2.1 Preparing the Primary and Standby Databases for HADR

After you have identified the HADR pair (i.e., the primary and standby databases), you need to enable archival logging on the primary database (see section 13.2.4.2, Archival Logging).

You also need to configure the database configuration parameters that are related to HADR on the primary and standby databases. Table 13.3 lists these parameters.

Table 13.3 HADR-Related Database Configuration Parameters

HADR-Related DB CFG Parameter	Description
HADR_LOCAL_HOST	Specifies the local host (i.e., TCP/IP server information) for HADR communication. Either a host name or an IP address can be used.
HADR_LOCAL_SVC	Specifies the TCP/IP service name or port number on which the HADR process accepts connections.
HADR_REMOTE_HOST	Specifies the TCP/IP host name or IP address of the secdondary HADR node.
HADR_REMOTE_SVC	Specifies the TCP service name or port number that will be used by the secondary HADR node.
HADR_REMOTE_INST	Specifies the instance name of the secondary server. Administration tools, such as the DB2 Control Center, use this parameter to contact the server.
HADR_TIMEOUT	Specifies the time (in seconds) that the HADR process will wait before determining that a communication attempt has failed.
HADR_SYNCMODE	Specifies the synchronization mode. It determines how primary log writes are synchronized with the standby database when the systems are in peer state (see section 13.11.2.3, Starting the Standby Database). Valid values are SYNC, NEARSYNC, or ASYNC (see section 13.11.3, Synchronization Modes).
HADR_DB_ROLE	Specifies the current role of a database (STANDARD, PRIMARY, or STANDBY) and whether it is online or offline.

13.11.2.2 Cloning the Primary Database

You can clone the primary database by taking a full database backup of the primary database, copy the backup image to the standby system, and restore it to a new or existing standby database. After the database restore, the standby database is placed in roll forward pending state. This means that the standby database will not be active to process any read or write transactions until it takes over the primary database role in the event of a failover.

Note that strict symmetry of table space and container configuration is required on the standby database. The name, path, and size of the containers must match the primary database. If any of the configurations do not match, HADR may fail to replicate the data to the standby database.

13.11.2.3 Starting the Standby Database

When the standby database is started, it enters the local catch-up state. Pending log records (if any) will be replayed on the standby database (see Figure 13.13).

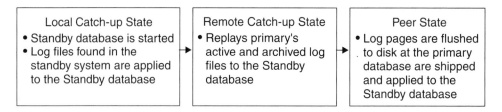

Figure 13.13　States of the standby database

When the end of any local pending log records is reached, the standby database enters the remote catch-up state. It replays log records from the primary database until the standby database is caught up. The primary database must be active for the standby database to be in the remote catch-up state.

When all of the log records on the primary system have been replayed, the primary and standby databases enter the **peer state**, which is when log records are shipped and applied to the standby database whenever the primary database flushes these log records to disk. You can specify one of the three synchronization modes to protect from potential loss of data (see section 13.11.3, Synchronization Modes).

13.11.2.4 Starting the Primary Database

When the primary database is started, the primary server waits for the standby server to contact it. If the standby server does not make a contact with the primary server after a period of time, HADR will not start. You can configure this timeout period using the HADR_TIMEOUT configuration parameter (see Table 13.3). This configuration avoids having two systems starting up as the primary server at the same time.

13.11.3 Synchronization Modes

Recall that when the HADR-enabled databases are in the peer state, log pages that are flushed to the log file on disk at the primary database are shipped and applied to the standby database. To indicate how log writing is managed between the primary and standby databases, you specify the synchronization mode. There are three synchronization modes: SYNC (Synchronous), NEARSYNC (Near Synchronous), and ASYNC (Asynchronous).

In **synchronous (SYNC) mode**, log writes are considered successful only when:

- Log records are written to the log files on disk on the the primary database.
- The primary database has received acknowledgement from the standby database that log records are successfully applied on the standby database.
- The log data is guaranteed to be stored at both sites.

Figure 13.14 shows how the log records are built on the primary server and sent to the secondary server. They are processed on both servers to keep the databases in synch. The application will not be able to proceed until both servers have been updated.

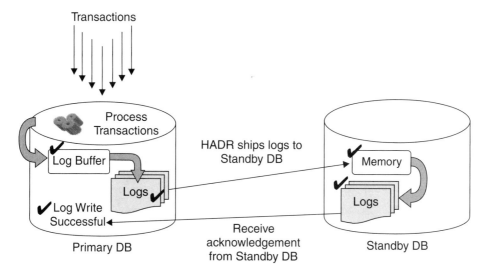

Figure 13.14   Synchronization mode: SYNC

Log records in the primary and standby database are almost (**NEARSYNC**) asynchronous because log writes are considered successful only when:

- Log records have been written to the log files on the primary database.
- The primary database has received acknowledgement from the standby database that log records are successfully written to main memory on the standby database.
- Loss of data occurs only if both sites fail simultaneously and if the target site has not transferred to nonvolatile storage all of the log data that it has received.

Figure 13.15 shows how the log records are built on the primary server and sent to the secondary server. As soon as the log record is received on the secondary database, the application can continue with other operations.

In **ASYNC** mode, the primary database does not wait for acknowledgement from the standby database. Log writes are considered successful only when:

- Log records have been written to the log files on the primary database.
- Log records have been delivered to the standby database; no acknowledgement is expected.
- A failure on the primary database host server, network, or standby database can cause log files in transit to be lost.

Figure 13.16 shows how the log records are built on the primary server and sent to the secondary server. As soon as the log record is sent to the secondary database, the application can continue with other operations.

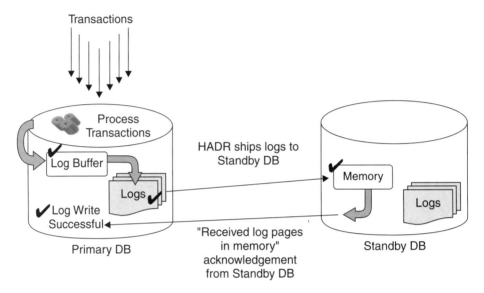

Figure 13.15   Synchronization mode: NEARASYNC

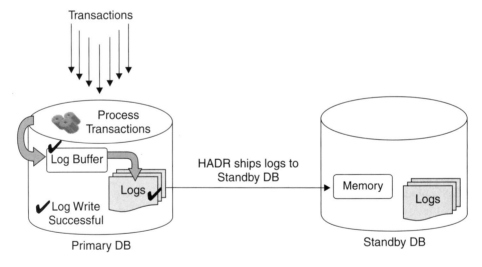

Figure 13.16   Synchronization mode: ASYNC

13.11.4 The HADR Wizard

As you can see, the HADR is a powerful feature that you can use to implement a high-availability solution. Like any other technology, it needs an interface so that users can exploit its features more efficiently. The HADR Wizard is user-friendly graphical tool that helps you set up, configure, and manage the HADR databases.

The HADR Wizard guides you through the tasks required to set up the HADR environment, stopping and starting HADR, and switching database roles in HADR. To launch the wizard, go to the Control Center, right-click on the database, and select **High Availability Disaster Recovery**. As shown in Figure 13.17, you can choose to set up or manage HADR.

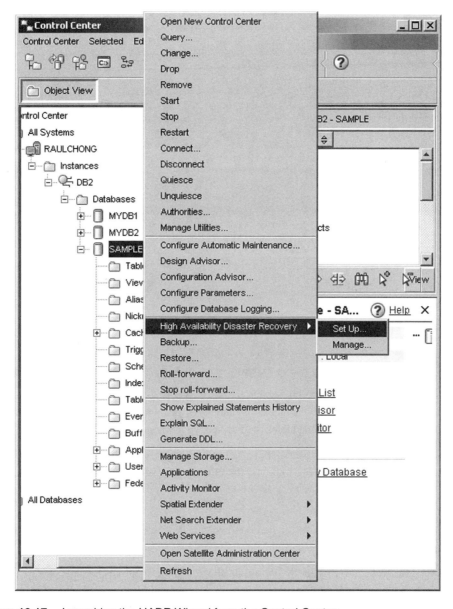

Figure 13.17 Launching the HADR Wizard from the Control Center

Choosing **Set Up** launches the HADR Wizard, as shown in Figure 13.18, which will step you through the process.

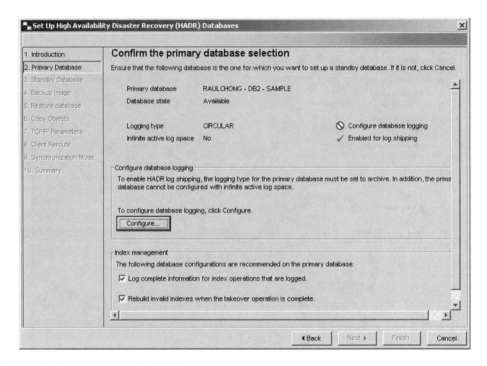

Figure 13.18   Setting up the HADR environment

13.12 Using DB2 Tools to Inspect the Health of Your Database

Both hardware and software problems can potentially corrupt data pages in your database. When a page is corrupted, its data becomes unusable, and users trying to access this page will receive an error. If a page in the system catalog tables is corrupted, your whole database may become unusable.

DB2 provides two tools to check for database corruptions and possibly fix them. One is **db2dart**, the database analysis and reporting tool, and the other tool is called the **INSPECT** tool.

13.12.1 The db2dart Tool

You can only use the **db2dart** tool when the database is offline, so no connections are allowed while the database is being inspected.

You can use **db2dart** to inspect the whole database, a table space in the database, or a single table. When the inspection ends, it presents the results in a nicely organized report, deposited in the directory where the **db2dart** command was issued (on Linux/UNIX), or the *db2_install_ dir\instance_name*\DART0000 directory (on Windows). The report has the name *dbalias.RPT*.

The syntax for the command is:

```
db2dart DBALIAS [OPTIONS]
```

Type **db2dart** from the command line to see the list of all available options.

The following are some ways you can use `db2dart`.

- To perform an inspection on all objects in the *sample* database, issue:
  ```
  db2dart sample
  ```
- To inspect table space USERSPACE1 in the *sample* database, issue:
  ```
  db2dart sample /TSI 2
  ```
  where **2** is the table space ID for table space *USERSPACE1*. Table space IDs can be found in the **LIST TABLESPACES** output.
- To inspect the *sales* table in the *sample* database, issue:
  ```
  db2dart sample /TSI 2 /TN "sales"
  ```

If **db2dart** reports some data pages being corrupted, restore the database using a good backup image.

If **db2dart** reports some index pages being corrupted, you can fix this instead of having to restore from a backup.

If **db2dart** reports an index is corrupted, take the following steps to fix it.

1. Mark the index invalid using:
   ```
   db2dart dbalias /MI /OI objectID of the index /TSI tablespaceID
   ```
   where both the `objectID` and `tablespaceID` can be found in the **db2dart** report.
2. Let DB2 automatically rebuild the index. When DB2 actually rebuilds this index depends on the INDEXREC database configuration parameter setting. Its values can be ACCESS, RESTART, or SYSTEM.
   - **ACCESS**: DB2 rebuilds invalid indexes when they are accessed again for the first time, after they have been invalidated by **db2dart**. With this method, the first user who accesses this index will experience a longer wait while the index is recreated.
   - **RESTART**: DB2 rebuilds invalid indexes when the database is restarted. With this method, the time taken to restart the database will be longer due to index re-creation, but normal processing is not impacted once the database has been brought back online.
   - **SYSTEM**: DB2 uses the setting in the INDEXREC at the database manager level.

> **NOTE** INDEXREC is available as a database configuration parameter and a Database Manager Configuration parameter. As a Database Manager Configuration parameter, the value of INDEXREC affects all databases that have INDEXREC set to SYSTEM. With this dual-level setting, you can choose to control the index recreation at instance level or at individual database levels.

13.12.2 The INSPECT tool

Unlike **db2dart**, the **INSPECT** tool runs while the database is online. The **INSPECT** tool inspects databases for architectural integrity and checks the pages of the database for page consistency. However, it cannot be used to mark an index invalid as can the **db2dart** tool.

The results file of the inspection is generated in the DB2 diagnostic data directory (i.e., where the db2diag.log file is). This is a binary file; you need to format it with the **DB2INSPF** command. If no errors are found, by default, the results file is erased after the inspect operation is complete, unless the **KEEP** option is used.

- To inspect the SAMPLE database and write the results to a file called *inspect.out*, issue:

```
CONNECT TO sample
INSPECT CHECK DATABASE RESULTS inspect.out
```

- To inspect the table space with table space ID *2* and keep the results and write it to the file *inspect.out*, issue:

```
CONNECT TO sample
INSPECT CHECK TABLSPACE TBSPACEID 2 RESULTS KEEP inspect.out
```

- To format the results file, issue:

```
DB2INSPF results_file output file
```

where *results_file* is from the **inspect** command.

13.13 CASE STUDY

You have just been assigned a new task: to clone the production database PROD1 on a Windows server to another Windows test server. These are the criteria:

- The cloned database name is TEST1.
- The containers for TEST1 must be redefined. They must reside on the D: drive of the test server.
- TEST1 must contain the most recent data in PROD1.

1. First, take a backup of the database PROD1. Because PROD1 is a 24x7 production database, it is not possible to perform an offline backup. Therefore, you decide to perform an online backup:

```
db2 backup db prod1 online to d:\temp
```

The backup image is created as:

```
D:\temp\PROD1.0\DB2\NODE0000\CATN0000\20040414\170803.001
```

2. Obtain the table space container information on PROD1. This information is needed to define table space containers for the test database.
    A. First, list all table spaces in PROD1, as shown in Figure 13.19.
    B. Then, list the containers for each table space, as shown in Figure 13.20.
    Since all three table spaces are SMS table spaces, all the containers are directories.
3. Transfer the backup image over to the test server. FTP the backup image, including the folders and directories starting at D:\temp, over to the test server.

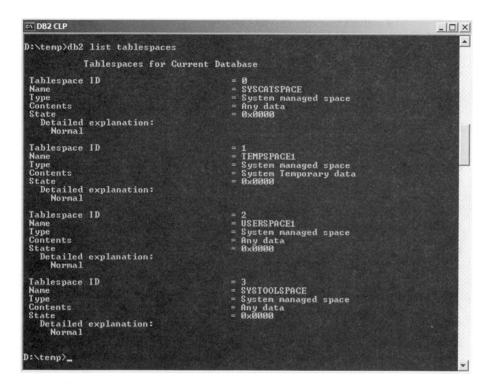

Figure 13.19   Getting table space information from PROD1

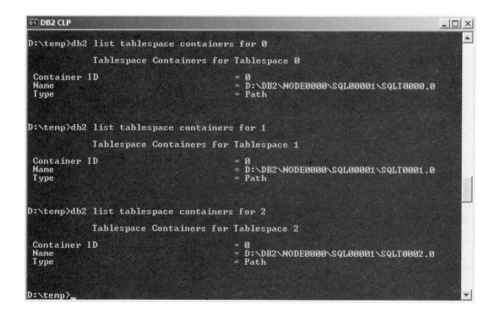

Figure 13.20   Getting container information from PROD1

4. Perform a database redirected restore and define the table space containers for database TEST1, as shown in Figure 13.21.

Figure 13.21   Performing redirected restore of PROD1 into TEST1

5. Perform a roll forward on the newly restored database TEST.

    A. At this point, you cannot connect to TEST1 yet. A connect attempt will receive the error SQL1117N.

    B. To roll forward, you need to find out which logs are needed. Run the **ROLLFORWARD DATABASE** command with the **QUERY STATUS** option (see Figure 13.22).

        Figure 13.22 shows the next log file to be read is S0000000.LOG. This means that you have to transfer all the logs in the active log directory of PROD1, starting at S0000000.LOG, to the active log directory of TEST1.

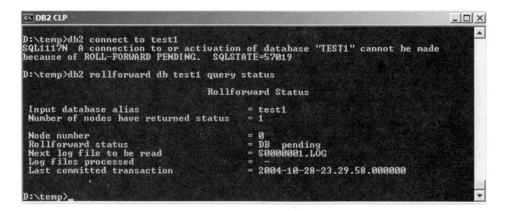

Figure 13.22   Finding out which logs are needed to perform roll forward

    C. To find out where the active log directory is for PROD1, issue the **GET DB CFG FOR**
       prod1 command. The active log directory is indicated as `Path to log files`.

```
Path to log files                    = D:\DB2\NODE0000\SQL00003\SQLOGDIR\
```

    D. The logs in this directory are: S0000000.LOG, S0000001.LOG, S0000002.LOG,
       and S0000003.LOG. Transfer all of these logs to the test server and into the active
       log directory of TEST1, which is on D:\DB2\NODE0000\SQL00001\SQLOGDIR\.
       (If you list this directory, you will see that it is currently empty.)

    E. Perform a roll forward operation on TEST1, as shown in Figure 13.23.

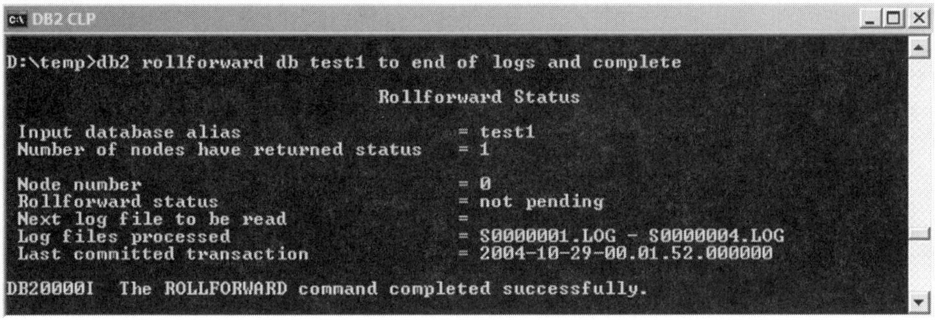

Figure 13.23   Performing the roll forward operation on TEST1

    6. Connect to TEST1 and verify that it contains the correct data.

13.14 SUMMARY

In this chapter you have learned the concepts of unit of work, (UOW), logging methods, and different recovery strategies.

A unit of work (UOW) is composed of one or more statements and completed by a **COMMIT** or **ROLLBACK**. If the UOW is interrupted in the middle, all statements executed up to that point will be rolled back. This ensures data integrity.

When a database is connected for the first time, DB2 allocates a number of primary logs, based on the setting in the LOGPRIMARY database configuration parameter. When there are not enough primary logs, DB2 allocates secondary logs, one at a time. When the maximum number of secondary logs is reached, specified by the LOGSECOND database parameter, DB2 encounters a log full condition. At this point, any uncommitted transactions are rolled back.

There are three types of database recoveries: crash, version, and roll forward recovery. Crash recovery and version recovery are the defaults. To enable roll forward recovery, you have to enable archival logging.

There are three logging methods in DB2: circular, archival, and infinite active logging. Circular logging is the default logging method. However, it does not support roll forward recovery.

Archival logging is enabled by setting the LOGARCHMETH1 database configuration parameter. Both archival logging and infinite active logging support roll forward recovery.

In DB2 Version 8.2, the new command **RECOVER DATABASE** combines both the **RESTORE** and **ROLLFORWARD** commands into one easy step. No backup image needs to be specified; the **RECOVER DATABASE** command will choose the best backup image possible to complete the recovery task.

Write suspend (aka suspended I/O) support offers a much faster way to perform database backups. This is achieved by taking an instantaneous disk copy of the primary database while it is in a write-suspend mode. During this time, all write operations on the database are suspended; however, other database functions still function normally. After the split mirror is completed, the database is returned to its normal state. No restore operation is needed to restore the split mirror into a new database. Instead, you use the **db2inidb** command to initialize the split mirrored database. There are three ways you can initialize the split mirror: as a clone database, a standby database, or a backup image of the primary database.

A new high-availability feature is introduced in Version 8.2: the High Availability Disaster Recovery (HADR) feature. The HADR setup requires both a primary server and a secondary server. The log pages that are flushed to the log file on disk at the primary database are constantly shipped and applied to the secondary database. When a failure occurs on the primary database, a takeover operation is initiated on the secondary database, which then becomes the new primary. Since the secondary database is already online, failover can be accomplished very quickly, resulting in minimal downtime.

DB2 provides two tools to inspect your database. The **db2dart** tool is an offline database analysis and reporting tool. In addition to inspecting a database, it can be used to mark an index invalid so it can be rebuilt. If your database is a 24x7 database, an inspection by **db2dart** is impossible. In that case use the **INSPECT** tool, which can be used while the database is online.

13.15 REVIEW QUESTIONS

1. Besides crash recovery, what are the other two types of recoveries?
2. In DB2 Version 8.2, you can back up the logs along with the database. What option allows you do that?
3. When are secondary logs created and destroyed?
4. What condition triggers the logs to be flushed from the log buffer to log files?
5. What is the maximum log space you can configure for a database?
6. What tool can you use to inspect a database while it is online?
7. What should you do when you find out that an index is corrupted?
8. How do you determine the minimum recovery time for a table space?
9. Which of the following requires manual archival and retrieval of log files?
   A. USEREXIT
   B. DISK

   C. LOGRETAIN

   D. VENDOR

10. A Unit of Work consists of one or more statements, and is terminated by which of the following?

   A. COMMIT

   B. TERMINATE

   C. RESET

   D. ROLL BACK

11. Which of the following is the default logging method used by DB2?

   A. Infinite logging

   B. Circular logging

   C. Archival logging

   D. Round-robin logging

12. Which of the following database configuration parameters specifies the size of log files?

   A. LOGPRIMARY

   B. LOGSECOND

   C. LOGFILSIZ

   D. LOGARCHMETH1

13. Which of the following database configuration parameters specifies a temporary target for archiving logs when the primary targets are not available?

   A. LOGARCHMETH1

   B. LOGARCHMETH2

   C. FAILARCHPATH

   D. LOGARCHOPT2

14. Given that you must restore a database from backup, which of the following objects must be available in order to recover the transactions performed after a backup was taken?

   A. Table space backups

   B. Buffer pools

   C. Logs

   D. Database snapshot output

15. Given the following database configuration information:

```
Number of primary log files (LOGPRIMARY) = 5
Number of secondary log files (LOGSECOND) = 5
Path to log files = C:\logsforDB1\
```

which of the following correctly lists the contents of the C:\logsforDB1 directory immediately after issuing the activate database command for the database, if log retain is *not* enabled?

   A. Directory of C:\LOGSFORDB1\

```
2004-03-10 06:06p 1,032,192 S0000000.LOG
2004-03-10 06:06p 1,032,192 S0000001.LOG
```

```
2004-03-10 06:06p 1,032,192 S0000002.LOG
2004-03-10 06:06p 1,032,192 S0000003.LOG
2004-03-10 06:06p 1,032,192 S0000004.LOG
```

B. Directory of C:\MYLOGS\

```
2004-03-10 06:06p 1,032,192 S0000001.LOG
2004-03-10 06:06p 1,032,192 S0000002.LOG
2004-03-10 06:06p 1,032,192 S0000003.LOG
2004-03-10 06:06p 1,032,192 S0000004.LOG
2004-03-10 06:06p 1,032,192 S0000005.LOG
```

C. Directory of C:\LOGSFORDB1\

```
2004-03-10 06:06p 1,032,192 S0000000.LOG
2004-03-10 06:06p 1,032,192 S0000001.LOG
2004-03-10 06:06p 1,032,192 S0000002.LOG
2004-03-10 06:06p 1,032,192 S0000003.LOG
2004-03-10 06:06p 1,032,192 S0000004.LOG
2004-03-10 06:06p 1,032,192 S0000005.LOG
2004-03-10 06:06p 1,032,192 S0000006.LOG
2004-03-10 06:06p 1,032,192 S0000007.LOG
2004-03-10 06:06p 1,032,192 S0000008.LOG
2004-03-10 06:06p 1,032,192 S0000009.LOG
```

D. Directory of C:\MYLOGS\

```
2004-03-10 06:06p 1,032,192 S0000001.LOG
2004-03-10 06:06p 1,032,192 S0000002.LOG
2004-03-10 06:06p 1,032,192 S0000003.LOG
2004-03-10 06:06p 1,032,192 S0000004.LOG
2004-03-10 06:06p 1,032,192 S0000005.LOG
2004-03-10 06:06p 1,032,192 S0000006.LOG
2004-03-10 06:06p 1,032,192 S0000007.LOG
2004-03-10 06:06p 1,032,192 S0000008.LOG
2004-03-10 06:06p 1,032,192 S0000009.LOG
2004-03-10 06:06p 1,032,192 S0000010.LOG
```

16. Which of the following activates infinite active log space?

   A. Logsecond = 0
   B. Logprimary = 0
   C. Logsecond =-1
   D. Logprimary = -1

17. Which of the following configuration parameters enables online backups?

   A. Logsecond = 0
   B. Logarchmeth1 = off
   C. Logarchmeth1 = logretain
   D. Mirror log path = userexit

18. Which of the following configuration parameters enables table space backups?

   A. Logsecond = 0
   B. Logarchmeth1 = off
   C. Logarchmeth1 = logretain
   D. Mirror log path = userexit

19. Which of the following is not allowed during a redirected restore?

   A. Change from DMS file to DMS raw containers

    B. Change from DMS file to SMS containers

    C. Change the number of containers in an SMS table space

    D. Change the number of containers in a DMS table space

20. Given a DB2 client in the Central time zone, and a DB2 server in the Eastern time zone, when the command `ROLLFORWARD DATABASE sample TO *timestamp* USING LOCAL TIME` is issued on the client server, which time is used?

    A. The time on the client

    B. The time on the server

21. Which of the following is not a valid option for the **db2inidb** command?

    A. Standby

    B. Mirror

    C. Snapshot

    D. Backup

22. To create a backup image of the source database using split mirror, which of the following options should be used?

    A. Standby

    B. Mirror

    C. Snapshot

    D. Backup

CHAPTER 14

The DB2 Process Model

ave you ever wondered what happens "behind the scenes" when your application connects to the database server? What handles the request? What actually does the work and returns you the results? When you check your system, you may see many DB2 processes. What are these processes, and what are they used for? Understanding the different types of DB2 processes and how DB2 works will help you determine the nature of a problem more easily.

In this chapter you will learn about:

- The DB2 process model
- The various types of DB2 processes
- Monitoring and tuning the usage of DB2 agents

14.1 THE DB2 PROCESS MODEL: THE BIG PICTURE

Figure 14.1 shows the DB2 engine process model. This illustrates what happens behind the scenes when a client application connects to a DB2 database.

As shown in Figure 14.1, a client application connects to the DB2 database server using one of the supported communication protocols.

- Local client applications connect to the database server using the Inter-Process Communication (IPC) protocol.
- Remote client applications connect to the database server using the TCP/IP, NetBIOS, or Named Pipes communication protocol.

> **NOTE** NetBIOS and Named Pipes are only supported on Windows platforms.

593

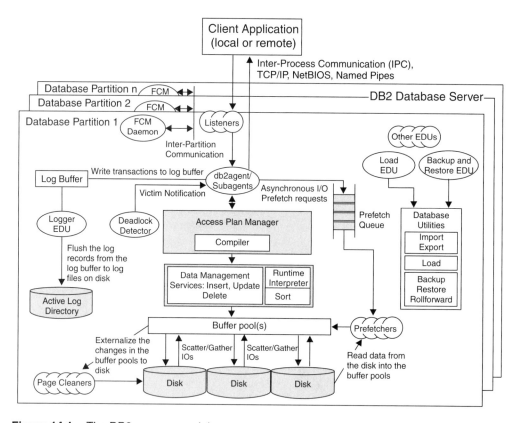

Figure 14.1   The DB2 process model

When a client application connects to the database, the connection request is first accepted by a process known as the **listener**. There are different listeners for different communication protocols:

- *db2ipccm* for local client connections
- *db2tcpcm* for remote TCP/IP connections
- *db2tcpdm* for TCP/IP discovery tool requests

The Configuration Assistant (CA) on the DB2 client makes discovery requests when it is searching the network for remote DB2 servers and their databases. The remote connection listeners are enabled when the DB2COMM registry variable and the appropriate Database Manager Configuration parameters are set (see Chapter 6, Configuring Client and Server Connectivity).

The *db2ipccm* listener is enabled by default; therefore no additional steps are required.

After the listener accepts a client application connection, it will assign a **coordinator agent**, *db2agent,* to work on behalf of that application. This agent will communicate with the application and handle all its requests. If the database server instance is multi-partitioned, or if

INTRA_PARALLEL is set to YES, the coordinator agent will distribute the work to a number of subagents, and its role changes to coordinating these subagents.

> **N O T E**   Both the subagents and coordinator agents work on behalf of the application. They both can be referred to as the **worker agents** for the application.

If the access plan provided by the **Access Plan Manager** specifies prefetching, then the worker agents send the prefetch requests to a **prefetch queue**. (**Prefetching** means that one or more pages are retrieved from disk in the expectation that they will be required by an application. Prefetching helps improve performance by reducing the I/O wait time.)

The prefetch request queue is monitored by processes called **prefetchers**, which take the requests from the queue and service each request by retrieving the required data from disk into the buffer pools.

The amount of data to retrieve for each prefetch request is determined by the prefetch size of the specific table space where the data is stored. (You can optionally specify this value in the **CREATE TABLESPACE** and the **ALTER TABLESPACE** statements, using the PREFETCHSIZE parameter.) If the prefetch size is not specified for a table space, then DB2 uses the value for the DFT_PREFETCH_SZ configuration parameter as the default. The default value is AUTOMATIC, which allows DB2 to calculate an appropriate prefetch size for a table space based on the extent size, the number of containers, and the number of physical spindles per container. This frees you from having to determine the appropriate value for the table space prefetch size. The number of prefetchers is determined by the NUM_IOSERVERS database configuration parameter.

Once the required data is in the buffer pools, the worker agents then perform the updates requested by the application. These updates stay in the buffer pools until a later time, when the **page cleaners** kick in and start writing the changes from the buffer pool to disk in batches. The number of page cleaners is determined by the NUM_IOCLEANERS database configuration parameter. (See Chapter 16, Database Performance Considerations, for information about how the number of page cleaners and prefetchers impact performance.)

All transactions made by the application are logged into DB2 transaction logs by the **logger** process. Logging ensures data recoverability (see the discussion on data recovery in Chapter 13, Developing Database Backup and Recovery Solutions).

There are other database processes that exist in a DB2 engine, such as the **load process** shown in Figure 14.1.

In a DPF environment, the same set of processes exists in each database partition. The **Fast Communications Manager** (FCM) processes (daemons) are responsible for inter-partition communications.

14.2 THE DB2 ENGINE DISPATCHABLE UNITS

Each circle shown in Figure 14.1 represents a DB2 process. The DB2 engine is where these processes live; hence these processes are called DB2 **Engine Dispatchable Units** (EDUs). Therefore, a coordinator agent, a page cleaner, and a subagent are all EDUs.

The EDUs are implemented as **processes** on Linux/UNIX platforms and as **threads** on Windows platforms. Unless explicitly indicated, we use the term *process* in this chapter to refer to both processes on Linux/UNIX and threads on Windows.

Figure 14.2 shows the hierarchy for some main DB2 EDUs.

Figure 14.2 shows a firewall between the client applications and the DB2 engine because the client applications run in a different address space from the DB2 engine. This way, if applications behave in an inappropriate manner, they will not overwrite DB2's internal buffers or files within the DB2 engine.

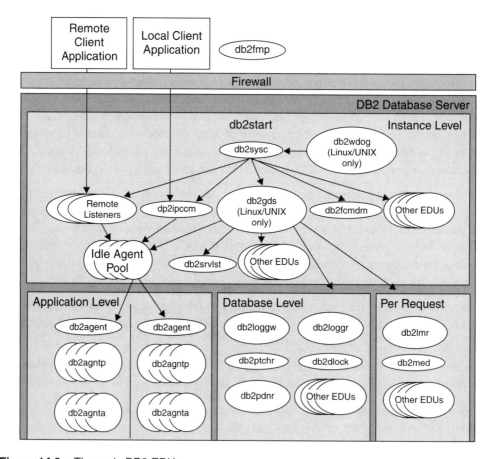

Figure 14.2   The main DB2 EDUs

The *db2fmp* process is the fenced-mode process; it is responsible for executing fenced-stored procedures and user-defined functions outside the firewall. If stored procedures and functions are defined as unfenced, then they will run within the same address space as the DB2 engine. By doing so, the performance of stored procedures and functions can be improved. However, there is an added potential risk to the DB2 engine: These stored procedures and functions can potentially overwrite DB2 internal buffers, causing DB2 to crash. This is why stored procedures and user functions should never run unfenced unless tested thoroughly.

In Figure 14.2, the EDUs are grouped in different levels. Let's look at what role each of them plays.

14.2.1 The DB2 Instance-Level EDUs

The core engine process is the DB2 system controller process, *db2sysc*. This is the first process created when the instance starts. The *db2sysc* process then spawns other processes to perform various tasks, such as the listeners, which listen for client connections.

Table 14.1 lists and describes the DB2 instance-level EDUs.

Table 14.1   The DB2 Instance-Level EDUs

Process Name	Description	Platform
db2cart	Determines when a log file can be archived and invokes the userexit process to do the actual archiving. There is one *db2cart* process per instance, but it only runs if there is at least one database in the instance that has USEREXIT enabled.	All
db2chkau	Used by the DB2 audit facility to log entries to the Audit log. It is only active if auditing has been enabled.	All
db2ckpw	Checks user IDs and passwords on the DB2 server. Since DB2 relies on operating system-level authentication, this process verifies the user ID and password when a user or application connects to a database on the server. This authentication will occur when authentication is set to SERVER or when a connection is made from a nonsecure operating system.	UNIX / Linux
db2disp	The DB2 agent dispatcher process. Dispatches application connections between the logical agent assigned to the application and the available coordinating agents when connection concentration is enabled.

This process will only exist when connection concentration is enabled. | All |

(continues)

Table 14.1   The DB2 Instance-Level EDUs *(Continued)*

Process Name	Description	Platform
db2fcmd	FCM daemon for handling inter-partition communications. One per server, per partition.	Multi-partitioned database environment only
db2fmcd	The fault monitor coordinator daemon. One per physical machine.	UNIX only
db2fmd	The fault monitor daemon that is started for every instance of DB2 that is monitored by the fault monitor. It is monitored by the coordinator daemon (*db2fmcd*), so if you kill the *db2fmd* process, *db2fmcd* will bring it back up.	UNIX only
db2fmtlg	Preallocates log files in the log path when the database is configured with LOGRETAIN ON and USEREXIT OFF. This is done so the engine process does not need to wait while switching from one log file to the next during normal processing.	All
db2gds	The DB2 Global Daemon Spawner. Starts all DB2 EDUs (processes) on UNIX. There is one *db2gds* per instance or database partition.	UNIX only
db2glock	Global deadlock detector. Coordinates the information gathered from the *db2dlock* process on each database partition to check for deadlock conditions that exist between database partitions. The *db2glock* process runs on the catalog partition of a multi-partitioned database.	Multi-partitioned database environment only
db2govd	The DB2 Governor, a reactive governing process that takes snapshots at the interval specified in the governor configuration file and checks the snapshot against all configured rules. If a rule is broken, the specified action is taken. This process only exists when the DB2 governor is enabled.	All
db2panic	The panic agent. Handles urgent requests after agent limits have been reached on any of the database's partitions.	Multi-partitioned database environment only
db2pdbc	The Parallel Database (PDB) Controller. Handles parallel requests from remote nodes.	Multi-partitioned database environment only
db2rebal	The rebalancer process. Called when containers are added to an existing table space and a rebalance of the existing data is required. This process performs the rebalance asynchronously.	All

(continues)

Table 14.1 The DB2 Instance-Level EDUs *(Continued)*

Process Name	Description	Platform
db2resyn	The resync manager process. Supports applications that are using two-phase commit.	All
db2srvlst	Manages lists of addresses for systems such as OS/390.	All
db2sysc	The main DB2 system controller or engine. Without this process, the database server cannot function.	All
db2syslog	The system logger process. Writes to the operating system error log facility. On UNIX, this must be enabled by editing the file syslog.conf. On Windows, DB2 will automatically write the Windows event log.	All
db2wdog	The DB2 watchdog. This process is required since processes in Linux and UNIX can only track their parent process ID. Each time a new process is started, *db2gds* notifies the DB2 watchdog. If any DB2 process receives a CTRL+C or other abnormal signal, the process sends the signal to the watchdog, and it propagates the signal to all of the other processes in the instance.	Linux and UNIX only
dlasync	A monitor for the DB2 Data Links (File Manager) servers. This process only exists if DB2 has been configured for data links.	Data Links only
db2ipccm	IPC communication manager. One per database partition. This is the inter-process communication listener for local client connections. A local client connection is a connection made from an application or the CLP within the same computer where the DB2 server is running.	All
db2tcpcm	TCP communication manager. It works as a communication listener for TCP/IP connection requests. When a connection request is received, the listener associates the connection with an agent and then resumes listening for more connection requests.	All
db2tcpdm	Communication listener for TCP/IP discovery requests. Discovery requests are made by the Configuration Assistant when it is searching the network for remote DB2 servers and their databases.	All

N O T E In a Database Partitioning Feature (DPF) environment, the same set of EDUs is created for each database partition.

Figure 14.3 shows the list of DB2 processes after an instance is started by **db2start**. The instance name is *db2inst1*, and it has two database partitions.

```
      root   29464         1   0  19:49:37    -  0:01  db2wdog 0
      root  418132         1   0  19:49:38    -  0:01  db2wdog 1
  db2inst1  121078    263592   0  19:49:46    -  0:00  db2pdbc 0
  db2inst1  135778    263592   0  19:49:46    -  0:00  db2ipccm 0
  db2inst1  263592     29464   0  19:49:39    -  0:00  db2sysc 0
  db2inst1  269678    394674   0  19:49:45    -  0:00  db2pdbc 1
  db2inst1  297878    263592   0  19:49:45    -  0:00  db2fcmdm 0
  db2inst1  308610    394674   0  19:49:45    -  0:00  db2resync 1
  db2inst1  315772    541832   0  19:49:47    -  0:00  db2srvlst 0
  db2inst1  321520    394674   0  19:49:45    -  0:00  db2ipccm 1
  db2inst1  324388    394674   0  19:49:44    -  0:00  db2gds 1
  db2inst1  341672    394674   0  19:49:44    -  0:00  db2fcmdm 1
  db2inst1  369054    394674   0  19:49:45    -  0:01  db2hmon 1
  db2inst1  394674    418132   0  19:49:40    -  0:00  db2sysc 1
  db2inst1  396446    394674   0  19:49:45    -  0:00  db2panic (idle) 1
  db2inst1  405400    263592   0  19:49:47    -  0:00  db2panic (idle) 0
  db2inst1  456718    263592   0  19:49:47    -  0:01  db2hmon 0
  db2inst1  519040    263592   0  19:49:47    -  0:00  db2resync 0
  db2inst1  541832    263592   0  19:49:41    -  0:00  db2gds 0
  db2inst1  573828    324388   0  19:49:45    -  0:00  db2srvlst 1
```

Figure 14.3   DB2 EDUs after an instance is started

Figure 14.3 shows that each partition has the same set of DB2 EDUs. The last column indicates the partition with which the EDU is associated. Note the *db2wdog* processes are owned by root, not the instance.

On AIX, Linux, and HP-UX, use the **ps −ef | grep *instancename*** command to display the DB2 processes owned by the instance. Alternatively, you can use the **db2_ps** command, which displays the DB2 processes under each database partition.

On Solaris, the **ps −ef** command only shows *db2sysc* for all processes (e.g., listeners, loggers, page cleaners, and prefetchers). To display the DB2 processes with their actual names, use the **db2ptree** command.

14.2.2 The DB2 Database-Level EDUs

When a database starts, it starts several processes to handle database-level tasks such as prefetching, logging, and page cleaning. These processes are spawned by the *db2gds* process on Linux/UNIX platforms and by *db2sysc* on Windows platforms.

Table 14.2 shows the DB2 EDUs at the database level.

Table 14.2 The DB2 Database-Level EDUs

Process Name	Description	Applicability
db2dlock	Local deadlock detector. One per database partition. Scans the lock list and looks for deadlock conditions. When a deadlock condition is encountered, one of the applications/transactions involved is chosen as the victim and rolled back.	All
db2estor	Copies pages between the database buffer pool(s) and extended storage. These processes appear only when extended storage is enabled for a database.	All
db2event	The event monitoring process. There is one *db2event* process per active event monitor, per active database. These processes capture the defined "events" and write to the output file specified for the Event Monitor.	
db2loggr	The database log reader. Reads the database log files during transaction processing (i.e., roll back and roll forward operations) and restart recovery.	All
db2loggw	The database log writer. Flushes log records from the log buffer to the log files on disk.	All
db2logts	Collects historical information about which logs are active when a table space is modified. This information is recorded in the DB2TSCHG.HIS file in the database directory. It speeds up table space roll forward recovery by enabling the skipping of log files that are not needed for the roll forward operation.	All
db2pclnr	The buffer pool page cleaners. Asynchronously writes dirty pages from the buffer pool(s) back to disk. (A dirty page is one that was changed after it was read into the buffer pool, and the image on disk is no longer the same as the image in the buffer pool.) Works to ensure that there is room in the buffer pools for new pages being retrieved for applications. When the page cleaners are "triggered," they all run at the same time. Once they complete their assigned work they sleep until triggered again. The number of page cleaners per database is configured by the NUM_IOCLEANERS database configuration parameter.	All
db2pfchr	The buffer pool prefetchers. Reads data and index information from disk and into the database buffer pool(s) before it is read on behalf of applications. Prefetchers perform this "read-ahead" asynchronously. The DB2 agents, acting on behalf of the applications, send prefetch requests which are serviced by the prefetchers. The prefetchers perform big-block I/O to read the data more efficiently. The number of prefetchers per database is configured by the NUM_IOSERVERS database configuration parameter.	All

Figure 14.4 shows the list of database-level EDUs after the *SAMPLE* database is started by a connection to the database. You can see that a set of database-level processes are created for each partition. For example, each partition has one db2loggr process, one db2dlock process, and three db2pfchr processes.

```
db2inst1   57846 324388    0 19:53:42    -  0:00 db2loggr (SAMPLE) 1
db2inst1   71504 541832    0 19:53:43    -  0:00 db2agent (idle) 0
db2inst1  128880 324388    0 19:53:43    -  0:00 db2event (DB2DETAILDEADLOCK) 1
db2inst1  132764 541832    0 19:53:43    -  0:00 db2pfchr 0
db2inst1  135778 263592    0 19:49:46    -  0:00 db2ipccm 0
db2inst1  169298 541832    0 19:53:43    -  0:00 db2pfchr 0
db2inst1  183970 541832    0 19:53:42    -  0:00 db2lfr (SAMPLE) 0
db2inst1  205302 324388    0 19:53:42    -  0:00 db2lfr (SAMPLE) 1
db2inst1  213500 324388    0 19:53:42    -  0:00 db2pfchr 1
db2inst1  218468 541832    0 19:53:43    -  0:00 db2pclnr 0
db2inst1  246144 541832    0 19:53:43    -  0:00 db2dlock (SAMPLE) 0
db2inst1  275236 324388    0 19:53:42    -  0:00 db2dlock (SAMPLE) 1
db2inst1  355768 324388    0 19:53:42    -  0:00 db2loggw (SAMPLE) 1
db2inst1  381136 541832    0 19:53:42    -  0:00 db2loggw (SAMPLE) 0
db2inst1  419484 541832    0 19:53:43    -  0:00 db2pfchr 0
db2inst1  439484 324388    0 19:53:42    -  0:00 db2glock (SAMPLE) 1
db2inst1  458448 324388    0 19:53:42    -  0:00 db2agntp (SAMPLE) 1
db2inst1  468242 324388    0 19:53:42    -  0:00 db2pclnr 1
db2inst1  483634 541832    0 19:53:42    -  0:00 db2loggr (SAMPLE) 0
db2inst1  492846 324388    0 19:53:42    -  0:00 db2pfchr 1
db2inst1  532004 324388    0 19:53:42    -  0:00 db2pfchr 1
db2inst1  546646 135778    0 19:53:42    -  0:00 db2agent (SAMPLE) 0
```

Figure 14.4   The database-level DB2 EDUs after the SAMPLE database is started

14.2.3 The Application-Level EDUs

Application-level EDUs are agents. After the listener process accepts a client connection, it takes a free agent, *db2agent*, from the idle agent pool. If no free agent is available, a new db2agent will be created. The db2agent becomes the coordinator agent for the application, and it will perform all database operations on behalf of the application. There are four types of DB2 agents.

- Coordinator agents
- Active subagents
- Associated subagents
- Unassociated agents

A **coordinator agent** (db2agent) coordinates the work on behalf of an application and communicates to other agents using the inter-process communication (IPC) protocol (for local connections) or remote communication protocol (for remote connections). Each connection request from client applications is allocated a coordinator agent.

Figure 14.4 shows that the db2agent process

```
db2inst1 546646 135778   0 19:53:42    -  0:00 db2agent (SAMPLE) 0
```

is assigned to a connection to the SAMPLE database. The SAMPLE in parenthesis indicates the database name that the db2agent is associated with. Note that this db2agent process is created by the db2ipccm process. (Its parent PID 135778 matches the db2ipccm process in Figure 14.3.) Because this is a local connection, db2ipccm was the responsible listener for accepting the connection, and it spawned this agent to handle this connection request.

There is one coordinator agent (i.e., the db2agent process) per connection, unless the connection concentrator is enabled. (We discuss the connection concentrator in section 14.5, The Connection Concentrator.) In a partitioned database environment, the coordinator agent exists on the partition that the application is connected to. In this example, it exists on partition 0 (this is indicated by the 0 beside *SAMPLE*), because this is the partition from where the connection request was issued.

In a DPF environment, or when the INTRA_PARALLEL Database Manager Configuration parameter is enabled, the coordinator agent distributes the database requests to an **active subagent**, *db2agntp*. These subagents perform the work and return the result set to the coordinator agent to return to the application.

In Figure 14.4, one subagent, *db2agntp*, is shown:

```
db2inst1 458448 324388   0 19:53:42    -  0:00 db2agntp (SAMPLE) 1
```

This is because db2inst1 is a multi-partition instance with two database partitions. This subagent works for the coordinator agent 546646 on database partition 1.

When a subagent completes its work it becomes an **associated** (idle) **subagent**. It changes its name from *db2agntp* to *db2agnta*, and it is returned to the application's agent pool. However, it is still associated with the application. When needed, it is called by the coordinator agent or the active subagents to service the same application again. Or it can be stolen by another application, if that application cannot find an idle agent or no more agents can be created (**MAXAGENTS** is reached). This improves performance by minimizing the creation and destruction of EDUs.

The idle db2agnta agents remain associated with the application as long as the total number of idle agents in the instance does not exceed the value of the NUM_POOLAGENTS Database Manager Configuration parameter. If the number of NUM_POOLAGENTS has already been reached, then the db2agnta process disassociates itself from the application and terminates. If subagents must be constantly created and reassociated to applications, performance suffers. (See Chapter 16, Database Performance Considerations, for a discussion on tuning of the NUM_POOLAGENTS parameter.)

Unassociated agents are idle agents (db2agent) not associated with any existing applications. They are ready for use by any incoming client connections, and can be called by any coordinator agents or active subagents to perform work.

Figure 14.4 shows an idle db2agent:

```
db2inst1  71504  541832   0 19:53:43      -  0:00 db2agent (idle) 0
```

Again, the number of idle agents is determined by the NUM_POOLAGENTS Database Manager Configuration parameter. The DB2 agent pool is shared by all databases in an instance, not just one database.

Table 14.3 lists the DB2 EDUs at the application level.

Table 14.3   The DB2 Application-Level EDUs

Process Name	Description	Applicability
db2agent	DB2 coordinator/coordinating agent that performs all database requests on behalf of an application. There is one db2agent process per connected application, unless the connection concentrator is enabled.	All
	If intra-partition parallelism is enabled, the db2agent process calls the DB2 subagents to perform the work, and they return the result set to the coordinator agent to return to the application.	
	In a partitioned database, the coordinator agent exists on the partition which the application connected to.	
db2agentg	The gateway agent for DRDA application requesters.	All
db2agnsc	The parallel recovery agent. During roll forward and restart recovery, performs the actions from the logs in parallel. This can improve recovery time in comparison to a serial recovery.	All
	Note: This process enables parallelism within logged transactions as well as between parallel transactions.	
db2agnta	An idle subagent used in the past by a coordinating agent and still associated to that coordinating agent process. Appears when the INTRA_PARALLEL dbm cfg parameter is set to YES or in a partitioned database environment.	All
db2agntp	A subagent that is currently performing work on behalf of the coordinating agent it is associated with. These processes provide intra-partition parallelism, that is, the ability to execute a query in parallel within a database instance/partition. Appears when the INTRA_PARALLEL dbm cfg parameter is set to YES or in a partitioned database environment.	All

14.2.4 Per-Request EDUs

Table 14.4 lists the per-request DB2 EDUs.

Table 14.4   The DB2 Per-Request EDUs

Process Name	Description	Applicability
db2bm	The Backup/Restore buffer manipulator. Reads from a table space during a backup operation and writes to a table space during a restore operation. One db2bm process per backup/restore buffer is configured on the **backup** or **restore** command.	All
db2fmp	Fenced processes that run user code on the server outside the firewall for *both* stored procedures and user defined functions. The db2fmp is always a separate process, but may be multithreaded depending on the types of routines it executes. **Note:** This process replaces both the db2udf and db2dari processes that were used in previous versions of DB2.	All
db2lbs	LOAD LOB scanner. Only used when the load tool is loading into a table with LOB columns. These processes scan the LOB object of the table and read the information back in.	All
db2lbm*X*	LOAD buffer manipulator. The last character (X') is a numeric identifier for the process. Writes loaded data to the database and can be involved in asynchronous I/O. There is always one, and often more, depending on a heuristic, which is based on the number of CPUs on the system and the number of containers being written to. This "intelligent default" may be overridden by the DISK_PARALLELISM modifier to the load command. Note: This asynchronous I/O is *not* the asynchronous file I/O supported by some operating systems; it just means there are separate processes writing the I/O—that other processes are formatting the data and are not tied up on I/O waits.	All
db2lfrm*X*	LOAD formatter process. The last character (X) is a numeric identifier. This process formats the input data into internal form. It is always present in a LOAD. An intelligent default is used, but can be overridden by the CPU_PARALLELISM modifier to choose the optimum number of CPUs.	All
db2lfs	Used when the table being loaded has long varchar columns. These are used to read and format the long varchar columns in the table.	All
db2lmr	The LOAD media reader process. Reads the load input file(s) and disappears once the input file(s) have been read completely—even before the entire load operation has completed.	All

(continues)

Table 14.4   The DB2 Per-Request EDUs *(Continued)*

Process Name	Description	Applicability
db2lmwX	The LOAD media writer processes. The last character (*X*) is a numeric identifier. These processes make the "load copy" if this option is specified for the **load** command. The load copy is essentially a backup of the data that was loaded into the table. These are the same as the media writers used by the **backup** and **restore** commands. There is one media writer invoked per copy session as described on the command line (you can create a load copy to multiple files). If there is no load copy, there is no media writer. They get input from the other processes in load depending on what the data type is, but typically every bit of data that gets written by a buffer manipulator will be passed on to the media writer. As with all the other processes they are controlled by the load agent.	All
db2lrid	Performs the index sort and builds the index RIDs during the LOAD. This process is not present in a nonparallel database instance, that is, if INTRA_PARALLEL is disabled. The tasks performed by this process are done by the formatter EDU in a nonparallel instance. This process performs four functions: synchronizes SMP, allocates Record IDs (RIDs), builds the indexes, and controls the synchronization of the LOAD formatter processes.	All
db2ltsc	The Load table scanner. Scans the data object for the table being loaded and reads the information for the Load tool. These are used during a Load append operation.	All
db2linit	The Load initialization subagent. Acquires the resources required on the database partitions and serializes the reply back to the load catalog subagent.	Multi-partitioned database environment only
db2lcata	The Load catalog subagent. Is executed only on the catalog partition and is responsible for spawning the initialization subagents and processing their replies, and storing the lock information at the catalog partition. The catalog subagent also queries the system catalog tables to determine which partitions to use for data splitting and partitioning. There is only one catalog subagent for a normal load job. The exception is when loads fail to acquire loading resources on some partitions. If setup errors are isolated on database partitions, the coordinator will remove the failed partitions from load's internal partition list and spawn a new catalog subagent. This process is repeated until resources are successfully acquired on all partitions, or failures are encountered on all partitions.	Multi-partitioned database environment only

(continues)

Table 14.4 The DB2 Per-Request EDUs *(Continued)*

Process Name	Description	Applicability
db2lpprt	Load prepartition subagent. This subagent pre-partitions the input data from one input stream into multiple output streams, one for each partitioning subagent. There is one pre-partitioning subagent per each input stream.	Multi-partitioned database environment only
db2lpart	The Load partition subagent. This subagent partitions the input data into multiple output streams, one for each database partition where the data will be written. You can configure the number of partitioning subagents with the PARTITIONING_DBPARTNUMS load option. The default number depends on the total number of output database partitions.	Multi-partitioned database environment only
db2lmibm	The Load mini-buffer manipulator subagent processes. Writes the partitioned output file if the PARTITION_ONLY mode is used for the load. There is one mini-buffer manipulator subagent per output database partition.	Multi-partitioned database environment only
db2lload	The Load subagent processes. Carries out the loading on each database partition, and spawns the formatters, ridder, buffer manipulators, and media writer EDUs and oversees their work. There is one load subagent for each output database partition.	Multi-partitioned database environment only
db2lrdfl	The Load read-file subagent processes. Reads the message file on a given database partition and sends the data back to the client. There will be a read-file subagent for each output partition, partitioning partition, and pre-partitioning partition.	Multi-partitioned database environment only
db2llqcl	The Load query cleanup subagent processes. Removes all of the load temporary files from a given partition. There is one cleanup subagent for each output partition, partitioning partition, and pre-partitioning partition.	Multi-partitioned database environment only
db2lmitk	The Load mini-task subagent processes. Frees all LOB locators used in a load from cursor call or a CLI load. There is one mini-task subagent per cursor/CLI load running on the coordinator partition.	Multi-partitioned database environment only
db2lurex	The Load user-exit subagent processes. Runs the user's file transfer command. There is one user-exit subagent for each load job using the `FILE_TRANSFER_CMD` option of the `load` command.	Multi-partitioned database environment only

(continues)

Table 14.4   The DB2 Per-Request EDUs *(Continued)*

Process Name	Description	Applicability
db2lmctk	Holds, releases, or downgrades locks held on the catalog partition as a result of the load.	Multi-partitioned database environment only
db2med	Handles the reading from and/or writing to the database table spaces for the **load**, **backup**, and **restore** commands, and writes the data in formatted pages to the table space containers.	All
db2reorg	Performs the new online-inplace reorg in DB2 Version 8.1. This works similar to a disk defrag tool; it places the data rows in the specified order.	All

Figure 14.5 shows the EDUs created during a database backup operation.

```
db2inst1  71504 541832   0 19:53:43    -  0:00 db2bm.546646.0 0
db2inst1 328336 541832   0 19:59:37    -  0:00 db2med.546646.0 0
db2inst1 541832 263592   0 19:49:41    -  0:00 db2gds 0
```

Figure 14.5   The DB2 EDUs responsible for backing up a database

14.3 TUNING THE NUMBER OF EDUs

DB2 controls the instance-level EDUs: db2sysc, db2gds, db2fcmd, db2wdog, and the listener processes. You can control some but not all of the EDUs at the database level. For example, you can tune the number of page cleaners (db2pclnr) and prefetchers (db2pfchr) with the database configuration parameters NUM_IOCLEANERS and NUM_IOSERVERS respectively.

At the application level, you can only tune the DB2 agents. The following Database Manager Configuration parameters control the number of different types of agents,

- MAXAGENTS indicates the maximum number of DB2 agents, both coordinator agents and subagents, available at any time.
- MAX_CONNECTIONS controls the maximum number of concurrent connections allowed to all the databases that share the same instance. These connections can be either active or inactive. An active connection means the application is doing a unit of work.
- MAX_COORDAGENTS indicates the maximum number of coordinator agents that can exist at any time. It must be set to a value less than or equal to MAXAGENTS. By default, MAX_CONNECTIONS is set to MAX_COORDAGENTS. This means that each connection has a coordinator agent assigned to it. When MAX_COORDAGENTS is set

less than MAX_CONNECTIONS, the connection concentrator is enabled (the connection concentrator is discussed in section 14.5, The Connection Concentrator).

- MAXCAGENTS controls the maximum number of DB2 agents that can be working at any time. In other words, it controls the number of active connections. An application, even with a coordinator or subagent agent assigned, cannot do any work if the number of active applications has already reached MAXCAGENTS. The agent of this application is put to sleep and will wake up when other agents complete their work and the number of active agents falls below the limit. By default, MAXCAGENTS is set to MAX_COORDAGENTS. Set this parameter to a value less than MAX_COORDAGENTS to limit the usage of system resources during times of peak processing.
- NUM_POOLAGENTS determines the maximum size of the idle agent pool. If more agents are created than is indicated by the value of this parameter, they will be terminated when they finish executing their current request rather than be returned to the pool.
- NUM_INITAGENTS determines the initial number of idle db2agents that are created in the agent pool at db2start time.

For example, assume the Database Manager Configuration file has these settings:

```
Max number of existing agents        (MAXAGENTS)      = 200
Agent pool size                      (NUM_POOLAGENTS) = 100(calculated)
Initial number of agents in pool     (NUM_INITAGENTS) = 0
```

Because NUM_INITAGENTS is zero, there will be no db2agent (idle) processes displayed at db2start time. If NUM_INITAGENTS had been set to 4 before the db2start time, then these processes would have shown after issuing a **db2start**:

```
db2inst1 35542 59814   0 16:25:57   -  0:00 db2agent (idle)
db2inst1 43096 59814   0 16:25:57   -  0:00 db2agent (idle)
db2inst1 49628 59814   0 16:25:57   -  0:00 db2agent (idle)
db2inst1 58170 59814   0 16:25:57   -  0:00 db2agent (idle)
```

After connecting to the SAMPLE database, the db2agent (SAMPLE) process appears. This process indicates there is in fact a connection to the SAMPLE database. If you issued the command

```
db2 connect reset
```

db2agent (SAMPLE) would become db2agent (idle). This is because NUM_POOLAGENTS is set to a number greater than zero, which means the agent will remain allocated in the pool even though it is idle. If NUM_POOLAGENTS had been set to zero, then after the **connect reset** command was issued, there would have been no db2agent process running.

14.4 MONITORING AND TUNING THE DB2 AGENTS

It is crucial to make sure that the number of agents you configure in the database manager is enough to service your applications. If an agent is needed but is not available, the application will get an error. If it is a new database and you are not sure what its workload is going to be, use the database Monitoring tools to get a sense of what the workload is like.

The database manager Snapshot Monitor will give you the most information on DB2 agent usage (use the **GET SNAPSHOT FOR DBM** command). Figure 14.6 shows a snippet of the database manager snapshot output.

```
              Database Manager Snapshot

Node type                                    = Enterprise Server Edition with
local and remote clients
Instance name                                = db2inst1
Number of database partitions in DB2 instance = 2
Database manager status                      = Active

Product name                                 = DB2 v8.1.0.64
Service level                                = s040321 (U488485)

Start Database Manager timestamp             = 04/22/2004
19:49:39.258796
Last reset timestamp                         =
Snapshot timestamp                           = 04/23/2004
15:04:29.606269

Remote connections to db manager             = 0
Remote connections executing in db manager   = 0
Local connections                            = 0
Local connections executing in db manager    = 0
Active local databases                       = 0

High water mark for agents registered        = 3
High water mark for agents waiting for a token = 0
Agents registered                            = 3
Agents waiting for a token                   = 0
Idle agents                                  = 2

Agents assigned from pool                    = 13
Agents created from empty pool               = 6
Agents stolen from another application       = 0
High water mark for coordinating agents      = 1
Max agents overflow                          = 0
```

Figure 14.6   Example of database manager snapshot output

When tuning MAXAGENTS, consider the *Max agents overflow* value. This is the number of times a request to create a new agent was received when the MAXAGENTS configuration parameter had already been reached. Increase MAXAGENTS if this value is not zero.

Remote connections to db manager and *Remote connections executing in db manager* indicate the number of remote connections and the number of remote connections that are currently active (i.e., they are processing a unit of work) respectively. If the number of remote connections is much larger than the number of active connections, that means most of the remote connections are idle.

This also applies to *Local connections* and *Local connections executing in db manager.* In this case, you may consider using the connection concentrator, which is explained in the next section.

The sum of *Remote connections to db manager* and *Local connections* gives you the total number of connections to the instance at the time the snapshot was taken.

The *High water marks for agents registered* indicates the highest number of coordinator agents and subagents being used concurrently, at some point in time.

Agents assigned from pool indicates the number of agents taken from the idle agents pool. *Agents created from empty pool* indicates the number of agents created because the idle agents pool was empty. If the ratio of *Agents created from empty pool* to the *Agents assigned from pool* is high, then you should increase NUM_POOLAGENTS.

The snapshot also shows the number of *Idle agents* and the *High water mark for coordinating agents.*

Use the snapshot frequently to analyze and get familiar with the type of workload on the instance. Setting the agents appropriately will save system resources and increase performance.

14.5 THE CONNECTION CONCENTRATOR

By default, each application is assigned a coordinator agent (MAX_CONNECTIONS = MAX_COORDAGENTS). Each agent operates within its own private memory and shares other memory sets with other agents. If an application connects to the database and does nothing, the resources associated with its coordinator agent are wasted. You can use the **connection concentrator** to avoid this.

The connection concentrator is enabled when MAX_CONNECTIONS is greater than MAX_COORDAGENTS. This means you can have more connections than the number of available coordinator agents. Each coordinator agent will service more than one connection.

When the connection concentrator is enabled, an application is in an active state only if there is a coordinator agent servicing it. Otherwise, the application is in an inactive state. Requests from an active application will be serviced by the database coordinator agent (and subagents in SMP or MPP configurations). Requests from an inactive application will be queued until a database coordinator agent is assigned to service the application (when the application becomes active). You can use the connection concentrator to control the load on the system.

For Internet applications with many relatively transient connections or any other applications with many relatively small transactions, the connection concentrator improves performance by allowing many more client applications to be connected. It also reduces system resource use for each connection.

When the connection concentrator is enabled, idle agents will always be returned to the idle agent pool, regardless of the value of the NUM_POOLAGENTS parameter. Therefore, more agents might be in the agent pool at any given time. Based on the system load and the time agents remain idle in the pool, agents might terminate themselves, as necessary, to reduce the size of the idle pool to the configured value.

14.6 COMMONLY SEEN DB2 EXECUTABLES

When you are running DB2, you will also see some additional executables on your server. Table 14.5 lists these.

Table 14.5   Commonly Used Executables

Process Name	Description	Applicability
db2	The DB2 Command Line Processor (CLP) foreground process. It is the interactive component of the DB2 CLP and parses DB2 commands and SQL statements.	All
	This front-end/back-end configuration does have some advantages for command line performance: The front-end handles the connection to the user, and the back-end interfaces with the database.	
	You can use CTRL+C/CTRL+Break to stop processing (i.e., when too many records are returned) without killing the connection to the database.	
db2bp	The persistent background process for the DB2 CLP; it is the process that actually connects to the database.	All
	Since the DB2 CLP allows OS as well as DB2 commands/statements, this background process is required.	
db2cmd	Similar to the db2 executable, but for Windows. Invokes a Windows command window. On Windows, parent threads cannot terminate their child processes when they are terminated. The DB2 CLP has a front-end and back-end process/thread; a cookie (launched from DB2CMD.EXE) ties these threads together on Windows so that the back-end process is terminated if the user exits or kills the front-end process.	Windows only
db2start	User command to start up the DB2 engine.	All
db2star2	The real db2start program.	All
db2stop	User command to stop the DB2 engine.	All
db2stop2	The real db2stop program.	All

14.7 ADDITIONAL SERVICES/PROCESSES ON WINDOWS

Because of the different architectures between Linux, UNIX, and Windows, you do see some slight differences between these operating systems. There are some extra services that you will likely see on your DB2 server if you are running on Windows (see Table 14.6).

Table 14.6   Other Windows Services/Processes

Process Name	Description
db2dasrrm.exe	The DB2 Admin Server process. Supports both local and remote administration requests using the DB2 Control Center.
db2dasstm.exe	The DB2 Administration Server tools database manager process. Stores and retrieves information from the tools database, if it has been set up on the DB2 server.
db2fmp.exe	Handles/executes all fenced stored procedures and user-defined functions.
db2rcmd.exe	DB2 Remote Command Service. Automatically handles inter-partition administrative communications.
db2licd.exe	The DB2 License daemon. Verifies that a correct DB2 license is installed on the server when DB2 is started.
db2sec.exe	Checks the user ID and password on the DB2 server on Windows. Since DB2 relies on operating system-level authentication, this process verifies the user ID and password when a user or application connects to a database on the server. This authentication will occur when authentication is set to SERVER or when a connection is made from a nonsecure operating system.
db2syscs.exe	The main DB2 system controller or engine on Windows. The EDUs are threads within this process. Note the *s* at the end for a Windows service.
IWH2SERV.EXE	The Warehouse Manager Center. This is installed as part of DB2 ESE, but is not part of the DB2 engine.

14.8 CASE STUDY

Diagnosing a Problem with the Help of DB2 Processes

The following real-life example shows how you can solve problems by reviewing the running DB2 processes of a system.

One afternoon, an AIX database server encountered a general slow-down in query response time. A DB2 list applications command did not show anything out of the ordinary running at the time. Before taking DB2 snapshots, we looked at the DB2 processes running on this AIX machine and found that the *db2rebal* process was running. This process performs a rebalancing of the data across containers when a container is added to a DMS table space. The DBA realized that earlier that day he had added one container to a table space containing a 40GB table. No action was required; when the rebalancing finished, the queries went back to its original good response time.

How to Control the Number of Connections by Setting the Number of DB2 Agents

Example 1

Consider an ESE environment with a single database partition in which 1,000 users on average are connected to the database concurrently. However, the number of connections that are actually active is 250 at the maximum. The transactions are short.

For this workload, you can enable the connection concentrator such that the database manager can allow up to 1,000 concurrent connections. You can set a maximum of 250 coordinator agents to handle the active connections at any one time. Without the connection concentrator, 1,000 coordinator agents are required to be created, one for each connection.

The following Database Manager Configuration parameters need to be set.

- Set MAX_CONNECTIONS to 1,000 to ensure support for the average number of 1,000 concurrent connections.
- Set MAX_COORDAGENTS to 250 to support the maximum number of 250 active concurrent transactions (assume MAXCAGENTS = MAX_COORDAGENTS).
- Set MAXAGENTS high enough to support all of the coordinator agents and subagents (where applicable) that are required to execute transactions on the partition.
- If INTRA_PARALLEL is OFF, set MAXAGENTS to 250, because there are no subagents in such an environment. If INTRA_PARALLEL is ON, set MAXAGENTS large enough to accommodate the coordinator agent and the subagents required for each transaction that accesses data on the partition. For example, if each transaction requires 4 subagents, MAXAGENTS should be set as follows: (1 coordinator agent + 4 subagents) x 250, which is 1,250.
- Set NUM_POOLAGENTS equal to MAXAGENTS to avoid the overhead of creating new agents.
- Set NUM_INIT_AGENTS to be the same as NUM_POOLAGENTS. This causes the database to create the appropriate number of agents when it starts instead of creating them before a given request can be handled.

Example 2

In a system for which you do not want to enable the connection concentrator but want to allow for 250 connected users at one time, set the Database Manager Configuration parameters as follows:

MAX_CONNECTIONS to 250

MAX_COORDAGENTS to 250

14.9 SUMMARY

In this chapter you learned a number of topics relating to the DB2 process model. A connection is first accepted by a process called a listener, and there are different listeners for different communication protocols. After an application connects to a database, a process is created and assigned to do work on behalf of the application. This process is called a coordinator agent (db2agent). In a partitioned database environment, or if intra-partition parallelism is enabled, the coordinator agent distributes work to subagents (db2agntp). These subagents perform the work and return the result to the coordinator agent to return to the application.

Since DB2 processes live within the DB2 engine, processes are also called DB2 Engine Dispatchable Units (EDUs). A coordinator agent, a subagent, a page cleaner, and a listener agent are all examples of EDUs. EDUs are implemented as processes on Linux/UNIX platforms and as threads on Windows Platforms.

The DB2 system controller process (db2sysc) is the first process created when an instance starts. The db2sysc process will then spawn other critical instance-level processes, such as the db2gds (only on Linux/UNIX), db2resyn, db2pdbc, db2cart, and others. The db2gds is the Global Daemon Spawner process—it spawns a lot of database-level processes.

There are four different types of DB agents: coordinator agents (db2agent), active subagents (db2agntp), associated idle subagents (db2agnta), and unassociated idle agents (db2agent (idle). Coordinator agents work on behalf of the application by communicating with other agents. Subagents are created in a DPF environment or when the INTRA_PARALLEL parameter is enabled. Associated subagents are nonactive agents (returned to the agent pool) that are still under the application coordinator agent's control. Unassociated idle agents are agents that are released by an application's coordinator agent (released to the agent pool) and thus can be used by any other application.

The number that the four types of agents can have are controlled by various Database Manager Configuration parameters, such as MAXAGENTS, MAX_COORDAGENTS, and NUM_POOLAGENTS. Tuning these parameters properly helps increase database performance. You can use the database manager Snapshot Monitor to check the usage of these agents, and then you can tune them accordingly.

Connection concentrator is enabled when MAXCONNECTIONS is greater than MAX_COORDAGENTS. When enabled, an application has to wait for a coordinator agent to become available to service it. Otherwise, it remains in an inactive state. This feature is useful when you want to limit the resources used by each connection, especially when you know these connections are often idle.

14.10 Review Questions

1. What command should you use to display the actual names of DB2 processes on Solaris (i.e., not just db2sysc)?
2. What is the db2fmp process, and why is it executed outside of the address space of the DB2 engine?
3. What DB2 process flushes the data in the buffer pool to disk?
4. What kind of environment do DB2 subagents exist in?
5. What happens to a subagent when it completes its work?
6. If MAXAGENTS is set to 100, does this mean there is a maximum of 100 agents per instance, or per database?
7. What are the four types of DB2 agents?
8. What tool can you use to monitor the DB2 agent usage?
9. If NUM_INITAGENTS=3 and NUM_POOLAGENTS=5, how many db2agntp processes will be created when an instance is started?
   A. 3
   B. 5
   C. 0
   D. 8
10. With the following settings, how many applications can execute concurrently?
```
MAXCONNECTIONS = 200
MAXCAGENTS = 100
MAX_COORDAGENTS = 200
```
   A. 100
   B. 200
   C. 300
   D. 500
11. In a partitioned environment with four partitions, how many DB2 system controller processes are started when the instance starts?
   A. 1
   B. 2
   C. 3
   D. 4
12. Which of the following parameters controls the number of idle agents?
   A. MAXAGENTS
   B. NUM_POOLAGENTS
   C. NUM_INIAGENTS
   D. MAXCAGENTS
13. With the connection concentrator disabled, how many db2agent processes are assigned to service an application that is connected to a database with four partitions?
   A. 1
   B. 2

    C. 3

    D. 4

14. Which of the following database configuration parameters controls the number of prefetchers?

    A. NUM_IOCLEANERS

    B. NUM_IOSERVERS

    C. NUM_INITAGENTS

    D. NUM_PREFETCHERS

15. Which of the following is the DB2 system controller process?

    A. db2wdog

    B. db2gds

    C. db2sys

    D. db2sysc

16. Which of the following is responsible for handling local client connections?

    A. db2ipccm

    B. db2tcpdm

    C. db2tcpcm

    D. db2local

17. Given the following Database Manager Configuration information:

```
Max number of existing agents           (MAXAGENTS) = 100
Agent pool size                  (NUM_POOLAGENTS) = 20
Initial number of agents in pool    (NUM_INITAGENTS) = 10
Max number of coordinating agents  (MAX_COORDAGENTS) = 100
Max number of client connections   (MAX_CONNECTIONS) = MAX_COORDAGENTS
```

what is the maximum number of concurrent connections possible to all databases in this instance?

    A. 10

    B. 20

    C. 100

    D. 200

18. Which of the following is not a DB2 agent process?

    A. db2agent

    B. db2agntp

    C. db2agnta

    D. db2agnti

19. In which of the following cases will the connection concentrator be enabled?

    A. MAX_CONNECTIONS = 10 and MAX_COORDAGENTS = 10

    B. MAX_CONNECTIONS = 10 and MAX_COORDAGENTS = 100

    C. MAX_CONNECTIONS = 100 and MAX_COORDAGENTS = 10

    D. MAX_CONNECTIONS = MAX_COORDAGENTS
       and MAX_COORDAGENTS = 1000

20. Which of the following processes will be seen when you enable the DB2 governor?

A. db2gov

B. db2govd

C. Governor

D. db2governor

The DB2 Memory Model

■ t is important that you understand how and when DB2 allocates and utilizes its memory to enable you to design and set up your applications optimally so they won't interfere with the database on the server.

In this chapter you will learn about:

- How and when DB2 allocates memory
- DB2's use of shared and private memory
- 32-bit and 64-bit considerations for DB2
- Optimizing Windows memory using AWE

15.1 DB2 MEMORY ALLOCATION: THE BIG PICTURE

DB2 allocates memory for three different types of operations.

- **Instance-level operations**: DB2 allocates memory for instance-level operations such as accepting connection requests, starting up support to activate a database, and for inter-partition communication if you have a multi-partition system. This is known as **instance-level shared memory** since it is shared by all databases in the instance and by all applications connecting to databases in the instance. Figure 15.1 shows the components that make up the instance-level shared memory in the top left corner (Per Instance Global Control Block).
- **Database-level operations**: DB2 also allocates a piece of shared memory for every database that has been activated or that has one or more connections. This memory is used for all access to the database, concurrency control on the database, and logging related to the database. This is known as **database-level shared memory** since it is shared by

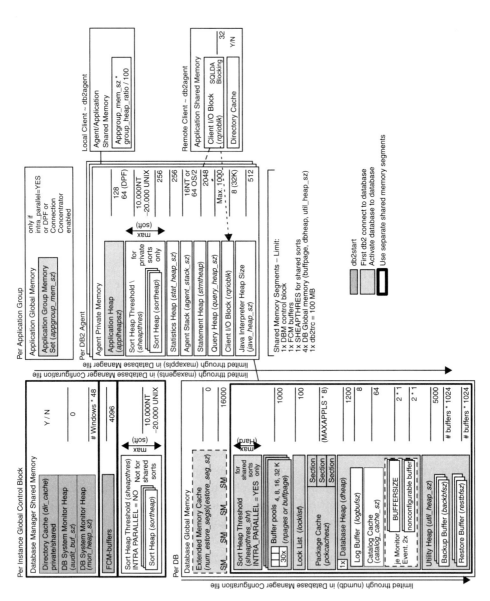

Figure 15.1 The DB2 memory model: the big picture

all applications that are connected to the database. The components that make up the database-level shared memory are shown in the bottom left corner of Figure 15.1 (Per DB).

- **Application/Agent-level operations**: For each connection to a database, the agents responsible for handling the requests for the application also need some memory. They need some shared memory for application control heap structures and some private memory for sorting, access plan generation, and so on. These memory areas are known as **application shared memory** and **agent private memory**. The components that make up the agent private memory are shown in the middle of Figure 15.1 (Per DB2 Agent).

DB2 allocates its instance-level shared memory for each instance that you start. This is the area on the top left side of Figure 15.1. For every database in the instance that has been activated or that has at least one connection, DB2 will allocate the database-level shared memory. This is the area on the bottom left side of Figure 15.1.

As long as one DB2 agent is connected to a database or is in the idle agent pool, DB2 will allocate and maintain the application shared memory. Every DB2 agent that is either working or in the idle agent pool will have its own agent-level private memory. Figure 15.1 illustrates this (Application Global Memory and Agent Private Memory).

15.2 INSTANCE-LEVEL SHARED MEMORY

When you start a DB2 instance using the **db2start** command, DB2 allocates the instance-level shared memory for the instance, and this remains allocated until you stop the instance using the **db2stop** command. The instance-level shared memory for the instance is shown in the top left corner of Figure 15.2. DB2 uses this memory to manage and coordinate database and agent activity for all applications running against all databases in the instance.

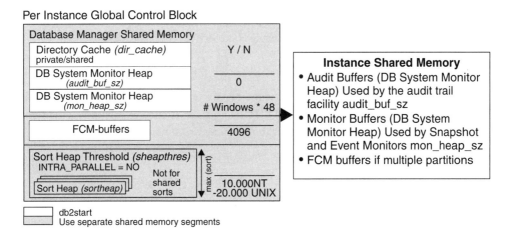

Figure 15.2   Instance-level shared memory

In a nonpartitioned DB2 instance, this memory contains information used by:

- The Snapshot and Event Monitors
- The audit logging facility
- The DB2 trace facility

In a partitioned DB2 instance, this memory also contains information used by the **Fast Communications Manager** (FCM), which is used for inter-partition communication. The amount of memory required for FCM communications depends on how you set up your multi-partition database system. If you have one partition per server, DB2 requires less memory for FCM since all communications use the TCP/IP interconnect. If you have more than one database partition within a server (also known as **logical partitions**), DB2 uses a segment of shared memory for FCM communications; this can greatly increase the amount of memory consumed at the instance level.

The Database Manager Configuration parameter *INSTANCE_MEMORY* controls how much memory can be allocated for the instance shared memory. By default this is set to automatic, which allows DB2 to calculate how much memory is required. If you want to limit or control the amount of memory that can be allocated, you can set this to a specific value. However, you need to be aware that this can impact performance, especially for a multi-partitioned database with logical partitions: setting too large a value can cause excessive paging, and too low a value can restrict the memory that DB2 can allocate.

If *INSTANCE_MEMORY* is set to *AUTOMATIC*, you can determine its effective value using the command:

```
db2 get dbm cfg show detail
```

If the instance is not started, this will only show the value AUTOMATIC, so remember to start the instance before running this command.

The following output of the **get dbm cfg** command shows that the instance memory is using 10,313 pages, or 42MB of memory (10,313 pages x 4,096 bytes per page).

```
Size of instance shared memory (4KB)
(INSTANCE_MEMORY) = AUTOMATIC(10313)          AUTOMATIC(10313)
```

The INSTANCE_MEMORY configuration parameter is only a limit for the instance shared memory, and typically it is not fully allocated. To find out the amount of memory actually used by the instance, use the DB2 memory tracker tool, **db2mtrk**:

```
db2mtrk -i -v
Memory for instance
  FCMBP Heap is of size 17432576 bytes
  Database Monitor Heap is of size 180224 bytes
  Other Memory is of size 3686400 bytes
  Total: 21299200 bytes
```

This example shows that although 42MB of memory is reserved for the instance shared memory set, only about 21MB is being used at the time **db2mtrk** is run. If the instance is not started, **db2mtrk** returns that no memory is being used.

> **N O T E**   The memory that DB2 allocates for the DB2 trace facility is
> not counted toward the INSTANCE_MEMORY configuration parame-
> ter. DB2 reserves this memory so that it can allocate it at any time in
> case you need to take a DB2 trace.

15.3 DATABASE-LEVEL SHARED MEMORY

When you issue the `activate database` command or connect to a database for the first
time, DB2 automatically allocates the database-level shared memory (see Figure 15.3). This
memory caches the object pages that are being manipulated to control concurrency on the rows
of data, ensure transactional integrity for all operations on the database, and so on.

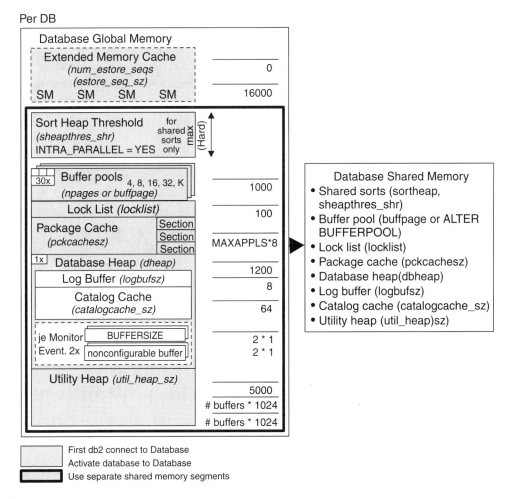

Figure 15.3   Database shared memory

The components of database shared memory include:

- The database buffer pool(s)
- The lock list
- The shared sort area (if intra-partition parallelism is enabled)
- The database heap, which also includes
    - The log buffer
    - The catalog cache
- The package cache
- The utility heap, which is used by processes such as backup and restore

15.3.1 The Database Buffer Pools

The database buffer pools area is usually the largest component of the database shared memory. As discussed in Chapter 7, Working with Database Objects, this is the area of memory where DB2 manipulates all regular and index data. A database must have at least one buffer pool, and it can have a number of buffer pools depending on the workload characteristics, database page sizes used in the database, and memory available on the system. Each individual buffer pool is sized independently, but DB2 allocates the total size of all buffer pools within the database shared memory area.

15.3.2 The Database Lock List

To control access to rows that are being read and written, DB2 must lock the rows until the operation completes. Information about each lock that DB2 obtains is stored in the database lock list until the lock is released. The LOCKLIST configuration parameter specifies the amount of memory that can be used to store the lock information. If this memory pool becomes full, DB2 performs **lock escalation** to free up some space in the lock list.

15.3.3 The Database Shared Sort Heap Threshold

If you enable intra-partition parallelism, DB2 may choose to perform a shared sort if it thinks using that method will be more efficient than a private sort. If DB2 performs a shared sort, it allocates the sort heap for the sort in database shared memory. The SHEAPTHRES_SHR configuration parameter limits the amount of shared sort memory that can be allocated for the database. If a new shared-sort request is made, and the allocation of the sort heap would exceed the shared sort heap threshold (SHEAPTHRES_SHR), DB2 will not allocate the sort heap and will perform an overflowed sort.

15.3.4 The Package Cache

For dynamic SQL, performance can be greatly improved if DB2 is able to reuse an already compiled access plan rather than having to perform the access plan generation. The **package cache** stores already compiled access plans so that they can be reused. Since multiple users can run the same applications, and therefore the same SQL statements, DB2 uses a shared package cache so that you can reuse an access plan even if it was originally compiled for another user. The size of the package cache is specified by the PCKCACHESZ configuration parameter.

15.3.5 The Utility Heap Size

DB2 does not allocate the utility heap when you first connect to or activate the database, but it is allocated if you perform a backup or restore operation. You need to be aware of this and plan for this, especially if you are working on a 32-bit operating system, which has very strict limits on the amount of shared memory that can be allocated. (32-bit and 64-bit memory models are described in sections 15.7 and 15.8, respectively.)

15.3.6 The Catalog Cache

The catalog cache is used to store previously accessed information such as object descriptions and privileges. In a multi-partitioned database, the catalog cache will be allocated on all partitions, but the information is not replicated. Each partition's catalog cache will contain information that has been previously accessed on that partition.

15.3.7 Database Logging Parameters

As you change data in your database, DB2 needs to log the changes so that it can:

- Roll back the changes if you issue the ROLLBACK statement
- Perform recovery operations if the server fails for any reason

To be able to perform well, DB2 cannot log the work that it is doing directly to disk, so DB2 uses a write-ahead logging algorithm to ensure that the changes are written to the log buffer (LOGBUFSZ) before they are made to the underlying index and data pages. DB2 also ensures that the log buffer is flushed to disk whenever a commit (or MINCOMMIT commits) occurs so that it is able to reapply any committed changes and can undo any uncommitted changes. This is discussed in more detail in Chapter 13, Developing Database Backup and Recovery Solutions.

The log buffer and the catalog cache are allocated within the database heap along with some other database-level control information. In addition, for every page in the buffer pools and extended storage, DB2 uses 12 bytes of memory in the database heap to store information about the state of the page.

15.3.8 Database Memory

The total amount of database shared memory allocated at a given time is the sum of all of these components. In DB2 Version 8 there is a new configuration parameter called DATABASE_MEMORY. If you install DB2 on a 64-bit operating system, you can change these configuration parameters dynamically, and DB2 can then extend or reduce the sizes of these shared memory areas. However, in 32-bit operating systems, once a segment of shared memory is allocated it cannot be extended or reduced. To overcome this limitation you can reserve extra database shared memory up to the operating system limit using the DATABASE_MEMORY configuration parameter. This will allow you to create new buffer pools or enlarge these memory areas dynamically.

If you want to figure out a good value to use for the DATABASE_MEMORY configuration parameter, you can set it to AUTOMATIC initially (which is the default). Then connect to the database and run the command:

```
get db cfg for dbname show detail
```

This command will show you how much memory is currently allocated in database shared memory area, and you can then determine what value to use based on this information. The following is a partial output of this command:

```
Size of database shared memory (4KB)(DATABASE_MEMORY=AUTOMATIC(177764)
```

This shows that there are 177,764 pages currently allocated in the database shared memory area.

As discussed earlier for instance-level memory, you can also use the **db2mtrk** tool to display the database shared memory used for your databases (you must specify **-I** on Windows; on UNIX, **-i** is optional):

```
db2mtrk -i -d -v
```

```
Memory for database: SAMPLE
    Backup/Restore/Util Heap is of size 16384 bytes
    Package Cache is of size 81920 bytes
    Catalog Cache Heap is of size 65536 bytes
    Buffer Pool Heap is of size 4341760 bytes
    Buffer Pool Heap is of size 655360 bytes
    Buffer Pool Heap is of size 393216 bytes
    Buffer Pool Heap is of size 262144 bytes
    Buffer Pool Heap is of size 196608 bytes
    Lock Manager Heap is of size 491520 bytes
    Database Heap is of size 3637248 bytes
    Other Memory is of size 16384 bytes
    Application Control Heap is of size 327680 bytes
    Application Group Shared Heap is of size 57344000 bytes
    Total: 67829760 bytes
```

Notice there are five buffer pool heaps allocated; the following are the four hidden buffer pools:

```
    Buffer Pool Heap is of size 655360 bytes
    Buffer Pool Heap is of size 393216 bytes
    Buffer Pool Heap is of size 262144 bytes
    Buffer Pool Heap is of size 196608 bytes
```

In this case if you run the statement

```
select * from syscat.bufferpools
```

you will get only one row returned, because the hidden buffer pools do not have entries in the buffer pool table.

To change this value and reserve some memory so that you can add a new buffer pool, or to increase the size of the lock list or log buffer dynamically, use the command:

```
update db cfg for dbname using database_memory 250000
```

15.4 APPLICATION-LEVEL SHARED MEMORY

DB2 only allocates application-level shared memory in a partitioned database environment, or when intra-partition parallelism or the connection concentrator is enabled. DB2 uses the application shared memory:

- For coordinating and sending messages between the DB2 agent processes that are working on behalf of an application
- To keep the state of the application when it gets moved to a logical agent when the connection concentrator is being used

15.4.1 Application Group Shared Memory

To facilitate easier and more efficient messaging and coordination of the agents working for the same application, DB2 arranges agents into **application groups** so that they can communicate using the **application group shared memory**. The application group memory is allocated in a database-level shared memory set, and the configuration parameter APPGROUP_MEM_SZ specifies its size.

Although this memory is used to speed up communication between agents working on the same application, DB2 does not create one application group for every application. DB2 can assign multiple applications to the same application group; the number of applications that can be assigned to an application group is calculated using:

```
appgroup_mem_sz / app_ctl_heap_sz
```

Within an application group, each application has its own **application control heap**. In addition, a portion of the application group shared memory is reserved for the **application group shared heap**. Figure 15.4 illustrates this.

Given the following database configuration:

```
Max size of appl. group mem set (4KB) (APPGROUP_MEM_SZ) = 40000
Max appl. control heap size (4KB)     (APP_CTL_HEAP_SZ) = 512
Percent of mem for appl. group heap   (GROUPHEAP_RATIO) = 70
```

let's examine the memory usage for applications connecting to this database.

- If the application group shared memory set is approximately 160MB:
  40,000 pages x 4K per page = 160MB
- If the size of the application group shared heap is approximately 114MB:
  40,000 x 70%= 28,000 4K pages = 114MB
- If the number of applications that can fit into this application group is 78:
  40,000/512 = 78

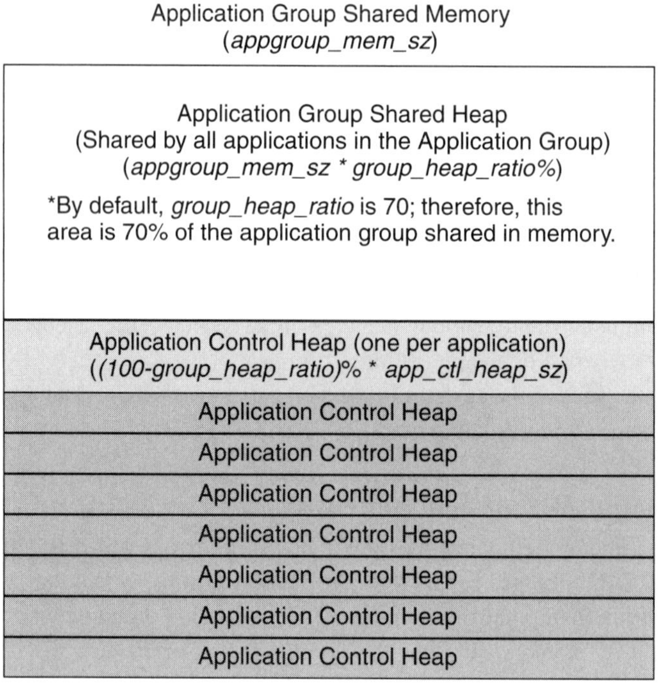

Application Group Shared Memory
(*appgroup_mem_sz*)

Figure 15.4   Application group shared memory

• If the application control heap for each of the applications is approximately 600K:
  (100–70)% x 512 = 153 4K pages = 0.6MB

The APP_CTRL_HEAP_SZ parameter is *not* the size of the individual application control heap for each application in the application group; it is only used to calculate the number of applications that can fit into an application group. The real application control heap size of each application is calculated using the formula:

  ((100 – GROUPHEAP_RATIO)% x APP_CTRL_HEAP_SZ)

As this formula shows, the larger that you set the GROUPHEAP_RATIO, the larger the application group shared heap will be and the smaller the application control heap for each application will be.

For the example configuration above, there are 400 applications connected to the database during the busiest time of the day. Since each application group can hold 78 applications, you will need 400/78, or 6 application groups, to be able to hold all 400 applications. Make sure that your system has enough memory to handle this; otherwise you may receive out of memory errors.

15.5 AGENT-LEVEL PRIVATE MEMORY

Each DB2 agent process also needs to acquire memory to perform its work. As you can see in Figure 15.5, they use memory to optimize, build, and execute access plans on behalf of the application, to perform sorts, to record cursor information such as location and state, to gather statistics, and so on.

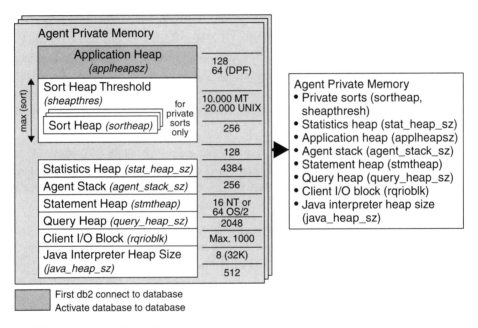

Figure 15.5 Agent-level private memory

When a DB2 agent is created, it allocates the minimum amount of memory that is required to do some basic work. As it works, it may allocate larger areas of these memory areas depending on the statements that are being processed, the number of cursors the application uses, and other functions. Once the DB2 agent allocates any of these memory heaps, it does not release the memory back to the operating system automatically, since the areas are normally reused over and over again. DB2 has chosen to do this for performance reasons so that you do not waste resources allocating and deallocating small pieces of memory all of the time.

15.5.1 Application Heap

The **application heap** stores a copy of the currently executing sections of the access plan for the application associated with the DB2 agent or subagent. The application heap is allocated when an agent or subagent is initialized for an application. The amount of memory allocated will be only what is needed to process the request that has been given to the DB2 agent or subagent. When a DB2 agent or subagent requires additional application heap to be able to process larger

SQL statements, DB2 will allocate additional memory, up to the maximum specified by the application heap size.

> **N O T E** If the database is partitioned, the executing sections of the SQL statements for the agents and subagents will be stored in the application control heap (APP_CTL_HEAP_SZ), not in the application heap.

15.5.2 The Sort Heap and Sort Heap Threshold

The **sort heap** (SORTHEAP) size specifies the maximum number of private memory pages to be used for private sorts, or the maximum number of shared memory pages to be used for shared sorts. If the DB2 optimizer chooses to perform a private sort, the sort heap size affects agent private memory. If the DB2 optimizer chooses to perform a shared sort, the sort heap size affects the database-level shared memory.

Each sort operation has a separate sort heap that is allocated as needed by DB2 where the underlying data is sorted. Normally DB2 will allocate a full sort heap; however, if directed by the optimizer, a smaller amount of memory than specified by the sort heap size may be allocated using the information provided by the optimizer and the database statistics.

For private sorts, the **sort heap threshold** parameter (SHEAPTHRES) is an instance-wide soft limit on the total amount of memory that can be used at any given time. When the total usage of private sort memory for a DB2 instance reaches this limit, the memory allocated for new private sort requests will be reduced by a factor of one half. Each time this happens, you will receive the following message in the db2diag.log:

```
Not enough memory available for a (private) sort heap of size <size of sortheap>.
Trying smaller size...
```

Chapter 17, Diagnosing Problems, discusses the db2diag.log file.

15.5.3 Query Heap

A **query heap** stores each SQL statement in the private memory for the DB2 agent executing the statement. The information stored in the query heap for an SQL statement includes the following:

- The input SQL descriptor area (SQLDA)
- The output SQLDA
- The statement text
- The SQLCA
- The package name
- The package creator
- The section number
- A consistency token
- The cursor control block for any blocking cursors

When an application connects to DB2, the initial size of the query heap allocated is a minimum of two pages, or the size of the application support layer heap (ASLHEAPSZ). If the currently allocated query heap is not large enough to handle the request, the query heap will be reallocated with a larger size that will handle the request, as long as it does not exceed the query heap size.

15.5.4 Client I/O Block Size

The maximum requester **I/O block size** is the maximum amount of data that can be sent back and forth between a DB2 client and server. Each agent process allocates the communication block in agent private memory for a DB2 instance; however, DB2 only uses what it needs up to this maximum size. If the application request or the output from DB2 is larger than the block size, the data will be split into multiple pieces and sent in multiple communication packets. The default maximum requester I/O block size is 32KB; the maximum size is 64KB.

15.5.5 Agent Stack

Each agent process uses the **agent stack** to process SQL statements. When an SQL statement is running, its sections are copied to the agent stack to be processed. Large, complex queries need a larger agent stack as they typically have much larger access plans with a large number of sections.

15.5.6 Java Interpreter Heap

The **Java Interpreter Heap** parameter determines the maximum size of the heap used by the Java interpreter started to service Java DB2 stored procedures and UDFs. This heap is used as a work area for the Java interpreter as it processes actions for the DB2 agent.

15.5.7 Statement Heap

The DB2 optimizer uses the **statement heap** as a work space as it examines and builds the access plan for an SQL statement. The statement heap is allocated when optimizing an SQL statement, and released once the access plan for the statement has been built. For applications using dynamic SQL, this work area is allocated and deallocated each time the statement is run in the application. Applications using static SQL statements only use this work area when the program is bound to the database.

15.5.8 Statistics Heap

The **statistics heap** is a memory area used by the `runstats` command to maintain and calculate the statistical information about tables and indexes. As `runstats` scans the table, it counts items, builds histograms for data distribution, and so on; this information is maintained in the statistics heap. When the `runstats` command completes, the information is then written to the catalog tables, and the statistics heap is freed.

15.6 THE MEMORY MODEL

You can now look at all of these memory areas together to see how they are related. Within each instance you can create more than one database, so for every active database there will be a database shared memory area that is allocated in memory.

For every application connected to a multi-partition database, or one configured either with intra-partition parallelism and/or using the connection concentrator, there will be an area of application shared memory allocated in memory. In addition, each DB2 agent process will have its own private memory area, as seen in Figure 15.6.

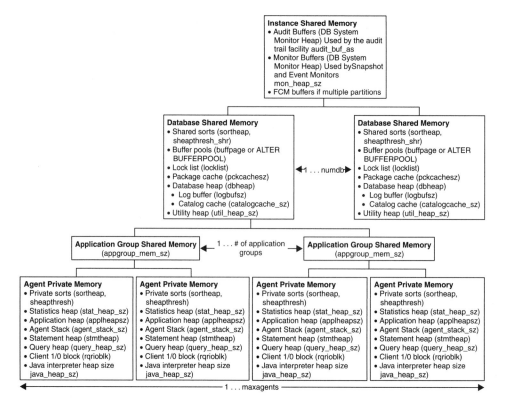

Figure 15.6   The memory model

15.7 32-BIT MEMORY MODEL CONSIDERATIONS

If you install DB2 on a 32-bit operating system, there are limitations to the maximum size of a shared memory segment that a process can allocate. Since each database has all of its shared memory allocated in the same segment, there is a limit on the total amount of shared memory that can be allocated per database.

In 32-bit AIX, there are a maximum of sixteen 256MB shared memory segments that can be addressed by a process. Of these sixteen segments, only seven can be used by DB2 for shared memory. By default, DB2 reserves one of these seven segments for optimizing memory-mapped I/O. If you have multiple logical partitions on the same server, DB2 also uses one of these seven segments for inter-partition (FCM) communications. DB2 lets you maximize the amount of memory available for the buffer pools and other shared memory components by allowing you to disable memory-mapped I/O and the FCM use of shared memory for inter-partition communication.

> **N O T E**   On AIX, memory-mapped I/O uses I-nodes to optimize access to files rather than tracking file handles.

To disable memory-mapped I/O, you can set the following DB2 registry variables to NO using the **db2set** command.

- DB2_MMAP_READ
- DB2_MMAP_WRITE

To force the FCM communications to use the network interconnect instead of shared memory for inter-partition communication between logical partitions, you can set the following DB2 registry variable to NO using the **db2set** command.

- DB2_FORCE_FCM_BP

The maximum addressable amount of shared memory for the 32-bit version of DB2 varies depending on the operating system. Table 15.1 lists the memory limits.

Table 15.1   The Maximum Addressable Amount of Shared Memory for the 32-Bit Version of DB2

32-Bit Operating System	Shared Memory Limit
AIX	1.75GB; 2GB if DB2_MMAP_READ and DB2_MMAP_WRITE are set to NO
HP/UX	800K
Linux	Kernel 2.3 or earlier: • 768KB if less than 2GB of real memory • 1.1GB if 2GB or more of real memory Kernel 2.4 or higher: • 1.75GB
Solaris	3.35GB
Windows NT/2000	• 2GB; 3GB if using Advanced Server and /3GB set in boot.ini • 64GB with AWE support requires that the DB2_AWE registry variable be set

15.8 64-Bit Memory Model Considerations

We suggest that you use DB2 on a 64-bit operating system whenever possible, since the limits discussed in the previous section do not exist. In addition, in a 64-bit environment, shared memory segments can be allocated and deallocated dynamically, making configuring and tuning of your DB2 server more dynamic and much easier.

DB2 currently supports the following 64-bit operating systems:

- AIX
- HP/UX
- Linux on AMD
- Linux on Intel (IPF)
- Linux on Power
- Solaris
- Windows 2003 Advanced Server

15.9 AWE Support with Windows

When working with Windows 2000, the total addressable memory can be up to 64GB; therefore, the maximum buffer pool sizes that can be created on Windows equals 64GB minus the memory used by the operating system and other DB2 memory allocations (assuming that the server is dedicated to DB2). The support for large memory addressing on 32-bit Windows is provided by the Microsoft Address Windowing Extensions (AWE). Through AWE, the Windows 2000 Advanced Server provides support for up to 8GB of memory addressing, while the Windows 2000 Data Center Server provides support for up to 64GB of memory.

To take advantage of memory addresses above 2GB, both DB2 and Windows 2000 must be configured correctly to support AWE. To address up to 3GB of memory, you must set the /3GB Windows 2000 boot option. To enable access to more than 4GB of memory via the AWE memory interface, you must set the /PAE Windows 2000 boot option. To verify that you have the correct boot option selected, under the Control Panel, select **System**, and then select **Startup and Recovery**. From the drop-down list you can see the available boot options. If the boot option you want is selected (/3GB or /PAE), then you are ready to proceed to the next task: setting up AWE support. If the option you want is not available, you must add the option to the boot.ini file on the system drive. The boot.ini file contains a list of actions to be done when the operating system is started. Add /3GB, /PAE, or both (separated by blanks) at the end of the list of existing parameters. Once you have saved this changed file, you can verify and select the correct boot option as described.

Windows 2000 also has to be updated to associate the right to *lock pages in memory* with the user ID that was used to install DB2. To set this, once you have logged on to Windows 2000 as the user who installed DB2, under the **Start** menu on Windows 2000 select the *Administrative Tools* folder, and then the *Local Security Policy* program. Under the local policies, you can select the user rights assignment for *lock pages in memory*.

DB2 also requires the setting of the DB2_AWE registry variable so you can take advantage of the larger memory addressing. You must set this registry variable to the buffer pool ID of the buffer pool that will be larger than 3GB and needs AWE support, as well as the number of physical pages and the address window pages to be allocated for the buffer pool.

The buffer pool ID is found in the BUFFERPOOLID column in the catalog view SYSCAT.BUFFERPOOLS. The number of physical pages to allocate should be less than the total number of available pages of memory, and the actual number chosen will depend on the working environment. For example, in an environment where only DB2 and database applications are used on the server, usually select a value between one half of the available memory up to one GB less than the available memory. In an environment where other nondatabase applications are also running on the server, these values will need to be reduced to leave memory available for the other applications. The number used in the DB2_AWE registry variable is the number of physical pages to be used in support of AWE and for use by DB2. The upper limit on the address window pages is 1.5GB, or 2.5GB when the /3GB Windows 2000 boot option is in effect.

15.10 CASE STUDY

You can use the tools available in DB2 to examine how much memory is being used by different DB2 operations.

To get the most useful information, start with a stopped DB2 instance. Running the memory tracker tool, **db2mtrk**, indicates that the instance is not running (see Figure 15.7)

```
C:\>db2stop
03/28/2005 13:39:29    0   0   SQL1064N  DB2STOP processing was successful.
SQL1064N  DB2STOP processing was successful.

C:\>db2mtrk -i -p -v
Tracking Memory on: 2005/03/28 at 13:39:31

Instance not started
```

Figure 15.7   Verifying that an instance is not running

Start the instance and see how much memory it will use (see Figure 15.8).

```
C:\>db2start
03/28/2005 13:47:08    0   0   SQL1063N  DB2START processing was successful.
SQL1063N  DB2START processing was successful.
```

Figure 15.8   Seeing how much memory an instance uses *(continues)*

```
C:\>db2mtrk -i -p -v
Tracking Memory on: 2005/03/28 at 13:47:10

Memory for instance

   Database Monitor Heap is of size 16384 bytes
   Other Memory is of size 7667712 bytes
   Total: 7684096 bytes


No active agents
```

Figure 15.8   Seeing how much memory an instance uses *(continued)*

The output in Figure 15.8 shows this particular instance consumes 7,684,096 bytes (7.3MB) when it is started.

If you activate a database, all of its shared memory, such as the lock list and buffer pool, will be allocated (see Figure 15.9).

```
C:\>db2 activate db samp82
DB20000I  The ACTIVATE DATABASE command completed successfully.

C:\>db2mtrk -i -p -v
Tracking Memory on: 2005/03/28 at 13:47:43

Memory for instance

   Backup/Restore/Util Heap is of size 16384 bytes
   Package Cache is of size 81920 bytes
   Catalog Cache Heap is of size 65536 bytes
   Buffer Pool Heap is of size 1179648 bytes
   Buffer Pool Heap is of size 655360 bytes
   Buffer Pool Heap is of size 393216 bytes
   Buffer Pool Heap is of size 262144 bytes
   Buffer Pool Heap is of size 196608 bytes
   Lock Manager Heap is of size 278528 bytes
   Database Heap is of size 3637248 bytes
   Database Monitor Heap is of size 180224 bytes
   Other Memory is of size 7733248 bytes
   Total: 14680064 bytes


No active agents
```

Figure 15.9   Verifying how much memory is allocated

The output in Figure 15.9 indicates that when this particular database is activated, 14,680,064 bytes (14MB) are consumed.

If you connect to the database, you will create a db2agent process, and this will also consume some memory (see Figure 15.10).

```
C:\>db2 connect to sample

   Database Connection Information

 Database server        = DB2/NT 8.2.0
 SQL authorization ID    = DSNOW
 Local database alias    = SAMPLE

C:\>db2mtrk -i -p -v
Tracking Memory on: 2005/03/28 at 13:49:12

Memory for instance

   Backup/Restore/Util Heap is of size 16384 bytes
   Package Cache is of size 81920 bytes
   Catalog Cache Heap is of size 65536 bytes
   Buffer Pool Heap is of size 1179648 bytes
   Buffer Pool Heap is of size 655360 bytes
   Buffer Pool Heap is of size 393216 bytes
   Buffer Pool Heap is of size 262144 bytes
   Buffer Pool Heap is of size 196608 bytes
   Lock Manager Heap is of size 278528 bytes
   Database Heap is of size 3637248 bytes
   Database Monitor Heap is of size 180224 bytes
   Other Memory is of size 7766016 bytes
   Total: 14712832 bytes

Memory for agent 2224
   Other Memory is of size 65536 bytes
   Application Heap is of size 131072 bytes
   Application Control Heap is of size 16384 bytes
   Total: 212992 bytes
```

Figure 15.10 Seeing how much memory an agent uses

In this case, the output in Figure 15.10 shows the agent consumes 212,992 bytes (208KB) of memory.

Let's execute some SQL statements and see how that affects the agent private memory allocation (see Figure 15.11).

```
C:\>db2mtrk -i -p -v
Tracking Memory on: 2005/03/28 at 13:56:02

Memory for instance

   Backup/Restore/Util Heap is of size 16384 bytes
   Package Cache is of size 262144 bytes
```

Figure 15.11 How executing SQL statements affects an agent's memory allocation *(continues)*

```
    Catalog Cache Heap is of size 65536 bytes
    Buffer Pool Heap is of size 1179648 bytes
    Buffer Pool Heap is of size 655360 bytes
    Buffer Pool Heap is of size 393216 bytes
    Buffer Pool Heap is of size 262144 bytes
    Buffer Pool Heap is of size 196608 bytes
    Lock Manager Heap is of size 278528 bytes
    Database Heap is of size 3637248 bytes
    Database Monitor Heap is of size 180224 bytes
    Other Memory is of size 7766016 bytes
    Total: 14893056 bytes

Memory for agent 2224

    Other Memory is of size 65536 bytes
    Application Heap is of size 212992 bytes
    Application Control Heap is of size 16384 bytes
    Total: 294912 bytes
```

Figure 15.11   How executing SQL statements affects an agent's memory allocation *(continued)*

As shown in Figure 15.11, the memory tracker tool indicates now that the agent's memory has grown to 294,912 bytes (288KB), an increase of 80KB from the output shown in Figure 15.10, due to an increase in the application heap (from 131,072 to 212,992 bytes). Since the statements would have been optimized to be run, their access plans would have been copied into the application heap as they were run.

Let's back up the database and see how that affects the memory used. Figure 15.12 shows a snapshot of **db2mtrk** while the backup is running, and Figure 15.13 shows it when it has completed. During the backup operation you can see that the backup/restore buffer is allocated.

```
C:\>db2mtrk -i -p -v
Tracking Memory on: 2005/03/28 at 13:59:19

Memory for instance

    Backup/Restore/Util Heap is of size 18432000 bytes
    Package Cache is of size 81920 bytes
    Catalog Cache Heap is of size 65536 bytes
    Buffer Pool Heap is of size 1179648 bytes
    Buffer Pool Heap is of size 655360 bytes
    Buffer Pool Heap is of size 393216 bytes
    Buffer Pool Heap is of size 262144 bytes
    Buffer Pool Heap is of size 196608 bytes
    Lock Manager Heap is of size 278528 bytes
    Database Heap is of size 3620864 bytes
    Database Monitor Heap is of size 16384 bytes
    Other Memory is of size 7864320 bytes
    Total: 33046528 bytes
```

Figure 15.12   Memory in use while a backup is running

```
C:\>db2mtrk -i -p -v
Tracking Memory on: 2005/03/28 at 14:01:08

Memory for instance

   Database Monitor Heap is of size 16384 bytes
   Other Memory is of size 7782400 bytes
   Total: 7798784 bytes

No active agents
```

Figure 15.13   Memory when a backup has finished

Once the backup completes, the backup/restore buffer gets released. Since this was an offline backup, it also releases the connection to the database, so the buffer pools, database heap, lock list, and other memory areas are also released.

15.11 SUMMARY

DB2 provides you with a very flexible way to configure your databases for optimal performance. By understanding how and when DB2 uses and allocates memory, you can tune your system to handle any workload.

For each instance you can control the instance-level memory for such things as the agents that work on behalf of your applications, the overall memory available for private sorts to ensure that you do not overwhelm your server, and for the memory available for inter-partition communications.

For each database you can control the size of each individual sort, the amount of space available for such things as locking and logging, as well as the size of the buffer pools available to retrieve data and index pages that need to be read and/or updated.

Now that you understand when and how these memory areas are allocated, and how they work together, you can better understand how changes to particular configuration parameters will impact the overall memory used on the system as well as how the configuration parameters will interact with each other.

15.12 REVIEW QUESTIONS

1. Which tools can be used to display the memory used by DB2, and how it is associated with the DB2 configuration parameters?
2. What database configuration parameter can reserve shared memory in a 32-bit environment to allow dynamic increases to the amount of shared memory used?
3. Which parameter can be increased in a dynamic SQL environment to allow applications to reuse the compiled statements of other applications?
4. Which of the sort heap thresholds is a hard limit?

5. What is the maximum amount of time that can elapse between one flush of the log buffer to disk and the next one?

6. How can you tell the current total amount of shared memory used by a database?

7. What is the largest client I/O block allowed by DB2?

8. What memory is allocated when you start your DB2 instance?

9. When is the database-level shared memory allocated?

10. For what purpose are the FCM buffers used?

11. How many buffer pools will a database have by default immediately after it is created?
    A. 1
    B. 2
    C. 3
    D. 4
    E. 5

12. Under which of the following conditions will application group memory not be used?
    A. DB2MEMDISCLAIM=ON
    B. INTRA_PARALLEL=ON
    C. Connection concentrator is enabled
    D. The database has multiple partitions

13. Which of the following is not part of the database shared memory?
    A. Lock list
    B. Shared sort heap threshold
    C. Package cache
    D. Statistics heap

14. Given the following configuration information:
    ```
    Max size of appl. group mem set (4KB)    (APPGROUP_MEM_SZ) = 10000
    Max appl. control heap size (4KB)        (APP_CTL_HEAP_SZ) = 512
    Percent of mem for appl. group heap      (GROUPHEAP_RATIO) = 30
    ```
    how large will the application group shared heap be?
    A. 3,000 pages
    B. 30,000 pages
    C. 300,000 pages
    D. 15,360 pages

15. Given the following configuration information:
    ```
    Max size of appl. group mem set (4KB) (APPGROUP_MEM_SZ) = 30000
    Max appl. control heap size (4KB)         (APP_CTL_HEAP_SZ) = 512
    Percent of mem for appl. group heap      (GROUPHEAP_RATIO) = 60
    ```
    if there are 300 applications, how many application groups will be needed?
    A. 1
    B. 5
    C. 6
    D. 10

16. Given the following configuration information:

```
Sort heap thres for shared sorts (4KB) (SHEAPTHRES_SHR) = 2000
Sort list heap (4KB)                         (SORTHEAP) = 256
```

how many concurrent shared sorts can occur within memory for this database?

A. 1

B. 5

C. 7

D. 8

E. Unlimited

17. Given the following configuration information:

```
Sort heap threshold (4KB)          (SHEAPTHRES) = 2000
Sort list heap (4KB)                 (SORTHEAP) = 256
```

how many concurrent private sorts can occur within memory for this database?

A. 1

B. 5

C. 7

D. 8

E. Unlimited

18. Which of the following is not part of the database manager shared memory?

A. DB2 trace

B. Event Monitors

C. DB2 audit facility

D. Buffer pools

19. Given the following output of the **get db cfg** command on a 32-bit DB2 instance:

```
Size of database shared memory (4KB) (DATABASE_MEMORY) = AUTOMATIC(75264)
```

how large would the DATABASE MEMORY need to be to allocate a new 16K page size buffer pool, with a size of 10,000 pages?

A. 75264

B. 85264

C. 100000

D. 125000

20. Given the following output of the memory tracker tool:

```
db2mtrk -i -p -v
Tracking Memory on: 2005/03/28 at 13:47:43

Memory for instance

   Backup/Restore/Util Heap is of size 16384 bytes
   Package Cache is of size 81920 bytes
   Catalog Cache Heap is of size 65536 bytes
   Buffer Pool Heap is of size 1179648 bytes
   Buffer Pool Heap is of size 655360 bytes
   Buffer Pool Heap is of size 393216 bytes
   Buffer Pool Heap is of size 262144 bytes
```

```
Buffer Pool Heap is of size 196608 bytes
Lock Manager Heap is of size 278528 bytes
Database Heap is of size 3637248 bytes
Database Monitor Heap is of size 180224 bytes
Other Memory is of size 7733248 bytes
Total: 14680064 bytes
```

which of the following is definitely not true for this database?

A. There is at least one application connected to the database.

B. A backup or restore is occurring.

C. The database has five user-created table spaces.

D. The instance has been started.

CHAPTER 16

Database Performance Considerations

Performance is probably the most important factor in databases and database applications. If performance was not important, people would simply create applications that store their data in flat files rather than purchase highly optimized relational database management systems.

Tuning a DB2 system to obtain optimal performance can be a lengthy process. Poor performance is usually a result of:

- Suboptimal system (hardware) design
- Suboptimal instance configuration
- Suboptimal database configuration
- Lack of proper maintenance
- Inefficient SQL

While you may not have a lot of control over the server and disks that are used for the database server, especially in a large UNIX shop, the hardware does have a big impact on the overall performance of the database system.

In this chapter you will learn about:

- The Database Manager (i.e., instance-level) Configuration parameters
- Database configuration parameters that have the largest impact on the performance of the system
- DB2 registry variables
- Maintenance operations that you must perform to ensure that the system continues to perform optimally once you have it running

16.1 PERFORMANCE FUNDAMENTALS

When you start designing, building, and tuning your database system, you need to try to balance the three main areas that affect your performance:

- CPU usage
- I/O utilization
- Memory usage

At least one of these three areas is affected by any change that you make, either in designing the system or tuning the system using the registry variables or DB2 configuration parameters. For example, increasing the size of one or more of your buffer pools will increase the memory consumption on the server, but it may then decrease the I/O that is required. By understanding how the various registry variables and configuration parameters impact the CPU usage, I/O, and memory usage, you will be better prepared to judge whether the changes will help the performance of the system.

Let's take another example. If you have a system that is already paging (or swapping) but is not doing a lot of I/O operations, increasing the size of the buffer pools will not be a good idea since this will further increase the paging operations but will not likely reduce the I/O much less than the current level. This change might actually reduce the overall performance of the system, so by thinking this through you can save time and effort in the tuning process.

16.2 SYSTEM/SERVER CONFIGURATION

The three commandments in designing your database server are

1. Ensure there is enough memory available.
2. Ensure there are enough physical disks to handle the I/O requirements.
3. Ensure there are enough CPUs to handle the workload.

16.2.1 Ensuring There Is Enough Memory Available

As discussed earlier in the book, all DB2 data and indexes are manipulated in the database buffer pools. The buffer pools are allocated in memory, so you need to ensure that you have enough real memory to hold the buffer pools that you have defined. If you have more buffer pool space defined than real memory, your system has to perform a lot of paging operations that have a very large negative affect on performance. While the buffer pools are normally the largest piece of DB2 memory used, there are other memory segments that DB2 also allocates, such as:

- Sort space
- The lock list
- Package cache
- Catalog cache
- Log buffer

N O T E For more information about other memory segments, refer to Chapter 15, The DB2 Memory Model. Chapter 15 also discusses the limitations imposed by 32-bit operating systems. With full 64-bit support in DB2 Version 8, and the gaining popularity and availability of 64-bit hardware, we recommend the use of 64-bit whenever possible, especially for the DB2 server.

Depending on your workload, allocate the available memory to different DB2 components. For a Decision Support System (DSS) or OLAP workload with large reports that scan vast amounts of data, the overall affect of the buffer pool is not as significant since DB2 typically has to scan a lot of data. In this type of workload, DB2 usually also needs to perform a number of sorts to help join and/or order the data. Therefore, in a DSS-type workload, try to divide your available memory evenly between the buffer pools and sort heaps.

Online Transaction Processing (OLTP) applications typically read and write a single row in the database, and therefore get a very big benefit if the data is already in the buffer pool. This type of workload is also good at keeping "hot" or often-accessed pages in the buffer pool for reuse. In addition, if you make the sort heap space too large, DB2 can sometimes favor a sort over an index scan, which has a negative affect on overall performance. Therefore, in an OLTP-type workload, dedicate approximately 75 percent of your available memory to the buffer pool and divide the rest among the sort heaps.

16.2.2 Ensuring There Are Enough Disks to Handle I/O

Do *not* size your disk requirements based on the disk capacity! In other words, if you have a 500GB database, do not buy only 500GB of disk. I/O performance comes from having enough physical disk drives to provide and sustain the throughput required for your workload. With the advent of 100GB and 200GB disks, it is easy to think that you simply need five disks to store a 1TB database. But when you want to read and scan your data, you have only five disks trying to supply all of the data to the processors to be read.

Having too few physical disks is the number one source of poor database performance, so do not get caught in this trap. Make sure that you have at least six to ten physical disks per CPU in your server; otherwise, you very likely will be building a system that will be I/O-starved and will constantly be waiting for I/O, and not working on processing your requests.

16.2.3 Ensuring There Are Enough CPUs to Handle the Workload

Just like a car, the bigger the engine, the faster it can go. In a computer the CPUs are the engine, and the power of the system depends on the number and speed of the CPUs. To handle a large amount of data and a number of concurrent users, you need to be sure that the system has enough CPUs so that you are not constantly utilizing 100 percent of the available CPUs.

It is important to strive for a balanced system that under normal operations is only consuming at most 80 percent of the available CPUs, so that you have room for spikes in activity such as month-end processing and morning application sign-ons.

16.3 THE DB2 CONFIGURATION ADVISOR

The Configuration Advisor is a tool that can be used to obtain an initial set of database configuration parameters. This tool can be run in either a graphical mode via the Control Center, or via command line.

Let's begin by covering how to use the Configuration Advisor via command line, and follow with the graphical version.

16.3.1 Invoking the Configuration Advisor from the Command Line

You can invoke the Configuration Advisor from the command line using the command `autoconfigure`. Figure 16.1 shows the syntax of the `autoconfigure` command.

```
>>-AUTOCONFIGURE--+----------------------------------------+----->
                  |           .----------------------------. |
                  |           V                          .  | |
                  '-USING----input-keyword--param-value-+-'

>--+------------------------------------+----------------------><
   |           .-DB ONLY----. |
   '-APPLY--+-DB AND DBM-+-'
            '-NONE-------'
```

Figure 16.1   The autoconfigure command

Table 16.1 lists and describes the input keywords.

Table 16.1   Input Keywords for the autoconfigure Command

Keyword	Valid Values [default]	Explanation
mem_percent	1–100 [80]	Percentage of memory to dedicate. If other applications (other than the operating system) are running on this server, set this to less than 100.
workload_type	simple, mixed, complex [mixed]	Simple workloads tend to be I/O intensive and mostly transactions, whereas complex workloads tend to be CPU-intensive and mostly queries.
num_stmts	1–1000000 [10]	Number of statements per unit of work.

(continues)

Table 16.1   Input Keywords for the autoconfigure Command *(Continued)*

Keyword	Valid Values [default]	Explanation
tpm	1–50000 [60]	Transactions per minute.
admin_priority	performance, recovery, both [both]	Optimize for better performance (more transactions per minute) or better recovery time.
is_populated	yes, no [yes]	Whether the database is populated with data.
num_local_apps	0–5000 [0]	Number of connected local applications.
num_remote_apps	0–5000 [10]	Number of connected remote applications.
isolation	RR, RS, CS, UR [RR]	Isolation level of applications connecting to this database (Repeatable Read, Read Stability, Cursor Stability, Uncommitted Read).
bp_resizeable	yes, no [yes]	Whether the buffer pools are resizable.

The **autoconfigure** command lets you apply the suggested changes to the database only (**DB ONLY**), the database and the database manager (**DB AND DBM**), or not apply the suggested changes at all (**NONE**).

You can also invoke the **autoconfigure** command as an option of the **CREATE DATABASE** command:

```
CREATE DATABASE mydb
      AUTOCONFIGURE using mem_percent 75 APPLY DB AND DBM
```

16.3.2 Invoking the Configuration Advisor from the Control Center

The Configuration Advisor asks you a series of questions about the database server, the nature of the workload, transactions, priority, connections, and isolation level to determine a starting set of database configuration parameter values. You can modify these parameters later to suit the production workload and for additional fine-tuning.

The following are the general steps for configuring a database for optimal performance using the Configuration Advisor.

1. Open the DB2 Control Center.
2. Select the database to be configured.
3. Choose the Configuration Advisor.
4. Complete each of the applicable wizard pages. Discussion of each page follows.
5. The *Finish* button is available once enough information has been supplied for the Configuration Advisor to configure performance parameters for the database.
6. Click *Finish* to get a list of suggested configuration parameters for the database.

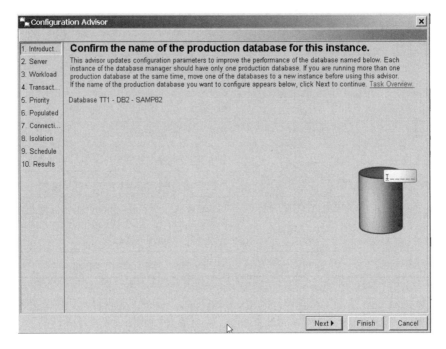

Figure 16.2   The Configuration Advisor Introduction page

As you can see in Figure 16.2, the Configuration Advisor takes you through step-by-step.

The Introduction page lists the database that is currently being examined (see Figure 16.2). Verify that the correct database is shown. If the correct database is not listed, you might have selected a different database by mistake. Close the Configuration Advisor by selecting *Cancel* and start again.

Use the Server page to specify what percentage of the server's memory is to be used by the database manager (see Figure 16.3). For a dedicated DB2 server, choose 100 percent; if other applications are also running on the server, set the value to less than 100 percent.

On the Workload page, indicate the type of workload for which the database will be used (see Figure 16.4). Indicate if the database is used mainly for queries (for a data warehousing environment), for transactions (for an order entry application), or a mixed workload (for a combination of queries and transactions).

Use the Transactions page to describe a typical SQL transaction for the database (see Figure 16.5). Indicate whether the average number of SQL statements per transaction is typically fewer than or more than 10. It is also important to give an indication of the transaction rate for the database.

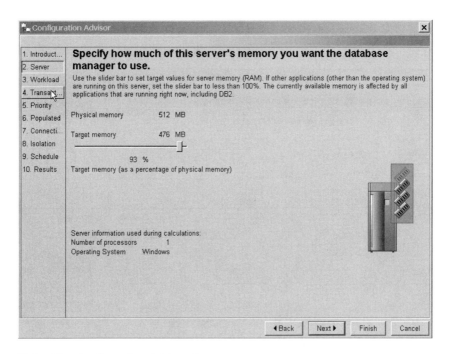

Figure 16.3 The Configuration Advisor Server page

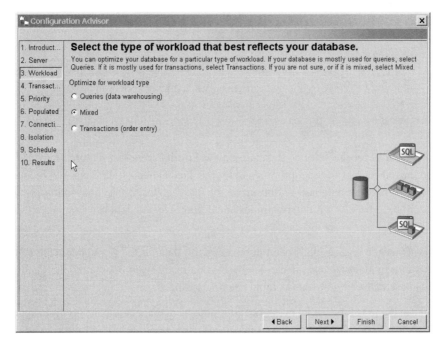

Figure 16.4 The Configuration Advisor Workload page

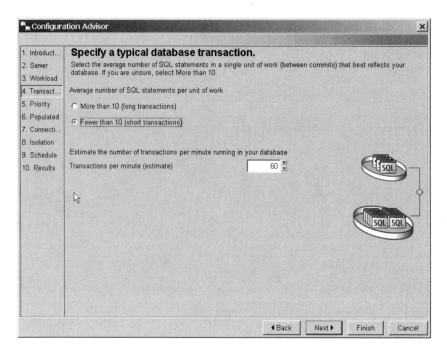

Figure 16.5   The Configuration Advisor Transactions page

> **N O T E**   Use the Snapshot Monitor with the **get snapshot**
> command (discussed in section 16.7, The Snapshot Monitor) to get an
> accurate measurement of the number of transactions per minute if the
> database is already operational.

Specify the priority for the selected database on the Priority page (see Figure 16.6). If the data-base is optimized for fast transaction processing, the database may take longer to recover in the event of an error. If the database is optimized for fast recovery time, transaction performance normally will be slower. If it is equally important to optimize both, choose to balance the optimi-zation of the two.

Indicate whether the database has been populated with data on the Populated page (see Figure 16.7). This is important because if the database has already been populated, the Configuration Advisor can use database statistics as input to its suggestions.

Indicate the average number of local applications and the average number of remote applications that will connect to the database on the Connections page (see Figure 16.8). If these numbers are not available and you don't have a good estimate, use the default values.

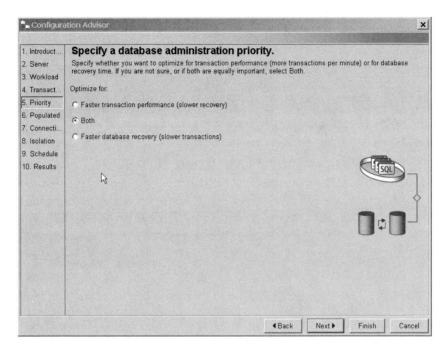

Figure 16.6 The Configuration Advisor Priority page

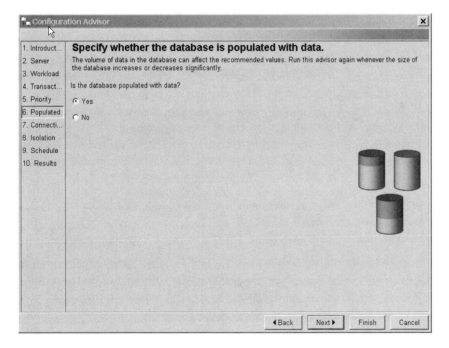

Figure 16.7 The Configuration Advisor Populated page

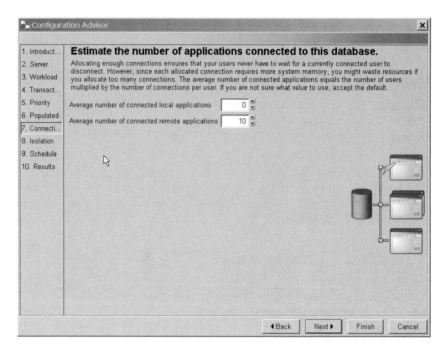

Figure 16.8   The Configuration Advisor Connections page

> Use the Snapshot Monitor to get an accurate measurement of the num-
> ber of remote and local applications that connect to the database.

Specify the isolation level that the applications will use to access the database on the Isolation
page (see Figure 16.9). If you use multiple isolation levels, specify the one that is used most frequently in the applications, or the one used by the most important application. Refer to Chapter 11,
Understanding Concurrency and Locking, for more information about isolation levels.

Specify whether a tools catalog database should be created to store information about scheduled
tasks on the Schedule page (see Figure 16.10). The Task Center is required for the DB2 scheduling function to be enabled, and it requires the tools catalog (see section 4.4.4, The Task Center).

The Results page displays the Configuration Advisor's recommended configuration parameter
settings based on the information provided (see Figure 16.11). You can choose to apply the suggestions immediately, or save them to a script so you can apply the changes later.

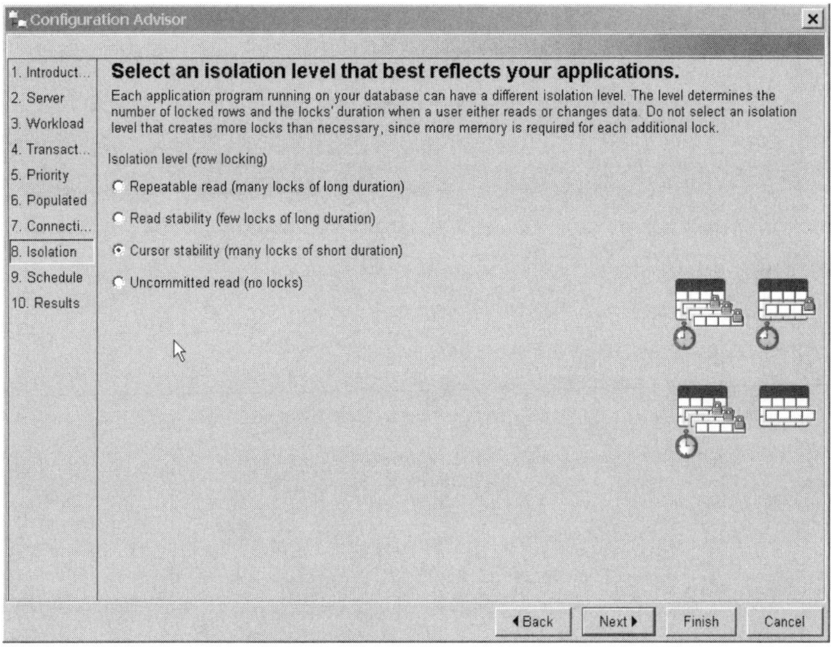

Figure 16.9 The Configuration Advisor Isolation page

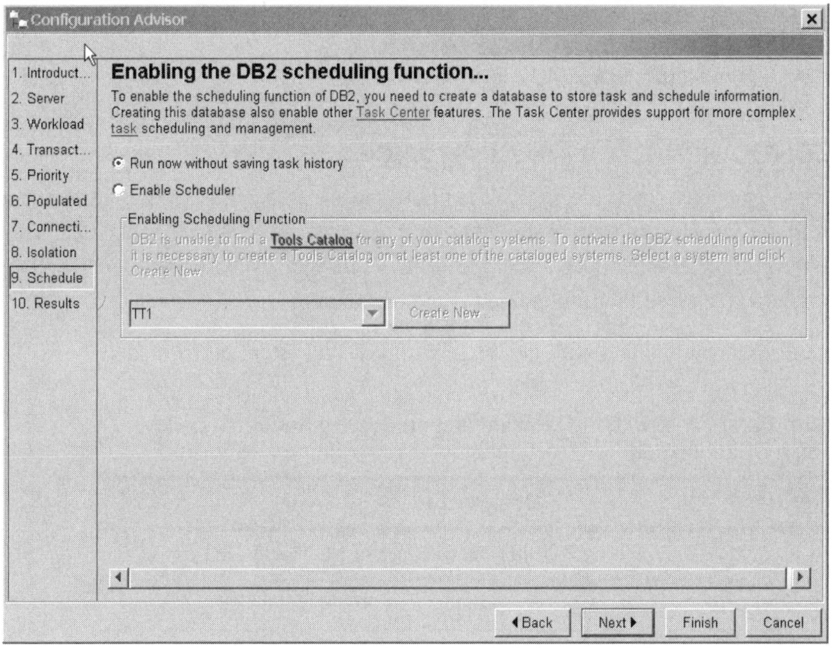

Figure 16.10 The Configuration Advisor Schedule page

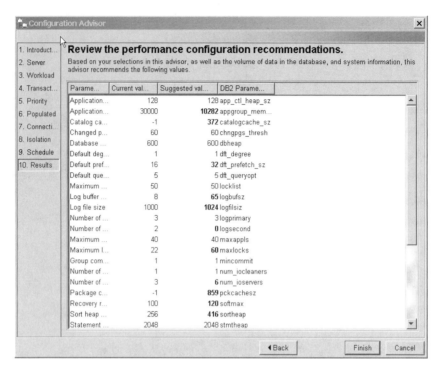

Figure 16.11   The Configuration Advisor Results page

16.4 CONFIGURING THE DB2 INSTANCE

The Database Manager (instance-level) Configuration parameters affect the performance of all databases in the instance and all applications that access databases in the instance. This section examines the parameters that have the biggest impact on the system performance and gives suggestions on how to choose the right value for the parameter.

Table 16.2 lists the parameters with the biggest impact on system performance.

Table 16.2   Parameters with the Most Impact on System Performance for Configuring a DB2 Instance

Parameter Name	Description
RQRIOBLK	Maximum requester I/O block size.
INTRA_PARALLEL	Enables intra-partition parallelism.
SHEAPTHRES	Sort heap threshold.
NUM_INITAGENTS	Initial number of agents in pool.
NUM_POOLAGENTS	Agent pool size.

16.4.1 Maximum Requester I/O Block Size

The **requester I/O block** is a piece of memory that is used to send data back and forth between the DB2 server and the clients where the applications are running. This memory block passes application requests from the client to the server and returns the result set from the server back to the client. DB2 allocates as much memory as it needs, up to the maximum requester I/O block size. If the application request or the result set is larger than the block size, the data must be split into multiple blocks. These blocks are then sent using multiple underlying communication packets.

By default, the maximum size of requester I/O block size is 32KB; its maximum size is 64KB. Since DB2 only allocates and uses what is required, it is good practice to increase this to the maximum of 64KB, especially if your application requests and/or the result sets generated by your applications are greater than 32KB. This results in less network traffic and normally allows result sets to be returned to the application more quickly.

To increase the maximum requester I/O block size to 64KB, use the command:

```
update dbm cfg using rqrioblk 64
```

16.4.2 Intra-Partition Parallelism

Intra-partition parallelism refers to the ability to break up a query into multiple parts within a single database partition and execute these parts at the same time. This type of parallelism subdivides what is usually considered a single database operation, such as index creation, database load, or SQL queries, into multiple parts, many or all of which can be executed in parallel within a single database partition. You can use intra-partition parallelism to take advantage of multiple processors of a symmetric multiprocessor (SMP) server.

It is important to note that intra-partition parallelism is not recommended for all workloads, even if you are running DB2 on an SMP server. In general, if your workload is mostly OLTP and is composed of a large number of simple SQL statements, you will get better overall performance by disabling intra-partition parallelism. If you are running mostly large, complex queries on an SMP server, you likely will gain from enabling intra-partition parallelism.

You can enable or disable intra-partition parallelism using the instance-level configuration parameter INTRA_PARALLEL as follows:

```
update dbm cfg using intra_parallel yes
```

or

```
update dbm cfg using intra_parallel no
```

16.4.3 Sort Heap Threshold

If you issue an SQL statement that includes an ORDER BY, GROUP BY, or DISTINCT clause, DB2 must either use an index to sort the data or perform a sort operation. DB2 will need to sort the data if you have not defined an appropriate index on one or more of the tables you are querying.

DB2 can perform either a private sort or a shared sort. If you have not enabled intra-partition parallelism, then DB2 can perform private sorts only. If you have enabled intra-partition parallelism, DB2 then can choose private or shared sorts, depending on which is more optimal.

DB2 creates and assigns each individual sort its own sort heap space. The sort heap threshold specifies the maximum amount of memory that can be simultaneously used for private sorts across all databases in the DB2 instance. When the total amount of private sort memory in use reaches the sort heap threshold, DB2 reduces the amount of memory that is assigned to subsequent sort operations. So in effect, the sort heap threshold is a soft limit, since DB2 can allocate more total sort space than the sort heap threshold specifies.

Set the sort heap threshold based on the size of your database sort heaps and the average number of concurrently executing applications. For example, if:

 • The sort heap for your database is set to 256 pages

and

 • Database monitor snapshots show an average of 20 concurrently executing applications

you should set the sort heap threshold to at least 5,120 pages (20 x 256 = 5120). Since some access plans do more than one sort operation, you may want to set the sort heap threshold to 10,240 pages. To set the sort heap threshold to this value, use the command:

```
update dbm cfg using sheapthres 10240
```

16.4.4 The DB2 Agent Pool

Since all database requests are handled by the DB2 agents, the agent configuration is very important to overall system performance. The two main configuration parameters that influence the agent operation are the agent pool size and the number of initialized agents.

Let's step through the interaction of applications, DB2 agents, and the agent pool using as an example a database that has not been activated and that has had no other connections (i.e., immediately after a **db2start** was issued). When an application requests a connection to the database, DB2 creates a db2 agent process (or thread on Windows) to handle the application's requests. There is some overhead involved in creating this agent process and with freeing it when the application disconnects from the database.

The goal of the agent pool is to eliminate the overhead of creating and deleting the agent processes for all applications. If you configure DB2 to use the agent pool, when your applications disconnect from the database, instead of deleting the agent process, it is placed in the agent pool for reuse by other applications. An agent in the agent pool is considered idle, since it is not working on behalf of an application.

When a subsequent application requests a database connection, DB2 will examine the agent pool to see if there is an available agent that can be reused. If there is, it is then associated with the application that needs it, and DB2 avoids the overhead of creating the agent process. The agent pool size (NUM_POOLAGENTS) specifies the number of idle agents that DB2 will maintain before ending the agent processes as they become idle.

In the above example, the number of initialized agents was zero (by default), so that the first connection to the database always needs to create the DB2 agent process. DB2 also allows you to prime the idle agent pool when DB2 is started so that you do not have the overhead of creating the first few agent processes. The number of initialized agents (NUM_INITAGENTS) specifies the number of idle agents to create in the agent pool when DB2 is started to optimize the initial database connection requests.

If your workload contains relatively few concurrent applications, you do not need to have a large idle agent pool, as this may waste resources if you create more agents than needed. If your workload contains a number of concurrent applications, you should have an idle agent pool that will avoid the cost of constantly creating and ending the agent processes.

To set the size of the agent pool to 64, use the command:

```
update dbm cfg using num_poolagents 64
```

To initialize 32 agents when DB2 is started to minimize the overhead of the initial application connect requests, use the command:

```
update dbm cfg using num_initagents 32
```

In this case, when the DB2 instance is started there will be 32 agent processes created in the idle agent pool. The first 32 applications (assuming that intra-partition parallelism is disabled for this example) will then use these agent processes. The 33rd application will find that there are no agent processes in the pool, so DB2 will create one for the application. This will continue for all subsequent applications unless one of the previous applications disconnects. If no applications disconnect, the idle agent pool will not be used. However, as applications disconnect from the database, DB2 will keep up to 64 idle agents in the pool to wait for reuse. If you had 100 applications connected, the first 64 would have their agents put into the pool as they disconnect. When the 65th application disconnects, its agent process will be terminated since the idle agent pool is already full.

16.5 CONFIGURING YOUR DATABASES

The database configuration parameters affect all aspects of your database performance and all applications that access the database. This section examines the parameters that have the biggest impact on system performance and provides suggestions on how to choose the right value for the parameter.

Table 16.3 lists the parameters with the biggest impact on system performance.

Table 16.3   Parameters with the Most Impact on System Performance for Configuring Your Database

Parameter Name	Description
AVG_APPLS	Average number of active applications.
MINCOMMIT	Number of commits to group.
LOGBUFSZ	Size of the log buffer.
SORTHEAP	Memory available for sorts.
SHEAPTHRES_SHR	Shared sort heap threshold.
LOCKLIST	Memory available to store lock information.
MAXLOCKS	Percent of lock list per application.
NUM_IOSERVERS	Number of I/O servers.
NUM_IOCLEANERS	Number of asynchronous page cleaners.
CHNGPGS_THRESH	Changed pages threshold before soft checkpoint.
SOFTMAX	Percent of log file before soft checkpoint.

The database buffer pools also have a very big impact on the performance of the database and its applications. You can choose the size of your buffer pools based on the default buffer pool size (BUFFPAGE), or you can size each buffer pool individually using the **create bufferpool** or **alter bufferpool** statements. (See section 8.5, Buffer Pools, for a detailed discussion of buffer pool usage.)

16.5.1 Average Number of Active Applications

The DB2 optimizer uses the value you set for the average number of active applications when it is determining the optimal access plans for statements in your applications. This number is used to determine the percentage of total system resources that each application can use.

Examine your current workload to determine the best setting for the average number of active applications. You can do this by taking database monitor snapshots at various times throughout the day and averaging the *Average number of concurrently executing applications* snapshot element. You can get this information for the sample database using either of the following commands:

```
GET SNAPSHOT FOR DATABASE
ON sample | grep -i 'Appls. executing in db manager currently'
```

or

```
SELECT appls_in_db2
FROM table(snapshot_database('sample', -1)) as snapshot_database
```

> **N O T E**   The Snapshot Monitor functions are discussed in detail in section 16.7, Snapshot Monitoring.

You can then set the average number of active applications for the database sample based on the snapshot information as follows:

```
update db cfg for sample using avg_appls 10
```

16.5.2 Database Logging

The log buffer is an area of memory that helps speed up the database logging process. DB2 writes information about all transactions to the log buffer and then flushes this buffer to disk periodically. This improves database performance since DB2 does not have to write every change to disk immediately. before making the changes in the database. This process is known as **write-ahead logging**. Remember that writing log records to disk is different than writing database changes to disk. Database changes are written (flushed) to disk either during buffer pool cleaning or when the buffer pool is full.

To ensure the integrity of your database, DB2 writes the log buffers to disk when:

- One or more transactions commit
- The log buffer is full
- One second has elapsed since the last log buffer flush

By default the log buffer is flushed to disk after every commit statement. However, for a database with a lot of concurrent applications, you can tell DB2 to wait to flush the log buffer until a specific number of commits occur. This number is known as the **number of commits to group** and is controlled by the MINCOMMIT database configuration parameter. When you set this parameter to a value greater than one, the applications that issue a commit may not return immediately because DB2 must ensure that the log buffer is written to disk before returning to the application. If you have many applications running very small, short transactions, you may see a slow down in the applications since they may wait up to one second for the commits to return. You can increase the number of commits to group for the sample database to a value of 5 using the command:

```
update db cfg for sample using mincommit 5
```

Since the log buffer is also flushed to disk when it becomes full, it is important to have a log buffer that is large enough that it is not constantly being written to disk. To increase the size of the log buffer for the *sample* database to 250 pages, use the command:

```
update db cfg for sample using logbufsz 250
```

16.5.3 Sorting

There are two database configuration parameters that affect sorting in your database applications. The database sort heap (SORTHEAP) specifies the maximum amount of memory that each individual sort can use.

You will not be able to have a large enough sort heap so that all sorts can occur in memory, especially for a large data warehouse. Therefore, you need to estimate the sort heap requirements for your system based on the EXPLAIN information for the queries being executed. The EXPLAIN output tells you if the optimizer has chosen to perform a sort to build the result set for your query. If there is a sort in the access plan, then in the sort portion of the access plan, there are two pieces of information:

- The average row size
- The estimated number of rows to be sorted

You can multiply these two values together to get a rough estimate of the memory required for the sort operation.

> **NOTE** Each row that is being sorted uses some extra space in the sort heap, so there is some overhead required to perform the sort.

You can set the sort heap threshold for the *sample* database as follows:

```
update db cfg for sample using sortheap 6400
```

As discussed earlier, private and shared sorts use memory from two different memory areas. The maximum amount of memory available for shared sorts (the shared sort heap threshold, SHEAPTHRES_SHR) within a database is allocated when the database is activated or when your first application connects to the database. When any shared sort occurs within the database it uses memory within this area. If there are already a number of shared sorts in process, and your application attempts to perform another shared sort, DB2 checks to make sure there is enough memory within this shared sort area. If there is enough memory available, the sort will be done as normal; if there is not enough memory available, the sort will be overflowed and DB2 creates a temporary table to perform the sort.

> **NOTE** Unlike the sort heap threshold, the shared sort heap threshold is a hard limit.

You can set the shared sort heap threshold for the *sample* database using the following command:

```
update db cfg for sample using sheapthres_shr 120000
```

16.5.4 Locking

When you are accessing data in a database, DB2 acquires locks as it is reading the data. The mode of the lock and the object that the lock is obtained on are determined by the isolation level of the application. No matter on which object the lock is held, DB2 needs to store and manage the information about all locks in the database. This information is stored in the database lock list. The lock list size (LOCKLIST) specifies the amount of memory that is available to store the lock information for the database. You can set the size of the lock list for the *sample* database using the command:

```
update db cfg for sample using locklist 2048
```

If the lock list becomes full, DB2 will perform **lock escalation**: the process where DB2 replaces a number of row-level locks with a single table lock. This can drastically reduce the amount of free space in the lock list for future lock requests.

Lock escalation can also occur when the number of locks held by a single application reaches or exceeds the maximum percent of lock list before escalation (MAXLOCKS). When an application reaches or exceeds this value, DB2 performs lock escalation by:

1. Examining the lock list for all locks held by the application to determine which database object has the most row-level locks held on it by this application,
2. Requesting a table-level lock on this table, and
3. Releasing the row-level locks once the table lock is granted.

The default setting for the maximum percent of lock list before escalation is 10 percent on UNIX and 22 percent on Windows and Linux. You may want to increase this, especially for databases with few applications, as this can cause premature escalation. To increase the maximum percent of lock list before escalation to 35 percent, use the command:

```
update db cfg for sample using maxlocks 35
```

16.5.5 Buffer Pool Prefetching and Cleaning

When DB2 agents are working to service your applications, they need to read and manipulate data within the database buffer pools. If the page that DB2 needs is not already in the buffer pool, it has to be read from disk and placed into the buffer pool before DB2 can scan or update the page.

DB2 can detect when your applications are reading pages and can read them into the buffer pool before your applications need them, saving the time the applications must wait to get its result set from DB2. This is known as **prefetching**. You can control the amount of prefetching that your system can perform by using the number of I/O servers (NUM_IOSERVERS) configuration parameter.

In the previous example the buffer pool is full, so when DB2 tries to read a page from disk into the buffer pool, DB2 must choose a spot in the buffer pool to place the new page. If there is a page already in this spot, DB2 will check the page to see if it has changed since it was placed into the buffer pool. If it has not changed, DB2 can simply replace this page with the new page. If it has changed, DB2 must first write the page back to disk since it cannot lose these changes. Only after the page has been written to disk can the new page replace it in the buffer pool.

To try to eliminate these wait conditions, DB2 periodically—and asynchronously—writes changed pages in the buffer pool back to disk. This is known as **buffer pool page cleaning**. You can control the amount of buffer pool page cleaning that your system can perform using the number of asynchronous page cleaners (NUM_IOCLEANERS) configuration parameter.

Prefetching is most efficient if your table spaces have more than one container, allowing DB2 to take advantage of parallel I/O. Base the number of prefetchers on the number of physical disks on which you have created table spaces for your database. If your database named *sample* has table space containers on 32 different physical disks, you can set the number of prefetchers for the database to 32 using the command:

```
update db cfg for sample using num_ioservers 32
```

If your applications perform a lot of update operations, increasing the number of asynchronous page cleaners will help to improve the overall performance of your database applications. If a system crashes due to a power failure or some other reason, this also helps to reduce the database recovery time because it keeps writing changes to disk instead of having a buffer pool full of a large number of changes.

Since all the page cleaners are triggered at the same time, having too many can overwhelm your system. As a general rule of thumb, do not configure more asynchronous page cleaners than there are CPUs in your DB2 server. For an eight-way SMP server, you can set the number of asynchronous page cleaners for the *sample* database to eight using the command:

```
update db cfg for sample using num_iocleaners 8
```

There are two different configuration parameters that let you control how frequently the page cleaners are triggered.

- The changed page threshold (CHNGPGS_THRESH) tells DB2 to trigger the page cleaners after any of the database's buffer pools is this percent used by pages that have changed since they were read into the buffer pool.
- The percent of the log file reclaimed before the soft checkpoint database configuration parameter (SOFTMAX) tells DB2 to trigger the page cleaners after this percent of any of the database log files has been filled by your transactions.

> **N O T E**   DB2 also triggers the page cleaners if a DB2 agent is attempting to place a page into the buffer pool and needs to write a changed page to disk before it can place the page in the buffer pool.

16.6 LACK OF PROPER MAINTENANCE

There are two important database maintenance operations that you need to perform on a regular basis.

- Reorganize your tables and indexes as they become unclustered due to INSERT, UPDATE, and DELETE statements.
- Keep the statistics on your tables and indexes current, especially as you add, change, or remove data from your tables.

The DB2 optimizer uses the statistics about your tables and indexes when it is building the access plan for the statements executed by your applications. If the statistics are out of date or show that the data is not clustered according to the indexes you have defined on the tables, the optimizer cannot choose the most efficient access plan.

Statistics about your database objects are stored in the database's system catalog tables. DB2 reads this information when the optimizer is building the access plan for one of your SQL statements. You can update this information with the current statistics by using one of these methods:

- Running the **RUNSTATS** utility
- Using the **LOAD** utility to load data into one of your tables
- Running the **REORGCHK** command

Use the **RUNSTATS** utility to gather new, updated statistics for tables and indexes after you have done any of the following:

- Reorganized a table or index
- Added a large number of rows to a table using the **LOAD** or **IMPORT** utilities
- Made a large number of changes to the data in the table using **INSERT**, **UPDATE**, or **DELETE** statements.
- Changed a table space's prefetch size

The reorganize utility clusters the data in the table so that it is in the same order as the index you specify. Be sure to specify the index that is most often used to join this table with other tables, and/or to access data in this table as a result of the SQL you are executing. To reorganize the table named *org* so that it is clustered in the same order as the index *orgx* on the table, use the command:

```
reorg table org index orgx
```

You can also reorganize a table using the Control Center by opening the tables list, selecting the table you wish to reorganize, and then right-clicking on the table and choosing the **Reorganize** option. This displays the dialog shown in Figure 16.12.

You can choose the index on which you wish to cluster the data, and also choose whether you want to perform an online or offline load. You can then open the *Schedule* tab and choose to

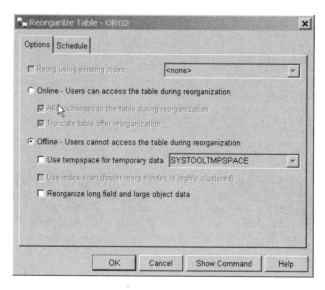

Figure 16.12   REORG utility options

either schedule the reorganization for a later time or run the reorganization immediately (see Figure 16.13). You can then select *OK*.

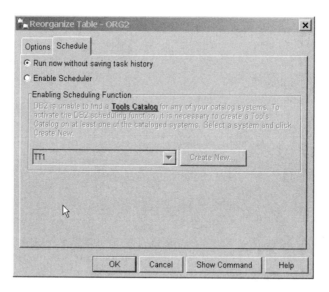

Figure 16.13   Scheduling a REORG

After reorganizing the table, be sure to capture the new statistics on the table. This is done using the command:

```
runstats on table johndoe.org
```

Since you also have at least one index on this table, you should capture the index statistics at the same time. Therefore it would be better to run the command:

```
runstats on table johndoe.org and indexes all
```

If this table contains a lot of data, and/or you have a lot of indexes defined, you should capture detailed statistics on the table and indexes. This is done using the command:

```
runstats on table johndoe.org
    with distribution and detailed indexes all
```

This provides the optimizer with the most complete statistics on the table data and indexes. You can also gather statistics using the Control Center. Open the tables list, select the table you wish to reorganize, right-click on the table, and choose the **Run Statistics** option. This displays the dialog shown in Figure 16.14.

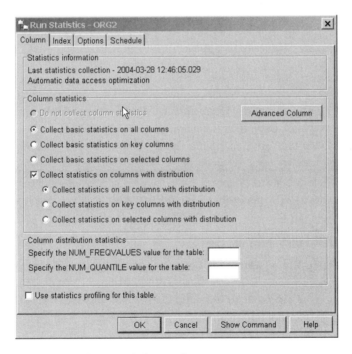

Figure 16.14   The RUNSTATS utility: Column tab

On the *Column* tab in this dialog you can tell DB2 whether you want to capture basic statistics or if you want to capture distribution statistics on the table. You can then go to the *Index* tab to choose the index on which you want the data clustered (see Figure 16.15).

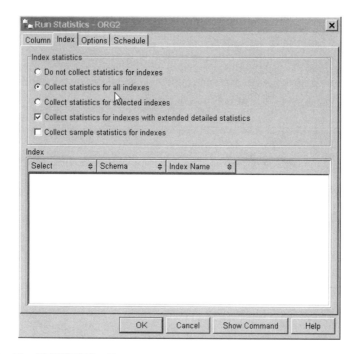

Figure 16.15   The RUNSTATS utility: Index tab

You can also specify if you want to capture detailed statistics that help the optimizer choose the most efficient access plans. Open the *Schedule* tab and choose to either schedule the run statistics operation for a later time or to run it immediately. You can then select *OK*.

> **N O T E**   Refer to Chapter 12, Maintaining Data, for more details
> about the **REORG, REORGCHK,** and **RUNSTATS** utilities.

16.7 THE SNAPSHOT MONITOR

To ensure that your system is performing optimally and to examine any issues that may arise, you normally will need to take DB2 snapshots. DB2 snapshots are like taking an X-ray of the various performance indicators within the DB2 engine, and just like doctors examine X-rays, you will examine the snapshot information.

Before capturing a snapshot, first determine what data you need the database manager to gather. Table 16.4 lists the information provided by the Snapshot Monitor, the monitor switch name, and the DBM parameter. If you want any of the following special types of data to be collected, set the appropriate monitor switches.

Table 16.4 Data Returned by the Snapshot Monitor

Group	Information Provided	Monitor Switch	DBM Parameter
Sorts	Number of heaps used, over-flows, sorts performance	SORT	DFT_MON_SORT
Locks	Number of locks held, number of deadlocks	LOCK	DFT_MON_LOCK
Tables	Measure activity (rows read, rows written)	TABLE	DFT_MON_TABLE
Buffer pools	Number of reads and writes, time taken	BUFFERPOOL	DFT_MON_BUFPOOL
Unit of work	Start times, end times, completion status	UOW	DFT_MON_UOW
SQL statements	Start time, stop time, statement identification	STATEMENT	DFT_MON_STMT
Timestamp	Timestamps for operations	TIMESTAMP	DFT_MON_TIMESTAMP

The switches corresponding to the information provided in Table 16.4 are all OFF by default, except for the switch corresponding to times and timestamp information, which is ON by default.

In Version 8, you can take a snapshot using either:

- The `get snapshot` command

or

- SQL SELECT statements against table functions

The SQL table functions are very powerful: You can use the power of the SQL language to gather only the information that you are interested in, and you can examine changes in the output over time.

Table 16.5 lists the different levels at which you can take snapshots.

Table 16.5 Levels for Taking Monitoring Snapshots

Level	Information Captured
Application	Applications.
Buffer Pool	Buffer pool activity.
Database	Databases.

(continues)

Table 16.5   Levels for Taking Monitoring Snapshots *(Continued)*

Level	Information Captured
Database Manager (Instance)	For an active instance.
Dynamic SQL	Point-in-time statement from the SQL statement cache for the database.
Lock	For locks held by applications against a database.
Table	For tables within a database.
Table Space	For table spaces within a database.

16.7.1 Setting the Monitor Switches

To capture snapshot information, the Snapshot Monitors must be enabled. You can enable them at either the instance or session level.

To enable the monitors at the instance level, you need to update the database configuration and set the monitor switch to ON:

```
update dbm cfg using DFT_MON_BUFPOOL ON
```

To enable the monitors at the session level, you can update the monitor switch directly:

```
update monitor switches using BUFFERPOOL ON
```

When you have set monitor switches at the session level, you can only take snapshots in the same session. Snapshots taken in one session will not pick up the monitor switch settings for other sessions. If you have set the instance-level monitor switch and stopped and restarted DB2, you can take snapshots in any session attached to the DB2 instance.

16.7.2 Capturing Snapshot Information

Since Version 8, you can capture snapshot information in two ways:

- Using the **GET SNAPSHOT** command
- Selecting from a snapshot table function

The **GET SNAPSHOT** command captures the requested snapshot information and writes the information to the screen or to an ASCII file. You then need to examine the output of the snapshot for the information that you are looking for. Since you access the snapshot table functions using SQL, you can select only the data you are interested in, store the data quickly into a history table, and so on.

To get a snapshot for all of the activity on the database *sample*, you would issue the command:

```
get snapshot for all on sample
```

To get the same information using the snapshot table function, you would use the statement:

```
SELECT *
  FROM TABLE(SNAPSHOT_DATABASE('SAMPLE',-1 )) as SNAPSHOT_DATABASE
```

For a complete list of the snapshot table functions, refer to the *DB2 UDB SQL Reference*.

16.7.3 Resetting the Snapshot Monitor Switches

The data returned by a Snapshot Monitor is based primarily on counters, and the counters are associated with a monitor switch. Monitor switches are initialized or reset when one of the following occurs.

- Application-level monitoring is used, and the application connects to the database.
- Database-level monitoring is used, and the first application connects.
- Table-level monitoring is used, and the table is first accessed.
- Table space-level monitoring is used, and the table space is first accessed.
- Issuing the **RESET MONITOR** command.
- Turning on a particular monitor switch.

You can reset monitor switches for the entire instance by issuing the command **reset monitor all**, and for a database by issuing the command **reset monitor for database** *database_name.*

16.8 EVENT MONITORS

While Snapshot Monitors let you "take a picture" of your system at a given time, Event Monitors allow you to collect information based on an event. A typical example is the case of deadlocks. Since it is very difficult to determine when a deadlock is going to happen, taking a snapshot at the right time is almost impossible. Instead, you can use an Event Monitor, which will automatically collect the deadlock information when it occurs. Event Monitors can also be used to collect static and dynamic SQL statements.

The following example shows a sequence of statements that illustrate how to collect Event Monitor information using commands.

```
(1) create event monitor mymon1 for database, statements write to file 'e:\temp'
(2) set event monitor mymon1 STATE=1
(3) select * from employee
(4) set event monitor mymon1 STATE=0
(5) drop event monitor mymon1
(6) db2evmon -path e:\temp
```

In the example, (1) is the statement used to create the Event Monitor *mymon1*, which specifically collects DATABASE and STATEMENTS events. Other events that can be collected are DEADLOCKS, TABLESPACES, BUFFERPOOLS, CONNECTIONS and TRANSACTIONS.

In (2), the Event Monitor is turned on. (3) is used as an example of an SQL statement that should be captured by the Event Monitor. In (4) the Event Monitor is turned off. In (5) the Event Monitor is dropped or deleted, and in (6) the collected information is analyzed with the command **db2evmon**, the command line version of the Event Analyzer.

Figure 16.16 shows part of the output of the **db2evmon** command after the previous sequence of statements were performed.

```
--------------------------------------------------------------------------
                         EVENT LOG HEADER
  Event Monitor name: MYMON1
  Server Product ID: SQL08020
  Version of event monitor data: 7
  Byte order: LITTLE ENDIAN
  Number of nodes in db2 instance: 1
  Codepage of database: 1252
  Territory code of database: 1
  Server instance name: DB2
--------------------------------------------------------------------------


--------------------------------------------------------------------------
  Database Name: SAMPLE
  Database Path: H:\DB2\NODE0000\SQL00003\
  First connection timestamp: 06/06/2005 03:10:25.965440
  Event Monitor Start time:   06/08/2005 02:49:26.271226
--------------------------------------------------------------------------

3) Connection Header Event ...
  Appl Handle: 249
  Appl Id: *LOCAL.DB2.016DC5204042
  Appl Seq number: 0014
  DRDA AS Correlation Token: *LOCAL.DB2.016DC5204042
  Program Name    : db2bp.exe
  Authorization Id: DB2ADMIN
  Execution Id    : DB2ADMIN
  Codepage Id: 1252
  Territory code: 1
  Client Process Id: 3048
  Client Database Alias: SAMPLE
  Client Product Id: SQL08020
  Client Platform: Unknown
  Client Communication Protocol: Local
  Client Network Name:
  Connect timestamp: 06/06/2005 03:11:27.082303

4) Statement Event ...
  Appl Handle: 249
  Appl Id: *LOCAL.DB2.016DC5204042
  Appl Seq number: 0014
```

Figure 16.16 Output of the db2evmon command *(continues)*

```
Record is the result of a flush: FALSE
-------------------------------------------
Operation: Static Commit
Package  :
Consistency Token  :
Package Version ID  :
Cursor   :
Cursor was blocking: FALSE
-------------------------------------------
Start Time: 06/08/2005 02:49:26.367666
Stop Time:  06/08/2005 02:49:26.379876
Exec Time:  0.012210 seconds
Number of Agents created: 1
User CPU: 0.000000 seconds
System CPU: 0.000000 seconds
Fetch Count: 0
Sorts: 0
Total sort time: 0
Sort overflows: 0
Rows read: 0
Rows written: 0
Internal rows deleted: 0
Internal rows updated: 0
Internal rows inserted: 0
Bufferpool data logical reads: 0
Bufferpool data physical reads: 0
Bufferpool temporary data logical reads: 0
Bufferpool temporary data physical reads: 0
Bufferpool index logical reads: 0
Bufferpool index physical reads: 0
Bufferpool temporary index logical reads: 0
Bufferpool temporary index physical reads: 0
SQLCA:
  sqlcode: 0
  sqlstate: 00000

5) Statement Event ...
  Appl Handle: 249
  Appl Id: *LOCAL.DB2.016DC5204042
  Appl Seq number: 0015

  Record is the result of a flush: FALSE
  -------------------------------------------
  Type     : Dynamic
  Operation: Prepare
  Section  : 201
  Creator  : NULLID
  Package  : SQLC2E03
  Consistency Token  : AAAAAJHR
  Package Version ID  :
  Cursor   : SQLCUR201
  Cursor was blocking: FALSE
  Text     : select * from employee
```

Figure 16.16   Output of the db2evmon command *(continues)*

```
-------------------------------------------------
Start Time: 06/08/2005 02:49:37.126020
Stop Time:  06/08/2005 02:49:37.163379
Exec Time:  0.037359 seconds
Number of Agents created: 1
User CPU: 0.000000 seconds
System CPU: 0.010014 seconds
Fetch Count: 0
Sorts: 0
Total sort time: 0
Sort overflows: 0
Rows read: 0
Rows written: 0
Internal rows deleted: 0
Internal rows updated: 0
Internal rows inserted: 0
Bufferpool data logical reads: 0
Bufferpool data physical reads: 0
Bufferpool temporary data logical reads: 0
Bufferpool temporary data physical reads: 0
Bufferpool index logical reads: 0
Bufferpool index physical reads: 0
Bufferpool temporary index logical reads: 0
Bufferpool temporary index physical reads: 0
SQLCA:
  sqlcode: 0
  sqlstate: 00000

-------------------------------------------------
...
```

Figure 16.16   Output of the db2evmon command *(continued)*

You can also create Event Monitors through the Control Center (see section 11.6.5, Event Monitoring, for an example).

16.9 THE DB2 OPTIMIZER

The DB2 optimizer, as stated in previous chapters, is the brain of DB2. The optimizer is a sophisticated and complex set of algorithms whose main objective is to calculate the fastest way to retrieve your data based on your database statistics.

The DB2 optimizer performs a number of tasks during the creation of the internal-compiled form of your SQL statements.

1. **Parse the query**. The optimizer's first task is to analyze the SQL query to validate the syntax. If it detects any syntax errors, the optimizer stops processing, and the appropriate SQL error is returned to the application attempting to compile the SQL statement. When parsing is complete, an internal representation of the query is created.

2. **Check the query semantics**. The second task of the optimizer is to further validate the SQL statement by checking to ensure that the parts of the statement make sense given

the other parts, for example, ensuring that the data types of the columns input into scalar functions are correct for those functions. Also during this stage, the optimizer adds the behavioral semantics to the query graph model, such as the effects of referential constraints, table check constraints, triggers, and views.

3. **Rewrite the query**. The optimizer uses global semantics provided in the query graph model to transform the query into a form that can be optimized more easily. For example, the compiler might move a predicate, altering the level at which it is applied, in an attempt to improve query performance. This particular process is called **general predicate pushdown**. Any changes made to the query are rewritten back to the query graph model.

4. **Optimize the access plan**. The SQL optimizer portion of the optimizer uses the query graph model as input and generates many alternative execution plans for satisfying the user's request. It estimates the execution cost of each alternative plan using the statistics for tables, indexes, columns, and functions, and chooses the plan with the smallest estimated execution cost.

   The optimizer uses the query graph model to analyze the query semantics and to obtain information about a wide variety of factors, including indexes, base tables, derived tables, subqueries, correlation, and recursion.

   The output from this step of the optimizer is an **access plan**, which provides the basis for the information captured in the **explain tables**. The information used to generate the access plan can be captured with an **explain snapshot**.

5. **Generate the executable code**. The optimizer's final step uses the access plan and the query graph model to create an executable access plan, or section, for the query. This code generation step uses information from the query graph model to avoid repetitive execution of expressions that only need to be computed once for a query. Examples for which this optimization is possible include code page conversions and the use of host variables.

   Information about access plans for static SQL is stored in the system catalog tables. When the package is executed, DB2 UDB will use the information stored in the system catalog tables to determine how to access the data and provide results for the query. It is this information that is used by the db2expln tool.

It is recommended that you run the **RUNSTATS** command periodically on the tables used in queries where you need optimal performance. The optimizer will then be better equipped with relevant statistical information on the nature of the data. If the **RUNSTATS** command is not run, or the optimizer determines that **RUNSTATS** was run on empty or near-empty tables, the optimizer may either use defaults or attempt to derive certain statistics based upon the number of file pages used to store the table on disk.

16.10 THE EXPLAIN TOOL AND EXPLAIN TABLES

The **explain** tool examines the access plan chosen by the DB2 optimizer for your SQL statements. Explain information must be captured before you can review it using one of DB2's explain tools. While the query is being compiled, the information can be captured into a file or special tables known as **explain tables**. DB2 uses explain tables to store access plan information so that users can see the decisions that the optimizer has made. These explain tables are listed in Table 16.6.

Table 16.6   Explain Tables

Table Name	Description
EXPLAIN_ARGUMENT	Represents the unique characteristics for each individual operator.
EXPLAIN_INSTANCE	Main control table for all explain information. Each row of data in the explain tables is explicitly linked to one unique row in this table. Basic information about the source of the SQL statements being explained and environment information is kept in this table.
EXPLAIN_OBJECT	Contains data objects required by the access plan generated to satisfy the SQL statement.
EXPLAIN_OPERATOR	Contains all the operators needed to satisfy the SQL statement.
EXPLAIN_PREDICATE	Identifies which predicates are applied by a specific operator.
EXPLAIN_STATEMENT	Contains the text of the SQL statement in two forms. The original version entered by the user is stored in addition to the rewritten version that is the result of the compilation process.
EXPLAIN_STREAM	Represents the input and output data streams between individual operators and data objects. The data objects themselves are represented in the EXPLAIN_OBJECT table. The operators involved in a data stream are represented in the EXPLAIN_OPERATOR table.

The explain tables have to be created before any explain information can be gathered. This is normally done automatically the first time you invoke Visual Explain from the Command Editor. If you need to create the tables manually, use the script file **EXPLAIN.DDL** located in the *misc* subdirectory of the SQLLIB directory. This file contains the definition of the explain tables. To create the explain tables, you can connect to the database and then run the following command:

```
db2 -tvf explain.ddl
```

The explain tool can be invoked with the EXPLAIN statement, which has the following syntax:

```
>>-EXPLAIN--+-PLAN SELECTION-+---+--------------------+---------->
            +-ALL------------+   '-+-FOR--+--SNAPSHOT-'
            '-PLAN-----------'     '-WITH-'

>--+----------------+--+------------------------+-------------->
   '-WITH REOPT ONCE-'  '-SET QUERYNO =--integer-'

>--+----------------------------------+------------------------>
   '-SET QUERYTAG =--string-constant-'

>---FOR--explainable-sql-statement---------------------------><
```

Note that:

- Specifying PLAN SELECTION, ALL, or PLAN are all equivalent.
- The WITH SNAPSHOT option captures snapshot and EXPLAIN data. Using this option Visual Explain can create a graph of the access path, and you can also query the appropriate tables for EXPLAIN data.
- The FOR SNAPSHOT option captures only snapshot data that can be used by Visual Explain. EXPLAIN data is not stored in any table.

If you don't specify any of these options, which is the default, only EXPLAIN data is collected. This will provide EXPLAIN data, but not snapshot data required by the Visual Explain tool. For example, the following statement populates the EXPLAIN tables with EXPLAIN and snapshot data for the query *select * from employee*:

```
EXPLAIN PLAN WITH SNAPSHOT FOR "select * from employee"
```

16.11 Using Visual Explain to Examine Access Plans

Once the EXPLAIN data has been stored in the explain tables, it can be queried or displayed using Visual Explain or other explain tools. This section describes how to use the Visual Explain tool to review and analyze an access plan.

Visual Explain is a graphical utility that gives the database administrator or application developer the ability to examine the access plan determined by the optimizer. Visual Explain can only be used with access plans explained using the snapshot option.

You can use Visual Explain to analyze previously generated explain snapshots or to gather explain data and explain dynamic SQL statements. If the explain tables have not been created when you start Visual Explain, it will create them for you. You can invoke Visual Explain either from the Command Center or Control Center.

From the Control Center interface, right-click on the database where your explain snapshots are stored.

The **Explain SQL...** option lets you gather explain data and show the graphical representation of a dynamic SQL statement. This is the easiest way to explain a single SQL statement.

Choosing the option **Show Explained Statements History** opens a window that lists all of the explained statements. In this view you will see the SQL statements and their cost in **timerons** (an estimate of database resources).

To examine an access plan in detail, double-click on the explained statement or highlight the entry of interest and use the menu to select **Statement Show access plan** in the Explained Statements History window.

All of the explain statements will be displayed in the Explained Statements History list, but only the explained statements with EXPLAIN SNAPSHOT information can be examined using Visual Explain.

The Visual Explain output displays a hierarchical graph representing the components of an SQL statement. Each part of the query is represented as a graphical object. These objects are known as **nodes**. There are two basic types of nodes:

- **OPERATOR** nodes indicate an action that is performed on a group of data.
- **OPERAND** nodes show the database objects where an operator action takes place. An operand is an object that the operators act upon. These database objects are usually tables and indexes.

There are many operators that can be used by the DB2 UDB optimizer to determine the best access plan. Figure 16.17 shows some of the operators used by Visual Explain. These operators indicate how data is accessed (IXSCAN, TBSCAN, RIDSCN, IXAND), how tables are joined internally (MSJOIN, NLJOIN), and other factors, such as if a sort will be required (SORT). You can find more information about the operators in the Visual Explain online help. The objects shown in a Visual Explain graphic output are connected by arrows showing the flow of data from one node to another. The end of an access plan is always a RETURN operator.

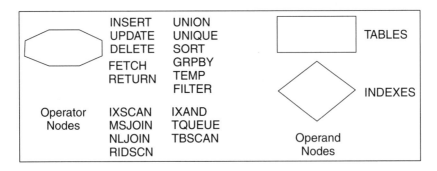

Figure 16.17   The explain operators

If your application is an OLTP-type application, and the explain plan for one or more of your queries indicates that DB2 is choosing a table scan, you should analyze the EXPLAIN data to determine the reasons why an index scan was not used. If you are administering a data warehouse, the most important thing to look for in the access plans is the type of join used. If you see that you are not using the optimal joins methods, examine the SQL statement and perhaps the partitioning keys and indexes to determine if you can change anything to allow collocation to occur in the joins.

16.12 CASE STUDY

In this case study assume that your database *POSDB* is supporting a point-of-sale system. Since you will be processing simple, single row selects, updates, and deletes, do not enable intra-partition parallelism. Check the INTRA_PARALLEL instance-level parameter to ensure it is disabled.

On Linux and UNIX you can use the **grep** tool to retrieve the intra-partition parallelism line as follows:

```
get dbm cfg | grep -I intra_parallel
```

The **-I** option after the **grep** command is used to ignore the case.

> **N O T E** On Windows you may need to parse the output manually. You can page through the output or redirect it to a file so you can search the file for the INTRA_PARALLEL string if needed.

If intra-partition parallelism is enabled, disable it using

```
update dbm cfg using intra_parallel off
```

Although you know there are 100 cash registers in your store, you do not know how many are normally active at the same time. To determine this information, capture some database manager snapshots over a period of time using the following statement:

```
SELECT rem_cons_in_exec , local_cons_in_exec,
   (rem_cons_in_exec + local_cons_in_exec) as total_executing
   FROM TABLE(SNAPSHOT_DBM(-1 ))
   as SNAPSHOT_DBM;
```

After capturing these snapshots over a period of time, calculate the average for the **total_executing** column in the output. If this average turns out to be 17, you can set the average number of active applications for your database to 17:

```
update db cfg for POSDB using avg_appls 17
```

You then notice that the performance of the system seems to slow down when there are a number of users using the application. Take a snapshot of the important performance related information using this statement:

```
SELECT
   db_name,
   rows_read,
   rows_selected,
   lock_waits,
   lock_wait_time,
   deadlocks,
   lock_escals,
   total_sorts,
   total_sort_overflows
   FROM table (snapshot_database ('POSDB ', -1) ) as snapshot_database
```

If this statement shows that a large percentage of the sorts are causing sort overflows, you need to examine the setting for your sort heap and sort heap threshold. Since intra-partition parallelism is disabled, there is no need to worry about the sort heap threshold for shared sorts.

```
get db cfg for posdb | grep -I sort
get dbm cfg  | grep -I sort
```

From the output of the above commands, look at the following lines in particular:

```
Sort list heap (4KB)                    (SORTHEAP) = 256
Sort heap threshold (4KB)               (SHEAPTHRES) = 1000
```

In this case you can see that the sort heap threshold is less than four times the value of the sort heap, so if there are more than three concurrent sorts, any subsequent sorts will have their sort heap reduced and are much more likely to overflow. Since the average number of concurrently executing applications you found earlier was 17, you should set the sort heap threshold to at least 17 times the sort heap. In this case you can choose 20 times the sort heap for ease of calculation (20 x 256 = 5120).

```
update dbm cfg using sheapthres 5120
```

Assume that you then retest the application and recapture the snapshots. In the snapshot you see that this did improve the percentage of overflowed sorts, but the percentage is still too high. Therefore, the sort heap itself is likely too small for the amount of data that is being sorted. If you then increase the sort heap, you should also increase the sort heap threshold accordingly to keep it at 20 times the sort heap.

> **NOTE** Having an excessively large sort heap makes sorts cost less to the DB2 optimizer, so do not increase the sort heap too much. Make this change iteratively, increasing the sort heap and sort heap threshold by small increments until you see the desired change in the percentage of overflow sorts and performance.

```
update db cfg for posdb using sortheap 400
update dbm cfg using sheapthres 8000
```

After retesting and recapturing the snapshots, you see that although this has improved the overall performance of your server, one of your applications still appears to be sluggish. Since this is specific to one application, it may be caused by poorly performing statements within the application. If the application is an embedded static SQL application, you can get the statements from your developers. If it is a dynamic SQL application, you can capture the SQL statements using the Snapshot Monitor or the Event Monitor.

You can run the application and then examine the performance of the SQL statements:

```
SELECT
(case
  when num_executions >0  then (rows_read / num_executions)
  else 0
end) as avg_rows_read,
(case
  when num_executions >0  then (rows_written / num_executions)
  else 0
```

```
end) as avg_rows_written,
(case
  when num_executions >0  then (stmt_sorts / num_executions)
  else 0
end) as avg_sorts,
(case
  when num_executions >0  then (total_exec_time / num_executions)
  else 0
end) as avg_exec_time,
substr(stmt_text,1,200) as SQL_Stmt
    FROM table (snapshot_dyn_sql ('sample', -1) ) as snapshot_dyn_sql
```

If you notice that there is one particular statement in the output of this SQL that has a long aver-age execution time and performs three sorts per execution, you can use the Design Advisor to help tune this statement. If you extract the statement text from the output above, and put it into the file *bad.sql*, you can run the Design Advisor from the command line using:

```
db2advis -d posdb -i bad.sql
```

If an index will help the performance of the query, the Index Advisor will tell you the definition of the index or indexes it recommends, as well as the new cost of the query and the percent improvement in the cost.

```
C:\temp>db2advis -d posdb -i bad.sql
Using user id as default schema name. Use -n option to specify schema
execution started at timestamp 2005-03-28-12.51.39.570001
found [1] SQL statements from the input file

Recommending indexes...
total disk space needed for initial set [    0.009] MB
total disk space constrained to         [   33.322] MB

Trying variations of the solution set.
Optimization finished.
  2  indexes in current solution
 [ 13.0000] timerons  (without recommendations)
 [  0.1983] timerons  (with current solution)
[98.47%] improvement
--
--
-- LIST OF RECOMMENDED INDEXES
-- ===========================
-- index[1],    0.009MB
   CREATE INDEX "DSNOW   "."IDX403281751440000" ON "DSNOW   "."ORGX" ("C1" ASC) ALLOW
REVERSE SCANS ;
   COMMIT WORK ;
   RUNSTATS ON TABLE "DSNOW   "."ORGX" FOR INDEX "DSNOW   "."IDX403281751440000";
   COMMIT WORK ;

-- RECOMMENDED EXISTING INDEXES
-- ===========================
-- ===========================
--
11 solutions were evaluated by the advisor
DB2 Workload Performance Advisor tool is finished.
```

You can run the **create index** and **runstats** statements from the Design Advisor output, and rerun your tests to make sure that this does improve you application's performance.

16.13 SUMMARY

This chapter covered the main factors that affect the performance of your database system: CPU usage, I/O utilization, and memory usage.

To configure DB2 for optimal performance, you need to understand how the database and Database Manager Configuration parameters impact your applications and the overall system. The Configuration Advisor can facilitate your tuning efforts with respect to parameter configuration.

Examining maintenance operations like **REORG** and **RUNSTATS** help keep the database running optimally, but you will also need to monitor you system using either the Snapshot Monitor or the Event Monitor to be sure it is running efficiently. If the snapshots indicate that a particular SQL statement is performing poorly, you can examine its access plan using the Explain tool.

> **N O T E** For more information about performance topics, we recommend *The Advanced DBA Certification Guide and Reference for DB2 Universal Database V8 for Linux, UNIX, and Windows* by Dwaine R. Snow and Thomas X. Phan (Prentice Hall, 2004).

16.14 REVIEW QUESTIONS

1. What isolation level acquires no row-level locks?
2. What is the maximum requester I/O block size?
3. How can you eliminate the need for the first connections to a database to create their own agent process?
4. When will a database's log buffer be written to disk?
5. When does lock escalation occur?
6. When can you capture the statistics about your tables and indexes?
7. What command can be used to remove overflow records from your tables?
8. What monitor switch is enabled by default in Version 8?
9. What command resets the counters reported by the database snapshot command?
10. What objects must exist in your database in order to use the visual explain tool?
11. Which of the following commands cannot update the statistical information about tables and indexes in your database?
   A. runstats
   B. load
   C. reorgchk
   D. import

12. Which of the following does not cause the log buffer to be written to disk?
    A. When the log buffer becomes full
    B. One second since the last time the log buffer was written to disk
    C. When applications issue MINCOMMIT commit statements
    D. When the percentage of the log buffer reaches SOFTMAX
13. When lock escalation occurs, row-level locks are converted to which of the following?
    A. Page-level locks
    B. Extent-level locks
    C. Table-level locks
    D. Table space-level locks
14. Which of the following configuration parameters allows DB2 to detect that pages are being read in order and automatically trigger prefetching?
    A. DETECT_PREFETCH
    B. SEQ_DETECT
    C. ENABLE_PREFETCH
    D. SCAN_DETECT
15. Which two of the following configuration parameters control when the page cleaners will be triggered to write dirty pages from the buffer pool to disk?
    A. NUM_IOCLEANERS
    B. SOFTMAX
    C. DIRTY_THRESH
    D. CHNGPGS_THRESH
    E. MAX_LOG
16. Which of the following commands will indicate that you need to reorganize your tables because they contain too many overflow records?
    A. reorgchk
    B. runstats
    C. inspect
    D. check
17. Which of the following SQL statements can cause an overflow record to be created by DB2?
    A. insert
    B. update
    C. delete
    D. reorg
18. Which of the following steps is not performed by the optimizer when building the access plan for an SQL statement?
    A. Query rewrite
    B. Check query semantics
    C. Parse the query
    D. Apply hints

19. Which of the following is not an operator that you will see in a DB2 access plan?

    A. IXSCAN

    B. TBSCAN

    C. RIDSCN

    D. DTSCAN

20. Given the following database configuration information:

```
Sort heap thres for shared sorts (4KB) (SHEAPTHRES_SHR) = 1000
Sort list heap (4KB)                        (SORTHEAP) = 256
```

what is the maximum number of concurrent shared sorts than can occur without causing the sort to overflow?

    A. 1

    B. 2

    C. 3

    D. 4

## CHAPTER 17

Diagnosing Problems

This chapter describes how to investigate problems you may encounter while working with DB2 and how to isolate them using diagnostic information. Once you isolate a problem, you can search for previously reported problems and identify workarounds.

In this chapter you will learn about:

- The big picture of DB2 problem diagnosis
- Obtaining more information about an error message
- Collecting diagnostic information: First Failure Data Capture (FFDC)
- The trace facility

17.1 PROBLEM DIAGNOSIS: THE BIG PICTURE

Figure 17.1 provides an overview of the actions that you can perform to investigate a problem further when working with DB2. The following sections describe the items in the figure in more detail.

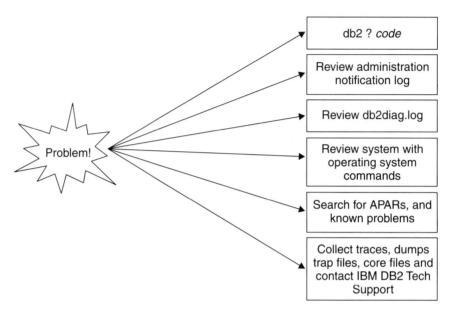

Figure 17.1   The big picture of problem diagnosis

17.2 HOW DOES DB2 REPORT PROBLEMS?

Typically when working with DB2, a problem is manifested by an error message. The error message may be reported immediately to the user, or it may be stored in some diagnostic file like the administration notification log or the db2diag.log (these diagnostic files are discussed in section 17.4, DB2 First Failure Data Capture).

Figures 17.2 and 17.3 show examples of DB2 reporting problems immediately after executing an operation. In Figure 17.2, after clicking on the instance *MYINST* in the object tree of the Control Center, getting the DB2 message SQL1032N indicates that this instance has not started.

In Figure 17.3, after entering the SQL statement **select from employee** in the CLP, getting the error SQL0104N indicates there is a syntax error in the statement (column names have not been specified).

Some problems may not report an error message. For example, if the DB2 instance hangs or the response time is very slow, you may need to run traces (see section 17.7, The DB2 Trace Facility).

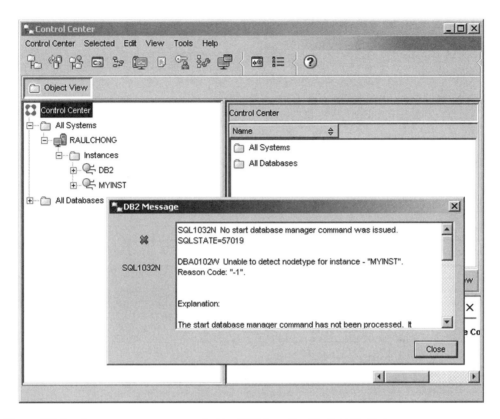

Figure 17.2   An error message reported by DB2 from the Control Center

Figure 17.3   An error message reported by DB2 from the CLP

17.3 DB2 Error Message Description

DB2 error messages are structured as follows:

CCCnnnnnS

where:

- *CCC* identifies the DB2 component returning the message. See Table 17.1 for a list of all components.
- *nnnnn* is a three- to five-digit error code.
- *S* is a severity indicator. When *S* has a value of *W*, it means a warning. When *S* has a value of *N*, it means it's an error (negative code).

Table 17.1 Error Message Component Description

Component	Message Source
ASN	Replication
CCA	Configuration Assistant
CLI	Call-level interface
DB2	Command Line Processor
DBA	Control Center and database administration utility
DBI	Installation or configuration
DWC	Data warehouse center
FLG	Information catalog manager
SAT	Satellite
SPM	Synch point manager
SQJ	Embedded SQLJ in Java
SQL	Database manager

To obtain more information about a code, you can use the help (**?**) command from the CLP as discussed in Chapter 4, Using the DB2 Tools. The help command lets you enter the error code in different ways. For example, if you want to get more information about SQLCODE -104, you can use any of the following:

```
db2 ? SQL0104N
db2 ? SQL104N
db2 ? SQL-0104
```

```
db2 ? SQL-104
db2 ? SQL-104N
```

The component keyword, in this case **SQL**, needs to prefix the error code. Negative numbers can be suffixed with the letter *n*. Figure 17.4 shows the output that displays when you use any of the above help commands.

Figure 17.4   Using the help (?) command

17.4 DB2 FIRST-FAILURE DATA CAPTURE

First-failure data capture (FFDC) is a general term applied to the set of diagnostic information that DB2 captures automatically when errors occur. This information reduces the need to reproduce errors to get diagnostic information. The information captured by FFDC is stored in the following files. (The DIAGPATH Database Manager Configuration parameter specifies the location of these files.)

- **Administration notification log**: When significant events occur, DB2 writes information to the administration notification log. The information is intended for use by database and system administrators. Many notification messages provide additional information to supplement the SQLCODE that is provided. The type of event and the level of detail of the information gathered are determined by the NOTIFYLEVEL configuration parameter. (The NOTIFYLEVEL parameter is discussed in the next section.)

On Windows systems, the DB2 administration notification log is not created as a separate file; instead, its entries are incorporated into the Windows event log and can be reviewed through the Windows Event Viewer.

On Linux and UNIX, the administration notification log for the instance is called *instance_name*.nfy.

- **db2diag.log**: Diagnostic information about errors is recorded in the db2diag.log text file. This information is more detailed than the administration notification log and is intended for DB2 technical support, but it can be useful for experienced database administrators. The level of detail of the information is determined by the DIAGLEVEL configuration parameter. (The DIAGLEVEL parameter is discussed in the next section.)
- **Dump files**: For some error conditions, extra information is logged in external binary files named after the failing process ID. These files have the file extension *xxx*, where *xxx* is the partition number. For single-partitioned environments, this extension is always *000*. Dump files are intended for use by DB2 technical support.
- **Trap files**: The database manager generates a trap file if it cannot continue processing because of a trap, segmentation violation, or exception. Trap file names begin with the letter *t* and have the file extension *TRP* on Windows systems and *xxx* on Linux/UNIX systems, where *xxx* is the partition number. These files are intended for use by DB2 technical support.
- **Core files** (Linux/UNIX only): When DB2 terminates abnormally, the operating system generates a core file. The core file is a binary file that contains information similar to the DB2 trap files. Core files may also contain the entire memory image of the terminated process. These files are intended for use by DB2 technical support.

17.4.1 The Database Manager Configuration Parameters Related to FFDC

The following Database Manager Configuration parameters are related to FFDC:

- DIAGPATH
- DIAGLEVEL
- NOTIFYLEVEL

17.4.1.1 The DIAGPATH Parameter

The DIAGPATH parameter specifies the fully qualified path in which DB2 puts the FFDC information. The default value for DIAGPATH is a null string. We recommend that you keep this default value. If you choose to change the value, we recommend that you use a centralized location, especially if there are multiple database instances.

When the value of DIAGPATH is a null string, the FFDC information is placed in the following locations.

- For Windows systems:
  - If the DB2INSTPROF environment variable is *not* set, the information is placed in DB2PATH*instance_name*. DB2PATH is the environment variable that indicates where DB2 is installed on a Windows system.
  - If the DB2INSTPROF environment variable *is* set, the information is placed in DB2INSTPROF*instance_name*,DB2INSTPROF is the environment variable that indicates the location of the instance directory. The DB2INSTPROF variable is normally not set, therefore instances on Windows are created under the directory specified in DB2PATH.
- For Linux/UNIX operating systems:
  - The information is placed in *$HOME*/sqllib/db2dump, where *$HOME* is the home directory of the instance owner.

We recommend that you clean out the DIAGPATH directory periodically to keep it from becoming too large.

17.4.1.2 The DIAGLEVEL Parameter

The DIAGLEVEL parameter specifies the type of diagnostic errors that will be recorded in the db2diag.log file. Table 17.2 lists the valid values for this parameter. The default level is 3. Increase the level to 4 if you want more information. However, be aware that the db2diag.log grows very fast at the 4 level due to the large amount of information logged.

Table 17.2   Values for the DIAGLEVEL Parameter

Value	What It Captures
0	No diagnostic data.
1	Only severe errors.
2	All errors.
3	All errors and warnings (this is the default).
4	All errors, warnings, and informational messages.

17.4.1.3 The NOTIFYLEVEL Parameter

The NOTIFYLEVEL parameter specifies the type of administration notification messages that are written to the administration notification log. On Linux/UNIX platforms, the administration notification log is a text file called *instance.nfy*. On Windows, all administration notification messages are written to the Event Log. The errors can be written by DB2, the Health Monitor, the Capture and Apply programs, and user applications. Table 17.3 lists the valid values for this parameter. You might wish to increase the value of this parameter to gather additional problem determination data to help resolve a problem.

Table 17.3   Values for the NOTIFYLEVEL Parameter

Value	What It Captures
0	No administration notification messages (this setting is not recommended).
1	Only fatal and unrecoverable errors.
2	Everything captured at NOTIFYLEVEL 1, plus conditions that require immediate attention from the system administrator or the database administrator. If the condition is not resolved, it could lead to a fatal error. Notification of very significant, non-error activities (for example, recovery) might also be logged at this level. This level captures Health Monitor alarms.
3	Everything captured at NOTIFYLEVEL 2, plus conditions that are nonthreatening and do not require immediate action but might indicate the system is not optimal. This level captures Health Monitor alarms, Health Monitor warnings, and Health Monitor attentions. This is the default.
4	Everything captured at NOTIFYLEVEL 3, plus informational messages.

17.4.2 db2diag.log Example

The following is an example of a db2diag.log entry at a diagnostic level of 3:

```
2004-06-01-18.30.19.884359-240 I1179921C311      LEVEL: Event
PID    : 163880            TID  : 1            PROC : db2star2
INSTANCE: db2inst1         NODE : 000
FUNCTION: DB2 UDB, config/install, sqlfLogUpdateCfgParam, probe:30
CHANGE  : CFG DBM: "Instance_Memory" <automatic> From: "3394" To: "2405"
```

Here is a breakdown of the entries in this db2diag.log:

- The message was generated at *2004-06-01-18.30.19.884359*.
- The process ID (PID) is *163880*.
- The thread ID (TID) is *1*.
- The process name is *db2star2*.
- The instance name is *db2inst1*.
- The partition (node) number is *0* as indicated by the field *NODE : 000*.
- The DB2 internal component identifier is *config/install*.
- The DB2 internal function identifier is *sqlfLogUpdateCfgParam*.
- The unique error identifier (probe ID) within the reported function is *30*. This indicates where in the DB2 source code the error or warning is logged. This information is used only by DB2 Technical Support.

The last part of the message entry is a message that often includes error codes, page dumps, or other detailed information. Sometimes this information will be complex, but usually it will give you an idea of the type of operation that is causing the failure, along with some supporting information to help the investigation.

17.4.3 Administration Notification Log Examples

The following is a sample administration notification log entry in the notification log on a UNIX system:

```
2004-06-01-18.30.22.941721   Instance:sylviaq   Node:000
PID:163880(db2star2)   TID:1   Appid:none
base sys utilities  DB2StartMain Probe:911

ADM7513W Database manager has started.
```

You interpret these entries the same way as you do the entries in the db2diag.log. This message is logged when the Database Manager Configuration parameter NOTIFYLEVEL is set at 3 and indicates that the instance has started.

On Windows, you need to open the Windows Event Viewer to view the DB2 administration notification log entries. From the Windows **Start** menu, choose **Administrative Tools** > **Event Viewer**. Figure 17.5 shows the Windows Event Viewer. The DB2 messages are displayed along with messages from other applications. The DB2 messages in the figure are displayed as *DB2-0* (where *DB2* is the instance name and *0* represents the partition number) in the Source column.

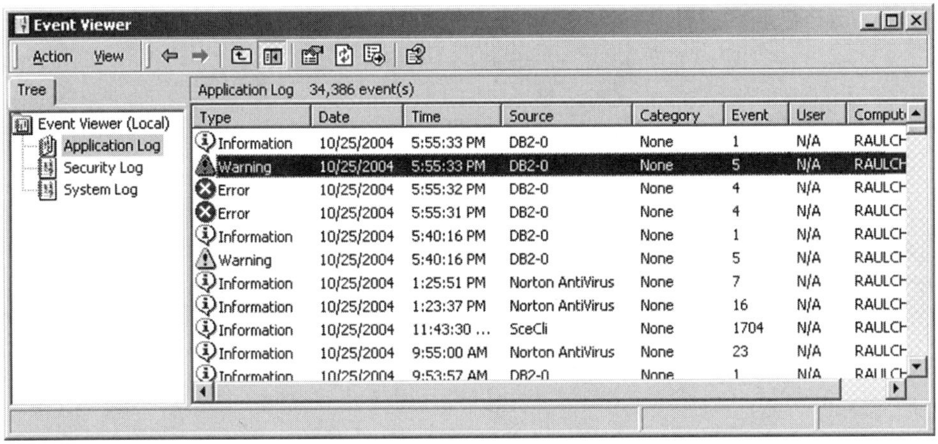

Figure 17.5   The Windows Event Viewer

The entry highlighted is a DB2 message at warning level. Double-click on it to display the entire message, as shown in Figure 17.6.

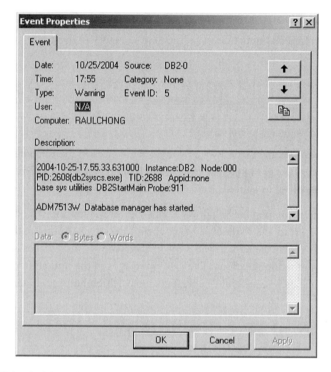

Figure 17.6   DB2 administration notification log entry on Windows

17.5 RECEIVING E-MAIL NOTIFICATIONS

If there is a SMTP server in your network, you can enable DB2 to send notification e-mails to you automatically through this SMTP server. This way, you do not have to monitor the administration notification log all the time: you will receive an e-mail when a problem occurs.

Note that you must set NOTIFYLEVEL to a value of 2 or higher for the Health Monitor to send any notifications to the contacts defined in its configuration. The HEALTH_MON Database Manager Configuration parameter must be set to ON (the default).

Follow these steps to enable DB2 to send notification automatically.

1. Add contact information with the **add contact** command. Use this command to add all the e-mail addresses that should receive notification e-mails from DB2. For example:

```
add contact sylvia type email address sylvia@youracme.com
```
You can also create a contact group using the **add contactgroup** command to contain all the individual contacts. To display the contacts who already have been added, use the **get contacts** command. Refer to the file *Command_and_SQL_Examples.pdf* on the CD-ROM accompanying this book for examples showing how to use these commands.

2. Update the health notification contact list using:

```
update notification list
      add contact contact_name_from_step_1
```

or

```
update notification list
      add group contact_group_name_from_step_1
```

Use the **get health notification contact list** command to display the contact list.

3. Update the CONTACT_HOST DAS parameter to indicate the host name or the IP address of the server where the contact information (from steps 1 and 2) is stored. For example:

```
update admin cfg using CONTACT_HOST prodserv1
```

4. Update the SMTP_SERVER DAS parameter to indicate the host name or the IP address of the SMTP server. For example:

```
update admin cfg using SMTP_SERVER smtpserv1
```

5. Restart the DAS using **db2admin stop** and **db2admin start**.

6. Make sure that the SMTP server is working. Also, the DB2 Health Monitor uses TCP/IP port 25, so port 25 must be open on the SMTP server. To test whether port 25 is open, from the DB2 server perform a telnet test as follows:

```
telnet SMTP_SERVER 25
```

If you get output similar to the following, then port 25 is enabled.

```
Trying...
Connected to <SMTP_SERVER>.
Escape character is '^]'.
220 <SMTP_SERVER> ESMTP Service (Lotus Domino Release 5.0.8) ready at Thu, 29
Apr 2004 13:21:49 -0400
```

If you do not get output like this or your session hangs, contact your network administrator to enable this port.

17.6 THE DB2SUPPORT TOOL

The **db2support** tool collects all diagnostic information, including the db2diag.log, dumps, and traps in one single file called *db2support.zip*. DB2 Technical Support usually requests this zip file. With this handy tool, you do not have to look for the diagnostic files manually.

The syntax of the **db2support** command is

```
db2support output_path -d db_alias options
```

This creates the file *db2support.zip* under *output_path* for the database *db_alias* after the command is completed. The following options are usually required when running the **db2support** command:

- **-g** collects all files under the DIAGPATH directory. This includes the db2diag.log, dump files, trap files, and the DB2 administration notification log.
- **-s** collects detailed hardware and operating system information.

Type **db2support -h** to get all the supported options.

In addition to the above information, this command also gathers standard information such as the database directory, application snapshots, and database snapshots.

17.7 THE DB2 TRACE FACILITY

Sometimes the information in the FFDC files is not enough to determine the cause of a problem. Under normal circumstances, you should only take a trace if asked by DB2 Technical Support. The process of taking a trace entails setting up the trace facility, reproducing the error, and collecting the data.

The command to turn on the DB2 trace is:

```
db2trc on options
```

Use **db2trc -h** to display all the available options. DB2 Technical Support usually requires you to perform the following steps to collect a trace.

1. Turn on the DB2 trace to collect the last 8MB of information in the trace:
   ```
   db2trc on -l 8M
   ```
2. Recreate the error.
3. Dump the trace information into a binary file:
   ```
   db2trc dmp db2trc.dmp
   ```
4. Turn off the DB2 trace:
   ```
   db2trc off
   ```
5. Format the trace dump file into a text file that sorts the records by process/thread:
   ```
   db2trc fmt db2trc.dmp filename.fmt
   ```
6. Format the trace dump file into a text file that sorts the records chronologically:
   ```
   db2trc flw db2trc.dmp filename.flw
   ```

17.8 SEARCHING FOR KNOWN PROBLEMS

Once you have collected some information about your problem, you can research if similar cases have been previously reported by other customers and learn about workarounds and fixes. These are the steps you can follow to resolve your problem.

1. First confirm if the product is working as designed by reviewing the DB2 documentation using the Information Center (http://publib.boulder.ibm.com/infocenter/db2help).
2. Search the Internet for problems reported by other DB2 users.
3. If your environment allows it, apply the latest FixPak, which you can download for free from the DB2 for Linux, UNIX, and Windows Technical Support site (www.ibm.com/software/data/db2/udb/support). The FixPaks are cumulative, and they also come with an aparlist.txt file describing the authorized program analysis reports (APARs) that were fixed with the FixPak. (An APAR is simply the official method that IBM uses to acknowledge a defect in the product.)

4. If you cannot apply the FixPak in your environment at the moment, besides reviewing the aparlist.txt file, you can also research for related problems in the DB2 Technical Support site. This site includes FAQs, technical notes, flashes, and you can also search for specific APARs.

5. Ask in DB2 forums or newsgroups like `comp.databases.ibm-db2` for problems similar to the one you are encountering. On CompuServe try **Go ibmdb2**.

6. If your research doesn't lead to any hits, and you suspect this is a defect issue, contact DB2 Technical support at 1-800-IBM-SERV.

17.9 CASE STUDY

You want to enable your DB2 database server running on Linux to accept client connections using TCP/IP. (This process is covered in Chapter 6, Configuring Client and Server Connectivity.) The first thing you need to do is to set the DB2COMM registry variable to TCPIP, for example:

```
db2set db2comm=tcpip
```

Then you stop and restart the instance for the setting of DB2COMM to take effect. However, when you start the instance again, you get the following message:

```
SQL5043N Support for one or more communications protocols failed to start
successfully. However, core database manager functionality started successfully.
```

You are not sure why this error would occur. You decide to look for more information about this error in the administration notification log, which is under the *$HOME*/sqllib/db2dump directory on Linux/UNIX systems. You open the file and the last entry in this file shows:

```
2004-06-07-16.24.57.229642   Instance:sylviaq   Node:000
PID:264502(db2sysc)   TID:1   Appid:none
common communication   sqlcctcpconnmgr Probe:50

ADM7006E The SVCENAME DBM configuration parameter was not configured. Update the
SVCENAME configuration parameter using the service name defined in the TCP/IP services
file.

2004-06-07-16.24.58.747410   Instance:sylviaq   Node:000
PID:442506(db2star2)   TID:1   Appid:none
base sys utilities   DB2StartMain Probe:911

ADM7513W Database manager has started.
```

The first message indicates that the SVCENAME parameter needs to be updated. The second message indicates that although the TCP/IP support failed to start, the instance is started regardless. This corresponds to the SQL5043N message.

You remember from Chapter 6 that to enable TCP/IP support on a DB2 server, you must also update the SVCENAME parameter to indicate the TCP/IP port number the DB2 instance is going to use. You execute the following command:

```
db2 update dbm cfg using svcename 50000
```

When you restart the instance, the error went away. The message you get is:

```
SQL1063N DB2START processing was successful.
```

17.10 SUMMARY

This chapter discussed how to diagnose problems encountered while working with DB2. DB2 reports problems using error messages and codes. The help (?) CLP command is a quick method to obtain more information about a particular error code.

The First Failure Data Capture (FFDC) is a generic term that refers to several diagnostic files that are generated or updated automatically by DB2, like the administration notification log or the file db2diag.log. Use the db2support tool to collect these diagnostic files automatically in a zip file called db2support.zip. For some types of problems, like hangs or crashes, DB2 Technical Support may ask you to collect a DB2 trace.

Check the DB2 documentation; it usually provides the answer to most problems. Otherwise, search for known problems on the DB2 Technical Support Web site.

17.11 REVIEW QUESTIONS

1. What does the ? command do?
2. An application developer tells you that he received an SQLCODE of -805. What command can you use to obtain more information?
3. What does FFDC stand for?
4. What is the name of the administration notification file in Windows?
5. What is the name of the administration notification file in Linux/UNIX?
6. How can you ensure the file db2diag.log captures the most information possible?
7. What does the db2support tool do?
8. What command is used to create a DB2 trace?
9. Where is the db2diag.log file placed by default for Linux and UNIX platforms?
10. What is the minimum NOTIFYLEVEL value required to receive e-mail messages?
11. Which of the following is used to determine where the administration notification log file will reside on UNIX?
    A. path
    B. adminpath
    C. diagpath
    D. notifypath
12. Which of the following is *not* a Database Manager Configuration parameter used for FFDC?
    A. NOTIFYME
    B. NOTIFYLEVEL
    C. DIAGLEVEL
    D. DIAGPATH

13. Which of the following levels for NOTIFYLEVEL only logs fatal and unrecoverable errors?
    A. 0
    B. 1
    C. 2
    D. 3
14. Which of the following commands can be used to update the parameter to indicate the host name of the SMTP server?
    A. update admin cfg using SMTP *hostname*
    B. update dbm cfg using SMTP *hostname*
    C. update admin cfg using SMTP_SERVER *hostname*
    D. update admin cfg using SMTP_SRV *hostname*
15. Which of the following files is not something a DBA would normally review to resolve a problem with DB2?
    A. db2diag.log
    B. Adminstration notification file
    C. The DB2 manuals
    D. Trap files
16. Which of the following is not collected with the db2support tool?
    A. db2diag.log
    B. Adminstration notification file
    C. Application log file
    D. Trap files
17. Which is the default value for DIAGLEVEL?
    A. 0
    B. 1
    C. 2
    D. 3
18. Which is the recommended value for DIAGLEVEL?
    A. 0
    B. 1
    C. 2
    D. 3
19. Which is the default value for DIAGPATH?
    A. SQLLIB
    B. DB2DUMP
    C. DUMP
    D. NULL

20. Which of the following is not needed to enable e-mail notification?

   A. Add contact information using the ADD CONTACT command.

   B. Update the health notification contact list.

   C. Update the CONTACT_HOST DAS parameter.

   D. Update the CONTACT_LIST_GROUP DAS parameter.

Solutions to the Review Questions

CHAPTER 1

1. IBM added the term "Universal" to reflect DB2's capability to store all kinds of electronic data including traditional relational data, as well as audio, video, text, and so on, and the support of a range of operating systems and hardware architectures.
2. Rational, DB2, WebSphere, Tivoli, and Lotus.
3. Yes. All the DB2 editions other than DB2 Everyplace have a set of core modules that are the same; therefore, an application that works with DB2 UDB Personal Edition will work against DB2 UDB Enterprise Server Edition.
4. No. DB2 Connect is required only in one direction: when connecting from a DB2 LUW to DB2 for z/OS or other host server like DB2 for iSeries, DB2 for VM, and VSE or DB2 for OS/390.
5. DB2 UDB Workgroup Server Unlimited Edition (WSUE) is most appropriate from a cost standpoint since it is licensed per CPU, not per user, while DB2 UDB WSE is licensed per user.
6. No. Federation support is built into the DB2 product for RDBMSs that are part of the IBM family, like IBM Informix.
7. A company migrating their production database from Oracle to DB2 may set up DB2 replication to replicate the data from the Oracle production server to the DB2 server. This approach lets developers at the company test their applications against the DB2 server with "real" data before switching completely to DB2.
8. No. Even though more than ninety percent of the code is common among these platforms, each platform has its own file used for installation for the appropriate platform.
9. The database partitioning feature (DPF) allows you to partition your data within a single server or across multiple servers running the same operating system. This provides for scalability.

10. Contact your IBM marketing representative, or call 1-800-IBM-SERV and indicate that you would like to buy a permanent license for your DB2 product.

11. **D**. The minimum software required on the Windows client is the DB2 runtime client. This is required to *run* any application, other than an application using the JDBC type 4 driver.

12. **D**. The application development (AD) client is required to *write* a JDBC application. To *run* the application, however, you may not need a client as in the case of the JDBC type 4 driver.

13. **B**. DB2 UDB Personal Edition is a fully functional server that is designed for personal use only. As such, it does not support connections from remote clients.

14. **C**. DB2 UDB Personal Edition is not considered a DB2 server since it cannot accept inbound (remote) connections from clients.

15. **B**. The application development client includes everything the Administration client has (including the graphical administration tools) in addition to libraries and tools used for application development.

16. **C**. DB2 Everyplace is a fully functional database that can be stored in mobile devices like PDAs. DB2 Everywhere is not a DB2 Edition, and DB2 Satellite Edition was merged with DB2 Personal Edition in Version 8.

17. **D**. DB2 Universal Developer's Edition (UDE) includes DB2 Connect Enterprise Edition, which allows the connection to host servers. It also includes all the DB2 LUW clients. Because this is a software development company, UDE is more convenient than DB2 UDB Enterprise Server Edition and it is cheaper.

18. **A**. A zSeries server with a LPAR running the Linux operating system can run DB2 UDB for Linux, UNIX, and Windows.

19. **A**. DB2 UDE (Universal Developer's Edition) includes DB2 Connect Enterprise Server Edition, which allows several clients to connect to DB2 for z/OS.

20. **B**. DB2 Warehouse Manager is one of the products under the Business Intelligence umbrella and can be used to help you understand your data to make better business decisions.

CHAPTER 2

1. They are classified in two categories: DB2 system commands and DB2 CLP commands.

2. For DB2 system commands use *command -h*. For DB2 CLP commands use **db2 ?** *command*.

3. The Information Center provides a fast search engine that lets you search all the manuals based on a keyword.

4. The **db2icrt** command creates a DB2 instance on the server where the command is run.

5. Every database has three default table spaces created automatically by DB2. These table spaces are:
   - SYSCATSPACE
   - TEMPSPACE1
   - USERSPACE1
6. The **db2ilist** command lists all instances that exist on a server, whether they are active or not.
7. When you install DB2 on a Windows server, the installation program will automatically create an instance named *DB2* on the server.
8. No. The DAS is required only to allow the use of graphical tools for remote administration.
9. The DB2 environment can be configured by changing values of parameters in different areas:
   - Environment variables
   - DB2 registry variables
   - The Database Manager Configuration (dbm cfg) file and database configuration (db cfg) file
10. Both the local database directory and system database directory are populated with the **CREATE DATABASE** command (not with the **catalog** command).
11. **C.** The **db2start** command starts the current DB2 instance.
12. **B.** The **db2set -all** command lists all of the currently configured registry variables.
13. **D.** The command **list db directory on C:** will examine the local database directory, which is not removed when the instance is dropped, and list all of the databases on that *drive/filesystem*.
14. **D.** You must catalog the database before you can connect to it. To catalog the database in this situation, you must specify the drive or directory where the local database directory exists. In this case it is C:, so use the command **catalog db sample on C:**.
15. **C.** You must set the DB2INSTANCE environment variable to the instance you want to work with, in this case *inst2*, so the command is **export db2instance=inst2**.
16. **D.** The DB2_FORCE_FCM_BP registry variable tells DB2 to use shared memory for inter-partition communication (FCM) and not to use the network.
17. **B.** The **db2_all** command runs the specified command on all database partitions in the database.
18. **B.** Federated support is turned on using the dbm cfg parameter FEDERATED.
19. **C.** DB2NODE.
20. **A.** The CURRENT DBPARTITIONNUM special register provides this information.

CHAPTER 3

1. Two methods are available: the DB2 Setup Wizard and Silent install.
2. Four methods are available: the DB2 Setup wizard, Silent install, the **db2_install** script, and the operating system's native install tools.

3. The default instance name is *db2inst1*. The user owner ID *db2inst1* is created as well. If *db2inst1* already exists, DB2 will try *db2inst2*, *db2inst3*, and so on.

4. An alternate FixPak contains all fixes, as does a regular FixPak, but the fixes are built into the product. Moreover, it is installed under a different directory, so DB2 treats it as a different product. This way you can have different DB2 FixPak levels for the same version on the same computer.

5. By default, three logs are generated under the /tmp directory: db2setup.his, db2setup.log, and db2setup.err. To redirect the logs to a different location, run the **db2setup** program with the **-l** option.

6. By default, two logs are generated under the My Documents\DB2LOG directory: db2.log and db2wi.log. To redirect them to a different location, run the **setup** program (from the DB2 installation media) with the **-l** option.

7. DB2ADMNS and DB2USERS.

8. You need to run the **db2iupdt** command for all of your DB2 instances after you install a DB2 FixPak to update the instance with the new libraries and to update the logical links to the installed libraries.

9. The following user rights are granted to the instance owner:
   • Act as part of the operating system
   • Debug programs
   • Create token objects
   • Increase quotas
   • Lock pages in memory
   • Log on as a service
   • Replace a process-level token

10. The user who is installing DB2 must have Local Administrator authority. If you want to have the DB2 Setup Wizard create a domain user account for the Instance owner or the DAS user, the installation ID must have the authority to create domain user accounts.

11. **B**. The DB2 Setup Wizard and the Silent install are the only two methods available on Windows.

12. **C**. A response file is a text file containing all the options to be used during the install process. Use this file as input during a silent install.

13. **C**. 50000 is the default

14. **D**. You need root authority.

15. **A**. The DAS User ID.

16. **B**. The db2_install script is not a valid method of installation on Windows.

17. **C**. The db2_install script.

18. **A**. db2setup -r *response_file*

19. **D**. The db2_install script.

20. **B**. Using a response file so you install DB2 interactively only once, and save the responses in a response file that you later use to install DB2 on the other machines.

CHAPTER 4

1. The Task Center lets you schedule scripts containing SQL statements and/or DB2 commands to be run at specific times.

2. There is no equivalent DB2 tool in the Linux/UNIX platforms. The Linux/UNIX *shell* would be equivalent to the DB2 Command Window.

3. The registry variable is DB2OPTIONS.

4. When you plan to copy a command or statement that has carriage returns and then paste it into the CLP, it is best to use this method.

5. The `terminate` command.

6. You can invoke Visual Explain from the Command Editor. Type a query, and then choose either the *Execute and Access plan* or *Access Plan* button.

7. The Development Center tool.

8. No. The Control Center can be used to administer DB2 for Linux, UNIX, and Windows databases as well as DB2 for OS/390 and z/OS databases.

9. The Journal keeps track of DB2 messages; therefore, review the Journal messages tab.

10. Access the Information Center from the Internet at http://publib.boulder.ibm.com/info-center/db2help.

11. **B** and **C**. You can enter SQL statements and DB2 CLP commands in the Command Line Processor (CLP) or in the Command Editor.

12. **B**. The default termination character is a semi-colon (;).

13. **E**. By default the CLP has autocommit enabled, and this causes the CLP to issue a commit statement automatically after every statement. Therefore, in this case, the CLP will issue a commit four times—after each entry in the input file.

14. **C**. The Health Center will alert you when actions in the database exceed thresholds for performance-related characteristics that you have defined.

15. **B** and **E**. The Memory Visualizer will track the memory used by DB2 on your system and will plot/graph this memory usage for you automatically if you desire. The `db2mtrk` tool is the command line interface to the same information, and it will provide the same information in a text-based report.

16. **A**. By default the CLP has autocommit enabled, which causes the CLP to issue a commit automatically after every statement. However, the +c flag tells the CLP to disable autocommit; therefore, in this case, the CLP will not issue a commit. Since there is no explicit commit statement, there will be no commits during the processing of this file.

17. **B**. To set a termination character you need to use the `-td` option, and to set the input file you need to use the `-f` option. However, if you specify a value for an option, you cannot string the options together. Therefore the correct answer is B.

18. **C and D**. `db2 ? SQL-911` is not commonly used, but it works. `db2 ? SQL911N` is most often used. Note that the *N* after the 911 is optional.

19. **D**. Repeat is not a DB2 CLP command and can't be run in interactive mode.

20. **C** and **D** are allowed from the CLP in interactive mode. **A** is not allowed since you cannot prefix the command with **db2** when in interactive mode. **B** is a DB2 system command, and it can only be executed from the Command Window or the Linux/UNIX shell.

CHAPTER 5

1. The DB2INSTANCE environment variable determines the current active instance.
2. You can set up your DB2 environment in Linux/UNIX by adding the db2profile (for the Bourne and Korn shells) or db2cshrc (for the C shell) in the .login or .profile initialization files. You should also modify the db2profile file to set the DB2INSTANCE variable to the name of the instance you want active by default.
3. db2set DB2COMM= -g
4. db2ilist
5. To create a new instance with the **db2icrt** command on Linux or UNIX you must have root authority.
6. To create a new instance with the **db2icrt** command on Windows you must have Administrator authority.
7. The **db2idrop** command will remove the DB2 instance from the list, and remove all DB2-related executables and libraries from the instance owner's home directory.
8. No. Executing the command once from any database partition will start all of the other database partitions.
9. Issue the **db2start** command with the **ADMIN MODE USER _userID_** option.
10. An attachment is required to perform operations at the instance level, while a connection is required to perform operations at the database level.
11. **C**. The **db2set -lr** command lists all of the registry variables that DB2 recognizes.
12. **A** and **D**. Sort heap threshold (SHEAPTHRES) and maximum query degree of parallelism (MAX_QUERYDEGREE) are both database manager (instance)-level configuration parameters.
13. **D**. Each instance is a separate DB2 operating environment, so errors in one instance cannot affect the other instances. Therefore, to ensure that problems that you normally encounter in development do not affect your production system, put these databases in separate instances.
14. **B**. To get the current, effective setting for each configuration parameter along with the value of the parameter the next time the instance is stopped and restarted, use the **show detail** option of the **get dbm cfg** command.
15. **D**. To update the DAS configuration use the command **db2 update admin cfg**.
16. **D**. To change the DAS configuration back to its default values, use the command **db2 reset admin cfg**.
17. **C**. **db2stop force** forces all applications off the databases and prevents new connections from happening. Then it stops the active instance.
18. **A**. The **list applications** command requires an instance attachment.

19. **D**. The **db2 get db cfg** command is used to review the contents of the database configuration (db cfg) file. If you are not connected to the database, you need to specify the name of the database in the command.

20. **B** and **D**. The values of YES and ON are equivalent, but a *1* is not allowed. Also, INTRA_PARALLEL is a Database Manager Configuration parameter; therefore, **D** is incorrect.

CHAPTER 6

1. The system database directory contains all the databases you can connect from a DB2 client machine.

2. To view the content of the database directory on the H: drive, you use the command **list db directory on H:**.

3. An entry type of *indirect* means that this entry corresponds to a local database.

4. To determine which port is being used, look for the string **db2_cDB2** in the *services* file.

5. APPC or TCPIP can be used as the communication protocol to connect from a DB2 Connect gateway to a DB2 for z/OS server.

6. DB2 Connect Enterprise Edition can be installed once on a gateway machine to allow all 1,000 clients to connect to the DB2 for iSeries server, while DB2 Connect Personal Edition is licensed only to be installed at the DB2 client machine.

7. To remove an entry from the DCS directory, you can use the command **uncatalog dcs db** *dbname*.

8. To remove an entry from the node directory, you can use the command **uncatalog node** *nodename*.

9. To remove an entry from the system database directory, you can use the command **uncatalog db** *dbname*.

10. When you have a huge network with many hubs, the "Search the network" method will take a long time, and it may not find the database you want because this method will only search your local network.

11. **D**. This command puts an entry into the node directory that points to the remote server and port that the instance will use for inbound connections.

12. **C**. DB2 ESE has built-in DB2 Connect functionality, so it can use the DCS directory along with the DB2 Connect products. Therefore, DB2 Personal Edition is the one that cannot use the DCS directory.

13. **B**. You should use the value specified in the SVCENAME parameter in the command as shown in B.

14. **C**. When a database is created, an entry of type *indirect* is inserted into the system database directory.

15. **A** and **B** are required. **A** specifies the port number used by the instance. **B** turns on the TCP/IP listener.

16. **D**. *Unknown discovery* is not a valid method. Search the network can be done using *known discovery* and *search discovery.*

17. **A**. At the DAS level at the server machine, you can prevent Discover for the DB2 server.

18. **D**. To disable a certain database to be discovered, you can disable the DISCOVER_DB database configuration parameter.

19. **C**. When a database is dropped, its entry is removed from the system and local database directory.

20. **B**. `DISCOVER=disable` is used to prevent a client machine from using the discovery method. In this case, the DB2 server is working as a DB2 client for other DB2 servers.

CHAPTER 7

1. **C**. Since no schema is explicitly specified, the schema will be the authorization ID for the connection. The authorization ID, also known as the connection ID, is the user ID used to connect to the database. Therefore, the table name will be *foo.t1*.

2. **B**. There is no object named IBMDEFAULTSPACE. When a database is created, DB2 creates the table spaces SYSCATSPACE, USERSPACE1, and TEMPSPACE1; the partition groups IBMCATGROUP, IBMTEMPGROUP, and IBMDEFAULTGROUP; and the buffer pool IBMDEFAULTBP.

3. **C**. An identity column ensures uniqueness, but only within a table. A sequence generates a unique value that is across the whole database and can therefore be used with multiple tables.

4. **D**. The statement `alter table t1 activate not logged initially with empty table` will delete all rows from the table and not log the deletions for the fastest response time. Table *t1* must have been created with the `activate not logged initially` clause for the `alter table` to work.

5. **B**. While you can enforce this by specifying the T or F constraint by creating a view (if all inserts are done using a view), this will not prevent you from inserting a different value if you insert into the table directly. To ensure that no other values are entered into this column, you need to define a check constraint.

6. **B**. The `CASCADE` option will delete all referenced rows in the child tables.

7. **B** and **D**. Both a unique constraint and a primary key constraint can be referenced by a foreign key constraint.

8. **C**. The statement inserting a value of 300 into the *productno* column will fail as this is an identity column GENERATED ALWAYS, so there will be two rows successfully inserted into the table.

9. **C**. The default precision and scale are 5, 0 if not explicitly specified in the `CREATE TABLE` statement.

10. **A**. INBETWEEN is not a type of trigger.

11. **C**. Each database has its own set of logs and system catalogs, and a schema is created within a database. However, the registry variables are set for all instances or at the instance level and control all databases in the instance.

12. **B**. The **CREATE TABLE** statement creates the table/data object for the database. Since there is a primary key clause in this statement, an index will also be created to support the primary key. This statement creates two objects.

13. **B**. There are two server names in the *db2nodes.cfg* file; therefore, the database is partitioned across two servers.

14. **A**. Data objects can be created in regular table spaces only.

15. **D**. You need to connect to the database and create the buffer pool with a 16K page size before you can create a table space with a 16K page size.

16. **A**. Only a table can be altered using the **ALTER TABLE** statement. You must drop and recreate an index, view, or schema to change its definition.

17. **A** and **B**. A package is stored in a database and contains the executable SQL statements and the access path the DB2 optimizer will choose to retrieve the data.

18. **D**. Object names must be unique within a schema, but since the schema is the high-level qualifier for the object name, objects can have the same name as long as they are in different schemas.

19. **B** and **C**. seq1.next and seq1.nextValue are not valid options.

20. **D**. A user temporary table space created with the **CREATE USER TEMPORARY TABLESPACE** statement is needed before global temporary tables can be declared. Global temporary tables are created with the **DECLARE GLOBAL TEMPORARY TABLE** statement.

CHAPTER 8

1. DB2 supports a database with up to 1,000 partitions.

2. The IBMDEFAULTBP buffer pool is created automatically in every database.

3. Since the row width is over 9,000 bytes, the table must be created in a table space with at least a 16K page size.

4. A table's data object in an SMS table space will be placed in a file with a .DAT extension.

5. The command **LIST TABLESPACES SHOW DETAIL** will display the number of used and free pages in each table space.

6. DMS table spaces are completely allocated when they are created.

7. SMS table spaces grow and shrink as the tables and indexes within them grow and shrink.

8. When a table has been defined with its data, index, and large objects in different table spaces, you cannot drop one of the table spaces without dropping the table first.

9. The block-based area of a buffer pool is used to improve performance of prefetching by allowing DB2 to read entire extents into contiguous pieces of the buffer pool.

10. The `get snapshot for tablespaces` command will show if and when a rebalance is occurring. It will show when the rebalance started and how many extents in the table space still need to be moved as part of the rebalance process.

11. **A**. DB2 supports 4K, 8K, 16K, and 32K page sizes.

12. **B**. Since the table spaces all use an 8K page size, they can all share a buffer pool with an 8K page size. However, since the system catalogs are created in a table space with a 4K page size, there must also be a buffer pool with a 4K page size. Therefore, the answer is 2.

13. **D**. Since there are 4 partitions, and with a 32K page size the maximum table space size is 512GB, the largest table could be 4 x 512GB or 2TB in size.

14. **D**. Under the /data directory, DB2 creates a directory with the instance name. The SQL*xxxxx* directories are created under the instance directory. Therefore, in this case, DB2 will create the directory *inst1* under the /data directory.

15. **A**. DB2 creates a directory with the partition number for that server under the /data/inst1 directory. Since partitions 2 and 3 are on server *mysrv2*, the directories will be NODE0002 and NODE0003.

16. **E**. By default DB2 Version 8 creates five subdirectories for the following:
    - The catalog table space
    - The temporary table space
    - Userspace1
    - The log directory
    - Event Monitor output

17. **B**. In this case, the database *sample* would use SQL00001. Sales would be placed in the directory SQL00002 and test in SQL00003. When the sales database is dropped, the SQL00002 directory is also dropped, and is then available in case other databases are created on the same drive or path. When the database *my_sales* is created, DB2 will reuse the SQL00002 directory.

18. **C**. Since the `create database` command was run on server *mysrv2*, the catalog partition will be on the partition with port number 0 on that server, in this case, partition 2.

19. **D**. You need to connect to the database and create the buffer pool with a 16K page size before you can create a table space with a 16K page size. Therefore, the correct answer is **D**.

20. **C**. The correct syntax is
```
CREATE BUFFERPOOL BP1
SIZE 150MB
        except on DBPARTITIONNUMS 1,2,3,4,5 size 100MB
```

CHAPTER 9

1. **A**. The condition of having *lastname* starting with the letter *P* returns two rows. However, the result set is further reduced to one row to obtain the only record that has a salary greater than $38,500.

2. **D**. Unknown values are identified by **NULL**. You verify the nullability of a value by checking **IS NULL**. The values `' '` and `" "` are known values of empty strings.

3. **C**. Selecting from an **UPDATE**, **DELETE**, or **INSERT** statement is an SQL enhancement available in DB2 Version 8.1 FixPak 4 or later. If the statement is executed on DB2 Version 8.1 with an earlier FixPak, it will fail. With FixPak 4 or later, the statement will execute the **DELETE** statement and return the number of rows removed.

4. **C**. An **INTERSECT** operation retrieves the matching set of distinct values (there are three distinct values) from the two columns. On the other hand, the **INTERSECT ALL** operator will return four rows because it returns all of the matching rows.

5. **C**. The UNIX command interpreter processes the `*` character, so to pass this character to DB2, you must enclose the command in quotes. To select all rows from a table you use the **SELECT *** syntax.

6. **D**. **FETCH FIRST *n* ROWS ONLY** limits the number of rows returned from a query. Use of the **OPTIMIZE FOR *n* ROWS** clause influences query optimization, based on the assumption that *n* rows will be retrieved. However, all rows of the result table will be retrieved.

7. **A**. `%` is used as a wildcard character in a **LIKE** clause of a **SELECT** statement.

8. **C** and **D**. Values to be inserted into the *employee* table must provide an *id* value in **INTEGER** data type, optionally provide a *name*, and *dept* must not be **NULL**. If no value is specified for *dept*, a default value *A00* will be used. You can choose to use the keyword **DEFAULT** to indicate that the default value defined in the table definition is used (in this case *A00*). Alternatively, simply do not specify a value for the column (as demonstrated in answers C and D).

9. **A**. Data is stored in no particular order. If data should be returned in certain order, the **ORDER BY** clause must be used.

10. **B**. The DB2 special register CURRENT DATE stores the date based on the time-of day clock at the DB2 server. To perform date and time calculations, simply add or subtract the number of years, months, days, hours, minutes, or seconds. For example:
```
CURRENT DATE + 3 YEARS + 2 MONTHS - 3 MINUTES
```

11. **B**.

12. **B**. The special register CURRENT DATE can be used to retrieve the current system date.

13. **A**.

14. **D**. There will be six rows:
```
col 1           col2
-------         ------
      2         Susan
      4         Mary
      5         Clara
      6         Jenny
      8         Tom
      9         Luisa
```

15. **C**. There will be two rows:

```
COL1         COL2                 COL1         COL2
-----------  -------------------- -----------  --------------------
          2  Raul                          2  Susan
          9  Glenn                         9  Luisa
```

16. **D**. There will be six rows:

```
COL1         COL2                 COL1         COL2
-----------  -------------------- -----------  --------------------
          2  Raul                          2  Susan
          -  -                             5  Clara
          -  -                             6  Jenny
          9  Glenn                         9  Luisa
          4  Mary                          -  -
          8  Tom                           -  -
```

17. **C**. There will be four rows:

```
COL1         COL2                 COL1         COL2
-----------  -------------------- -----------  --------------------
          2  Raul                          2  Susan
          4  Mary                          -  -
          8  Tom                           -  -
          9  Glenn                         9  Luisa
```

18. **C**. There will be four rows:

```
COL1         COL2                 COL1         COL2
-----------  -------------------- -----------  --------------------
          2  Raul                          2  Susan
          -  -                             5  Clara
          -  -                             6  Jenny
          9  Glenn                         9  Luisa
```

19. **B**. There will be two records successfully inserted into the employee table:

```
EMPNO   SALARY
------  -----------
000999            -
001000            -

  2 record(s) selected.
```

20. **E**. There were 10 records and 2 more were inserted, so there will be 12 records after executing the statement.

CHAPTER 10

1. DB2 relies on operating system security and does not store user IDs and passwords in the database.

2. DB2 also supports Kerberos security service. Starting with DB2 Version 8.2, you can also write your own security service as plug-in. The plug-in will be loaded at instance startup.

3. When a new package is bound to the database, for example, when creating an SQL stored procedure, BINDADD is required.

4. He must have CONNECT privileges to connect to the database and CREATETAB privileges to create a new table in the database. Because he is trying to create a table that has a different schema than the authorization ID (i.e., *bob*), he must have IMPLICIT_SCHEMA privileges if schema *mary* does not already exist. If it does exist, then CREATEIN privileges on the schema *mary* is needed. In addition to all of the above, *bob* also needs to have USE privileges on the table space *ts1*.

5. DB2 SYS* authorities must be set to a user group. The command will be executed successfully, but *bob* will not receive the authority. It must be set to the group *dba* like this:
```
update dbm cfg using sysctrl dba
```

6. First, a local group, for example, called *db2dba*, defined on the DB2 server is required. Second, add the global group *glbgrp* as a member of the local group *db2dba*. Third, update the Database Manager Configuration parameter to set SYSADM to *db2dba*.

7. The first type is called untrusted clients, which do not have a reliable security facility. The second type is called trusted clients, which have a reliable security facility. The third type is called DRDA clients, which are clients on host systems with reliable security facility.

8. CREATETAB is granted to PUBLIC implicitly when a database is created. To allow only *bob* to create tables in the database, you must first revoke CREATETAB from PUBLIC and GRANT CREATETAB to *bob*.
```
REVOKE CREATETAB FROM PUBLIC;
GRANT CREATETAB TO USER bob;
```

9. Regardless of the SQL statements performed in the program, *bob* only needs EXECUTE privileges on the package. *Mary* needs the associated privileges to perform all the SQL statements in the program. In addition, BINDADD is required to bind the new package to the database.

10. Since TRUST_ALLCLNTS is set to NO, only trusted clients can be authenticated on the client. Windows ME is not a trusted client, so users from this OS must be authenticated on the server.

11. **B**. The default authentication takes place on the server, so in this case the user ID will be authenticated on the DBX1 server.

12. **C**. The SERVER_ENCRYPT authentication type encrypts only the user ID and password that is sent during an authentication request; it does not encrypt the data.

13. **A**. Since TRUST_ALLCLNTS is set to YES, users are authenticated on the client to see if they do exist.

14. **A** and **D**. Both SYSADM and DBADM authorities allow read/write access to tables.

15. **D**. If you choose, you can encrypt the user ID and password as it is passed from the client to the server. In Version 8.2 you can also encrypt the data for more security.

16. **A**. The user who wants to create or drop an event monitor must hold either SYSADM or DBADM authority.

17. **B**. Only SYSMON does not have the ability to take a DB2 trace.

18. **C**. When a privilege is revoked from a user, it does not cascade to users who received privileges from this user. Therefore, be careful who you give WITH GRANT OPTION permission to. In this example, Barney, Wilma, and Betty will have the privileges.

19. **D**. By default, PUBLIC is granted use of a table space when it is created. Therefore, to ensure only the group *grp1* can use the table space you must revoke use of the table space from PUBLIC.

20. **C**. CREATETAB is a database level privilege; therefore, information about its grantee is stored in the SYSCAT.DBAUTH table.

CHAPTER 11

1. Increasing MAXLOCKS (the percentage of the lock list that an application can use before escalation occurs) and increasing LOCKLIST can reduce the chances of getting lock escalations.

2. When a user performs a read operation, by default DB2 attempts to lock the rows with share locks. Once a share lock is acquired, concurrent users will not be able to make changes to the rows. However, concurrent read is allowed. In this example, Sam may have set the isolation level as UR, so DB2 will not acquire any row lock. This may result in uncommitted data within the same transaction as described here.

3. Databases: **CONNECT TO** *dbname* **IN EXCLUSIVE MODE**
   Table spaces: **QUIESCE TABLESPACE FOR TABLE** *tabname* **INTENT FOR UPDATE**
   Tables: **LOCK TABLE** *tabname* **IN EXCLUSIVE MODE**

4. U lock is compatible with S and NS lock only. (Refer to the Row lock mode compatibility chart in Figure 11.23.)

5. It means that the current transaction has been rolled back because of a lock timeout.

6. It means that the current transaction has been rolled back because of a deadlock.

7. There are two database configuration parameters that can cause locks to be escalated. Make sure LOCKLIST is sufficiently large. If LOCKLIST is full, lock escalation will occur. Next check if MAXLOCKS is set appropriately. This value defines the percentage of the total LOCKLIST permitted to be allocated to a single application. If any application holds locks more than this percentage, lock escalation will also occur. If both values are set appropriately, you may want to check the isolation level used in the application or maybe the application design.

8. DB2 comes with various troubleshooting and diagnosing tools. Those that are particularly useful for locking-related information are the **list applications** command, the Snapshot Monitor, snapshot table functions, Event Monitors, Activity Monitors, and the Health Center.

9. Application handle 14 is currently in a lock-wait status. It has been waiting for locks for 6507 ms. The dynamic SQL statement that this application is executing is **SELECT * FROM org**. It is requesting an IS lock on the table *org*.

10. By default, DB2 acquires row-level locking. Unless a lock escalation is required, table lock will not be requested. In this case, it is most likely that the table *employee* was altered to perform table-level locking rather than row-level locking. If row-level locking is the desired behavior, Mike can issue the following statement:

```
ALTER TABLE employee LOCKSIZE ROW
```

11. D. Cursor With Hold is not a DB2 isolation level.

12. B. DB2 does not obtain page-level locks. If lock escalation occurs, a number of row-level locks will be turned into a table-level lock.

13. B. If you do not specify the isolation level for your application, DB2 defaults to cursor stability.

14. D. Since repeatable read must guarantee the same result set within the same unit of work, it retains locks on all rows required to build the result sets. Therefore, this typically causes many more locks to be held than the other isolation levels.

15. A. Uncommitted read obtains an intent none (IN) table-level lock, but does not obtain row-level locks while scanning your data. This allows DB2 to return uncommitted changes since it does not have to wait for locks on rows.

16. A. Uncommitted read allows access to changed data that has not been committed.

17. C. The read stability isolation level allows new rows to become part of the result set, but does not allow rows to be deleted that are part of the result set until the transaction completes.

18. B. The **WITH** isolation clause will change the isolation level for the statement to the specified value.

19. C and E. You can set the lock size for a table to be either an individual row or the whole table. For batch operations that update a large number of rows in a table, it is sometimes beneficial to set the lock size to the table level first.

20. B. The option **NOT WAIT** specifies that the application will not wait for locks that cannot be obtained immediately.

CHAPTER 12

1. The load utility supports CURSOR as the input. The cursor must be already declared before the load utility is invoked. The entire result of the query associated with the specified cursor will be processed by the load utility.

2. When the load utility is invoked in INSERT mode, one needs INSERT privileges on the target table. If REPLACE mode is used, INSERT and DELETE privileges on the target table are also required.

3. Rows that do not comply with the table definition will not be loaded and placed in the dump file. Therefore *stockdump.dmp* contains:

```
20, "BBB", -
40, "EEE", x
```

4. Rows that violated the unique constraint will be deleted and inserted into the exception table. Therefore *stockexp* has the following row:

```
30, "DDD", 4
```

5. The table will be in CHECK PENDING state because only unique constraints are validated during the load operation. If a constraint is defined in the table like the CHECK constraint in the example, the utility will place the table in CHECK PENDING statement. You need to issue the **SET INTEGRITY** command to validate the data before the table is available for further processing.

6. The table will be accessible after the **import** command is successfully executed. No other command is required because data is already validated during the import operation.

7. The command will generate the DDL for all objects in the database *department*, the **UPDATE** statements to replicate the statistics on all tables and indexes in the database, the **GRANT** authorization statements, the **UPDATE** statements for the Database Manager Configuration and database configuration parameters, and the **db2set** statements for the registry variables. The output will be stored in the file *db2look.sql*.

8. The step that Bob missed is to REBIND the packages. Packages for static and SQL stored procedures are created at compile time. When the packages are bound to the database, data access plans are determined. Since the large amount of data is inserted into the database and database statistics have been updated, data access plans for these packages are still based on the outdated statistics. A REBIND of all packages that already exist will ensure that the latest statistics are used, hence more optimal data access paths.

9. He can either increase the size of the log files (or the number of logs) sufficiently large enough to hold all the changes made during the import. Alternatively, he could include the **commitcount** option:

```
import from largeinputfile.ixf of ixf
    commitcount 1000
    messages import.out
    create into newtable in datats index in indexts
```

10. The option **insert_update** means that the utility will add imported data to the target table or update existing rows with matching primary keys. Therefore, the table must already exist with primary keys. Otherwise, the import will fail.

11. **C** and **E**. The load and import tools can read ASCII data from an input file and then insert them in a table in your database.

12. **E**. Only the import tool can insert records from an input file into a view. The load tool can only add data to a table, not a view.

13. **D**. DB2 does not support the XLS format. For column delimited data, use the WSF format.

14. **D**. The default column delimiter is a comma, so you need to modify the column delimiter as in answer D to import this data successfully.

15. **C**. While you can export from a view and import into a view, you cannot load into a view. You must load into the base table(s) directly.

16. **B**. **db2relocatedb** can be used to rename a database.

17. **C**. The load utility can capture statistics on all data added to the table during a load operation.

18. **B** and **D**. By default, the load utility locks the target table for exclusive access until the load completes. If the `allow read access` option is specified, it allows read access to data already existing in the table before the load was run. However, you cannot see the newly loaded data until the load completes.

19. **B**. The import utility can create the table if it does not exist and if the input file is in the IXF format.

20. **B**. PCTFREE = –1 means PCTFREE value for a table page is 0. With this setting, the import utility will not leave free space on the data pages. However, the load utility can do so by specifying the options **INDEXFREESPACE**, **PAGEFREESPACE**, and **TOTALFREESPACE**. The REORG utility will leave free space on the data and/or index pages based on the value of PCTFREE of the tables and indexes. This is especially important for tables with a clustering index.

CHAPTER 13

1. Besides crash recovery, DB2 also supports version recovery and roll forward recovery.

2. You can backup the transaction logs along with the database by using the **INCLUDE LOGS** option in the **BACKUP DATABASE** command.

3. Secondary logs are created when needed and are destroyed when the database is restarted.

4. Log buffer is flushed to log files when the log buffer is full or when the MINCOMMIT number of commits has been issued. Note that MINCOMMIT is a database configuration parameter.

5. The maximum log space you can configure for a database is 256GB.

6. You can use the **INSPECT** command to inspect a database while it is online.

7. You can either restore from a good database backup or use the **db2dart** tool to mark the index invalid. Depending on the value of the INDEXREC database parameter, the index will be recreated either when the database is restarted or when the index is being accessed for the first time.

8. You can find out the minimum recovery time for a table space by using the **LIST TABLSPACES SHOW DETAIL** command. The time is shown in UTC time.

9. **C**. The LOGRETAIN database configuration parameter can be used to enable archival logging. When a log file is no longer active, it should be manually archived to a backup device to avoid the log path being filled up. In addition, you also need to manual retrieve those archived log files when they are required in case of recovery.

10. **A**. COMMIT or ROLLBACK (one word) can be used to complete or rollback a unit of work.

11. **B**. Circular logging is the default logging method used by DB2.

12. **C**. You can use the LOGFILSIZ parameter to customize the size of the log file.

13. **C**. FAILARCHPATH specifies a path to which DB2 will try to archive log files if the log files cannot be archived to the archive destinations.

14. **C**. Roll forward recovery replays the transactions in the database logs to recover any transactions after the backup was performed.

15. A. DB2 does not allocate the secondary logs until they are needed, so they would *not* be allocated immediately after activating the database. DB2 also starts numbering the logs using the number 0, so the correct answer is A.

16. C. Infinite active logging is activated by setting log second to −1.

17. C. Archival logging must be enabled in order to perform online backups. Archival logging is enabled by setting LOGARCHMETH1 to a value other than OFF.

18. C. Archival logging must be enabled in order to perform online backups. Archival logging is enabled by setting LOGARCHMETH1 to a value other than OFF.

19. B. You cannot change from DMS to SMS or SMS to DMS using a redirected restore.

20. B. When using local time, it is always local relative to the server.

21. D. Backup is not a valid option of the db2inidb command.

22. B. You can use the Mirror option to create a backup image of a source database.

Chapter 14

1. The **db2ptree** command. On Linux/UNIX platforms, you can also use the **ps -ef** command.

2. The db2fmp process is the fenced-mode process for fenced UDFs and stored procedures. **Fenced** means it is executed outside of the address space of the DB2 engine. Should it misbehave, it is not able to overwrite DB2 internal buffers.

3. It is the DB2 page cleaner process, db2pclnr.

4. Subagents exist in partitioned database environment, or the database manager parameter intra-parallel = ON.

5. If the total number of idle agents in the instance is less than NUM_POOLAGENTS, then the subagent changes its name from db2agntp to db2agnta and it is returned to the idle agent pool. However, it is still associated with the application. When needed, it is called by the coordinator agent, or the active subagents, to service the same application again. Or it can be stolen by another application, if that application cannot find an idle agent or no more agents can be created (**MAXAGENTS** is reached).

6. Per instance. The MAXAGENTS is a Database Manager Configuration parameter.

7. The four types of agents are: coordinator agents (db2agent), active subagents (db2agntp), associated idle agents (db2agnta), and idle agents (db2agent (idle)).

8. You can use **dbm snapshot**.

9. **C.** The NUM_INITAGENTS controls how many db2agent processes are created at instance startup time, not the db2agntp processes.

10. **A.** The number of applications that can execute concurrently is controlled by MAXCAGENTS.

11. **D.** There is one db2sysc process per partition.

12. **B.** NUM_POOLAGENTS controls the number of idle agents.

13. **A.** There is one coordinator agent (db2agent) per connection, and it exists on the partition where the application is connected to. The other partitions have the db2agntp processes.

14. **B**. NUM_IOSERVERS controls the number of prefetches.
15. **D**. db2sysc is the DB2 system controller process.
16. **A**. The db2ipccm handles local client connections.
17. **C**. Since MAX_COORDAGENTS is set to 100, the maximum number of concurrent connections for this instance is 100.
18. **D**. Coordinating agents are named db2agent, active agents are named db2agntp, and idle agents are named db2agnta or db2agent, depending on whether they are associated with a coordinating agent. The process db2agnti does not exist.
19. **C**. The connection concentrator is enabled when MAX_CONNECTIONS is greater than MAX_COORDAGENTS. This means you can have more connections than there are the number of available coordinator agents.
20. **B**. The governor uses the process db2govd.

CHAPTER 15

1. The memory tracker and memory visualizer tools display DB2's memory usage at the instance, database, and agent levels.
2. The DATABASE_MEMORY configuration parameter allocates more shared memory than actually used to allow for the increase of the buffer pools, lock list, and so on, or for the creation of new buffer pools.
3. The package cache allows for the sharing and reuse of packages between applications.
4. The shared sort heap threshold is a hard limit for the concurrent amount of memory that can be used for shared sorts.
5. The log buffer is flushed to disk:
    • When it is filled
    • When MINCOMMIT commits occur
    • Or every one second
   depending on which occurs first. Therefore, the longest time period between flushes of the log buffer is one second.
6. If the DATABASE_MEMORY configuration parameter is set to AUTOMATIC, you can connect to the database and at any time issue the **GET DB CFG FOR *dbname* SHOW DETAIL** command. It will show AUTOMATIC(*nnnnnn*), and *nnnnnn* will be the actual amount of used memory.
7. The largest size you can set for the client requester I/O block is 64KB.
8. The instance-level (database manager) shared memory is allocated when you run the **db2start** command.
9. The database shared memory is allocated when the database is activated or when the first connection to the database is made.
10. The Fast Communications Manager (FCM) buffers are used for inter-partition communication.

11. **E**. There will be the IBMDEFAULTBP, plus the four hidden buffer pools for a total of five buffer pools.

12. **A**. Application group shared memory is used for partitioned databases, databases using intra-partition parallelism, and when the connection concentrator is enabled.

13. **D**. The statistics heap is allocated in agent private memory.

14. **A**. The application group shared heap is calculated by multiplying the application group memory size by the percentage of memory for the application control heap, and therefore equals 10,000 x 30% or 3,000 pages.

15. **C**. Each group can hold 30,000/512 or 58 applications. Therefore, you will need 6 groups to hold the 300 applications.

16. **C**. Since 2000 / 256 = 7.81, there can be a maximum of 7 concurrent shred sorts within this database.

17. **E**. DB2 does not limit the number of concurrent private sorts in memory; it reduces the sort heap allocated once the sort heap threshold is reached, so there is no limit.

18. **D**. The buffer pools are database specific, and therefore are not part of the database manager shared memory.

19. **D**. Since the 10,000 16K pages would use an additional 40,000 4K pages, the minimum size for the shared memory would be 115,264 pages, but of the options given, you would need to set the database memory to 125,000 pages for the CREATE BUFFER-POOL statement to be successful.

20. **A**. There are no applications connected to the database.

CHAPTER 16

1. Uncommitted read applications acquire an IN lock on the table but no row-level locks.

2. The maximum requester I/O block size is 64K.

3. You can configure DB2 to create some agent processes when DB2 is started by setting the NUM_INITAGENTS parameter to a value greater than zero.

4. To ensure the integrity of your database, DB2 writes the log buffers to disk when:
   • One or more transactions commit
   • The log buffer is full
   • One second has elapsed since the last log buffer flush

5. Lock escalation will occur when:
   • The database lock list becomes full
   • Any one application uses more than the MAXLOCKS percent of the lock list

6. You can capture table and index statistics:
   • By running the **runstats** utility
   • When loading data into one of your tables
   • By running the **reorgchk** utility

7. The **reorg** command not only reclusters the data in the table, but it also removes embedded free space by deleting rows and eliminating overflow records.

8. The timestamp monitor switch is enabled by default (it is used by the health monitor).
9. The `reset monitor all` command will reset all of the database monitor counters.
10. You need to create the explain tables to use the Visual Explain tool.
11. **D**. The `import` command cannot capture statistics.
12. **D**. The SOFTMAX configuration parameter controls the percentage of a log file that is filled before the page cleaners are triggered to write dirty pages from the buffer pool(s) to disk.
13. **C**. When DB2 performs lock escalation, it converts row-level locks to a table-level lock.
14. **B**. The configuration parameter sequential detection (SEQ_DETECT) allows DB2 to detect sequential page reads and trigger prefetching.
15. **B** and **D**. The page cleaners are triggered when the percentage of dirty pages in any one buffer pool reaches CHNGPGS_THRESH, or when applications write enough information to the logs to reach SOFTMAX percentage of any log file.
16. **A**. `reorgchk` will indicate if a reorg is suggested based on a number of conditions. One of these conditions is the number of overflow records in the table.
17. **B**. An overflow record is created when a row in a table is updated, a varchar column is updated, and its length increases so much that it can no longer fit on the same page.
18. **D**. DB2 does not support hints, as they are not needed due to the efficiency of the DB2 optimizer.
19. **D**. DTSCAN is not an operator used by DB2.
20. **C**. The shared sort heap threshold is a hard limit, and an attempt to start the fourth concurrent shared sort would cause that sort to overflow; therefore, the answer is C.

CHAPTER 17

1. The `?` is the help command that can be issued from the CLP. It provides a description of the error.
2. You use the command `db2 ? sql0805n` to get more information.
3. FFDC stands for first failure data capture.
4. There is no administration notification file in Windows. Administration notification logs are provided as part of the Windows Event Viewer.
5. The administration notification file in Linux/UNIX is *instance_name*.nfy.
6. To capture the most information possible, set the DIAGLEVEL Database Manager Configuration parameter to 4.
7. The db2support tool captures all the necessary information that DB2 Technical Support needs to research a problem.
8. The command `db2trc` is used to capture DB2 traces.
9. db2diag.log is located in the directory *$HOME*/sqllib/db2dump, where *$HOME* is the home directory of the instance owner.
10. To receive e-mail notification messages, you must use NOTIFYLEVEL 2 at least.

11. **C**. All FFDC information, including the administration notification log, is kept in the path specified by the Database Manager Configuration parameter DIAGPATH.

12. **A**. NOTIFYME is not a database manager configuration parameter.

13. **B**. NOTIFYLEVEL = 1 only logs fatal and unrecoverable errors.

14. **C**. SMTP hostname is defined in the database manager configuration file.

15. **D**. Trap files are normally reviewed only by DB2 Technical Support.

16. **C**. Application log file is not collected with the db2support tool.

17. **D**. 3 is the default DIAGLEVEL.

18. **D**. DIAGLEVEL 3 is the recommended value which is also the default value for DIAGLEVEL.

19. **D**. DIAGPATH is set to NULL by default.

20. **D**. CONTACT_LIST_GROUP is not a DAS parameter.

Use of Uppercase Versus Lowercase in DB2

Table B.1 identifies which kinds of commands, parameters, objects, and data are case-sensitive in DB2 UDB for Linux, UNIX, and Windows and gives examples.

Table B.1   Table B.1 Case-Sensitivity Requirements in DB2

Category	Description	Examples

DB2 system commands (including the *db2* executable)	You can treat DB2 system commands like any other program or application launched from the operating system.
	
	On Windows, the case does *not* matter.
	
	On Linux and UNIX, the case *does* matter, and since all DB2 system commands are named in lowercase, you need to issue the commands in lowercase.
		These work in Linux, UNIX, and Windows:
		`db2`
		`db2start`
		`db2ilist`
		These only work in Windows:
		`dB2`
		`db2STARt`
		`DB2ILIST`

CLP commands	You can invoke CLP commands from the DB2 Command Line Processor, the DB2 Command Window (Windows only) and the Command Editor. These tools do *not* care about the case of the command.	These work in Linux, UNIX, and Windows:
		`list applications`
		`LIST apPLicatIONs`
		Or if working with the CLP in non-interactive mode:
		`db2 list applications`
		`db2 LIST apPLicatIONs`

(continues)

Table B.1   Table B.1 Case-Sensitivity Requirements in DB2 *(Continued)*

Category	Description	Examples

SQL statements	You can invoke SQL statements from within an application or tool like the CLP. DB2 tools do *not* care about the case of the SQL statement.	These work in Linux, UNIX, and Windows:
		`select * from employee`
		`SELECT * frOM emPLOYee`

	When you create database objects, you can specify the object name in any case. However, DB2 usually stores names in the DB2 catalog in uppercase unless you use double quotes enclosing the object name when you create the object.[a]	These work in Linux, UNIX, and Windows:
		`create table Tab1 ...`
		`create table taB1 ...`
		(*TAB1* will be stored in the DB2 catalog tables)
		`create table "taB1"`
		(*taB1* will be stored in the DB2 catalog tables)

DB2 registry variables	Case-insensitive on all platforms.	These work in Linux, UNIX, and Windows:
		`db2options`
		`DB2optIOns`

DB2 configuration parameters	Case-insensitive on all platforms.	These work in Linux, UNIX, and Windows:
		`INTRA_PARALLEL`
		`intra_PARAllel`

User data stored in the database	DB2 stores the data in your database exactly the way you inserted it.	In Linux, UNIX, and Windows, if you issue:
		`insert into mytable`
		`(col2) values ('RAul')`
		Then column *col2* in table *mytable* will have the value *RAul*, just as it was inserted.

Database object names or any system data already stored in DB2 catalog tables	Typically any database object names or system-related data stored implicitly by DB2 itself is in uppercase. However, the object name can be in mixed case if it was created using double quotes.[a]
	
	Keep this in mind when you refer to these objects in a query.
		In Linux, UNIX, and Windows if you issue:
		`create table t1 (col2 integer)`
		t1 will be stored as *T1* and *col2* will be stored as *COL2* in DB2 catalog tables.
		If double quotes enclose the object:
		`create table "t1" (col2 integer)`
		t1 will be stored as *t1* and *col2* will be stored as *COL2* in DB2 catalog tables.

a. Using the CLP in Windows to create an object in mixed case by using double quotes will not work. Use the Command Editor instead.

IBM Servers

able C.1 provides a simplified overview of the servers that IBM offers. For detailed information, go to the IBM Servers Web site at www.ibm.com/servers/.

Table C.1 IBM Servers

	Server Name	Operating System	Processor
Distributed Platform Servers	xSeries	Windows, Linux	Intel
	eSeries	Windows, Linux	AMD
	pSeries	AIX, Linux	POWER
Mid-Range Servers	iSeries	i5/OS, OS/400, Linux (on a separate LPAR)	POWER
Mainframe Servers	zSeries	z/OS, OS/390, Linux (on a separate LPAR)	zSeries Application Assist Processor (zAAP)

Using the DB2 System Catalog Tables

his appendix describes how to use the DB2 system catalog tables. You will learn about:

- The different types of system catalog tables
- How to extract useful information from the system catalog tables
- How to perform *what-if* analysis of query performance

DB2 SYSTEM CATALOG TABLES

Each DB2 database has a set of tables called the **system catalog tables**. DB2 creates these tables when a database is created. They contain definitions of database objects (for example, tables, views, indexes, and packages), security information about the type of access that users have to these objects, and statistical information about the tables in the database.

DB2 automatically updates these tables when SQL Data Definition Language (DDL) statements are issued. For example, when you create a table, DB2 enters the definition of the table into the SYSIBM.SYSTABLES table. When you create an index, DB2 enters the index definition into the SYSIBM.SYSINDEXES table. DB2 uses these catalog tables to keep track of what exists in the database and their statistics. You cannot explicitly create or drop these tables, but you can query and view their contents.

DB2 creates the system catalog base tables under the SYSIBM schema. All of the table names have the prefix *SYS*, for example, SYSTABLES, SYSVIEWS, and SYSTABLESPACES. DB2 also creates a set of read-only views for the SYSIBM tables under the SYSCAT schema. These views contain the same or a subset of the information in the SYSIBM base tables, but the view names do not have the *SYS* prefix. For example, SYSCAT.TABLES is a view defined for the SYSIBM.SYSTABLES table, SYSCAT.VIEWS is a view defined for the SYSIBM.SYSVIEWS table, and SYSCAT.TABLESPACES is a view defined for the SYSIBM.SYSTABLESPACES table.

In addition to the SYSIBM tables and the SYSCAT views, DB2 defines the following database objects in the system catalog.

- A set of routines (functions and procedures) in the schemas SYSFUN and SYSPROC.
- A set of updatable catalog views in the SYSSTAT schema. The updatable views contain statistical information that is used by the optimizer. The values in some columns in these views can be changed to test query performance (see section D.3, How to Use the SYSSTAT Tables to Perform What-if Modeling and Analysis).

To display the names of all the system catalog tables and views along with their creation time, use the **LIST TABLES FOR SYSTEM** command. To display tables or views by their schema names, use the **LIST TABLES FOR SCHEMA** *schemaname* command, where *schemaname* is any valid schema, for example, SYSIBM, SYSCAT, SYSFUN, SYSPROC, or SYSSTAT.

HOW TO EXTRACT INFORMATION FROM THE SYSTEM CATALOG TABLES

When working with a database, sometimes you ask the following questions.

- How many buffer pools are there in the database and what table spaces use them?
- Are there any Event Monitors and are they active?
- What are the privileges given to users of this database?

You can answer all of these questions and more by querying the system catalog tables or views. In general, there is at least one system catalog table, and therefore one system catalog view, for each database object type. Table D.1 lists some of the system catalog views. For example, if you want to know about all the tables in the database, query the SYSCAT.TABLES view. If you want to know about all the indexes, query the SYSCAT.INDEXES view.

Table D.1   System Catalog Views

Database Object	SYSCAT System Catalog View
Table	TABLES
View	VIEWS
Index	INDEXES
Data type	DATATYPES
Column	COLUMNS
Table space	TABLESPACES
Buffer pool	BUFFERPOOLS

(continues)

Table D.1   System Catalog Views *(Continued)*

Database Object	SYSCAT System Catalog View
Package	PACKAGES
Constraints	CHECKS
Referential integrity	REFERENCES
Partition groups	NODEGROUPS
Partition group definitions	NODEGROUPDEF
Stored procedures	PROCEDURES
Sequences	SEQUENCES
Event Monitors	EVENTMONITORS

The following examples show how you can extract useful information from the SYSCAT views. A database connection is required.

Example 1: Extracting Buffer Pool Data

To find out how many buffer pools are in the database and their information, issue the statement:

```
SELECT * FROM SYSCAT.BUFFERPOOLS
```

Figure D.1 shows sample output for this command. In this database, only one buffer pool is defined, IBMDEFAULTBP. This is the default buffer pool DB2 creates when the database is created. The buffer pool has an ID of 1. Its size is 1MB (250 pages x 4096 bytes per page). ESTORE (Extended Storage) is not enabled for this buffer pool.

BPNAME	BUFFERPOOLID	DBPGNAME	NPAGES	PAGESIZE	ESTORE	. . .
IBMDEFAULTBP	1	-	250	4096	N	

Figure D.1   Sample buffer pool information

> **N O T E**   For detailed descriptions of all the columns in system catalog tables and views, search for the table/view name in the DB2 Information Center or refer to the *SQL Reference Manual*, Volume 1.

You can get the same information using the Control Center, as shown in Figures D.2 and D.3.

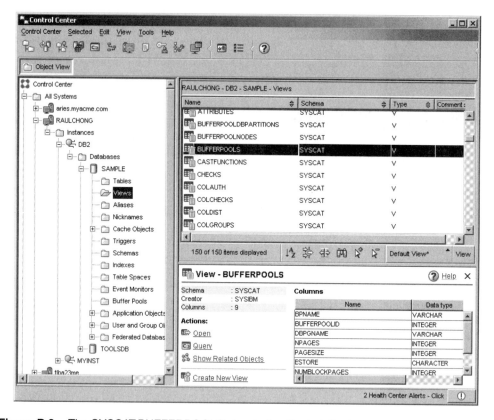

Figure D.2   The SYSCAT.BUFFERPOOLS view in the Control Center

From the Control Center, expand the *All Systems* folder until you find the database you want. All system catalogs tables (the SYSIBM tables) and user tables are stored in the *Tables* folder. All system catalog views (the SYSCAT views) and user-defined views are stored in the *Views* folder. Open the *Views* folder to display all the views. The contents of the selected folder in the left pane are displayed in the top right pane.

In the top right pane, click on the view you are interested in. The definition of the view is displayed in the bottom right pane of Figure D.2. In this example, it is the SYSCAT.BUFFER-POOLS view.

Double-click on the view name to display its contents (or right-click on the view name and select **Open**). Figure D.3 shows the contents of the SYSCAT.BUFFERPOOLS view.

Note that the information in Figure D.3 is the same as the output of the **SELECT * FROM SYSCAT.BUFFERPOOLS** statement (see Figure D.1).

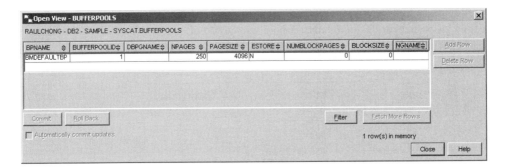

Figure D.3   Contents of the SYSCAT.BUFFERPOOLS view

Example 2: Determining Which Table Spaces Use the Buffer Pool

To find out which table spaces use the buffer pool found in Example 1, you need to query the SYSCAT.TABLESPACES view. Use the **DESCRIBE TABLE** command to display the columns defined in the view; then you can issue queries to display the contents of the columns you are really interested in. For example, the **DESCRIBE TABLE SYSCAT.TABLESPACES** statement displays the output shown in Figure D.4.

Column name	Type scema	Type name	Length	Scale	Null
TBSPACE	SYSIBM	VARCHAR	128	0	No
DEFINER	SYSIBM	VARCHAR	128	0	No
CREATE_TIME	SYSIBM	TIMESTAMP	10	0	No
TBSPACEID	SYSIBM	INTEGER	4	0	No
TBSPACETYPE	SYSIBM	CHARACTER	1	0	No
DATATYPE	SYSIBM	CHARACTER	1	0	No
EXTENTSIZE	SYSIBM	INTEGER	4	0	No
PREFETCHSIZE	SYSIBM	INTEGER	4	0	No
OVERHEAD	SYSIBM	DOUBLE	8	0	No
TRANSFERRATE	SYSIBM	DOUBLE	8	0	No
PAGESIZE	SYSIBM	INTEGER	4	0	No
DBPGNAME	SYSIBM	VARCHAR	128	0	No
BUFFERPOOLID	SYSIBM	INTEGER	4	0	No
DROP_RECOVERY	SYSIBM	CHARACTER	1	0	No
REMARKS	SYSIBM	VARCHAR	254	0	Yes
NGNAME	SYSIBM	VARCHAR	128	0	No

Figure D.4   Columns defined in a table

In Figure D.4, the columns you really need are the TBSPACE and BUFFERPOOLID columns. Issue

```
SELECT TBSPACE, BUFFERPOOLID FROM SYSCAT.TABLESPACES
```

to see the results shown in Figure D.5. You can see that there are four table spaces in the database, and all of them are using the buffer pool with an ID of 1. From Example 1, you know this buffer pool ID corresponds to the IBMDEFAULTBP buffer pool.

TBSPACE	BUFFERPOOLID
SYSCATSPACE	1
TEMPSPACE1	1
USERSPACE1	1
SYSTOOLSPACE	1

Figure D.5   Contents of the TABSPACE and BUFFERPOOLID columns

You can obtain the same information by displaying the contents of the SYSCAT.TABLESPACES view in the Control Center.

Example 3: Checking for Privileges and Authorization

A user with user ID *guest* complains that he is not able to insert any rows into a table called SYLVIAQ.TABLE1. The first thing you need to know is whether the user *guest* has the authority to insert into SYLVIAQ.TABLE1.

You are not sure which SYSCAT view contains the table privilege information. Therefore, you issue the **LIST TABLES FOR SCHEMA SYSCAT** statement to display all the available SYSCAT views, and hope to see one that might give you the table privilege information.

You browse through the output and find a table called TABAUTH. This might be the table you are looking for. You issue

```
DESCRIBE TABLE SYSCAT.TABAUTH
```

to display its contents. Figure D.6 shows the output.

Figure D.6 displays the contents of the SYSCAT.TABAUTH view. The view contains 13 columns: GRANTOR, GRANTEE, GRANTEETYPE…UPDATEAUTH. The DELETEAUTH column contains information about whether a user has DELETE privileges. Likewise, the INSERTAUTH column contains information about whether a user has INSERT privileges. You issue the following statement to find out what privileges the user *guest* has on SYLVIAQ.TABLE1:

```
SELECT * FROM SYSCAT.TABAUTH WHERE GRANTEE = 'GUEST'
```

As you can see in Figure D.7, the INSERTAUTH column has a value *N*. This means that the user *guest* does not have insert privileges; therefore, he cannot insert any rows. Note the SELECT-AUTH column has a value *Y.* This means the user has SELECT privileges for the table SYLVIAQ.TABLE1.

Column name	Type schema	Type name	Length	Scale	Nulls
GRANTOR	SYSIBM	VARCHAR	128	0	No
GRANTEE	SYSIBM	VARCHAR	128	0	No
GRANTEETYPE	SYSIBM	CHARACTER	1	0	No
TABSCHEMA	SYSIBM	VARCHAR	128	0	No
TABNAME	SYSIBM	VARCHAR	128	0	No
CONTROLAUTH	SYSIBM	CHARACTER	1	0	No
ALTERAUTH	SYSIBM	CHARACTER	1	0	No
DELETEAUTH	SYSIBM	CHARACTER	1	0	No
INDEXAUTH	SYSIBM	CHARACTER	1	0	No
INSERTAUTH	SYSIBM	CHARACTER	1	0	No
SELECTAUTH	SYSIBM	CHARACTER	1	0	No
REFAUTH	SYSIBM	CHARACTER	1	0	No
UPDATEAUTH	SYSIBM	CHARACTER	1	0	No

Figure D.6   Output of the DESCRIBE TABLE command

GRANTOR	GRANTEE	GRANTEETYPE	TABSCHEMA	TABNAME	CONTROLAUTH	ALTERAUTH	...
SYLVIAQ	GUEST	U	SYLVAIQ	TABLE1	N	N	

Figure D.7   User privileges in a table

You can get the same information using the Control Center. First, browse through all the views in the *Views* folder, then identify the SYSCAT.TABAUTH view and display its contents.

Now you know how to query the system catalog tables to get the information you need. If you prefer, you can use the Control Center to display the contents of the system catalog tables without having to issue any SQL statements.

HOW TO USE THE SYSSTAT TABLES TO PERFORM WHAT-IF MODELING AND ANALYSIS

Because DB2 maintains the SYSIBM and SYSCAT system catalog tables and views, they are read-only. However, you can update the SYSSTAT views. This is a special set of views that you can use to update database statistics. The information contained in these views affects how the DB2 optimizer chooses access plans when executing a query.

For planning purposes, you can change the statistical information in the SYSSTAT tables so that they do not reflect the actual state of tables and indexes. This lets you:

- Model query performance on a development system using production system statistics.
- Perform what-if query performance analysis by examining various possible changes to the query access plan.

You must have explicit DBADM authority for the database to modify statistics for tables and indexes and their components. That is, your user ID must have DBADM authority in the SYSCAT.DBAUTH table.

Table D.2 provides information about the system catalog tables that contain catalog statistics and the RUNSTATS options that collect specific statistics.

Table D.2   Table Statistics (SYSCAT.TABLES and SYSSTAT.TABLES)

		RUNSTATS Option	
Statistic	**Description**	**Table**	**Indexes**
FPAGES	Number of pages being used by a table.	Yes	Yes
NPAGES	Number of pages containing rows.	Yes	Yes
OVERFLOW	Number of rows that overflow.	Yes	No
CARD	Number of rows in a table (cardinality).	Yes	Yes[1]
ACTIVE_BLOCKS	For MDC tables, the total number of occupied blocks.	Yes	No

1. If the table does not have any indexes defined and you request statistics for indexes, no new CARD statistics are updated. The previous CARD statistics are retained.

The Yes or No in the RUNSTATS Option column indicates whether you need to execute the **RUNSTATS** command on the table, the indexes, or both to collect the statistics specified in the Statistic column. For example, if you want to collect the statistics on FPAGES, you must execute the **RUNSTATS** command on both the table and indexes. On the other hand, if you want to collect the statistics for OVERFLOW, you need to execute the **RUNSTATS** command on the table only.

Let's walk you through a what-if scenario: If the EMPLOYEE table had a lot more rows that it has now, which access plan would the DB2 optimizer choose?

First, you collect the statistics on the EMPLOYEE table using the **RUNSTATS** command:

```
RUNSTATS ON TABLE SYLVIAQ.EMPLOYEE
```

After it is completed, obtain the statistics by querying the SYSSTAT.TABLES view:

```
SELECT * FROM SYSSTAT.TABLES
WHERE TABSCHEMA = 'SYLVIAQ' AND TABNAME = 'EMPLOYEE'
```

Figure D.8 shows the output.

TABSCHEMA	TABNAME	CARD	NPAGES	FPAGES	OVERFLOW	. . .
SYLVIAQ	EMPLOYEE	32	2	2	0	

Figure D.8 Statistics for the EMPLOYEE table

In Figure D.8, the CARD column indicates that the EMPLOYEE table currently has 32 rows. To update the statistics for the EMPLOYEE table to reflect a bigger table, issue:

```
UPDATE SYSSTAT.TABLES
   SET CARD   = 10000,
       NPAGES = 1000,
       FPAGES = 1000,
       OVERFLOW = 2
   WHERE TABSCHEMA = 'SYLVIAQ' AND TABNAME = 'EMPLOYEE'
```

After this is completed, you can run your query against the EMPLOYEE table and get the access plan in text-based format using the **db2exfmt** command, or in graphic format using the Visual Explain GUI tool (see Chapter 4, Using the DB2 Tools).

You must be careful when manually updating catalog statistics: arbitrary changes can seriously affect the performance of subsequent queries. You can use any of the following methods to revert your changes back.

- ROLLBACK the unit of work in which the changes have been made (assuming the unit of work has not been committed).
- Use the RUNSTATS utility to recalculate and refresh the catalog statistics.
- Update the catalog statistics to indicate that statistics have not been gathered. (For example, setting column NPAGES to –1 indicates that the number-of-pages statistic has not been collected.)
- Replace the catalog statistics with the data they contained before you made any changes. This method is possible only if you used the **db2look** command to capture the statistics before you made any changes.

In some cases, the optimizer may determine that some particular statistical value or combination of values is not valid, and it will use the default values and issue a warning. Such circumstances are rare, however, since most of the validation is done when updating the statistics.

Tables D.3 through D.8 briefly describe the rest of the updatable SYSSTAT views.

Table D.3   Column Statistics (SYSCAT.COLUMNS and SYSSTAT.COLUMNS)

Statistic	Description	RUNSTATS Option	
		Table	Indexes
COLCARD	Column cardinality.	Yes	Yes[1]
AVGCOLLEN	Average length of a column.	Yes	Yes[1]
HIGH2KEY	Second highest value in a column.	Yes	Yes[1]
LOW2KEY	Second lowest value in a column.	Yes	Yes[1]
NUMNULLS	Number of NULLs in a column.	Yes	Yes[1]
SUB_COUNT	Average number of subelements.	Yes	No[2]
SUB_DELIM_LENGTH	Average length of each delimiter separating each subelement.	Yes	No[2]

1. Column statistics are gathered for the first column in the index key.
2. These statistics provide information about data in columns that contain a series of subfields or subelements that are delimited by blanks. The SUB_COUNT and SUB_DELIM_LENGTH statistics are collected only for single-byte character set string columns of type CHAR, VARCHAR, GRAPHIC, and VARGRAPHIC.

Table D.4   Multicolumn Statistics (SYSCAT.COLGROUPS and SYSSTAT.COLGROUPS)

Statistic	Description	RUNSTATS Option	
		Table	Indexes
COLGROUPCARD	Cardinality of the column group.	Yes	No

The multicolumn distribution statistics listed in Tables D.5 and D.6 are not collected by RUN-STATS. You can update them manually, however.

Table D.5   Multicolumn Distribution Statistics (SYSCAT.COLGROUPDIST and SYSSTAT.COLGROUPDIST)

Statistic	Description	RUNSTATS Option	
		Table	Indexes
TYPE	F = Frequency value. Q = Quantile value.	Yes	No
ORDINAL	Ordinal number of the column in the group.	Yes	No
SEQNO	Sequence number n that represents the nth TYPE value.	Yes	No
COLVALUE	The data value as a character literal or a null value.	Yes	No

Table D.6 Multicolumn Distribution Statistics 2 (SYSCAT.COLGROUPDISTCOUNTS and SYSSTAT.COLGROUPDISTCOUNTS)

Statistic	Description	RUNSTATS Option	
		Table	Indexes
TYPE	F = Frequency value. Q = Quantile value.	Yes	No
SEQNO	Sequence number *n* that represents the *n*th TYPE value.	Yes	No
VALCOUNT	If TYPE = F, VALCOUNT is the number of occurrences of COLVALUEs for the column group identified by this SEQNO. If TYPE = Q, VALCOUNT is the number of rows whose value is less than or equal to COLVALUEs for the column group with this SEQNO.	Yes	No
DISTCOUNT	If TYPE = Q, this column contains the number of distinct values that are less than or equal to COLVALUEs for the column group with this SEQNO. Null if unavailable.	Yes	No

Table D.7 Index Statistics (SYSCAT.INDEXES and SYSSTAT.INDEXES)

Statistic	Description	RUNSTATS Option	
		Table	Indexes
NLEAF	Number of index leaf pages.	No	Yes
NLEVELS	Number of index levels.	No	Yes
CLUSTERRATIO	Degree of clustering of table data.	No	Yes[2]
CLUSTERFACTOR	Finer degree of clustering.	No	See [1,2]
DENSITY	Ratio (percentage) of SEQUENTIAL_PAGES to the number of pages in the range of pages occupied by the index.[3]	No	Yes
FIRSTKEYCARD	Number of distinct values in the first column of the index.	No	Yes
FIRST2KEYCARD	Number of distinct values in the first two columns of the index.	No	Yes
FIRST3KEYCARD	Number of distinct values in the first three columns of the index.	No	Yes

(continues)

Table D.7   Index Statistics (SYSCAT.INDEXES and SYSSTAT.INDEXES) *(Continued)*

		RUNSTATS Option	
Statistic	**Description**	**Table**	**Indexes**
FIRST4KEYCARD	Number of distinct values in the first four columns of the index.	No	Yes
FULLKEYCARD	Number of distinct values in all columns of the index, excluding any key value in a type-2 index for which all record identifiers (RIDs) are marked deleted.	No	Yes
PAGE_FETCH_PAIRS	Page fetch estimates for different buffer sizes.	No	See [1,2]
SEQUENTIAL_PAGES	Number of leaf pages located on disk in index key order, with few or no large gaps between them.	No	Yes
AVERAGE_SEQUENCE_PAGES	Average number of index pages accessible in sequence. This is the number of index pages that the prefetchers can detect as being in sequence.	No	Yes
AVERAGE_RANDOM_PAGES	Average number of random index pages between sequential page accesses.	No	Yes
AVERAGE_SEQUENCE_GAP	Gap between sequences.	No	Yes
AVERAGE_SEQUENCE_ FETCH_PAGES	Average number of table pages accessible in sequence. This is the number of table pages that the prefetchers can detect as being in sequence when they fetch table rows using the index.	No	Yes[4]
AVERAGE_RANDOM_FETCH_ PAGES	Average number of random table pages between sequential page accesses when fetching table rows using the index.	No	Yes[4]
AVERAGE_SEQUENCE_F ETCH_GAP	Gap between sequences when fetching table rows using the index.	No	Yes[4]
NUMRIDS	Number of record identifiers (RIDs) in the index, including deleted RIDs in type-2 indexes.	No	Yes

(continues)

Table D.7 Index Statistics (SYSCAT.INDEXES and SYSSTAT.INDEXES) *(Continued)*

| Statistic | Description | RUNSTATS Option | |
		Table	Indexes
NUMRIDS_DELETED	Total number of RIDs marked deleted in the index, except RIDs on leaf pages on which all record identifiers are marked deleted.	No	Yes
NUM_EMPTY_LEAFS	Total number of leaf pages on which all record identifiers are marked deleted.	No	Yes

1. Detailed index statistics are gathered by specifying the DETAILED clause on the RUNSTATS command.
2. CLUSTERFACTOR and PAGE_FETCH_PAIRS are not collected with the DETAILED clause unless the table is of a respectable size. If the table is greater than about 25 pages, then CLUSTERFACTOR and PAGE_FETCH_PAIRS statistics are collected. In this case, CLUSTERRATIO is –1 (not collected). If the table is a relatively small table, only CLUSTERRATIO is filled in by RUNSTATS while CLUSTERFACTOR and PAGE_FETCH_PAIRS are not. If the DETAILED clause is not specified, only the CLUSTERRATIO statistic is collected.
3. This statistic measures the percentage of pages in the file containing the index that belongs to that table. For a table having only one defined index, DENSITY should normally be 100. DENSITY is used by the optimizer to estimate how many irrelevant pages from other indexes might be read, on average, if the index pages were prefetched.
4. These statistics cannot be computed when this table is in a DMS table space.

Column distribution statistics (listed in Table D.8) are gathered by specifying the WITH DISTRIBUTION clause on the **RUNSTATS** command. Note that distribution statistics *cannot* be gathered unless there is a sufficient lack of uniformity in the column values.

Table D.8 Column Distribution Statistics (SYSCAT.COLDIST and SYSSTAT.COLDIST)

| Statistic | Description | RUNSTATS Option | |
		Table	Indexes
DISTCOUNT	If TYPE = Q, the number of distinct values that are less than or equal to COLVALUE statistics.	Distribution[1]	No
TYPE	Indicator of whether row provides frequent-value or quantile statistics.	Distribution	No
SEQNO	Frequency ranking of a sequence number to help uniquely identify the row in the table.	Distribution	No
COLVALUE	Data value for which frequency or quantile statistics is collected.	Distribution	No
VALCOUNT	Frequency with which the data value occurs in columns. For quantiles, the number of values is less than or equal to the data value (COLVALUE).	Distribution	No

1. DISTCOUNT is collected only for columns that are the first key column in an index.

Table D.9   Function Statistics (SYSCAT.FUNCTIONS and SYSSTAT.FUNCTIONS)

Statistic	Description
IOS_PER_INVOC	Estimated number of read/write requests executed each time a function is executed.
INSTS_PER_INVOC	Estimated number of machine instructions executed each time a function is executed.
IOS_PER_ARGBYTE	Estimated number of read/write requests executed per input argument byte.
INSTS_PER_ARGBYTES	Estimated number of machine instructions executed per input argument byte.
PERCENT_ARGBYTES	Estimated average percent of input argument bytes that the function will actually process.
INITIAL_IOS	Estimated number of read/write requests executed only the first/last time the function is invoked.
INITIAL_INSTS	Estimated number of machine instructions executed only the first/last time the function is invoked.
CARDINALITY	Estimated number of rows generated by a table function.

Setting Up Database Connectivity for DB2 UDB for z/OS and DB2 UDB for iSeries

In Chapter 6, Configuring Client and Server Connectivity, you read about several connectivity scenarios where DB2 UDB for Linux, UNIX, and Windows behaved as the client. In this appendix, you will learn scenarios where DB2 UDB for z/OS and DB2 UDB for iSeries behave as the clients. In some of the scenarios, DB2 UDB for Linux, UNIX, and Windows behaves as the server.

The appendix is divided into two parts.

- Part I covers connectivity involving DB2 UDB for z/OS Version 8.
- Part II covers connectivity involving DB2 for iSeries Version 5.2.

PART I: SETTING UP DATABASE CONNECTIVITY FOR DB2 UDB FOR z/OS

In this section, you will learn to set up these three connectivity scenarios:

- From a DB2 for z/OS client to a DB2 for Linux, UNIX, and Windows server
- From a DB2 for z/OS client to a DB2 for iSeries server
- From a DB2 for z/OS client to a DB2 for z/OS server

The DB2 Connect software is not required in these scenarios.

> **N O T E** In Chapter 6, Configuring Client and Server Connectivity, we mentioned that APPC is supported when connecting from a DB2 for Linux, UNIX, and Windows client to a host server. However, inbound connections using APPC from a host client into a DB2 for Linux, UNIX, and Windows server is not supported. TCP/IP is assumed for all the scenarios described in this appendix.

The Communications Database

Before describing the different connectivity scenarios, we need to explain what the Communications Database (CDB) is. The CDB consists of several updatable system tables where connectivity information is stored in the host. In previous versions of DB2 UDB for z/OS, it used to be a separate database; currently, it is part of the Catalog. The CDB tables are only used by DB2 UDB for z/OS when it behaves as a client (Application Requester). Figure E.1 shows the relevant CDB tables used for a TCP/IP connection with several rows inserted.

In Figure E.1, we have highlighted a few related cells to explain two common cases that will help you understand how to populate the CDB tables.

SYSIBM.LOCATIONS

LOCATION CHAR(8) Not NULL Primary key	LINKNAME CHAR(8) Not NULL Foreign key	IBMREQD CHAR(1) Not NULL with default 'N'	PORT CHAR(32) Not NULL with default	TPN VARCHAR(64) Not NULL with default
Name of database you want to connect from DB2 z/OS client. This is a primary key.	Link to table SYSIBM.IPNAMES.	Use default values.	Port number of the DB2 server machine you are trying to connect. If left blank, the default is 446. It can also contain a service name as defined in the *services* file of this client machine.	Use default values.
SAMPLE	MYUDBLNK		50000	
SAMPLE2	MYUDBL2		50000	
TORISC6	MY400LNK		446	
MEXICO	MY390LNK		447	

SYSIBM.IPNAMES

LINKNAME CHAR(8) Not NULL Foreign key	SECURITY_OUT CHAR(1) Not NULL with default 'A'	USERNAMES CHAR(1) Not NULL with default	IBMREQD CHAR(1) Not NULL with default 'N'	IPADDR VARCHAR(254) Not NULL with default

Figure E.1   The CDB tables for a TCP/IP connection *(continues)*

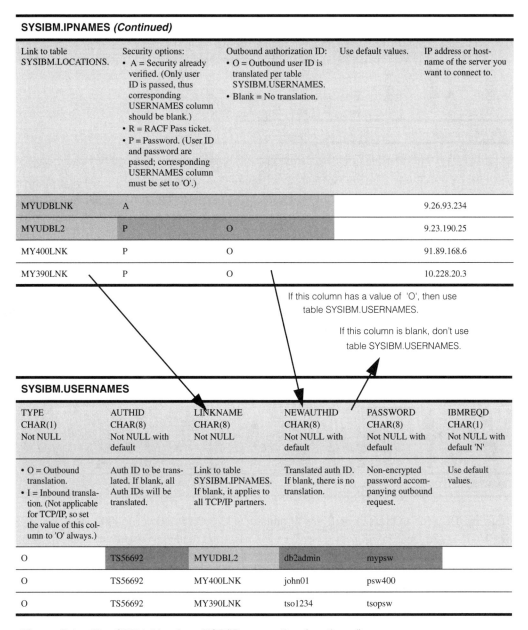

Figure E.1   The CDB tables for a TCP/IP connection *(continued)*

In the first case, let's assume the DB2 for z/OS client is trying to connect to the SAMPLE database. DB2 for z/OS will first join the first row of SYSIBM.LOCATIONS with the first row of SYSIBM.IPNAMES given that the LINKNAME column is the same (with value MYUDBLNK). This is shown next.

SYSIBM.LOCATIONS					SYSIBM.IPNAMES			
LOCATION	LINKNAME	IBMREQD	PORT	TPN	SECURITY_OUT	USERNAMES	IBMREQD	IPADDR
SAMPLE	MYUDBLNK		50000		A			9.26.93.234

Thus, the DB2 for z/OS client will use IP address 9.26.93.234 and port 50000. Also, because SECURITY_OUT = A (already verified), it will only pass the user ID to the server given that authentication has already been performed at the client when logging on to TSO. Note as well that the USERNAMES column is blank. This should normally be the case when SECURITY_OUT = A, and it means there is no need to look into the SYSIBM.USERNAMES table. At the DB2 for Linux, UNIX, and Windows server, the database manager configuration parameter AUTHENTICATION must be set to CLIENT in order for these settings to work.

For the second case, let's assume the DB2 for z/OS client is trying to connect to the SAMPLE2 database. DB2 for z/OS will join the second row of SYSIBM.LOCATIONS, the second row of SYSIBM.IPNAMES, and the first row of SYSIBM.USERNAMES given that the LINKNAME column is the same (with value MYUDBL2). This is shown next.

SYSIBM.LOCATIONS					SYSIBM.IPNAMES				SYSIBM.USERNAMES				
LOCATION	LINKNAME	IBMREQD	PORT	TPN	SECURITY_OUT	USERNAMES	IBMREQD	IPADDR	TYPE	AUTHID	NEWAUTHID	PASSWORD	IBMREQD
SAMPLE2	MYUDBL2		50000		P	O		9.23.190.25	O	TS56692	db2admin	mypsw	

Thus, the DB2 for z/OS client will use IP address 9.23.190.25 and port 50000. Also, because SECURITY_OUT = P, it will pass a user ID and a password to the server because authentication will be performed at the server. Note as well that the USERNAMES column has a value of O. This should normally be the case when SECURITY_OUT = P, and it means there is a need to look into the SYSIBM.USERNAMES table for the user ID and password. The columns AUTHID, NEWAUTHID, and PASSWORD show the mapping between the TSO ID and the ID and password combination that will be passed to the server. At the DB2 for Linux, UNIX, and Windows server, the database manager configuration parameter AUTHENTICATION must be set to SERVER in order for these settings to work.

For this example, we assumed the second DB2 for Linux, UNIX, and Windows server had a database called SAMPLE as well (not SAMPLE2). However, because the LOCATION column of the SYSIBM.LOCATIONS table is a primary key, and because there was already an entry for

SAMPLE for the first row of SYSIBM.LOCATIONS, the only way to put an entry in the table is to first create an alias to the database in the DB2 for Linux, UNIX, and Windows server as follows:

```
db2 catalog db sample as sample2
```

Then we could add an entry in SYSIBM.LOCATIONS for SAMPLE2.

Now you have learned how to read and populate the CDB tables. Let's discuss the three different connectivity scenarios.

Scenario 1: DB2 for z/OS Client to DB2 for Linux, UNIX, and Windows Server

Figure E.2 shows the overview for the scenario described in this section.

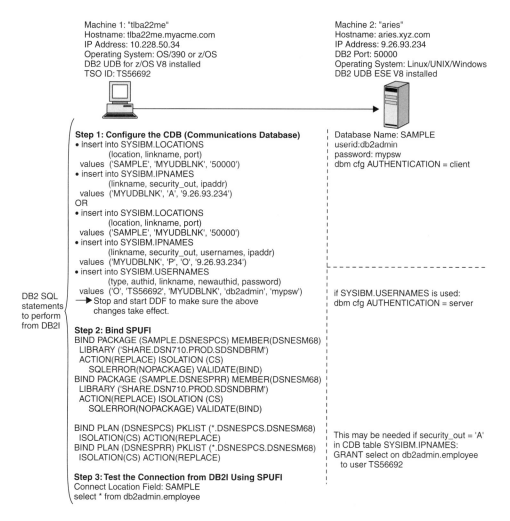

Figure E.2   DB2 for z/OS client to DB2 for Linux, UNIX, and Windows server

Table E.1 presents the list of commands required to set up this connection.

Table E.1 DB2 for z/OS Client to DB2 for Linux, UNIX, and Windows Server

Commands to Run on Machine 1 (*tlba22me*) DB2 for z/OS	Information You Need to Obtain from Machine 2 (*aries*) DB2 for Linux, UNIX, and Windows to Perform the Commands on Machine 1
Step 1: Configure the CDB (Communications Database)	

Option 1:
 	
`INSERT INTO SYSIBM.LOCATIONS`
`(location, linkname,port) VALUES`
`('SAMPLE','MYUDBLNK', '50000')`
 	
`INSERT INTO SYSIBM.IPNAMES`
`(linkname, security_out, ipaddr )`
`VALUES    ('MYUDBLNK', 'A',`
`'9.26.93.234' )`
 	
Note:
 	
MYUDBLNK is an arbitrary name used to link tables SYSIBM.LOCATIONS and SYSIBM.IPNAMES.
 	
When SECURITY_OUT = A, authentication has already been verified at this machine.
	1. *SAMPLE* is the database in machine 2 that you want to connect from the z/OS machine. If you don't remember the database name, you can issue from the CLP the command:
	
	`list db directory`
	
	and look for any entries with a directory entry type of `indirect`. These entries would correspond to local databases in your machine.
	
	2. For this example:
	
	`9.26.93.234` = the IP address of machine 2
	
	`50000` = the port used for DB2
	
	To find out the port used, issue this command from the CLP:
	
	`get dbm cfg`
	
	Then look for the parameter SVCENAME.
	
	If the value of SVCENAME is not the port number but a string, look in your system for the file *services* and grep for this string, which is normally based on your DB2 instance name. For example, if your instance name is *db2inst1*, you will normally find a corresponding entry like this:
	
	`db2cdb2inst1      50000/tcp`
	
	You can find the *services* file at /etc/services in Linux/UNIX and at *X*:\WINNT\System32\drivers\etc\services in Windows.
	
	3. The DBM configuration parameter AUTHENTICATION should be set to CLIENT for option 1, when column SECURITY_OUT is set to A. It should be set to SERVER for option 2, when this column is set to *P*.
	
	4. For this example:
	
	db2admin = user ID as defined on machine 2
	
	mypsw = password as defined on machine 2

(continues)

Table E.1 DB2 for z/OS Client to DB2 for Linux, UNIX, and Windows Server *(Continued)*

Commands to Run on Machine 1 (*tlba22me*) DB2 for z/OS	Information You Need to Obtain from Machine 2 (*aries*) DB2 for Linux, UNIX, and Windows to Perform the Commands on Machine 1
Option 2: ``` INSERT INTO SYSIBM.LOCATIONS (location, linkname,port) VALUES ('SAMPLE', 'MYUDBLNK', '50000') INSERT INTO SYSIBM.IPNAMES (linkname, security_out, usernames, ipaddr) VALUES('MYUDBLNK', 'P', 'O', '9.26.93.234') INSERT INTO SYSIBM.USERNAMES (type, authid, linkname, newauthid, password) VALUES ('O','TS56692','MYUDBLNK', 'db2admin','mypsw') ``` Note: MYUDBLNK is an arbitrary name used to link tables SYSIBM.LOCATIONS, SYSIBM.IPNAMES, and SYSIBM.USERNAMES. A value of P for the security_out column implies that authentication will be performed at server machine 2. TS56692 is the TSO ID on this mainframe machine 1 client.	
To make sure the changes to the CDB take effect, restart DDF (**-stop ddf**, **-start ddf**). This may not be necessary if you have entered a *new* entry in the CDB.	

(continues)

Table E.1   DB2 for z/OS Client to DB2 for Linux, UNIX, and Windows Server *(Continued)*

Commands to Run on Machine 1 (*tlba22me*) DB2 for z/OS	Information You Need to Obtain from Machine 2 (*aries*) DB2 for Linux, UNIX, and Windows to Perform the Commands on Machine 1

Step 2: Bind SPUFI

| ```
BIND PACKAGE (SAMPLE.DSNESPCS)
MEMBER(DSNESM68)
LIBRARY
('SHARE.DSN710.PROD.SDSNDBRM')
ACTION(REPLACE)
ISOLATION (CS)
SQLERROR(NOPACKAGE)
VALIDATE(BIND)

BIND PACKAGE (SAMPLE.DSNESPRR)
MEMBER(DSNESM68)
LIBRARY
('SHARE.DSN710.PROD.SDSNDBRM')
ACTION(REPLACE)
ISOLATION (CS)
SQLERROR(NOPACKAGE)
VALIDATE(BIND)

BIND PLAN (DSNESPCS)
   PKLIST (*.DSNESPCS.DSNESM68)
   ISOLATION(CS)
   ACTION(REPLACE)

BIND PLAN (DSNESPRR)
   PKLIST (*.DSNESPRR.DSNESM68)
   ISOLATION(CS)
   ACTION(REPLACE)
``` | *SAMPLE* is the database in machine 2 that you want to connect from the z/OS client machine.<br><br>The user ID performing the bind should have been granted the appropriate authorization/privileges. |

Note:

DSNESPCS is the package to bind for the SPUFI application with isolation Cursor Stability. DSNE-SPRR would be for isolation Repeatable Read.

The library specified contains DBRM member DSNESM68 (for the SPUFI application) and is dependent on how DB2 was set up in your system.

After the packages have been bound against server machine 2, the PLAN has to be bound. Using * in the package list guarantees the PLAN is bound in all locations.

(continues)
```

Table E.1   DB2 for z/OS Client to DB2 for Linux, UNIX, and Windows Server *(Continued)*

Commands to Run on Machine 1 (*tlba22me*) DB2 for z/OS	**Information You Need to Obtain from Machine 2 (*aries*) DB2 for Linux, UNIX, and Windows to Perform the Commands on Machine 1**
Step 3: Test the Connection from DB2I Using SPUFI	
Make sure to specify the *connect location* field as SAMPLE. Then issue the following command: `SELECT * FROM db2admin.employee` Note: There is no connect statement issued from SPUFI, but there is a specific field where you put the location you want to connect to. Note as well that the user ID and password are stored in the CDB.	When configuring the CDB using option 1 (when column SECURITY_OUT = A), you would be passing the TSO ID to the DB2 for Linux, UNIX, and Windows server. For this example, the TSO ID is *TS56692*. Thus, in order to access a table for `SELECT`, you would need to do this: `GRANT select ON db2admin.employee TO USER TS56692`

Table E.2 provides troubleshooting hints for connectivity problems.

Table E.2   What to Check If You Cannot Connect

Client Machine *tlba22me*	**Database Server *aries***
`ping aries.xyz.com` This command can be performed from the TSO Command Processor (assuming the hostname was used instead of the IP address itself in the SYSIBM.IPNAMES table).	`aries.xyz.com` = the host name of the database server If you cannot ping, there may be problems with the DNS. Try pinging the IP address.
`ping 9.26.93.234` This command can be performed from the TSO Command Processor.	`9.26.93.234` = the IP address of the database server This command will confirm whether or not there are problems with the network.

No corresponding information required on this machine.	1. Is DB2 started? If not, run **db2start**.
	2. Is DB2COMM set to TCPIP?
	
	Check by executing the following command:
	
	`db2set -all`
	
	If this registry variable is not set, you should execute:
	
	`db2set db2comm=tcpip`
	
	Then issue a **db2stop/db2start** command to make sure the change takes effect.

(continues)

Table E.2   What to Check If You Cannot Connect *(Continued)*

Client Machine *tlba22me*	Database Server *aries*
No corresponding information required on this machine. *(continued)*	3. Is SVCENAME set to the port number or service name specified in the *services* file of this server machine? Check this parameter from the CLP by issuing this command: `get dbm cfg`
If you used a service name instead of the port number in your SYSIBM.LOCATIONS table, make sure the entry is correct in the *services* file at the client machine.	No corresponding information required on this machine.
`netstat` This command shows all connections and port numbers and their statuses. It can be performed from the TSO Command Processor.	`netstat -a -n` This command shows all connections and port numbers and their statuses. Issue it from your command prompt.

> **N O T E**   DB2COMM and SVCENAME are set up automatically during the installation of DB2 for Linux, UNIX, and Windows for the default instance. Any other new instance created after installation with the **db2icrt** command will not have these parameters set up.

> **N O T E**   DB2 will check the *services* file on the machine where the DB2 command is issued.

Scenario 2: DB2 for z/OS Client to DB2 for iSeries Server

Figure E.3 shows the overview for the scenario described in this section.

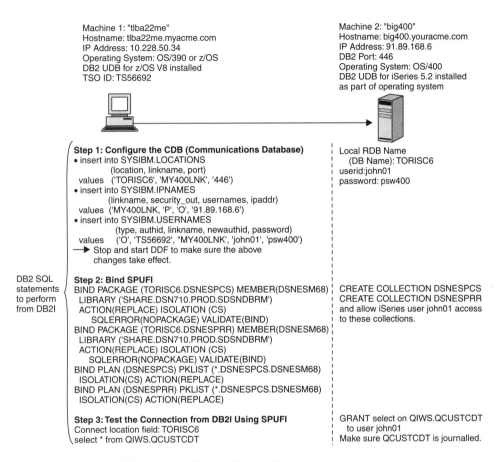

Figure E.3   DB2 for z/OS client to DB2 for iSeries Server

Table E.3 presents the list of commands required to set up this connection.

Table E.3   DB2 for z/OS Client to DB2 for iSeries Server

Commands to Run on Machine 1 (*tlba22me*) DB2 for z/OS	Information You Need to Obtain from Machine 2 (*big400*) DB2 for iSeries to Perform the Commands on Machine 1
Step 1: Configure the CDB (Communications Database)	

`INSERT INTO SYSIBM.LOCATIONS`
`(location, linkname,port) VALUES`
`('TORISC6','MY400LNK', '446')`
 	
`INSERT INTO SYSIBM.IPNAMES`
`(linkname, security_out,`
`usernames, ipaddr )`
`VALUES   ('MY400LNK', 'P', 'O',`
`'91.89.168.6' )`
 	
`INSERT INTO SYSIBM.USERNAMES (type,`
`authid, linkname,`
`newauthid, password) VALUES ('O',`
`'TS56692', 'MY400LNK', 'john01',`
`'psw400')`
 	
Note:
 	
MY400LNK is an arbitrary name used to link tables SYSIBM.LOCATIONS, SYSIBM.IPNAMES, and SYSIBM.USERNAMES.
 	
When SECURITY_OUT = P authentication will be performed at server machine 2.
 	
TS56692 is the TSO ID on this mainframe machine 1 client.
	1. *TORISC6* is the local RDB name.
	
	In order to determine the local RDB name, contact your iSeries administrator who can issue the command:
	
	`WRKRDBDIRE`
	
	When the *Work with Relational Database Directory Entries* panel appears, the administrator can find the desired value in column *Relational Database* that maps to the column *Remote Location* with a value of `*LOCAL`.
	
	2. For this example:
	
	91.89.168.6 = IP address of machine 2
	
	446 = the port used for DB2
	
	Port 446 is the default value for the DRDA service. It is very unlikely this port is changed.
	
	3. For this example:
	
	john01 = user ID as defined on machine 2
	
	psw400 = password as defined on machine 2

To make sure the changes to the CDB take effect, restart DDF (`-stop ddf`, `-start ddf`) This may not be necessary if you have entered a *new* entry in the CDB.	No corresponding information required on this machine.

(continues)

Table E.3 DB2 for z/OS Client to DB2 for iSeries Server *(Continued)*

Commands to Run on Machine 1 (*tlba22me*) DB2 for z/OS	Information You Need to Obtain from Machine 2 (*big400*) DB2 for iSeries to Perform the Commands on Machine 1

Step 2: Bind SPUFI

| ```
BIND PACKAGE (TORISC6.DSNESPCS)
MEMBER(DSNESM68)
LIBRARY
('SHARE.DSN710.PROD.SDSNDBRM')
ACTION(REPLACE)
ISOLATION (CS)
SQLERROR(NOPACKAGE)
VALIDATE(BIND)

BIND PACKAGE (TORISC6.DSNESPRR)
MEMBER(DSNESM68)
LIBRARY
('SHARE.DSN710.PROD.SDSNDBRM')
ACTION(REPLACE)
ISOLATION (CS)
SQLERROR(NOPACKAGE)
VALIDATE(BIND)

BIND PLAN (DSNESPCS)
   PKLIST (*.DSNESPCS.DSNESM68)
   ISOLATION(CS)
   ACTION(REPLACE)

BIND PLAN (DSNESPRR)
   PKLIST (*.DSNESPRR.DSNESM68)
   ISOLATION(CS)
   ACTION(REPLACE)
``` | ***TORISC6*** = the local RDB name<br><br>In order to bind the packages, you first need to create the collections:<br><br>```
CREATE COLLECTION DSNESPCS
CREATE COLLECTION DSNESPRR
```<br><br>Then grant iSeries user john01 the appropriate authorization/privileges against the collection. |

Note:

DSNESPCS is the package to bind for the SPUFI application with isolation Cursor Stability. DSNE-SPRR would be for isolation Repeatable Read.

The library specified contains DBRM member DSNESM68 (for the SPUFI application) and is dependent on how DB2 was set up in your system.

After the packages have been bound against server machine 2, the PLAN has to be bound. Using * in the package list guarantees the PLAN is bound in all locations.

(continues)

Table E.3   DB2 for z/OS Client to DB2 for iSeries Server *(Continued)*

Commands to Run on Machine 1 (*tlba22me*) DB2 for z/OS	Information You Need to Obtain from Machine 2 (*big400*) DB2 for iSeries to Perform the Commands on Machine 1
Step 3: Test the Connection from DB2I Using SPUFI	

Make sure to specify the *connect location* field as TORISC6. Then issue the following command:
 	
`SELECT * FROM QIWS.QCUSTCDT`
 	
Note:
 	
There is no connect statement issued from SPUFI, but there is a specific field where you put the location you want to connect to. Note as well that the user ID and password are stored in the CDB.
 	
Issue this query for testing purposes. The sample table QIWS.QCUSTCDT is normally available after installation of iSeries unless it was removed or not set up by your iSeries administrator.
	Grant the appropriate **SELECT** privilege to the user:
	
	`GRANT select ON QIWS.QCUSTCDT`
	`         TO USER john01`
	
	Also, most tables in iSeries are automatically journalled, but the QCUSTCDT sample table is not, so make sure to journal it.

Table E.4 provides troubleshooting hints for connectivity problems.

Table E.4   What to Check If You Cannot Connect

Client Machine *torisc6*	Database Server *tlba22me*
`ping big400.youracme.com` This command can be performed from the TSO Command Processor (assuming the hostname was used instead of the IP address itself in the SYSIBM.IPNAMES table).	`big400.youracme.com` = the host name of the database server If you cannot ping, there may be problems with the DNS. Try pinging the IP address.
`ping 91.89.168.6`	`91.89.168.6` = the IP address of the database server This will confirm whether or not there are problems with the network.
No corresponding information required on this machine.	Since the database server is DB2 UDB for iSeries, check: Is DDM started? If not, execute the following: `STRTTCPSVR SERVER(*DDM)`

(continues)

Table E.4 What to Check If You Cannot Connect *(Continued)*

Client Machine *torisc6*	Database Server *tlba22me*
If you used a service name instead of the port number in your SYSIBM.LOCATIONS table, make sure the entry is correct in the *services* file at the client machine.	No corresponding information required on this machine.
`netstat` This command shows all connections and port numbers and their statuses. It can be performed from the TSO Command Processor.	`netstat` This command shows all connections and port numbers and their statuses. It can be performed from the OS/400 Main menu, options 6 -> 5 -> 10 -> 7 -> 3.

Scenario 3: DB2 for z/OS Client to DB2 for z/OS Server

Figure E.4 shows the overview for the scenario described in this section.

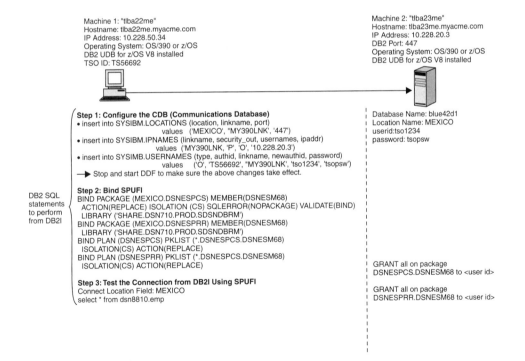

Figure E.4 DB2 for z/OS client to DB2 for z/OS server

Table E.5 presents the list of commands required to set up this connection are given in the next table.

Table E.5   DB2 for z/OS Client to DB2 for z/OS Server

Commands to Run on Machine 1 (*tlba22me*) DB2 for z/OS	Information You Need to Obtain from Machine 2 (*tlba23me*) DB2 for z/OS to Perform the Commands on Machine 1
Step 1: Configure the CDB (Communications Database)	

`INSERT INTO SYSIBM.LOCATIONS`
`(location, linkname,port) VALUES`
`('MEXICO', 'MY390LNK', '447')`
 	
`INSERT INTO SYSIBM.IPNAMES`
`(linkname, security_out, usernames,`
`ipaddr )`
`VALUES  ('MY390LNK', 'P', 'O',`
`'10.228.20.3' )`
 	
`INSERT INTO SYSIBM.USERNAMES`
`(type, authid, linkname,`
` newauthid, password)`
`VALUES ('O', 'TS56692', 'MY390LNK',`
`'tso1234','tsopsw')`
 	
Note:
MY390LNK is an arbitrary name used to link tables SYSIBM.LOCATIONS, SYSIBM.IPNAMES, and SYSIBM.USERNAMES.
When SECURITY_OUT = P authentication will be performed at server machine 2.
TS56692 is the TSO ID on this mainframe machine 1 client.
	1. *MEXICO* is the location name for the DB2 for z/OS subsystem in this machine 2 that you want to connect from the other DB2 for z/OS client.
	2. For this example:
	10.228.20.3 = the IP address of machine 2
	447 = the port used for DB2
	To find out the port used, contact your DB2 for OS/390 and z/OS administrator, who can check the MVS syslog for message DSNL004I. "TCPPORT" in that message contains the port to use. Also, the **-DISPLAY DDF** command provides this information.
	3. For this example:
	tso1234 = the user ID as defined on machine 2
	tsopsw = the password as defined on machine 2

To make sure the changes to the CDB take effect, restart DDF (`-stop ddf, -start ddf`) This may not be necessary if you have entered a *new* entry in the CDB.	No corresponding information required on this machine.

(continues)

Table E.5 DB2 for z/OS Client to DB2 for z/OS Server *(Continued)*

Commands to Run on Machine 1 (*tlba22me*) DB2 for z/OS	Information You Need to Obtain from Machine 2 (*tlba23me*) DB2 for z/OS to Perform the Commands on Machine 1

Step 2: Bind SPUFI

| ```
BIND PACKAGE (MEXICO.DSNESPCS)
MEMBER(DSNESM68)
LIBRARY
('SHARE.DSN710.PROD.SDSNDBRM')
ACTION(REPLACE)
ISOLATION (CS)
SQLERROR(NOPACKAGE)
VALIDATE(BIND)


BIND PACKAGE (MEXICO.DSNESPRR)
MEMBER(DSNESM68)
LIBRARY (
'SHARE.DSN710.PROD.SDSNDBRM')
ACTION(REPLACE)
ISOLATION (CS)
SQLERROR(NOPACKAGE)
VALIDATE(BIND)


BIND PLAN (DSNESPCS)
   PKLIST (*.DSNESPCS.DSNESM68)
   ISOLATION(CS)
   ACTION(REPLACE)


BIND PLAN (DSNESPRR)
   PKLIST (*.DSNESPRR.DSNESM68)
   ISOLATION(CS)
   ACTION(REPLACE)
``` | *MEXICO* is the location name for the DB2 UDB for z/OS subsystem in this machine 2 that you want to connect from the other DB2 UDB for z/OS client.

The user ID performing the bind should have been granted the appropriate authorization/privileges.

This may also be required to run the packages:

```
GRANT ALL ON PACKAGE
         DSNESPCS.DSNESM68 TO user_id

GRANT ALL ON PACKAGE
         DSNESPCS.DSNESM68 TO user_id
``` |

Note:

DSNESPCS is the package to bind for the SPUFI application with isolation Cursor Stability. DSNESPRR would be for isolation Repeatable Read.

The library specified in the bind package command contains DBRM member DSNESM68 (for the SPUFI application). This library location will vary depending on how DB2 was set up in your system.

After the packages have been bound against server machine 2, the PLAN has to be bound. Using * in the package list guarantees the PLAN is bound in all locations.

(continues)
```

Table E.5   DB2 for z/OS Client to DB2 for z/OS Server *(Continued)*

Commands to Run on Machine 1 (*tlba22me*) DB2 for z/OS	Information You Need to Obtain from Machine 2 (*tlba23me*) DB2 for z/OS to Perform the Commands on Machine 1
Step 3: Test the Connection from DB2I Using SPUFI	
Make sure to specify the *connect location* field as MEXICO. Then issue the following command: `SELECT * FROM dsn8810.emp` Note: There is no connect statement issued from SPUFI, but there is a specific field where you put the location you want to connect to. Note as well that the user ID and password are stored in the CDB. Issue this query for testing purposes. The sample table *dsn8810.emp* is normally available after installation of DB2 for OS/390 and z/OS unless it was removed or not set up by your mainframe DBA. The example uses Version 8 *emp* table. If connecting to a DB2 for OS/390 and z/OS Version 7 subsystem, use table *dsn8710.emp* instead.	Make sure the user executing the query has the appropriate authorization/privilege, for example: `GRANT select ON dsn8810.emp TO USER tso1234`

Table E.6 provides troubleshooting hints for connectivity problems.

Table E.6   What to Check If You Cannot Connect

Client Machine *tlba22me*	Server Machine *tlba23me*
`ping tlba23me.myacme.com` This command can be performed from the TSO Command Processor (assuming the hostname was used instead of the IP address itself in the SYSIBM.IPNAMES table).	`tlba23me.myacme.com` = the host name of the database server If you cannot ping, there may be problems with the DNS. Try pinging the IP address.
`ping 10.228.20.3` This command can be performed from the TSO Command Processor.	`10.228.20.3` = IP address of Database Server This will confirm if there are problems or not with the network.
No corresponding information required on this machine.	1. Is DB2 started? If not, execute `-start db2`. 2. Is DDF started? If not, execute `-start ddf`.

(continues)

Table E.6 What to Check If You Cannot Connect *(Continued)*

Client Machine *tlba22me*	Server Machine *tlba23me*
If you used a service name instead of the port number in your SYSIBM.LOCATIONS table, make sure the entry is correct in the *services* file at the client machine.	No corresponding information required on this machine.
`netstat` This command shows all connections and port numbers and their statuses. It can be performed from the TSO Command Processor.	`netstat` This command shows all connections and port numbers and their statuses. It can be performed from the TSO Command Processor.

PART II: SETTING UP DATABASE CONNECTIVITY FOR DB2 UDB FOR ISERIES

In this part, you will learn to set up these three connectivity scenarios:

- From DB2 for iSeries client to DB2 for Linux, UNIX, and Windows server
- From DB2 for iSeries client to DB2 for z/OS server
- From DB2 for iSeries client to DB2 for iSeries server

The DB2 Connect software is not required in these scenarios.

Scenario 1: DB2 for iSeries Client to DB2 for Linux, UNIX, and Windows Server

Figure E.5 shows the overview for the scenario described in this section.

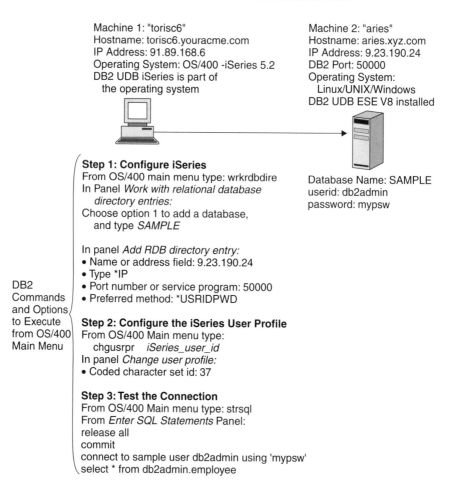

Figure E.5   DB2 for iSeries client to DB2 for Linux, UNIX, and Windows servers

Table E.7 presents the list of commands required to set up this connection.

Table E.7   DB2 for iSeries Client to DB2 for Linux, UNIX, and Windows Server

Commands to Run on Machine 1 (*torisc6*) DB2 for iSeries	Information You Need to Obtain from Machine 2 (*aries*) DB2 for Linux, UNIX, and Windows to Perform the Commands on Machine 1
Step 1: Configure iSeries	
From the OS/400 Main menu, type: `wrkrdbdire` After you press Enter, this command will bring up the *Work with Relational Database Directory Entries* panel.	No corresponding information required on this machine.
From the *Work with Relational Database Directory Entries* panel: • Choose Option 1 to add a database. • Type the database name: *SAMPLE*.	*SAMPLE* is the database in this machine 2 that you want to connect from the iSeries machine. If you don't remember the database name, you can issue from the CLP the following command: `list db directory` and look for any entries with a directory entry type of `indirect`. These entries would correspond to local databases in your machine.

In the *Add RDB Directory Entry* panel, specify:
 	
• Name or address field: *9.23.190.24*
• Type: *IP
 	
Note:
 	
The hostname could have been used instead of the IP address.
 	
After you specify *IP for the TCP/IP protocol and press Enter, other choices will appear:
 	
• Port number or service program: *50000*
• Preferred method: *USRIDPWD
 	
Note:
 	
The default port number is *DRDA, which means port 446.
 	
The service name as defined on this machine 1 (client) could have been used instead of the port number.
 	
The default authentication method is *ENCRYPTED, which only works between iSeries machines, thus *USRIDPWD is used.
	For this example:
	
	9.23.190.24 = the IP address of machine 2
	
	50000 = the port used for DB2. To find out the port used, issue this command from the CLP:
	
	`get dbm cfg`
	
	Then, look for the parameter SVCENAME. If the value of SVCENAME is not the port number but a string, then look in your system for the file *services* and grep for this string, which is normally based on your DB2 instance name. For example, if your instance name is *db2inst1*, you will normally find a corresponding entry like this:
	
	`db2cdb2inst1      50000/tcp`
	
	You can locate the *services* file at /etc/services in UNIX and *X*:\WINNT\System32\drivers\etc\services in Windows.

(continues)

Table E.7   DB2 for iSeries Client to DB2 for Linux, UNIX, and Windows Server

Commands to Run on Machine 1 (*torisc6*) DB2 for iSeries	Information You Need to Obtain from Machine 2 (*aries*) DB2 for Linux, UNIX, and Windows to Perform the Commands on Machine 1
Step 2: Configure the iSeries User Profile	
For this example we logged on to the iSeries machine with a user ID of *jmascare*. We need to change the profile for this user so that the CCSID value is not the default of 65335 but something else, like 37 (US English). There is no codepage conversion supported for CCSID 65335. From the OS/400 Main menu, type: `chgusrprf jmascare` This command will invoke the *Change User Profile* panel. Then, specify the coded character set ID as 37.	No corresponding information required on this machine.
Step 3: Test the Connection	

Start the Interactive SQL tool from the OS/400 Main menu by typing:
 	
 `strsql`
 	
 From the *Enter SQL Statements* panel, type:
 	
 `release all`   (Press Enter)
 `COMMIT`   (Press Enter)
 `CONNECT TO sample`
 `    USER db2admin`
 `    USING 'mypsw'`   (Press Enter)
 `SELECT * FROM`
 `    db2admin.employee`   (Press Enter)
 	
 Note:
 	
 The password needs to be passed in single quotes in order to maintain its case. Using double quotes for the user ID as shown below also works:
 	
 `CONNECT TO sample`
 `    USER "db2admin"`
 `    USING 'mypsw'`   (Press Enter)
	For this example:
	
	 db2admin = the user ID as defined on machine 2
	
	 mypsw = the password as defined on machine 2

Table E.8 provides troubleshooting hints for connectivity problems.

Table E.8   What to Check If You Cannot Connect

Client Machine *torisc6*	Database Server *aries*
`ping aries.xyz.com` This command can be performed from the OS/400 Main menu (assuming the hostname was used instead of the IP address itself in the *Add RDB Directory Entry* panel).	`aries.xyz.com` = the host name of the database server If you cannot ping, there may be problems with the DNS. Try pinging the IP address.
`ping 9.23.190.24` This command can be performed from the OS/400 Main menu.	`9.23.190.24` = the IP address of the database server This will confirm whether or not there are problems with the network.

No corresponding information required on this machine.	1. Is DB2 started? If not, run **db2start**.
	2. Is DB2COMM set to TCPIP?
	Check by executing the following command:
	`db2set -all`
	If this registry variable is not set, you should execute:
	`db2set db2comm=tcpip`
	and then issue a **db2stop/db2start** command to make sure the change takes effect.
	3. Is SVCENAME set to the port number or service name specified in the *services* file of this server machine?
	Check this parameter from the CLP by issuing:
	`get dbm cfg`

If you used a service name instead of the port number in your **Add RDB Directory Entry** panel, make sure the entry is correct in the *services* file at the client machine.	No corresponding information required on this machine.
`netstat` This command shows all connections and port numbers and their statuses. It can be performed from the OS/400 Main menu, options 6 -> 5 -> 10 -> 7 -> 3.	`netstat -a -n` This command shows all connections and port numbers and their statuses. Issue it from your command prompt.

Scenario 2: DB2 for iSeries Client to DB2 for z/OS Server

Figure E.6 shows the overview for the scenario described in this section.

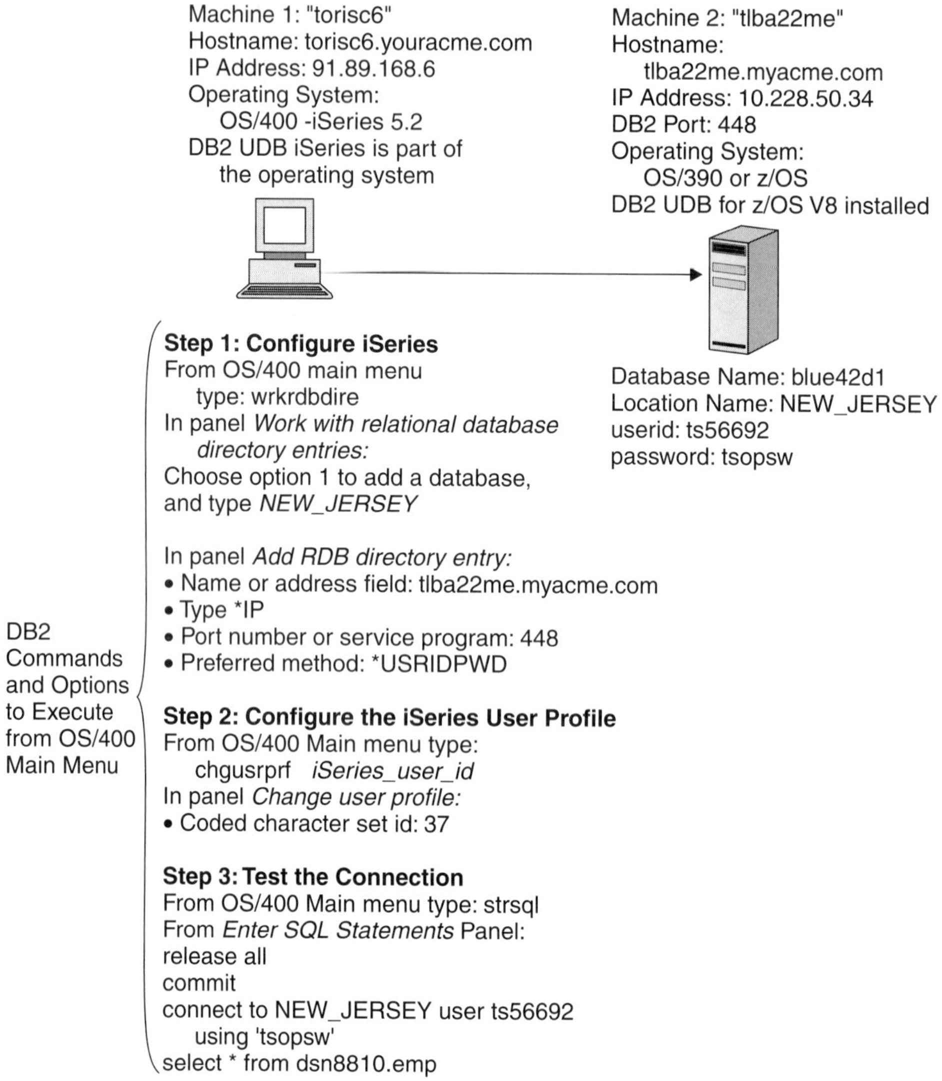

Machine 1: "torisc6"
Hostname: torisc6.youracme.com
IP Address: 91.89.168.6
Operating System:
    OS/400 -iSeries 5.2
DB2 UDB iSeries is part of
    the operating system

Machine 2: "tlba22me"
Hostname:
    tlba22me.myacme.com
IP Address: 10.228.50.34
DB2 Port: 448
Operating System:
    OS/390 or z/OS
DB2 UDB for z/OS V8 installed

DB2 Commands and Options to Execute from OS/400 Main Menu

Step 1: Configure iSeries
From OS/400 main menu
    type: wrkrdbdire
In panel *Work with relational database
    directory entries:*
Choose option 1 to add a database,
and type *NEW_JERSEY*

Database Name: blue42d1
Location Name: NEW_JERSEY
userid: ts56692
password: tsopsw

In panel *Add RDB directory entry:*
• Name or address field: tlba22me.myacme.com
• Type *IP
• Port number or service program: 448
• Preferred method: *USRIDPWD

Step 2: Configure the iSeries User Profile
From OS/400 Main menu type:
    chgusrprf   *iSeries_user_id*
In panel *Change user profile:*
• Coded character set id: 37

Step 3: Test the Connection
From OS/400 Main menu type: strsql
From *Enter SQL Statements* Panel:
release all
commit
connect to NEW_JERSEY user ts56692
    using 'tsopsw'
select * from dsn8810.emp

Figure E.6   DB2 for iSeries client to DB2 for z/OS Server

Table E.9 presents the list of commands required to set up this connection.

Table E.9 DB2 for iSeries Client to DB2 z/OS Server

Commands to Run on Machine 1 (*torisc6*) DB2 for iSeries	Information You Need to Obtain from Machine 2 (*tlba22me*) DB2 for z/OS to Perform the Commands on Machine 1
Step 1: Configure iSeries	
From the OS/400 Main menu, type: `wrkrdbdire` After you press Enter, this will bring up the *Work with Relational Database Directory Entries* panel	No corresponding information required on this machine.
From the *Work with Relational Database Directory Entries* panel: • Choose Option 1 to add a database. • Type the database name: ***NEW_JERSEY.***	***NEW_JERSEY*** is the location name of the DB2 for z/OS subsystem you want to access on machine 2. To find out the location name, contact your DB2 for z/OS administrator, who can check the MVS syslog for message DSNL004I. "LOCATION" in that message contains the location name to use. Also, the **-DISPLAY DDF** command provides this information.
In the *Add RDB Directory Entry* panel, specify: • Name or address field: `tlba22me.myacme.com` • Type: *IP Note: The IP address could have been used instead of the hostname. After you specify *IP for the TCP/IP protocol and press Enter, other choices will appear: • Port number or service program: ***448*** • Preferred method: *USRIDPWD Note: The service name as defined on this machine 1 (client) could have been used instead of the port number. Versions other than DB2 for iSeries 5.2 may not have some of these choices.	For this example: ***tlba22me.myacme.com*** = the host name of machine 2 ***448*** = the port used for DB2 Though the example shows port 448, port 446 is normally the default value. To find out the port used, contact your DB2 for OS/390 and z/OS administrator, who can check the MVS syslog for message DSNL004I. "TCPPORT" in that message contains the port to use. Also, the **-DISPLAY DDF** command provides this information.

(continues)

Table E.9   DB2 for iSeries Client to DB2 z/OS Server *(Continued)*

Commands to Run on Machine 1 (*torisc6*) DB2 for iSeries	Information You Need to Obtain from Machine 2 (*tlba22me*) DB2 for z/OS to Perform the Commands on Machine 1
Step 2: Configure the iSeries User Profile	
For this example we logged on to the iSeries machine with a user ID of jmascare. We need to change the profile for this user so that the CCSID value is not the default of 65335 but something else, like 37 (US English). There is no codepage conversion supported for CCSID 65335.	No corresponding information required on this machine.

From the OS/400 Main menu, type:

```
chgusrprf jmascare
```

This command will invoke the *Change User Profile* panel. Then specify the coded character set ID as 37.

Step 3: Test the Connection

Start the Interactive SQL tool from the OS/400 Main menu:	For this example:
	ts56692 = the user ID as defined on machine 2

```
strsql
```
From the *Enter SQL Statements* panel, type:

tsopsw = the password as defined on machine 2

```
release all    (Press Enter)
COMMIT    (Press Enter)
CONNECT TO NEW_JERSEY
     USER ts56692
     USING 'tsopsw'    (Press Enter)
SELECT * FROM dsn8810.emp    (Press Enter)
```

Note:

The password needs to be passed in single quotes in order to maintain its case. Using double quotes for the user ID as shown below also works:

```
CONNECT TO NEW_JERSEY
     USER "ts56692"
     USING 'tsopsw'    (Press enter)
```

The **SELECT** query is using the sample table *dsn8810.emp* for Version 8. If connecting to a DB2 for OS/390 and z/OS Version 7 subsystem, use table *dsn8710.emp*.

Table E.10 provides troubleshooting hints for connectivity problems.

Table E.10   What to Check If You Cannot Connect

Client Machine *torisc6*	Database Server *tlba22me*
`ping tlba22me.myacme.com` This command can be performed from the OS/400 Main menu (assuming the hostname was used instead of the IP address itself in the *Add RDB Directory Entry* panel).	`tlba22me.myacme.com` = the host name of the database server If you cannot ping, there may be problems with the DNS. Try pinging the IP address.
`ping 10.228.50.34` This command can be performed from the OS/400 Main menu.	`10.228.50.34` = the IP address of the database server This will confirm whether or not there are problems with the network.
No corresponding information required on this machine.	Since the Database server is DB2 UDB for OS/390 and z/OS, check: 1. Is DB2 started? If not, execute `-start db2`. 2. Is DDF started? If not, execute `-start ddf`.
If you used a service name instead of the port number in your *Add RDB Directory Entry* panel, make sure the entry is correct in the *services* file at the client machine.	No corresponding information required on this machine.
`netstat` This command shows all connections and port numbers and their statuses. It can be performed from the OS/400 Main menu, options 6 -> 5 -> 10 -> 7 -> 3.	`netstat` This command shows all connections and port numbers and their statuses. Issue this command from *option 6 Command* in the main ISPF menu.

Scenario 3: DB2 for iSeries Client to DB2 for iSeries Server

Figure E.7 shows the overview for the scenario described in this section.

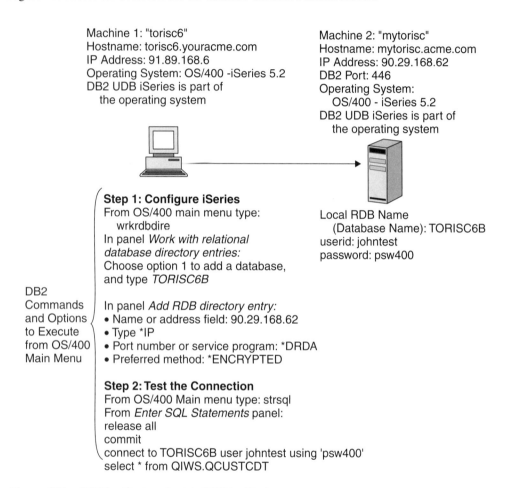

Machine 1: "torisc6"
Hostname: torisc6.youracme.com
IP Address: 91.89.168.6
Operating System: OS/400 -iSeries 5.2
DB2 UDB iSeries is part of
    the operating system

Machine 2: "mytorisc"
Hostname: mytorisc.acme.com
IP Address: 90.29.168.62
DB2 Port: 446
Operating System:
    OS/400 - iSeries 5.2
DB2 UDB iSeries is part of
    the operating system

DB2
Commands
and Options
to Execute
from OS/400
Main Menu

Step 1: Configure iSeries
From OS/400 main menu type:
    wrkrdbdire
In panel *Work with relational
database directory entries:*
Choose option 1 to add a database,
and type *TORISC6B*

In panel *Add RDB directory entry:*
• Name or address field: 90.29.168.62
• Type *IP
• Port number or service program: *DRDA
• Preferred method: *ENCRYPTED

Step 2: Test the Connection
From OS/400 Main menu type: strsql
From *Enter SQL Statements* panel:
release all
commit
connect to TORISC6B user johntest using 'psw400'
select * from QIWS.QCUSTCDT

Local RDB Name
    (Database Name): TORISC6B
userid: johntest
password: psw400

Figure E.7   DB2 for iSeries client to DB2 for iSeries server

Table E.11 presents the list of commands required to set up this connection.

Table E.11 DB2 for iSeries Client to DB2 iSeries Server

Commands to Run on Machine 1 (*torisc6*) DB2 for iSeries	Information You Need to Obtain from Machine 2 (*mytorisc*) DB2 for iSeries to Perform the Commands on Machine 1
Step 1: Configure iSeries	
From the OS/400 Main menu, type: `wrkrdbdire` After you press Enter, this will bring up the *Work with Relational Database Directory Entries* panel.	No corresponding information required on this machine.
From the *Work with Relational Database Directory Entries* panel: • Choose Option 1 to add a database. • Type the database name: *TORISC6B*.	*TORISC6B* is the local RDB name you want to access on machine 2. In order to determine the local RDB name, contact your iSeries administrator, who can issue the command **WRKRDBDIRE**. When the *Work with Relational Database Directory Entries* panel appears, the administrator can find the desired value in column *Relational Database* that maps to the column *Remote Location* with a value of **LOCAL*.
In the *Add RDB Directory Entry* panel, specify: • Name or address field: *90.29.168.62* • Type: *IP Note: The hostname could have been used instead of the IP address. After you specify *IP for the TCP/IP protocol and press Enter, other choices will appear: • Port number or service program: **DRDA* • Preferred method: *ENCRYPTED Note: *DRDA is equivalent to entering port 446. This value is very unlikely to be changed. *ENCRYPTED authentication works between iSeries machines. Versions other than DB2 for iSeries 5.2 may not have some of these choices.	For this example: *90.29.168.62* = the IP address of machine 2 **DRDA* = the port used for DB2 *DRDA is equivalent to port 446 and is the default value.

(continues)

Table E.11   DB2 for iSeries Client to DB2 iSeries Server *(Continued)*

Commands to Run on Machine 1 (*torisc6*) DB2 for iSeries	Information You Need to Obtain from Machine 2 (*mytorisc*) DB2 for iSeries to Perform the Commands on Machine 1
Step 2: Test the Connection	

Start the Interactive SQL tool from the OS/400 Main menu:
 	
`strsql`
 	
From the *Enter SQL Statements panel*, type:
 	
`CONNECT TO TORISC6B`
`    USER   johntest`
`    USING 'psw400'   `(Press Enter)
`SELECT * FROM QIWS.QCUSTCDT` (Press Enter)
 	
Note:
 	
The password needs to be passed in single quotes in order to maintain its case. Using double quotes for the user ID as shown below also works:
 	
`CONNECT TO TORISC6B`
`    USER "johntest"`
`    USING 'psw400'   `(Press Enter)
	For this example:
	
	johntest = the user ID as defined on machine 2
	
	psw400 = the password as defined on machine 2

Table E.12 provides troubleshooting hints for connectivity problems.

Table E.12   What to Check If You Cannot Connect

Client Machine *torisc6*	Database Server *mytorisc*
`ping mytorisc.acme.com` This command can be performed from the OS/400 Main menu (assuming the hostname was used instead of the IP address itself in the *Add RDB Directory Entry* panel).	*mytorisc.acme.com* = the host name of the database server If you cannot ping, there may be problems with the DNS. Try pinging the IP address.
`ping 90.29.168.62` This command can be performed from the OS/400 Main menu.	*90.29.168.62* = the IP address of the database server This will confirm whether or not there are problems with the network.
No corresponding information required on this machine.	Since the Database server is DB2 UDB for iSeries, check: Is DDM started? If not, execute the following command: `STRTTCPSVR SERVER(*DDM)`

(continues)

Table E.12 What to Check If You Cannot Connect *(Continued)*

Client Machine *torisc6*	Database Server *mytorisc*
If you used a service name instead of the port number in your *Add RDB Directory Entry* panel, make sure the entry is correct in the *services* file at the client machine.	No corresponding information required on this machine.
`netstat`	`netstat`
This command shows all connections and port numbers and their statuses. It can be performed from the OS/400 Main menu, options 6 -> 5 -> 10 -> 7 -> 3.	This command shows all connections and port numbers and their statuses. It can be performed from the OS/400 Main menu, options 6 -> 5 -> 10 -> 7 -> 3.

Diagnosing DB2 Connectivity Problems

Figure F.1 illustrates what happens when you issue a **CONNECT TO** *database* statement. It also shows how the system database, node, and DCS directories are used during the process.

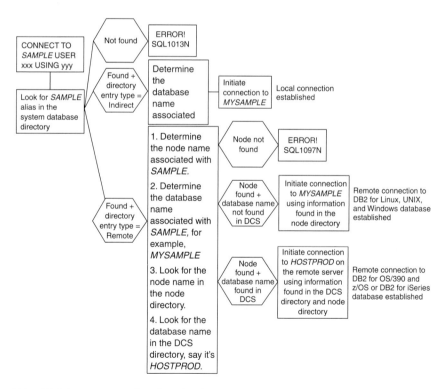

Figure F.1   Database connection flowchart

For example, when the **CONNECT TO SAMPLE** statement is issued, DB2 first looks for the database *alias* SAMPLE in the system database directory. This is the alias used for the database with the name MYSAMPLE. If the alias is not found, you get an SQL1013N error. If it is found, DB2 checks if this is a local or remote database. If it is a local database, DB2 initiates a connection to the database MYSAMPLE. If it is a remote database, DB2 checks the node directory to retrieve information about the remote server and then initiates a connection to the server.

The flowchart in Figure F.1 shows what is involved to establish a database connection. Follow this chart to diagnose connection problems more easily.

DIAGNOSING CLIENT-SERVER TCP/IP CONNECTION PROBLEMS

SQL30081N Communication error and *SQL1013N Database not found* are the most common connection errors. If either of these errors occurs, you need to verify the server and client configurations.

- On the server, verify that the DB2 instance is properly set up to accept client connections.
- On the client, verify that the node directory, database directory, and in the case of a host connection, the DCS directory, are set up correctly.

F.0.1 Verifying the Server Configuration

At the database server, follow this procedure to verify its configuration.

1. Verify that the database exists by issuing one of the following commands at the server:

   `list db directory`

   or

   `list db directory show detail`

   Figure F.2 shows the output for the `list db directory` command.

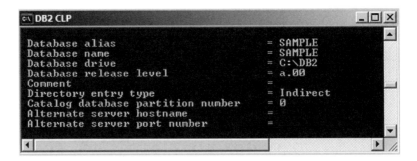

Figure F.2   Verifying that a database exists on the server

Figure F.2 confirms that the SAMPLE database resides locally on this server since the *Directory entry type* field has a value of *Indirect*. If the database resides on a different server, this field would have a value of *Remote*, which is not what you would want to see.

2. Check the DB2COMM registry variable to verify that the correct communication protocol is specified by using the **db2set -all** command (see Figure F.3).

Figure F.3 Checking the DB2COMM registry variable on the server

Figure F.3 shows that DB2COMM is set to TCPIP; therefore, the server is ready to listen for TCP/IP requests.

3. Verify that the appropriate configuration parameters are set in the Database Manager Configuration file. Issue the **get dbm cfg** command and examine the following.

• If DB2COMM=TCPIP, then SVCENAME must be set.
• If DB2COMM=NETBIOS, then NNAME must be set.

In Figure F.4, you can see that the SVCENAME is set to a service name, db2c_DB2.

Figure F.4 Verifying that SVCENAME or NNAME is correctly set on the server

If SVCENAME is set to a service name instead of a port number, confirm that the value listed there is mapped to a unique port number in the operating system's services file. For example:

```
db2c_DB2    50000/tcp    # Connection port for DB2 instance db2inst1
```

If this line is not already in the services file, use a text editor to add it.

After you have made sure that you can connect locally on the server and that the server is set up correctly to accept client connections, verify the client configuration.

F.0.2 Verifying the Client Configuration

At the client, follow these steps to verify its configuration.

1. Verify that the server connectivity information has been correctly entered in the node directory by using the `list node directory` command.

    The service name in the client's node directory is a port number that matches the port number referenced by the SVCENAME on the server. For example, the SVCE-NAME on the server is set to *db2c_DB2*, as shown in Figure F.4, and as we saw, this mapped to port 50000 in the server's services file. Therefore, the client needs to specify port 50000 in the node directory, as shown in Figure F.5.

Figure F.5   Checking the node directory on a client

    Alternatively, the client can specify a service name instead of the port number in the node directory. However, this service name is to be defined at the client services file, not the server services file. For example, the node directory can have the service name *db2conn*. If this is the case, then in the client's services file, you must set *db2conn* to 50000:

    ```
    db2conn      50000/tcp
    ```

2. Verify that you can ping the host name exactly as it appears in the node directory. If you cannot, that means there is problem connecting to the server. Try to ping the IP address of the server. If that works, then recatalog the node using the IP address instead of the host name and try again.

    To recatalog the node directory, you need to first uncatalog the existing node:

    ```
    uncatalog node nodename
    ```

3. Even if the client can reach the server, it does not necessarily mean that the client can access the port to connect to databases on the server. Sometimes, for security reasons, the server port is not open to client connections, or the port is not enabled at all. To test if a port is accessible, you can telnet to the port as follows:

    ```
    telnet hostname or ip address 50000
    ```

If DB2 is listening on that port on the server, you will see the Telnet window open, but it will hang, since DB2 is not configured to respond to the `telnet` command. This means that you have indeed reached that port on the server.

If you get an immediate error, this means that either:

- The server is not listening on this port. Refer back to section F.1.1, Verifying the Server Configuration, to resolve this.
- The port is behind a firewall and is not reachable by clients. Contact your network administrator for assistance.

4. Confirm that the correct database values appear in the database directory using the `list db directory` command. The database *name* in the client's database directory must match the database *alias* in the server's database directory (see Figure F.6).

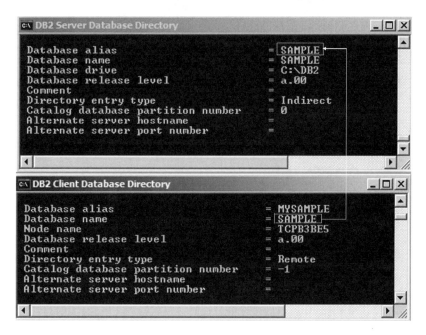

Figure F.6   Verifying that the database name in the client database directory matches the database alias on the server

If the database resides on a host server, verify the DCS directory. Using the `list dcs directory` command, ensure that the database name in the database directory matches the database name in the DCS directory (see Figure F.7). The target database name in the DCS directory must be the Location name if the host server is DB2 for z/OS and OS/390, or the RDB name if the host server is DB2 for iSeries.

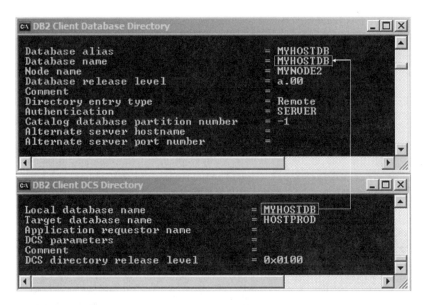

Figure F.7   Verifying that the database name in the database directory matches the database name in the DCS directory

Figure F.8 displays a flowchart for diagnosing client-server connectivity problems. It summarizes what we have discussed so far. The client is a DB2 client; the server can be either a DB2 UDB server or a DB2 Connect gateway.

Figure F.9 displays a flowchart for diagnosing client-host connectivity problems.

In Figure F.9, the client has at least DB2 Connect Personal Edition installed (review Scenario 3 in Chapter 6).

For a three-tier configuration where a DB2 Connect gateway works as the middle tier, the diagnosing path splits into two parts. First, you need to make sure the connection is working from the Connect gateway to the host database. For this, use the flowchart in Figure F.9. Second, for the client-gateway connection, use the flowchart in Figure F.8.

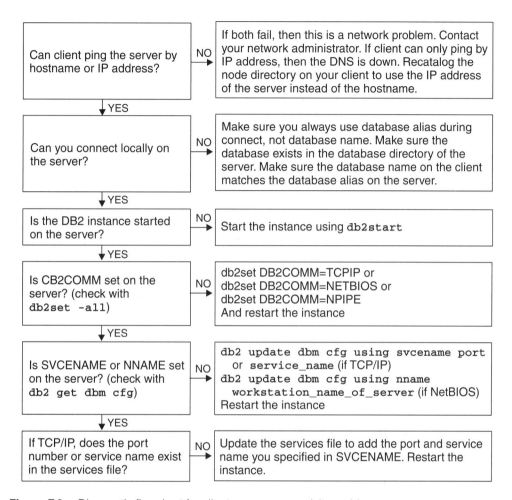

Figure F.8   Diagnostic flowchart for client-server connectivity problems

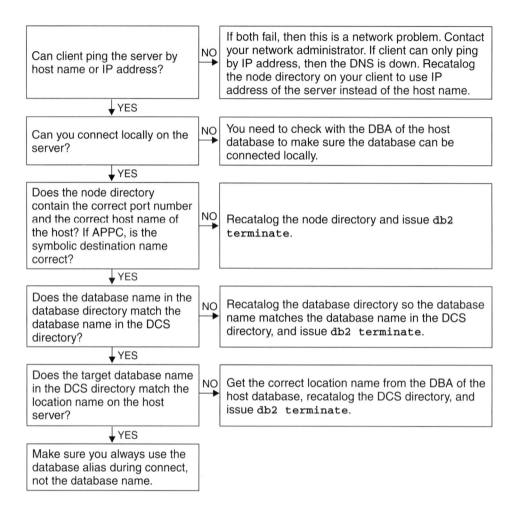

Figure F.9   Diagnostic path for client-host connection problems

Resources

This section lists the Web site resources referenced in this book as well as additional resources, including traditional course offerings, computer-based training courses, free tutorials, and other information. The document *WebsiteResources.txt* provided on the CD-ROM accompanying this book contains all the Web sites listed in this section so that you can copy and paste the URLs directly into your browser.

Table R.1 lists the Web site resources referenced in this book. It provides a brief description of the Web site and notes the chapter where it was referenced.

Table R.1 Web Sites Referenced in This Book

Resource Name	Description	URL	Chapter
IBM on-demand (glossary) Web page	Descriptions of terms used for on-demand businesses	www.ibm.com/e-business/ondemand/ us/toolkit/glossary_a.html	1
DB2 for Linux, UNIX, and Windows main Web page	Information about DB2 products	www.ibm.com/software/data/db2/ udb/	1
IBM DB2 Support Web site—FixPaks	Place to obtain DB2 clients and FixPaks	www.ibm.com/software/data/db2/ udb/support.html	1
The DB2 Information Center	Search engine for searching in the DB2 manuals	http://publib.boulder.ibm.com/ infocenter/db2help	4
IBM DB2 Installing and Administering a Satellite Environment Version 8	Information about satellite environments	www.ibm.com/support/ docview.wss?rs=71&context=SSEPG G&q1=satellite+database&uid=pub1 gc09482300&loc=en_US&cs=utf-8 &lang=en+en)	4
Internet's Requests for Comments (RFC)	Technical and organizational notes about the Internet	www.rfc-editor.org/rfc.html	10
DB2 Recovery Expert Multiplatform Tool	This tool recovers dropped objects	www.ibm.com/software/data/ db2imstools/db2tools/ db2recovexpert.html	13

(continues)

Table R.1   Web Sites Referenced in This Book *(Continued)*

Resource Name	Description	URL	Chapter
IBM Software Support Handbook	Guidelines for working with DB2 Technical Support	http://techsupport.services.ibm.com/ guides/handbook.html	17
DB2 Documentation (on the DB2 Technical Support Web site)	PDF versions of the DB2 manuals	www.ibm.com/cgi-bin/db2www/data/ db2/udb/winos2unix/support/ v8pubs.d2w/en_main	17
Search for DB2 known problems (within DB2 Technical Support Web site)	Searches APARS, fixes, and whitepapers	www.ibm.com/software/data/db2/ udb/support.html	17

Table R.2 lists other books of interest we have mentioned in this book.

Table R.2   Other Books Referenced

Book Information	Chapter
Zamil, Janmohamed, Clara Liu, Drew Bradstock, Raul Chong, Michael Gao, Fraser McArthur, and Paul Yip. *DB2 SQL PL: Essential Guide for DB2 UDB on Linux, UNIX, Windows, i5/OS, and z/OS*. Boston: Prentice Hall. 2004.	7
Snow, Dwaine R. and Thomas X. Phan. *Advanced DBA Certification Guide and Reference for DB2 Universal Database V8 for Linux, UNIX, and Windows*. Boston: Prentice Hall. 2004.	16

In addition to reading this book to prepare for the DB2 database administration certification exams, there are free tutorials you can take. Table R.3 lists the IBM Professional Certification program Web site and the tutorial Web sites for all available certification exams.

Table R.3   IBM Certification Program and Tutorials Web Site

Web Site Name	URL
IBM's Professional Certification Program	www.ibm.com/certify
DB2 Fundamentals Certification (Exam 700) Tutorial	www.ibm.com/developerworks/db2/library/tutorials/ db2cert/db2cert_V8_tut.html
DB2 DBA Certification (Exam 701) Tutorial	www.ibm.com/developerworks/db2/library/tutorials/ db2cert/701_prep.html
DB2 Application Development Certification (Exam 703) Tutorial	www.ibm.com/developerworks/offers/lp/db2cert

Table R.4 lists some of the traditional classroom courses for DB2 database administration and performance tuning offered by IBM Learning Services. For more information, see the DB2 Education Web site at www.ibm.com/software/data/education.html.

Table R.4   Course Offerings

Course Number	Course Name
CF201	DB2 UDB Database Administration Workshop for Linux
CF211	DB2 UDB Database Administration Workshop for UNIX
CF231	DB2 UDB Database Administration Workshop for Windows NT
CF241	DB2 UDB EEE for UNIX Administration Workshop
CF261	DB2 UDB EEE for Windows NT Administration Workshop
CF271	DB2 UDB Database Administration Workshop for Sun Solaris
CF411	DB2 UDB Performance Tuning and Monitoring Workshop
CF441	DB2 UDB EEE for UNIX Performance Monitoring and Tuning Workshop
CF451	DB2 UDB Advanced Administration Workshop
CF481	DB2 UDB Advanced Administration for Experienced Relational DBAs
CF491	DB2 UDB Advanced Recovery and High Availability Workshop
CG241	DB2 UDB Enterprise-Extended Edition for DB2 UDB Enterprise Edition DBAs

Table R.5 lists the Computer-Based Training (CBT) courses available (they are free) and their URLs.

Table R.5   Computer-Based Training Offerings

Course Number	Course Name	URL
CT28D	DB2 UDB Administration Fastpath Course for Version 8	www.ibm.com/software/data/education/ct28v8.html
CT10	DB2 UDB Programming Fastpath Course	www.ibm.com/software/data/db2/ct10crs

Table R.6 lists resources that provide articles, books, whitepapers, brochures, and so on about DB2. It also includes information about news groups.

Table R.6   DB2 Technical Resources and News Groups

Resource Name	Description	URL
DeveloperWorks	DB2 articles of interest	www.ibm.com/developerworks/db2
IBM Redbooks	Free books about IBM technology	www.redbooks.ibm.com
DB2 Technical Materials Library	Books, whitepapers, brochures, consultant reports, technology overviews, and so on	www.ibm.com/software/data/pubs/
DB2 News Group	News, forums about DB2	comp.databases.ibm-db2
DB2 on CompuServe	News, forums about DB2	Go ibmdb2

Table R.7 lists resources about magazines, news, and e-mail services.

Table R.7   DB2 E-mail Services and Periodicals

Resource Name	Description	URL
DB2 Magazine	A magazine about DB2. Each issue contains a variety of features on technical and business topics for the DB2 community, plus columns with tips and techniques on data mining, programming, system administration, content management, and more. The magazine is available in print as well as on the Web.	www.db2mag.com
DB2 UDB News	Subscribe to receive notification of new FixPaks and other DB2 service news.	www.ibm.com/software/mailing-lists
DB2 Today	Each monthly issue describes the latest offers, downloads, events, Web-based seminars, product news, and more. Subscribe to receive via e-mail.	www.ibm.com/software/data/db2today/

You can participate in user groups and DB2 conferences to keep up to date with the latest new features or version of DB2. Table R.8 lists the two most popular resources.

Table R.8   DB2 User Groups and Conferences

Resource Name	Description	URL
International DB2 Users Group (IDUG)	DB2 user group organization	www.idug.org/
DB2 and other IBM Technical Conferences	Technical conference with sessions of interest about DB2 and other products	www.ibm.com/services/learning/conf/us/index.html

For IBM Business Partners, Table R.9 lists the relevant Web sites.

Table R.9   IBM Business Partners Information

Resource Name	Description	URL
IBM PartnerWorld Home Page	Home page for IBM Business Partners support	www.developer.ibm.com
Virtual Innovation Center (VIC)	IBM VICs provide free education and technical and marketing support to business partners. Free registration is required.	www.virtualinnovationcenter.com/login.html

Glossary

A

access path
The method that the database manager selects for retrieving data from a specific table. For example, an access path can involve the use of an index, a sequential scan, or a combination of the two.

access plan
The set of access paths that the optimizer selects to evaluate a particular SQL statement. The access plan specifies the order of operations to resolve the execution plan, the implementation methods (such as JOIN), and the access path for each table referenced in the statement.

access profile
Contains information a client workstation needs to catalog a remote database stored on a DB2 UDB server.

access token
An object that describes the security context of a process or thread. The information in the token includes the identity and privileges of the user account associated with the process or thread.

active log
The primary and secondary log files that are currently needed for recovery and roll back.

Activity Monitor
The DB2 tool that assists database administrators (DBAs) to monitor application performance and concurrency, resource consumption, and SQL statement usage of a database or database partition. It provides predefined views of application, statement, and SQL cache activity. DBAs can choose to view live monitor data and can record monitor data for further analysis. The tool also gives recommendations to resolve resource utilization problems.

address space
The actual memory that an active program uses. See also **buffer pool**.

Address Windowing Extensions (AWE)
A Windows API that lets user applications use physical non-paged memory beyond the 32-bit virtual address space and have window views to this physical memory from within the application's virtual address space. The AWE API also contributes to both system and application performance.

administrative authority
SYSADM and DBADM authority levels that have full privileges for instance resources and database resources, respectively.

administrative authorization

The process by which DB2 obtains information about the authenticated user, such as the database operations the user may perform and which data objects the user may access.

administration notification log

A list of user-friendly, national language messages that should help database administrators resolve minor issues. Also known as the *DB2 notify log*.

administrator

A person responsible for administrative tasks such as access authorization and content management. Administrators can also grant levels of authority to users.

Advanced Peer-to-Peer Networking (APPN)

An extension to SNA that features distributed network control, dynamic definition of network resources, and automated resource registration and directory lookup.

Advanced Program-to-Program Communication (APPC)

A protocol that allows interconnected systems to communicate and share the processing of programs. APPC supports Systems Network Architecture and uses the Logical Unit (LU) 6.2 protocol for establishing sessions between systems.

after trigger

A trigger activated after the triggering SQL operation has completed. The triggering operation can be an **INSERT**, **UPDATE**, **DELETE**, `fullselect`, or **SIGNAL SQLSTATE** statement.

agent

A separate process or thread that carries out all the DB2 requests made by a particular client application.

alert

A signal representing the state of an object (such as a database, table space, or instance).

alias

An alternative name used to identify a table, view, database, or nickname. An alias can be used in SQL statements to refer to a table or view.

ambiguous cursor

A cursor is ambiguous if all of the following conditions are true:

- The **SELECT** statement is dynamically prepared.
- The **SELECT** statement does not include either the **FOR READ ONLY** clause or the **FOR UPDATE** clause.
- The LANGLEVEL bind option is SAA1.
- The cursor otherwise satisfies the conditions of a deleteable cursor.

An ambiguous cursor is considered read-only if the BLOCKING bind option is ALL; otherwise, it is considered deleteable.

American National Standard Code for Information Interchange (ASCII)

An encoding scheme that represents character strings in many environments, typically on personal computers and workstations. See also **EBCDIC** and **Unicode**.

authorized program analysis report (APAR)

A term used in IBM for a description of a problem. It is formally tracked until a solution is provided.

API

See **application programming interface**.

APPC

See **Advanced Program-to-Program Communication**.

APPL

A VTAM network definition statement used to define a DB2 for z/OS and OS/390 to VTAM application program that uses SNA LU 6.2 protocols.

application

A program or set of programs that performs a task; for example: payroll, inventory management, and word processing applications.

Application Development Client

An application development product that lets applications developed on a client workstation access remote database servers, including host relational databases, through the DB2 Connect products.

application ID

A unique string that is generated when an application connects to a database or when DB2 Connect receives a request to connect to a DRDA database. An identifier is generated when the application connects to the database. This ID is known on both the client and the server and can be used to correlate the two parts of the application.

application name

The name of the application running on the client that identifies it to the database manager or DB2 Connect. The client passes the application name to the server to establish the database connection.

application programming interface (API)

A functional interface that allows an application program written in a high-level language to use specific data or functions of the operating system or another program, such as a database management system. In DB2, APIs enable most of the administrative functions from within an application program.

application requester

The component on a remote system that generates DRDA requests for data on behalf of an application. An application requester accesses a DB2 database server using the DRDA application-directed protocol.

application server

In DB2 for z/OS and OS/390, the target of a request from a remote application. In the DB2 environment, the distributed data facility (DDF) provides the application server function for accessing DB2 data from remote applications.

APPN

See **Advanced Peer-to-Peer Networking**.

archived log

The set of log files that is closed and is no longer needed for normal processing. These files are retained for use in roll forward recovery. See also **active log**.

ASCII

See **American National Standard Code for International Interchange**.

AST

See **automatic summary table**.

asynchronous

Without a regular time relationship; unpredictable with respect to the processing of program instructions.

asynchronous I/O

The nonsequential processing of read and write requests across multiple disks.

attach

To remotely access objects at the instance level.

authentication

The process of validating a supplied user ID and password against a security facility.

authority

A user's access and ability to perform high-level database management operations such as maintenance and utility operations. A user's authority level is used with privileges to control access to the database and its database objects.

authorization

The process by which DB2 obtains information about the authenticated user, such as the database operations the user may perform and which data objects the user may access.

authorization ID

A string that can be verified for connecting to a DB2 UDB and to which a set of privileges is applied. An authorization identifier can represent an individual, an organizational group, or a function, but the DB2 UDB does not determine this representation. The authorization ID is defined in an external security facility that DB2 supports.

autocommit

To automatically commit the current unit of work after each SQL statement.

automatic configuration parameters

A set of configuration parameters whose values can be changed automatically by the database manager to reflect the current resource utilization.

automatic summary table (AST)

A summary table defined such that changes made to the underlying tables cascade to it immediately without the need for a **REFRESH TABLE** statement.

autonomic computing system

A computing system that manages, repairs, and protects itself.

AWE

See **Address Windowing Extensions**.

B

backout

The process of undoing uncommitted changes that an application process has made. A backout may be necessary if an application process fails or in a deadlock situation. See also **roll back**.

backup

A copy of a database or table space that can be stored on a different medium and used to restore the database or table space in the event of failure or damage to the original.

backup pending

The state of a database or table space that prevents an operation from being performed until the database or table space is backed up.

base table

A table created with the **CREATE TABLE** statement. A base table has both its description and data stored in the database.

before trigger

A trigger that is activated before the triggering SQL operation has completed. The triggering operation can be a **fullselect**, **SIGNAL SQLSTATE**, or **SET** transition variable SQL statement.

BID

See **block identifier**.

binary large object (BLOB)

A sequence of bytes with a size from 0 bytes to 2GB minus 1 byte. This string does not have an associated code page and character set. BLOBs can contain image, audio, and video data.

bind

To convert the output from the SQL compiler to a usable control structure, such as an access plan, application plan, or package. During the bind process, access paths to the data are selected and some authorization checking is performed.

bind file

A file the precompiler produces when the **PRECOMPILE** command or the respective API is used with the **BINDFILE** option.

bit data

Data with character type CHAR or VARCHAR that is not associated with a coded character set and therefore is never converted.

BLOB

See **binary large object**.

block

(1) A string of data elements that is recorded or transmitted as a unit.

(2) A set of contiguous data pages in a buffer pool.

(3) A set of consecutive pages on disk.

block-based I/O

A database manager method of reading contiguous data pages from disk into contiguous portions of memory.

block fetch

A DB2 function that retrieves (fetches) a large set of rows together. Using block fetch can significantly reduce the number of messages sent across the network. Block fetch applies only to cursors that do not update data.

block identifier (BID)

An entry that is stored along with a key value in the leaf node of a block index. This identifier references a particular block in a multidimensional clustering table.

block index

An index that is structured in the same manner as a traditional record identifier (RID) index, except that at the leaf level the keys point to a block identifier (BID) instead of a RID.

block locks

The locking of a block within a multidimensional clustering environment.

block map

A bitmap that contains an array of block states, one for each block in the multidimensional clustering table.

block size

Specifies the number of pages in a block and is equal to the extent size. Also known as *block factor.*

blocking

An option specified when binding an application. It allows caching of multiple rows of information by the communications subsystem so that each **FETCH** statement does not require the transmission of one row for each request across the network.

buffer manipulators

The processes used in backup and restore operations to read from or write to the database. By default, a single buffer manipulator is used; however, this can be overridden by using the **parallelism** option of the **BACKUP DATABASE** or **RESTORE DATABASE** commands.

buffer pool

An area of memory into which database pages are read, modified, and held during processing.

built-in function

A strongly typed, high-performance function that is integral to DB2 UDB. A built-in function can be referenced in SQL statements anywhere that an expression is valid.

C

cache

A buffer containing frequently accessed instructions and data. It is used to reduce access time.

caching 3

The process of storing frequently used results from a request to memory for quick retrieval until it is time to refresh the information. DB2 UDB provides many forms of caching, such as directory caching and package caching.

call-level interface (CLI)

A callable API for database access that is an alternative to an embedded SQL API. In contrast to embedded SQL, the CLI does not require precompiling or binding to a database; instead, it provides a standard set of functions to process SQL statements and related services at runtime.

cardinality

The number of rows in a database table.

cascade delete

The way DB2 UDB enforces referential constraints when it deletes all descendent rows of a deleted **parent row**.

CASE expression

An expression that allows another expression to be selected based on the evaluation of one or more conditions.

case-insensitive search

A search that does not consider the case of the string being searched.

cast function

A function that converts instances of a source data type into instances of a different target data type. In general, a cast function has the name of the target data type and has one argument whose type is the source data type. Its return type is the target data type.

catalog

A set of tables and views maintained by the database manager. These tables and views contain information about the database, such as descriptions of tables, views, and indexes.

catalog node

See **catalog partition**.

catalog partition

In a partitioned database environment, the database partition where the catalog tables for the database resides. Each database in a partitioned database environment can have its catalog partition on a different database partition server. The catalog partition for a database is automatically created on the database partition server where the **CREATE DATABASE** command is run.

catalog table

A table in the DB2 UDB catalog that is automatically created when a database is created. These tables contain information about the database and definitions of database objects, such as user tables, views, and indexes, as well as security information about the authority that users have on these objects. You cannot explicitly create or drop a catalog table, but you can query and view its contents using the catalog views.

catalog view

A SYSCAT or SYSSTAT view on the catalog table.

CDB

See **communications database**.

cell

A unique combination of dimension values. Physically, a cell is made up of blocks of pages whose records all share the same values for each clustering column.

character conversion

The process of changing data from one character coding representation to another.

character large object (CLOB)

A sequence of characters (single-byte, multibyte, or both) with a size ranging from 0 bytes to 2GB minus 1 byte. In general, character large object values are used whenever a character string might exceed the limits of the VARCHAR type. Also called *character large object string*.

character set

A defined set of characters, for example, 26 unaccented letters A through Z.

character string

A sequence of bytes that represent bit data, single-byte characters, or a mixture of single-byte and multi-byte characters.

character string delimiter

The characters enclosing character strings in delimited ASCII files that are imported or exported.

CHECK clause

In SQL, an extension to the **CREATE TABLE** and **ALTER TABLE** statements that specifies a table check constraint.

check condition

A restricted form of a search condition used in check constraints.

check constraint

A constraint specifying a check condition that is not false for each row of the table on which the constraint is defined.

check integrity

The condition that exists when each row in a table conforms to the check constraints that are defined on that table. Maintaining check integrity requires DB2 to enforce table check constraints on operations that add or change data.

check pending

A state which a table can be placed in. Only limited activity is allowed on the table, and constraints are not checked when the table is updated.

checkpoint

A point at which the database manager records internal status information on the log. The recovery process uses this information if the subsystem terminates abnormally.

circular log

A database log in which records are overwritten if they are no longer needed by an active database. Consequently, if a failure occurs, lost data cannot be restored during forward recovery.

clause

In SQL, a distinct part of a statement, such as a **SELECT** clause or a **WHERE** clause. (e.g., `SELECT * FROM employee WHERE empno='000010'`).

CLI

See call-level interface.

client

Any program (or workstation that a program is running on) that communicates with and accesses a database server.

client profile

A profile that configures clients using the Import function in the Configuration Assistant. It can contain database connection information, client settings, CLI or ODBC common parameters, and configuration data for local APPC or NetBIOS communication subsystems.

CLOB

See **character large object**.

CLP

See **command line processor**.

clustered index

An index whose sequence of key values closely corresponds to the sequence of rows stored in a table. The degree to which this correspondence exists is measured by statistics that the optimizer uses. Synonym for *partitioning index*.

clustering block index

A block index that is automatically created for a particular dimension when the dimension is defined on a multidimensional clustering table. This index maintains the clustering of data along that dimension, together with the other dimensions that are defined on the table. Also known as a **dimension block index**.

code page

A set of assignments of characters to code points.

code point

A unique bit pattern that represents a character in a code page.

code set

International Organization for Standardization (ISO) term for code page. See **code page**.

coded character set

A set of unambiguous rules that establishes a character set and the one-to-one relationships between the characters of the set and their coded representations.

collating sequence

The sequence in which the characters are ordered for sorting, merging, comparing, and processing indexed data sequentially.

collocated join

The result of two tables being joined when the tables reside in a single-partition database partition group in the same database partition, or when they are in the same database partition group and have the same number of partitioning columns, the columns are partition-compatible, both tables use the same partitioning function, and pairs of the corresponding partitioning key columns participate in the equijoin predicates.

column data

The data store that is stored in a DB2 column. The type of data can be any data type supported by DB2.

column distribution value

Statistics that describe the most frequent values of some column or the quantile values. These values are used in the DB2 optimizer to help determine the best access plan.

column function

(1) An operation that derives its result using values from one or more rows.

(2) A function that performs a computation on a set of values rather than on a single value.

command

A way to start database administration functions to access and maintain the database manager.

Command Line Processor (CLP)

A character-based interface for entering SQL statements and database manager commands.

commit

The operation that ends a unit of work by releasing locks so the database changes made by that unit of work can be perceived by other processes. This operation makes the data changes permanent.

commit point

A point in time when data is considered to be consistent.

common table expression

An expression that defines a result table with a name (a qualified SQL identifier). The expression can be specified as a table name in any **FROM** clause in the **fullselect** that follows the **WITH** clause.

communications database (CDB)

A set of tables in the DB2 for z/OS and OS/390 catalog that establishes conversations with remote database management systems.

comparison operator

Comparison operators are $\not<$ (not less than), $<=$ (less than or equal to), $\neq$ (not equal to), $=$ (equal to), $>=$ (greater than or equal to), $>$ (greater than), and $\not>$ (not greater than).

composite block index

An index that contains only dimension key columns and maintains the clustering of data over insert and update activity in a multidimensional clustering (MDC) table.

composite key

An ordered set of key columns in the same table.

compound SQL statement

A block of SQL statements that are executed in a single call to the application server.

concurrency

The shared use of resources by multiple interactive users or application processes at the same time.

configurable configuration parameters

A set of configuration parameters containing information that can be changed.

configurable online configuration parameters

A set of configuration parameters whose values can be changed while the database manager is running.

Configuration Advisor

A graphical tool that can be used to obtain an initial set of database configuration parameters. This tool can be run from the command line or in a graphical mode from the Control Center.

Configuration Assistant

A graphical tool that can be used to configure and maintain the database objects that you or your applications will be using. With this tool, you can work with existing database objects, add new ones, bind applications, set Database Manager Configuration parameters, and import and export configuration information.

configuration file

A file that contains the values specified for configuration parameters. These parameters specify the resources that are allocated to the DB2 products and to individual databases as well as the diagnostic level. There are two types of configuration files: the Database Manager Configuration file for each DB2 instance and the database configuration file for each individual database. Database Manager Configuration parameters are stored in a file named *db2systm*. Database configuration parameters are stored in a file named *SQLDBCON*. In a partitioned database environment, each database partition has its own database configuration file, but all partitions that participate in the instance use the same Database Manager Configuration file.

configuration parameter

A parameter whose value limits the resources that can be used by the database manager or database. Some configuration parameters are informational and display characteristics about the environment that cannot be changed.

connection

(1) An association between an application process and an application server.

(2) In data communications, an association established between functional units for conveying information.

connection concentrator

A process that allows applications to stay connected without any resources being consumed on the DB2 host server. Thousands of users can be active in applications, while only a few threads are active on the DB2 host server.

constant

A language element that specifies an unchanging value. Constants are classified as string constants or numeric constants.

constraint

A rule that limits the values that can be inserted, deleted, or updated in a table.

container

(1) A physical storage location of the data, for example, a file, directory, or device.

(2) See **table space container**.

container tag

A container tag uniquely identifies the database and table space that the container (an allocation of physical storage, such as a file or a device) is part of.

contention

A situation in which a transaction attempts to lock a row or table that is already locked.

Control Center

The DB2 graphical interface that shows database objects (such as databases and tables) and their relationship to each other. You can perform the tasks provided by the various tools in the Control Center, such as Replication Center, Health Center, Task Center, and Journal.

Coordinated Universal Time (UTC)

Synonym for *Greenwich Mean Time*.

coordinator agent

The agent that is started when the database manager receives a request from an application. The agent remains associated with the application during the life of the application. This agent initiates subagents that work for the application.

coordinator node

See **coordinator partition**.

coordinator partition

The database partition server to which the application originally connected and on which the coordinating agent resides.

correlated subquery

A subquery that contains a correlated reference to a column in a table that is outside the subquery.

correlation name

An identifier that designates a table or view within a single SQL statement. The name can be defined in any **FROM** clause or in the first clause of an **UPDATE** or **DELETE** statement.

cost

The estimated total resource usage that is necessary to run the access plan for a statement (or the elements of a statement). Cost is derived from a combination of processor cost (in number of instructions) and I/O (in numbers of seeks and page transfers).

counter

A representation of information that is cumulative up until the sample is taken. The counter counts values that increase, such as the number of deadlocks. Counters are reset when you stop and restart an instance or database.

country/region code

The two-character representation for the country or region to establish monetary, date, and numeric formatting.

crash recovery

The process of bringing a database back to a consistent and usable state after a failure.

CS

See **cursor stability**.

cumulative backup

See **incremental backup**.

current path

An ordered list of schema names that is used to resolve unqualified references to functions and data types. In dynamic SQL, the current function path is set by the CURRENT PATH special register. Static SQL defines it in the **FUNCPATH** option for the **PREP** and **BIND** commands.

current working directory

The default directory of a process from which all relative path names are resolved.

cursor

A named control structure that an application program uses to point to a specific row within some ordered set of rows. The cursor is used to retrieve rows from a set.

cursor blocking

A technique that reduces overhead by retrieving a block of rows in a single operation. These rows are cached while they are processed.

cursor sensitivity

The degree to which database updates are visible to the subsequent **FETCH** statements in a cursor. A cursor can be sensitive to changes made with *positioned* **UPDATE** and **DELETE** statements that specify the name of the cursor. A cursor can also be sensitive to changes made with *searched* **UPDATE** and **DELETE** statements, or with cursors other than this cursor.

cursor stability (CS)

An isolation level that locks any row accessed by an application's transaction while the cursor is positioned on the row. The lock remains in effect until the next row is fetched or the transaction is terminated. If any data is changed in a row, the lock is held until the change is committed to the database.

D

daemon

A system process that provides a specific service to applications or users.

DAS

See **Database Administration Server**.

Data Control Language (DCL)

A language used to control access to the DB2 database manager for an instance. Statements such as **GRANT**, **REVOKE**, and **CONNECT** are DCL statements.

Data Definition Language (DDL)

A language for describing data and its relationships in a database.

Data Manipulation Language (DML)

A subset of SQL statements that manipulates data. Most applications primarily use DML SQL statements, which are supported by the DB2 Connect program. **SELECT**, **INSERT**, **UPDATE**, and **DELETE** statements are similar across the IBM relational database products.

data mart

A subset of a data warehouse containing data that is tailored and optimized for the specific reporting needs of a department or team. A data mart can be a subset of a warehouse for an entire organization, such as data that is contained in online analytical processing (OLAP) tools.

data mining

The process of collecting critical business information from a data warehouse; correlating the information; and uncovering associations, patterns, and trends.

data source

In a federated system, typically a relational DBMS instance and one or more databases supported by that instance. However, there are other types of data sources that you can include in your federated system, such as flat-file databases and table-structured files.

data type

In SQL, an attribute of columns, literals, host variables, special registers, and the results of functions and expressions.

data warehouse

(1) A subject-oriented nonvolatile collection of data that supports strategic decision making. The warehouse is the central point of data integration for business intelligence. It is the source of data for data marts within an enterprise and delivers a common view of enterprise data.

(2) A central repository for all or significant parts of the data that an organization's business systems collect.

Data Warehouse Center

The component of DB2 UDB that provides both the graphical interface and the software behind it that enables you to work with the components of the warehouse. You can use the Data Warehouse Center to define and manage the warehouse data and the processes that create the data in the warehouse.

Database Administration Server (DAS)

A service or a process that assists the Control Center and Configuration Assistant when working on administration tasks.

database administrator (DBA)

A person responsible for the design, development, operation, security, maintenance, and use of a database.

database agent

A representation for the physical process or thread that will do the actual work inside the database engine.

database client

A workstation that accesses a database on a database server.

database configuration file

A file created when a database is created; it resides where that database resides. There is one configuration file per database. Its parameters specify, among other things, the amount of resources to be allocated to that database. You can change the values for many of the parameters to improve performance or increase capacity. Different changes may be required, depending on the type of activity in a specific database.

database configuration parameter

A parameter whose value limits the system resources that a database can use.

database connection services (DCS) directory

A directory that contains entries for remote host databases and the corresponding application requester used to access them.

database directory

A directory that contains database access information for all databases to which a client can connect.

database engine
The part of the database manager that provides the base functions and configuration files needed to use the database.

database function
The relationship between a set of input data and a set of result values.

database log
A set of primary and secondary log files consisting of log records that record all changes to a database. The database log rolls back changes for units of work that are not committed and recovers a database to a consistent state.

database-managed space (DMS) table space
A table space whose space is managed by the database.

database management system (DBMS)
Synonym for *database manager.*

database manager
A computer program that manages data by providing the services of centralized control, data independence, and complex physical structures for efficient access, integrity, recovery, concurrency control, privacy, and security.

Database Manager Configuration parameter
A configuration parameter that is established when the instance is created. Most Database Manager Configuration parameters affect the amount of system resources that will be allocated to a single instance of the database manager, or they configure the setup of the database manager and the different communications subsystems based on environmental considerations.

database manager instance
(1) A logical database manager environment similar to an image of the actual database manager environment. It is possible have several instances of the database manager product on the same workstation. Use these instances to separate the development environment from the production environment, tune the database manager to a particular environment, and protect sensitive information.

(2) The DB2 code that manages data. An instance has its own databases (which other instances cannot access), and all its database partitions share the same system directories. It also has separate security from other instances on the same computer.

database name
The identifying name that a user provides as part of the **create database** command or application programming interface. A database name must be unique within the location in which it is cataloged.

database node
See **database partition**.

database object

(1) An association within a database to anything that can be monitored.

(2) Anything that SQL can create or manipulate. Tables, views, indexes, packages, triggers, and table spaces are database objects.

database partition

In a partitioned database environment, a part of the database that consists of its own user data, indexes, configuration files, and transaction logs.

database partition group

In a partitioned database environment, a named set of one or more database partitions. This term replaces the term **nodegroup**.

database partition server

In a partitioned database environment, an occurrence of DB2 that is recorded in the *db2nodes.cfg* file.

Database Partitioning Feature (DPF)

The feature of DB2 UDB Enterprise Server Edition to work with a partitioned instance.

database request module (DBRM)

A data set member created by the DB2 for z/OS and OS/390 precompiler and that contains information about SQL statements. DBRMs are used in the bind process.

database server

The target of a request from a local application or an intermediate database server. In the DB2 environment, the distributed data facility provides the database server function to access DB2 data from local applications or a remote database server that is acting as an intermediate database server.

database system monitor

A collection of APIs that collect information regarding the state of the database system at the instance, database, and application levels. This information is stored in data elements, which can be examined by taking point-in-time snapshots or by using the Event Monitor to log system activity over a period of time.

DATALINK

An SQL data type that enables logical references from the database to a file stored outside the database.

datetime value

A value of the data type DATE, TIME, or TIMESTAMP.

DB2 Application Development Client (DB2 AD Client)

A collection of tools that help developers create database applications.

DB2 client

Allows access to a remote database without knowing its physical location. The DB2 client determines the location of the database, manages the transmission of requests to the database server, and returns the results.

DB2 command

An instruction to the operating system to access and maintain the database manager. For example, DB2 commands allow a user to start or stop a database and to display information on current users and the status of databases.

DB2 Connect

A product that enables client applications to read and update data stored on host and iSeries servers.

DB2 control server

A DB2 UDB system that contains the satellite control database, *SATCTLDB*.

DB2 Data Links Manager

A DB2 feature you can order separately that enables your applications to manipulate data residing in both unstructured files and in the relational database management system (RDBMS). The DB2 Data Links Manager enables DB2 UDB to manage unstructured files as though they were stored directly in the database, and it provides the integration between the RDBMS and the external file systems through extensions to DB2 UDB.

DB2DC

See **Development Center**.

DB2 extender

A program you can use to store and retrieve data types beyond the traditional numeric and character data, such as image, audio, and video data and complex documents.

DB2 Net Search Extender

A program that provides full-text retrieval through a DB2 stored procedure. The Net Search Extender is primarily optimized for performance, and it can be particularly advantageous in applications where search performance on large indexes and scalability according to concurrent queries are important factors.

db2setup utility

A utility that guides users through the installation process with a graphical interface and online help. You can use this utility to create or assign groups and user IDs, create a DB2 instance, and install product messages. Default values are provided for all required installation parameters.

DB2 Spatial Extender

A program that creates a geographic information system.

DB2 Text Extender
A full text retrieval system integrated in DB2 UDB that provides powerful search features enhanced by additional rich linguistic functionality for applications with highly structured documents. This is particularly useful when the information need is complex, and the quality and precision of the search result are key issues over and above system response times.

DB2 tools catalog
A set of tables or files maintained by the database tools (Data Warehouse Center, Control Center, Task Center, Information Catalog Center) that contains information about the processes and tasks that DB2 runs, such as loads, reorgs, database maintenance processes, data movement processes, and the associated schedules, logs, and dependencies.

DB2 tools metadata
The information about the processes and tasks that DB2 runs, such as loads, reorgs, database maintenance processes, data movement processes, and the associated schedules, logs, and dependencies. The DB2 tools metadata is contained in the DB2 tools catalog.

DB2 XML Extender
A program that is used to store and manage XML documents in DB2 tables. Well-formed and validated XML documents can be generated from existing relational data, stored as column data, and the content of XML elements and attributes can be stored in DB2 tables.

DBA
See **database administrator**.

DBA utility
A tool that lets DB2 users configure databases and database manager instances, manage the directories necessary for accessing local and remote databases, back up and recover databases or table spaces, and manage media on a system using a graphical interface. The tasks provided by this tool can be accessed from the DB2 Control Center.

DBCLOB
See **double-byte character large object**.

DBCS
See **double-byte character set**.

DBMS
See **database management system**.

DBRM
See **database request module**.

DDF
See **distributed data facility**.

DDL
See **Data Definition Language**.

deadlock
A condition under which a transaction cannot proceed because it is dependent on exclusive resources that are locked by another transaction, which in turn is dependent on exclusive resources that are in use by the original transaction.

deadlock detector
A process within the database manager that monitors the states of the locks to determine if a deadlock condition exists. When it detects a deadlock condition, the detector stops one of the transactions involved in the deadlock. This transaction is rolled back and the other transaction can proceed.

Decision Support System (DSS)
In the Information Catalog Center, a system of applications that help users make decisions. This kind of system lets users work with information that is presented in meaningful ways; for example, spreadsheets, charts, and reports.

declared temporary table
A table that holds temporary data and is defined with the SQL statement `DECLARE GLOBAL TEMPORARY TABLE`. Information about declared temporary tables is not stored in the DB2 catalog, so this kind of table is not persistent and can be only used by the application process that issued the `DECLARE` statement.

degree of parallelism
The number of concurrently executed operations that are initiated to process a query.

delete rule
A rule associated with a referential constraint that either restricts the deletion of a parent row or specifies the effect of such a deletion on the dependent rows.

delimited ASCII (DEL)
A file format that contains a stream of ASCII characters separated by row and column delimiters.

delimited identifier
A sequence of characters enclosed within quotation marks ("). The sequence must consist of a letter followed by zero or more characters, each of which is a letter, digit, or the underscore character.

delimiter
A character or flag that groups or separates items of data.

delta backup
A copy of all database data that has changed since the last successful backup (full, incremental, or delta) of the table space in question. A delta backup is also known as a **differential** or **noncumulative**

backup image. The predecessor of a delta backup image is the most recent successful backup that contains a copy of each of the table spaces in the delta backup image.

denormalization

The intentional duplication of columns in multiple tables whose consequence is increased data redundancy. Denormalization is sometimes necessary to minimize performance problems and is a key step in designing a physical relational database design.

dependent

In SQL, an object (row, table, or table space) that has at least one parent.

dependent foreign key table

A table of a given table that has at least one foreign key constraint referencing the given table.

dependent immediate materialized query table

A dependent materialized query table that is defined with the **REFRESH IMMEDIATE** option.

dependent materialized query table

A materialized query table that references a given table directly or indirectly (for example, from a view) in its materialized query table definition.

dependent row

A row containing a foreign key that matches the value of a parent key in the parent row. The foreign key value represents a reference from the dependent row to the parent row.

dependent table

A table that is a dependent in at least one referential constraint.

dependent table space

A table space that contains a dependent of a parent table.

Development Center

A DB2 component that provides a graphical interface for building, testing, and deploying stored procedures and user-defined functions. Features include a server view, an integrated SQL debugger, export and import wizards, and an editor.

differential backup image
See **delta backup**.

dimension

A data category, such as time, accounts, products, or markets. The elements of a dimension are referred to as *members*. Dimensions offer a very concise, simple way of organizing and selecting data for retrieval, exploration, and analysis. Dimensions also represent the highest consolidation level in a multidimensional database outline.

dimension block index

In multidimensional clustering, a block index that is automatically created for a particular dimension when the dimension is defined in an MDC table. This index maintains the clustering of data along that dimension, together with the other dimensions defined in the table.

dimension table

The representation of a dimension in a star schema. Each row in a dimension table represents all of the attributes for a particular member of the dimension.

disaster recovery

The activities that are required to restore the database in the event of a fire, earthquake, vandalism, or other catastrophic events. Typically, disaster recovery requires that you restore the entire database, so if a major disaster occurs, a full database backup is available from a standby site.

distinct type

A user-defined data type that is internally represented as an existing type (its source type), but is considered to be a separate and incompatible type for semantic purposes.

distributed data facility (DDF)

A facility that provides the application server function for accessing DB2 data from remote applications on DB2 for z/OS.

Distributed Relational Database Architecture (DRDA)

The architecture that defines formats and protocols for providing transparent access to remote data. DRDA defines two types of functions: the application requester function and the application server function.

distributed unit of work (DUOW)

A unit of work that allows SQL statements to be submitted to multiple relational database management systems, but no more than one system per SQL statement.

DML

See **Data Manipulation Language**.

DMS table space

See **database-managed space table space**.

DNS

See **Domain Name Server**.

domain

A part of a network that is administered as a unit with a common protocol.

domain name

The name by which TCP/IP applications refer to a TCP/IP host within a TCP/IP network. A domain name consists of a sequence of names separated by dots. For example: www.ibm.com.

Domain Name Server (DNS)
A TCP/IP network server that manages a distributed directory that maps TCP/IP host names to IP addresses.

double-byte character large object (DBCLOB)
A data type consisting of a sequence of double-byte characters, with a size ranging from 0 bytes to 2GB minus 1 byte, that can be used to store large double-byte text objects. This kind of string always has an associated code page.

double-byte character set (DBCS)
A set of characters in which each character is represented by two bytes. These character sets are commonly used by national languages, such as Japanese and Chinese, that have more symbols than can be represented by a single byte.

double-precision floating point number
In SQL, a 64-bit approximate representation of a real number.

DPF
See **Database Partitioning Feature**.

DRDA
See **Distributed Relational Database Architecture**.

DSS
See **Decision Support System**.

dual log path
A secondary log path that maintains duplicate copies of online archived files and the active log.

DUOW
See **distributed unit of work**.

dynamic SQL
SQL statements that are prepared and executed at runtime. In dynamic SQL, the SQL statement is contained as a character string in a host variable and is not precompiled.

E

EBCDIC
A coded character set of 256 8-bit characters that represents textual data. It is typically used on zSeries and iSeries servers.

embedded SQL
SQL statements coded within an application program.

encoding scheme
A set of rules to represent character data.

escape character
See **SQL escape character**.

Event Analyzer
A monitoring tool that provides information about the database events that have taken place. An Event Analyzer is used with the Event Monitor file to assess and record performance information.

Event Monitor
A database object that monitors and collects data on database activities over a period of time. For example, starting the database might be an event that causes an Event Monitor to track the number of users on the system by taking an hourly snapshot of authorization IDs using the database.

exception table
(1) A user-created table that reflects the definition of the table being loaded.

(2) A table that holds rows that violate referential constraints or checks constraints that the CHECK DATA utility finds.

exclusive lock
A lock that prevents running executing application processes from accessing data.

executable statement
An SQL statement that can be embedded in an application program, dynamically prepared and executed, or issued interactively.

execution time
The elapsed runtime of a query. This is the time between the start and the end of the query execution.

exit routine
A program that receives control from another program to perform specific functions.

explain
To capture detailed information about the access plan that was chosen by the SQL compiler to resolve an SQL statement. The information describes the decision criteria used to choose the access plan.

explain snapshot
(1) A collection of information that is compressed when an SQL statement is explained.

(2) A capture of the current internal representation of an SQL query and related information. This information is required by the Visual Explain tool.

explainable statement
An SQL statement for which the explain operation can be performed. Explainable statements are **SELECT**, **UPDATE**, **INSERT**, **DELETE**, and **VALUES**.

explained statement

An SQL statement for which an explain operation was performed.

explained statistics

Statistics for a database object that was referred to in an SQL statement when the statement was explained.

explicit privilege

A privilege that has a name and is held as the result of **SQL GRANT** and **REVOKE** statements, for example, the SELECT privilege.

export

(1) To copy data from database tables to a file using formats such as PC/IXF, DEL, WSF, or ASC.

(2) In the Information Catalog Center, to populate a tag language file with information catalog contents for use with another program.

export utility

A transaction utility that extracts data from a table.

expression

An SQL operand or a collection of operators and operands that yields a single value.

Extensible Markup Language (XML)

A text-based tag language that is used for document processing and for publishing information on the Web.

Extensible Stylesheet Language (XSL)

A language for specifying stylesheets for XML documents. XSL consists of two parts: a language for transforming XML documents and an XML vocabulary for specifying formatting semantics.

Extensible Stylesheet Language Transformation (XSLT)

An XML processing language that converts an XML document into another document in XML, PDF, HTML, or other format.

extent

An allocation of space within a container of a table space to a single database object. Data for any table will be stored on all containers in a table space in a round-robin fashion. This balances the data across the containers that belong to a given table space. The number of pages that the database manager writes to one container before using a different one is called an extent.

extent map

A metadata structure stored within a table space that records the allocation of extents to each object in the table space.

external function

A function for which the body is written in a programming language that takes scalar argument values and produces a scalar result for each invocation.

external name

The name of an executable file for a stored procedure or user-defined function that is written in a host programming language.

external procedure

An application program written in a host language, possibly containing SQL statements, that can be started with the **SQL CALL** statement.

external routine

A function, method, or procedure written in a host language and that possibly contains SQL statements.

F

fact table

(1) In a DB2 OLAP Server, a table, or in many cases a set of tables, that contains all data values for a relational cube.

(2) A relational table that contains facts, such as units sold or cost of goods, and foreign keys that link the fact table to each dimension table.

Fast Communications Manager (FCM)

A group of functions that provide inter-partition communication support.

federated database

In a federated system, the database that is within the federated server. Users and applications interface with the federated database. To these clients, the data sources appear as a single collective database in DB2.

federated server

The DB2 server in a federated system. Any number of DB2 instances can be configured to function as federated servers. You can use existing DB2 instances as your federated server, or you can create new ones specifically for the federated system.

federated system

A special type of distributed database management system (DBMS). A federated system lets you query and manipulate data located on other servers. The data can be in database managers such as Oracle, Sybase, Informix, and Microsoft SQL Server, or it can be in lists or stores such as a spreadsheet, Web site, or data mart. A federated system consists of a DB2 instance that operates as a server, a database that serves as the federated database, one or more data sources, and clients (users and applications) who access the database and data sources.

fenced

Pertaining to a type of user-defined function or stored procedure that is defined to protect the database manager from modifications by the function. The database manager is isolated from the function or stored procedure by a barrier.

fetch

An SQL action that positions a cursor on the next row of its result table and assigns the values of that row to host variables.

fixed-length string

A character or graphic string whose length is specified and cannot be changed.

foreign key

A column or set of columns that refers to a parent key. In a relational database, a key in one table that references the primary key in another table.

forward recovery

A process that rebuilds a restored database or table space to a specified point in time by applying the changes recorded in the database log.

fragmentation

The separation of the index into pieces as a result of inserts and deletions in the index.

free space

The total amount of unused space in a page. The space that is not used to store records or control information is free space.

full outer join

The result of an SQL join operation that includes the matched rows of both tables being joined and preserves the unmatched rows of both tables.

fullselect

A subselect, a values-clause, or a number of both that are combined by set operators. Fullselect specifies a result table. If a **UNION** operator is not used, the result of the fullselect is the result of the specified subselect.

function

A mapping, embodied as a program (the function body) and invoked by means of zero or more input values (arguments). Functions can be user-defined, built-in, or created by DB2.

G

General Parallel File System

A high-performance, shared-disk file system that provides fast data access to all nodes in a cluster of servers.

generated column

A column that is derived from an expression that involves one or more columns in the table.

governor

See **resource limit facility**.

GPFS

See **General Parallel File System**.

grant

To give a privilege or authority to an authorization identifier.

graphic character

A DBCS character.

graphic string

A sequence of DBCS characters.

grid computing

A type of distributed computing that collects and shares resources in a large network to simulate one large, virtual computer.

group

(1) A logical organization of users that have IDs according to activity or resource access authority.

(2) In a satellite environment, a collection of satellites that share characteristics such as database configuration and the application that runs on the satellite.

H

HACMP

See **High Availability Cluster Multiprocessor (HACMP)**.

hash partitioning

A partitioning strategy that applies a hash function to the partitioning key value to determine the database partition to which the row is assigned.

Health Center

The DB2 graphical interface that shows the overall state of the database environment and all current alerts. From the Health Center, you can get details about alerts and recommended resolution actions.

heterogeneous replication

Replication between DB2 and non-DB2 relational databases.

High Availability Cluster Multiprocessor (HACMP)

Any hardware environment with multiple processor nodes that supports the takeover of operations on one processor by another.

host

In TCP/IP, any system that has at least one Internet address associated with it.

host computer

(1) In a computer network, a computer that provides services such as computation, database access, and network control functions.

(2) The primary or controlling computer in a multiple-computer installation.

host language

Any programming language in which you can embed SQL statements.

host variable

In an application host program, a variable that is referred to by embedded SQL statements. Host variables are programming variables in the application program and are the primary mechanism for transmitting data between tables in the database and application program work areas.

HTML

See **Hypertext Markup Language**.

Hypertext Markup Language (HTML)

A markup language that uses tags to specify the format of a document on the Web. These tags define the page layout, graphics, and hypertext links within the document and to other documents on the Internet.

I

identity column

A column that provides a way for DB2 to automatically generate a numeric value for each row inserted into the table. Identity columns are defined with the **AS IDENTITY** clause. A table can only have one identity column.

idle agent

A database agent that currently does not have a database connection or an application attachment.

implicit privilege

(1) A privilege that accompanies the ownership of an object, such as the privilege to drop a synonym one owns or the holding of an authority, such as the privilege of SYSADM authority to terminate any utility job.

(2) A privilege that is granted to a user who has the privilege to execute a package on data objects used within the package that does not require granted explicit privileges.

import

(1) To copy data from an external file, using formats such as PC/IXF, DEL, WSF, or ASC, into database tables. See also **export**.

(2) In the Information Catalog Center, to read the contents of a tag language file to initially populate the information catalog, change the information catalog contents, or copy the contents of another information catalog.

import utility

A transactional utility that inserts user-supplied record data into a table.

incremental backup

A copy of all database data that has changed since the most recent successful full backup operation. This is also known as a *cumulative backup image*, because a series of incremental backups taken over time will each have the contents of the previous incremental backup image. The predecessor of an incremental backup image is always the most recent successful full backup of the same object.

index

A set of pointers that are logically ordered by the values of a key. Indexes provide quick access to data and can enforce uniqueness on the rows in a table. When you request an index, the database manager builds the structure and maintains it automatically. The database manager uses indexes to improve performance and ensure uniqueness.

index key

The set of columns in a table that determines the order of index entries.

individual privilege

A privilege that is granted to a single data object.

indoubt

The status of a unit of recovery. If the database manager fails after it finishes its phase 1 commit processing and before it starts phase 2, only the commit coordinator knows if an individual unit of recovery is to be committed or rolled back. At an emergency restart, if the database manager lacks the information that it needs to make this decision, the status of the unit of recovery is *indoubt* until the database manager obtains this information from the coordinator. More than one unit of recovery can be indoubt at restart.

indoubt resolution

The process of resolving the status of an indoubt logical unit of work to either the committed or the roll back state.

indoubt transaction

A transaction in which one phase of a two-phase commit completes successfully but the system fails before a subsequent phase can complete.

inflight

A status of a unit of recovery.

information catalog

A collection of metadata, managed by the Information Catalog Center, containing descriptive data (business metadata) that helps users identify and locate data and information available to them in the organization. An information catalog also contains some technical metadata.

informational configuration parameter

A type of configuration parameter that holds information that cannot be modified.

inheritance

The passing of class resources or attributes from a parent class downstream in the class hierarchy to a child class.

initialization fullselect

The first fullselect in a recursive common table expression that gets the direct children of the initial value from the source table.

inner join

A join method in which a column that is not common to all of the tables being joined is dropped from the result table.

inoperative package

A package that cannot be used because a function it depends on has been dropped. Such a package must be explicitly rebound.

inoperative trigger

A trigger that depends on an object that has been dropped or made inoperative or on a privilege that has been revoked.

inoperative view

(1) A view no longer usable because the SELECT privilege on a table or view that the view is dependent on is revoked from the definer of the view.

(2) An object on which the view definition is dependent was dropped (or possibly made inoperative in the case of another view).

insert rule

A condition enforced by the database manager that must be met before a row can be inserted into a table.

insert trigger

A trigger that is defined with the triggering SQL operation `INSERT`.

instance

(1) A logical DB2 extender server environment. You can have several instances of DB2 extenders server on the same workstation, but only one instance for each DB2 instance.

(2) See also **database manager instance.**

instance-owning partition

The first database-partition server that is installed in a partitioned database environment.

interactive SQL

A set of SQL statements that is provided through an interface such as the Command Center or Command Line Processor. These statements are processed as dynamic SQL statements. For example, an interactive **SELECT** statement can be processed dynamically using the **DECLARE CURSOR**, **PREPARE**, **DESCRIBE**, **OPEN**, **FETCH**, and **CLOSE** statements.

inter-partition parallelism

A single database operation (for example, index creation) that is executed in parallel across the partitions of a partitioned database.

inter-process communication (IPC)

A mechanism of an operating system that allows processes to communicate with each other within the same computer or over a network.

inter-query parallelism

The ability of multiple applications to query a database at the same time. Each query executes independently of the others, but DB2 runs all of them at the same time.

intra-partition parallelism

The subdivision of a single database operation (for example, index creation) into multiple parts, which are then executed in parallel within a single database partition.

intra-query parallelism

The ability to process parts of a single query at the same time using either intra-partition parallelism, inter-partition parallelism, or both.

invalid package

A package that depends on an object that has been dropped.

I/O parallelism

See **parallelism**.

IP address

A 4-byte value that uniquely identifies a TCP/IP host.

isolation level

(1) A security feature that determines how data is locked from other processes while it is being accessed. See also **repeatable read**, **read stability**, **cursor stability**, and **uncommitted read**.

(2) An attribute that defines the degree to which an application process is isolated from other concurrently executing application processes.

J

Java Database Connectivity (JDBC)

A set of database APIs used in the Java programming language. These APIs allow access to database management systems from Java applications using callable SQL, which does not require the use of an SQL preprocessor. The JDBC architecture lets users add modules, called *JDBC database drivers*, that link the Java application to their choice of database management systems at runtime. Applications do not need to be linked directly to the modules of all the supported database management systems.

JDBC driver

A program included with database management systems to support the JDBC standard access between databases and Java applications.

join

An SQL relational operation that retrieves data from two or more tables based on matching column values.

Journal

The destination pages from which you can view all available historical information about task history, database history, PM alerts, messages, and the notification log.

Journaled File System (JFS)

The native file system in the AIX operating system.

K

Kerberos

A network authentication protocol that provides strong authentication for client/server applications.

key

A column or an ordered collection of columns that is identified in the description of a table, index, or referential constraint. The same column can be part of more than one key.

keyword

(1) One of the predefined words of a computer, command language, or an application.

(2) A name that identifies an option used in an SQL statement.

L

large object (LOB)

A sequence of bytes with a size ranging from 0 bytes to 2GB minus 1 byte. It can be any of three types: binary large object (binary), character large object (single-byte character or mixed), or double-byte character large object (double-byte character).

large table space

A table space that can store only long strings, large objects (LOBs), or index data.

latency

The time required for updates made to a replication source to appear in a replication target.

leaf page

A page containing pairs of keys and record identifiers that points to actual data.

left outer join

The result of a join operation that includes the matched rows of both tables being joined and preserves the unmatched rows of the first table.

list prefetch

An access method that takes advantage of prefetching even in queries not accessing data sequentially. A list prefetch is done by scanning the index and collecting record identifiers before any data pages are accessed. These record identifiers are then sorted, and data is prefetched using this list.

load copy

A backup image of data previously loaded and that can be restored during roll forward recovery.

load module

A program unit that is suitable for loading into main storage for execution. A load module is the output of a linkage editor.

load utility

A nontransactional utility that performs block updates of table data.

LOB

See **large object**.

LOB locator

A mechanism that allows an application program to manipulate a large object (LOB) value in the database system. A LOB locator is a simple token value that represents a single LOB value. An application program retrieves a LOB locator into a host variable and can then apply SQL functions to the associated LOB value using the locator.

local database

A database that is physically located on the workstation in use.

local database directory

A directory where a database physically resides. Databases that are displayed in the local database directory are located on the same node as the system database directory.

locator

See **LOB locator**.

lock

(1) A means of serializing events or access to data.

(2) A means of preventing uncommitted changes made by one application process from being perceived by another application process and for preventing one application process from updating data that is being accessed by another process.

lock escalation

The response that occurs when the number of locks issued for one agent exceeds the limit specified in the database configuration. This limit is defined by the MAXLOCKS configuration parameter. During a lock escalation, locks are freed by converting locks on rows of a table into one lock on a table. This is repeated until the limit is no longer exceeded.

locking

The mechanism used by the database manager to ensure the integrity of data. Locking prevents concurrent users from accessing inconsistent data.

log

(1) A file that records changes made in a system.

(2) See also **database log**.

log file

(1) A record that monitors a database's activity. Log files are essential to the backup and recovery process.

(2) A file that is produced by the Information Catalog Center when it imports a tag language file into the information catalog. This file records the times and dates when the import process started and stopped and any error information for the process.

logical agent

An agent that represents the client or application connection.

logical operator

A keyword that specifies how multiple search conditions are to be evaluated (AND, OR) or if the logical sense of a search condition is to be inverted (NOT).

long string

A variable-length string whose maximum length is 32700 bytes.

long table space

See **large table space**.

M

maintenance window

A user-defined time period for running only required automatic maintenance activities.

mass delete

The deletion of all rows in a table.

massively parallel processing (MPP)

The coordinated execution of a single request either by multiple single-processor computers in a shared-nothing environment (in which each computer has its own memory and disks) or by symmetric multiprocessor (SMP) computers (in which multiple processors in each computer share memory and disks). Both environments require that all computers are linked together in a high-speed network.

materialized query table

A table whose definition is based on the result of a query and whose data is in the form of precomputed results taken from the one or more tables that the materialized query table definition is based on.

MBCS

See **multibyte character set**.

MDC table

See **multidimensional clustering table**.

merge

To update and insert new content into a table.

metadata

Data that describes the characteristics of stored data; descriptive data. For example, the metadata for a database table might include the name of the table, the name of the database that contains the table, the names of the columns in the table, and the column descriptions, either in technical terms or business terms. Database catalogs and information catalogs contain metadata.

migration

(1) The process of moving data from one computer system to another without converting the data.

(2) Installation of a new version or release of a program to replace an earlier version or release.

monitor switch

A database manager parameter manipulated by the user to control the type and quantity of information returned in performance snapshots.

MPP

See **massively parallel processing**.

MQT

See **materialized query table**.

multibyte character set (MBCS)

A set of characters in which each character is represented by 1 or more bytes. Contrast with **double-byte character set** and **single-byte character set**. See also **ASCII**, **EBCDIC**, and **Unicode**.

multidimensional

In the DB2 OLAP Server, pertaining to a method of referencing data through three or more dimensions. An individual data value in a fact table is the intersection of one member from each dimension.

multidimensional clustering (MDC) table

A table whose data is physically organized into blocks along one or more dimensions, or clustering keys, specified in the `ORGANIZE BY DIMENSIONS` clause.

multidimensional database

In the DB2 OLAP Server, a nonrelational database into which you copy relational data for OLAP analysis.

multisite update

Distributed relational database processing in which data is updated in more than one location within a single unit of work.

multitasking

A mode of operation that provides for concurrent performance or interleaved execution of two or more tasks.

N

nested savepoint

A savepoint that is included or positioned within another savepoint. Nested savepoints allow an application to have multiple levels of savepoints active at a time and allow the application to roll back to any active savepoint as desired.

nested table expression

A fullselect in a `FROM` clause (surrounded by parentheses).

network address

An identifier for a node in a network.

network addressable unit (NAU)

The origin or the destination of information transmitted by the path control network. An NAU can be a logical unit (LU), physical unit (PU), control point (CP), or system services control point (SSCP).

Network File System (NFS)

A client/server application that lets all network users access shared files stored on computers of different types. Users can manipulate shared files as if they were stored locally on the user's own hard disk.

Network Identifier

In a z/OS or OS/390 environment, the network identifier that is assigned by IMS or CICS, or if the connection type is RRSAF, the z/OS and OS/390 RRS unit of recovery identifier (URID).

Network Information Service (NIS/NIS+)

On AIX, a central record of passwords, nodes, and related data that can be used with the DB2 Administration Server to administer user and group names.

network name

In SNA, a symbolic name by which users refer to a network addressable unit (NAU), a link station, or a link.

network node (NN)

In APPN, a node on the network that provides distributed directory services, topology database exchanges with other APPN network nodes, and session and routing services.

Network Node Server

An APPN network node that provides network services for its local logical units and adjacent end nodes.

network-qualified name

The name by which an LU is known throughout an interconnected SNA network. A network-qualified name consists of a network name identifying the individual subnetwork and a network LU name. Network-qualified names are unique throughout an interconnected network. Also known as the *network-qualified LU name* or *fully qualified LU name*.

network services

The services within network addressable units that control network operation through SSCP-to-SSCP, SSCP-to-PU, SSCP-to-LU, and CP-to-CP sessions.

New Technology File System (NTFS)

One of the native file systems in Windows NT and later operating environments such as Windows 2000.

NFS

See **Network File System**.

nickname

(1) In a federated system, an identifier in a query that refers to an object at a data source. The objects that nicknames identify arc referred to as *data source objects*. Examples of data source objects include tables, views, synonyms, table-structured files, and search algorithms.

(2) A name defined in the DB2 Information Integrator that represents a physical database object (such as a table or stored procedure) in a non-DB2 relational database.

NID

See **network identifier**.

NIS/NIS+
See **Network Information Service**.

NN
See **network node**.

node
(1) In communications, an end point of a communications link, or a junction common to two or more links in a network. Nodes can be processors, communication controllers, cluster controllers, terminals, or workstations. Nodes can vary in routing and other functional capabilities.

(2) In hardware, a uniprocessor or symmetric multiprocessor (SMP) computer that is part of a clustered system or a massively parallel processing (MPP) system. For example, RS/6000 SP is a MPP system that consists of nodes connected by a high-speed network.

(3) An obsolete term for database partition.

node directory
A directory that contains information that is necessary to establish communications from a client workstation to all applicable database servers.

nodegroup
An obsolete term for **database partition group**.

noncumulative backup image
See **delta backup**.

non-DB2 relational database server
An Informix database server or a relational database server from a vendor other than IBM.

non-delimited ASCII (ASC)
ASC file format is also known as fixed-length ASCII file format because each column length in the file has the same length as defined for the corresponding column definition in the table.

nonleaf page
A page that contains keys and page numbers of other pages in the index (either leaf or nonleaf pages). Nonleaf pages never point to actual data.

normalization
The process of restructuring a data model by reducing its relations to their simplest forms. It is a key step in the task of building a logical relational database design. Normalization helps avoid redundancies and inconsistencies in your data. An entity is normalized if it meets a set of constraints for a particular normal form (first normal form, second normal form, and so on). See also **denormalization**.

notification log
See **administration notification log**.

NTFS

See **New Technology File System**.

null

A value that indicates the absence of information.

nullable

The condition in which a value for a column, function parameter, or result can have an absence of a value.

O

object

Anything that can be created or manipulated with SQL, for example, tables, views, indexes, or packages.

ODBC

See **Open Database Connectivity**.

ODBC driver

A driver that implements ODBC function calls and interacts with a data source.

offline backup

A backup of the database or table space that is made while the database or table space is not being accessed by applications. During an offline backup, the backup database utility acquires exclusive use of the database until the backup is complete.

offline maintenance

Maintenance activities that can occur only when user access to a database is interrupted.

offline restoration

A restoration of a copy of a database or table space from a backup. The restore database utility has exclusive use of the database until the restore is completed.

OLAP

See **online analytical processing**.

OLTP

See **online transaction processing**.

on-demand business

An enterprise whose business processes—integrated end to-end across the company and with key partners, suppliers and customers—can respond with speed to any customer demand, market opportunity, or external threat.

online analytical processing (OLAP)

In the DB2 OLAP Server, a multidimensional, multi-user, client-server computing environment for users who need to analyze consolidated enterprise data in real time. OLAP systems feature zooming, data pivoting, complex calculations, trend analysis, and modeling.

online transaction processing (OLTP)

A class of program that facilitates and manages transaction-oriented applications, typically for data entry and retrieval transactions in a number of industries, including banking, airlines, mail order, supermarkets, and manufacturers.

online backup

A backup of the database or table space that is made while the database or table space is being accessed by other applications.

online index creation

The process of creating a new index while allowing the underlying table and any previously existing indexes to be read and updated by concurrent transactions.

online index reorganization

Reorganizing indexes on a table while allowing the table and existing indexes to be read and updated by concurrent transactions.

online maintenance

Maintenance activities that can occur while users are connected to a database.

online restoration

A restoration of a copy of a table space while applications are able to access the tables in other table spaces.

Open Database Connectivity (ODBC)

An application programming interface (API) that allows access to database management systems by using callable SQL, which does not require the use of an SQL preprocessor. The ODBC architecture lets users add modules, called *database drivers*, that link the application to their choice of database management systems at runtime. Applications do not need to be linked directly to the modules of all the supported database management systems.

operand

An entity on which an operation is performed.

operator

An action that must be performed on data, the output from a table, or an index when the access plan for an SQL statement is executed.

optimized SQL text

SQL text, produced by the explain facility, that is based on the query actually used by the optimizer to choose the access plan. This query is supplemented and rewritten by the various components of the SQL compiler during statement compilation. The text is reconstructed from its internal representation and differs from the original SQL text. The optimized statement produces the same result as the original statement.

outer join

(1) A join method in which a column that is not common to all of the tables being joined becomes part of the result table.

(2) The result of a join operation that includes the matched rows of both tables that are being joined and preserves some or all of the unmatched rows of the tables being joined.

overflow record

An updated record that is too large to fit on the page it is currently stored in. The record is copied to a different page and its original location is replaced with a pointer to the new location.

overloaded function name

A function name for which multiple functions exist within a function path or schema. Those within the same schema must have different signatures.

ownership privilege

Control privilege that allows all privileges for the owned data object.

P

package

A control structure produced during program preparation that is used to execute SQL statements.

page

(1) A block of storage within a table or index whose size is 4096 bytes (4KB).

(2) A unit of storage within a table space (4KB, 8KB, 16KB, or 32KB) or index space (4KB). In a table space, a page contains one or more rows in a table. In a LOB table space, a LOB value can span more than one page, but no more than one LOB value is stored on a page.

parallelism

The ability to perform multiple database operations at the same time.

parameter marker

A question mark (?) that appears in a statement string of a dynamic SQL statement. The question mark can appear where a host variable might appear if the statement string was a static SQL statement.

parameter name

A long identifier naming a parameter that can be referenced in a procedure or user-defined function.

parent key

A primary key or unique key that is used in a referential constraint. The values of a parent key determine the valid values of the foreign key in the constraint.

parent row

A row that has at least one dependent row.

parent table

A table that is a parent in at least one referential constraint.

partitioned database

A database with two or more database partitions. Each database partition stores a subset of table data for each table that resides on it.

partitioning key

An ordered set of one or more columns in a given table. For each row in the table, the values in the partitioning key columns determine on which database partition the row belongs.

partitioning map

A vector of partition numbers that maps a partitioning map index to database partitions in the database partition group.

partitioning map index

A number that is assigned to a hash partition or range partition.

path

(1) In an operating system, the route through a file system to a specific file.

(2) In a network environment, the route between any two nodes.

PC version of Integrated Exchange Format (PC/IXF)

IXF data interchange architecture is a generic relational database exchange format that lets you move data among DB2 databases.

performance snapshot

Performance data for a set of database objects that is retrieved from the database manager at a point in time.

phantom row

A table row that can be read by application processes executing with any isolation level except repeatable read. When an application process issues the same query multiple times within a single unit of work, additional rows can appear between queries because of the data being inserted and committed by application processes that are running concurrently.

plug-in

A dynamically loadable library that DB2 UDB uses to carry out user-written actions that involve the database.

point of consistency
A point in time when all the recoverable data that a program accesses is consistent. The point of consistency occurs when updates, insertions, and deletions are either committed to the physical database or rolled back.

precision
In numeric data types, the total number of binary or decimal digits, excluding the sign. The sign is considered positive if the value of a number is zero.

precompile
To process programs that contain SQL statements before they are compiled. SQL statements are replaced with statements that will be recognized by the host language compiler. The output from a precompile process includes source code that can be submitted to the compiler and used in the bind process.

predicate
An element of a search condition that expresses or implies a comparison operation.

prefetching
Prefetching pages means that one or more pages are retrieved from disk in the expectation that they will be required by an application. Prefetching index and data pages into the buffer pool can help improve performance by reducing the I/O wait time. In addition, parallel I/O enhances prefetching efficiency.

prepare
(1) To convert an SQL statement from text form to an executable form by submitting it to the SQL compiler.
(2) The first phase of a two-phase commit process in which all participants are requested to prepare for commit.

prepared SQL statement
In SQL, a named object that is the executable form of an SQL statement processed by the **PREPARE** statement.

primary database
In High Availability Disaster Recovery (HADR), the main database, which is accessed by applications. Applications apply updates to the primary database, and those updates are propagated on the standby database by using log shipping.

primary key
A unique key that is part of the definition of a table. A primary key is the default parent key of a referential constraint definition. It is a column or combination of columns that uniquely identifies a row in a table.

primary log

A set of one or more log files used to record changes to a database. Storage for these files is allocated in advance.

principal

An entity that can communicate securely with another entity. In Kerberos, principals are represented as entries in the Kerberos registry database and include users, servers, computers, and others.

private memory

Memory allocated for a program/process when that process is performing work. This memory is only accessible by the program or process that allocated it.

privilege

The right to access a specific database object in a specific way. Privileges are controlled by users with SYSADM (system administrator) authority, DBADM (database administrator) authority, and by creators of objects. For example, privileges include rights to create, delete, and retrieve data from tables.

procedure

See **stored procedure**.

pseudo deleted

A key that is marked as deleted but has not yet been physically removed from the index page.

public authority

The authority for an object granted to all users.

Q

query

A request for information from the database based on specific conditions, such as a request for a list of all customers in a customer table whose balance is greater than $1,000.

query optimization class

A set of query rewrite rules and optimization techniques for compiling queries.

query optimizer

A component of the SQL compiler that chooses an access plan for a data manipulation language statement by modeling the execution cost of many alternative access plans and choosing the one with the minimum estimated cost.

quiesce

To end a process by allowing operations to complete normally while rejecting any new requests for work.

quiesce point

A point at which data is consistent as a result of running the DB2 UDB QUIESCE utility.

R

RDB

See **relational database**.

RDBMS

See **relational database management system**.

read-ahead prefetching

A method of prefetching pages by looking ahead in a scan, which results in an asynchronous retrieval of pages even though those pages are not located sequentially on disk.

read-only

Pertaining to data that can be read but not modified or deleted.

read stability (RS)

An isolation level that locks only the rows that an application retrieves within a transaction. Read stability ensures that any qualifying row that is read during a transaction is not changed by other application processes until the transaction is completed, and that any row changed by another application process is not read until the change is committed by that process.

rebind

To create a package for an application program that was previously bound. For example, if an index is added for a table that is accessed by a program, the package must be rebound for it to take advantage of the new index.

record

The storage representation of a single row of a table or other data.

record identifier (RID)

A 3-byte page number followed by a 1-byte slot number that is used internally by DB2 to uniquely identify a record in a table. The RID contains enough information to address the page in which the record is stored.

record identifier pool

In DB2 UDB for z/OS and OS/390, an area of main storage above the 16MB line that is reserved for sorting record identifiers during list prefetch processing.

record length

The sum of a length of all the columns in a table, which is the length of the data as it is physically stored in the database. Records can be fixed or variable in length, depending on how the columns are defined. If all columns are fixed-length columns, the record is a fixed-length record. If one or more columns are variable-length columns, the record is a variable-length column.

recoverable log

A database log in which all log records are retained, so if there is a failure, lost data can be recovered during forward recovery.

recovery

The process of rebuilding a database or table space that has become unusable because of a hardware or software failure, or both. The process includes restoring a backup image and can also include rolling database logs forward in time.

recovery log

See **database log**.

recovery pending

A state of the database or table space when it is restored from a backup. While the database or table space is in this state, its data cannot be accessed.

recursive common table expression

A common table expression that refers to itself in a **FROM** clause from the fullselect. Recursive common table expressions are used to write recursive queries.

recursive query

A fullselect that uses a recursive common table expression.

referential constraint

The referential integrity rule that the nonnull values of the foreign key are valid only if they also appear as values of a parent key.

referential integrity

The state of a database in which all values of all foreign keys are valid. Maintaining referential integrity requires the enforcement of a referential constraint on all operations that change the data in a table where the referential constraints are defined.

regular table space

A table space that can store any nontemporary data.

relational database

A database that can be perceived as a set of tables and manipulated in accordance with the relational model of data. Each database includes a set of system catalog tables that describe the logical and physical structure of the data, a configuration file containing the parameter values allocated for the database, and a recovery log with ongoing transactions and archivable transactions.

relational database management system (RDBMS)

A collection of hardware and software that organizes and provides access to a relational database.

remote database

A database that is physically located on a system other than the one in use.

remote unit of work (RUOW)

A unit of work that lets a user or application program read or update data at one location per unit of work. Remote unit of work supports access to one database within a unit of work. An application program can update several remote databases, but it can only access one database within a unit of work.

repeatable read (RR)

An isolation level that locks all the rows in an application that are referenced within a transaction. When a program uses repeatable read protection, rows referenced by the program cannot be changed by other programs until the program ends the current transaction.

replication

The process of maintaining a defined set of data in more than one location. It involves copying designated changes from one location (a source) to another (a target) and synchronizing the data in both locations.

Replication Center

A graphical interface that lets you define, operate, maintain, and monitor the replication environment. It is part of the DB2 Administration Client tool suite.

Request For Comments (RFC)

A set of technical and organizational notes about the Internet (originally the ARPANET), beginning in 1969. Memos in the RFC series discuss many aspects of computer networking, including protocols, procedures, programs, and concepts, as well as meeting notes, opinions, and sometimes humor.

requester

The source of a request to access data at a remote server. Also, the system that requests the data.

reserved word

(1) A word that is used in a source program to describe an action to be taken by the program or compiler. It must not appear in the program as a user-defined name or a system name.

(2) A word that has been set aside for special use in the SQL standard.

resource limit facility (RLF)

A portion of DB2 UDB for z/OS and OS/390 code that prevents dynamic manipulative SQL statements from exceeding specified time limits. Also known as the *governor*.

response file

An ASCII file customized with the setup and configuration data that will automate an installation. The setup and configuration data must be entered during an interactive install, but with a response file, the installation can proceed without any intervention.

response file generator

A utility that creates a response file from an existing installed and configured DB2 UDB product. You can use the generated response file to recreate the same setup on other computers.

restore

To rebuild a damaged or corrupted database or table space from a backup image produced with the BACKUP utility.

restore set

A backup copy of a database or table space plus zero or more log files which, when restored and rolled forward, bring the database or table space back to a consistent state.

result set

The set of rows that a stored procedure returns.

result table

The set of rows produced by the evaluation of a **SELECT** statement.

revoke

To remove a privilege or authority from an authorization identifier.

RID

See **record identifier**.

RID pool

See **record identifier pool**.

right outer join

The result of a join operation that includes the matched rows of both tables being joined and preserves the unmatched rows of the second join operand.

roll back

To restore data changed by SQL statements to the state at its last commit point.

roll forward

To update the data in a restored database or table space by applying changes recorded in the database log files.

roll forward recovery

A process started by the roll forward utility to recover a database by applying transactions recorded in the database recovery log file.

routine

A user-defined method, user-defined function, or stored procedure.

row

The horizontal component of a table that consists of a sequence of values, one for each column of the table.

row lock

A lock on a single row of data.

RR

See **repeatable read**.

RS

See **read stability**.

RUOW

See **remote unit of work**.

S

satellite

A DB2 UDB server that is a member of a group of similar DB2 UDB servers. Each satellite in the group runs the same application and has a similar configuration to support the application.

Satellite Administration Center

A user interface that provides centralized administrative support for satellites.

satellite control server

A DB2 UDB system that contains the satellite control database, *SATCTLDB*.

savepoint

A named entity that represents the state of data and schemas at a particular point in time within a unit of work.

savepoint level

A distinct scope that is used for reference and interaction between savepoint-related statements.

SBCS

See **single-byte character set**.

scalar fullselect

A fullselect that returns a single value—one row of data that consists of exactly one column.

scalar function

A function that optionally accepts arguments and returns a single scalar value each time it is invoked. A scalar function can be referenced in an SQL statement wherever an expression is valid.

scale

The number of digits in the fractional part of a number.

schema

A collection of database objects such as tables, views, indexes, or triggers that define a database. A database schema provides a logical classification of database objects.

scrollable cursor

A cursor that can be moved in both a forward and a backward direction.

scrollable result set

A result set associated with a scrollable cursor that allows the application to fetch rows and to fetch previously fetched rows again.

search

To request the display of objects that meet user-specified criteria.

search condition

A criterion for selecting rows from a table. A search condition consists of one or more predicates.

secondary log

A set of one or more log files used to record changes to a database. Storage for these files is allocated as needed when the primary log is full.

section

The segment of a plan or package that contains the executable structures for a single SQL statement. For most SQL statements, one section in the plan exists for each SQL statement in the source program. However, for cursor-related statements, the **DECLARE, OPEN, FETCH,** and **CLOSE** statements reference the same section because they each refer to the **SELECT** statement named in the **DECLARE CURSOR** statement. SQL statements such as **COMMIT, ROLLBACK,** and some **SET** statements do not use a section.

self-referencing constraint

A referential constraint that defines a relationship in which a table is a dependent of itself.

self-referencing row

A row that is a parent of itself.

self-referencing subquery

A subselect or fullselect within a **DELETE, INSERT,** or **UPDATE** statement referring to the same table that is the object of the SQL statement.

self-referencing table

A table that is both a parent and dependent table in the same referential constraint.

sequence

A database object independent of any one table that automatically generates unique key values based on initial user specifications.

sequential prefetch

A mechanism that triggers consecutive asynchronous I/O operations. Pages are fetched before they are required, and several pages are read with a single I/O operation.

serialization

(1) The consecutive ordering of items.

(2) The process of controlling access to a resource to protect the integrity of the resource.

server

In a network, hardware or software that provides facilities to other stations, for example, a file server, a printer server, or a mail server.

service name

A name that provides a symbolic method of specifying the port number to be used at a remote node. The TCP/IP connection requires the address of the remote node and the port number to be used on the remote node to identify an application.

set operator

The SQL operators **UNION, EXCEPT,** and **INTERSECT** that correspond to the relational operators union, difference, and intersection. A set operator derives a result table by combining two other result tables.

shared memory

Shared memory is an efficient means of passing and sharing data between programs/processes. One program or process will create a memory portion which other processes (if permitted) can access.

single-byte character set (SBCS)

A character set in which each character is represented by a one-byte code.

single-precision floating point number

A 32-bit approximate representation of a real number.

slice

The set of blocks that contain pages with data having a certain value of one of the clustering dimensions.

SMS table space

See **system-managed space table space**.

SNA

See **Systems Network Architecture**.

snapshot

A record of the current state of the database environment.

socket

A communications handle used by TCP/IP.

soft checkpoint

The process of writing some information to the log file header. This information determines the starting point in the log if a database restart is required.

source program

A set of host language statements and SQL statements processed by an SQL precompiler.

source table

A table that can be a base table, a view, a table expression, or a user-defined table function.

source type

An existing type that internally represents a distinct type.

special register

DB2 special registers are memory registers that allow DB2 to provide information to an application about its environment. They can be referenced in SQL statements. Examples are USER and CURRENT DATE.

SQL

See **Structured Query Language**.

SQL Assistant

A wizard that is available in several DB2 UDB tools and centers that generates SQL statements graphically.

SQLCA

See **SQL communication area**.

SQL communication area (SQLCA)

A set of variables that provides an application program with information about the execution of its SQL statements or its requests from the database manager.

SQL connection

An association between an application process and a local or remote application server.

SQLDA

See **SQL descriptor area**.

SQL descriptor area (SQLDA)

(1) A set of variables that is used in the processing of certain SQL statements. The SQLDA is intended for dynamic SQL programs.

(2) A structure that describes input variables, output variables, or the columns of a result table.

SQL escape character

The symbol that is used to enclose an SQL delimited identifier. The escape character is the quotation mark, except in COBOL applications, where the user assigns the symbol to be either a quotation mark or an apostrophe.

SQL function

A function that is implemented entirely by using a subset of SQL statements and SQL PL statements.

SQLJ

A three-part standard for supporting embedded SQL in Java programs (Part 0), defining and calling Java stored procedures and user-defined functions (Part 1), and using database structured types in Java (Part 2).

SQL method

A method that is implemented entirely by using a subset of SQL statements and SQL PL statements.

SQL PL

See **SQL procedural language**.

SQL procedural language (SQL PL)

A language extension of SQL that consists of statements and language elements to implement procedural logic in SQL statements. SQL PL provides statements for declaring variables and condition handlers, assigning values to variables, and for implementing procedural logic.

SQL procedure

A procedure that is created by running the **CREATE PROCEDURE** statement and is implemented entirely in SQL PL. An SQL procedure is called by running the **CALL** statement.

SQL return code

Either SQLCODE or SQLSTATE.

standard database

In High Availability Disaster Recovery (HADR), a database that is neither the primary nor the standby. A standard database is not configured for HADR.

standby database

In High Availability Disaster Recovery (HADR), a copy of the primary database. Updates to this database occur by rolling forward log data that is generated on the primary database and sent to the standby database.

star schema

A type of relational database schema that is composed of a set of tables comprised of a single, central fact table surrounded by dimension tables. Star schemas are used by the DB2 OLAP Server and are often created in the Data Warehouse Center.

statement

An instruction in a program or procedure.

statement savepoint

An internal savepoint mechanism that ensures that either all the updates or none of the updates are applied to the database at the completion of an SQL statement.

static SQL

SQL statements that are embedded within a program and are prepared during the program preparation process before the program is executed. After being prepared, a static SQL statement does not change, although values of host variables specified by the statement can change.

statistics profile

A file that contains all of the options information that specifies which statistics are collected for a table when using a particular **RUNSTATS** command logic.

stored procedure

(1) An application program, possibly containing SQL statements, that can be invoked with the **SQL CALL** statement.

(2) A user-written application program that can be started by using the **SQL CALL** statement.

string

A sequence of bytes that might represent characters.

strong typing

A process guarantying that only user-defined functions and operations defined on a distinct type can be applied to that type. For example, two currency types, such as Canadian dollars and U.S. dollars, cannot be directly compared, but a user-defined function can be provided to convert one currency to the other and then do the comparison.

structure

A name that refers collectively to different types of DB2 UDB objects, such as tables, databases, views, indexes, and table spaces.

Structured Query Language (SQL)

A standardized language for defining and manipulating data in a relational database.

structured type

A data type that is a named collection of attributes (standard data types or other structured types), which allows for greater semantic control than predefined types.

subagent

A type of agent that works on subrequests. A single application can make many requests, and each request can be broken into many subrequests. Therefore, there can be multiple subagents that work on behalf of the same application. All subagents working for the application are initiated by the initiating agent for that application.

subordinate agent

See **subagent**.

subquery

A **SELECT** statement within the **WHERE** or **HAVING** clause of another SQL statement; a nested SQL statement.

subselect

The form of a query that does not include an **ORDER BY** clause, an **UPDATE** clause, or **UNION** operators.

subset

To replicate data from part of a source table, rather than from the entire table, to a target table. Data can be subset by rows or by columns.

summary table

A specialized type of materialized query table whose fullselect contains a **GROUP BY** clause that summarizes data from the tables referenced in the fullselect.

superuser

A user who has various system control authorities above and beyond that of the ordinary user. In UNIX environments, the standard superuser is root.

sync point

See **point of consistency**.

synchronous

Pertaining to two or more processes that depend on the occurrences of specific events, such as a common timing signal.

system administrator

(1) The person at a computer installation who designs, controls, and manages the use of the computer system.

(2) A DB2 UDB user with SYSADM authority.

system authority

SYSCTRL and SYSMAINT authority levels with full privileges for managing the system but without the ability to access the data.

system catalog

See **catalog**.

system database directory

A directory containing entries for every database that can be accessed using the database manager. The directory is created when the first database is created or cataloged on the system.

system-managed space (SMS) table space

A table space whose space is managed by the operating system. This storage model is based on files that are created under subdirectories and managed by the file system.

system monitor

See **database system monitor**.

Systems Network Architecture (SNA)
An architecture that describes the logical structure, formats, protocols, and operational sequences for transmitting information units through networks, and also operational sequences for controlling the configuration and operation of networks.

T

table
A named data object consisting of a specific number of columns and some unordered rows.

table check constraint
See **check constraint**.

table collocation
In a partitioned database environment, a state that occurs when two tables are stored in the same database partition group and have the same number of compatible partitioning keys. When this happens, DB2 UDB can choose to perform the join or subquery processing at the database partition where the data is stored.

table expression
An expression that creates a temporary result table from a simple query. For example, a table expression might be a query that selects all the managers from several departments and further specifies that they have over 15 years of working experience and are located at the main branch.

table function
A function that optionally accepts arguments and returns a table to the SQL statement referencing it. Table functions can be referenced only in the **FROM** clause.

table lock
A lock on a table of data.

table space
An abstraction of a collection of containers into which database objects are stored. A table space provides a level of indirection between a database and the tables stored within the database. A table space has space on media storage devices assigned to it. The data, index, long field, and LOB portions of a table can be stored in the same table space, or can be individually divided into separate table spaces.

table space container
An allocation of space to a table space. Depending on the table space type, the container can be a directory, device, or file.

table space high water mark
The table space high water mark is the first page after the highest page number that has been allocated within the table space.

task

In the Task Center, a unit of work and its associated schedule and task actions. Tasks can be set to run on schedules and can perform various actions based on the success or failure of the task. DB2 UDB scripts, operating scripts, and warehouse steps are all examples of tasks.

Task Center

The DB2 UDB graphical interface for organizing task flow, scheduling tasks, and distributing notifications about the status of completed tasks.

TCP/IP

See **Transmission Control Protocol/Internet Protocol**.

TCP/IP port

A 2-byte value that identifies a TCP/IP network application within a TCP/IP host.

temporary table

A table that holds temporary data. For example, temporary tables are useful for holding or sorting intermediate results from queries that contain a large number of rows. The two kinds of temporary tables, which are created by different SQL statements, are the *created temporary table* and the *declared temporary table*.

temporary table space

A table space that can store only temporary tables.

territory code

A code used by DB2 UDB to preset the default collation order for an SBCS database and to establish monetary, date, time, and numeric formatting that is specific to a country, region, or territory.

throttled utilities

Utilities with a limit placed on the resources that would otherwise be consumed. The degree to which the resources are limited is based on the current workload of the system. Supported utilities include backup, restore, and table space reorganization.

timeron

A unit of measurement that gives a rough relative estimate of the resources, or cost, required by the database server to execute two plans for the same query. The resources calculated in the estimate include weighted processor and I/O costs.

timestamp

A data type that contains a seven-part value that consists of a date and time expressed in years, months, days, hours, minutes, seconds, and microseconds.

Tivoli Storage Manager (TSM)

A client-server product that provides storage management and data access services in a heterogeneous environment. TSM supports various communication methods, provides administrative facilities to manage the backup and storage of files, and provides facilities for scheduling backups.

transaction

An atomic series of SQL statements that make up a logical unit of work. All of the data modifications made during a transaction are either committed together as a unit or are all rolled back as a unit. Synonym for **unit of work**.

transaction manager

A function that assigns identifiers to transactions, monitors their progress, and takes responsibility for transaction completion and failure recovery.

transition table

A temporary table that contains all the affected rows of the subject table in their state before or after the triggering event occurs. Triggered SQL statements in the trigger definition can reference the table of changed rows in the old or new state.

transition variable

A variable that is valid only in FOR EACH ROW triggers. It allows access to the transition values for the current row. An old transition variable is the value of the row before the modification is applied; the new transition variable is the value of the row after the modification is applied.

Transmission Control Protocol/Internet Protocol (TCP/IP)

An industry standard, nonproprietary set of communications protocols that provide reliable end-to-end connections between applications over interconnected networks of different types.

trigger

A database object associated with a single base table or view that defines a rule. The rule consists of a set of SQL statements that run when an insert, update, or delete database operation occurs on the associated base table or view.

truncation

The process of discarding part of a result from an operation when it exceeds memory or storage capacity.

trusted clients

DB2 clients with reliable security facilities like Windows 2000, AIX, z/OS, and Linux.

TSM

See **Tivoli Storage Manager**.

tuple

A synonym for a row in a table.

two-phase commit

A two-step process by which recoverable resources and an external subsystem are committed. During the first step, the database manager subsystems are polled to ensure that they are ready to commit. If all subsystems respond positively, the database manager instructs them to commit.

typed table

A table in which the data type of each column is defined separately or the types for the columns are based on the attributes of a user-defined structured type.

U

UCS-2

Universal Character Set, coded in 2 octets, which means that characters are represented in 16-bits per character.

UDF

See **user-defined function**.

UDT

See **user-defined type**.

unambiguous cursor

A cursor that allows a DBMS to determine whether blocking can be used with the answer set. A cursor that is defined **FOR FETCH ONLY** or **FOR READ ONLY** can be used with blocking, whereas a cursor that is defined **FOR UPDATE** cannot.

uncommitted read (UR)

An isolation level that allows an application to access uncommitted changes of other transactions. The application does not lock other applications out of the row that it is reading, unless the other application attempts to drop or alter the table.

unfenced

Pertaining to a type (characteristic) of a procedure, user-defined function, or federated wrapper that is defined to run in the database manager process. When this type of object is run (using the **not fenced** clause), the database manager is not protected from changes made by this object.

unfenced routine

A type of user-defined function or stored procedure that is defined to be run in the database manager process. There is no protection for the database manager from changes by this routine.

Unicode

An international character-encoding scheme that is a subset of the ISO 10646 standard. Each character supported is defined using a unique 2-byte code.

uniform resource locator (URL)

A sequence of characters that represents information resources on a computer or in a network such as the Internet. This sequence of characters includes the abbreviated name of the protocol that accesses the information resource and the information used by the protocol to locate the information resource.

union

An SQL operation that combines the results of two **SELECT** statements. Unions are often used to merge lists of values that are obtained from several tables.

unique constraint

The rule that no two values in a primary key or key of a unique index can be the same. Also referred to as *uniqueness constraint.*

unique index

An index that ensures that no identical key values are stored in a table.

unique key

A key that is constrained so that no two of its values are equal.

unit of work (UOW)

A recoverable sequence of operations within an application process. At any time, an application process is a single unit of work, but the life of an application process can involve many units of work as a result of commit or roll back operations. Synonym for **transaction**.

Universal Coordinated Time

The international time standard. 00:00 UTC is midnight in Greenwich, England.

untrusted clients

DB2 clients that do not have a reliable security facility such as Windows 98, Windows ME, and Classic Mac OS.

update rule

A condition enforced by the database manager that must be met before a column can be updated.

UR

See **uncommitted read (UR)**.

URL

See **uniform resource locator**.

user-defined function (UDF)

A database object that is created with the **CREATE FUNCTION** statement. All functions that are not built-in functions are user-defined functions.

user-defined type (UDT)

A data type that is not native to the database manager and was created by a user. In DB2 UDB, the term **distinct type** is used instead of user-defined type.

user exit program

A program written by a user that receives control at predefined user exit points. When a user exit program is invoked, the database manager passes control to the executable file. Only one user exit program can be invoked in a database manager instance.

user mapping

In a federated system, the association between the authorization ID at the federated server and the authorization ID at the data source. User mappings are needed so that distributed requests can be sent to the data source. User mappings are created when a user's authorization ID to access the federated database differs from the user's authorization ID to access a data source. Use the **CREATE USER MAPPING** statement to define the association and the **ALTER USER MAPPING** statement to modify a user mapping that you have already created.

UTC

See **Universal Coordinated Time**.

UTF-8

Unicode Transformation Format, 8-bit encoding form, which is designed for ease of use with existing ASCII-based systems. The CCSID value for data in UTF-8 format is 1208.

UTF-16

Unicode Transformation Format, 16-bit encoding form, which is designed to provide code values for over a million characters and is a superset of UCS-2. The CCSID value for data in UTF-16 format is 1200.

V

value

(1) The alpha or numeric content of a field or variable.

(2) The smallest unit of data manipulated in SQL.

(3) A specific data item at the intersection of a column and a row.

variable

A data element that specifies a value that can be changed.

variable-length string

A character, graphic, or binary string whose length is not fixed but can range within set limits. Also referred to as a *varying length string*.

version recovery

The restoration of a previous version of the database, using an image that was created during a backup operation.

view

(1) A logical table that consists of data generated by a query. A view is based on an underlying set of base tables, and the data in a view is determined by a **SELECT** statement that is run on the base tables. Contrast with **base table**.

(2) A way of looking at the information about or contained in objects. Each view might reveal different information about its objects.

Visual Explain

A tool that provides a graphical interface for database administrators and application programmers to display and analyze detailed information on the access plan of a given SQL statement. The tasks provided by this tool can be accessed from the Control Center.

volatile table

A table for which SQL operations choose index access whenever possible.

W

warehouse

See **data warehouse**.

Web service

A modular application that performs specific tasks and is accessible through open protocols such as HTTP and SOAP.

WebSphere MQ

A family of IBM licensed programs that provides message queuing services.

Windows global group

A global group exists only on a domain controller and contains user accounts from the domain's SAM database. That is, a global group can only contain user accounts from the domain on which it is created; it cannot contain any other groups as members. A global group can be used in servers and workstations of its own domain and in trusting domains.

Windows local group

A local group can include user accounts created in the local accounts database. If the local group is on a machine that is part of a domain, the local group can also contain domain accounts and groups from the Windows NT domain. If the local group is created on a workstation, it is specific to that workstation.

worksheet format (WSF)

WSF files are Lotus 1-2-3 and Symphony worksheets that the database manager supports.

wrapper

In a federated system, the mechanism that the federated server uses to communicate with and retrieve data from the data sources. To implement a wrapper, the federated server uses routines stored in a library called a *wrapper module*. These routines allow the federated server to perform operations such as connecting to a data source and retrieving data from it iteratively. The DB2 UDB federated instance owner uses the **CREATE WRAPPER** statement to register a wrapper for each data source that is to be included in the federated system.

X

XML
See **Extensible Markup Language**.

XSL
See **Extensible Stylesheet Language**.

XSLT
See **Extensible Stylesheet Language Transformation**.

Z

z/OS
An IBM operating system for the IBM eServer product line that supports 64-bit real storage.

Index

About the CD-ROM

The CD-ROM included with this book contains the following:

- IBM® DB2® Universal Database™ Enterprise Server Edition Version 8.2 for Windows® Operating Environments (see the Note).
- Several color figures in GIF format that appear in black and white in the book.
- Useful scripts to capture snapshots for monitoring and tuning your DB2 system.
- Reference materials in PDF format with descriptions of database manager and database configuration parameters, and examples of DB2 commands and SQL statements.
- A subset of the book's Resources section in text format so you can easily copy and paste URLs into your browser.

> **NOTE**   The version of DB2 on this CD-ROM runs on:
>
> - Windows NT Version 4 with Service Pack 6a
> - Windows 2000 Professional, Standard Server, Advanced Server, and Datacenter Servers. Windows 2000 Service Pack 2 is required for Windows Terminal Server.
> - Windows Server 2003 (32-bit and 64-bit).
> - Windows XP Professional Edition (*not* Home Edition).
>
> It is an Evaluation version that is valid for six months after installation. See Chapter 3, Installing DB2, for installation instructions.
>
> If you would like to run DB2 on Windows XP Home Edition, download the DB2 Personal Edition install image from the DB2 for Linux, UNIX, and Windows main Web page (www.ibm.com/software/data/db2/udb/).

We encourage you to print the figures included on the CD-ROM so that you can refer to them without needing to have the book with you.

CD-ROM Warranty

IBM Press warrants the enclosed CD-ROM to be free of defects in materials and faulty workmanship under normal use for a period of ninety days after purchase (when purchased new). If a defect is discovered in the CD-ROM during this warranty period, a replacement CD-ROM can be obtained at no charge by sending the defective CD-ROM, postage prepaid, with proof of purchase to:

Disc Exchange
IBM Press
Pearson Technology Group
75 Arlington Street, Suite 300
Boston, MA 02116
Email: AWPro@aw.com

IBM Press makes no warranty or representation, either expressed or implied, with respect to this software, its quality, performance, merchantability, or fitness for a particular purpose. In no event will IBM Press, its distributors, or dealers be liable for direct, indirect, special, incidental, or consequential damages arising out of the use or inability to use the software. The exclusion of implied warranties is not permitted in some states. Therefore, the above exclusion may not apply to you. This warranty provides you with specific legal rights. There may be other rights that you may have that vary from state to state. The contents of this CD-ROM are intended for personal use only.

More information and updates are available at:

www.phptr.com/ibmpress